CODLINE'S CHILD

Wilbert Snow; portrait by Wilson Irvine, ca. 1928 (photo by Wm. L. Fortin)

Codline's Child

THE AUTOBIOGRAPHY
OF

Wilbert Snow

WESLEYAN UNIVERSITY PRESS

Middletown, Connecticut

Chapter 20, "The Robert Frost I Knew," first appeared in slightly longer form in *The Texas Quarterly*, Vol. XI, No. 3, Autumn 1968. The author is grateful to its editors for assigning the copyright to him. This chapter contains:

Portions of poems from *The Poetry of Robert Frost* edited by Edward Connery Lathem. Copyright © 1938, 1930, 1969 by Holt, Rinehart and Winston, Inc. Copyright © 1936, 1956, 1958 by Robert Frost. Copyright © 1964, 1967 by Lesley Frost Ballantine. Reprinted by permission of Holt, Rinehart and Winston, Inc.

Letters from *Selected Letters of Robert Frost* edited by Lawrance Thompson. Copyright © 1964 by Holt, Rinehart and Winston, Inc. The letter beginning "Jimminy Criquetts Bill . . . " was first published in *The Texas Quarterly*, Autumn 1968; copyright © 1968 by Holt, Rinehart and Winston, Inc. Reprinted by permission of Holt, Rinehart and Winston, Inc.

Letters from Wallace Stevens included in Chapter 21, "Other Poets," copyright © 1974 by Holly Stevens.

Library of Congress Cataloging in Publication Data

Snow, Wilbert, 1884–
    Codline's child.

    1. Snow, Wilbert, 1884–   I. Title
PS3537.N683Z5   813'.5'4[B]   73–15008
ISBN 0–8195–4069–2

Manufactured in the United States of America
FIRST EDITION

*Dedicated to the Memory of
my Father and Mother*

Contents

Illustrations

Acknowledgments

My thanks go first to the Wesleyan Class of 1927. At their fortieth reunion in 1967 they voted to give their contribution to the Alumni Fund that year to me to be used for clerical help and research in writing the story of my life. Having accepted this fund, I was bound to see it through, though it took several years instead of the expected one.

My thanks are due also to Wyman Parker, Librarian of Wesleyan University, for encouragement when I grew weary, and to three of his assistants—Joan Jurale, Brian Rogers, and Edmund Rubacha—who have helped so much in research. Thanks go also to the staff of the State Library in Hartford for the recovery of bills and resolutions that came up when I was Lieutenant Governor in 1945; to members of the Bowdoin College Library staff for the corrections they have made in my memories of college years; to Mrs. Ned Larrabee for helping me to recall my days at Reed College; to Mrs. E. Lingle Craig for garnering the memories of my days at Indiana University where Stith Thompson, Robert Telfer, and Herman Wells the former President of the University poured pitchers of Hoosier hospitality over my head. My thanks go also to my secretaries who have successfully deciphered my wretched handwriting, especially to Sally Downes, a young woman of unlimited patience; and to Bob Burns of the Rockland (Maine) *Courier Gazette* for digging out records of my Snow ancestors.

Lastly, I want to thank all those individuals and organizations who have permitted me to include here several previously unpublished letters from writers I have known, as well as poems, letters, and the like by other hands reprinted from copyright sources. Acknowledgments of all these borrowings are made in proper form elsewhere in this book.

CODLINE'S CHILD

CHAPTER 1

Island Yankee

There may be in an island birth
A need unknown to inland men,
Need for an armistice with earth
To let salt tides flow in again.
"Dust to dust" was spoken when
The race had not yet found the sea;
A deeper call has come since then—
Salt brine to blood for men like me.

I WAS born on the island of White Head at the western entrance of Penobscot Bay in the state of Maine, the third boy in the family. When the birth seemed imminent, my mother urged, "Forrest, it's time to call the doctor!"

"Good God, how can I call Hitchcock? I haven't paid him for last time." He paced from window to window. "Remember? He came in a snowstorm and was marooned on this island two whole days. He had a good time duck hunting, but all the same. . . ."

My mother waited, and the pains increased. "Forrest, see if you can get Codline Foster." So a midwife attended, and midwives in those days did not bother to record births. Years later, when I needed a passport, I had to find an elderly citizen of the village to testify to the town clerk that I was born on April 6, 1884. My older brother is sure that the year was '83. So the first important fact with which a man should begin the story of his life is in my case clouded with uncertainty. At least I am sure of the place.

White Head Island is a wooded eminence of eighty acres. One side is on the calm waters of Penobscot Bay; the other, dominated by a lighthouse and a Coast Guard station, faces the turbulent Atlantic. In July fog often hangs over the island for weeks. As a child, walking through the mist and hearing the clang of the bell buoy a quarter of a mile off and the dismal fog whistle on the headland sounding its deep blasts every thirty seconds, I experienced the feeling of being pursued by malignant forces, that I later discovered expressed so well in Goethe's tragic poem *The Erl-King*.

On sunny days the island is a delight. The cove on the ocean side has layer upon layer of white granite ledges. The big waves roll in, concealing beneath their rise and fall a tremendous force that meets the rock with a crashing explosion and sends green water and spray high into the air. A child creeps as near the water as he dares, watching for the big ninth wave that will flood the ledge and send him racing back, screaming with fear and delight.

The contrasting aspects of that island shaped my character. The turbulent waves of the outer side symbolized my desire to take this old world by its topknot, "shatter it to bits—and then / Remold it nearer to the Heart's desire"; while the calm waves of the inner side symbolized my longing for quietude, peace, and contemplation among birds, animals, and northern green woods.

My parents furnished a further contrast in my heredity. My mother was a vivid, dark-eyed Irish colleen whose parents had come across the ocean in a Black Ball liner. My father was a sober tenth-generation descendant of the Bay Colony's earliest settlers.

My parents were both born on April 2, one in 1859, one in 1860, my father on White Head Island, and my mother in St. John, New Brunswick. The coincidence of birth dates was one of the bonds that drew them together. My father was a severe puritanical man inclined to govern his seven children with the iron rod of discipline. My mother was full of gaiety, humor, and wit and was inclined to wait on her children, especially her five sons, beyond the call of duty or good sense.

I knew both of my grandmothers but never saw either one of my grandfathers. The poem in the *Third Reader* which began "Over the river and through the wood / To grandmother's house we go . . ." struck me as correct, for I suspected from my own experience that the grandfather was no longer living. The joke of the semi-illiterate letter-writer apologizing for his bad English by writing "Excuse grammar, grandpa's dead," hit me harder by its accuracy than by its humor. Years later, studying paintings of the Holy Family in European galleries, I was not surprised to find many beautiful portrayals of Christ's grandmother Anne, but not one picture that I can remember of his grandfather.

The grandfather on my mother's side, Michael Quinn, was a stonemason and from all accounts an excellent one. When the potato famine of the '40's struck Ireland, he and his wife Mary crossed the Atlantic and settled in St. John, New Brunswick. Mary's mother's two brothers, Hugh and James, came with them. Hugh was a sailor addicted to the bottle. He called on my mother once years later, but was too deep in his cups to give any accurate family information. James was the agent of a trading company which dealt extensively in Indian wares and artifacts. His job was bringing goods from the Indian trading station north of the city to ships at St. John's wharf, a job which necessitated carrying on his person a large amount of money. One night he was robbed and murdered and his body thrown into the St. John River. His mother sought help from every available source to find the body. After days of fruitless search she in desperation went to a fortune-teller, who told her to make a small basket out of reeds and rushes, place a lighted candle in it, and set it adrift on the river. Under the exact spot where the basket came to a stop, she would find her son's body. She carried out these instructions to the letter. Accompanied by her family and many half-doubting curious neighbors, she anxiously followed the candle downstream. When the basket veered toward a bend in the bank and finally came to rest against a growth of alders, they drew near, hardly daring to look down into the water. A bold neighbor stepped in, peered about, and shouted, "Here he is!"

The Quinns had three children, Katherine, Hugh, and Agnes, all of whom were born in St. John. Soon after the birth of the third child an epidemic of diphtheria carried off the father, Michael Quinn, at the age of twenty-seven. This would have left his wife and children alone and friendless had it not been for Michael Fleming.

Fleming had grown up in Dublin, Ireland. As a young man in his teens he became engaged to a pretty colleen of that city. Arrangements were made for the wedding, a priest was secured, the wedding cake was baked. At the last moment Mike got a bad case of "buck fever." Everyone was assembled at the church; it was time for Mike to appear, but the trembling boy panicked and set off on foot for Waterford. There he got a job in the quarries and took his washing, as the other bachelors did, to a lively, high-spirited young woman, the

Widow McGraw. He married the widow and later they joined the group that included Michael and Mary Quinn and sailed for New Brunswick. After the death of Michael Quinn, Fleming became the guide and friend of the Quinn family.

Stone workers of New Brunswick soon heard of the high wages paid to stonecutters and quarrymen at Dix Island and other centers on the Maine coast. With Michael Fleming as advisor and helper, the widow Quinn and her three children came to Spruce Head, Maine. She put her children in the village school and went to work in a big boarding house that was filled with teamsters, blacksmiths, and stone workers. She made beds, swept floors, washed dishes, and helped with all the endless chores. She told me that Mr. Sawyer, the manager and owner, would allow her only one match with which to light twenty kerosene lamps. She carried twisted pieces of bark and paper to light before her one match should burn out.

A few hundred yards below this boarding house a long point of land thrust a prong into the sea. It was one of the beauty spots of the region with magnificent spruce woods, a sandy beach, and an unparalleled view of Penobscot Bay with schooners and yachts sailing by. People from all over the county came there for Sunday picnics. Among these visitors was a widower named Patrick Gray, who cast an eye on the young Widow Quinn, soon proposed marriage, and carried her off to his lonely home in Thomaston.

My mother was the eldest of Mary Quinn's three children. She was ten years old when she came to the States. She attended the village school, married my father at nineteen, reared seven children, and spent all of her short life in their service. She was five feet two in height, had sparkling brown eyes that deepened to black when she was emotionally stirred. She had an olive complexion, and faced life with a warm heart and a sweet, wistful smile. When the village boys were whooping it up on the night before the Fourth of July, they knew just where to find a hearty welcome at midnight with coffee, lively talk, and laughter. She had five boys and two girls and said many times she wished they were all boys, girls were so hard to bring up. She had an excellent reading voice. There seemed to be tears in it. Her reading of Goldsmith's "Traveller" convinced me that it was a better poem than the better-known "Deserted Village." When the snow was too deep for sliding down hill she read to us, a chapter a night, Harriet Beecher Stowe's *Uncle Tom's Cabin*, and at the death of little Eva, she had every one of us in tears.

She loved flowers, had a green thumb, and rejoiced in seeing things grow. Her morning glories twined all over our piazza, and became my favorite flower. Of all the roses she planted, the pale moss rose was always her favorite. When I was seven years old she and I set out a linden tree, which after eighty years is still flourishing. She lent a gaiety to church gatherings, and at the village supper that followed the Thanksgiving hunting contest, she was proud to be the wife of an excellent shot who was usually on the winning side.

On $40 a month, with seven children to feed and clothe, she had little time and less money for the amenities of life. It was only once in every three years that she could have enough for cloth for a new dress. She rarely went the eight miles to Rockland, the city nearest to our village.

Payday with its check of $125 came four times a year. As soon as it arrived and my father had his day off from the Coast Guard station, he went by mail stage to Rockland. Reaching home at night, he was loaded down with manila rope, nails, second-hand books, shell-loading tools, and fishing tackle—some of which he could not afford to buy. Many of these items he bought at a store called H. H. Crie's. Another store he patronized was H. H. Stover's. When he came home without bringing his wife anything pretty, she would upbraid him and accuse him of running into debt at H. H. Crie's, H. H. Stover's, H. H. Dondis's, H. H. Tuttle's—and rattle off a list of H. H.'s that nobody had ever heard of. Thus between her tears one could catch the Irish sense of humor that softened the chastisement. She deserved a richer, fuller life, and I myself have wept many times thinking about her impoverished deprivation. She died at forty-six of cerebrospinal meningitis, a short time before the medical profession discovered a serum to cure that disease. This early death seemed to me to crown the hazards and discomforts that marked her life.

The second member of my mother's family, Uncle Hugh, was a wanderer over the earth. He would take a job, work for a season, get tired of it and give it up. He would come to our house, stay for a few days, and then be off again. He went to bed, I remember, in his underclothes, and they were always red and sweaty. He and mother were very fond of each other. At her prodding he would tell us about living in the forecastle of a Canadian schooner with nothing but "bully beef" to eat, or about the beauty of the Blue Ridge Mountains of Virginia where he lived one summer and got mixed up with a Southern belle. His descriptive powers were remarkable. When he told us about the majesty of Niagara Falls, we could feel the rushing of the water and hear the thunder of the great stream crashing into the gorge.

He closed his aimless career by enlisting in the American Army, and was shipped off to the Philippines to fight against the insurrection of Aguinaldo. He must have served well as he was promoted from private to corporal, but was finally killed and buried at Iloilo on the island of Panay. Along with many other American soldiers, he was laid to rest in a cemetery where cement coffins were placed in rows on top of the marshy ground.

During World War II I asked my son John, who was a pilot in the Army Air Corps based near Manila, to go to Iloilo and take a look at Uncle Hugh's grave. He located the cemetery but not his uncle's casket; in that damp climate the outer layers of the cement had crumbled and the names were not decipherable.

The third and youngest member of the family was Aunt Aggie. She had big blue eyes like her mother, a heavy mop of dark brown hair, and a sharp nose. She always wore an inquisitive look as if she were seeking something that was just eluding her. She chose me to be her favorite, and indulged me more than was good for a child. For example, if I had picked up a stray dog and no one else wanted it, she would take it in even if it were not house-broken, just for me.

She married a widower who was much older than herself and who treated her more like a child than a wife. In early life he had been a sailor and sea captain, but later had joined the Coast Guard station. Once he took his wife and myself with him on a trip to Boston on a stone sloop named the *Jenny Lind*. The first night out I slept in the forecastle and acquired both bedbugs and cockroaches. My legs were in torment. An old sailor took pity on me, filled a tub full of salt water, and made me stand in it until some of the ache had subsided. A hundred times I have remembered gratefully the kindness of that old tar.

On our arrival in Boston I made a bee line for Austin Stone's Museum, where a great checker player hidden behind a partition, and using an iron dummy to move the pieces, was ready to take on anyone willing to compete with him. At thirteen I considered myself the champion checker player of Spruce Head. The Boston champion did not scare me a bit. I had to pay twenty-five cents a game, and if I licked him I would be presented with the fabulous sum of five dollars. I tried three times and each time went down to defeat. I came back to the *Jenny Lind* and my Aunt Aggie, humiliated.

Aunt Aggie and Uncle Ernest would bring their little girl Helen to visit us every Sunday and stay all day. One Sunday I wanted Aunt Aggie to see me fly my new kite. I knew it was the Sabbath but that was the only day she could come; so I put up my kite in a lovely southwest breeze, tied the string to an apple tree, and went into the house to fetch her. She came out, looked long and hard at the kite, and admired it to my satisfaction. I was trying to untie the string from the tree when it slipped through my fingers and the kite went sailing out over the bay. I doubt if there was ever a more grief-stricken boy than I was at that hour. Even Aunt Aggie failed to comfort me. I felt certain that God was punishing me for flying my kite on Sunday, such was the Calvinistic atmosphere that overshadowed my childhood.

When a new minister came to town it was an event. One winter a little man named Reverend Moffat arrived and my Aunt Aggie headed the committee to welcome him. The chapel was decorated with flowers and the odor of the birchwood fire vied with them for fragrance. There were about fifty people present, including a dozen impatient youngsters wondering how long before the cake and ice cream would be served. Aunt Aggie had neglected everything else for two days preparing for the welcome. Meanwhile Uncle Ernest had procured a bottle of whiskey and was celebrating the occasion in his own preferred way. He stayed at home until near the end of the party, then strayed over to the doorway leading into the chapel. He looked the assembly over and recognized all but one. In a moment of silence he pointed his right hand toward the newcomer and said, in a voice that could be heard all over the room, "Who in the name of God is that?" My aunt, whose number one enemy was King Alcohol, retired to the kitchen, chagrined and humiliated.

As she grew older Aunt Aggie hated more and more the task of getting up in the morning to build a fire. No one had central heat. The cold of the winters seemed to penetrate her more deeply than the rest of us. At last she declared that her husband must leave the Coast Guard station, come to Spruce Head, and be there to start the fire on winter mornings. Her declaration came one year before her husband would be eligible to retire on half-pay. She said she could not last out another year. With great misgiving Uncle Ernest came home to stay. Those were the days before old-age pensions and unemployment insurance. All a man had was what he had saved, and only about one in a hundred put by enough to retire on. As a result, the last days of this couple were difficult. Uncle Ernest managed to get through them with the help of whiskey and the old ballads he loved to sing. One of his favorites was a bawdy song called "The Little Cabin Boy," a lad whom the captain of a ship in the China trade had taken along with him. The boy turned out to be a girl, who presented the Captain with a baby before the end of the voyage. Uncle Ernest would sing this only when there were no womenfolk at home. Another was the story of "The Princess Royal," a ship which was chased by pirates and got away. The singing seemed to go better when there was whiskey on Uncle Ernest's breath.

Meanwhile Aunt Aggie had her barn moved out by the side of the road and started a small store selling notions, dress goods, soft drinks, and candy. At first she made a success of the venture. Then another woman started a rival store, and that was too much in a small village of three hundred inhabitants. Death came to Aggie as a welcome guest. Her husband took on a night watchman's job and other chores of that nature until he, too, began to realize that "Death was the poor man's dearest friend," as Robert Burns put it, and he went to join Aunt Aggie.

On the other side of my family the name of Snow is found in New England from 1623, when Nicholas Snow came over on the *Ann* and married Constance Hopkins who had arrived on the *Mayflower*. A descendant of Nicholas named Isaac moved to Maine and settled first in Harpswell and later in Brunswick. His third son Elisha, the most colorful and interesting of my ancestors, husband of four wives and father of nineteen children, was the "founding father" of South Thomaston. There, in 1767 or soon after, he started a sawmill on the Wessaweskeag River and later a grist mill; he opened a general store, took out a license to retail liquors, and became owner of some two thousand acres of land.

When the Revolutionary War began, the town organized a Committee of Safety, with Elisha Snow as one of the nine members. But when the British won an overwhelming victory at what is now Castine and began to roam the coast with ruthless privateers, Elisha thought further resistance to England useless and sided with the Tories. When Benjamin Burton and General Peleg Wadsworth (Longfellow's grandfather), who were the leading military men of the area, were captured by the British and imprisoned at Castine, the men who carried out the mission stopped at Snow's home to find out just where the two patriots were lodging, and stopped again at his house on the way back.

Things must have been difficult for this convinced Tory when the Revolution ended; but in 1784 the Reverend Mr. Case, a dedicated minister of the Gospel, wrought a change in the life of the town and in the life of Elisha Snow. Before this date no minister had been settled, no religious society organized, and no public worship maintained. The sincerity of Mr. Case and his effective preaching brought about a big revival and succeeded in establishing a Baptist church. Among the converts were Snow's wife and four children—and above all, Elisha Snow himself, whose conviction became so strong that he felt impelled to become a preacher himself and devote his life to the ministry.

But he could not well compete in South Thomaston with his mentor Mr. Case; and besides, there were many townsfolk who hated his Toryism. So he withdrew to begin his labors as a preacher in a distant town. Some years later, when Case had departed for another parish, he returned to his old home. Then, as a local chronicler put it, he "was soon enabled, by his zeal, self-humiliation, and vehement eloquence in prayer and preaching, to gain the confidence, which he ever retained, of his townsmen and neighbors."

The Baptist society under the care of Elder Snow continued to prosper. The men of the parish in 1796–1797 built the first church in the region, a building that housed the congregation for more than a century. A religious awakening commenced under his auspices, rapidly spread, and soon became the greatest revival the region had ever experienced. Not far from 150 persons were baptized and received into the church. The prize convert to the Baptist faith was a Mr. Baker, then a Methodist minister, who was rebaptized (probably, this time, by immersion) and ordained as the colleague of Elder Snow. He did not believe in foreordination and election (i.e., salvation for a chosen few) as Snow did. A violent difference arose between them which nearly wrecked the parish. In spite of their differences Snow seems to have retained a brotherly affection and charity for his colleague, and used to pray earnestly that he might be reclaimed; using, on one occasion, the following language: "Take him, O Lord, and shake him over the pit of everlasting fire, till he shall see the error of his way; but God, *don't* let him fall in!"

So it was that Elisha Snow started the first sawmill, the first grist mill, the first grocery and liquor store, and built the first church in this region of Maine. He had enough energy and persuasiveness to live down his adherence to the British cause during the Revolutionary period, and to establish himself as a leading citizen of the town. He came within two months of living ninety-three years, and left a group of descendants—including two sons, Elisha Jr. and Isaac, who fought their country's enemies in the undeclared French war of 1799 and in the War of 1812—who, in spite of their distaste for his Tory sympathies, revere his memory.

My own grandfather, Elisha Snow IV, was the first child of the original Elisha's seventh son Isaac. He was called by many people of Rockland "the black sheep of the Snow family." He married Mary Sawtelle of Camden and by her had ten children. Soon after her death in 1858, my grandfather abandoned the children and strayed to White Head Island, where he met Elizabeth Norton, a young woman in her early twenties. Her father owned most of White Head Island, the Brown Islands, and Norton Island, which was named for him. He raised sheep and cattle and was one of the more prosperous men of the region. He and his wife were strong Baptists, rowing to the mainland every Sunday to attend a three-hour service in an unheated church at Wiley's Corner. We can imagine their feelings when they found that Elisha Snow had, as the Irish side of my family would say, "taken advantage of their daughter's innocence." We have here all the signs of a shotgun marriage. Elisha and Elizabeth stole away to Marion, Massachusetts, near the Cape, and were married there on Christmas Day, 1859. Back in Maine, a son was born on April 2, 1860. No doubt many eyebrows were raised!

As with many shotgun marriages, this one was of brief duration. The bride was thirty-four years younger than Elisha; they had little in common. When the baby was six months old, Elisha left, seeking fresh woods and pastures new. Discreditable stories hang about his name— how he got a job at the lighthouse, secretly sold part of the government supply of whale oil, and was dismissed in disgrace; how he shipped on a coasting vessel and was lost at sea. Neither of these tales is true; the fact is that, as I discovered in the Knox County records, he died in his bed in Rockland, Maine, in 1877, aged eighty years. Of course I have never heard his side of the story. One thing is certain: if it hadn't been for his misdemeanors and indiscretions, neither my father nor myself would have had a chance to experience the light of the sun and the "obscuration of the earth."

I used to question my father about my grandfather and he always put me off with no response or an unsatisfactory evasion. Not until I dug into the record for this book did I know why.

The baby, as you know by now, was my father, Forrest. He had a rough time growing up. On the first of February of 1864 his mother applied for and received a divorce and the custody of the child. Soon afterward she married Henry Metcalf, a man nearer her own age. The little boy and his stepfather did not get on well. The child was sent on long visits to various relatives. He went to school one winter at Ingraham's Hill, near Rockland, and another year he was with his maternal Aunt Annie, wife of the Reverend Greenfield Bowie, who suffered under the nickname of Green Buoy.

Young Forrest's happiest days were spent with his grandfather Norton on White Head Island. He loved to sail and as soon as he got enough money he bought a sloop named *Onaway*. Sailing off Round Pond one day, he was hit by a squall which upset his boat. She was heavily ballasted and started to sink. Luckily, he had a very sharp jackknife and cut the painter of his towboat just as the sloop was beginning to drag it under. Later, when he had boys of his own, he warned them never to go in a boat without a jackknife.

A major crisis in his life came when he was nearing fifteen. At the time he was living with his mother and stepfather on White Head. Metcalf rigged up several haddock trawls and took Forrest with him to tow, cut bait, and help with all the work. He showed his dislike of the boy by finding constant fault with whatever he did. One day Metcalf became so enraged with what he called Forrest's stupidity that he tied him to a rope, kicked him overboard, and hauled him astern the rest of the way home. By the time they arrived at the cove, Forrest had worked up some pretty hot anger of his own. He ran to the boat, took a ten-foot ash oar, struck Metcalf a heavy blow and knocked him flat. Within the hour, the boy ran away from home, walked to Tenants Harbor, and signed with Captain Will Sherer as cook on a sloop bound for the West Indies. Many times I have talked with Sherer about that trip. He told me that my father was faithful, cheerful in every sort of weather, added a note of youth and cheer to the voyage, and ultimately developed into a fine cook.

I have talked to my grandmother a great deal about Metcalf. He was an unusually strong man, and had two rows of teeth where the rest of us have one. By him she had one daughter who grew to be an unusually attractive woman. Dissatisfied with fishing life along the coast, Metcalf went to sea and became a mate on a barkentine out of Rockland. In those days large vessels carried two mates, one to carry on the regular routine of the work of the ship, and the other to maintain discipline as a "hatchet man." Metcalf was the "hatchet man" on this ship. One day he got into a dispute with a young emotional Irish sailor, who stabbed him to death with a knife. The sailors in the fore-castle stood by their buddy, picked up Metcalf, and threw him over-board. My grandmother told me that the night he was killed she had a long black umbrella standing in the corner of the living room which for no explainable reason fell out of the corner into the middle of the floor. She checked later and found out that the umbrella fell on the very hour her husband was stabbed.

The men in the forecastle of the ship vehemently asserted to the captain that Metcalf's behavior was brutal beyond all reasonable lim-its. As a result, the case was never brought to trial and it was gen-erally understood that the young Irish sailor acted in self-defense.

My grandmother lived in our home during her last days. She died in 1911, aged seventy-nine. Her tombstone stands in a small, neglected graveyard in South Thomaston. Tall grass, bushes, and even trees grow over the graves. The place is entirely surrounded by an automobile junk yard. Grandmother's stone, standing alone in the high grass, reads: "*Elizabeth Metcalf, daughter of Joseph Norton,*" not as one would expect, "*Elizabeth, wife of Henry Metcalf.*" Since her father was dead, this lettering must have been at her own request. It tells briefly the story of her life.

My father had Saxon-blue eyes, high cheek bones, and reddish brown hair. These were inherited from his Norton mother. He was about 5 feet 9 inches in height, with large shoulders and a wide breast. The top part of his body indicated enormous strength; the lower part tapered off. In fact, he was built much like the famous Australian prizefighter Bob Fitzsimmons.

I have thought much about my father since I started this book. He never had a fair chance in life. His father left the island before he was a year old. His stepfather was a brute. What schooling he had was miscellaneous and intermittent. A one-room schoolhouse at Owl's Head and another at Georgetown taught him the three R's and that's about all. I may be wrong in saying that he never had a fair chance. He was never *given* a fair chance but he seized whatever came his way. For example, he learned to handle a sextant and quadrant on his first trip to sea at fourteen. All his skills he had to learn himself, by watching others and by trial and error. With no teaching whatever he learned carpentry and could build a boat or a house. He could dig a well and stone it up. He could build a brick chimney, plaster a room, and lay up the stone walls of a cellar.

He married at eighteen and had seven children in fourteen years. He loathed the work at the Coast Guard station but stuck to it for the sake of his wife and children. At the earliest opportunity he left the year-round job at the station and became the "seventh man," the extra man taken on in the dangerous winter months. During his six months of freedom, he built sailboats and rowboats, rigged up trawls for haddock and cod, and spent long days fishing and lobstering. One year he built a craft that was half sloop, half dory, twenty feet long with two sails and a jib. With her he could sail out into the bay and set six tubs of trawl. The boat had a centerboard, could head well up to windward in a breeze, and proved herself able to weather a hurricane. Once my father and oldest brother went out and got caught in a September gale, and when night came down my mother thought they were both lost. I recall her pacing the wharf wondering what she would do if the two were drowned. The boat endured the gale and arrived at the wharf at midnight with the largest catch of haddock my father had ever brought in. I have recorded this episode in a poem entitled "Vigil."

In the long summer months my father had time to be with his boys, time to teach them how to handle a small boat in a squall, how to tie a codfish hook, to walk in the woods with a gun and to aim just ahead of a flying seabird in order to bring it down. He was a better shot than any of his boys. Not content with a 16- or 12-gauge gun, he insisted on having a 10-gauge, which we boys called his cannon. His favorite sport was hunting for seabirds on the outer ledges. We started this in October when the air was crisp and cool and kept it up until Thanksgiving and beyond.

Father was a great reader and brought home books every time he went to Rockland—books he could not afford. His taste in reading ran to biography, history, economics, and politics. He started out as a staunch Republican but toward the end of his life his mind veered toward Eugene Debs and Socialism. He regarded the dining table as the center of the home and during meals insisted on talking about politics and current events.

He was proud of his grandfather's prowess in saving a captured ship from the enemy and sailing her into the port of Machias. He admired his great-grandfather Elisha the first, even though he was a

Tory. His silence about his own father is understandable in the light of what I later dug out of the local archives. I feel that my father must have resolved to live a life that contrasted about 100 per cent with that of his old dad. He told me that he got drunk once in his life, and was horrified to find himself reduced to the level of a beast.

Although his schooling was scrappy, his religious education was taken care of by his mother, his grandfather Norton, and the Reverend Greenfield Bowie. He accepted the Puritan discipline of "Thou shalt not's" and gave his children a strict religious upbringing.

On his days off the station my father often took me on walks. On one of these I saw a sight that still haunts me—a blacksnake had succeeded in charming a song sparrow and was holding it between his jaws. Father suddenly picked up a big pasture rock and threw it so forcibly at the snake's head that the bird dropped out of the snake's mouth and flew away. The inexpressible joy that event gave me is with me yet. How I admired Dad's exact throwing arm!

On one foggy day—a day when the fog was so thick that you couldn't see twenty-five feet ahead—I was out in a boat alone catching cunners for my father's lobster bait. I was doing so well that I forgot to come home for supper. My father got worried, thought I was lost, and began searching for me. At last he found me between Burnt Island and Spruce Head, hauling up my trap and landing a boatload of fish, utterly oblivious of time. He beckoned me to come ashore, put his arm around me—a thing not done in our family—and wept with joy to find I was safe and alive. That was the first time I realized that he loved me. As I look back on it now, I realize how completely we refrained from any outward display of emotion in our relations with each other. That is the dark aspect of our New England heritage—something negative that gives a leaden restraint to our lives.

It seems to me as I review and ponder my father's life that all the finer qualities of his ancestry were embodied in him.

CHAPTER 2

Childhood at White Head and Spruce Head

Methinks an island would be the most desirable of all landed property,
for it seems like a little world by itself; and the water may answer instead of the atmosphere that surrounds planets

—Hawthorne

I LIVED on the island of White Head until I was seven, and my memories of life during those early years are still vivid. I recall a field
full of buttercups and daisies. My older brother George would put me
in a little four-wheeled cart and haul me over the field. I reached for
buttercups rather than for daisies, a choice that seemed odd to my
parents. The lowly buttercup, however, glowed brightly for me, and
I buried my face in bunches as large as my small fists could hold. Beside the house there was a balm o'Gilead tree. I knew that it was different from all the other evergreens; the odor was spicy and strong.
I crushed a tip in my hands and the fragrance, fresh and clean, lasted
until Mother washed it off.

West of our shore were three small islands, known as Brown's
Islands, connected with White Head by a "gut" where the flats were
bare at low tide. Our cow spent much of her time over on these island, believing, as humans do, that distant fields are greener, and
when she came home to be milked at sunset, the tide in this gut was
often high and the cow would have to swim. I loved to go to the
shore and watch her swim across.

After Grammy Fleming died, Uncle Mike moved in with us. He
loved children, and when he was not working on the quarries he
spent much of his time with our boys. He used to go to Rockland for
a bottle of whiskey Saturday afternoon and come home waving his
cane and singing Irish ballads. One night Mike came home late feeling especially happy. Spying our green parrot in the hallway as he en-

tered, and wanting Polly to share his joy, he filled the two feeding cups on the sides of the cage with whiskey. Next morning Polly was lying on her back, dead. That needless death sank deep and Sunday was dark all day.

Mike brought home a book one week end and promised fifty cents to the boy who first read it through. It was Henty's *Hannibal, The Carthaginian*—a tough assignment for a six-year-old. With my mother's help, I had been reading since I was three, but my vocabulary was no match for Henty's. Yet there was that shiny half-dollar! Fifty cents was an enormous amount of mony. Normally we measured out our wealth in pennies. I determined to win the prize and kept doggedly at the task, struggling with the heavy style and big words. Hannibal became to me a Robert E. Lee character, more attractive than Scipio, as Lee in our own history is personally more attractive than Grant. It took me ten days to finish the book and become joyful owner of the big round silver coin.

I recall, too, letting a new white piglet out of its pen. I watched it nosing its way along the fence, looking for a way out, and I pitied it. The pig ran for the shore, waded into the cold Maine water, and started to swim. It dug its two forefeet into its throat, tore the throat open, and began to bleed. Andrew Wiley, a neighboring lobster catcher out hauling his traps, saw it struggling in the water, took it on board, and brought it in. Before he reached our cove the pig was dead. My father scolded me, pointing out what a loss it was to the family, and would have spanked me had he not seen tears of sorrow and remorse streaming down my face. I felt like a murderer and could think of nothing but that dead pig for the whole long day.

Another island memory was the visit of about fifteen birch bark canoes, loaded with Penobscot Indians from the reservation at Old Town, sixty miles up the river. Our mother took us down to see them. They landed on a beach below our house and started to dig clams for their annual clambake. The chief's canoe had a beautiful red rug spread on the floor and a big stuffed Arctic owl fastened to the bow. To me the sight was breathtaking. The Indians dug three or four bushels of clams. On the coals of a huge driftwood fire they piled rockweed, then clams, and then rockweed to cover. The clams were steamed rather than baked and had a smoky flavor. I wondered how those Indians knew that our shore had the best clamming beach in this entire region. My admiration was mixed with fear, for I had heard that Indians stole white children and carried them off to their wigwams. When one of the Indian girls tried to make friends with me, I backed off and would not let her get near me, to the amusement of a number of young Indian boys. We stayed at the beach not more than a half-hour, but the dark-skinned Indians, their canoes—the first I had ever seen—and the mountain of steamed clams made a strange and never-to-be forgotten picture.

Another memory was the wreck of the *Ella F. Bartlett,* a schooner that dragged her anchors and piled up on the northeast end of Hay Island, just north of White Head. The schooner was thrown up high and dry. The Coast Guard men rescued the captain and his crew and lodged them in a government boathouse on the White Head shore about three hundred yards from our house. They stayed perhaps ten days. To me they were all heroes, although to others they probably were just the "bilge water of the ship of state." They made me want to be a sailor when I grew up. I visited them morning, noon, and night. One sailor took a shine to me and gave me my first work of art. He took a wooden box that measured about fifteen inches by ten and glued to its surface small pieces of hard wood of various shapes, colors, and sizes, fitting them neatly together. He was an expert with a jackknife and succeeded in making this wooden box a thing of beauty. My admiration for his handiwork was so intense that he gave it to me. No other present up to that time impressed me like this. It was my treasure chest; in it I put my choicest belongings; around it my imagination built many sea stories. When I left the island at seven for the mainland, I saw to it that my precious box was not left behind.

Lodged in my mind is a picture of my father as he looked on a cold winter night. Like all the other Coast Guardsmen he had to stand watch and punch the clock. The clocks were carried on the men's shoulders. The keys used to punch them were chained to hardwood posts, one on each side of the island. The watches were of four hours each, and the clocks had to be punched once an hour. They were examined by the captain the following morning, to see that each one had been punched on time. On the 4:00 to 8:00 P.M. watch, my father would drop in to see the family between punches. On a zero night when snow was falling and the wind blowing, his moustache was covered with little icicles, his hat was white with sleet and snow, and his cheeks were bright red. He was all in all a new version of Santa Claus—a Santa much more vigorous and purposeful than the jolly one of Clement Moore's creation. In this terrible weather he had to be more alert than usual, for these were the nights when the lime coasters, the lumber carriers, and other vessels were in danger of coming ashore and breaking up on the ledges.

More enduring than all these impressions was my awareness of the sea. It enveloped the island and enveloped me. Its music reached my inner as well as my outer ear. Even now, when I am away from it, my dreams bring it back. It is my natural element. I feel more at home there than on land. It is not only the biggest thing, it is the greatest thing on the planet; and once it grips you there is no leaving it for long. As I later wrote:

> It thundered on my inner ear at birth
> And was the tuning fork my ancestry
> For countless generations had obeyed
> To pitch their song of life to, when in need.

In my seventh year, when there were six children in my family, four of whom needed schooling, we moved from the island to Spruce Head village. For five hundred dollars my father sold the island house that he had built and the five acres of land deeded to him by his grandfather. On a half-acre lot near the chapel he built a new house with six rooms, a cellar, a low attic, and a piazza. Until we grew up and went away, this was home. One other child was born here, making seven in all. My father continued to work at the Coast Guard station on the island, a post he hated but could not afford to leave. The salary was $40 a month, and living on $40 a month was a task that tried my mother's soul. But we had a cow that gave us butter and milk, and a pig for winter meat. We had hens, good layers, black Wyandottes at that. In summer we could catch fish and pick berries of all kinds—blueberries, huckleberries, wild strawberries, raspberries, and blackberries. There were also gooseberries (my mother's favorite) and wild plums. In winter we dug clams and hunted rabbits. For fuel we cut wood on shares in neighboring wood lots, one cord for the owner and one for us. We could pay part of our taxes by shoveling snow on the town roads. But with all that we felt ourselves exceedingly poor. We lacked money.

Our house, with ten in the family, was too small for comfortable living. Upstairs were three bedrooms. In the smallest the two oldest boys shared a double bed. In another room was a double bed for three boys and a cot for Uncle Mike. In the largest room stood two double beds, one for my parents and one for the two girls. My father was at home only during the day on his weekly day off. After the noon meal, Father and Mother would retire to her room "for a nap," they said. If the weather permitted we were encouraged to go outside, "not to disturb them."

Father was paid quarterly and the money never lasted until the next payday. The last few weeks my mother would skimp along, borrowing a little here and there from neighbors. Cardboard soles in our shoes kept our feet off the ground; if a patch gave way another patch covered it; aching teeth were pulled; haircuts were taken care of by my father. Yet my sister Cora, the youngest of us, has no recollection of living in poverty. We were never really hungry, and since nearly all the village was in the same boat, there was no sharp contrast to arouse dissatisfaction.

Our diet through the winter was far from balanced. We had no fresh fruit or green vegetables. The staff of life was fish and potatoes. The dried, salted fish was freshened by simmering in water several hours. Salt pork was cut into small cubes and "tried out." The crisp brown cubes and the fat were poured over the fish and boiled potatoes. Day after day this was our food. Anyone who complained was silenced with this:

> Fish and potatoes
> The fat of the land,
> If you can't eat that,
> You can starve and be damned.

George, the oldest, who always sat next to mother, was not rugged like the others. He would not go swimming with us; the water was too cold. One winter morning, cutting bait for my father's trawls, he fainted and had to be carried into the house. Dr. Horne came, put a stethoscope on his chest, and told mother she must face up to the fact that George would not be with us long. (He lived eighty-nine years.)

Frank was the rugged one. At eight he could handle a pair of ash oars almost as well as my father. He was a thoroughgoing extrovert who loved a fight. He was a handsome child, the one that people noticed and admired. (In this listing of sons, I followed Frank.)

Hugh was the runt of the family, but made up for his small size by the extraordinary skill of his hands with tools and machines. His was a gentle, unselfish nature.

Maynard, the youngest boy, was the most cheerful member of the family. He greeted each new day with enthusiastic optimism. Whatever went wrong yesterday was sure to go right today. He was a born salesman. If we had any old guns, shell-loading machines, or other articles we wanted to get rid of, Maynard could persuade a buyer that the article was worth a good price and sincerely believe every word he said.

Mary Agnes, the older sister, had her father's blue eyes and her mother's dark hair. She inherited her father's toughness of character. Her Irish grandmother, for whom she was named, said of her when she was a young lady, "She could be trusted in a barracks." She was an excellent reader and used to go around reading to old crippled, house-bound women. How they sang her praises!

Cora, the youngest, had both the blue eyes and light hair of her father. She had a full realization that she was the baby of the family and was entitled to special privileges. She was a sweet attractive child and my special pet.

The schooling in the village was meager. There was a one-room schoolhouse with woodshed and privies in back and only one teacher to handle about forty-eight youngsters. On the first day in school my brothers and I, as newcomers, were obliged to engage in a fight. That was the initiation. The older boys saw to it that a seven-year-old like myself was pitted against another of his same age and height. After a few blows in imitation of John L. Sullivan we threw ourselves into each other's arms and became friends. Three seven-week terms were all the village could afford. The teacher was paid from seven to ten dollars a week. She was "boarded round" at various houses in addition to her salary.

My first teacher was Abigail Walters, who was stout, jolly, and good-natured toward her pupils who in those days were called "scholars," forty-eight "scholars" aged five to fifteen! We were happy with her, but she was attracted to a young widower in town, Peter Aagerson, an easy-going intelligent Dane, the boss in a stone quarry, and after one term of teaching she married him and became one of the important ladies in the village.

My second teacher was a Mrs. Whalen, whose name fitted her conception of her major duty. One day when she left the room, I stood behind her desk, aping her voice and words and brandishing her ruler. Returning quickly, she heard my mockery, seized the ruler, and struck me down to the floor. I was knocked out for a moment but soon recovered and apologized. She too married, reared a large family, and died at the age of ninety-nine.

Another teacher was Hattie Walters, a dedicated woman. She urged many of us to go on with our education, even if we had to leave Spruce Head. The seed, for the most part, fell on barren ground, but her ambition for our advancement was so fervent, so sincere that we all loved her. She was stricken with consumption and died in her early thirties.

Our next was a man, Ralph Wiggin, and he brought something new to the village schoolhouse, two pairs of boxing gloves. After four o'clock he gave the older boys lessons in the "manly art of self-defense." Inasmuch as our one major contact with the great outside world was our interest in prizefighting, this was a welcome innovation.

We liked Wiggin so much that we were sorry when he was out-fought by Ed Cowing, who had been a professional boxer in his youth, and, it was rumored, had had the gloves on with our number one hero of the prize ring, John L. Sullivan. He heard of Wiggin's boxing gloves, and shortly after four o'clock one day he showed up at the schoolhouse and proceeded to put on the gloves with our popular young teacher. No boxers of the prize ring ever had a more attentive audience. The two men squared away between our school desks and the potbellied stove. The bout was shortlived. After a few preliminary movements, Cowing landed a haymaker on Wiggin's nose. The blood began to spurt and the bout was over.

Our next teacher, Mary B. Grant, sister of the White Head light-house keeper, was an educational innovator. She was old and gray, but her sparkling brown eyes and her cheery smile showed her to be very much alive. She was a graduate of Castine Normal School, a de-voted teacher who looked upon educating the young as her country's most important function. She saw clearly that eight grades reciting separately in reading, writing, spelling, arithmetic, history, and ge-ography would require forty-eight periods each day with only five minutes for each class. This was folly. She organized the school into three groups plus the beginners. This meant that twelve-year-olds re-cited with ten-year-olds and seven-years-olds with nine, etc. Under this system, she could devote at least fifteen minutes to each class.

Since the classes were small, the work could be handled. The new program drew moans and groans from those students who had to step down, but their groans were offset by the glee of those in the lower echelons who were raised up a notch. It was a humiliating experience for some of the older students, but they soon saw the advantage of the longer recitation periods.

We had one more man teacher, Ralph Hanscom, the son of a Methodist minister. He had run out of money, left college, and was working for the wherewithal that would help him get back. His "morning exercises" (Bible reading and prayer) were longer than usual. He picked out the dramatic stories of the King James Version of the Old Testament and read them well. After this, we all repeated together the Lord's Prayer. Hanscom was the only teacher I recall who could make these morning exercises exciting. Instinctively interested in the humanities, he loved poetry and painting, and he hung on the walls of the schoolroom reproductions of paintings by Rembrandt, Raphael, Rubens, and Titian—inferior prints given in exchange for Star Soap wrappers, but they were a revelation to us. He set us all to drawing and hung on the schoolroom walls the sketches he liked best. One morning I saw that he had pinned up one of mine—a pencil drawing of a squirrel on a fallen tree in the woods. I was so pleased with his favorable comments that I resolved to be an artist when I grew up, an artist like Titian, no less! He made me want to visit art galleries and see the originals of these masterpieces. To this teacher I probably owe my habit of visiting art galleries in whatever city I happen to be.

Recess was a happy time. The boys lined up in two teams, one on each side of the schoolhouse, and played a game called "haley over." A ball was thrown from one side of the schoolhouse over the roof and caught by a boy on the other side. The receivers could not see the ball as it was thrown and never knew over what part of the roof it would appear. It was a desperately exciting game.

On each Friday afternoon to close out the week there was a more serious game—a spelling match. Two older pupils—a boy and a girl, both good spellers—acted as captains and alternately chose the members of their teams. Each tried to secure the best spellers. The teacher at first would start with easy words and move quickly on to those more difficult. If one missed, he was transferred to the opposing team. After twenty minutes the rules changed for the "spell-down." Now if you missed you had to go back to your seat. As the half-hour period drew

to a close, big words like "embarrassment" were chosen and the casual-
ties were heavy. A few superior spellers would hang on, the words
growing harder and harder until a word like "renaissance" floored
everybody but one. He was declared the winner.

One afternoon when all but two boys, one on each side, had fallen
by the wayside, the word offered was *"hospice."* The boy who had
to spell this word was the son of a livery stable keeper. "Hospice" to
him meant only one thing, pronounced in Maine style. He hesitated,
blushed, shuffled his feet, started with *h-o-s-s* when roars of laughter
cut him off and he sank into his seat. Village memories are long. Years
later a friend got a rough tumbling by asking him, "Joey, how do you
spell *hospice?*"

The girls seemed to enjoy their lessons. Most boys passed the time
as easily as possible. The larger boys, models for us youngsters, would
often take a paper-covered "dime novel" such as *Kit Carson* or *The
Hairy Man of the Demon's Den* and fit it into the middle of their ge-
ographies, pretending that they were studying the sources of the
Amazon River or the capitals of Europe. Other boys might spend the
time drawing a man in a dory aiming a gun at a flock of coots flying
past. At fourteen, most of these boys had had enough of schooling
and went to work lugging drills on the quarry, working in the boarding houses, peddling papers, or bringing together a string of lobster
pots for the sheddering season. They found school dull, the lessons
hard, and even the leisure time uninteresting. If a teacher had put any
gaiety in the school program, she would have been suspect.

When the *Abbie S. Walker* came in to the Spruce Head wharf, the
boys were there. The Negro sailors, the captain inspecting the water
barrels on deck, the horses hauling the loaded dumpcarts to the end
of the wharf, the noise of the tumbling granite as the bodies of the
carts were raised and the load dumped, the shriller noise as the blocks
struck the steel-lined dump chutes, thrown in by the men who counted
aloud as they threw—all this, combined with the yodeling of sea gulls
a hundred yards off shore, made a pageant that no red-blooded boy
would want to miss. Add to this the growling commentaries of the old
men who had been to sea on square-riggers and who despised fore-
and-afters. I heard one old sailor declare vehemently that he would
rather be hanged on board a square-rigger than die a natural death on
board a fore-and-after!

When all this happened during school hours, the older boys instinctively felt that there was more education outside than within four walls and a ceiling, and would slip away to the wharf at recess. They expected that the palms of their hands would be cut hard by a ruler when they returned, but they took the risk, and after school ran back to the wharf to get another glimpse of the big three-master and accept her standing invitation to climb the shrouds to her masthead.

Another part of my early education came from our second Bible —*The Maine Farmer's Almanac*. There I learned about "fates, destinies, odd sayings, the Sisters Three and such branches of learnings," as Shakespeare once expressed it. In the *Almanac* we learned all about the quarterly changes of the moon. In miserable weather we did not look for relief until the moon had entered upon a new phase. This the *Almanac* promised, and it was usually right. In winter when the *Almanac* said, "Heavy snow should be expected about this time," the notice gave several days leeway in order that the prognosticator might not lose his shirt. Our *Almanac* studies forced us to learn the signs of the zodiac in order that we might know under what constellations we were born. My father reinforced this knowledge by teaching us this:

> The Ram, the Bull, the Heavenly Twins
> And next the Crab, the Lion shines,
> The Virgin and the Scales;
> The Scorpion, Archer, and Sea Goat,
> The man that bears the Watering Pot,
> And the Fish with glittering tails.

Although I cannot remember one of the pious rhymes I learned when I "spoke pieces" at Sunday School celebrations, I find myself able to recall this poetic monster perfectly. And of course we all had to know "Thirty days hath September" and "Red sun at night" and other such weather rhymes.

Almanac readers as a rule have little faith in scientific reports from the weather bureau. These are people who observe whether the wild geese go south early in the fall or later; who notice whether the fur of the foxes is thicker than usual in any given year. They take notice of the changes in the Gulf Stream and in sun spots, in the courses of tides and the position of the stars, but cast grave doubts on the reports of the U. S. Weather Bureau, noting with pleasure every time they go wrong.

Sex education was picked up at odd times around the village. A group we called the "Unbelievers," who were skeptical about religion or too lazy to shave and change their clothes, spent Sunday afternoon loafing on settees beside an old abandoned livery stable. It was a strange place for a sensitive boy to learn "the facts of life," but that was my school. My father was too modest or too Puritanical to bring up such matters at home. I recall a tin peddlar who had just been married, and the needling that went on the following Sunday. They asked how he enjoyed his first honeymoon night. His reply, "I didn't know it went so slarnting," brought guffaws from the crowd. Some of the young men hesitated to acquaint the young boys with sex, but a few went out of their way to shock us. The shocking was not too successful, for half of the time we did not know what they were talking about. Every now and then phrases such as "polite as a whore at a christening," spoken in a rich Irish brogue, had the effect of poetry. Today boys of twelve know more about "the facts of life" than I did at sixteen. My major interest as a boy was in the tall tales of hunting, fishing, and hairbreadth escapes of young men in their late teens out sailing in squally northwest breezes. But there was a strong Freudian element in the village as I look back on it, much of which escaped me. Such lines as "Ambrose in the bushes hid / To see what Joe Mackellar did" appealed to me as a rather jolly couplet, and that's about all. When two of the old "sisters" at prayer meeting sang with eyes closed and beatific expressions on their faces such a stanza as:

> Perfect submission, perfect delight
> Visions of rapture now burst on my sight
> Angels descending bring from above
> Echoes of mercy, whispers of love

they seemed to be getting a very special joy out of the old hymn. Looking back, it strikes me now that these old ladies were remembering trips to the woods or the blueberry fields with boys eager and ready for love.

Boys with work to do have less time than others for mischief. After school meant home chores for the Snow boys. Because he had many sons to do the work and cordwood was an expensive item, our father bought stumpage very cheaply and sent us into the woods to cut it. The stumpage which he bought for as little as $6 a half-acre was mostly green alders, with here and there a birch or rock maple. We chopped it all down, had it hauled out by a neighbor who owned a horse and woodsled. To me this was an exciting experience. One does not feel cold in winter woods when the sun is shining. The fra-

grance of green boughs, the singing chickadees and the brilliant blue
jays, the crisp wholesome winter air, the sounds of other woodchop-
pers nearby—all this was enough to make me want to be a woodchopper for the rest of my life. There is no better exercise, no work more
healthy. By always having a fireplace in my home I have managed to
keep a sawhorse and a chopping block busy in the back yard and have
seen to it that my children and grandchildren know and meet the
challenge of a wood pile.

On my first assignment in the woodlot I experimented with a
cigar. It made me first dizzy, then sick unto death. I stumbled home
and told my mother what I had done. She tucked me into bed and
brought me a cup of tea in a little white and gold cup that she used
in such emergencies. In a few hours I was myself again.

To improve house heating, my mother put green alders into the
kitchen oven at night and baked them dry. The next morning they
gave the kitchen a quick warming start. Their peculiar fragrance filled
the house.

Each week on his day off, just before he left for the station in the
afternoon, my father would write out and paste up in the kitchen the
names of those who were to do the chores. One of the three older boys
had to lug in wood and keep the woodbox full; one had to fetch water
from the well and keep two pails from going dry; one had to feed the
hens and fetch in the eggs. The following week these tasks would be
assigned in a different order. The woodbox task was the hardest, for
that job included sawing four-foot pieces of spruce and birch and
alder into stove lengths before bringing them in. Our bucksaw always
seemed to be dull, although we poured porpoise oil on the blade
every day to make it slip more easily through the wood. We wasted
the rare oil shamelessly, but what we really needed was a modern
bow saw with an improved Swedish cutting blade.

Another hard task my boyhood knew was turning the grindstone
when father wanted to sharpen a scythe. He would first pour water on
the stone and then with one hand on each end of the blade he would
press down and down, harder and harder. I turned the wheel with
all the strength I could command, and he kept on pressing down until
finally he brought me to a halt. "Haven't you got more strength than
that?" I would feel ashamed, change hands, and start turning the
wheel once more. He poured on water and pressed the blade on the
stone again, harder and harder until I was again brought to a halt. I
thought it would never, never end.

But this hardship had compensations. A few minutes later I breathed in the fragrance of the grass as he laid it low. I loved the sound of the blade of the scythe, expertly whetted by my father. "Magic casements opening on the foam" were mine as I watched him cut down the daisies, buttercups, and clover, listened to the song-birds at their morning chorus and to the old ocean making its daily assault on the shore.

Work was no hardship when it was done for someone outside the family and meant a little cash in the pocket. When I was eleven Silas Hall, who kept the village livery stable, hired me to take care of his three horses. He said he was getting too old to climb up in the loft and pitch down hay, open the crocus bags and deal out the corn and oats, too old to curry and harness the horses, at least during the win-ter. He offered me a dollar and a quarter a month to clean the stable and feed the animals every day, Sunday included. I also had to keep them properly groomed for people who might want to hire a horse and buggy for a trip to Rockland. Every now and then a man drove down from the city with a rig of his own. He usually had business with the company store on the island. I would go with him to the ferry, drive his horse back to my stable and in the afternoon drive down and fetch him. I sometimes had difficulty handling these strange horses! Once in a while for this service I was tipped ten cents or even a quarter. I wish I could say that I gave this money to my mother, but I am afraid Fronie Hall's candy counter got it!

Through this terribly underpaid labor I learned to know and love horses. Whenever I had a chance to go to Rockland I went down to Berry Brothers stable to look at the thoroughbreds and racehorses one could always find there. Later, when I entered World War I, I saw to it that I was assigned to a horse-drawn artillery outfit, know-ing well that working with horses would relieve the monotony of army life.

One of the greatest experiences of my early years was my awaken-ing to poetry. In the attic of our home there was a book entitled *Swin-ton's Sixth Reader*. Unlike the earlier readers, largely of prose, this presented a group of American poets, arranged with a biographical sketch, followed by poems. The book included Bryant, Poe, Emerson, Longfellow, Whittier, and Lowell. I used to go to the attic on rainy days and read the poems aloud. Poe's *Ulalume* lifted me out of Spruce Head and landed me on the banks of the "dark tarn of Auber." Whit-tier's *Snow Bound* brought me into a world where falling snow makes the whole world a planet of beauty. The first four lines of Emerson's *Concord Hymn* and the last stanza of Longfellow's *Building of the Ship* intensified my love for my native land. I found the world of poetry so enthralling that I began to look upon "the cool element of prose" as a second-best dwelling place for the spirit. I even resolved to write some poems of my own, and have been carrying out that resolve all the rest of my life. I was hooked.

I have an idea that country children learned more out of school than in. The seacoast village was our school, for the world beyond interested us only on the occasion of prizefights and murder trials. Of these we mastered every detail.

Two murder trials occupied the minds of New England during my childhood, and both left indelible impressions. The Lizzie Borden trial brought neighbors nightly to our home for discussions that ran on and on and on. The *Boston Globe* covered the case in depth, and that was the one daily paper the village knew. The picture of Lizzie walking up the aisle of the courtroom with the pastor of her church on one arm and the superintendent of the Sunday School on the other was dramatic. Some in our living room scoffed at this picture; others viewed it with reverential awe. My father insisted that the children should be spared the gory details of the murder, and on these nights sent us off to bed earlier than usual. We went up to bed but instead of crawling under the warm woolen blankets we all sat in the dark on the frigidly cold front stairs and listened to the talk. The cold penetrated our bones and set our teeth chattering, but the awesome details excited our brains, and though we shivered, we were determined to hear it all.

Another murder occurred on the barkentine *Herbert Fuller*. Captain Nash, his wife, and the second mate were brutally murdered with an axe one night in the after cabin while the ship was sailing with an eight-knot breeze in the mid-Atlantic. Suspicion fell on Thomas Bram, the first mate, who may have intended to take over the ship and sell her and her cargo to Cuban insurgents. He was bound over by the grand jury. Suspicion also fell on Charlie Brown, the man at the wheel when the murders were committed. Brown, as a very young man in the Netherlands, had gone out of his head for two weeks and fired a gun through a window at an imaginary enemy. The Knox County defense lawyers for Bram laid heavy stress on Brown's mental history and possible guilt. All this happened in December, when the nights were long and seacoast people were more than normally willing to sit late and talk. One critical issue centered on whether the man at the wheel would have had time to leave his post, descend into the after cabin, murder three people, and get back before the ship luffed up into the wind. This would take about eight mintues at least. Some ship captains who testified on this crucial point were people we knew, people whose ships often anchored in our own harbor, therefore the trial was about people and places familiar to us. In both trials of this case—and there were two, one in Canada and one in Boston—Charlie Brown was exonerated and Bram found guilty of murder in the first degree.

Still another murder stirred the village more than these, for it happened right in our own back yard. In the police records it stands described as an accidental death, but the whole village called it murder.

The "guilty" man was Fred Rackliffe, probably the most remarkable man among us. He knew birds, animals, and fish—better, the secretary of the Maine Natural History Society once told me, than any member of the Audubon Society. He was very skillful in stuffing and mounting birds and animals, making them appear alive. In the stuffing process he learned to take arsenic and became an addict. This drug may have dulled his moral sense. He lived among us; we used his skills, but somehow no one really liked him. He had no close friends. He managed to get himself a wife, Aunt Cyn Norton's sister, and went with her one evening through the woods to visit her sister. On the way back his gun went off and she was instantly killed. The news spread rapidly. The next day hundreds from all over the county traveled through March mud on winding roads to Rackliffe's secluded home. He led them to the scene, showed them where a fallen tree stretched across the path, told them that he put his gun down to help his wife over and when he picked it up, it accidentally went off and put a charge of buckshot through her heart and lungs.

Late that afternoon the coroner, Dr. Judkins, stood on the steps of the house and addressed the crowd: "If any of you folks have any suspicion of foul play in this case, speak now." He paused. No answer. "Again I say, if any of you can shed any light on how this death occurred, the time to speak up is now. The Grand Jury will listen to any evidence you can bring in." There was a long, dramatic silence. No one spoke out.

In their hearts the people, knowing Fred, felt more than suspicion. They believed with certainty that he had deliberately shot his wife. Why was he carrying a loaded gun in the woods at night? But there was no proof, and the thought of testifying before a grand jury was frightening. Ten days later the neighbors hung on his doorknob a round-robin note which read: "You are hereby commanded to get out. If you don't we'll strip you of your gear and make your life miserable in every way we can." He heeded the message and disappeared.

Some years later he returned with another wife and set up housekeeping in an upstairs apartment. One night he asked her to go downstairs and bring up some article he had forgotten. She tripped over a codline stretched across the top stair and fell headlong to the bottom. She died a few days later. Who tied the codline across the stair?

It is amazing how this Bluebeard got himself another wife, but he did. After living with her a while, he pleaded poverty and got her admitted to the poor farm. After that, he lived alone in an old scow drawn up on the beach near our summer camp. One day he sold me some lobsters and said, "Wilbert, don't tell anyone that you are paying me money. The town will make me take my wife home. I'm shed of her now and I want to stay shed!"

As I have already said, prizefighting was our number one interest in the outside world. The grownups looked upon John L. Sullivan as the greatest fighter who ever lived. He held the heavyweight championship for ten years, and when Corbett defeated him, they all thought it was because he had been drugged or was the victim of some other foul play. This group knew all about the ring generalship, solar plexus punches, boxing skill, and all the details of the prize ring. In these matters they were experts and handed down all their knowledge to the younger generation. We could not wait for the *Boston Globe* the day following a heavyweight bout. We kept Aunt Sophronia in her store late in the evening until the result of every heavyweight championship bout came over her telephone, the only one in the village. In no other field were the grownup people of Spruce Head so well versed.

Our sixty-odd families lived in story-and-a-half frame cottages built fairly close to the street. There was a mixture of nationalities—Scotch, Irish, swamp Yankees, Scandinavians, and a few Danes tossed out after the Schleswig-Holstein upheaval—these comprised our village. Of Jews there was none. The first Negroes I ever saw were sailors on the *Abbie S. Walker*.

Most of the villagers enjoyed gathering at the store, the dance hall, and the church, and a great deal of visting went on from house to house. Occasionally we found we harbored an oddball, a loner. One of these was Rube Wiley, who shipped as a sailor at fourteen, went to Boston, and joined the crew of a Marblehead racing yacht. In one of the races, Rube's yacht was lagging behind. This worried him. He finally got up courage to go aft and tell the captain what the matter was and how it could be remedied. His earnestness was so convincing the captain let him take charge. He ordered the ballast moved forward and the sails trimmed to his liking. The yacht picked up speed and crossed the line a winner. The owner was delighted and offered Rube a hundred dollars a month as a master mate, but Rube said "No!" and came home. News of this excited and exasperated the village. My father asked him why he turned down such a wonderful offer. He replied, "I want to keep my independence. I don't take no orders from no one." Thereafter he lived in a Friendship sloop anchored in Emery's channel, and became a nautical hermit. He would eat enough for four men at one meal, and then go three or four days without eating at all. He seemed rugged and healthy, a bit too corpulent perhaps, but strangely alone. He caught enough lobsters to meet his needs. He kept his Friendship sloop in perfect condition; she was his wife and family, but he never combed his hair or changed his clothes, and conversed only with those whom he had known as boys. One day there was no smoke coming from his cabin's chimney; a neighbor went aboard and found him stretched out dead.

Three years before we moved to the village, the people had felt the need of religion, banded together, and built a Union Chapel. It was to be used by all religious denominations, but after one Mass the Catholic Bishop of Maine forbade the Rockland priest to come again. (John XXIII had not yet arrived.) So our chapel became Protestant, although Catholics attended, and the Methodist and Baptist ministers from St. George and South Thomaston took over on alternate Sundays.

Theological disputes were common. We wrestled with the problem of free will and determinism as though we were professional philosophers. A "remnant" held meetings in the chapel twice a week, but the majority of the population stayed away. In March, after the long winter, when tempers were pretty much on edge and people who had been living too close together arrived at the stage of hating one another, traveling preachers appeared and conducted services every night for two or three or even four weeks. These revivalists interested everyone in the village and attracted people from places far off in the woods. The revival hymns used by Sankey and Moody were sung by all, whether they could carry a tune or not. Each service was divided into three parts. The first was a sermon on some text like "Prepare to meet thy God," in which the preacher made us feel that Death was just around the corner, and that we should "get right with God and do it now." After the preacher was through, individuals in the audience testified to the faith, and then sinners were called to come forward and be saved. While penitents were gathering at the altar, the preacher would start up the old hymn, "Just as I Am Without One Plea" in a subdued tone and the verses would be taken up by the believers and repeated over and over. It was a deeply emotional hour. Enthusiastic helpers urged sinners to repent. I heard one old sister talking to Simon Harrington, a farmer from the backwoods, pleading with him to come forward and be saved. His firm reply, "Aunt Nancy, I'm *past redemption!*" had a terrible effect on me. I felt I was looking into the eyes of a lost soul. Only a Dante could express my terror.

These revivals were the great religious events of my childhood, and I regret to be obliged to record the human failings that often crept into them. One spring, two men arrived out of nowhere and opened our chapel for nightly services. One preached the Word and the other sang hymns. The singer (we learned later) was a common sailor named Collins who had shipped on board two-masted lime-carriers. As he approached middle life, he found living in the cold forecastle in winter a bit too rough, so he joined up with the preacher. He had an attractive tenor voice and stressed sentimental hymns such as "Where Is My Wandering Boy Tonight" and "The Ninety and Nine." His companion was a man who called himself DeMerit, a name which fitted him perfectly. In his very recent secular life, he had been a horse-jockey and auctioneer. He had a very good speaking voice, read the Scriptures well, and knew how to hold the attention of an audience. At these meetings he wore a long black Prince Albert coat obtained from some auction he had presided over or from some second-hand clothing store. Collins also wore a long black coat and a black bow tie. This garb persuaded us that they were men "of the cloth," which for the time being they were. Both men kept straight faces as they nightly reminded us that Death is no respecter of persons. They passed the contribution box and exhorted us all to come forward and be saved. Collins, weeks later, boasted to my older brother that he had come out of that revival with a bag of coins worth at least fifty dollars, enough to keep him through the summer.

Another revivalist I recall was Linendoll (sinners called him "Linen-drawers"), a soft-spoken ladies'-man type who apparently spent his life avoiding hardships. He took over the best bedroom in one of the leading homes in town and of course had his board and room free. This procedure was taken for granted at all these revivals. One night when it was 13 degrees above zero, the wind was piercing and blew gusts of snow between the house and the outhouse two hundred yards below in the field. In the night the preacher felt an urgent call of nature, grabbed out of a bureau drawer a large silk stocking belonging to his hostess, used it as a dumping ground, and shoved it under the bed. He neglected to dispose of it before leaving town. The lady of the house, embittered by this foul act, was unable to keep it from the neighbors who rocked with laughter when they heard it. The village skeptics had an unexpected chance to say, "I told you so."

We knew the preacher spoke the truth when he warned, "Death is just around the corner"—for death by drowning on our seacoast occurred altogether too often. I recall father's sudden return home one morning after he had tried in vain to resuscitate two men who had fallen from their boat. There was, in those days, no bridge between the mainland and Spruce Head Island. Rather than wait to be ferried over in a rowboat and then walk a mile to the quarries on the farther side of the island, many workers sailed over in the morning and back at night. It added pleasure to the long day. Two men, William Waldron and his son, had reached the island cove in their wherry; the son went forward to furl the sail; the boat tipped over, and the two men were drowned.

Ellis Maker's son Herbert, and a partner of his named Smith, were camping and lobstering on a Mussel Ridge island three miles away. One evening, sailing home after a trip to the mainland grocery store, they were struck by a squall and thrown into the water. Herbert was drowned, but air had caught under Smith's oilskin blouse and kept him afloat until the Coast Guard arrived and rescued him.

Two glassblowers, a man and wife, came to town and put on a show every night for nearly two weeks. Each evening people were admitted to the hall without charge. The man gave a short talk on the art of blowing glass and then the two of them blew lovely patterns for us to admire and purchase. Their charges were small and they did a thriving business. On the second Sunday of their visit they wanted to go sailing, and Ben Burton, a teen-age stripling, said he would take them in his small catboat. It was a windy Sunday. Ben was a novice at sailing. The wind, northwest, was punctuated with squalls, which were dangerous to a boy who did not know when to let off the sheet and turn his bow into the wind. About two hundred yards off Long Point, the catboat was struck by a squall and tipped over. Ben clung to the boat as he had been taught to do and was rescued by the Coast Guard. The glassblower took his wife upon his back and swam for shore. He almost made it. Within twenty yards of the beach, the man's heart gave out, and the two of them drowned.

The world I was brought up in was a man's world. Women were considered a necessary burden on a man's life. As one man put it, "A dog is a man's natural companion, a woman is a man's unnatural companion." At the very time that most American men were treating their women too much like the "cat that was killed with kindness," the men of Spruce Head were fashioning their lives in the true 18th-century British style of masculine domination. Not one woman played in the Spruce Head band; not one was a member of the Gun Club or took part in our joyous Thanksgiving shoots; not one went swimming with the boys except occasionally my sister Cora. Not a woman took part in sloop-boat races—the climax of our Fourth of July celebration. The women prepared the dinners on these gala occasions and probably got some pleasure out of their culinary masterpieces, but their role was largely that of cook and servant. I look back with shame on the way the women of our village were treated. If a man were caught helping his wife with housework he was looked down upon as a weakling, "a damned sissy!"

The people had marital troubles enough but divorce was practically unknown. It was too expensive. A man, fed up with a shrew, might put an ad in the local paper, "I hereby give notice that from this date I will no longer be responsible for any bills contracted by my wife," then flee to the woods and hole up in some buddy's shack. There were some unusual cases, as for example, the man who was allergic to sea air and became a woodchopper in Maine's north woods while his wife, who was allergic to inland air, spent her days with her sister, the lightkeeper's wife, on White Head Island.

One morning as I was walking to the post office, a woman chased her husband out of the house and threw the coal hod after him. (She probably had been compelled to lug the coal in herself and had had "enough.") He escaped the coal hod but met up with a neighbor who asked what the commotion was all about. He replied, "Me and the old woman have been having *words.*"

The women weren't entirely downtrodden and without resources. Now and then one would catch and hold our attention. The postmistress and keeper of the village store was an old maid named Sophronia Hall. The second story was a hall which was rented for parties and dances. She knew the financial standing of everybody in town. Her telephone had no booth for privacy and she listened to all the conversations. When a new contract came for building a Portsmouth dry dock or a Chicago post office out of Spruce Head granite, she was the first to get the news and spread it. She bobbed her hair forty years before that custom became the vogue. She smoked a pipe in her dark back office when smoking by women was not considered respectable. She would wait for the town fathers to gather around the stove after the evening meal and light up their pipes. As soon as their smoke had filled the room sufficiently, she would light up, thinking that a little more smoke would not be noticed. No one was deceived.

"Fronie," as we called her, was a woman of violent moods. "Manic depressive" may have described her, but we had not heard the term. When her good mood was on, she would give us anything we wanted, tell stories and reminisce about the "olden days." But when her vile mood had taken over, it was not quite safe for a young boy to enter the premises.

Her favorite tale was of a barn dance she attended when she was a young girl of seventeen, something difficult for us to imagine. When the evening festivities were at their liveliest, she was romping through the Boston Fancy with John Blethen, who later became the leading citizen and the wealthiest man in town. As the couples were galloping all together through the movement known as "Down the Center," the double doors at the end of the barn flew open and she and John were swept out onto a pile of cow manure. They were chagrined but could not help joining the boisterous guffaws of the crowd. The laughing girl had a sudden appeal for John. He drew her around the corner and proposed marriage. She sensed that that was no time and no place for such a proposal and shook her head, no. She had turned down a chance to marry the leading prospect in town, and spent the rest of her life in single blessedness. Alas for Fronie!

There were no septic tanks and no sewers in our village. Each home had a backhouse that had to be cleaned out once a year. For three years, when I was between ten and thirteen, I did this chore for Fronie. Each time she gave me five dollars, and five dollars to me then was far more than five hundred would be to me now. In those days no lime was thrown over the dung to make the task easier for the shoveler. Each time I became deathly sick, but I needed the five dollars so desperately that I saw the job through. I have no words to express the horror of those two or three hours each year. I would lie on my stomach and throw up when there was little or nothing to yield. After the job was over, I would go to the Mill Cove for a swim and to Patten Point to smell the fragrance of fir trees and bayberry bushes. A few years later in high school when I read of the harpies in Virgil's *Aeneid* with their loathsome, stinking breaths, the terrible stench of Fronie's backhouse came back so vividly my somach tightened with pain.

Our own outhouse was not so bad as Fronie's, for we had a bucket of dirt to throw in to bury the odor. That didn't help the cold. Going to that spot in the dead vast and middle of a zero night was a supreme hardship. The cold night wind would creep up under the barn and assail our thighs until we were chattering and shivering and almost out of breath. How we dreaded that Spartan experience! Even the slum children in the ghettos today have it better than we did in this respect.

Aunt Fronie was a great reader. As a young lady, she once rode to Rockland to hear Robert Ingersoll give a lecture on "The Mistakes of Moses." The lecture was well phrased and Bob Ingersoll uncommonly eloquent. She became a disciple of Ingersoll there and then, bought all his books, and even went so far as to buy and read Tom Paine's *Age of Reason*. Her folks were Baptists who believed that the Scriptures, even the imaginative, poetic sections, should be taken literally. Her break with her family on these religious grounds was a crisis in her life. She became the black sheep of the family, even though she lavished presents, vacation trips, and other favors on them all.

She was the only one in the village who spent hours on her meals. She would not eat our blue mud clams but insisted on having white sand clams. She loved flounders when they first came out of the mud in March and paid well for them. Many a time I sat on Cowing's wharf suffering the assaults of the cold March winds to catch her a mess. She knew all about mushrooms, the edible and the poisonous. On Sundays while all the rest of her family were in church, she roamed the dark wooded areas where chanterelles could be found. She was about the only person in town who ate pâté de fois gras—or even knew that it existed. She clipped new recipes out of the *Boston Globe* and tried them out. Years later when I discovered an excellent restaurant in New York or Paris, I thought of Fronie and wished she might have sampled their offerings.

As she neared eighty and the close of her career as postmistress, storekeeper, and village mother, she seemed to lose interest in her work. She would order goods and forget to open the packages. She spent more time in her back room smoking and less time on the job. Finally her creditors insisted that she hire a helper. Each man hired quit when one of her periodic rages swept over her. Finally a patient, good-natured young man, Tom Maker, stuck to the job. He found that she had let too many ne'er-do-wells have goods they couldn't pay for and there was no possibility of collecting. She was forced into bankruptcy and became a charge of the town. The selectmen decided that Fronie, a village institution, should not be sent to the poorhouse several miles away; they boarded her out with some old friends whom she had known for years. Neighbors remembered her many favors and brought in clams, lobsters, and ears of corn for her. Toward the close, she read her Bible daily but did not forget to read Bob Ingersoll, whose writing had illumined her life.

One of Aunt Fronie's frequent visitors was Dan Elwell's wife. She was called Polly Dan to distinguish her from another Polly Elwell in the village. One day working in the garden, Polly Dan stumbled over a big rock and sprained her leg. The postmistress telephoned for Dr. Hitchcock, who took a good look at her leg, probed the muscles, and said, "Aunt Polly, I'll bet that's the dirtiest leg in all Knox County." "How much will you bet?" asked Polly. "I'll bet five dollars." "All right, it's a deal," she said. Thereupon she took off her other shoe and stripped down her stocking. "I washed that one because I knew you were coming." The doctor lost money, but he had a story which he loved to tell for the rest of his life.

A mile away was a settlement known to us as Makertown. These people rarely came to the village, but when they came, they showed the rest of us what good talk was like. They were poor far beyond the poverty we ourselves knew. The original Maker, Tenant, for whom Tenants Harbor is named, came from Gloucester in the eighteenth century to cut tall spar timber for the King's fleet. He married an Indian princess, according to his grandson, and raised ten children. As a result, Indian features were not an uncommon sight in our village, for these ten children married and reared children of their own.

The Makers were people who could not adjust to ordinary men's work habits. They loved to fish, hunt, and smoke pipes, but they did not like to go every day to a job at seven in the morning and work until five at night. They were regarded as a lower brand of goods by the thrifty, path-keeping, habit-loving English stock. Crèvecoeur has written about these people who live on the outskirts of villages and towns, and in one chapter of his *American Farmer* calls them the typical Americans, i.e., a breed that differs from anything known in Europe. "Once a hunter, farewell to the plough," he writes of these people.

They were shiftless; their homes often had rags stuffed in the windows; screen doors hung on broken hinges all winter; grass around the sagging doorsteps was never mowed; but we liked them for their humor. Brightest of all the Makers was Uncle Ben. He was the laziest man in town, and enjoyed that distinction. Once when three loafers were lingering in the company store, Uncle Ben asked one of them if a fish was an animal. One of the boys said, "Yes." "By what criterion do you make that judgment?" The boy, fresh from school said, "Anything which has a backbone is an animal." "Well," said Uncle Ben after a pause, "if that is the case, then I'm no animal."

The word "criterion" was a big word for that village, but Ben loved big words. He kept a copy of Webster's school dictionary always at hand. One day a gentleman from the city came to the village to look over some shabby cottages he owned. One of these had been overhauled during the early spring. He drove up in a shining buggy with a smart bay mare to inspect the work. We boys flocked around, admiring the man's overcoat, the buffalo robe, and the bay horse who held her head high and pawed like a thoroughbred. Uncle Ben was with us. "Well, Uncle Ben," said the man, "this old place is certainly being rejuvenated, isn't it?" "I think, John, that *renovated* is the word you are looking for." The story was added to the village ditty box of anecdotes, and finally the man of property told it as a joke on himself.

On rainy days the quarrymen often spent more time in the company store than they did in the quarry. The work was on a dangerous slope and the rain made everything slippery. Ben noted the slippery chains and the dangerous ledges and headed for the company store.

Four or five others followed him hoping to get him to talking. They found Paris Rackliffe holding forth deploring the state of the nation. Grover Cleveland, he declared, was a menace to America. The Democratic Party was still the party of slavery. The Union was heading for complete destruction. This tirade over, Paris got up and hurried back to the stone sheds.

"Well, Uncle Ben, what do you think of Paris Rackliffe?"

"It's like this, Charles," he replied, "Paris and me know all there is to know in this world."

"How do you make that out?"

He straightened up. "It's like this. Paris Rackliffe knows everything there is to know in the world except one thing, namely, that he's a damned fool, and I know that!—and that's the sum total of human knowledge!"

To counteract the drinking in the village there was a temperance organization known as the I. O. G. T., the Independent Order of Good Templars (the drunks called it "I Often Get Tight"). Many joined and "took the pledge." The officers of the organization wore purple hoods and observed a solemn ritual in their meetings. A good deal of social prestige was connected with the group. My Aunt Agnes, whose husband was a bit too fond of a nip, was a strong temperance advocate, and offered to pay my initiation fee if I would join. The fee was fifty cents, and that was a lot of money. I accepted her offer. The organization held a big annual convention in one of the cities of the state and each chapter was entitled to send two delegates. The local lodge paid their traveling expenses, but even so, it was not easy to get members to go. The men were busy working at the quarries and stone sheds or hauling lobster pots and could not spare the time. At one convention in Portland, the only delegates our lodge, known as Starlight Lodge, was able to send were two octogenarians, Uncle Ben Maker and Joe MacKellar. MacKellar was a bachelor who was a justice of the peace and a renowned orator. He had run as a candidate for the state legislature on the Greenback ticket and won.

At the convention, the representatives of each lodge were called upon to stand and show themselves and one delegate was to make an appropriate report about the condition of his chapter. These two old codgers stood up. Ben asked Joe to speak, and Joe asked Ben. They did an Alphonse and Gaston act for a few minutes and Joe finally sat down. Ben cleared his throat and sang out, "Fellow delegates, we are here to represent the youth and beauty of Starlight Lodge." A surge of laughter stopped him short. The story was retold a hundred times to anyone who would listen. When the home folks heard it, they wondered which one represented the beauty and which the youth!

Uncle Ben grew feeble in his late eighties, but he smoked his pipe as much as ever. One day he found the long eight-mile walk to the city wearing on him and turned off into a field to lie down and rest. The embers from his pipe burned a hole in his jacket. As he slept on, the fire crept through his clothes and burned his body so badly that he was found dead a few hours later. The funeral drew people from all the neighboring region, and almost everyone there remembered some witty saying, some capital response he had made, and all agreed that Spruce Head would be a poorer place without him.

In the course of the year, certain village rituals were observed. One of these, called "taking away the banking," came in April. We had no central heat in our homes. Most of us burned wood in two stoves, one in the kitchen and one in the living room. Each morning we started from scratch to warm the house, and on cold mornings this was a Spartan venture. To mitigate the cold weather, we cut spruce boughs and banked the four sides of the house. When these were taken away in April, each house furnished the makings of a big bonfire. We boys begged our neighbors to stretch the program out, and have the bonfires on different nights. My father, apparently tired of the long Maine winter, took his banking away in March. His premature bonfire inspired me to write a lyric on the subject entitled "Taking Away the Banking," one stanza of which reads:

> We tugged at big ends of the bottom brush
> The small ends as reluctant to let go
> As winter was himself, although the rush
> Of warmth, once started, was an overflow
> Of sunny days, bluebirds, and brooklets racing
> Like children from worn mothers, tired of chasing.

Two holidays we celebrated extravagantly: Christmas and the Fourth of July. We opened the Fourth with a parade of "horribles" (we called them "fantastics") at mid-morning. The "Spirit of '76" usually led the procession with fife and drum. Behind them were crazily dressed boys and girls whose gay spirits made up for their nondescript costumes. Witches, clowns, cowboys, Indians, soldiers, Aunt Chloes, dogs, and wagons made up the parade.

At noon the whole village assembled on the shore for a fish chow-

(above left) Forrest Snow; (above right) Katherine Quinn Snow; (below)
Parents and children: l. to r., Maynard, Mary Agnes, George, Frank, Wilbert,
Hugh; beside father, Cora

(above left) The little boy at four; (above right) The high school student; (below) Thomaston High's third baseman (third from left, standing) with his teammates

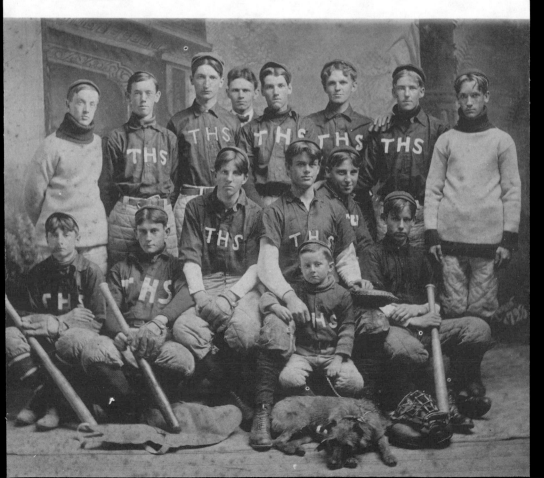

der or lobster stew. To while away the time before dinner, the grown-up men usually played horseshoes. A few veterans could pitch a "ringer" or a "leaner" at almost every throw, and these champions were looked upon as heroes. The climax of the celebration came after dinner when the lobster boats (many of them Friendship sloops) squared away for a race. Three or four men were experts in handling small boats, and watching them perform was a delight. On good summer days we could depend on a southwest breeze every afternoon. As the hour of three approached, the whole crowd grew tense with expectation. The judges and timers watched seriously while the sloops maneuvered, jockeying for a good start across the line. To a boy with imagination and good health, it was the climax of a glorious holiday.

Another ritual was the November slaughter of the family pig. Many families bought a shoat in the spring, fattened him all summer, and had him killed at Thanksgiving. As a rule, the pig grew to be a family pet, and when the time arrived to have him killed, a sombre group gathered to witness the tragedy. Rufus Kinney was called in to administer the *coup de grace*. I hated to go to these butchering parties, but I hated still more to be called a "sissy." The pig would be let out of the pen, two or three men would grab him by the legs and trip him. Rufe got down on his knees with a long sharp sheath knife. Apparently sensing what was going to happen, the pig squealed to the top of his lungs. The knife was inserted deep into the animal's throat and poor piggie continued squealing until exhausted by loss of blood. On most of these occasions, Rufe would be afflicted with a "Charley horse" in the middle of the operation, and stumble around on one foot, rivaling the pig's squeals with groans of his own. This, to many of the boys, was the highlight of the event, and when we re-enacted the scene for our own entertainment, our imitation of Rufe's affliction was the climax of our act. Why many of us attended such a sadistic and revolting spectacle, I never was able to make out. But it was one of our village practices and we were always a part of it.

The Christmas festival was an even greater event. Everyone, Christian and pagan alike, took part. We cut two magnificent spruces and set them up in the chapel, one on each side of the pulpit. Their fragrance filled the room. For two days, the women filled red net bags with candy, popcorn, and nuts, one for every child in town. Both trees were trimmed with strings of popcorn and cranberries and at the top of each a silver star.

On the night before Christmas the chapel was crowded. Wagons from the backwoods lined the village street. The horses, well blanketed against the cold, were tethered to heavy round iron weights placed in the road.

The exercises started with a familiar Christmas hymn, "O Little Town of Bethlehem," in which the audience heartily joined. Then came the unpleasant feature of the evening, the chore of "speaking pieces." It was right here I learned that "Hell is more than half of Paradise," for I was shy and sensitive and dreaded to face a crowded congregation. I don't recall a single poem I had to recite on any of these occasions, but I know I hated it. I do recall four lines from a "poem" my sister Agnes recited:

> At length his journey over
> And free from care and sin
> With joy and gladness on his head
> The Pilgrim enters in.

She recited the first two and a half lines but was held up by some psychological block after the word "gladness." She paused, closed her eyes, put her hand to her forehead—then burst out: "On his head the pilgrim enters in." The audience, thinking that was a strange way to enter the pearly gates, broke into hearty laughter. My bewildered sister blushed and ran weeping off the stage. One woman wanted her to go back and recite the verse correctly, but Aggie said "No." She wanted only to get home and hide.

After this torture came a Santa Claus in the style of Clement Moore, fat and jolly, in a red suit with a long white beard. It was considered an honor to be chosen for this task, and the young man designated tried hard to be a little jollier and funnier than those who had gone before. His ambition was often frustrated by some child who refused the present offered him, screaming, "I don't want a book! I want a jackknife!" The children of most families had one present on this occasion. A few well-to-do families couldn't resist giving their little ones three or four, while the ragamuffins from the outskirts of the village received only the candy and popcorn bag allotted to everyone. Our family of seven had one modest present each.

During the winter there were two big shooting contests, one at Thanksgiving and one at Christmas. Two well-known hunters chose sides until all our nimrods were accounted for. The teams then hurried to the woods or the sea for game. Each bird and animal counted 100, 200, or 300 points depending upon the size and scarcity. A wild goose or a fox would count 1000, but these were rarely brought in at the six-o'clock deadline.

We boys knew all the hunters. We watched their departure in the morning and their return at night. We longed for the time when we could have a double-barreled gun and participate in these exciting affairs. The team that lost had to pay for the dinners of the team that won. Tables were spread out on wooden "horses" in Fronie's hall, and as six o'clock neared, the atmosphere was tense. Who was going to surprise us with game that counted heavily—perhaps a wild goose or a fox? Which side was going to win?

Meanwhile, the women were bringing chicken, roast beef, and pork to the tables, and the odors aroused the appetites of little boys and led them into temptation. The watching women screamed, "You kids let that food alone!" The fiercer ones grabbed a chicken leg or a spare rib; the less daring had to wait. Finally all the hunters were in, the points tallied, the winning team announced, and the cheering over. A short blessing was offered by the minister, and the feast was on. To a country boy from ten to fifteen, hunting and fishing were the chief attractions. We made squirrel traps hoping to secure and tame one of these woodland creatures. We caught them but although we tried, we never succeeded in taming one. We did capture a crow, tamed him, then killed him by overfeeding. We captured an owl and tried to make a pet of him, but he got out of the cage and flew away one dark night. We set snares for rabbits, and these our mothers were glad to have for stew.

As soon as we were thirteen, we were allowed to have guns and became real hunters. We shot rabbits, partridges, sandpipers, and plovers, including marsh hens (which we always pronounced "mash-hens") and brought them home for food. Once in a great while we shot a woodcock, which my father called the most foolish and most tasty of all birds. We agreed that he was the best for eating, but the breast of a partridge was a close second. Wild black ducks were a rarity, but now and then we brought a pair home, and they were stuffed and baked for a choice Sunday dinner. Coots (our name for scoter) were considered by most women of the village too fishy for eating, but my mother discovered a way to get much of the fishiness out. She simmered them on the back of the stove all night in a dish of saleratus water, and when she had baked them in the oven surrounded with carrots and onions, we found no fault with them. Once when we had two coots and two chickens on our table, we boys, to Mother's great surprise, preferred the coots. In our region of the bay, there were four kinds of coots, i.e., the early little gray, the patch-head, the butter-bill, and the white-wing; and they all had good feathers for pillows and feather beds.

To hunt for seabirds we started at dawn to row in a thirteen-foot dory to the Stallion, a half-tide ledge two miles away. We set our decoys twenty yards off the rock, hauled up and hid our dory, then dropped behind a ledge just as the birds began to come. We shot some, rowed off and picked them up, then crouched on the ledge for more. The sun was just coming up, the calm water was full of sequin-spotted patches of color. On one of these occasions the beauty of the bay so overcame me that I knocked off shooting and had eyes only for that eerie light over the ledges, the bay and the islands. My father said, "Hey, pick up that gun!" I hardly heard him. I knew that

> A bigger game was calling, with a cry
> More piercing than the cry of coots and old-squaws
> Circling above us—quarry more elusive
> Then hunters for blue goose or wild sea eagles
> Or even ibises could ever know.

On another evening we sailed down to Metinic Green Island in a Friendship sloop, anchored off Hog Island, and waited for daybreak. Again we set our decoys and the sea ducks and drakes came in great numbers. We came back with about thirty birds, and the neighbors flocked around to see them. We were young braves, returning after a successful hunt, and we accepted the homage of the old men, the squaws, and the children. Life was rugged but good.

Fishing as well as hunting was an exciting experience for a boy in a seacoast town. My father had six tubs of trawl with six hundred hooks on each one. In summer I would go with him and cut bait. The bait was herring and I cut each one into three or four pieces, filled a bucket, and shoved it along for my father to put onto the hooks. We usually went to the Mussel Ridge Islands, three miles away, stayed overnight on Mink Island with Freeman Elwell, a friend of my father's, and the next morning at sunrise sailed or rowed to the Green Islands four miles farther out in the bay. After all the trawls were set, we anchored for an hour. That was the hour I looked forward to. We baited our handlines and tried our luck. Within a few minutes we hauled in haddock and cod. One day I hooked a fish so hard to pull in

I thought I had at least a thirty-pounder. I finally landed him, but was disappointed to see a fish of about seven pounds *hooked by the tail*. He had been swimming down with all his might as I was hauling up with all mine. A few minutes later I hooked a big cod, and got him halfway up when he broke away. I hauled the line in; the hook was gone. This was a calamity. A few lost hooks meant a trip to Rockland and good money spent to replace them. My father said, "Here, fish with my line and I'll bend on a new hook." He had nothing but scorn for a fishhook with an eye in the end for threading the line. He insisted they were designed for landlubbers. He used nothing but a snood hook around the end of which strands of the line were tightly fastened with eight or ten half-hitches. That made the barbed end of the hook stand out at an angle and catch more fish. While he was bending a new hook on my line, I hauled aboard a fourteen-pound cod with my lost hook in his throat. Thus, I got the big cod and saved my hook at one stroke.

On the way home we gutted the fish and immediately attracted the gulls. By some miraculous instinct, they arrived—first one or two, then four or five, then fifty, and then three or four hundred. These graceful creatures added the crowning touch to the expedition. They didn't care how near the boat they came. The fish livers were their favorite delicacy. They fought over a liver until the last scrap was swallowed. Then on they came for more. Their sulphur bills, blue wings, and white breasts made them seem the loveliest of God's creatures.

For the less adventurous people of the village, smelting was the favorite way to fish. Smelt frequented the coves and inlets where brooks full of minnows ran into the sea. It was these minnows they came for, although they would as soon bite a garden worm or a bloodworm out of the clam flats. Our fishing poles were usually slim green alders, our lines, stout black thread furnished by our mothers. The bobbers were cork stoppers. The hooks we had to buy at one cent each. The sinker was a piece of lead hammered and cut to size. The creel was a grape basket with a hole in the cover just big enough to shove a smelt through. That was protocol, although once in a while some greedy fisherman would bring along a galvanized iron ten-quart pail. The fishing ground of the village was the Mill Cove that ran inland for nearly half a mile. The fish began to bite at about half-tide and kept it up until high water. After the tide turned the smelt instinctively felt it was time to leave and the catch dropped off abruptly. The smelt is an uncertain creature. I have known them to bite ravenously after the tide had begun to ebb. The colder it was, and the more disagreeable the weather, the faster they would bite. Bitter cold rainy nights were good smelting times, although our fingers were almost too stiff to bait the hooks. To taste right, smelts should be eaten the day they are caught. Out of a market they taste of the mud flats. But there is no better meal on earth than a mess of fresh smelts cooked right.

As children, our play followed a rather fixed pattern through the year. In March we would take advantage of the high winds and fly homemade kites; in April we cut poles and built stilts so that we could walk high above the muddy roads; in May we played marbles, jumped rope, and rolled hoops which usually were the cast-off iron rims of old wagon wheels.

All summer we went swimming in the Mill Cove, which had sedge and cut-grass along its sides and mud in its bottom. On afternoon high tides, when the wind was southwest—as it usually was in fair summer weather—fifteen or twenty of us would show up for a swim. On these afternoons, the water was warm. All morning the sun had been pouring down on the mudflats, warming the slowly incoming water to about 70 degrees, and we were all there to enjoy it. We had no bathing suits. Some of the boys wore no underclothes in summer. Speed in getting undressed was somehow regarded as a great virtue. To shame the slow members of our gang, someone would shout, "Last one undressed got to fuck a leaf!" Although some of us were too young to understand what this desperate punishment meant, the threat would put speed into us and we would literally tear our clothes off to avoid the penalty.

On bright sunny mid-summer days some of us, impatient, went down to the mouth of the cove to accompany the tide as it rolled in. We ran around in the mud and got ourselves completely splattered with the stuff. There were "honeypots" in the cove (our local word for quicksands) and these were truly dangerous. Every once in a while a boy would sink into one and we would have to pull him out. The admonition "Don't go in swimming alone" had a special meaning for us, for in our cove there was a fate worse than getting drowned. One spot in the cove, where a cow got mired and died, was pointed out to us repeatedly. On these afternoons we needed more than a swim when high tide arrived; we needed a complete body cleaning. These were great afternoons. I am always skeptical when I read that lobster catchers, fishermen, and sailors on the Maine coast never learn to swim. The legend does not apply to our village.

After the late fall rains, the meadows would freeze over and we enjoyed skating. To me this was the best of all winter sports, and I have kept it up all my life. One year we dammed up a brook about half a mile from the village, dammed it at a spot where it ran into a culvert under a town road. The rains descended, the thermometer went below freezing, and we were blest with a veritable lake that reached back into the meadow and permitted us to skate in and out among the alders. The selectmen of the town should have condemned our project because we had blocked drainage on a highway, but they let us alone, and we had a month of sheer joy on the pond we ourselves had made.

Social life in the village was skimpy. With no radio, no television, no motor boats, and only one telephone, we were socially stranded and left on our own. Very few possessed a horse and buggy. The rest were lucky if they got over the unpaved road to Rockland twice a year. The village store was the social center for the men. The women did a great deal of visiting from house to house over a cup of tea. The man-talk around Fronie's stove sooner or later drifted to the Civil War. One old soldier, somewhat of a reader, defended George B. Mc-Clellan as the best general that Lincoln ever had. He had Robert E. Lee's word for it. McClellan was dismissed, he contended, because he was a Democrat. The others, two of whom had fought under McClellan, insisted that he was too much of a Hamlet, never could make up his mind. So the battle raged almost every night.

On Saturday nights there were dances in Fronie's hall. Respectable girls were not supposed to attend; some of them did, however. On these occasions, a local fiddler would call off the movements of the Boston Fancy, Portland Fancy, Smith's Hornpipe, Virginia Reel, Lady of the Lake, and other square dances. Sprinkled through the program were waltzes, one-steps, and schottisches for the more sophisticated. The square dances would sometimes get noisy, especially if the hour were late and the bootleg liquor had begun to take effect. Visitors from nearby villages might steal a partner that a local boy considered his own and things would begin to simmer. In the end, two or three visitors would be thrown downstairs. On rare occasions there would be a general fist fight.

Occasionally entertainment arrived from the outside. One day a man walked up the village street with a bear, "a trained bear," he announced. A crowd quickly gathered. The bear could stand on his hind legs, bow, and dance; that was about all. The man passed his hat and gathered a few pennies and nickels. Before he left, I rode on the bear's back and acquired a supply of lice and bedbugs that kept my mother busy for two days.

Another form of American entertainment that reached our village was the minstrel show, often called "blackface." A white man impeccably dressed would occupy the center of the stage with a row of black men behind him. The program consisted of witty dialogue between the white leader and the two Negroes at either end, interspersed with songs sung by the whole troupe. The humor in the performance was furnished by the Negroes. Like the Uncle Remus stories of Joel Chandler Harris, the repartee revealed the wit and wisdom of the Negro, but the opposition of colored people, who felt that their race was being degraded by these performances, led to their removal from the American stage.

In spite of all this activity on land and sea, my childhood was not a wholly happy one. My sensitivity did not jibe well with a village of rough workingmen. When husbands were turned against wives, or wives against husbands, I was hurt. Some of this sharp speech I know now was spicy satirical or ironical humor and was undoubtedly altogether wholesome as an outlet. Often it was a game husband and wife were playing to see which could hurl the sharpest barb. To me it was angry and ugly, and it saddened me.

I was hurt by the way men talked about girls and women. Full of idealism, I tended to glorify the attractive girls of the community. I was unduly shy and worshipped from afar. This shyness tended to intensify my adoration. I looked at their shapely backs, expecting at any time to see the prettiest of them sprout wings. When some disgruntled male said, "They are all bitches," I would wonder how any man could think or say such a thing. I was Endymion looking at the moon and enjoying it from a distance. Like Shelley, I was "feeding on the Aereal kisses/Of shapes that haunt thought's wildernesses." I was too shy to come close to these lovely girls and deeply afraid of becoming entangled with one of them. I had known some boys who were dragged into shotgun marriages and the married state did not look attractive to me. When a young man brought his bride home to be inspected, the usual verdict was, "Another poultice!" While a few couples separated, most of them fought it out in double harness. Observing these families carefully, I was forced to decide that peace and satisfaction were not to be found in marriage. (Later, much later, I had reason to change my mind.)

My unhappiness was increased by the death of my earliest playmate just across the street, Fred Burton, who died suddenly of diphtheria when he was about nine. I mourned weeks and months and could not understand why the life of my happy playmate had to be snuffed out. Religion did not lift the gloom. I lived next door to the church, was naturally religious, but was repelled by the edict against dancing, smoking, playing cards, and other joys of village life. Gloom sat upon the faces of most of the faithful churchgoers, and gloom seemed to be the requisite for a good religious life. The Calvinism that pervaded the village brought on a duodenal ulcer I had to live with for ten years. My father passed on to his children the rigid faith and grim rules of conduct his grandfather had taught him.

On Sundays we were supposed to sit indoors and read the Bible. By reading three chapters a day and five on Sunday, we could read it through in a year. On Sundays, we were also permitted to read such books as John Bunyan's *Pilgrim's Progress* and *Drummond's Natural Law in the Spiritual World*, both of which I found rather interesting.

The only out-of-door exercise our parents permitted on Sunday was walking to the graveyard. This exercise was not as lugubrious as it sounds, for if the day were sunny, the whole village would be out, making the walk a social event. The cemetery was about half a mile from the village, a quiet nook surrounded by beautiful woods on three sides. Lovers did not find it difficult to slip off into the shrubbery among the fir trees every now and then.

We were not permitted to go out sailing on Sundays no matter how fair the breeze, nor to go in swimming. At dinner my father would walk around the table and inspect the back of each boy's head. If there was a wet rim on the hair, the boy was taken out to the barn and spanked with a flat cudgel. I look upon this rigidity now as the dying gasp of the Puritanism in our family. It was Ralph Waldo Emerson who later snatched me out of this Slough of Despond, and the first time I visited Concord and looked upon his home I was moved to tears of joy thinking of what he did to emancipate me. I said over and over again the lines that first stirred me to revolt:

> They reckon ill who leave me out;
> When me they fly, I am the wings;
> I am the doubter and the doubt,
> And I the hymn the Brahmin sings.

CHAPTER 3

Lobster Catcher

Our village school was ungraded. When the older children had finished the sixth reader, they had completed the curriculum. What next? Lobstering, deep-sea fishing, sailoring on a lime coaster, or work in the quarries and stone sheds? No one thought of further education. My choice was lobster fishing. My father built me a thirteen-foot "double-ender," an open boat whose stern was pointed like the stem, a shape extremely useful when a man got caught in the breakers where it was unsafe to turn around and he could either push forward or pull back to escape being hurled onto the ledges. The "make and break" engine for small boats had been invented but had not yet reached our village. A man rowed standing up, with oars in oarlocks (we called them rowlocks) or in wooden tholepins raised on posts a foot and a half above the gunnel. On stormy days he wore oilskins and a sou' wester; on good days a petticoat barvel, a loose oilskin skirt permitting the free circulation of air around the body.

My older brother Frank was already fishing with a string of sixty pots, all a young man could handle with a rowboat. My father helped me build sixty of my own. He showed me how to start with a flat rectangular base, then bend spruce boughs in a semicircle, three to a trap, and push the ends of the boughs into holes drilled in the sills. Across the boughs we nailed laths three-quarters of an inch apart. The open ends were closed with a net called a "pothead" in the center of which was a hole held open by a circle of bent spruce or iron, through which the lobsters crawled to reach the bait impaled upon an iron spike in the center of the trap. The hole was drawn back toward the center, creating an easy ramp leading the lobster in, at the same time making it hard for him, once in, to get out.

In the sixty-five or seventy years since that time, many fishermen

53

have discarded the boughs and have built rectangular pots, but the design of the head has not changed. The boughs were hard to come by, as only island spruce produces the boughs that bend easily. We called them "cat spruce" because when you cut into them the odor was like that of cat's urine. All the materials for the rectangular pots can be found today in a lumber yard. No visit to a wooded island with all its dark green beauty is called for. The curved pots are more pleasing to the eye, but not so easy to stack on the boat or in piles when brought ashore to dry out.

My brother would haul his sixty pots and be home before dinner time—eleven o'clock. It would always take me from one to two hours longer to haul my sixty. I "wasted" my time looking at the rocks and islands, observing the colors on the sea, and studying the daily variation of the tides. These colors, especially when "the wind sprang up and sang along the wine-dark sea" as Homer phrased it, continually interested me—as did the ever changing tides, the eel grass, kelp, wild ducks, and sea gulls. They helped shape the direction much of my poetry was to take later.

One morning I put a black lobster in a bucket and watched every detail of his shedding. The fleshy body inside had grown and provided itself with a new pink shell, at this point rather thin and pliable. As it continued to grow and swell it exerted pressure against the old outer black shell. Something had to give! The old shell split up the back, like Peggotty bursting her buttons or like a fourteen-year-old boy trying to get himself into his thirteen-year-old coat. The energy in the new enlarged lobster is so great that it is able to pull itself out of the old shell. The limp watery new claws and legs are drawn slowly out. Even the threadlike new antennae are drawn out. Once free, all these various parts begin to swell and harden, and the result is a lobster an inch or two longer than the one that occupied the old shell. I laid the outworn cast-off shell in the bow of the boat and fetched it home as a souvenir. Years later in the University of Utah when a young man handed me a theme about sitting all day in the Wasatch Mountains watching a rattlesnake shedding his skin, I felt that here was a boy after my own heart and gave him an A.

Our life settled into a daily routine. We spent the forenoon hauling our sixty pots, and the afternoon catching bait. In those years there were millions of cunners (known in some areas as bergalls) in our arm of the bay, and we rigged up a contraption for catching them.

We fastened a bowl-shaped net to a large iron hoop, which was hinged on opposite sides so that it could be folded into a semicircle and the net closed. We baited it with black lobster or smashed-up crabs the cunners liked, then lowered the hoop to the bottom with ropes attached to the center of each semicircle. We watched over the side of the boat until we saw twenty or thirty cunners hovering above our appetizing bait, then gave a quick yank and pulled the iron rims together. Some fish escaped, but we usually landed five or ten good cunners at each haul.

For a change of bait we used flounders, fish we captured by spearing them at low water, using a long pole tipped with a sharp-pointed piece of iron about a foot long. The best bait was herring out of the fish weirs, but those cost thirty cents a bushel, and that was more than we could usually afford to pay. Because thirty cents a bushel was a steep price, we often resorted to the illegal method of torching. The weir owners had a law put through the Maine legislature which prohibited the use "of any inflammable substance in liquid form" for catching fish within the state's coastal waters. This law was aimed directly at the lobster catchers, who enjoyed the sport as well as the profit that came from torching two or three hundred bushels of herring in a single night.

The method was as follows. With wire we tied a cotton batting roll to one end of an iron rod and fastened the free end tightly to the bow of a dory. The cotton batting reached out over the water two feet beyond the gunnel. Two men sat and rowed while one man stood ready in the bow with a dip net. He poured kerosene on the cotton batting, touched it off with a match, then stood and watched for the herring to swim to the light. The two oarsmen would speed up their rowing. The faster they rowed the more furiously the herring gave chase and boiled up under the light. The man standing in the bow dipped until the dory was loaded. Then the three returned to their Friendship sloop and unloaded the catch. Off again they went for another load. It was grim, grueling work but very exciting, especially to a young boy of fourteen or fifteen. When we returned home after a big catch, day would be breaking along the eastern horizon. Tired as I was, I couldn't get enough of what Homer called "the rosy-fingered dawn." He saw it as a tramp. I saw it as an innocent violator of the law. Too many people never see it at all.

Successful nights of torching herring were rare. Often there were not enough fish in the cove to pay for our effort. Again, fish wardens would lurk around to catch us and fine us. The first night after someone had discovered a new inlet crowded with herring, lobster catchers would gather in crowds, just as miners were attracted by the hint of a new gold strike in Alaska. Everybody would be there. As the tidings spread, the fish wardens often got the word and managed to be on hand watching for us.

If we had an especially prosperous week of lobstering, we would buy a dory load of herring and salt them down in hardwood barrels. It was generally agreed in lobster-catcher circles that the lighter you salted them the better they would fish. As a result of this light salting, the stench from the barrels assailed the air for many yards around. The smell of rotting fish would often saturate the boat and the man's clothing. It would bury itself in the wood of the oars, the handle of the gaff, and everything connected with the business, if one were not immaculately clean in his habits. It so clung to a man's hair, fingernails, clothing, and boots that his wife would almost hate to see her spouse come home. If divorces were as plentiful then as they are now, the lobster-catcher wives of our seacoast village would have furnished sociologists another interesting chapter on marital estrangements. Luckily a few of our married lobster catchers were neat and clean in their personal habits. One man, at his wife's instance, salted his herring deeply and avoided the stench altogether. These tidy men spent hours washing down their boats, digging out the spaces under cleats and timbers, removing particles of rotten fish, and bailing out the last drop of gurry-saturated bilge water. Then they'd go home to wash and put on clean clothes. These were exceptions. The others were so careless that people had to keep to windward of them when engaged in a neighborly chat, and they were a continual source of annoyance to their families, sitting down to supper without even washing their hands.

Every now and then we would catch a big seed lobster, i.e., a female crustacean with thousands of eggs under her tail. We were required to sell these to the *Grampus,* a government boat that cruised up and down the coast to buy them and dump them into a big well in the boat's center. The eggs were hatched in this well and went through the many holes that punctuated the bottom. Biologists tell us that the female lobster produces every two years from three thousand to more than seventy thousand eggs, according to her age and size, and secretes a glue which fastens them in a solid mass to the swimmerets, or fins, under her tail. She carries her eggs from ten to eleven months, flexing her tail to enclose them in a kind of pocket when eels and other hungry enemies draw near. Then comes the hatching period which lasts about seven days. During the nights only, as a safety measure, she agitates her tail and disperses the tiny young in clouds as they emerge from the eggs. Not until the spring or summer of the following year will she spawn again. Ichthyologists tell us that the new larvae are only one-third of an inch long, with big green eyes. They lack swimmerets and paddle along the surface of the water with hair-fringed legs, snapping up drifting food particles. Many are eaten by herring, menhaden (better known to us as porgies), and other fishes. The larvae molt three times in their first fifteen to eighteen days. By this time those that survive are back on the bottom, one-half inch long and resemble small adults. When they are a year old, they are two or three inches long and have molted from fourteen to seventeen times. They mature and become "count," i.e., marketable, lobsters when they are about three years old.

Lobsters became fewer and fewer along the coast. The *Grampus* method was declared a failure. Practically all of the larvae washed out of the *Grampus*'s well were eaten by fishes before they reached the bottom. (My father, who had been opposed to the *Grampus* program, now had a chance to say "I told you so.")

A new plan was devised. The seed lobsters were immediately thrown back overboard where they were caught. This method worked. The lobster industry experienced a boom. Today the bottom in places crawls with lobsters in the fall of the year. Between July 15 and December 15 almost any good lobster fisherman can earn a hundred dollars a day. In my lobstering days one-half a counter to a pot, amounting to three dollars for the day's work, was considered a triumph. Now three or four count lobsters to a pot is something to talk about. The price of shedders in my day was seven cents apiece. Today it is at least seventy. As a result of the change from the *Grampus* method, the number of lobster fishermen in this region increased more than fourfold. From a poor man's occupation it became a business of men who paid income taxes and took winter trips to Florida, an undreamed-of situation at the turn of the century.

Lobster catchers in my day were not entirely respectable. We built our traps in the barn and hid our buoys behind the woodshed.

Hardship overtook us in later October. Fall winds would be cold and often our wet mittens would freeze while we rowed from one pot to another. Life became grim and Spartan. A chill stiffened our muscles and reached to the very marrow of our bones. The second week in November we took our traps ashore, a few every day, until they were all up. There would be a respite for us until March, when we started our spring fishing. In the meantime we knitted potheads and bait bags, mended our gear on good days, and went hunting.

Hunting sea birds and land game was an integral part of our lives. We enriched the kitchen larder and enjoyed the sport as much as boys today enjoy basketball. By the time a boy was twelve years old he was supposed to own a gun (my father fixed the age at thirteen). It was often a boy's most prized possession.

Before thirteen we did some trapping. We would find a rabbit path, pick out a place along the path where there were alders, bend one over the path and fasten it there. Then with a length of slender wire we fashioned a noose. We formed half the wire into a circle and bent the end around the middle of the wire. The other end we bent around the alder in such a way that the loop hung just about where the head of the rabbit would come as he loped along on his nightly round. If the bunny shoved his head into the loop, efforts to escape would only draw the wire tight and he would struggle until he was dead. In a wood half a mile from our home I once caught a large male rabbit. I saw the struggle he had been through, saw the blood upon the snow, how his eyes bulged out in his straining effort to free himself, and I was overcome with grief. I resolved then and there never to use a snare again. I was not sentimental about it. We needed the rabbits for food, but I resolved to subject them to a shorter, easier death with a shotgun.

There were times when I could not use even the more merciful shotgun. One February morning I was walking in the woods on the lookout for game. It was a calm day. Not a breath of wind was stirring. A white rabbit was hopping silently among the green alders over pure white snow. Big snowflakes were zigzagging down. February was telling me, "I, too, can produce beauty." The hare and the mystical landscape made such an impression on me that I could not stain Beauty with Death.

When a neighbor died in the village it was customary for friends to drop in and stay all night until the day of the funeral. There were usually three or four in attendance at these wakes. When I was fifteen I sat up one night with three men to keep watch over the corpse of Asbury Rackliffe. The three were Tom McKellar, a devout Baptist; Adam Kirkpatrick, a disciple of Bob Ingersoll; and Cyrus Rackliffe, a hunter and fisherman, who had lost his leg in an accident, and whose strong personality dominated the party. Our talk soon turned to the endlessly fascinating subject of life after death. Tom, a hard-shelled Baptist, said he thought the Bible contained all the answers one needed. Adam, a skilled stonecutter and a sportsman, was the skeptic. He told us about Ingersoll and Tom Paine and was well acquainted with Fitzgerald's translation of the *Rubaiyat*. He proceeded to quote:

> Oh threats of Hell and Hopes of Paradise!
> One thing at least is certain—*This* Life flies:
> One thing is certain and the rest is Lies;
> The Flower that once has blown for ever dies.

Cyrus had kept still for a long time. He took his wooden leg off, threw it under the haircloth sofa, turned to Adam and said, "That may be true of a flower, Adam, but I'm not quite sure about humans. And now I'm going to tell you something I almost never talk about. The night before I lost my leg we had made plans for a gunning trip to the outer islands. That night my father's clock which hadn't struck for ten years up and struck one just as plain as I am speaking.

"I turned over and went to sleep and dreamed that the air was full of little birdshot—number 9 or 10 I reckon—and I was breathing them into my throat and lungs. The pain was so powerful it woke me up. I was a soggy mess of sweat. I woke up Emily and told her what had happened. She said, 'It must be a presentiment.' I thought that over and said, 'I'll not go out cooting tomorrow no matter how fair the day is.'

"The next morning the boys came over and called me. I lifted a window and said, 'I'm not going.' 'Why not?' they said. 'It's a wonderful day.' So I, like a fool, up and told them why. Then they called out 'Superstitions! Bogeyman!' and things like that. I became ashamed of myself and said, 'All right, boys, I'll go.'

"We hadn't been out an hour when I saw a loon come up just ahead of us. I reached for my old Parker, grabbed her by the muzzle, and pulled her toward me. Something caught the hammer. She went off and blowed the gunnel of the boat and a piece of my leg to smithereens.

"That didn't cure me none of hunting. The night the *Portland* went down, I was packing tollers into my dory for a gunning trip to the Green Islands and a voice behind me spoke up and said, 'Don't go, Cyrus.' I looked around to see who was there and there wa'n't nobody. This time I didn't go and both of you know that if I had a' gone I couldn't have come through alive. That was the worst storm that ever swept this coast."

When Cyrus got through I think he had convinced us all that "There are more things in heaven and earth, Horatio, / Than are dreamt of in your philosophy." Few nights in my life stand out so vividly in memory.

During these three years the family rented a cottage on White Head Island, built a wharf in the "Old Cove," put out a hauling line, and erected a fish flake for drying out the cod and haddock we brought in and salted. (Cod and haddock were so plentiful during my childhood that it was not uncommon to find one trapped in a lobster pot.) A few hand-lining trips to the fishing grounds plus these occasional strays took care of our winter fish needs. The hand-lining was sport for us youngsters. We kept careful count of the number and size of the fish each boy landed on any given expedition, and the boy who caught the most was champion for the day. A better combination of utility and pleasure would be hard to find.

My mother and the younger children moved off the island the first week in September. Father went back to the Coast Guard station. Frank and I kept bachelor's hall until the middle of November. Then we too would call it a day, stack our traps, haul up our double-enders, and live with the family on the mainland until March, when we moved back again for spring fishing. This was our routine for three years.

What did I get out of those three years? First, I discovered living out of doors was so much better than living in a cramped place of four walls and a ceiling. I discovered that islands have different smells, and that knowledge helped me when I was lost in a thick fog. I discovered that the rote on the ledges has a different sound on each shore. The rote on the Brown's Island ledges charmed me then and still does after many, many years. It is music that stirs me deeply. Those three years of lobstering, outdoors eighteen hours a day in unpolluted air, probably did more for my health and longevity than anything else in my life.

CHAPTER 4

High School Education

DURING the third summer of my lobstering my mother began to worry about the education of her children. She was not satisfied with the short terms of the one-room village school, and two of her boys had finished the limited course there. A few years earlier, the Norton family had hired a two-masted schooner and a scow and sailed to Portland in order that their children might have good schooling. The force behind this hegira—a really epic undertaking—was my great-aunt Cyn (shortened from Asenath.) Her husband, Horace Norton, was an easy-going bookworm, perfectly willing to dream his life away on the island. But Aunt Cyn sensed both the economic and the social values of an education. Her life was wrapped up in her children and her will was strong enough to break down any barriers, including poverty, that stood in her way. This move occasioned a great deal of talk in the village, both for and against, but when she and her family sailed away in that two-master dragging the scow piled high with their household goods, Aunt Cyn Norton became a heroine everybody was proud of.

All this was in my mother's mind when she said, "I am going to Thomaston. You children will have better schools. We'll live with my mother." She closed our village house, hired a hayrack drawn by two horses, and moved with the four younger children to grandmother's home on Gleason Street in Thomaston. My oldest brother, George, was away on Hurricane Island learning the stonecutter's trade. Frank and I remained on the island lobstering, and kept bachelor's quarters. We lived on "short" lobsters, clams, and fish for the most part. The smack *Hattie and Nelly* commanded by Captain Cushman of Friendship came once every two weeks to buy our lobsters and sell us whatever groceries we needed. In mid-November we hauled up our traps and joined the family at Thomaston.

What school should we attend? The Thomaston High School, an outgrowth of the old Thomaston private academy, had a rugged curriculum. The college course offered four years of Latin, four of mathematics, three of Greek, plus a specified number of English classics required by colleges for admission. That was the course I resolved to try. The other less exacting course was for students who were leaving school at the end of four years.

Would the high school accept us? "What grades did you complete at Spruce Head?" asked Albert Cole, the high school principal. "I don't know," I answered. "We didn't have grades." "You are two months late. I hope you realize that." He pondered while we waited apprehensively for his decision. "Tell you what I'll do. You come here for a month and if you can handle the work I'll keep you on. If not, I'll send you back to the ninth grade grammar."

"O.K.," I said. "O.K.," said Frank. Thus we began our handicapped program. Ralph Cushing, a classmate, helped me with beginner's Latin. He drilled me on declensions, vocabulary, and conjugations until I was exhausted. One classmate who hated Latin went around singing a bawdy quatrain:

> Amo, amas, I loved a lass
> And she was young and tender;
> Amas, amat, I laid her flat
> And tickled her feminine gender.

An understandable outlet, perhaps, for an unwilling boy compelled to learn a language in which he had no interest, to please parents ambitious to send him to college.

I worked every night until eleven o'clock and Saturday nights until twelve. In Milton's words, "I lived laborious days and scorned delights," and before many weeks I was up with my class. I had sense enough to see that the orderly program of Latin grammar shed some needed light upon the disorderly, illogical subject known as English grammar, and my work in English composition took on an added interest.

My brother Frank, in the meantime, had discovered a greater joy than any I had known—the joy that comes to a teen-ager when he first discovers the pleasures of a fascinating girl. While I was punishing my slow mind learning Latin and algebra, he was enjoying the "first fine careless rapture" and long-drawn-out good-nights that go with a fresh young lassie. At the time I did not envy him, for although

I was approaching seventeen, I had not yet awakened to sex and girls. I could only enjoy at second hand the eagerness that was in Frank's eyes when he was going out for a date. He had discovered something fairer and lovelier than Latin, Greek, or mathematics. At the end of a month he was sent back to the ninth grade of the grammar school and I was told that I could stay on in high school. Frank had a quick mind—ever so much quicker than my own—but school to him was dull in comparison with all extracurricular activities. When school ended in June we were both back with our double-enders and our lobster pots.

Moving to Thomaston had not worked out well. The house on Gleason Street was too small for a large family. There arose the old problem of two women under one roof—the Chinese symbol for war. There was also the absence of my father on the Coast Guard station. He found it too difficult on his day off each week to make the journey to Thomaston and be back on White Head Island by six o'clock. So we moved back to our Spruce Head village home but spent our summers at the cottage on White Head.

My best friend and dearest companion, Ralph Elwell, was home from his first year at Bucksport Seminary, where he had distinguished himself in both athletics and scholarship. During the summer he and I put on a debate in Fronie's hall on the subject of immigration, a live question nationally at the moment. I argued for letting down the bars and living up to the motto inscribed upon the Statue of Liberty. He argued for closing the gates and keeping the Greeks, Slavs, and Italians as well as the Orientals from becoming American citizens. Strange as it may seem, we filled the hall, and after our preliminary clearing of the decks the whole assembly entered into the debate. The most vociferous members of the audience were for keeping the "furriners" out, and I was made to understand that I was on the unpopular side of the question, a stance that became habitual with me later! One man said in a loud voice, "They can't even speak no English!" It was a "no decision" debate; otherwise I would have been swamped. As I look back on it, the interesting thing was that two brash teen-age kids were able to fill the hall and stir the village up on the question of immigration.

Ralph was a magnificent example of American youth. He was a skillful athlete, an excellent marksman with a shotgun, a delightful companion in every way, and a heart-warming friend. During his sophomore year he was internally injured while playing football, came home and bled to death. Blood transfusion was then unknown. If it had been available, he could have been saved. His death saddened my whole life.

During that summer on the island a honeymoon couple in a sailing yacht anchored off our White Head shore known as the Old Cove, and came to our cottage for drinking water. I was at a table in the back yard struggling with Caesar and the bridge he was building across the Rhine. I had determined to finish the Gallic Wars during the summer. The bride had majored in Latin at Wellesley and became interested in my project. For nearly a week she came ashore every day and worked with me. We finished building the bridge, learned about what domestic animals and pets the Gauls had in their homes, explored the rites of the Druid religion, and struggled every afternoon with the inverted sentence structure of the Latin tongue. Some of her bridal joy must have rubbed off on me, for I accomplished more that week than I had in the whole month before. This summer study enabled me to go into the third-year Latin class in the fall.

September came, and with it a crisis in my life. The shedders were beginning to crawl and the lobstering was profitable. I needed money desperately for a suit of clothes and other things a high school boy should have. I wanted to play on the baseball team, for I had had good luck on the Spruce Head nine against Clark's Island, South Thomaston, and other rivals. My father wanted me to tend my traps, earn more money, and go back to high school late, as I had the previous year. Mr. Cole warned me that I was to begin Greek and plane geometry in September and should be back at school on time. My mother agreed with Mr. Cole. It was up to me to decide, and the decision was one of the hardest I ever made—at least up to that moment. Aside from all the arguments pro and con, I had discovered that the sea and the tides, the rock islands and gulls had become almost indispensable to my life. To leave them all and go to a lonely unheated room at my grandmother's house in Thomaston was not an engaging prospect. I found myself crying, trying to make up my mind, and watched the teardrops as they fell into the bottom of my double-ender. After much debate with myself I finally decided to go back to Thomaston on Labor Day. I would come home on week ends, take in my traps gradually, and stow away my gear. I did all this during the month of September, and sold my double-ender for fourteen dollars.

That winter was a cold one, and I lived a Spartan life in my grandmother's second story. There was no heat upstairs, and my step-grandfather said "No!" when I suggested a stove. I still studied every night until eleven and Saturdays until twelve. I learned to keep fairly warm by hauling extra quilts and blankets up over my shoulders and head. Even then my hands were white with cold and I found it difficult to use a pen or pencil. To make my bleak existence still more grim, I turned all the upstairs mirrors back to the wall because I disliked my homely face with its big nose and high cheekbones. I was not un-like the medieval monks who felt that they had to mortify the flesh in order to glorify the spirit.

The English teacher in that school, Miss Emma Fountain, knew and loved the great masterpieces of English literature, and she could communicate her enthusiasm to her pupils. She first introduced us to Shakespeare's *Julius Caesar*, and I was so deeply impressed by this play that I could say almost the entire five acts by heart. Here was something greater than all the poetry in Swinton's Sixth Reader. While going through this play, Miss Fountain gave us a tough assignment. In Act III, Scene 2, Brutus and Cassius are about to explain why Caesar has to be killed. Brutus takes over on the spot, and says, "Those that will follow Cassius, go with him." Miss Fountain asked us to write what Cassius had to say to the plebeans that followed him to another part of the city. That night, in an attempt to match Mark Antony's great oration, I wrote out a speech full of bombast, rhetoric, and fustian, and read it to the class the next day. The other eleven members had wisely refused to attempt the assignment. My "masterpiece" is lost, and if it were here it would merely show the reader how bad imitations of Shakespeare can be. But Miss Fountain was delighted with my effort and I became one of her cherished pupils.

I am sorry to say I went back on her before the year was over. We later studied *The Merchant of Venice*, and she asked each one of us to learn ten lines by heart and recite them at our next meeting. At recess we ganged up on her and decided that we would all learn and recite the identical lines. We chose the Prince of Morocco's opening speech in Act II, Scene 1. She called on the first pupil and heard:

> Mislike me not for my complexion,
> The shadow'd livery of the burnisht sun
> To whom I am a neighbour . . .

She turned to the second member of the class and heard the same "Mislike me not . . ." Miss Fountain's own complexion had changed color by the time she got to number four. She saved me until the last, expecting, I imagine, some relief. I was torn in my loyalties but decided to go along with my class and burst out:

> "Mislike me not for my complexion,
> The shadow'd livery of the burnisht sun . . ."

Before I had finished my ten lines she called out sharply, "Class dismissed!" I felt really sorry for my teacher and tried to show it in the look I gave her as I was leaving the room. High school students can be cruel on occasion—but all in all they are not yet sophisticated and give their good teachers more affectionate appreciation than any other group I know of. This warmth of theirs is the teacher's greatest reward for casting his lot with secondary school work.

At the turn of the century dropouts were so common that nobody paid them any special attention. This was true in grammar school as well as high school. Unskilled labor was so much in demand that boys could always find something to do. One of my favorite classmates, Harris Shaw, dropped out and moved to Boston. He was intent on becoming a church organist and a teacher of piano. To keep himself alive and pay for his music lessons he cleaned out furnaces by the dozen and did other menial work. He succeeded in achieving his ambition and was the organist for many years in the Universalist Church of Boston, as well as a fine piano teacher. He had a studio on Huntington Avenue right next, I remember, to the studio of Carrie Jacobs Bond, who wrote "When You Come to the End of a Perfect Day." On my many trips to and from Maine I visited him and we cemented our friendship. He was a skillful mimic, and when talking about a friend he could give a perfect illustration of his speech, gestures, and facial expression. If he had become an actor instead of a musician he would, I think, have been a great success. But he loved music and lived in its demanding, satisfying, and absorbing world. Yet he never outgrew a boy's delight in pranks. He amused children by unhinging his jaws and making his chin and nose come together. Children who saw this trick never forgot it, and never forgot him.

Another boy who should have been a Thomaston classmate, a friend I cherished, was snatched away from public schools and sent to Philips Andover Academy. He was Albert Gould, the son of A. P. Gould, one of the leading criminal lawyers of Knox County. Albert developed into one of the finest raconteurs I have ever known. We renewed our friendship at Bowdoin College, worked on the Bowdoin *Quill* together, and had many grand hours sailing on the George's River and Penobscot Bay. He became an admiralty lawyer in Boston, an enthusiastic yachtsman, and the donor of a fine boat he had built for the Grenfell Mission in Labrador, a mission in which he had served during a summer vacation. The biggest and finest ship in the Grenfell fleet today, I recently learned, is named the *Albert T. Gould.*

On my way to the high school I passed groups of grammar school children and noticed one particularly beautiful little girl. When I found her name was Addie Bushnell, memories began to stir, memories of a doctor of that name, famous for storytelling, who used to come to Spruce Head when home remedies failed. Jerome Bushnell was an itinerant "pennyroyal doctor" who had served in the medical corps during the Civil War. He had a feeling for words, possessed an immense vocabulary, and used it telling extravagant tales of his Civil War experiences. He would tell about sawing the legs and arms off Northern soldiers after the chloroform had given out, embroidering the bloody details until his listeners would squirm, cry out, and beg him to stop. He knew the old soldiers of Spruce Head and told me tales about them I had never known. He told me that Ed Cowing, who was given up for dead after the second battle of Bull Run, came crawling into camp long after midnight with a broken-stemmed clay pipe in his mouth and a bullet in his lungs. He told me that our Frank Tower was a real soldier who distinguished himself at the battle of Antietam. It often seemed to me that he knew every last Civil War soldier in Knox County.

I began to call at the home. This family was not one of the most cultured in town, but it was the one I loved to visit. A good-looking girl and a storytelling father made hours seem like minutes when I was there. There was no privacy; I always met with the whole family. Even now I cannot say which attracted me more—Addie's girlish charms or her father's yarns.

Addie became an actress in a stock company and played the lead in such melodramas as *East Lynne* and *The Old Homestead.* Whenever she was playing in a nearby town I would go to see her act and take her out to supper. A beautiful woman, good talk and laughter, what an evening! She married a fellow-trooper named Manning and they had one son. One night while acting in Boston her voice, which was always a bit husky, gave out completely and she was forced to leave the stage. Undaunted, she began to write novels and plays, and her first novel about the private lives of Thomaston sea captains in foreign parts had considerable success, a *succès de scandale*. Greenwood's painting, "Sea Captains Carousing at Surinam," would have made a good illustration for the book. It brought down upon Addie the wrath of the widows and daughters of Thomaston captains, who thought of their men as dignified and blameless gentlemen. For a time she lived in Hollywood, wrote dialogue for films, and acted in mob scenes.

One day years later I read in a newspaper that Addie Bushnell had returned East and was living on Iranistan Avenue in Bridgeport. I wrote her a long letter full of warm appreciation and affection, recalling Thomaston days and the many happy evenings sitting with her and listening to her father's talk. I told her that her spirit that would not accept defeat had been an inspiration to me. A letter came in response—but the Addie Bushnell in Bridgeport was not my Addie. I wrote back asking for the return of the letter. The woman replied, "No, I will keep the letter. I will type off a copy and send it to you if you wish." I have often wondered about this woman. Was she so forlorn that this warm effusion, though not meant for her, was a comfort to her in her loneliness?

The real Addie came back to Thomaston some years later when I was out West and spent her last days in the old home on Beechwood Street, writing and directing plays that were put on by local amateurs. She was a brave spirit and died without ever knowing how much she enriched my life.

All summer following my sophomore year I worked hard on Latin, history, and particularly Greek. Greek grammar was a difficult chore and Xenophon's *Anabasis* which followed was not much better. But Homer's *Iliad* was a sheer joy. Unlike Latin with its inverted sentence structure and its ablative absolutes, the Greek moves along with the straightforward ease of French. In Homer I discovered a great storyteller, a poet whose imaginative figures came straight out of nature and common life. In Book II, I made a poetic discovery. During a summit conference of the generals a snake comes out from under a plane tree, climbs up and devours eight sparrows and their mother. In the movement of the Greek line I could see that Homer's syllables were catching the lively, kinetic movement of the snake. The description and the thing described merged into one. It was there that I saw the greatness of poetry and its superiority over the "cool element of prose." Years later, when I read in an essay of Oscar Wilde's that "the two greatest pleasures in this life are reading the Greek page and speaking the French tongue," I was inclined to agree with him.

The weeks of study paid off. In September I was admitted to the senior class. So many had dropped out that there were only eight girls and two boys left in the class. The girls were extremely attractive. One of them, Mary McPhail, became a lifelong friend. The beauty of this group, a Baptist, became engaged to a devout Roman Catholic. Religion was a barrier they somehow could not negotiate. The boy had a certain distinctive whistle he used when he wanted her to come out and take an evening walk with him. Twenty years later I happened to be in Thomaston calling on old friends, and while walking along Main Street I was startled to hear that same odd whistle and to see the same girl a few minutes later emerge from the house and join him. Neither ever married.

When cold weather came I moved to my grandmother's front room downstairs and set up a small wood stove for warmth and cheer. Several boys called to spend evenings in talk. Thus my rigid program of the year before was eased somewhat. I was also an enthusiastic member of the baseball team. I played third base and did fairly well at bat, and enjoyed the journeys to neighboring towns. As a result I have been an avid follower of the great American sport, rooting for the Red Sox through thick and thin.

My grandmother, who was too lame to walk upstairs, used to hobble into my room and tell me about life in Waterford, Ireland, city of the most delicate lace and the finest glass in the world. She told me often of the nightmare steerage trip across the Atlantic in a Black Ball liner. When she caught me hard at work she would sigh and say, "In my family it was Rosie who had all the brains and all the beauty," then she would sigh again. One day I asked her, "What became of Rose?" "She went to Boston and married a man by the name of Fitzgerald— Richard Fitzgerald. She and her husband had a nephew who became a great politician. He was mayor of Boston time and time again. Instead of making long speeches at the rallies," she said, "he would sing 'Sweet Adeline.' They called him Honey Fitz."

My step-grandfather spent most of his time reading the daily papers, particularly reports of murders and murder trials. In the most famous murder trial of Knox County (Pearson calls it one of the great murder cases in America), the Hart-Meservey case, he was foreman of the jury that exonerated Meservey who was first indicted, and he followed all the proceedings of the jury that convicted Hart, the second suspect. A poorly written but much read book of the period, *An Innocent Man in a Felon's Cell*, which asserted the innocence of Hart, he read over and over. Hart's guilt or innocence was debated even in my own time. In his old age Job Montgomery, the Camden lawyer who defended Hart, wrote a long article for the *Courier-Gazette*, our local paper, elaborating on Hart's confession of guilt to him, which finally settled the matter. But this was long after my step-grandfather died.

At the high school the principal had put on the shelves in the back of the room a number of "Great Books," classics of American and English literature. Any student who had finished his assignment was permitted to explore these books. One day I stumbled upon a copy of Bulfinch's *Mythology* edited by Edward Everett Hale, the famous Boston clergyman who had written *The Man Without a Country*. To me this book was a revelation. Like the Bible, it was an interpretation of man's life upon earth. I devoured it day after day and wished that someday I might have a Bulfinch of my own.

Another book I discovered there was Benjamin Franklin's *Autobiography*. It so impressed me that I decided to make his "rules of life" my own. It was an expurgated edition. Later on I bought an unexpurgated edition and discovered that some of his advice to young men was a bit shocking to a boy brought up in Puritan New England. Other books which hit me hard at this time was Carlyle's *Heroes and Hero Worship* and Hawthorne's *House of the Seven Gables*. It was while reading this last book that I discovered the difference between journalism and writing that possesses style. Hawthorne became my hero. Cowper's *Task* ought to be added to this list for its quiet realistic genre pictures and its sententious aphorisms.

On these shelves I found copies of the Bowdoin *Orient*. Reported in one was a speech by Thomas Brackett Reed, Speaker of the House of Representatives, on the occasion of his receiving an honorary degree from the college. The speech impressed me profoundly and gave me a desire to go to his college. The general trend of his remarks was that we do a great deal toward lifting intelligent individuals into places of eminence, but when are we going to do something to lift up the masses themselves to a higher level of culture? I read the speech many times and it haunted me for years.

While in Thomaston I discovered a type of human being new to me, George Langtry Crockett. He was a whirlwind of activity. As a young doctor he got mixed up in an abortion case and fled the country, finding refuge in the West Indies. He expected to be called back to stand trial—the girl had died—but never was. While waiting in the southern states for his trouble to blow over, he visited the Hermitage and fell in love with Andrew Jackson, of whom he wrote a short life that was full of rhetorical eloquence. He converted me to the belief that Jackson's "Proclamation Against Nullification" in which he declared "the Federal Union, it must be preserved" is one of our country's great state documents. In due time he came back to Thomaston, began to practice medicine once more, and took over the leadership of the Democratic Town Committee. He announced a series of public lectures on Jackson, and through these lectures enlarged his following and put new life into the Democratic Party of Knox County, a party which had given up trying to win elections and only as a matter of form put two or three names on the county ballot.

He became a well-known and much-talked-about man. He and his wife did not move in the best society, for the story of his malpractice was still whispered about. He had a loud speaking voice and an oratorical stage manner that drew crowds to hear him. In a hard-fought campaign he was his own hatchet man and spared no one. He visited all the towns of the county, rejuvenated the slumbering Democrats, insisted on a full county ticket, and defeated the Republicans at the next state election and in every other county election for the next twelve years. In Republican Maine this was a Herculean achievement.

Dr. Crockett's contemporary political hero was William Jennings Bryan, whom he succeeded in bringing to Knox County during the mer of 1898. A dozen of us Spruce Head boys walked eight miles before breakfast to hear him. There was no hall big enough to hold the audience, so they stood in the open space in the courthouse square.

Dr. Crockett loaned me unusual books such as Gail Hamilton's *Life of Blaine* and Burton's *City of the Saints*, books not in favor with nice people. He also acquainted me with Emerson. He listened rather patiently to the verses I was writing, and offered some pertinent criticism.

When I married a Knox County girl years later I put the doctor's name near the top of the list of those I wanted invited to the wedding. But my bride's mother, thinking a man who had the reputation of being an abortionist was not respectable, refused to invite him. Between the hour of our wedding and the hour of our departure on the train, I slipped into his home and told him how much I owed to him and how keenly I wanted him to be present at my wedding. "I've been up against this all my life," he said. "I'm used to it." But his next words showed how embittered he was by his social ostracism. "Your wife's mother has no reason to feel superior to me. She kept her husband so deeply in debt all his life that he was glad to die!" Then, "Never mind, Bill. Don't let it bother you."

Another type of orator I encountered during high school days was Endicott Hastings, a layman of the Thomaston Methodist Church. For two years I tended the huge furnace of this church—filling its capacious maw every evening with great shovelfuls of coal. My pay for this work was fifty cents a week. I often stayed over from seven to eight to attend prayer meeting. Hastings was a gigantic man who I believe could have danced in a medieval coat of armor. He had an overpowering voice. When he spoke in prayer meeting his voice rose as if he were addressing the House of Commons. But his theme was always himself. As a young man, he told us, he was drunk every week end and sobered up just in time to go to work Monday morning. "During those week ends," he said, "I was not a man but a beast. I visited houses of ill fame, tasted the lips of scarlet women, and sank down into the depths of degradation, a lost soul! But Christ redeemed me!" (He had been converted during a great revival which shook the town.) He spoke with such fervor and such power that the silence which followed was awesome and overwhelming. He made the same speech almost every week for thirty years.

Another man whose influence I felt in my high school days was the Reverend William Newcomb, the pastor of the Baptist Church. He was a member of the School Committee, the only one who ever called at the high school to see how the teachers and students were getting on. He was something of a philosopher, read books on evolution, and pondered long over the much debated question of science versus religion.

He was a forgetful man, and stories of his lapses of memory entertained the town. For example, he once went on a trolley ride to Rockland, and decided to have a luncheon at one of the city restaurants. At the conclusion of the meal he reached into his vest pocket where he always carried his money and discovered that he had no change, not even a tip for the waitress. He assured the manager that he would bring over payment the next day. When he got home, he found he had put a second vest on over the one containing the money.

Another Newcomb story that people loved concerned a funeral on the outskirts of town. An old grandfather had died and Mr. Newcomb by some misunderstanding thought it was the mother. He chose as his Bible text, "She hath done what she could" and went on to extoll the virtues of the mother and the wife in mellow tones. Fortunately for him, the mother had a magnificent sense of humor. I once heard her say, "I bet I'm the only woman in Knox County who ever listened to her own funeral oration." These lapses endeared Newcomb to his friends.

I often dropped into his study and talked with him about religion. Like young Omar I was having some theological doubts, and he was the one man in town who was most interested in talking over these matters with young inquirers. Looking back, I marvel at the time this man was willing to spend with me, and the serene patience he manifested when I told him about my concern. I recall telling him that if the bulk of the human race went to Hell I wanted to go there also. I knew it was a terrible thing to say but it was the way I felt. I told him that the idea of the "remnant" preserved in the Old Testament and the "few who are chosen" in the New was repulsive to me. He laughed at that and said, "You ought to be a preacher if you are that much interested in the human race."

On another occasion I told him that the tortured death on the Cross was an ugly means of salvation, borrowed from the human sacrifices of the ancient pagan religions. Moreover, "a fountain filled with blood, drawn from Emanuel's veins" could not signify cleansing. I wished more than anything else that Jesus had chosen more attractive symbols in presenting his mission to the world. Newcomb said, "That is the aesthetic side of you coming out. You see the importance of Beauty more than you do the importance of Sacrifice. But you will change when you get older and see life more clearly."

One afternoon Mr. Newcomb told me of an experience he had in Andover Theological Seminary. One night about ten o'clock he was reading a dull text on Christian Apologetics when all at once, tears came to his eyes and the room was filled with white clouds. He wondered what was happening to him. He pounded the side of his head with his left hand, looked again at the page he was reading, and realized that there was nothing in the text that could move a man to weeping. The next day he received a telegram from Canada telling him that his father was dead. Making a careful check, he learned that his father had died at ten o'clock the previous night.

The months sped by and we came to the last weeks of school. This was a happy time, mixed with some doubt and fear of what lay ahead. I had thought a little about going to college, which meant Bowdoin —for Thomaston was a Bowdoin town, and sons of the leading families had followed one another there. Hawthorne and Longfellow were graduates of the college, both in the same class, and that was a lodestone for me. Henry Beveridge, already a junior, gave me a glowing account of campus life. Ralph Cushing had left high school, taken intensive private lessons in Latin and Greek, and had already completed two years there. He urged me to come to college. But that required money. I had none; my relatives had none; and that settled the matter.

We seniors had long talks together. We seemed to be clinging to our high school days, making the most of each one. We chose a class motto, in Latin of course. It was short, "In Medias Res," meaning that we were about to enter the great world of men and affairs. Edith Wilson, a straight A girl, was chosen by the faculty to be valedictorian, and my good friend Mary McPhail was salutatorian. I, number three, was chosen to deliver an oration. The class prophet and historian were selected by ballot. I wrote a class poem, a sin of versification which I hope will never see the light of day. Someone else wrote the class song, set to an old tune.

I was the first person from Spruce Head to finish high school. On the night of graduation a goodly number of village friends and neighbors hired a haywagon drawn by two horses and drove to Thomaston. This pleased me more than anything else that occurred that night. It made me resolve to speak my oration loud enough for my somewhat deaf Uncle Ernest to hear. The oration called for the rebuilding of our American merchant marine. After depicting past glories and deploring the low state into which it had fallen, I ended by forecasting the day when the American flag "will be flying in every port and our American bottoms will dominate the Seven Seas!" This climactic outburst brought tremendous applause, to the entire satisfaction of my hometown folks.

When it was all over, I climbed into the haywagon along with the Spruce Headers and rode home, not knowing what I was going to do next.

CHAPTER 5

Country School Teacher

THE summer following my graduation I got a job boxing stone on the Spruce Head Island quarry. I was paid $1.35 for a nine-hour day. I worked with a man named Clark who knew exactly the encasement needed to keep the corners and edges of a piece of finished granite from being chipped off in transit. I soon caught on to the technique and became proficient at it. There were about three hundred men working in the quarries, the stone sheds, and the blacksmith shops, and the whole place was a beehive of noisy activity.

Before I had time to settle into the routine came July 12. This was Orangemen's Day, a time for the Protestant Irish Ulsterites to put on a demonstration. About ten o'clock that morning a group of North Irish quarrymen, some with orange sashes and orange flowers in their buttonholes, got together and began singing:

> Ten thousand Micks lay down their picks
> Ten thousand more to slaughter,
> Ten thousand Micks lay down their picks
> At the battle of the Boyne water . . .

They always managed to get two syllables out of "Boyne," calling it "Boy-yun." By the time the singing ended a group of unmistakably Irish Catholic patriots had gathered and, organizing a phalanx, charged the Orangemen. Fists flew in all directions. "Papists!" "John Bull's lackeys!" and other insults were thrown about even more rapidly than the fists. Before the fighting had gone too far a straw boss rushed in and yelled, "Cut this out, or I'll see to it that your pay is docked!" That had a sobering effect on both groups. Those able to do so slunk away growling and went back to their work. As a teen-age boy, I was delighted with this break in the day's routine.

At first I rather liked the work, but before long it became extremely monotonous. Why was it, I asked myself, that the stonecutters working side by side with us enjoyed the luxury of an eight-hour day at $2.80, over twice as much as we were getting for a nine-hour day? The answer was that they had a union and we had not. So I took it upon myself to call the quarrymen together and urge them to organize a union. One old man said, "But they are skilled workers and we are not. Only skilled workers can have a union." I said, "No such thing! We do the hard work. We drill and blast out the stone, and when they get through with it, we box it for shipment. Our work is *just* as important as *theirs* and more hazardous." My pleadings got nowhere with the men, but they did reach the ears of the head boss, who quietly told me my services would no longer be required after Saturday night. I quit work a strong believer in unions.

Once more I was out of a job and didn't know where to turn. Within a few days I received a letter from Gilford B. Butler, chairman of the school committee of the town, asking if I would consider teaching the Bassick School. It was an ungraded school of about thirty pupils. The term began in mid-August and ran for ten weeks. This early start was for the benefit of the pupils from the outlying districts who could not negotiate the big snowdrifts of midwinter. The school would reopen in the spring for another ten weeks. The pay was six dollars a week. I could live at home, take a cold lunch for the noon meal, and enjoy the blessings of a three-mile walk each day. I accepted.

Each day I came to school early to start the fire and warm the room before the children arrived. The older boys lugged in wood, and the older girls helped with the sweeping and dusting. The master's desk was on a raised platform at the end of the room. On its edge, facing the pupils, were two wooden brackets holding a smoothly whittled birch rod. In this session it was rarely used. A similar instrument had once been used on me unmercifully when I had mimicked a teacher, and I resolved to "spare the rod."

I followed in part the program of Mary B. Grant and put the children in three groups instead of eight grades. I lengthened the recess periods both morning and afternoon and played baseball with the boys for a half-hour in both sessions. We took on neighboring teams Saturdays and I went to all the games. I took the whole school on a nutting expedition one day and brought down on my head the condemnation of their parents. One woman said, "We aren't paying him to romp in the beech woods with the children." On Hallowe'en we had an evening party and performed most of the feats mentioned in Robert Burns' "Halloween" plus some additions, such as bobbing for apples. The children had a wonderful time and remembered it for years.

How tired I was at the end of the first week! I walked home wearily, dropped into the swing chair in our front yard, too exhausted to come in and eat my supper. After that first week the "all gone and tired feeling" never returned.

One girl in the school was taking work in the primary class for the fourth straight year. She was a "retarded" child unable to learn her ABC's. I didn't know how to cope with this problem and encouraged her to stay at home on every snowy or even overcast day, but she was strong and persisted in coming.

I established the custom of making those who did not finish their lessons stay a half-hour after school, review their assignments, and recite to me. The plan worked well for everyone but Bertha, an uncommonly attractive, blue-eyed little child. She stayed the half-hour, pouted, acted sullen, and refused to look at a book. As a teen-aged male, I could not bring myself to take the ruler to such a pretty little girl, so at the end of the half-hour I let her out with the rest.

I studied the entire school from my raised platform and noted how many of them had Indian features. Some of their grandfathers or great-grandfathers had married or cohabited with the original native stock. They were ashamed of the Indian outcropping; it was never discussed.

Among the pupils was a girl named Flora Jackson, whose father had died at forty leaving five children. There were no widows' pensions, no unemployment insurance, no help of any kind except the miserable pittance the town fathers chose to allot. She had a brother a year older than herself, and there were three smaller children about six, seven, and eight. When school closed for the day, this girl of thirteen bundled the children up, especially on snowy, stormy days, for the half-mile walk home, and was so gentle in her loving care of them that she won my affectionate admiration. She was a sweet, sensitive child who loved poetry and appreciated everything I was trying to do for the school. She later became the village postmistress, married well, and had a fine family of her own.

Looking back, I feel certain that that three-mile walk every day was a health builder. In high school I had worked harder than a boy should, with too little time for relaxation and pleasure. Those walks on dirt roads, partly through woods with branches reaching to the sky, not only strengthened my body but uplifted my spirit. A sunrise delighted me. I observed all five acts of a glorious sunset. "Beauty born of murmuring sound" came to life in the moving water of brooks and the rote of ocean tides. These good things of life were mine in spite of my poverty.

At the end of the term, Mr. Butler told me they would like to have me teach the spring session of the Timber Hill School at Owl's Head, with a magnificent advancement to seven dollars a week.

Gilford B. Butler was born on a well-managed farm in the Buttermilk Lane section of South Thomaston. It was said that he carried eggs to market for his mother when he was a boy, charged her one cent a dozen for the service, and saved each one of those pennies. He was educated at Boston University, practiced law in Rockland, made money, and saved it. He joined the Rotary Club but refused to pay for Rotary dinners. If the Club had a well-known speaker, he would eat a sandwich in his office and turn up at the dinner in time to hear the address. He had several sweethearts but failed to marry any one of them. Marriage cost too much.

When Butler died in his seventies, he left an estate worth more than $300,000. In his will, he left the bulk of his estate to his nieces in California, adding "I hope they will have as much fun spending it as I had earning it." But he also left $35,000 to help pay for a new elementary school the town was then building, stipulating that it be called "The Guilford B. Butler School," the name to be displayed in letters at least one foot high. All this the town fathers gladly carried out.

I accepted Butler's offer to teach at Timber Hill, and on the Sunday afternoon before school began, walked the dirt road eight miles carrying a dress-suit case with a few changes of clothing and some books. A sea captain's wife, Mrs. Knott Emery, who turned out to be my father's half-sister Ada, had already agreed to give me board and room for three dollars a week.

I knocked at the front door and heard her call out, "Scrape off your shoes on that old rug!" She had not seen me yet, but I surmised at once that she was more intersted in the condition of my shoes than she was in me. She escorted me to a room on the second floor. On a bureau in one corner was a big bowl and a pitcher full of water. Here I was to wash and shave. There was no heat in the room. One zero day later on I asked if I could come downstairs and shave in the kitchen. She said forcefully, "No, not in *my* sink!" So I went back, broke the ice in the pitcher, and shivered through a miserable half-hour. Aunt Ada belonged to that group of New England women known as "nasty neat." They do not believe that "cleanliness is next to godliness;" they go further and give cleanliness the place of honor.

On Monday morning at 8:45, I arrived at the Timber Hill schoolhouse to face about forty "scholars," a half-dozen of whom were in their teens and ready for ninth-grade work. My first encounter, however, was with an immaculately dressed gray-haired woman named Isabel Lattie, who taught the Timber Hill School for twenty-odd years. She regarded it as her own prerogative and had no intention of giving it up. She had been officially discharged by Mr. Butler but the notice did not take. What was I to do—a teen-aged boy up against an articulate, determined Irish schoolmarm who was probably over sixty but looked very much younger?

As the children poured into the room I could see that they were caught by the dramatic situation facing them, and when the two of us began talking you could hear a pin drop.

I said to her, "So you intend to stay here?"

She answered, "I do," as solemnly as if she were taking an oath with her hand on the Bible. I smiled and looked her straight in the face. There was no response, no yielding. With an air of deadly earnestness she sat down at the teacher's desk. The attention of the children was so complete that I could feel the silence. I bestirred myself and said, "Well, you take the math and science and I'll take the reading and history."

"But I prefer the reading and history," she said; "I love poetry."

"All right," I replied, "then you take the reading and history, and I'll take the math and science."

I then suggested that we adopt the Mary B. Grant program and divide the children as far as possible into groups of three grades.

"No," she said, "I'll have none of that. It wouldn't be fair to all the children."

"All right," I said, "call out your first class." She was proud of the work she had done with the second-graders, and called them to come forward and recite.

I listened to her with great interest, hoping I might learn something valuable from an experienced teacher. My close attention began to annoy her so I turned to my arithmetic class. Instead of taking up the lesson, I decided to get acquainted with the children. I asked their names, found out where they lived, what they were interested in, and got them to talking about themselves. Miss Lattie listened and could not help registering a towering disgust with the way I handled my first class.

For three days our antiphonal teaching program continued. On the morning of the fourth day, Isabel did not show up. Our dialogue was ended. Difficult as it had been, I felt sorry for the woman. There were no teachers' pensions in Maine in 1902 (they date from 1913) and old-age assistance had not even been suggested. All an old teacher could do was live with relatives, or join her cronies in retirement, pooling her small savings with theirs, or go "over the hill to the poorhouse." I felt that something ought to be done to improve this situation. At the grass roots I was learning something about my country and forming political opinions.

On the fourth day I reorganized the school, keeping the primary class as it was, combining the reading, arithmetic, and grammar classes into three groups, and providing an advanced English literature class and an algebra class for four older pupils who should have been sent away to a high school or academy.

On the fourth day also I had my first case of discipline. A hulking boy named Harold Philbrook got up to stretch and then began walking around in the aisles for exercise. I politely asked him to sit down, and he replied, "I'll sit down when I get damn good and ready." I saw that he was out to defy me. He weighed about 200 pounds and I only 160, but from my brothers I had learned something about boxing. I took my ruler, went up to him and said, "Hold out your right hand." He replied, "Right hand nothing." I made a lunge for him and hit his extensive derriere with my ruler. He immediately came at me like a raging bull. I was more agile than he, dropped my ruler, and backed away from his short-reaching, flinging fists. Either he or I was going to be the master in that school and my anger mounted. He was strong but overly fat and clumsy. Suddenly I saw an opening and socked him a left-hand punch on the point of the chin. Before he recovered from this blow, I hit him a right on the side of the face. When he saw that I could handle him, he slunk back into his seat. From that moment on I had no trouble at all with discipline. This boy Philbrook later joined the police force in Rockland and rendered that city excellent service.

As a result of that encounter I started having ten minutes of calisthenics each morning after we got through with Bible reading and the Lord's Prayer. I felt that other children besides the Philbrook boy needed some stretching.

I soon discovered that the Baptist Church dominated the social as well as the religious life of Owl's Head. They had prayer meetings once a week which I attended. The leading man in the church and the community was Bradford K. Emery (no relation to Aunt Ada's husband). He was a Bull of Bashan if ever there was one. He believed in a literal interpretation of the Scriptures. He was as rigid in his theology as the Catholics he despised. To him the Catholic Church was the "whore of Babylon" and its monks and nuns were "whited sepulchres" even though they dressed in black. In his testimony at prayer meetings, he often repeated the words, "One faith, one Lord, and one baptism"—meaning baptism by immersion, and leaving no shadow of a doubt about which denomination held the one true Christian faith.

He was a successful farmer, worked from sunrise to sunset daily on his rocky farm, and was sufficiently well-to-do to send his son to Colby College and to medical school. He did not believe in higher education for his girls. One extremely attractive daughter, Katherine, was afflicated with a nervous condition which baffled the family doctor. A new young doctor in Rockland suggested that she go to Boston and consult a famous physician skilled in nervous diseases. Her father hesitated because of the expense, but when Katherine failed to improve he gave her the money for the trip. I selfishly hated to see her go, for she was so beautiful that I would often cross the street just to have one glimpse of her.

While she was in Boston in a hospital, she was visited by a Christian Science missionary. Her acquaintance with this woman blossomed into friendship and the two became devoted to each other. Katherine then joined the Mother Church. At Christmas she wrote that she was coming home. News of her going over to Mary Baker Eddy had already reached the community and stirred it to the foundations. Her apostasy preyed deeply on her father's mind. Love for his daughter vied with loyalty to his church. The church won. When Katherine arrived home, he stood in the doorway and refused to let her enter the house. This event shook me more than anything that occurred while I was at Owl's Head. It haunted my mind so completely that I finally wrote a poem about it.

At the end of the term I said good-bye with regrets. I realized as never before the inadequacy of education in Maine—twenty weeks a year in a one-room schoolhouse; outhouses filthy, the boys' section jackknife-carved with obscene graffiti; potbellied stoves able in cold weather to heat only the front half of the room; underpaid and overworked teachers trying to manage on six, eight, or ten dollars a week —all this showed that people were giving lip service to education, and that was all.

I wondered whether other states were doing any better by their teachers and pupils. A National Education Association meeting to be held in Boston on July 6, 7, and 8 would give me a chance to find out. Like other New England teachers, I was urged to attend and I resolved to go.

On my way to Boston, I decided to stop over in Brunswick and take the Bowdoin College entrance examinations. It was a brash thing to do, but teenagers are not afraid to do brash things. Candidates for the freshman class were assembled in Memorial Hall. In the large main room were fifty to seventy-five small octagonal tables—one for every candidate. Proctors paced up and down the hall looking every minute for cheaters. I had never known an examination so searchingly supervised. I translated passages from Caesar, Cicero, and Virgil easily enough. Then I came upon a Latin story I had never seen before. That gave me a little trouble. I turned one English paragraph into Latin. The Greek of the *Anabasis* covering so many *stages* and so many *parasangs* was easy. Passages from the Iliad were not difficult. At the end of three hours, one proctor with a loud voice cried out, "Sign your names and hand in your bluebooks." As I walked out, I looked around at the portraits of Bowdoin worthies hanging on the walls. I longed to belong to their world.

The next day I struggled with mathematics and English literature for another three hours, walked to the railroad station, and took a train to Boston. Arriving late, I sought out a flophouse and got an overnight bed for twenty-five cents. The next morning I walked up Huntington Avenue, found where my classmate and friend Harris Shaw had his studio, told Harris why I had come to Boston, cleaned up, and went with him to Thompson's Spa for breakfast.

The first session of the NEA, held July 6, 1903, at Mechanics Hall opened with an invocation delivered by none other than one of my great heroes, Edward Everett Hale, editor of the Bulfinch Mythology that had opened my eyes to the human revelations of Greek mythology. I felt toward him much the same as one of my grandsons feels now toward Carl Yastrzemski. His appearance was not disappointing. He looked like the plaster of Paris reproductions of the poet Homer invariably on view in American high schools at the turn of the century. He must have been eighty years old.

The main speaker was Charles W. Eliot, president of Harvard and president of the NEA. He was tall, dignified, and touched with the quality of greatness. One side of his face was disfigured by a large red birthmark, but his personality was so commanding and his nobility of character so evident that one forgot all about his disfigurement. He argued that the educated man of the twentieth century would need a knowledge of both science and the humanities to equip himself for the demands of modern life.

I looked around at the large audience and saw that it was composed almost entirely of girls and women. There was an amazingly small scattering of men, most of whom were administrators—principals of high schools, grammar schools, and the like.

Word was passed along the aisles that a lady from Waltham would like to have some of us come to dinner at her home. Buses to take us there were provided. A St. Louis teacher said to me, "Let's go out and see where Waltham watches are made. The woman inviting us is the wife of the general manager." This girl was older than I but I liked her breezy Western manner and said, "All right, let's go." On the way she told me about her school in St. Louis, told me how much she enjoyed teaching, and only wished that Missouri would pay a decent wage like New York and New Jersey. When I told her what my salary was, she refused to believe me. "You're kidding!" I agreed to swear to my wage on a stack of Bibles, and she still refused to believe. "No one would pay only seven dollars a week; no one would work for that."

By this time we had arrived at the magnificent lawn of the grand lady and were ushered to our tables. I had never seen a sight like this before. On each of the long tables were several big bouquets of roses beautifully arranged in low white vases. I was so overwhelmed by these roses that I don't recall one thing that we ate. I only remember that it was a sumptuous dinner and that there were roses everywhere. I resolved then and there that if I ever had the means I would raise roses and have them on my table—a resolve I later carried out.

The next day I went alone out to Concord and stood by "the rude bridge that arched the flood." Daniel French's minute-man statue had not yet been erected. The brook was much smaller than I had imagined, but the memory of the "embattled farmers" who once stood there thrilled me. I experienced a still greater emotion when I stood before the house of Emerson and remembered what his emancipated utterances had meant to me. I repeated: "Nor knowest thou what argument / Thy life to thy neighbor's creed has lent," recalling the day I first met with and devoured his illuminating essays and poetry. I knew then I had hit upon a germinal mind and had discovered the best that America had to offer. As I stood before the house I was moved to tears and was glad that I he 1 come alone. I took a good look also at the Old Manse and thanked Heaven for Hawthorne. I had not yet discovered Thoreau, otherwise I would have had another shrine to visit. That day at Concord gave me a sense of elation a young man feels when a "new planet swims into his ken."

I was now determined to go to college even though I didn't have the money to go with. When I got home and announced my intention, the news made quite a stir. "He'll never make it," one grocery store loafer said, "it takes money to go to college, and he haint got any." Another one said, "He's got a lot of stick-to-it-ive-ness in him and maybe he'll make it." "I doubt it," said another. "Nobody out of this village ever went to college. College is something for rich folks, not for people like Foss Snow's family."

When I went over and told my somewhat deaf Uncle Ernest that I was going to college, he said, "What's that?" I raised my voice and repeated, "Uncle Ernest, I'm going to college!" He stood up, nervously looked me over and said, "Well, I'll be God damned!"

The women took it differently. They met and decided to make me a patchwork quilt of woolen squares sewed together. Like Joseph's coat, it was a creation of many colors. In the center of each square was embroidered the name of the woman or girl who had made it. There were about sixty squares in the quilt. They figured it would help keep me warm on cold winter nights. It was an odd gift, but I appreciated it and still have it. They also gave me a fine edition of the King James version of the Bible, which I have kept to this day.

CHAPTER 6

Bowdoin College

SEPTEMBER arrived and I braced myself for college. I had already received notice of my acceptance as a member of the forthcoming freshman class. I threw my dress-suit case out in the rain one night to make sure it wouldn't look too new. I dried it off and packed it with my new Bible, my patchwork quilt, a toothbrush, two changes of underwear, an extra pair of stockings, one necktie, Franklin's *Autobiography*, and a picture of my family. These were not enough to fill it. I had a shabby overcoat, no raincoat, no extra suit of clothes, in fact not much of any worldly goods at all. My father gave me $50; that was more than he could really afford, for his house was already mortgaged and his salary of $40 a month in winter was inadequate for his family. He was able to help now only because the shedders were crawling well that September. Out of my two school jobs I had saved another $50. I bought my fare on the Maine Central Railroad and enjoyed the ride from Rockland to Brunswick—a distance of about fifty miles.

My favorite cousin, Bill Norton, had already completed his first two years at Bowdoin. He had a summer job at a hotel in Chocorua, New Hampshire, and would not be back for nearly two weeks. He made me promise that I would not pledge myself to any fraternity until I had talked matters over with him. This promise was not easy to keep. My freshman roommate, Ensign Otis, had pledged himself to Kappa Sigma and he was asked by his brothers to make a pitch for me. I told him of my promise and he left me alone. Pledging in those days was an aggressive and brutal ritual. If a man was a star athlete or otherwise gifted, some fraternity would get hold of him and hide him away until they got the pledge button in his coat lapel. It was called the lead-pipe method of pledging, and the innocent freshman was the victim. Fraternity men in those days spoke of nonfraternity men, in the ancient Greek fashion, as "Barbarians." But the real barbarians were the rushing squads whose duty it was to fill the house quotas and thus keep the dining room budget solvent. As a matter of fact I didn't want to join any fraternity at all because of the expense, but I was annoyed for a week by these "storm-troopers" rushing into 18 Winthrop Hall at all hours of the day and night regaling me with the glories of their fraternities. It was a period of harassment and I was glad when it was over.

Some of the interclass hazing carried on at Bowdoin in my day seems sadistic to me now. There was the nightshirt parade, a ceremony in which all the freshmen had to line up in their nightshirts, their hands on the shoulders of the man ahead, and walk under the windows of the three dormitories while the upper classmen poured hundreds of buckets of water upon their heads. The first five minutes of this treatment were distressing. After that one didn't care how much he was drenched. The ceremony ended with a clash downtown between the freshmen and the "yaggers" of the city, in which rocks and bottles and any other handy missiles were used as ammunition in a near-riot. There were no fatalities but many injuries. I was bruised and cut with rocks and went to the infirmary to be patched up.

I remember only one other general hazing experience. The sophomores got together a number of boats and ferried all of the freshmen to a small island in the Kennebec River below Brunswick, known as Cow Island. They left us there to get off as best we could. We milled around for a while, then tore off the big door of an abandoned barn, used rocks for hammers, nailed some old roof beams under the door, and made ourselves a raft. Before the sun was up we had ferried every freshman off. We walked back to the college, sat down triumphantly on the campus, and yelled and sang defiance to the sophomores.

Tuition at Bowdoin was $75 a year, and I paid half of it the day I arrived in Brunswick. As soon as Bill Norton came back he pledged me to his fraternity, Beta Theta Pi, and saw to it that I landed a job in the house waiting on tables. After buying my textbooks I was pretty much on the rocks financially. A senior told me that college boys now and then served as substitutes for preachers who were ill or out of town. So I went to the Y.M.C.A. leader and told him that I was available. Without questioning my qualifications as a "man of the cloth," he landed me three $10 pulpits in nearby towns and one $20 pulpit in Bath. I didn't feel right about accepting these "divine services," but like some old Spruce Head evangelists I was driven to it by a lack of money.

In my room at 18 Winthrop Hall many boys gathered to talk, box one-minute rounds, and burn the midnight oil. One of these was a fraternity brother named Charles Hawksworth, who was fascinated by the Arctic and got me to reading everything I could find about Eskimos, the northern ice fields, and so on. Others were interested in philosophy and religion, discussed the old problem of free will and determinism and "came out by the same door where in we went." A few thought they were wise to the woman question and burst out with the key line, "I learned about women from her," from Kipling's popular poem "The Ladies." I personally knew little about women. I only knew that I was going to keep them out of my life until I had had some adventure. At a smut session one night an upper classman came in and read us lines from Walt Whitman's "Children of Adam." They all thought it was dirty poetry but I wasn't sure. After they had left I took down *Leaves of Grass* and read a portion of the verses the upper classman had laughed at: "Through you I drain the pent-up rivers of myself. / In you I wrap a thousand onward years." There was a dignity about the movement and the sound of these lines that impressed me. "This isn't smut," I said to myself. "This is real poetry." I kept on reading the book until two o'clock in the morning and became a convert to the "Good Gray Poet." That was a strange approach to a poet but it was mine.

Toward the close of my freshman year my financial situation was desperate. I had not paid my fraternity dues. I had not paid the second half of my tuition. I didn't know where to turn. Just then I heard of a school committee in Cundy's Harbor, about twelve miles away, who were in desperate need of a teacher. In this coastal school of forty-eight "scholars" two teachers had been kicked out of the school one after the other by the older boys and had refused to continue. There were seven weeks left in the term. When I appeared as a candidate, they fairly begged me to take the job and offered me $11 a week and board. I agreed to take the school providing they would let me have a week or ten days off in June to take my final exams at the college. Finally they gave in, and I became the third Cundy's Harbor teacher that spring.

I started out by making a speech. I regretted the fact that they had already kicked two fine teachers out, reminded them that theirs was an uncommonly large one-room school which required some semblance of order. I urged them to cooperate with me in making the rest of this session a worth-while experience for us all. I didn't dare put in the Mary B. Grant system of three classes each in reading, grammar, arithmetic, history, etc., fearing that such an innovation might cause a third eruption. I boarded across the way from the schoolhouse at the home of a widow, who was surprised to find me all in one piece at the end of the first imperfect day. As a matter of fact, the three roughneck sons of lobster catchers who had given most of the trouble to my predecessors were surprised to have a lobster catcher for a teacher. We talked shop—potheads, bait bags, toggles, torching herring, spearing flounders, and all the rest—and soon became friends. There was no need to think about discipline after the first day.

While I was at Cundy's Harbor the college was preparing to celebrate the centennial of Nathaniel Hawthorne's birth. Bliss Perry, the editor of the *Atlantic Monthly*, was to make the Centennial Address and I determined to go. So I walked the twelve miles to Brunswick and listened to the excellent paper in which Perry called Hawthorne the Hamlet of the New England Renaissance writers. I visited with my fraternity brothers until after midnight, and then walked back to my boarding house, arriving just as the stars were fading.

Twenty-one years later the college was celebrating the centenary of the famous class of 1825—the class of Longfellow and Hawthorne— and I was one of the three speakers on that occasion. The others were Edward Page Mitchell, editor of the New York *Sun* and the author of the most popular Bowdoin song *Phi Chi*, and Bliss Perry. On the stage while the crowd was assembling I told Perry of my twenty-four-mile walk to hear his essay on Hawthorne. He said, "That is the greatest compliment I have ever received."

Bowdoin in my freshman year had three terms of twelve weeks each ending at Christmas, Easter, and June. Fortunately I was blessed with a remarkable memory and could do well on examination questions that covered only a twelve-week term. While at Cundy's Harbor I kept up on the reading in all four of my classes and was ready for the term examinations when they came. I finished my freshman year with good grades—thirteen A's, five B's, and one C—in mathematics, the blind spot in my mental equipment.

I picked up a few odd jobs during the summer and enjoyed sailing a new boat my father had built. She was equipped with a large mainsail and a jib, plus a Mianus engine which could be used if the wind dropped out. Sailing her around the bay was my number one pleasure of that vacation.

Fall approached and I didn't have enough money to return to college. John Woodard, a grocery store keeper of South Thomaston, became interested in me and said he would endorse my check for $50 or even $100 if I wanted to borrow from the Rockland bank. But that wasn't necessary, for at the same time Gilford Butler offered me a job to teach the South Thomaston High School for $12.50 a week. He said he would start the session in August so that I could go back to college without losing too many weeks.

A one-room, one-teacher grammar school was a common thing in Maine. But a one-room, one-teacher high school was something else again. There were about twenty-eight students in that school and they deserved a better opportunity. I taught Latin, algebra, geometry, history, English composition and literature. The mathematics kept me up until midnight every weekday night. The other subjects I was able to take in my stride.

While teaching this high school I attended a Maine teachers' convention in Bangor. The highlight of those meetings was a speech by William DeWitt Hyde, the president of Bowdoin. He seemed to have the same vision as Charles W. Eliot, who wanted America to wake up and do far more than it was doing in the field of public education. I was stirred to the depths by his earnestness and his eloquence. Riding home on the train I discovered that he was sitting alone in the same car. I wanted desperately to tell him how profoundly I was stirred by his address, and finally summoning all the courage I could muster, I went to his seat and spoke my piece. He received me kindly and asked my name. I told him I was a sophomore at Bowdoin, and was teaching school to earn enough money to get back.

"What were your freshman grades?" he asked. I told him. He took a notebook out of his pocket and wrote something down. Five days later I had a letter from him telling me to come back to college and I would have a scholarship to take care of a good share of my expenses for the next three years. That meeting assured me that I would complete my college education.

I finished my high school chore and went back to Bowdoin the first week of November, over a month behind in my courses. In languages the handicap was serious but not insurmountable. As a freshman I had enjoyed Livy's *History of Rome*, especially the attempts of Hannibal to defeat Scipio. I had enjoyed still more the odes of Horace. Their subject matter, their perfect technical finish, their unforgettable phrases—all these made my discovery of Horace the major scholastic event of my freshman year. I was now ready to enjoy Catullus, Juvenal, Tibullus, and the dramatists Plautus and Terence. This course in Latin poetry was taught by a young instructor, Kenneth Sills, who had a genuine enthusiasm for the classics and who was later chosen to be the president of the college.

In French I enjoyed getting acquainted with Racine and Molière under Professor Henry Johnson, who was nearer to being a man of letters than anybody we had at Bowdoin. He made a translation of Dante's *Commedia* which was published by the Yale University Press, an excellent blank-verse translation of Hérédia's sonnets, and had written a book of original poetry entitled *Where Beauty Is*. As an extracurricular chore he took groups of students through the rooms of the Bowdoin Art Building and made comments on the few good paintings and sculptures that the college possessed. As a young man he had visited the Louvre and other European galleries, and he wanted the college to establish an Art Department and let him teach art rather than French. The President told him that the college was too poor to afford that "luxury." Calling art a luxury hurt Johnson to the quick. One day during this period he felt so deeply about his rejection that he went home and wrote an ironic poem to the President which began, "I thank thee, Baal, now that I have fed," indicating his contempt for a job that provided him with a living but denied expression to his aesthetic interests.

The day I returned to Bowdoin for sophomore work I went to call on a young professor named William T. Foster. He had received his A.B. and A.M. degree from Harvard, had made a marked success at Bates as a teacher of debating, and was inaugurating a daily theme course, modeled on the Harvard course taught by Barrett Wendell, which I wanted to take. I told him my story. He listened with sympathetic interest, told me to go ahead and make up the number of themes I was lacking, and said he would exact no penalties for their lateness. I soon discovered that Emerson was his hero as well as my own. He quoted sentences from Emerson's "Nature," "Compensation," and "Self-Reliance" with great gusto during the class periods. He taught debating as well as English and wrote a textbook entitled *Argumentation and Debate*, which dominated the teaching of this subject for about thirty years. He told me later that the royalties from that one book paid for the college education of his four children.

Debating public questions was a vital course at Bowdoin, and Foster made it more vital than it had been before. We were continually reminded that three Bowdoin men had simultaneously held three key positions in the Federal government only a few years earlier: Thomas B. Reed, Speaker of the House; Melville W. Fuller, Chief Justice of the Supreme Court; and Eugene Hale, Majority Leader of the Senate. A major event each year in my day was "The Bradbury Debate," in which six boys, three on a side, debated some current national question. The three winners got about $50 apiece, and the losers about $30 each. I managed to be on the winning team during both my junior and senior years. My desperate and every present need for money was for me the driving force in these two events.

Henry Leland Chapman, of the English department, was the popular professor of this period. He began his career as a Congregational minister but discovered that he liked the English poets better than he liked homiletics or eschatology and came back to his alma mater to instill a love of Chaucer, Shakespeare, and the Romantic poets in the hearts of Bowdoin men. This he did with marked success. Of all the professors of my day at Bowdoin he was the most beloved.

The literary-inclined students were full of Carlyle (especially his *Heroes and Hero Worship*) and John Ruskin. A very few of the more advanced thinkers were enthusiastic over Ibsen and Sudermann. The more sophisticated boys reveled in the *Rubaiyat of Omar Khayyam*. One classmate of mine, Ned Pope, could recite it by heart. Every now and then his family would send him a small roast pig. A favored few of us were invited to the feast. We ate the roast while listening to our host's recitation of the *Rubaiyat*.

Apart from the few who read Carlyle, Ruskin, and the *Rubaiyat*, most thinking students in my time looked upon science as the white-haired boy of the intellectual world. The Darwinian theory was still occupying the student's mind, and Thomas Huxley's interpretation and popularization of Darwin occupied the center of the college world. I was caught in the maelstrom and decided I would major in biology and learn the secrets of life and death. I hung on for two years. Professor "Pinkey" Lee was impressed by my seriousness and gave me higher grades than I deserved. One day when I was looking at spirogyra under a microscope and drawing on a paper what I saw there, Lee came up to me and said, "Snow, you aren't drawing what you see under that microscope; you are drawing what you imagine. You don't belong here. You belong in the arts. I hope you got something out of these courses, but you must major elsewhere." I knew he was telling the truth, and I decided to shift to English.

"Pinkey" Lee had been to the Galapagos Islands on a scientific expedition and loved to tell about his experiences there. He admired the work of Darwin and got us all to reading the *Voyage of the Beagle.* He was a member of my fraternity and enjoyed mingling with the boys. His son Richard, in a class below mine, became one of my warmest friends. He and a classmate named Morrison hired a sloop-boat and sailed along the Maine coast. The boat was hit by a squall and capsized, and both boys were drowned. The father, with a horse and buggy, traveled in and out along the coast for weeks trying to find some trace of these two. The sorrow in his eyes when I met him on this search was deeper than any sorrow I had ever looked upon. I, too, was a mourner and wrote the following verse:

> The leaves are dead! 'Tis joy to feel
> Their rustle here beneath my feet,
> The golden rays through sunset glades
> Waft dreams of countries more complete,
> Leaves are not dead to me.
>
> The moon is dead! My chamber wall
> Is hallowed by its mystic light
> The mellow gleam of old romance
> Shines in to speed the hours of night,—
> The moon's not dead to me.
>
> My friend is dead! His soul went out
> And left its impress on my own.
> Now Life's more clear, the Change less drear,
> I'll reap where his clean hands have sown,—
> He is not dead to me.

I became well acquainted with Roswell Ham, teacher of French German, and later Russian. He was the most thorough drillmaster I have ever encountered. When I got through with his beginning French course I felt that I had a thorough grounding in the elements of the language. He possessed the nineteenth-century German scholar's attention to detail and was a great corrective for students like myself who tended to ignore the minutiae of thorough investigation. His wife enjoyed contact with undergraduates and invited a group into her home each week for poetry reading, literary discussion, and refreshments.

She was a devout Catholic and tried to make us see how much superior Father Tabb and Francis Thompson were to the Protestant poets of the time. She rated Santayana above Emerson as a philosopher, but her appreciation of his beautiful style made her blind to his skepticism. She was a charming hostess and brought a great deal of pleasure into the lives of green country boys. They learned at the same time what to do with a napkin and how to hold a teacup.

The professor who realized the homesick freshman's plight and sought to help him find his way into college life was Wilmot Brookings Mitchell. He taught us elocution and made us learn and deliver before the class such pieces as "Toussaint L'Ouverture" by Wendell Phillips, "Spartacus to the Gladiators" by Elijah Kellogg, and such other displays of eloquence that were extremely popular in nineteenth-century America. Our favorite was "Spartacus," for it was written by a Bowdoin man. When Kellogg was a timid undergraduate he was compelled to compose and deliver before the class an original oration. He kept putting the assignment off and at the eleventh hour locked himself in his room and composed this "masterpiece." It was taken over by the makers of textbooks and became nationally famous. It was delivered before a thousand schools and won a thousand prizes. This type of literature Professor Mitchell loved. All his criticisms were really appreciations.

Mitchell also taught a course in logic, using Jevons' famous book as his text. We learned to repeat by heart the mnemonic verses "Barbara, Celarent, Darii, Ferioque, prioris, etc., etc.," and armed with their formulas we were able to examine arguments and detect fallacies. He made deductive logic look very shaky. "All men are mortal; Socrates was a man; Socrates was mortal" seemed to me to be the only example of deduction that could stand up under examination. The others, such as "All birds fly," "All fishes swim," invariably fell by the wayside.

A classmate and friend, Lorenzo Baldwin, was even more interested in logic than I was. He and I got John Stuart Mill's *Logic* out of the library and compared it with Jevons'. We read Leibnitz together and laughed at his *monads* (to him, an infinite group of souls, each of which reflected the universe). In all this study I sensed the limitations of syllogistic logic, and realized that there must be other paths into the House of Truth. I was driven back to Emerson's poetry, then to Dante and the metaphysical poets of the seventeenth century. I felt that the intuitive perception rising out of man's emotions would help him to see deeper into life than he would ever know through syllogistic reasoning. I felt that poetry would help him to penetrate deeper into the secrets of existence than all objective rational intellectual processes.

Another young professor that some of us loved was Charles T. Burnett, professor of psychology. Psychology was a new subject in colleges and didn't know whether it wanted to be treated as a science or as one of the humanities. The drift of Burnett's mind was aesthetic; he had written his Ph.D. thesis at Harvard on Boethius' *Consolations of Philosophy*, and he shied away from treating his subject as a cold scientific offering. He had a gift of friendship. He married Sue Winchell, a sister of one of my classmates. Their home life was an oasis to many a Bowdoin undergraduate. Burnett played the piano and his wife the cello. Music lovers spent many a pleasant evening at their home and lucky were the persons who were invited to their dinner parties. Sue was an unusually excellent cook. She could prepare exotic dishes and add a touch to plain dishes that made them seem exotic.

The dominating figure on the campus was William DeWitt Hyde, a Congregational minister who came to the college when he was twenty-eight and spent his life there as a teacher and administrator. There was a touch of the poet in him and a good deal of the philosopher. His course in philosophy for seniors, the only one he offered, was a must for any student interested in the problems of philosophy and religion. The essence of that course was summarized in a book he published in 1904 entitled *From Epicurus to Christ*, which had one chapter each on Epicureanism, Stoicism, Platonism, Aristotleanism, and Christianity. Sixty-five years later it was reprinted as a paperback and put in circulation among college bookstores under the new title *Five Great Philosophies*. I have asked many times what other American college president, if any, can match that performance. In his course he added anecdote, illustration, and example that made the subject come vividly to life.

It was apparent that Hyde loved teaching philosophy more than he loved administrative work. But as an administrator he did a great deal to enhance the wealth and reputation of the college. Once when a group of Bowdoin men were meeting with President Teddy Roosevelt one of the group ventured to say, "We think that Hyde is one of the best small college presidents in the country." Teddy immediately replied, "Yes, I agree with you but you must leave out the word *small*." Hyde's defense of the four-year B.A. College, written for *The Outlook*, is worth quoting even today:

To be at home in all lands and all ages; to count Nature a familiar acquaintance, and Art an intimate friend; to gain a standard for the appreciation of other men's work and the criticism of your own; to carry the keys of the world's library in your pocket, and feel its resources behind you in whatever task you undertake; to make hosts of friends among the men of your own age who are to be leaders in all walks of life; to lose yourself in generous enthusiasms and cooperate with others for common ends; to learn manners from students who are gentlemen, and form character under professors who are Christians, —this is the offer of the college for the best four years of your life.

In appearance Hyde was a short man—about 5 feet 9 inches, with gray eyes that became blue when he grew animated, a swarthy complexion framed in a black beard. In my first letter home to my mother I told her that he looked just like the picture of James Russell Lowell in the school readers.

Along with his virtues there was a Puritanical element in Hyde. An example is the fact that he vetoed Edgar Allan Poe as a candidate for the Hall of Fame. I asked him how he could possibly turn down such a great poet, and he replied, "I cannot hold up a dissolute man for high honors. It would have a bad effect on the young of America."

At the end of my sophomore year I became a book agent. Orison Swett Marsden was the editor of *Success Magazine*, a publication that gloried in the capitalistic system and encouraged its readers to leave their rags and enter into riches. He had written a series of articles on men who had made good, and bound them in book form. This book, plus a year's subscription to the magazine, was my offering. I went from house to house in the northern Maine towns of Kingman, Mattawamkeag, Passadumkeag, and Molunkus, making a pitch for subscriptions and sales.

At Kingman I made the acquaintance of Dr. Beverly Summerville, an Englishman who loved poetry and felt a deep loyalty toward England and Queen Victoria. He had collected all the verses written in commemoration of the Queen's Diamond Jubilee, the damnedest accumulation of versified tripe that I have ever read, and that includes reams of undergraduate verse. The doctor didn't seem to care at all about the quality of the works, only the subject matter counted. He loved the queen and gloried in her seventy-five-year reign. I spent many hours driving with him all over the region. He taught me how to sell my product. He would drop me off at the home of a fairly well-to-do woman, urge me to impress upon her the inspiration and spur to ambition the book would be to her children, and get her to sign on the dotted line. Then, by the doctor's direction, I would proceed to the next house along the road. All I would have to do there, he said, was to show the signature of the first woman. Not to be outdone, the second woman would sign whether she could afford it or not. Within a few weeks I had made $200.

I was doing so well that I could not understand why the words "Go home! Go home!" sounded in my ears each night. The doctor said I was hearing the sound of the moaning of the wind. For recreation I went fishing and one night paid admission to a traveling dog show. Even there the words "Go home! Go home!" kept ringing in my ears. I finally gave up and went home, to find my mother dying of cerebral meningitis. I sat on the edge of the bed and had a good long talk with her. She died the next day, only forty-six years old. In her death I felt more than ever the cruelty and injustice of the world.

Back at college, I decided to do some extracurricular reading on my own. It was then that I discovered Herman Melville, who in 1905 was 100 per cent unknown in this country. During my sophomore year the library of the college was moved from its overgrown resting place at the back of the college chapel to the newly built Hubbard Library. Help was inadequate and hundreds of books were left on the floor for nearly two semesters before they were all in place. I went in and looked these volumes over and found one named *Omoo* and another named *Typee* by an unheard-of author. These books of travel and adventure fascinated me. I read and enjoyed them, and put them back. Three years later at the Columbia Graduate School I became well acquainted with Carl Van Doren, who already felt himself something of an authority on American literature. One day he was praising the narrative gift of DeFoe as shown in *Robinson Crusoe*. I spoke up and said, "It isn't a damn bit better than *Omoo*." "What in hell is *Omoo*?" Carl asked. I said it was a book written by a fellow nobody ever heard of named Melville. He got interested, looked Melville up, became wildly enthusiastic—especially over *Moby-Dick*—and determined to bring Melville into the light. He went to a publisher (I think it was the firm that put out the Everyman series) and got them to bring out a new edition of this neglected author. A few years later he was teaching English in the Columbia Graduate School, and had three young men doing their Ph.D. theses on Melville. One of these, R. M. Weaver, discovered the author's *Billy Budd, Foretopman*, written in longhand and never published, a long short story which in my opinion is the finest thing Melville ever wrote.

One spring Professor Sills brought a friend of his from Harvard to give us a poetry reading. The man was Melvin T. Copeland, and his reading was from the poems of Kipling. Copeland was the finest reader I had ever heard. He made every syllable count. He knew how to pack a pause, and he made the verse of Kipling appear much finer than it really was. To the intelligentsia, Kipling's verse was something below the level of poetry. But to me, that day, Kipling was a poet and a good one. The hour was over before I knew it, and I went across the campus in a daze with "Mandalay" ringing in my ears. Slight as it must seem to a reader, to me it was a major experience.

About this time I became aware of Wordsworth. His poetry expressed for me a recognition of the relation of man to nature. The *Prelude* struck me as one of the great achievements of English poetry. His work was more than poetry; it was an immersion into the mind of man and a hint of the unexplored region which the new science of psychology was attempting to chart. There was something satisfying about it, something restoring to one's spirit. When I participated in the Bowdoin Class of 1868 Prize Speaking Contest, which meant $75 for the winner—a program in which an undergraduate had to compose and deliver an original essay—I chose for my subject "The Message of Wordsworth." The leading judge was the editor of the *Youth's Companion*, a short-story writer named C. A. Stephens. As chairman of the committee, he said, "We liked all of your fine declamations, but the congealed judgment of our Committee awards the prize to Mr. Snow." At that moment I was stone broke and I owed a bill at the college—which was clamoring for attention. I was forced to believe that the stars in their courses were favoring me that night.

Another memorable moment to me was my awakening to the poetry of Edwin Arlington Robinson. My cousin Bill Norton had taken *Captain Craig* out of the library, and he and I spent a large part of one night in the spring of 1905 reading and examining this long poem. Robinson was then unknown to the average poetry reader, but Norton and I decided back there in 1905 that America had produced a really great poet.

The spirits of Hawthorne and Longfellow were still moving among the branches of the Bowdoin pines. My love of poetry impelled me to write something of my own, something good enough to appear in our literary magazine, the *Quill*. The editor-in-chief was Frank Seavey, who later became an English professor at Tufts. I sought him out, introduced myself, and told him I wanted to write for the *Quill*.

He said, "Send me some of your stuff and let me look it over." I sent him a ballad titled "Sailor Song," about two common sailors who shipped on the first trip of a new schooner—one had a glorious experience, and the other a miserable time. I ended it with a moral. President Hyde stopped me on the campus one day and told me he liked it. I was delighted, but I know now that the verse was a first draft, carelessly written, and had no literary value. I think that Hyde, a preacher, liked it for its moralizing.

I kept on with the *Quill*, was the business manager my junior year and the editor-in-chief my senior year. As business manager I ran the magazine deeply in debt. There was no financial aid from the college. The only money we had, aside from subscription, came from ads we solicited from local merchants—barbershops, laundries, ice cream parlors, banks, and bookstores. I was probably a poor solicitor, and it would have taken a supersalesman to convince businessmen of the value of space in our little literary magazine. It took me five years to pay the printer. I borrowed money on the Brunswick bank and Professor Mitchell endorsed the note every six months until the debt was paid. That was my major course in vocational guidance. I found out then and there that I had no skill in business, and business had no use for me.

The only material reward I ever obtained out of the *Quill* was a big shore dinner. One of my fraternity mates, William T. Johnson, showed me a letter he had received from a soliticious uncle who asked him why he didn't participate in some extracurricular activity like the *Orient*, the *Quill*, debating, etc. He said to me, "If you will write something for the *Quill* and sign my name to it, I'll treat you to a shore dinner at New Meadows Inn." The temptation was so great that I wrote an eight-line poem, "Life," and signed his name to it. The boy's uncle was apparently satisfied. A week after the poem appeared in the *Quill* he sent his nephew a generous check.

In my junior year a number of us who were interested in literature and creative writing formed an organization called The Coffee Club. It consisted of six or seven undergraduates and two members of the faculty. We adopted literary names for ourselves, names like Dante, Dr. Johnson, Stevenson, Rip Van Winkle, met once a week and read original stories, poems, essays, and reviews, and criticized one another's productions. It was a lively organization. We thought we were imitating the great coffee houses of England in the eighteenth century.

We had a good time showing our "works," but our productions were a far cry from those we endeavored to imitate. The two professors in the group, Kenneth Sills and W. B. Mitchell, attended our meetings faithfully and joined in the programs. We looked to them for criticism but about all we got was encouragement. As Milton phrased it, "old Damoetas loved to hear our song." These two were not old but they were too generous in their praise.

When there was talk of forming a Socialist Club, I was enthusiastic and jumped in. We declared for public ownership of public utilities, the abolition of wage slavery, the recognition of labor unions, and the conservation of national resources. We discussed these issues at length, but our major contribution was bringing Jack London to the campus.

Lecturers at Bowdoin were expected to come to the platform dressed in a tuxedo or at least in a long Prince Albert coat. Jack appeared in square-toed workingmen's shoes, a flannel shirt, no coat, and no tie. This garb was offensive to "proper" people. None of his gifts as a storyteller showed up on the platform. He spoke in a flat, even tone with no change of pitch or emphasis. He briefly explained the Socialist theory, then spent the rest of the hour telling tales of deprivation, squalor, and suffering imposed by capitalists on the poor of California.

The next day, before a college audience, Jack debated with President Hyde on "Capitalism versus Socialism." Hyde asked many questions Jack could not answer, tied him up in knots, and won the debate. Our club was embarrassed, but we did not lose faith in our principles.

The second day of Jack's visit I took him and his wife to the Walker Art Building to show him our few treasures. (The building itself is a treasure, one of Stanford White's little masterpieces.) As we entered the building the first thing that struck our eyes was a portrait of a beautiful young woman. Mrs. London looked at it long and carefully and then burst out, "Why, that looks just like Jack's first wife!" When the Bowdoin wives heard of this, they were shocked. Why, it is hard in this day to understand, but the ladies of Bowdoin, with their rigid code of proper social behavior, could not tolerate such a "want of good breeding," such a "lack of sensitivity," such an "exhibition of poor taste!" The one thing remembered later about Jack London's visit to the campus was his wife's simple remark.

One day during my junior year it was rumored about the campus that Carrie Nation, the crusader for Prohibition, was coming to town. She had been lecturing at Waterville, was heading south, and would have to change cars at Brunswick. About a hundred of us showed up and when her train rolled into the station we gave her three rousing cheers. Some of us crowded around the car as she got off, and continued cheering. One of my classmates named Haines was smoking a cigarette. She rushed up to him, snatched the cigarette out of his mouth, threw it on the ground, stamped her foot on it, and said, "Young man, don't make a stinkpot of yourself." This act excited us still more. She looked to me something like a dowdy, middle-aged housewife, although her eye was brighter and her jaw more pronounced than most. She carried the hatchet as a symbol of her mission —which was summarized in a poem by Vachel Lindsay entitled "The Saloon Must Go." As I came nearer to her and looked her in the eye, I could see, to my surprise, that she was really enjoying herself at this brief contact. Her usual act of breaking plate-glass windows and bottles in hotels and liquor stores strikes me now as an excellent example of the American tendency to go to extremes.

Another side of my college activity centered around debating. We had class debates in Professor Foster's course, and these explored the economic and political issues that were current in our state and nation at the time. Looking back, it is amazing to see how free we were from international complication. The Monroe Doctrine was our shield and buckler, and freedom from "entangling alliances" our watchword. Now and then an international question would arise, such as the appeal for America to intervene in the Belgian Congo when King Leopold's agents were perpetrating horrors on the Negroes of that region. We debated that question many times. The negative speakers would warn the audience that if America intervened we would become a world power and lose our greatest asset as a country, our sublime isolation. In answer to this the affirmative would almost invariably say, "World power! World power! America became a world power when Cornwallis surrendered at Yorktown!" These ringing words sounded so magnificently that they usually tipped the scales in favor of the affirmative.

In Foster's class we usually had two speakers on each side of a question. I recall one debate on the Smoot-Hawley tariff bill. I launched a devastating attack against it and defied my opponents to name one instance in which this bill *lowered* the tariff on anything. Thereupon one of my opponents arose and read off three things that were lower than they were in the previous tariff bill—"jute, barbed wire, and putty." This man had done his homework so thoroughly that he amazed the whole class. His name was Harold Burton, and he later became a justice of the U. S. Supreme Court. His father was dean of M.I.T., his aunt an eccentric artist who dwelt alone in a studio on T Wharf in Boston, and his brother Felix Arnold, one of my favorite classmates, who later became a fine architect. At Deer Isle, Maine, his uncle, Mr. Hitz, had a speedy yawl and took me sailing with him during the summer of my junior year when I lived on that island.

My summer on Deer Isle was an unusual experience. President Hyde stopped me on the campus one spring day and asked me to come see him the following afternoon. I thought he was going to bring up the subject of my unpaid bills. But no, he merely wanted to know if I would go to Sunset, Deer Isle, and take over a church for the summer. He said he thought I should go into the ministry as my profession. My impulse was to say No, but Hyde had done so much for me I found *No* difficult to say. The pay was to be $20 a week and the parish would take care of my board in a hotel named "The Firs." With great reluctance and only as a favor to Hyde, I said I would go. I took along a Bible, the Book of Common Prayer, Browning and Tennyson and the metaphysical poets of the seventeenth century. The local people furnished the choir, and the congregation was about one-half natives and one-half "summer folks." My first Sunday was a nightmare. The night before I could not sleep. I felt like a hypocrite because the life of a clergyman had no appeal for me. I was not even a member of a church although I had always gone to Union Chapel services at home and to the Methodist and Baptist services in Thomaston. I was a preacher without any credentials and the hungry sheep could not expect to be fed by such a shepherd as I. I felt sorry for them.

That first Sunday I gave them an exposition of Browning's poem *Christmas Eve.* The two hymns I asked the choir to sing were "Lead Kindly Light"—which expressed how I felt—and Whittier's "Dear Lord and Father of Mankind, Forgive our Foolish Ways." I closed the service promptly on the hour, went to the rear of the church, and shook hands with everyone present. Fortunately for me I had a sincere love of people; they sensed it, and that was what saved me throughout the summer.

I was expected to make parish calls. People did not know what to say to me, so they brought out albums containing pictures of their families and collections of postcards showing places they had visited. These pastoral calls confirmed me in my determination not to be a preacher.

On Deer Isle I had many heroes who knew nothing of my existence. These were the men who worked as sailors on the racing yachts built by John Brown Herreshoff in the '90's—the *Vigilant*, *Defender*, and *Columbia*. To me as a boy these boatmen were competing for the most prized trophy in the world. They were chosen because they could maneuver a Friendship sloop from one lobster pot buoy to another with consummate skill. They knew just how far to leeward one had to be before putting the tiller down and shooting up toward a waiting buoy. They knew just how much allowance had to be made for the swift-running tide. Tacking back and forth in head winds, they learned just how to change from one hitch to another without losing any wind out of their sails. Their quickness of movement contrasted noticeably with the slow, deliberate movements of the British tars working on Lord Dunraven's challengers. (Later on, to the disgust of coastal men, college boys were chosen by the New York Yacht Club for these coveted competitions.) I often hung around the grocery store mornings— they were early risers—just to hear them tell about their experiences on the *Vigilant* and the *Defender*.

One day a member of my parish, a lobster catcher, was drowned. While hauling a pot a warp broke and he was pitched headlong overboard. The petticoat barvell he was wearing was pulled up over his head. He was trapped and could not get his hands free to swim ashore. I was asked to preach his funeral sermon. This was too much for me to take. I knew that if I stood above that man in the coffin and looked down on him I would go to pieces emotionally. (A lobster catcher I knew and loved, Dave Elwell, had drowned back of White Head in the same way as this man.) All this came upon me heavily and I asked the family if I, a young green preacher, might get someone else to preach the sermon. They agreed, so I took a walking trip hunting for a preacher. I found one near Stonington, in the Church of Latter-Day Saints, told him my predicament, offered to pay for the service. He agreed to come and help out. I did not know at the time that the Latter-Day Saints and the Mormons were one and the same. When I got back to Bowdoin in the fall I met President Hyde and the college preacher, Herbert Jump. Both of them had heard the story of my getting a Mormon to preach a Congregational funeral sermon and called it the joke of the year.

During my last two years I was the bell-ringer of the college, a job which paid for my tuition. At 6:55, six days a week, I had to get out of my bed, run over to the chapel, and wake the college up. At 7:40 I had to ring it again for daily chapel, an exercise presided over by one of the professors which lasted from 7:45 to 8:00. Each hour of the day from 8:00 to 3:00 I had to leave my class five minutes before the hour was up and ring the bell to let the college know the classroom period was over. We had no electric bells in classrooms in those days. If anything in the world was designed to bring order and discipline into a young man's life, this should have been it. But alas! I was forever impervious to all discipline and never learned the first principles of an orderly existence. This heavy burden was a chore that had to be done. I did it from a sense of duty and monetary necessity, and when it was over the discipline it should have achieved was over also.

One day at the beginning of my senior year I stopped by to see the President, who had asked me to drop in at four. This time he made a strange request. He said he would like me to go and live in 21 Appleton Hall with a boy named Libby, whose father was a distinguished lawyer in Portland, Maine, and a former president of the American Bar Association. The father was very anxious that his son should have a college degree, but the son was having a peripatetic love affair with a chorus girl. I had a congenial roommate, Ami Roberts, whom I didn't want to leave, but the President was so persuasive telling me that I would have a steadying influence on this young man that I finally agreed to go.

I moved to 21 Appleton and for several days had the room all to myself. At the end of the week Libby appeared and we had a good talk. He was an attractive young man of nineteen, and was having his first big love affair. He showed me several pictures of his girl. She was a shapely blonde and a beauty, and to him the only thing in the world that mattered. She was to be in Providence the next week and he spent much of his time looking over train schedules. He glanced at his textbooks, picked them up, opened the front covers of each one, and then carefully laid them back on the table. None of them had any appeal for him. I thought of my brother Frank having his first love affair in Thomaston. Libby's expression, manner, and attitude toward scholastic assignments were much the same. Both boys were lost to the world of scholarship but they had found a richer world and were happy dwelling in it. So I had 21 Appleton Hall all to myself. Libby appeared once more, stayed over night, and was off to Chicago. After six weeks I went back to Maine Hall to live with my friend Ami Roberts.

At Commencement I was chosen one of three seniors to deliver an essay. The subject I decided upon, "Matthew Arnold, Honest Doubter," showed that I was still preoccupied with religion. This time I did not win the prize.

A few of us had become so attached to the college that we were loath to leave it. Four or five of us stayed over for nearly a week after Commencement, reminiscing, discussing, criticizing, and evaluating what those four years had meant to us and what we intended to do in life.

My drive for money had kept me away from athletics and social life but I felt no bitterness on that account. I had wanted to play baseball and run the 440 race. I had wanted also a richer social life, but at every college dance I invited only my sister Cora, an excellent dancer, who understood my impoverished state. The joys of college life had to be secondary. At least their deprivation left no scars. There were things to be done to improve American life, books to be written to enlarge the scope of American literature, and I, a brash senior in a small college, wanted to play a part in both. These were not the best four years of my life, but I return to the campus as often as possible and my love for the college has increased rather than diminished with the years.

CHAPTER 7

The Big City: N.Y.U. and Columbia

To leap from the position of student in a small New England college in June to teacher in a big university in September was an unorthodox jump, but that was my experience after graduation. Archibald Bouton, teacher of debating and public speaking at New York University, was going on a year's sabbatical leave and was looking for a substitute. But to his great surprise none of the English graduate students in the universities round about wanted anything to do with public speaking or debating.

In desperation Bouton wrote for help to the Reverend Herbert Jump, an Amherst classmate, who now was the minister of the Bowdoin College Church. Jump had seen me in action, and wrote that I might be able to take over the work even though I lacked graduate-school training.

The job was offered to me and I accepted it. I was to receive $500 a year and a suite of rooms in Helen Gould Hall on University Heights. The Chancellor of the University, a Scotchman named McCracken, was carrying on the reputation of his nation for thrift! I had to give one course in English 1, one in public speaking, one in argumentation and debating, and in addition coach all the University debates. It was further stipulated that I was to take some graduate work at Columbia. This meant much riding up and down on the subway, offering me a chance to observe the people of the great city of New York.

My first class was an ordeal. I wrote out a six-thousand-word essay which summarized all I had to say about the subject of English composition. I was shy, embarrassed, and really frightened. Without looking up once, I read this essay to the class. My Maine Coast accent at the time was so pronounced that very few understood what I was saying. Luck was with me! Before I got down to the last page the bell rang and the students mercifully moved out. When the class met again two days later, I was able to look them in the eye and discovered that most of the them were sons and daughters of first-generation immigrants. At the end of the hour a few stopped to talk. One of these was an attractive German girl—a blonde whom I could not help admiring.

Another was a Russian who had spoken ill of the Czar's government, had been put in prison for a week and then taken out in a field to be hanged. The importunate pleading of the boy's uncle, plus a little money, induced the hangman to let the young man escape into the woods. He reached the coast and shipped as a sailor to New York. His adventures furnished subject matter for his themes, which were absorbing in spite of his difficulty with the English language.

Talking with him one day I mentioned having seen the great Nazimova play in Ibsen's *A Doll's House*. He asked, "Would you like to meet her?" Would I! That night we went to the theatre after the performance and knocked at her dressing room door. This was a wholly new experience for me. I would not have dared to go alone. We found her very friendly, quite simple and unaffected. Her Russian accent gave an added appeal to her speech. I don't remember one word she said or one word we said, but we came away exhilarated, wrapped in the aura of her charm.

In my public speaking class I took the students one at a time for fifteen minutes. I recalled the old definition of a gentleman as a man who does not have to raise his voice to be heard, and told them that this was my prescription for a public speaker. Can you deliver what you have to say without shouting? If so, you will be effective and secure results. This one-man-at-a-time program in the one and only auditorium the University possessed usually kept me late into the afternoon and put me on a collision course with Reinald Werrenrath, a recent graduate with a lovely baritone voice, who needed the auditorium for practice at the same time. He later became a nationally famous singer. Another recent graduate was Deems Taylor, a bosom crony of Werrenrath, who made his name in the world of music as a critic and the composer of scores for Lewis Carroll's *Through the Looking Glass* and Edna St. Vincent Millay's *King's Henchman*. His father, professor of education at N.Y.U., invited me to his home many times to hear these two young musicians entertain the household guests.

The head of the English department, Francis Hovey Stoddard,

was a fine teacher, a wit, and a delightful table companion. He had written a book on Romanticism, and had edited Scott's *Ivanhoe*—an accomplishment that brought him, he told me, handsome royalties. I managed to lunch with him three days a week. One day an enthusiastic young colleague of his rushed over to our table and said, "My book is selling so well the publishers are getting out an edition in Braille for the blind!" Stoddard pondered for a minute and then said with a smile, "I always thought your book was written for the blind."

My immediate superior was a Bowdoin man named Arthur Huntington Nason. He was the most conventional human being I have ever known. He lived by the book, in this case *Manners, Culture and Dress of the Best American Society* or some similar guide to etiquette. He wore a Van Dyke beard and spent much time each morning grooming it. For afternoon calls he wore a long coat, a colorful vest, and a Windsor tie. No matter how exciting the conversation became, he would leave after twenty minutes, as prescribed by "the rules." He composed sentimental poems and played the guitar. Ritual somehow took charge of his life and that which was beyond ritual he relegated to second place. He took me under his wing and tried to teach me his program of social manners and practices. I was the poorest pupil he ever had, for I would forget his admonitions as rapidly as he could expound them. He finally gave me up.

A young mathematics teacher, Pearley Thorne, began teaching at N.Y.U. the year I arrived. He was a Maine man, a graduate of Colby, and a congenial companion. He had a sly sense of humor and characterized our fellow teachers at N.Y.U. rather neatly and without bitterness. He and I were both homesick for Maine and spent many hours together. On Thanksgiving Day we walked about 140 blocks down to the theatre district and took in a musical comedy called *The Girls from Holland* by Reginald DeKoven, a popular and widely acclaimed composer of the period. (His song "O Promise Me," from *Robin Hood*, has probably been sung at American weddings more than any other composition.)

When the Knickerbocker Trust Company failed on October 21, 1907, I experienced for the first time a panic in the financial world. I went downtown and watched the people standing in line all night at Whitney's Bank and Trust Company hoping the bank would open in the morning so they could get their money. One couple feared the loss of all the money they had saved for their old age. Another woman was deeply worried about the money she had saved for her children's education; still another, the money put aside for her crippled husband's surgery. Four days later J. P. Morgan loaned $25 million on the Stock Exchange just before the close of the day, thereby checking the demoralization in the market and starting a sharp rally. At the same time John D. Rockefeller placed in the Street a sum for loaning at 6 per cent and is said to have further assisted by lending bonds to the government depository institutions for use as collateral against the money obtained from the national Treasury. These gestures showed that the big capitalists were more influential and dependable in a crisis than the government. I felt that something ought to be done and phrased a debating question which I thought would help. My proposition was: "That the U.S. Government should establish a Federal bank similar to the Reichsbank of Germany to meet financial crises." Our tight bond-secured currency, I decided, was a failure. It possessed no elasticity. We needed a Federal currency that could be expanded in an emergency. I got several colleges to take on this question for debate.

Joseph French Johnson, dean of the College of Commerce, Accounts and Finance, a downtown branch of New York University, became interested in my question, called on me, and offered me an opportunity to teach business English and debating in his new school, which had only six hundred students but would, he said, soon have six thousand. I could do graduate work on the side and give whatever courses I wanted to. He said the school had a great future and I could help build it. I thanked him for his offer but replied I was a country-oriented person and wanted to get back to the country as soon as possible. I wanted to see pussy willows and violets growing in the spring.

Stoddard knew I was going to have this offer, and when he heard that I was refusing it, he turned on me savagely and gave me hell. He said, "You know Bouton is coming back, and here is a chance in the city far better than most. You are a damn fool to turn down an offer like that. Johnson is a big man and you would love working with him. You are acting like an idiot!"

He upbraided me so violently that I walked out on him. A week later he apologized and invited me to dine with him at the Century Club where we had a gourmet dinner of planked shad. He introduced me to two literary luminaries, Hamilton Wright Mabie, an editor of the *Outlook*, and Thomas Janvier, a fiction writer who was having a great vogue at the time. Both of these "greats" are now almost entirely forgotten.

One of my students had an aunt, a bluestocking, who was interested in the arts and in young people who were aspiring to be poets and painters. She took me under her wing and introduced me to the Pen and Brush Club, where creators and would-be creators spent Sunday afternoons drinking tea and talking about their wares and the shortcomings of our civilization. There I met Angela Morgan, a young poet, more beautiful than Maxine Elliott because of her greater sensitivity and delicacy of expression. I made a date with her and called on her the following Thursday evening.

She was living in an apartment with her mother, an enormous woman who overflowed an armchair in a corner of the room. She sat there like a Buddha, motionless, with her eyes half-closed, seemingly lost in meditation. She acknowledged my presence with a brief nod, then returned to her contemplation. We passed into the next room where Angela told me that her mother was looked up to by many people as a prophetess. They brought her their troubles, she listened motionless, not appearing to hear, then murmured words of advice and they went away comforted. To me the woman was uncanny and disturbing.

Angela began to read her poems. As she read, her face lighted up, her eyes flashed, and the poems seemed much better than they were. How could I do otherwise than praise them? But as she was egostically wrapped up in her verse, so was I egostically wrapped up in mine. I too wanted a sympathetic listener. So we did not coalesce like "perfect music unto noble words."

When I rose to go, she held onto my hand, drew nearer, and lifted her face. I brushed her lips with a light kiss. "Is that the best you can do? That is no kiss at all!" She took down Browning's poems and read from "In a Gondola" the verses that compare the kiss of the moth with the kiss of the bee. "You know only the moth kiss. Now we'll have a bee kiss!" She clasped both arms around my neck and gave me an exciting demonstration. I was not slow to learn! I went home feeling elated over the experience, but all the same I never went back to that apartment. I shied away from the eerie mother.

Angela and I had some dates walking in Central Park, but I had no money for suppers or the theatre and we drifted apart—although we never were really together. When she died in 1957 and *The New York Times* gave her age as eighty-three, I knew for the first time that she was ten years older than I. She had published ten volumes of verse, one of short stories, and one novel. She had quite a bit of recognition in her day, and she sent me forth better equipped to deal with the female of the species!

On some week ends I would go downtown and walk block after block observing the people and imagining myself to be Walt Whitman looking at and checking his beloved Mannahatta. I would even try to write Walt Whitman—like poems of the great city. One example which I have somehow managed to keep, entitled "New York City, 1908," begins:

> I love to wander alone through the streets of the populous city,
> City teeming with workers and loafers from Old World nations.
> Before me visions of joy and brotherhood rise in succession:
> With joy I walk in the morning to the scenes of its busiest traffic
> Whose sights and sounds imbue me with a sweet medicinal secret . . .

On one of these downtown walks I was held up by two thugs, one of whom told me to put up my hands. At Bowdoin I had spent one semester on boxing three times a week; I had learned how to punch, counterpunch, and roll with the blow. I moved in quickly, gave the man a knockout blow in the jaw which sent him sprawling into the street. I then ran just as fast as I could for the nearest subway station. I was trembling and frightened when I dropped my ticket in the box and pushed through the gate onto the uptown platform.

My two graduate courses in Columbia were the history of rhetoric under George Rice Carpenter and the history of the drama under Brander Matthews. Carpenter was a Vermont Yankee who took a personal interest in each one of his graduate students. He had written a life of Whittier and was completing a life of Whitman—both fine, scholarly works. He was one of the very few professors who encouraged me to write poetry. The others told me to forget that nonsense and get down to the real business of scholarship.

Brander Matthews was a free-lance writer and Blue Book socialite who felt ill at ease in a scholar's gown. He urged us not to read his book on the history of the drama. He may have been afraid that we might find his lectures a rehash of the book. Remarks he made in class which had nothing to do with the course added spice to the hours. He told us that he played pool and billiards with Mark Twain and made us wish that we, too, might have a close-up of the great man. He insisted that *Pudd'nhead Wilson* was Twain's greatest book. He told us about the eccentricities of actors and actresses he knew personally, and made us wish that we could have seen Booth play *Hamlet*, or Mrs. Fiske as Becky Sharp in *Vanity Fair.*

I left N.Y.U. with regret. I was young and struggling with the same problems that faced my students. I was so young that two fraternities rushed me for membership in their ranks. Remembering the Bowdoin Coffee Club of a year previous, I started a Coffee Club at N.Y.U. When I was off to Maine on a Christmas vacation, the Club changed its name to the Andiron Club. Professor Nason became deeply involved, and changed it from a group of undergraduates reading and criticizing each other's stories, poems, and essays to a scholarly organization with national status. It continued in this fashion for many years and put out a magazine now and then filled with learned contributions.

The week before I left the University, an informal group gave a dinner in my honor. Most of these were boys I had worked with in debating and their dinner party came to me as a great surprise. My English class on the last day made me a present of a group of pre-Shakespearean Elizabethan plays. Through these volumes, I became acquainted with John Webster and sensed his worth as a poet. I was embarrassed and touched by these unexpected gestures of appreciation. They confirmed me in feeling that I might succeed as a teacher.

Early in the spring of 1908, I had a letter from Bowdoin informing me that I had been chosen to receive its first Longfellow Fellowship for graduate study. The year 1907 was the hundredth anniversary of Longfellow's birth. At the June commencement, Longfellow's three daughters, "grave Alice, and laughing Allegra, and Edith with golden hair," were all present. They combined financial resources to present the college with a fellowship in their father's name. The income from that endowment amounted to $500—or $41.69 a month. I accepted the honor and decided to continue my studies at Columbia.

That summer at home I had a long relaxing vacation. I took long walks in the woods, sailed my father's small sloop-boat among the islands, caught haddock and cod with a handline, and wrote snatches of verse as they came to me. I was not a methodical writer. I could not write in cold blood; I always waited for the spirit to move. When winds of the spirit blew through me as summer breezes blow through a birch tree, I got out my pen and jotted down the thoughts that came to mind. Even though it was spontaneous inspiration it was usually poor stuff. Whether the result turned out well or ill, I found the creative experience exhilarating beyond any other activity.

My father, now retired from the Coast Guard on half-pay, had changed. After my mother's death, he spent a great deal of time reading. Some left-wing magazines I had brought into the house caught his attention and he subscribed to one of them. He saw the rich growing richer and the poor growing poorer and felt strongly the need of a more equitable distribution of wealth. In brief, he was leaning toward Eugene Debs and the Socialist program. I was surprised and pleased at the change. We had more in common than before.

On my way back to New York City, I was urged to stop over at Cambridge and call on Miss Alice Longfellow. As the senior member of the three daughters of the poet, she wanted to see the first recipient of the Longfellow Fellowship. With fear and trembling, I rang the doorbell of the famous home on Craigie Street. A moment later "grave Alice" appeared, reached out her right hand, and gave me a hearty welcome. She was a thin, elderly-looking woman (all women over thirty-five were elderly to me) with gray hair, blue eyes like her father's, neatly and becomingly dressed. I liked her face and her wistful smile. She asked me if I were going to study in Europe. I said, "No. I have begun my graduate work in English at Columbia, and would like to continue it at least until I get a master's degree." "I am disappointed," she said. "My father enjoyed Göttingen and I was hoping you would go there." I was tactful enough not to tell her that I, at that moment, was deep in Walt Whitman and felt that American poets should saturate themselves with their native land. Whitman had made me a fanatic on that notion.

She took me over the house, showed me where her father wrote at a desk standing up, showed me a pair of andirons in the fireplace that had belonged to Lafayette, an inkstand that once belonged to Samuel Taylor Coleridge, and many other mementoes and keepsakes. We talked about her father's poetry, and she was delighted to find that I knew a great deal of it by heart. We talked about the other Cambridge worthies, and when we came to Oliver Wendell Holmes she said, "But his brother John was a finer man and a better writer." I wondered whether she had ever had a love affair with John. I could think of no other explanation. She grew younger as she became more animated and when I left, she followed me out into the yard, clasped my hand heartily and wished me a good year. Some of her father's charm still lingered in the old house on Craigie Street.

Arriving in New York City, I settled down as a Columbia graduate in 527 Hartley Hall. My roommate was Paul Simpson, whose brother Tom and cousin Lorenzo Baldwin had been among my dearest Bowdoin classmates and friends. The Simpsons had two attractive sisters—Ada, a brunette beauty, and Lillian, who had read widely and could hold her own easily in a conversation with young men of literary tastes. Their home in Newburyport was a place I loved to visit. Paul was doing his undergraduate work at Columbia in order that he might enjoy the cultural life of the great metropolis.

I had not been around Columbia long before I ran into Carl Van Doren—a fine-looking, bright, brown-eyed young man who was ambitious to do something worth while in the field of American literature. Most English professors at this time regarded the writings of native authors as unworthy of careful attention. American literature courses were few and far between. American folksongs were so completely neglected that when John Lomax first showed his collection of cowboy ballads to an English professor at the University of Texas and asked him what he should do with them, the professor said. "Throw them into the waste basket!" Had Lomax done so, we might have lost forever "The Buffalo Skinners" and others of our best Western ballads. Luckily, many young students like Lomax and Van Doren were training their sights on the American scene.

Carl and I had long walks and long talks together. Like Johnson and Savage in the eighteenth century, we swore "to stand by our country" and do something for its literature. I admired his enthusiasm, his whole-hearted interest in American life and letters, his way of saying "Yes" to life, and his warm gift of friendship. He and I and two other graduate students were anxious to write and to sell our wares to American magazines. Together one night we agreed that the first to sell a poem, a story, or an essay would have to treat the others. I won by selling a poem to the *Smart Set* for the whole sum of three dollars. The verse was entitled *Fate* and read:

> He plied his pen for the sons of men,
> To lessen their toil and woe,
> But the poor buffoons ignored his runes
> Till his hopes in life sank low.

> When he tested the fears of the quickening years
>   And wary of moralists grew,
> He sang one day an aimless lay,
>   And it echoed the whole world through.
>
> So the work that he wrought for human thought
>   Men spurned with a pitying look,
> While the random play of a lazy day
>   They claimed and called his book.

"Come on, fellows," I called. "The treat's on me!" Away we went to supper. We had a great evening. The bill, alas, was three times three dollars! What could I do but grin and see it through?

My income from the Longfellow Fellowship was $41.67 a month. On the last three days of each month I was always broke. This was not alarming because poverty had been my close companion for years. I soon found my way to a barroom on 113th Street that specialized in fine cheeses—bel paese, roquefort, edam, camembert, and brie. I would order a five-cent glass of beer, pick it up, and move over to the cheese table. The bartender, a gentle, soft-spoken Irishman, was sometimes alone and he and I had good talks. He sensed my need and would often turn his back and let me devour cheese and bread as I wanted. In a few days another $41.67 would arrive and I would return to the Columbia dining hall and my courses.

One of these was Anglo-Saxon, whose grammar struck me as an undecipherable Chinese puzzle but whose word hoard sank deep into my mind and influenced markedly my vocabulary. When I had a choice, I began (not *initiated*) the practice of dropping (not *eliminating*) the Latin derivative in favor of the simpler Saxon word. I enjoyed poems like *The Seafarer* and *Widsith* with their alliteration of form and intensity of theme. (Ezra Pound's recording of *The Seafarer*, incidentally, is worth a trip to the Harvard poetry room.) My teacher, Professor Harry Morgan Ayres, was young, thoroughly alive, and gave the impression that he enjoyed teaching Anglo-Saxon.

The next semester I had William W. Lawrence, a Bowdoin man, as my teacher of *Beowulf*. He had a touch of the poet himself and was sensitively aware of the purple passages of that undying story in verse. Lawrence gave me his ticket to several Carnegie Hall concerts and on one occasion two tickets to a Columbia dance. Here was my one chance to take a girl to a dance.

Ashley Thorndike, head of the English Department, took me

through Shakespeare's tragedies. The first semester he asked me to do a paper on three hundred years of *King Lear* criticism. In this study I made a discovery which was entirely new to me but which is probably well known to many of my readers: namely, that critics of literature are not as objective or detached as they claim to be; each merely reflects the mood of his generation. The critics of the Restoration, for example, had no reverence for Shakespeare. They were perfectly willing to turn *Lear* into a comedy and marry off Cordelia happily in the last act. To Romantics, on the other hand, everything Shakespeare wrote was above criticism. They were not offended by his punning on his name in a sonnet or shocked by the "extrusion of Gloucester's eyes," as Dr. Johnson phrased it, on the London stage. Before I made this study I thought that the French poet who called literary critics "monkeys in a zoo picking lice off each other" was going a bit too far. But after poring over three hundred years of *King Lear* criticism I felt there was something to be said for his devastating pronouncement.

The second semester Thorndike asked me to do a paper on "The Stage History of Romeo and Juliet." I had to search out the number of times it was played, the length of each run, and other factual details of each showing. I thought a more stupid assignment could not be devised by the brain of man. So I went into rebellion and built my essay after the old tale of the king who offered his daughter to the suitor who could entertain him with the longest story. One young man kept repeating "and then one locust went in and carried off one grain of corn, and then another locust went in and carried off another grain of corn," and so on, hour after hour. After a thousand locusts had carried off a thousand grains of corn and there was no end in sight, the king could stand it no longer. "Enough!" he cried. "Take my daughter and be off with you!" In my paper I repeated "The tragedy of *Romeo and Juliet* was played again . . . " at the beginning of each paragraph. A dozen repetitions were both irritating and wearisome.

In my own defense I must say that I searched the books in the Columbia library, accumulated a mass of details, learned for the first time that Otway's *Venice Preserved* was merely a rewrite of the Shakespearean play, and ended my long paper with the couplet, "And ne'er was thesis writ with greater woe, / Than this of Juliet and Romeo!" —a rhyme that I forgot I ever wrote until Carl Van Doren reminded me of it ten years later.

Professor Thorndike summoned me to his office and rebuked me for misusing the Longfellow money. I told him of my dislike of the Ph.D. system. I called it a German invention, designed to turn an art into a science. I said that Ph.D. theses like "Color Words in Thompson's *Seasons*," "The Dative in Chaucer," "The English Sonnet in the Eighteenth Century" when hardly any sonnets written were worth speaking about, seemed to me a waste of a man's time.

To my great surprise Thorndike agreed with my indictment in part but added that if I wanted to be a college teacher of English and desired any advancement, or hoped someday to be a full professor, I would have to "dig the ditch." Because of my outrage in the *Romeo and Juliet* paper he neither passed me nor failed me in his course. He simply wrote N. M. (i.e., no mark) as his rating for my year's work. Later on we met often at Wesleyan during Commencement week and became good friends.

Joel Elias Spingarn gave a course in seventeenth-century criticism which I elected because he had written an unusually thorough book on the subject. In class he was uneven. He would doddle along on footnotes for seven or eight lessons and then wake up and deliver and excellent, most interesting lecture. Then he would relapse into another two weeks of innocuous desuetude and comment on time-killing details. He must have observed the boredom on my face during the dull class hours, for he flunked me both semesters. I learned from him that criticism of other people's criticism was not my dish of literary tea. This conviction overflowed in a long poem of mine entitled "Zeb Kinney on College Professors."

Years later (in 1923, to be exact) I took this satire out of storage, fixed it up a bit, and sent it to Carl Van Doren, who was then editor of the *Century Magazine*. (His wife Irita was poetry editor of *The Nation*.) He replied:

Dear Bill:

Zeb Kenney is a joy. I accept him with shouts. There will be a check in your hands shortly.

Irita is very sore she didn't get the poem.

Carl.

I also took a course in seventeenth-century poetry with William Porterfield Trent, a Southerner with a great deal of charm, and a lover of good verse. He was at work gathering materials for a definitive life of DeFoe. We all looked forward to its publication but it was never completed. His strength subsided, his wife died, and he finally lost interest and fell by the wayside. In all the many colleges where I have been I have come upon scholars like Trent. Some were keen at collecting material but had no gift for putting it together. Some used their unfinished opus as an excuse for getting time off for travel abroad. Some used it as an excuse for early retirement. All the while the book was lying around gathering dust. It always seemed to be lurking in the back alleys and by-ways of the professor's mind—a conversation piece and nothing more. I was prompted to define a professor as a man who was always getting ready to write a book.

The most thought-provoking course I had at Columbia had little to do with my major. It was James Harvey Robinson's course on the intellectual history of Europe, which was later published in book form under the title *The Mind in the Making*. Robinson impressed on us the importance of taking a critical attitude toward life. This theme was in sharp contrast with President Hyde's philosophy. Hyde wanted us to have faith in something and enthusiasm for something if we wanted to make anything of our lives. Robinson labored to instill in us the importance of a critical examination of every creed and ism. He swept over the great upheavals, revivals, and movements of a thousand years and bore down on their pitfalls and quicksands. He emphasized the needless deaths that the Church had caused by its inquisitions and took a special delight in enumerating the detailed horrors and slavery that attended the Children's Crusade. He emphasized the need of Plato's "sweet reasonableness" in examining the edicts of the church and state. He made us distrust emotional decisions and cleave to critical insight. Where Hyde would urge a man to plunge, Robinson would caution him to hold back. I kept the two men and their philosophies in my mind for many years and finally saw how they might complement each other.

During this Columbia period I became acquainted with Nordica, the grand opera singer. The mother of my friend Lorenzo Baldwin was her companion and mistress of the wardrobe, and she saw to it that we met the diva. Nordica was a native of Farmington, Maine, and her real name was Lillian Norton. She had a genealogist working on her ancestry and told me that she was a distant cousin of my grandmother Norton. She traced her own ancestry back to Charlemagne. Was this to offset the fact that her father had been for many years the town drunk in Farmington? Young Lillian resolved to be an opera singer. She studied in New York, worked hard, and became the first American to learn and sing the great Wagnerian operas. She wanted to help me and asked what she could do. I said I would like to raid a good larder now and then. Thereupon she gave me a key to her home in Ardsley-on-the-Hudson and told me to drop in and tell the servants to dig me up a good meal—which I did, but only once.

She gave a concert in Carnegie Hall for which she reserved a box for Baldwin, myself, and a few others. As a final encore she sang "The Last Rose of Summer." By this time (1909) her own summer as an opera singer had passed and she, as singers often do, was giving a series of "farewell appearances" across the country. Five years later she embarked on a concert tour around the world, became ill, and died on Thursday Island off Australia under grim and distressing circumstances. I wept as I heard the story from Lorenzo's mother.

During the winter Carl Van Doren and I saw Maud Adams at her best in a production of Barrie's *What Every Woman Knows*. We also attended a matinee of a play entitled *The Passing of the Third Floor Back*, in which the leading character is a thinly disguised Christ. The audience that afternoon was so deeply impressed by this performance that no one hurried on the way out to the street; in borrowed humility, each one wanted his neighbor to precede him. The mood of the Master seemed to have settled on us all.

One night for a dollar I purchased a standing-room ticket for *Il Trovatore*. Caruso and Emma Eames sang the leads and the performance was so thrilling that I forgot that I was standing. There was a crystal clarity in Eames' voice joined with tremendous power, and Caruso's farewell song to Leonora was little short of heartbreaking. I wanted very much that winter to see such plays as the rarely presented Shakespeare's *King John* and worked my way in to this and other performances by carrying a spear in the background or helping to change the sets.

Kate Douglass Wiggin, a Maine writer who received an honorary degree from Bowdoin and took every Bowdoin aspirant to authorship under her wing, spent her summers writing in Bar Mills, Maine, and her winters in New York enjoying plays, operas, and art exhibits. She gave many delightful teas and dinners to which she invited a host of friends and acquaintances. In these days her *Rebecca of Sunnybrook Farm* was a long-time best-seller. At one tea she told me she was having a big dinner the following Sunday, showed me the guest list, and asked me to choose my dinner companion. Without a moment's hesitation I chose Maxine Elliott, a Maine-born girl and a beauty, whose career as an actress was then at its height. I spent that week planning conversation with her! The day came when I found myself seated at the great table with Maxine at my side. I started our talk with a glorification of Maine. In those days I disliked the big city and was full of nostalgia for the Maine coast. She herself was born in Rockland, eight miles from my home, and I expected a cozy reaction. Instead she clammed up, took on a dour look, and finally said, "I hate the place and have no intention of ever going back." Clouds and darkness descended upon me and I felt rebuked. I wished I had asked to sit beside someone else. But she was a beauty and I could still look on and admire. Years later when I read that delightful book *My Aunt Maxine* written by her niece Diana Forbes-Robertson Sheehan, I understood and sympathized with her reaction. Her parents had not been socially accepted by the first families of Rockland. Memories of cruel slights embittered her. Her father's one big venture, a ship of his own, ran aground on a hidden ledge on its first trip and was lost. The ship was not insured and her father was ruined. No wonder she hated the place!

It is evident that my shyness was wearing off and that my interest in women had taken a leap forward! In addition to the famous names, Nordica, Kate Douglas Wiggin, and Maxine Elliott, there was one other woman in my life that winter, a young woman more on my own level of age and experience. She was Katherine Van Allen, a girl who had come from upstate to New York City to further her career as a portrait painter. She had a magnificent head, a winning smile, and brown eyes that sparkled when she talked. Yet she was more like a mother than a sweetheart. She and I spent many hours in art musems. They were about the only thing I could afford to take a girl to, and fortunately I enjoyed them as much as going to a play. She found that the men who came to her studio were often more interested in her person than in her painting, and some were difficult to handle when they came for sittings. Finally she closed her studio and took a job as a teacher of art in a city high school. I used to go walking with her and told her a great deal about my home village at Spruce Head. She said she would like to go there in the summer and paint scenes along the coast. When college closed I found her a place to board with my aunt, who lived next door to my father. She made friends with my sister, went sailing with my brothers, and took long walks with me, but nothing further came of this friendship. At the end of the summer she went back to New York, I went on to Bowdoin as an instructor, and we drifted apart. I never knew what became of her. But I cherished her watercolor of a Spruce Head cove, which she had given me, until it was ultimately burned in the East Hall Wesleyan fire.

The school year came to an end. Although I had earned enough credits in course for an M.A. degree, my thesis had not been accepted and I was leaving as I had entered, a mere bachelor of arts. Yet the year was one of growth in many ways. My major effort had been spent writing verse. I composed a long blank-verse poem of four hundred lines entitled "The Agony in the Garden," in which I put words in Christ's mouth pleading for a less horrendous way than the way of the cross to call the attention of the world to himself and his mission. The blood and torture of his death offended my aesthetic sense. I believed that his message of forgiveness and brotherly love, if put into practice, could redeem the race and cure society of its ills. The poem was never published.

CHAPTER 8

Academic Tramp

In spite of my ungraceful exit from Columbia, I was going back to my alma mater to teach debating and English for a year. The salary of the debating teacher, Professor William T. Foster, was $2200 a year. I was offered half of that amount for teaching his courses, and he was to take the other half, go to Columbia Graduate School, and work for a Ph.D. in education. All this had been worked out by President Hyde. I was to have a room in Foster's home on Federal Street and be a help to his beautiful wife Bess and their two young children, Russell and Barrie. I was expected to furnish the sense of security a man in the house contributes. I tended the furnace, rolled out the trash barrels, fixed faulty gadgets, ran errands, and played with the children. My role was similar to that of Thoreau in Emerson's home when the latter went abroad for a year.

Few things are more attractive to an exiled New Englander than the road that leads him back home. At Bowdoin Hyde was still the president and most of my old teachers still active. I was attracted to the home of Professor Henry Johnson, who was then completing his translation of Dante's *Commedia*. He encouraged me in my ambition to write poetry and urged me to see what I could do with various stanzas and meters. Under his friendly eyes I began a poem in the Spenserian measure entitled "A Northeaster" which was not finished and published until seventeen years later. He was a great smoker and had a special pipe set aside for me to use whenever I dropped in, which was three or four times a week. His wife, brought up in Thomaston, Maine, was a Wellesley graduate, a woman of delightful wit and humor, and an accomplished cook. A young instructor counted himself lucky if he were favored with an invitation to one of her dinner parties. The dinners were always formal, the black tie a must. After dessert the English custom of a half-hour of male talk before joining the ladies was always observed. Then came coffee in the parlor served in tiny fragile cups. (The country boy was learning his manners!) In spite of the formality, the parties were gay with lively discussion and witty banter that went on until midnight.

It was a friendly faculty and I enjoyed their company. There was a leisurely atmosphere on the Bowdoin campus which a man like myself could enjoy. The ultimatum "publish or perish" had not yet reached Brunswick. There was much social life, many dancing parties, singing parties, amateur dramatics, and the like. The strain which later visited too many American colleges was conspicuous here by its absence.

I did some hard work too. Sometime during that fall Columbia University, from which I had stolen away under a dark shadow, wrote me that I had sufficient credits for an M.A degree and that if I would write a satisfactory thesis and send it along for their consideration, they would send me an M.A. diploma in June 1910. At this moment a new novelist was having a great vogue. His name was William De Morgan, and he had up to that time written four "three-decker" novels: *Joseph Vance, Alice-for-Short, Somehow Good,* and *It Can Never Happen Again.* In a way De Morgan was a reincarnation of my favorite novelist, Charles Dickens, and I decided that my thesis would be an analysis and a commentary on these four books. Under Bess Foster's prodding I stuck to my task, wrote the thesis, and sent it to the head of the Columbia English Department. They pronounced it satisfactory and in June sent me the promised diploma.

All this I owe to Bess Foster who took me under her wing, mothered me, and made me feel myself a member of the family. She loved fresh air and kept the bedroom windows up in the dead of winter. Many a night when the snow blew in and covered the counterpanes of her two little boys I got up and closed their windows to keep them from being buried in the snow. I took Mrs. Foster to the college dances whenever my sister Cora could not come. She had an abrupt manner that offended many of her acquaintances, but those who saw the woman of goodwill behind the abruptness saw a person to love and cherish. We became lifelong friends.

I still had no Ph.D. and no intention of trying to get one. I was interested in the flesh and blood of literature, not in the bones.

My debating work went well. I recall one debate that year with two young men from Wesleyan University, George Brengle and Arthur T. Vanderbilt. I had revived my subject of two years earlier on the need of a more flexible currency in America, so deeply did I feel on the matter. Bowdoin won the decision of the judges by a 2 to 1 margin, but as a coach I honestly felt that the Wesleyan boys were more skillful than mine. One of these boys, Arthur Vanderbilt, became a nationally famous lawyer and president of the American Bar Association. Many years later when I went to Wesleyan as a teacher these young men saw to it that I was made an honorary member of their class of 1910.

On April 6, 1909, Commander Peary, one of the most famous of Bowdoin alumni, discovered the North Pole. He had made seven trips into the Arctic, suffered untold hardships, had had his toes frozen, but his strength of will had continued until he achieved his goal.

Bowdoin decided to have a big celebration in his honor. The college assembled in the old Congregational Church; President Hyde made a memorable address; Professor Chapman read a poem, and Peary responded with a brief but effective reply. The Governor and other State of Maine leaders, not content to have Bowdoin alone celebrate Peary's triumph, organized a committee and put on another show in Portland. John Kendrick Bangs, a humorist of the period, who spent his vacations in Maine and called himself a "son of Ogunquit," was the chairman of the exercises. No hall was big enough to hold the crowd, so we all assembled at the Longfellow monument in the center of Portland. The Governor, a short stout man named Fernald, made the opening speech and eloquently referred to the lonely hours Peary had spent under the "*Aurelia* Borealis." (From that hour on the Governor was nicknamed Aurelia.) Other notables spoke briefly. On the speakers' stand were Peary, President Hyde, and Matt Hensen, a magnificent specimen of Negro who went clear to the Pole with Peary and was probably all in all the most resourceful man on many of these seven expeditions. Alluding quietly to the controversy then raging as to whether Dr. Cook or Peary was the first to reach the Pole, Bangs remarked, "We know now that Peary was first, for we have it in black and white!"

That year I shared sections of a course in English composition with a young man fresh out of Yale. His name was James L. McConaughy. He belonged to my fraternity. His office in Hubbard Hall was next door to mine, and we became good friends. In many of our long-drawn-out "bull sessions" he upheld the cause of conformity and I the cause of nonconformity. My convictions were verging toward Socialism and I did not lower my voice when expressing my opinions. Many years later, in 1946 to be exact, he and I were destined to run against each other as candidates for the governorship of Connecticut. He won.

Toward the end of the year I discovered that my nonconformity was depriving me of a great opportunity. In the spring of the year it was rumored that Mr. Foster was going to be the first president of a new college in Oregon. The news made quite a stir on the campus, and left a vacancy I wanted.

President Hyde called me in and we had a long talk. He asked me where I acquired such radical ideas. I told him they came straight out of my life. A father trying to raise a family on $40 a month; a summary dismissal because I tried to form a quarrymen's union; a salary of $6 a week teaching school; a fine faithful schoolteacher thrown to the wolves after a life of service with no pension to help her through her twilight years; two girls, one in Bassick School and one in the Owl's Head school, entering on a prostitute's career because their fathers were dead and their mothers were "on the town"—all these came straight out of my life and not out of books on political theory. "But Bowdoin," he said, "is a very conservative college. The trustees and leading alumni want on the faculty not only gentlemen, but conscious gentlemen. You could survive all right in a place like Chicago University where they can stand John Dewey, but you couldn't expect to survive here. I'll see that you get some good calls elsewhere." I left this conference brokenhearted. But Hyde had done so much for me that I could not bring myself to hate him.

Hyde saw to it that I had a good job offered me in the fall—an instructorship in English and debating in Williams College, substituting for Professor Byron J. Rees who was going abroad for a year. Here I was to teach one course in eighteenth-century prose, one in the Anglo-Saxon language, one in freshman English; I was also to coach all the debating. To fit myself for Anglo-Saxon I went to the Harvard Summer School and elected that one course. It was taught by a man who had no real feeling for Anglo-Saxon literature as my Professor Ayres of Columbia had. He was a pedant from Vermont substituting for the summer session. He could make dullness duller than "minutes of the last meeting."

When I arrived in Williamstown I discovered that not enough students were electing Anglo-Saxon to justify giving it as a course. So I took over a course in the Bible as literature, a "gut" course which had been taught by a Presbyterian minister named Spring who was retiring on account of ill health.

I fell in love with the Berkshire countryside and said if I couldn't live by the sea, here was the place I would choose. Graylock, which Emerson once called a "serious mountain," overshadowed the town, commanded one's attention, and appeared to shed its benediction over the college. The beauty of the place and the climate "far above sea level" attracted wealthy residents whose estates clustered around the town. Among them were Mrs. Parmalee Prentice, daughter of John D. Rockefeller; the novelist Edith Wharton; and a Mr. Procter, of Procter and Gamble's wealthy corporation, who drove into town in an English coach with well-groomed English horses and an announcer up front to sing out his arrival. If Mr. Procter had any other marks of distinction I never heard about them. Perhaps this was enough.

The head of the English Department and the man in charge of English composition was Carroll Lewis Maxcy. He was a martinet to end all martinets. He called the freshman English teachers together and informed us that *exposition* was the important thing in writing and that we were to spend our semester on that subject. I suggested the importance of poetry for freshmen. He gave me a withering look and repeated, "The organization of expository writing is the important thing." With this he handed us sheets of essays he had organized, analyzed, and briefed, and told us to hand them over to the class. These were all marked up with notations, made by an orderly mind, such as "1, A, (1), (a), X, Y, Z," etc. It all looked like Sanskrit to me. At one point in the discussion I said, "Professor Maxcy, if this is the way we are going to proceed, I suggest it would be cheaper to hire secretaries to handle this work." George Dutton, a fellow instructor, looked over toward me and smiled agreement but he was tactful enough to keep still. I had made an enemy without fully realizing it. Later, when I left Maxcy's office, I left the door ajar instead of closing it completely. The next day I got a letter from him saying, "Next time you leave my office please close the door." I had certainly made an enemy.

The man in charge of the literature division, Lewis Perry, was a refreshing contrast. When I went to see him and asked how I should teach eighteenth-century English literature, he went down cellar and brought up several bottles of Pilsner beer and said, "Drink this, and teach the course in your own way." If better pedagogic advice was ever given to a young instructor, I have yet to hear it.

The Perry family fascinated me. Bliss, the editor of the *Atlantic Monthly*, was a man of great charm who wrote delightful essays. Lewis, whom I once heard read Browning's "Blot on the 'Scutcheon" better than I ever thought it would be read, left Williams and became the headmaster of Phillips Exeter Academy, a post he retained until his retirement. Grace, the sister, who never married, spent much time while I was there filling and trimming kerosene lamps. She was afraid, she said, that if she put electricity into the home lightning would strike it.

The father, Adam Nathan Perry, interested me most of all. He was no longer living but his spirit was all over the place. He was the first American professor to teach political science as a college course. That was in 1865. He wrote a history of Williamstown and Williams College that was quite different from the usual town chronicles. He not only called a spade a spade but he told what was on the spade. The book shocked the old Williamstown families and they did their best to suppress it.

I was fascinated by a marginal note of his I found in an *Anthology of Williams Poetry*. Among the verses in the book was a sonnet called "Opportunity" written by John J. Ingalls when he was a sophomore at Williams. This sonnet, which was Theodore Roosevelt's favorite American poem, reads as follows:

> Master of human destinies am I!
> Fame, love, and fortune on my footsteps wait.
> Cities and fields I walk; I penetrate
> Deserts and seas remote, and passing by
> Hovel and mart and palace—soon or late
> I knock unbidden once at every gate!
> If sleeping, wake—if feasting, rise before
> I turn away. It is the hour of fate,
> And they who follow me reach every state
> Mortals desire, and conquer every foe
> Save death; but those who doubt or hesitate,
> Condemned to failure, penury, and woe,
> Seek me in vain and uselessly implore.
> I answer not, and I return no more!

At the bottom of the page Perry had written, "Young Ingalls has this day written a sonnet. It is a fine piece of work and will doubtless live in American Literature, but it is godless in every line!"

One of my fine debating students, James P. Baxter, started a curriculum reform that stirred the campus. In our college paper, *The Williams Record*, he made an attack on prerequisites. Before a man could take a course in Shakespeare, for example, he must have had English 1, English 13, English 26, etc., etc. Before a student could take a course in philosophy he must have had a course in logic and one or two others. These prerequisites were designed in part by the older professors to insure themselves small classes. They were tired to death of correcting hundreds and hundreds of papers—most of which were regurgitations of things they had said in class. Harry Garfield, the president, was alarmed by Baxter's crusade, called a special meeting of the faculty, and said, "Now, gentlemen" (he always began his faculty meetings by calling us gentlemen), "what shall we do with this young man?" One testy professor replied, "Throw him out." Another man said, "I wouldn't be in a hurry to do that. There may be something in what he says about too many prerequisites." Another said, "We don't want brash under-graduates to come here and tell us how to run our college." To this a young professor said, "It's his college as well as ours." After much of this discussion one man said, "I move that the President be empowered to appoint a committee to look into, evaluate, and report on the subject of prerequisites in our curriculum." More discussion followed. Finally the motion was put and carried by a rather slim majority.

After a month's deliberation the committee reported; the curriculum was overhauled; the prerequisites were reduced to a minimum. Twenty-five years later to my great joy this brash young man was elected president of Williams College!

One faculty family, the Salters, were especially good to me. The husband played the college organ. The wife, Mary Turner Salter, was primarily interested in composing music. Her "Cry of Rachel" with its persistent repetition of "Death, let me in" was a moving composition. Mrs. Salter showed me a letter she received from Madame Schumann-Heink saying that she liked singing this song as an encore better than anything else in her repetoire. They had a daughter, Edith, a student at Vassar whom I enjoyed taking out to games and dances. I worked hard on some of her assignments in Horace's *Odes*, I remember, and when she was home on vacation helped her translate them into live English. When our relations took a more intimate turn I shied away from her because I wanted definitely to travel alone. I had no Ph.D., no security whatsoever; I was supporting my sister Cora in Parsonsfield Seminary; and I was not a candidate for matrimony. She took me more seriously than I took her and frightened me immensely during the Easter recess by visting my home in Spruce Head. My father's second wife (he married again after eight years of living alone) was charmed by Edith, but I myself was looking for an exit. We corresponded with each other for a few years. Her last letter demanded to know "where I stand with you, Bill Snow, and what I have to expect, if anything." My reply was not satisfactory, and she finally married a professor in the English Department of the college.

A cousin of Edith's, Margaret Morton, who lived in the Salter household that year, intrigued me far more than Edith. She had a fancy equal to that of a James Barrie character, and an imagination that overwhelmed me. But she was engaged to a young man on the faculty named Mears, and that was that. Margaret and I carried on a correspondence even after I had gone to the Alaskan wilds. Shortly after her second child was born she died. News of her death darkened my life.

A young German professor of philosophy named Warbecke and I determined to bring George Santayana to the campus. I wanted him to come and read his poetry (which I greatly admired); Warbecke wanted him to give us a talk on philosophy. Santayana agreed to come and read an essay he was working on entitled "Shelley, Angel or Devil." This satisfied us both. As a meeting place we chose a fraternity house whose fireplace was designed by Augustus Saint-Gaudens, and whose living room, furnished in paneled oak, exuded an English baronial atmosphere. The author came and read his manuscript in a low, monotonous voice before a gathering of faculty and students. To matter-of-fact people in the audience like Professor Maxcy the performance was a bore. To Santayana fans it was a rare and exhilarating evening. The next day the three of us took a long walk around the town, visited the library, and engaged in much talk of poetry and philosophy with emphasis on Shelley.

An experience that touched me more deeply that winter was a visit to the campus by Dr. A. Wakefield Slaten, a preacher who came to Williams to tell students and faculty that God was dead. He urged us to "eliminate the word God from our vocabulary, rather than keep it and give it a new meaning." He assured us that "that which has been referred to a conscious, divine purposive will is rather to be referred to the interactions of unconscious physical and chemical forces." In his peroration he quoted St. Paul's well-known words, "When I became a man, I put away childish things"—including, of course, the childish and obsolete concept of a Supreme Being.

That lecture haunted me day and night for nearly a week, and revealed to me all over again what a religious person I was. As a result, I sat down one night and wrote a long rebuttal of his arguments for the Williams College paper. The last two paragraphs read as follows:

> Men with excess of caution and bridled imagination have, it seems to me, little to give a college community like ours. We are too cautious already. We exercise our imaginations too little and too circumspectly. We need someone to tell us to fling a filament of faith out into the unknown, trusting that it may some day catch on somewhere, and lift the world to a higher plane.
>
> As Santayana says, "It is not wisdom to be only wise / And on the inward vision close the eyes, / But it is wisdom to believe the heart." Man's emotional and intuitive nature reaches over and beyond his rational nature and demands a religious outlet. Men like Slaten only try to stifle it.

A few memories of Williams linger. One is Mountain Day when all classes were suspended and we went up Graylock to revel in the autumn scenery and renew contact with Nature, camp out all night, hear a fox bark. Another is the fellowship of young instructors like Theodore Hewitt, Brainard Meers, Roy Hack, and George Dutton. Another is the portrait of Mark Hopkins in the faculty room with its compelling intensity of gaze.

I recall the contrast between the inferior houses of the Williams professors and the magnificent fraternity houses of the students. Last of all I remember the country-club atmosphere of the place. Most of the boys came from well-to-do families. They dressed well and lived well. The faculty were underpaid and furnished a striking contrast. I once got in wrong by saying, "This faculty is divided into two parts, those who drink tea with Mrs. Parmalee Prentice and those who do not." Mrs. Prentice gave expensive presents to faculty members she liked. I recall a magnificent lamp she presented to the Warbeckes. In many ways she was Lady Bountiful. President Harry Garfield was a charming man with an even more charming wife, but the college needed, I felt, a dynamic leader like Harper to overhaul its entire structure and lead it closer to the mainstream of American life. There was a vacancy in English when I left but people like Professor Maxcy had no idea of giving it to a man like me.

One day during the summer I had a letter from the president of Miami University in Oxford, Ohio, asking if I would accept an instructorship in debating and English at his college. He said I had been highly recommended by President Hyde of Bowdoin. The salary would be $1200. If I would accept, he urged me to come out and get settled a week or ten days before the college opened, which I did. I had ten days talking with students who were to be in my debating class and enjoying the marvelous elm trees which grow in that part of Ohio. To me they were breathtaking in their majesty and peace.

I also spent much time with a retired professor named Andrew Hepburn, whom I was delighted to meet and know. He believed that Thomas Gray was the neglected poet of English literature, and wanted to do something to put his magnificent poetry and letters back into circulation. He told me his early teaching career was spent at Virginia Military Institute and that reading casualty lists in the early battles of the Civil War was like calling the roll of his classes. The old professor interested me so much that I wrote a character sketch of him and sold it to *The Christian Register,* a Unitarian magazine of Boston, for $15.

I loved the elm trees and the country and the students so much that I was struck dumb when the President called me in after ten days and said he would give me $80 if I would pack up and go home. I hauled myself together and asked, "What have I done to deserve this?" The President replied, "You talk too plainly with undergraduates about politics and religion." "But President Hughes," I said, "I thought that was what a college was for."

Stunned for a moment, he said, "Well, I am a chemist, this is my first year as President, and I don't want anyone on my faculty who is going to rock the boat. You look to me like a boat-rocker, and I would rather you'd leave."

"All right," I said, "give me the $80 and I'll go."

"Never mind your room bill," he said. "I'll settle for that." As I went out of the room he called me back. "I wish you would read onto a record your poem that I saw in the *Youth's Companion* recently which begins, 'The leaves are dead!' I would like to turn it on and listen to it now and then." He brought out a small disk and an old "His Master's Voice" machine. I obliged him and left. Looking back, I think now that I was establishing some kind of professional record for length of stay on a job. But I was a sad boy at the time, too sad to think of any humorous reactions.

It was a humiliating defeat. Bowdoin, Williams, Miami, three strikes! I decided to go to New York, lay seige to the English faculty of Columbia, and get a job. The decision made me feel better. I took a ticket on the Pennsylvania Railroad expecting to find the beautiful Horseshoe Bend region soothing to my sore spirits. But scenery failed me for the first time. I was wrapped in the folds of wretchedness and felt myself a hopeless failure. When my friends in New York greeted my story with roars of laughter, I brightened a little, but I was still without a job.

A telegram from Alaska, which my sister Cora forwarded from Maine, reached me and changed my life.

CHAPTER 9

My Alaska

WHEN I was a child I read a Sunday School library book entitled *Three Boys in the Wild Northland.* It described the magnificent scenery of Alaska, the abundance of fish and game, and the strange life of the Eskimo boys who enjoyed an unbroken holiday fishing, hunting, and racing dog teams. I resolved that some day I would go to that wonderful country.

The telegram I now held in my hand could make that dream come true. It offered me a job as Eskimo teacher and reindeer agent at Council City on the Seward Peninsula at a salary of $1100 a year. It was signed by Charles W. Hawksworth, the Bowdoin friend and fraternity brother with whom I had talked so much about the North. After his graduation in 1906 he found himself at Point Barrow, Alaska, teaching the natives and looking after their welfare. He found the work fascinating and resolved to give his life to it. Now he was asking me to join him. All my gloom and disappointment left me. Here was an exciting new prospect opening up! Quickly I sent a telegram of acceptance, told Cora to pack up my things, and as soon as possible started for Seattle, where I would take a steamer to Nome.

The overland train took me across the flat Middle West. Chicago did not please me; ugly business buildings, vulgar displays of wealth, shortcuts to riches and reputation stood out and shrieked at you from every corner. At Omaha the Missouri River was a yellow stream, muddy and shallow. What a disappointment to one who knew the wide blue Penobscot, Kennebec, and Hudson! What we saw of Wyoming was a barren stretch of flat land, with now and then a sheepherder living in an isolated shack, spending his summer and fall in the lone company of sheep. In Idaho were great barren tablelands and lofty gray mountains looming up in the distance—some of them covered with snow, all of them beautiful.

(above left) The "academic tramp" at Williams, 1910 (photo by Kinsman); (above right) Jeannette Simmons, ca. 1912 (photo by White); (below) Old-line Democrats, average age 82, at Vinalhaven, 1912

(above left) Eskimo reindeer herders with their animals, Seward Peninsula, ca. 1911; (above right) A play by Ewen MacLennan at Council City, winter 1911–1912: identifiable actors include Wilbert Snow (in parka and mukluks), Ole Olson (the man in blackface), MacLennan (in white sweater), Lou Welch (with lorgnette), "Classy" the roadhouse chef (with false mustache and white trousers); (below) Council City on the Neukluk (photo by Lomen Brothers)

I tired of the scenery and turned my attention to my fellow-travelers, who were a friendly lot. We all became interested in a middle-aged woman who told us frankly that she was going west to join a man she had never seen. She had found him through a matrimonial bureau. He promised to marry her and sent her a railroad ticket to The Dalles, Oregon. She was a sweet little woman, somewhat apprehensive about the whole thing, and we were anxious to see how she fared. We could hardly wait for the train to reach The Dalles. When it finally did, the whole carful of us jumped out to get a look at the husband. Alas for us all, he was not there! Our last view was that of a wild-eyed, bewildered woman waiting on a strange platform for a husband she had never seen, and we speeding on through the night.

We reached Seattle the third day of October 1911. I went to the Frye Hotel to await the departure of the steamship *Senator* for Nome a week later. Seattle was a growing city, full of bustle and boom. It was rightly called the winter capital of Alaska. The gold rush had quickened the city's growth, and now coal had been discovered in that northern territory. Everyone I talked to had been to the Alaskan gold country. One man had lost $12,000 in four months; another had made $100,000 just as quickly. Others had gotten business ventures going well in the mining towns and then had sold out to get back to "God's country." The Alaskan flavor gave Seattle a distinction all its own.

Third Avenue on Saturday night was a picturesque sight. All sorts and conditions were assembled there. Japs and Chinamen from the Orient, Indians from the backwoods hereabouts, miners going and coming, Eskimos, painted ladies—all crowded the board sidewalk. The unpaved street was full of horse-drawn wagons and the two-wheeled carts of vendors shouting their wares. "Right here, young feller! Don't miss the chance of a lifetime. Razors! Corn plasters! A toy for the baby! Wind it up and see it jump!" The bars were wide open, music blaring.

William Carlos Williams thought he knew America and wrote a book called *In the American Grain*. His friend Ezra Pound told him that he did not know the country because he had always lived in the East and had seen nothing of the "Whoop" of the West. I was experiencing the "Whoop"!

My ship for Nome got started the morning of October 10. The weather was perfect and we moved along a glassy sea. The hills around Puget Sound were dimmed by a haze that seemed always to surround them. I could not tell, in the distance, where the mountains left off and the ocean began. The effect was impressionistic and very lovely.

On board our ship were few passengers. A half-dozen soldiers going to Fort Wrangel, a few nuns, a few women with their children returning to their husbands in Nome, some unattached men like myself—that was the list.

One of the passengers was a Mr. Prosser, an invalid shopkeeper of Nome, who told me he had found it more profitable to batten off miners than to be one. He and two companions had kept a roadhouse at the foot of the Skagway Pass and the prices they charged travelers were unbelievable. Unashamed of this, he told me how a villain named Soapy Smith had made *his* pile. Soapy was a saloon keeper on the Yukon Trail. After a new customer had had a few drinks, Soapy would tell him about a bald-headed eagle he had out in the back yard. "Would you like to see him?" Soapy asked. If the customer said Yes, he was escorted out through the back door where a hired thug bashed him over the head, sometimes killed him, took whatever money was on his person, and then buried him. The sheriff finally caught up with this gangster and put a slug through his head. Mr. Prosser claimed that he himself had barely escaped Soapy's clutches.

We had twelve days and twelve nights of voyaging from Seattle to Nome, with no stops between. One seaman who signed on and came aboard at Seattle was seasick on most of the trip. I told Captain Scoby that I would stand watch for him. When we went through Unimak Pass in the half-light early hours of the morning, we ran into a flock of birds. As the bow of our ship plunged downward, the birds rose and scattered in all directions. They appeared like specks before my eyes, and for a moment I thought something was going wrong with my sight.

There was much bad weather and one terrific storm, so fierce that Captain Scoby did not leave the wheelhouse all night. He kept the *Senator* head on into the wind, fearing that she would turn over if she got caught in the trough of the sea. The next morning the wind abated, but only a few passengers showed up for breakfast. Two nuns did appear; they looked white and drawn with weariness. One of them said, "Captain, we prayed all night for you and the ship." Scoby replied gruffly, "It would have been better for you both if you had got a good night's sleep."

When our steamship arrived at Nome, we found no dock or wharf;

several had been built, but none could survive the first big Behring Sea storm. We had to lay to about 150 yards from the shore and send the passengers and freight ashore in a car that traveled on a rope, something like a mammoth Coast Guard breeches buoy that would carry fifteen or twenty people at one time. I had been told that I would be disappointed in Nome. Not with the view from the boat deck! It was a Sunday morning in October and the snow-capped hills behind the stretch of brown tundra looked beautiful to my sea-weary eyes. Beyond the hills the light blue sky was almost white and the whole effect was strikingly Japanese.

The disappointment came when I crossed over to the shore and beheld the dingy streets and still more dingy cabins of that once famous mining camp. Buildings were scattered haphazardly along Main Street as though they had been spilled out of a dice cup. They were obviously temporary structures, whose builders never intended to settle down and live there. They meant to stay just long enough to get a "home stake," that is, enough money to go back and live on. At one end of the street was a big stockade, behind which a large dwelling housed the "ladies of the evening." At the other end of the street was a steam-heated public toilet which one could use if he had a twenty-five-cent ticket. The tickets were sold at several places around town and they circulated as legal tender. One could buy candy, cigars, milk for the baby—anything at all with toilet tickets. This heated "rest room" was a great institution in a below-zero country.

Between the stockade and the public toilet were the Barrel Bar, the Malemute Saloon, various stores, the offices of the two local papers, the *Nome Nugget* and the *Industrial Worker*, and two makeshift hotels. In one of these I waited for transportation to Council on the Neukluk River, a hundred miles north. I called on Walter Shields, who had charge of the reindeer herds and the native schools on the Seward Peninsula. He was my boss. He explained what my duties would be, but as they figure largely in later pages, there is no need to give details here.

Another Sunday had come before we got started on the trail for Council. The wait of seven days was trying to me, but to the people I met in Nome it was of no consequence. In Alaska, time was an unimportant consideration. To the Eskimos, the real owners of the land, time and space were abstractions unrelated to life. The white men coming into the country soon acquired the same attitude.

On the trek, I had the dubious fortune to travel with Bill Black, an odd "number" who knew the trail thoroughly and who had mined and teamed in the country for nine years. He came from Idaho, where he had been mixed up in a jealous brawl and had been accused of killing a man. For this he was tried and acquitted. He left his wife "Outside" and came north at the time of the Nome gold rush.

Black was the roughest roughneck I ever met. He was a short, muscular man. His face was swarthy, his eyes black and piercing, and he wore a short bristly beard that made him look like a pirate. He was brutal to his horses—so much so, I was told, that one of the Percherons on his team deliberately put his head under water and committed suicide. It was a strange story, but after seeing the way Bill beat two of his horses on this trip I did not disbelieve it. He had a low opinion of women. One night he said, "The only way to keep a woman straight is to have one baby on her back and one in her belly all the time." A harsher pronouncement, I thought, was inconceivable. To him a woman was a bitch, no more.

No one was disturbed by the fact that we started on a Sunday morning. Sunday was no more and no less than any other day here. In summer the miners worked four months, in winter they loafed eight. No wonder that they worked every day without rest all summer.

Our outfit consisted of three wagons drawn by four horses each. On one of these wagons there were two tons of freight. The others were somewhat lighter. A soft spell of weather began just before we started and we hoped it would remain until our journey's end. There was a chill in the air and we needed thick underclothing, heavy shoes, arctics, overcoats and raincoats. Mukluks and parka would have been better but a "cheechako," as a newcomer was styled, could seldom enjoy such luxuries. Our trail—in no sense a road, merely a track marked by metal stakes driven into the ground here and there—for the first thirty miles extended along the Behring Sea. All along the way were the ruins of miners' cabins, mute and lonesome reminders of the days when the stampede was on and when everyone thought that a claim staked on the beach would bring a fortune. In the ruin of these huts, stretched for miles along the shore, one could read the old, old story of the delusive quest which obsessed the human race even before the Argonauts sought the Golden Fleece.

At times the trail was so bad that we were compelled to go down into the sea. Imagine the horses up to their knees in water, the rolling breakers, the wild weird desolate country where surface is all tundra and no trees, the sun very dim over the light green sea and going down at three-thirty—then you may sniff a bit of the excitement that was mine on my first day out.

The sun was beginning to descend as we arrived at Cape Nome. I knew that our leader was anxious about rounding the cape and wondered why. The cape rises precipitously out of the sea, and heavily laden teams must go along a beach cluttered with heaps of driftwood brought in by the ocean streams flowing north through the Behring Strait. Several years earlier a man had built a toll road with a sea wall around the cape at an expense of $11,000. But the road failed to pay and was abandoned, waves pounded at the sea wall, and the road became a mishmash of loose stones. Every minute we expected the horses would break their legs. Some of the men walked ahead and pushed aside the worst of the movable rocks. At one place the wheels of the heaviest wagon caught around a tree stump, which had to be cut away with an axe before we could move on.

As soon as we had rounded the cape, we noticed the stars. They had come out as they can come out only in the northern land. There is none of that impressionistic blur which we notice beneath southern skies; there is a classic clearness that is cold and crystalline and as beautiful as sparks of phosphorescence in a fisherman's dipnet. Later that night I saw the Northern Lights as I had never seen them before —great splashes of white light moving in the northern sky; a geyser spurting up oceans of white foam; an immense Roman candle set off by the gods—none of these word pictures is adequate.

After fifteen miles of travel, we arrived at Cape Nome Roadhouse. "Roadhouse" was the term universally used for eating and lodging houses on all the Alaskan trails. Its sign was a bottle of whiskey called "hootch." Our approach was greeted by the wail of a pack of malemute dogs. Once inside, the lady of the house planted a bottle on the table, saying, "Here, boys, have some hootch." While the others drank the whiskey, undiluted of course, I inspected my first roadhouse. An oilcloth-covered table, canned food, bunks upstairs for beds, candles for lights—the whole house called to my mind Edward Lear's famous nonsense verse:

> Two old chairs, and half a candle,
> One old jug without a handle,—
>   These were all his worldly goods:
>   In the middle of the woods,

> These were all the wordly goods,
> Of the Yonghy-Bonghy-Bò,
> Of the Yonghy-Bonghy-Bò.

Ham, eggs, and baked beans were put steaming hot on the table and we all ate as if we had never known any stomach trouble except hunger. The first day on the trail made us all weary, and early to bed we went.

At five we were up and out once more. The morning sunrise was indescribably lovely. The early sun made the trail stakes glow like incandescent lamps and the tundra shine like brown silk.

At noon we ate at the Port Safety Roadhouse. At this place a few dreamers lingered, expecting to see the spot grow into a great seaport town. Fifty of the finest wolf-dogs in Alaska were kept here, and a copy of the Nome Kennel Club's constitution and bylaws was the Bible. The dogs of this country were not pets to be stroked or patted. They were half-wild and were purely business animals, indispensable to the winter work of the country.

Here we consumed five hours getting our horses, wagons, and selves over the ferry. The current was swift, and a stampede among the twelve horses would have made an end to this story.

At Solomon we had to cross a shorter ferry. And here we ate a wonderful dinner at the famous Solomon Roadhouse. This house supported the luxury of a bar, where twenty men would drink beer and whiskey and shake dice until the next mining season opened in June.

The next day we had to cross the Solomon River about two hundred times. The trail led along its banks. Now it would be decent traveling on one side, now on the other. At times in crossing, the horses would go into water up to their bellies and the low forewheels of the wagons would be completely submerged. It began to snow and grow bitterly cold, and we prepared for squalls. At night we reached East Fork Roadhouse after a zigzag journey of fourteen miles, covered in eight hours.

After that came our big day. There were no houses between East Fork and Council, and we had to make the whole distance of thirty-two miles in a single day or stay out under the stars in our sleeping bags. The men were up feeding the horses at two-thirty. We breakfasted at three-thirty and hit the trail at four. It was piercingly cold and we looked forward to a hard day. But the morning star was as big as a basket and the mountains in the distance were glimmering white. My heart grew warm when I saw that Council, my head-quarters, was to be in the world of mountains and timber. Ice was forming on the Fox River, making it hard for the horses to ford it over and over again. At times we had to travel straight down the river, for the banks were too steep for mounting.

We were now in the heart of the ptarmigan district. Ptarmigan are about the size of a partridge. Their feet are like a partridge's in summer but are covered with furlike feathers in winter. The birds circled around us in flocks of tens and hundreds. I shot all I wanted and Bill Black shot more.

At noon we fed our horses by the side of the trail, built a camp-fire, roasted ptarmigan without any salt to give it savor, ate sandwiches and warmed condensed milk, then set out on the final lap. We finished at seven o'clock, thirty-two miles, fifteen hours on the road.

Council, hopefully called a city, was actually a village of two hundred natives, three hundred white men, nine married white women, and a few single women one did not speak of. The town had been much larger during the days of the gold rush, consequently there were a number of empty houses.

I was met on my arrival by the telephone operator, a Mr. Kinne, who pointed to a cabin on the river bank and told me that was to be my lodging. On the ground floor were two rooms, one large general kitchen–living room and a bedroom. Upstairs was a good-sized bed-room which I chose for mine. For furnishings there were four chairs, two beds, and a few miscellaneous items. A few years earlier two miners had lived there. I was attracted to the house by the skull of a mammoth that lay on the front door steps, preserved by the lime deposits found in these northern soils. Outside the back door was a supply of firewood for the kitchen range and the potbellied stove that stood in the center of the living room. Two large chunks properly placed would keep the fire going all night. That was important. The government agent had stocked the kitchen shelves with a goodly supply of coffee, tea, rice, cans of beef, condensed milk, and the like. At this time a duodenal ulcer was keeping me thin and I had to be careful about what I ate and drank. Food was not high on my list of values. The best part of a meal to me was conversation, and at the Red Cross Drug Store and the roadhouse I found an abundance of good talk.

On my second night in town, I discovered that I was talking too much. At the roadhouse I was asking the men sitting there with me where they had lived Outside, how long they had been in the territory, and why they had left the States. A tall, square-shouldered Scotchman came up and took me outdoors. "Young man," he said, "the questions you ask are not asked in this country. Some of these boys got into trouble Outside and had to skedaddle. Some deserted their families, some were jailbirds, others are remittance men. So please lay off the questioning." I thanked him and asked his name. "Ewen MacLennan," he replied. "Scotchman by way of Vancouver." We went back in, sat down together, and found that we both loved poetry and tried our hands at writing it. He loved Robert Burns and could recite verse after verse of Sir Walter Scott. We became great friends.

My first job was to get ready for the opening of school. The schoolhouse was an abandoned miner's shack made of logs, with chinks between which had to be plugged up. I made a wooden box, mixed mortar, and began to fill the chinks. A few of the older Eskimo boys helped me. In the midst of this work I had to leave them and run about three hundred yards to answer a telephone call from Nome. I urged the boys to keep on filling the cracks while I was away, for the mixture would soon harden.

When I got back half an hour later all the boys were seated in a circle singing "The Old Rugged Cross" at the top of their lungs. The cement still in the box was rock hard.

I started with twelve pupils. As the autumn months grew colder, more and more Eskimos moved into town and I finally had thirty-eight.

W. T. Lopp, who directed the Eskimo education program from an office in Seattle, had begun his career as a missionary, and he insisted that each school should open every day with Bible reading and prayer. Each day I read the Song of Solomon, all seven chapters from beginning to end. To me it is the greatest love poem in the world, and the translators of the King James version certainly recognized its magnificence. As for the Eskimo children, they did not have enough English to realize what was going on. I'm not proud of this reminiscence, but it does show that my emotional life was " a spring shut up, a fountain sealed," too long. Activity was my salvation.

I was expected to close my school occasionally, call on other schools, and report to Mr. Shields. I visited one whose teacher was proud to be a graduate of the Carlisle Indian School. She expected me to be properly impressed. When I entered she had just dismissed the

"Second Reader" group. They had apparently done well so she called them out again. The lesson was about "The Cat's Birthday Party." She began by asking them what the story was about. They replied, "Kush kuk! Kush kuk!"—the Eskimo word for cat. "And what are they having?" The children became silent and stared at me instead of at the book. I wondered what the children would answer, knowing that the word "birthday" had no meaning for them. Time for them was not measured in months or years. "Baby born big snowstorm" or "Man die salmon come up river" was as near as they could come to setting a date. They had no birthdays. The teacher persisted, "Can't anyone tell me what they're having?" A boy on the end of the row raised his hand. "Yes, Tahar," she nodded, "what *are* they having?" Tahar shouted, "Kittens!"—to my delight and to the consternation of the teacher. The answer was more than a delight, it was a revelation of the primitive thinking of a primitive race.

At another school I visited the children were speaking pieces. During these recitations I became impressed by the fact that K is the dominating letter in the Eskimo alphabet. Almost every Eskimo word begins with K or ends with K. One boy I recall recited the well-known two-line poem by Robert Louis Stevenson; but his version went:

> The world is so full of a number of thinks,
> I am sure we should all be as happy as kinks.

The teacher said, "Kootook, can't you ever learn to pronounce the *ng* sound correctly?"

I said, "Please be easy on this boy, for to me his version is better than the original. Anyone who doesn't agree has another *think* coming."

The readers used in these schools were a slight improvement on McGuffey's. There were no such monstrosities as:

> When wicked children mocking said
> To an old man *Go Up Bald Head*
> God was displeased with them and sent
> Two bears which them in pieces rent.

Yet that would be better understood by the Eskimo child than such sentences as these from his own reader: "The lady has a fan. It is a nice fan. Have you a fan?" Eskimo children did know what a bear was, but they knew nothing of either a lady or a fan.

In a moment of indignation I sat down and began to make "An

Eskimo Primer." I took my work over to Nome and showed it to the Lomen brothers, who sold cameras and photographic equipment, and who were excellent photographers. One of the Lomen boys became interested and said he would prepare pictures for my "Primer" such as a pair of mukluks, a dog team, a kayak, an *immusee* (soapstone dish), an *umiak* (skin boat), a brown bear, a parka, etc. But the Lomens soon became interested in a larger project, namely selling reindeer meat to the people Outside. My own activities widened and multiplied, and the project of the "Primer" was abandoned. But I still think the book should be written—I hope it has already been done.

Kinne, the telephone operator, showed a personal interest in everyone in Council. He was a male gossip who loved to pry into the lives of others. One day he called me into his office and told me I needed a housekeeper. He knew a young Scotchwoman from Nome named Mackay, who was working at the Morrison Roadhouse in Council cooking, washing dishes, and doing all other heavy chores about the place. Morrison himself was a Scot, hard to get along with. "She asked me," said Kinne, "to find her an easier place. She won't expect a large wage. She'll cook and keep your house tidied up."

"Send her along," I said. "I'll be very little company for her. I don't spend much time at home, and when I am at home, I'm reading. If she'll come for what I can pay, I'll give her a try."

I found her to be a woman of about twenty-five or thirty, with a strong Scotch burr and a very serious manner. I settled her in the downstairs bedroom. I told her I'd be away all day and most evenings too. I explained that she would be visited fairly often by Eskimos asking for tea, coffee, rice, and other staples the office at Nome had sent me to give to the "deserving poor." I gave her the names of the families who should have the food and how much to give each one.

The first night after supper I went off to visit friends. The second night I was called out to care for a sick Eskimo. (I was the doctor for the Eskimos as well as the teacher and reindeer agent. The government had supplied me with a book on the treatment of common diseases.) The third night I could see that my housekeeper was lonesome, restless, and pouty. I stayed home and had a talk with her. She told me she was born in Aberdeen, that her mother was left a widow early in life, and that she had had only a few years of schooling. She had come to America in the steerage and had landed in Canada. She heard people talking excitedly about a gold strike on the Nome beaches in Alaska and decided to go see the place. At Nome she did the work of a housemaid, found it monotonous, and drifted over to Council and the Morrison Roadhouse.

The reader may find it hard to believe, but I did not think of her as a bed companion, not even in a cold Alaskan winter. One night I came home from a visit and found her clad like a Bali girl, bare from the waist up. When I came in she acted a bit surprised, reached for a wrap that wasn't there, smiled, and said "You're home early tonight!" I answered "Yes" and went upstairs. I had resisted many much more attractive females, was full of ideals and dreams, and was never able to make the grade in a house of prostitution. That winter I was reading Aristotle's *Ethics* with Muirhead's comments, also Plato's *Republic*, and I spent much time thinking those books over, marking them up, and making notes. I was in no mood to dally with a Scotch lady in whom I had no emotional interest, even if she did have what Alaskans of that time called "a good shelf."

The woman stood me for two weeks and then ran off to Nome without saying good-bye. That chapter in my life closed with both a bang and a whimper, and all the people of Council were vastly amused.

My job as amateur doctor to the Eskimos made me acquainted with Dr. Curtis Welch, who later became famous all over the United States and Canada. In fact, it was thirteen years later, in January 1925, when the plight of Nome, winter-bound and stricken with diphtheria, and the dramatic dash of the dog-mushers rushing serum six hundred miles from Nenana, the end of the Canadian railroad, thrilled the American people as no other news of the winter did. The story was given front-page headlines, and all over the country we followed the progress of the dogs along the trail. In this story one man stood out, Dr. Curtis Welch, the only M.D. in the entire region. Next to Leonard Seppalla, the dog-musher who was hastening the serum over the trail, the name of Dr. Welch was on everybody's tongue. He was a man of quick decisions, with a will of iron and a capacity for getting things done.

Curtis Welch was a New Haven boy. After graduation from Yale he studied medicine, received his degree, and set out for the West. In San Francisco he did intern work and met Miss Lula James, whom he afterward married. He was in the midst of the San Francisco earthquake, and had an exciting experience in a hospital which caught fire. The doctor and Miss James, with the help of two or three others, saved every patient on the third floor; and when the last of these was brought out, the smell of fire was on their clothes.

In another Western city, Dr. Welch became disgusted with his profession. He saw men who were bluffs making great names for themselves, and honest surgeons who lacked the spectacular in their make-up held back in secondary places. He growled about all this unfairness, and finally in a characteristic moment of spirited decision, renounced his practice and went to Alaska. If quackery were to be the price, he refused to play the game.

It was in Alaska that I met him in 1911, and he and I became fast friends. Welch was the doctor for the white people, but practice was the one thing he wanted to get away from. He and a Dr. Ramsay owned the Red Cross Drug Store, but both men were far more interested in their claims on Ophir Creek than they were in their practice. They did dispense drugs enough to support their dog teams and keep the wolf (a real wolf) from the door.

I learned to know him while I was trying to persuade him to take over my Eskimo medical cases. For a long time he refused to be interested in the natives. Finally a case came up which I could not diagnose. I told the doctor about the pain the Eskimo was continually suffering. What to do with him was a question I insisted on his answering. He agreed to see the man, called it a case of hydrocele, and made a brilliant operation on the patient. That broke the ice. Other native patients followed; and finally I got him to take care of all the medical work in that part of the Seward Peninsula. From that day until his retirement, he did invaluable work among the Eskimos.

On the personal side, the doctor was the soul of hospitality. He had few friends, for he made friends slowly, but those he had, "and their adoption tried," he grappled to his "soul with hoops of steel." His dog team was his great hobby when I first knew him, and his devotion to his leader "Bang" was not unlike the fondness of a doting father for a first-born son. His drugstore was a meeting place for the village that winter; and visitors from Nome, Candle, Golovin Bay, and other places on the Peninsula found the Red Cross Drug Store a good substitute for the social life they were missing. Impromptu gatherings at the Red Cross discussed literature, politics, religion, the best kind of poker to play, the best kind of drink, or any other subject that demanded attention. The doctor was not much of a literary "shark"; but the night I received my "Sourdough Papers," Welch was called upon

for remarks and surprised everyone present by reciting from memory
a stanza from his favorite poem, Longfellow's "Skeleton in Armor":

> Many a wassail-bout
> Wore the long Winter out;
> Often our midnight shout
>   Set the cock crowing,
> As we the Berserk's tale
> Measured in cups of ale,
> Draining the oaken pail
>   Filled to o'erflowing.

A more appropriate stanza to characterize the life men lived in those
faraway pre-Volstead days it would be hard to find in the whole range
of literature.

Night after night, eight or ten of us would meet at the Welches'
home over the drugstore to sing ballads. Mrs. Welch presided over
the piano and usually made the selections. Ballads like "Casey Jones"
and "Jesse James" were sung with special gusto. In the midst of the
singing someone would run across the street to the roadhouse and
bring in the drinks.

We listened at midnight for the "malemute chorus." One dog
would signal the arrival of midnight by sounding off with a long wolf
cry. Others would follow in rapid crescendo and soon all the dogs in
the village were howling, full fortissimo. It lasted about ten minutes.
I suspect it was a warming-up exercise. It occurred so close to the
midnight hour that one could set his watch by it. It stirred me to write
the following sonnet:

THE MALEMUTE MIDNIGHT CHORUS

> The hum of frogs in plaintive minor keys,
> The loon's lone autumn cry across the reach,
> The wailing wintry winds through giant trees,
> And pounding waves upon a darkling beach,
> Are notes of joy compared to that drear sound
> That sings from out the wolf-dog's lonely throat,
> Arousing others till the din profound
> Has tuned the North to one big funeral note.
>
> One cannot doubt the damned souls faring forth
> Have taken lodgement in that piteous plea,
> Condemned to fill the weird and beauteous North
> Each midnight with grim wails of agony;

> One doubts not that the ugliest notes of Hell
> Were mixed to yield that melancholy yell.

One evening we decided to sing some old familiar hymns instead of ballads. Dr. Welch's father had been a strict Methodist who compelled his children to go to church and prayer meetings where they learned all the old favorites. One that Curt called for was a fine old hymn containing these lines:

> See, the stream of living waters
> Springing from eternal Love,
> Well supply thy sons and daughters
> And all fear of want remove;
> Who can faint while such a river
> Ever flows their thirst to assuage?
> Grace which like the Lord, the Giver,
> Never fails from age to age.

Dr. Welch came over to my chair and said, "I love that old word 'assuage,' don't you, Bill? It's a rare word."

"Yes," I said, "I like it but I imagine it can be found in many hymns."

"I'll bet you a dollar you can't find it in any other."

"All right," I said, "I'll take your bet." Thereupon I searched through book after book of Gospel hymns and failed to find "Assuage" in any but this one. So I gave him the silver dollar—which he accepted after examining it carefully.

When the hymn-singing subsided, Dr. Ramsay, who had been out in a back room equipping himself with a long black cape and a prayer book, came into the room holding the book with his hands folded in a precise clerical manner, and intoned solemnly in a bishop's voice, "He pardoneth and absolveth all those who truly repent and unfeignedly believe His Holy Gospel." It was impressive. Harry Riley, over from Nome that night, sighed and said, "I feel forgiven. Now we can start drinking all over again"—which we proceeded to do.

When an injured man was brought in from the mines, all the social side of the doctor would vanish utterly. He would have two or three men at work as assistants, and demanded immediate response to every order. Eskimo or white, a man who had made a strike or just a "shovel-stiff"—all were alike to him. He was efficiency itself when an operation was demanded, and possessed that additional touch which goes beyond efficiency and lifts a science into an art.

Mrs. Welch was more responsible than her husband for the success of the talkfests and singfests at the drugstore. She loved to have people around her just as a Frenchwoman loves to keep a salon. In a village of three hundred men and nine women, social life was a difficult matter to arrange. She kept open house and gleaned all the fun she could from people who dropped in. John Dexter from Golovin Bay was a frequent visitor. Fox Ramsey, English gentleman, remittance man, dog fancier, and generous supporter of the Sweepstakes Races as well as all worthy charities, "honored" her with his presence three or four times a year. Judge Murane from Nome added dignity to some of her gatherings. Fred Ayer, manager of Ophir Creek and Blue Goose Mine, and his wife Elsie, people of uncommon social charm, were intimate friends who showed up often. Rex Beech's old piano played by Mrs. Welch furnished the music, and she was frequently helped out by Billy Elms, who dropped in with his violin from winter diggings four miles from town.

Mrs. Welch was born in Indiana, but when she was eight her family moved to Anaheim, California. As a young lady she met Madame Modjeska and told her she wanted to be an actress. She joined the company but did not show a marked talent for the stage. At Modjeska's advice she decided to train for a nursing career.

She loved pioneer life. She could drive a dog team and once won an amateur race from Solomon to Council. She had a deep affection for Curt's team, and when it was destroyed, she mourned as much as if she had lost a child. That disaster happened in this way: The Welches had taken their dogs to be boarded out at the town of Safety, on the shore. One day there were unusually high tides that increased each hour. When giant waves began to pound the shore, mounting higher and higher, the family caring for the dogs could think of only one place where they would be safe from the approaching tidal wave —the tower room of a wireless station. They left the dogs in that room and ran for their lives. Several hours later, when the waves had receded, the husband returned. He climbed the high tower to check on the dogs. There he found that they had apparently started fighting and had not stopped until they were all dead. When the message came over the telephone, Curt buried his face in his hands and Lou began to cry.

Lou's brother Earl came up in 1911 and became a winter caretaker for the Wild Goose mining property. He loved the fishing and hunting and the free life in the wild as much as his sister, but his wife couldn't endure it, and complained until he agreed to return to the States. When they stopped at Council to say good-bye, the wife was all happy smiles, telling what a good job Earl had in Sacramento, how they could have a car now, go to the movies, and live like other people. Earl was very sober. Lou caught him standing, looking back at the hills he was leaving. There was the free life he loved! She felt deep pity for them both.

Curtis Welch died in Pasadena in 1945. Lou retired to a senior citizens' home. She kept up a lively correspondence with her old Alaska friends until her death at nearly ninety years of age. She had learned how to live, how to roll with the blows, and how to endure uncomplainingly to the end.

The first tragedy of that winter occurred when a much loved teamster, Jack Harney, froze to death between Ophir Creek and Council. He was on his way home from the Blue Goose dredge, about four miles away, when a blizzard struck and the thermometer plunged to 40 degrees below zero. His two horses and the wagon arrived in town without a driver. A searching party found Harney sitting under a big Sitka spruce frozen to death. No one could understand why he left his wagon.

Two miners came to me and asked if I would conduct the funeral. Remembering that I had a copy of the Book of Common Prayer tucked away somewhere, I consented. (Now I had four jobs: minister, doctor, teacher, and reindeer agent.) I asked Paul Schwarz, a Jew, and Mrs. Welch, a Humanitarian, to help me with my two favorite hymns, Cardinal Newman's "Lead Kindly Light" and Whittier's "Dear Lord and Father of Mankind." Harney's friends came out of their winter quarters in a body, each one wearing a black arm band, and took seats together in the Arctic Brotherhood Hall, the only building we had for such a ceremony. They were a picturesque crew. Most of them rarely showed themselves in the village. During their hibernation in a big barracks-like building at the edge of the town they did some reading, played cards, made bets, got into fights, and waited for the oncoming of spring. They were taken care of by a Spanish-American named Henricus, a fine-looking man of superior tact and intellect, who grubstaked them. I marveled at his gift for handling these unruly men. It was he, of course, who furnished the arm bands.

I read the burial service and called upon the men to join me in saying the Lord's Prayer. They started out all right but got stuck in the middle and fell silent. I had to finish it alone.

Harney's friends had dug a grave for him on a hill behind Council, a Herculean task in that temperature and that frozen ground, and we all went there for the final portion of the ceremony. The zero weather made the committal service and the lowering of the home-made spruce coffin a difficult rite, but we saw it through.

After the ceremony, one of Harney's friends came to me with a roll of bills the men had gotten together, and offered them to me for performing the rites. I shook my head. "What will I do with it?" he asked. "Send it to the Catholic priest in Nome," I replied, "and ask him to say prayers for the repose of Jack's soul." When I got home that night I found my dining room table covered with bottles of Pabst Blue Ribbon beer, which was regarded as something very special. I accepted this gift as a tribute to Harney. His friends could do nothing for him; their need to express their sorrow spilled over on me.

The death of Jack Harney was a grim reminder of the fickleness of this land and the "hair-breadth 'scapes" one was apt to encounter there. I myself had two close-to-death experiences—one at the beginning and the other near the end of the winter. In November I was invited to spend the week end with Earl James and his wife at Ophir Creek. I wanted very much to see this creek, whose No. 7 claim yielded more gold than any other single mining claim in our country's history. I borrowed a dog team from a friendly Swede named Hanson —a team of only five dogs—and started about noon. I had to drive out from Council about four miles, cross over a ridge of "mountains"— they were really little more than hills—turn right, proceed up the valley two miles, and there find the Ophir Creek dredge and mining buildings. I never reached my destination. Instead of crossing the mountains into the valley, I went over a spur of hills to the right of the main ridge. I drove on and on and found no buildings. Snow was beginning to fall and I was lost. I circled round and round, moving without knowing it continually to the right. I finally ended up at the Neukluk River, on which Council was located. At the frozen river I could not tell which direction was which. Luckily for me, I recalled what a miner had told me two nights before in the barroom of Morrison's Roadhouse: "If you ever get stuck on the river and want to find which is up and which is downstream, dig into the ice and find out which way the Arctic willows are slanting, for they always slant down-stream." I made two soundings in order to be doubly sure. I noticed, too, that the river here was much wider than it was in Council. Trusting that the willows were telling me the truth, I set out upstream for Council.

In the meantime, Mrs. Welch had telephoned her brother at Ophir Creek and found that I had never arrived. My friends got busy and built an enormous bonfire in the middle of the street in the hope that I might see the smoke and flames. There were no strong winds blowing and the thermometer was above zero. Luck was with me. After nearly three hours, I could see that the river was narrowing, and at the end of four hours I arrived in town—one of the happiest, tiredest hours of my life.

Late in April I was driving a reindeer from Golovin Bay to Council. I drove on the frozen river, for there were no roads. The sun was lengthening the days and the ice on the river was beginning to melt. My reindeer was performing beautifully and the sunlight on the landscape made the trip a delight. When I was within three miles of Council, the ice broke and my reindeer fell through and began to sink. The snapbuckle below his hind legs had to be unsnapped; otherwise he could do nothing but wallow around and drown. So without reckoning the outcome, I jumped into the water with him and unsnapped the buckle. Fortunately for me the ice on the river had frozen in layers. Under three feet of water was another layer of ice. But for that, both of us would have gone to the bottom of the swift-flowing river. I got back onto the ice, took hold of the rein under his neck, and encouraged him to leap out. My eyes met his and he knew exactly what I wanted. He put his two forefeet up on the ice and gave himself a lunge forward. But the first attempt failed. He sank back into the river. I talked to him, encouraged him, tightened my handgrip on the rein under his neck, and begged him to try again. Once more he put his forefeet on the ice, gave a big lunge forward, and this time he came clear out onto the ice. Was I glad to see him back on the surface! I praised him, patted him, and thanked him with my eyes. I was wet all over, but the April sun was warm and wetness didn't matter. At supper I saw to it that my reindeer had a "super" helping of choice reindeer moss for his evening meal. That night when men at the barroom said, "It was good enough for you; it proves that you should have taken dogs and not reindeer on that trip," I thought of my friend the deer and could not give them a civil answer.

A month or so later I went once more on the the the river—this time with Cyclone Hanson and Gus Aspen, who were hired to clear a wide towpath on the river bank for the horses that were to haul barges loaded with provisions from Golovin Bay to Council. Supplies were getting low and the eggs were too rotten to eat. The people could hardly wait for the first ship that could be legally permitted to enter the Behring Sea. When the ship did arrive, I was amazed to discover that the first cargo hauled up the river was 100 per cent liquor! The miners certainly believed in putting first things first.

On this trip downriver I was merely the guest of these two men. I brought with me fishing tackle and a twelve-gauge shotgun. While they worked, I tramped the wooded area looking for fish and game. Suddenly I came upon a small cinnamon bear. He stood up on his hind legs like a circus bear and trained his little eyes on me. I stood up on my hind legs and stared at him. We were about twenty-five or thirty feet apart. My gun was loaded but I did not dare shoot at him, for all I had with me was shells loaded with small number 8 shot, which would merely have aroused his anger. So I just stood there and looked him in the eye. It was a terrible moment. Three minutes standing there seemed like three hours. Finally he turned to the right and walked back into the woods. I turned and walked rapidly toward the river bank. Cyclone Hanson said, "You look white. What's the matter?" I told them, and their laughter was so hearty that it could have been heard on the other side of the river—that is, if there had been anyone on the other side to listen, which there was not. To Gus and Cyclone it was a laughing matter, but to me it was one more "hairbreadth 'scape."

On one occasion when I had a rifle loaded for bear I didn't shoot. I was about three miles below Council near a large spruce tree that cast its shadow on the river. I saw a mother bear on her knees in the middle of the stream fishing for salmon. She would let the fish go swimming by until she saw one she wanted; then she would reach out her paw, bring the fish in range of her teeth, give it a heave with her mouth, and throw it on the bank where her two small cubs were waiting. She never missed once. I was her fascinated audience; I did not have the heart to shoot. I looked to see what the cubs would do. One of them sniffed at the salmon, pawed it a little, and waited for mother to come ashore. When the mother had landed four or five of these silver beauties she came up out of the water, tore a salmon to pieces, and fed her cubs. I was ashamed to tell this story when I got back to town for fear they would call me a sentimental sissy.

My failure to shoot was not wholly due to humanitarian sentiment. The year before, on this same spot, a man with a rifle shot a bear. The animal had just enough life left in him to rush forward, clutch the man's body, tear his breast entirely off so that his heart and lungs were exposed, then fell dead. The bear and man were lying dead a few feet apart when a friend of mine reached the spot. He said the man's dog was so fierce guarding his master that no one dared come near. They had to shoot the dog before they could recover the man's body.

Walter Shields, with headquarters in Nome, was my boss. He was deeply interested in the reindeer but cared little about the schools. He dreamed of the time when the reindeer would be the number one industry of Alaska. And he wanted me to see a village of Eskimos uncontaminated by white civilization.

Early in December Shields drove his dog team to Council, took me aboard, and with sleeping bags we set out for a deep wooded area toward Golovin Bay and well back from the river. Night came early and we built a snow house. He was a clever workman; he knew just how to carve out blocks of frozen snow, fit them together, and make an igloo. Inside we had nothing but a Sterno lamp to keep us warm but it was sufficient. Over the Sterno he warmed up a can of baked beans and heated coffee. That was our supper. His malemute dogs kept warm huddled together outside the igloo.

These dogs were blessed with both hair and fur, whereas dogs Outside have only hair. I wasn't long in the country before I learned how supremely important dogs were. Their great strength was coupled with tremendous endurance. They would pull to the last breath. I have known a reindeer's strength to play out before reaching its destination, and I once myself had to pull the sled the rest of the way. We were instructed by the government to make our official trips with reindeer, but Shields this time insisted on a dog team!

The second day we arrived in a village of four or five houses and moved into a god-sized log cabin, the home of an attractive young Eskimo, a reindeer herder, and his more attractive wife. That night when it came bedtime the Eskimo took me by the arm, led me over to the corner of the large room where his wife had already slipped into bed, looked me in the eye, stretched out his hand toward her, and offered me the pleasure of her company that night. This was the last word in free-hearted hospitality. But my Puritanical upbringing surged into the foreground; I thanked my host in the politest way I knew how, took him warmly by the arm, and told him this was his bed and his wife. If any reader thinks I feel pride in what I refused that night, he is 100 per cent mistaken. Today I feel, with Yeats, that "I was young and foolish and now am full of tears."

This village was far from the white man's roadhouses with their wine and women. Here the Eskimos lived as they had in the old days, except for their reindeer, an imported gift from Uncle Sam. The herds which we inspected before leaving for home were in prime condition.

Two months of sunless weather, an oversupply of leisure, and the monotony of winter life in the deep cold had made everyone eager for a lively Christmas celebration. As the holiday approached, the out-lying population came mushing into town, their malemutes swelling the midnight chorus of the dogs. Morrison, the proprietor of the road-house, put on a two-bartender shift to serve the boys day and night.

The roadhouse barroom, the town's social center, was an exciting rendezvous all week. New mustaches and beards, grown in the hills, were the butts of many a jest. A few of the more volatile were already drinking too heavily and had to be restrained. Bear furs were brought into town and presented to the ladies. Everyone felt that a white woman who was willing to live under the Arctic Circle through the winter was deserving of special consideration. Each one of the nine women became a nucleus around which a group of males revolved.

Two of these women directed the activities. Four men, at their request, went to the woods and brought back two beautiful spruces. Within an hour these trees were set up in the Arctic Brotherhood Hall and decorated with tinsel and spangles. It was decided to have festivi-ties on Christmas Eve for the "white" children and on Christmas night for the natives.

The dinner at the roadhouse on Christmas Eve was sumptuous. Fresh-killed caribou steak was the *pièce de résistance*; and for those who were averse to the game taste of the native animals there were storage meats of all varieties. Classy, the roadhouse chef—he went by only the one name—from time to time came into the dining room, beamed on his handiwork, and tossed jokes across the tables in a loud voice. His boisterous jollity loosened other tongues, and the room was soon a hubbub of gaiety.

After the big dinner, all the whites and half-breeds met at the A. B. Hall. During the first part of the evening the school children sang carols and received presents. At nine they went home and the grownups cleared the hall for a miners' dance. The scarcity of women made dancing a real problem. Of the nine women in the village only seven danced—only three danced well—and the orchestra demanded the services of one of these as pianist. For the men who did not or could not dance, card tables were set up, and draw poker at moderate stakes was the favorite game. If a man succeeded in getting one dance with a woman during the evening he counted himself lucky. Men who liked dancing inordinately danced with each other. The flowing bowl made this type of dancing fairly enjoyable. A magnificent cube of ice with one side chipped out served as the bowl. It was filled with dry champagne. Every man had to make a special contribution to finance this staggering luxury.

The violinist, a man who had struck gold on the creek that winter, was the pivotal point of the orchestra. Whenever he came to town, he always urged upon his comrades the philosophy of the half-jag as the golden mean of the true drinker. This night, during the intermission, he left the dance hall and failed to reappear. Impatient dancers, searching, found him lying across his bed with his beloved violin on his breast. Attempts to rouse him proved beyond any doubt that this time he had exceeded the limits of his philosophy. The dancers growled their disappointment, but the card playing went on until long after midnight.

Sleep was the order of the day for everyone on Christmas. In the evening we again went to the A. B. Hall, this time to give our little brown brothers a good time. As government man, I was Santa Claus and called off the presents. Some of the gifts the Eskimos hung for each other were incredible. For example, a favorite present was a bottle of castor oil. The chief staple of the Eskimo diet was seal oil, a commodity which had a rancid smell and taste caused by the fact that it was tried out in the midsummer sun. Castor oil had the oily properties the natives loved without the rancid taste. Another present was the No. 2 Blake steel trap with long chain attached—the trap we used on the Outside to catch mink and muskrat. The natives used these traps on their annual spring squirrel hunt—one of their big events. Many white men, anxious to hang remembrances to the Eskimo women who had made mukluks and parkas for them, or who had mended their socks, often did not know, or could not spell out, the Eskimo name; so they marked the packages in faltering handwriting using the village nickname. Imagine keeping a straight face while calling off a present for "Hannah Cook," "Rabbit's Mother," or "Cross-Eyed Jim's Wife"! After a half-hour of this I was so hysterical that I had not only forgotten all about my homesickness, but was accused by the chambermaid of being half-seas-over.

After the exercises the Eskimos came forward with a program for the white men. They began with games in which there was a great deal of horseplay. One game especially delighted the audience. Two young men came to the center of the stage with their hands fastened together behind them and tried to wrestle. They tripped and tumbled over one another, and laughed immoderately at the laughter of the audience. A first Eskimo act must bring laughter to the audience; otherwise, the tribe feels itself disgraced. Next, two old Eskimos gave a demonstration of lighting a fire without matches.

Then came the Eskimo dances. The drummer took his place at the center of the stage and began to tune up. The drum, the only musical instrument, was made by stringing the intestine of a seal across a bent piece of wood like a barrel hoop. One peculiar feature was that the drummer struck the hoop rather than the head of the drum. Eskimos came out and danced, singing while they went through their movements. For costumes they wore parkas hung here and there with the small bones of birds and animals, which rattled as they danced. About the hoods feathers of eagles and ravens fluttered colorfully. Some of the dancing was in masks as grotesque as the faces on totem poles. To an outsider the songs sounded like chants, made up partly of words and partly of meaningless sounds, like our own "fol-de-dol-de-do." The rhythm of the music was distinct, although the major and minor scales as we know them were unknown to the Eskimo. A wail, a chant, a falling and rising tone like the sound of wind through November trees or the sound of waves on the shore—this was Eskimo music. Some of it was deeply appealing, and comes back into one's mind over and over again like the strains of a great hymn.

The dancing is individual. Although the dancers often come out

in pairs or in groups, they do not touch one another. Some of the
dances represent the flight of birds; others picture a whale hunt or a
seal hunt. Others express little else than abandon to whatever emotion
seizes the dancer. Sometimes a desire to disrobe becomes the ruling
passion, and by the time the dance is ended he or she has little or
nothing on. In the seal hunt dances, the acting is so realistic that one
Eskimo's face takes on the veritable expression of the seal being pursued. The scratching on the ice near the blow hole; the shooting of
the small harpoon; the triumph; all these live before our eyes. The
Eskimos themselves are easily hypnotized, and one feels during this
dance that the natives are actually living over their experiences on the
Behring Sea.

During the dances, a few enterprising miners went about and
collected ten dollars for prizes, five for the best woman dancer and
five for the best male. A committee was appointed and winners were
chosen. For some reason this put a damper on the closing minutes
of the exercise. The evening broke up in a savage grumbling and
muttering among the natives that we could not understand.

I went to my cabin wondering what had caused the mutiny, and
half-suspecting that their communal feeling had been violated by the
white man's climax of competition. Then Garfield, the young leader of
the tribe, came softly in. His step was gentle, but anger was burning
in his eyes. He had been to the Carlisle Indian School for two years
and understood white men's ways. "Ah-neo," he began—Ah-neo is
Eskimo for Snow—"do you know you spoiled our Christmas with your
prizes?" "Yes," I replied, "I guessed as much, but why were you all so
outrageously angry?" "Don't you savvy? These dances are our religion.
Giving prizes is all same as giving prizes in white man's prayer meeting for white man who makes best prayer." Then I realized the full
extent of our blunder.

Between Christmas and New Year's I got a telephone call from
Superintendent Shields asking me to go to Ip-ni-choo-ik on the Behring
Sea to inspect the reindeer herd and see if the people there were alive
or dead. It was an official trip so I had to use a reindeer. I loaded my
sled, took Andrew Apogruk as my Eskimo guide, and started out. The
first day we covered thirty-five miles when we came across an abandoned cabin, and Andrew said, "We sleep here." I uncovered a ham,
some storage eggs, and bacon. Andrew said, "Bring inside, wolves

here tonight." I brought the meat in, found that the Sterno was working well, melted some snow for tea, and cooked supper. We loaded our rifles and got ready for the timber wolves. At midnight we could hear them crying and our reindeer snorted with fear. "Will they come near?" I asked Andrew. "Depend on how much they hungry." I looked out and thought I saw a wolf, but it may have been a bush swaying in the night wind. The howling stopped, but the reindeer was still restless. Andrew dozed off but I could not close my eyes until morning. Then I had two good hours of sleep.

The second day when we got to within five miles of Ip-ni-choo-ik, Andrew said, "I go back." He pointed to the direction across the bay and left me. Why he deserted me so abruptly I never could understand. Perhaps he wanted to call on a relative or friend nearby. At any rate, he walked off. After my reindeer had traveled a mile and a half he too failed me. He fell down. I pulled him up and he fell down again. Where we had stopped the night before there was no reindeer moss for my deer to eat; the load was heavy and he was all played out. Perhaps Andrew saw this coming. In any case, I turned myself into a pack animal, adjusted the harness around my shoulders, and pulled the sled four miles into town.

When I arrived in Ip-ni-choo-ik, a hunter had just brought in a good-sized seal. Everybody was cutting a slice of it. I took my sled knife, cut off an ample piece, and started at once to cook it over a driftwood fire. I was never hungrier and never ate meat that was so tender and easy to digest. The Eskimos stood around and laughed at me like children looking at an animal eating in a zoo.

These people were not living in igloos. They had dug holes into the side of a hill and made their dwelling places underground. It was a good way to combat the cold winds that blew off the Behring Sea. I spent two quiet, comfortable nights in one of these homes. The only drawback was that where the snow melted, the water ran down from the ceiling. They had not conquered that discomfort.

In the morning I inspected the reindeer herd. It was one of the first on the Seward Peninsula. The Eskimo herders were watching over it and keeping the wolves away. We rounded up, branded (i.e., sliced the ears), and parceled out the new young deer to the four best young men in the tribe, then marked the remainder for the government.

The young men gave me lessons in driving reindeer. It was hard with one rein, and was a wonderful exercise for the wrist. When the deer I was driving bolted for the side of a hill, upset the sled, and threw me off, they laughed loud enough to frighten the seals in the Behring Sea. But I was young and enjoyed the upset as much as they.

That night a baby was born, and having just left two Christmas parties, I felt I was having another one with all the necesesary ingredients—winter, reindeer, a new baby. I dashed off a poem:

CHRISTMAS IN ALASKA

On oceans of Alaskan snow
He saw stars big as sunflowers glow,
The Northern Lights their kin below.

And on a hill by Behring's strand
He saw a thousand reindeer stand,
Herded by natives of the land.

And from a birthing-hut nearby
He heard a baby's earliest cry;
No doctor, nurse, nor any one
To help that mother swathe her son.

While Eskimos stood round and smiled
He mused on Mary and her Child,
And thought, touch earth, no matter where,
Some portion of *Noel* is there.

For the return trip the tribe loaned me a fine strong reindeer. I needed no guide as I planned to go back the long way, following the shore of Norton Sound and Golovin Bay, then up the Neukluk River to Council. All went well until the second day, when I could see a storm coming. I hurried along. The sky grew black and the wind picked up. I was fearful of being caught without shelter for the night, but I was lucky enough to reach the Dexter Roadhouse before the storm broke. This saved my life as it turned out to be a four-day blizzard.

John Dexter (the Dextra of Rex Beach's *The Spoilers*) had come from Newburyport. One day on Golovin Bay, the ice he was standing on broke off and began drifting out to sea. An Eskimo woman named Molly saw his predicament, called three boys, put them in a skin boat with herself, and rescued him. The lower part of his body was frozen and he never completely recovered the full use of his legs.

Dexter had a good claim at Ophir Creek and it brought him a goodly amount of gold. With this he married Molly, went Outside, and hired a private train to take her and a few of his Alaskan cronies across the country to New England and back. This private journey made good publicity which John thoroughly enjoyed. But Molly did not care much for the Outside.

Molly was the most intelligent and reflective Eskimo woman I met on the Seward Peninsula. While I was caught at John's roadhouse in that four-day blizzard, she and I had many serious talks. She would point out to me one man over in a corner absorbed in a novel, another man reading Mark Twain's *Roughing It* and chuckling over Mark's drolleries. She turned to me and said, "White man have the best time. He read and read and we—we just sit and mope and wait for good weather."

John and Molly had lost their only child, a pretty little girl who showed marked artistic talent. John sent her Outside to an art school. She enjoyed the work, improved her art, but felt alone and out of place in the States. She came back to Alaska, contracted tuberculosis, and died in her early teens. Some of her paintings were hung in the roadhouse. In two of them she had caught the tone and spirit of the Seward Peninsula landscape.

A four-day storm in Alaska is a great experience. Picture a big barnlike room in a roadhouse. A blizzard is raging outside, and has been raging for two days. The snow has drifted and blocked the trails; no one has any ambition to venture out. What few books and magazines there are have been pawed over until they no longer hold any interest. The phonograph records have become as stale as the books, with the exception of one. At a certain place in this record a dog jumps out from behind the Yukon stove and lets out a wail. Why this strange performance no one can answer. No other record has any effect on him. Everyone must put on this record and see for himself before he is satisfied.

The Eskimo women, following Molly Dexter's lead, have taken out their beadwork. They are the calmest, most undisturbed group in the big house. John Dexter wants to tell once more about his visit to Elbert Hubbard at East Aurora. When he tires of this he wants to discuss religion, especially the immortality of the soul. The other white men are restless. They are mail-carriers, dog-mushers of various types, and missionaries just returned from a church celebration farther up on the Seward Peninsula, with whom the others do not feel at home. The mushers go out to see the dogs four or five times; more often than is necessary. After loosening a chain here, patting a head there, growling out their troubles in a series of half-finished sentences, they stroll back to the roadhouse. The lead dogs tug at their chains, begging for salmon. The wolflike wail that dies away as the mushers close the roadhouse door tells their disappointment.

Mealtime breaks the monotony. John has an air about him that makes him the perfect host. There is conversation at his table, often good conversation. At the close of the meal I ask him if the Eskimos have any religion. "As much as we have," he replies, "and about the same. Do you know the Eskimo story of Creation?"

"No."

"Then get Ptarmigan to tell it to you as soon as you get back to Council." (Ptarmigan was the medicine man or shaman of the Fish River tribe among whom I spent most of my time.)

"All right, I will. Do these Eskimos here in the roadhouse know any good stories?" I inquire.

"Do they? Try them out."

There were about a dozen young Eskimos on the premises who washed dishes, cleaned floors, and lugged in wood. That night I gathered them about me in the dining room. I told them I wanted a story and took out my pencil and notebook. At first they just stood around and laughed at me. John broke the ice by calling for the fox story. "Nah-pee-gan, he tell it," they all shouted. And Nah-pee-gan told me the story. He lined it out sentence by sentence in Eskimo and then translated into English. When his wordings were unsatisfactory to the others, they broke in. In the fox story, for example, my translator used the word "nur-ik-shuck" (food) in the phrase "food enough to last all winter." Two sticklers for exactness shouted out the correction, "neah-gee," which would make the statement read "*meat* enough to last all winter." Then followed an argument in Eskimo which raged fast and furious like the storm outside. Some of the quicker minds were fluent with idioms which carried over the exact meaning. The slower ones felt that the idiom-slingers were taking too many liberties; hence talking, correcting, arguing. Sometimes when the argument waxed hot, the seal-oil smell on their bodies made me wish I had never begun the storytelling.

For three days more the blizzard raged, and for three nights I went on with my transcribing. On the second night the Eskimos were around the table before John and I had disposed of our caribou steaks. Even the dog-mushers became interested, and really enjoyed the performance when the Eskimos were rising to the height of a tough argument. Personally I didn't care how long the blizzard continued. Through that storm, some of us were getting a glimpse of an unwritten literature, and through the literature the souls of a primitive people.

In all, I collected ten or a dozen stories in those evenings—stories of animals, of fishes, of men, of supernatural beings. I include only one of them here—a short one:

THE MAMMOTH

A long time ago a mammoth used to walk in the earth through the gravel between the overburden and the bedrock. This mammoth's name was Kee-lee-gee-vuk. When he came out of the land into the sea, the track he left behind through the land became a river. Sometimes in walking from an inland lake to the sea, he would cut a river so wide and deep that it would drain the lake dry. Once when a man saw the mammoth going in that strange fashion through the earth he shot it, saying, "I will shoot you in the heart." He fired his arrows toward the animal and then turned away. On the following morning he went out to look for the mammoth. He found Kee-lee-gee-vuk standing on the grass dead. When the man touched him he fell down to the ground. It was like pushing a stone through the gravelly earth. Then the man skinned Kee-lee-gee-vuk.

When he had finished skinning Kee-lee-gee-vuk, the Eskimos built a campfire in that place. They piled up a large heap of dry wood to roast the animal. Next they put a piece of the mammoth meat on the fire. The fire strangely and suddenly went out. The people were all dumbfounded, but an old man of the tribe saw what was the matter. He left the crowd and went around the shore. Under the overburden he found what he was seeking, some heavy, age-old, long-buried wet wood. He brought this old buried wood to the place and built it into a fire. Then he put the meat of Kee-lee-gee-vuk on it. This time the fire burned all right, and the people had a wonderful feast.

While taking down that story, I didn't know what it meant. When I finally got it through my head that it took prehistoric wood to cook prehistoric meat, I realized it was another illustration of the old adage, "It takes a crow to catch a crow."

When I returned to Council, Ptarmigan, the shaman of the Fish River tribe, told me the Eskimo version of how the world began:

THE CREATION

In the beginning the Universe was made up of a big moving mist. Out of this moving mist arose the crow, the sacred bird. The crow picked up in his mouth a piece of this thickening mist and, after flying about in the air, dropped it on the earth. As it touched the earth it swelled and took the shape of a woman. This woman conceived and brought forth a man child. High up in the *inne* [igloo] of the mother and child the crow then placed two balls of phosphorescent light, like the will-o'-the-wisp balls that float over the marshes at twilight, but warned the mother not to touch them and not to let the child play with them. The child, seeing the phosphorescent glow, cried for these balls of light; and the mother, not without misgivings, let him have them. In his play he dropped one of the balls. It immediately scattered into many, many pieces and became the stars. Then he dropped the other, which broke into two pieces, one becoming the sun and the other the moon. Thus broke light and understanding on the earth. The Great Spirit's messenger, the sacred crow, then had to mete out some form of punishment for the disobedience. So he caused a great cold wave to sweep once a year over the earth. This great cold wave became the long Arctic winter.

The Eskimo women fascinated me. In a cabin near the schoolhouse in Council lived Isaac and his wife. Isaac was a cripple. His wife spent her time making mukluks, which she sold to white men, who could pay more than Eskimos. She crimped the soles of these boots by chewing them into shape with her teeth—a tough task when the leather was hard and stubborn. Eskimo teeth as a rule are white and good to look at, but hers were worn to the gums. She knew a great many Eskimo songs whose tunes meant nothing to me when I first heard them. Later they haunted me. I caught myself humming them over and over. If I had only had a recording machine—but alas! I had none.

Once I was held up by a blizzard for two days at the Fish River Roadhouse ten miles from Council. One of the servants there, a very intelligent girl named Mary, had within the week given birth to a baby that was the talk of the house. I went into the back room to get a good look at the child. I said, "That doesn't look like an Eskimo baby." Mary said, "No, that's miner's baby. We marry too much together. No good. Bad in the head! Bad in body too." These women had no Puritanical feelings whatsoever and knew very little about romantic love. Many of them were deliberately trying to improve their stock, and that is why seventeen out of eighteen children in the so-called white school in Council were half-breeds. I found Mary interesting and wanted to stay awhile and talk with her. But when I saw her cleaning the child exactly the way a female dog cleans her pups (she had neither paper nor cloth) I could stand it no longer and made a beeline for the bar.

While Eskimos know little about romantic love, they have something closely akin to it. One of the prettiest girls in Council was besieged by a suitor. When he became too aggressive, she picked up her belongings and traveled to Nome. He followed her there and pressed his case. She left him and went to Little Diomede Island in the Behring Sea. He followed her and she moved to Big Diomede Island. He chased her over there on the ice and she went across the Straits to Golovin Bay. Finally convinced that he wanted her desperately, she gave in and mated with him. The rank and file of Eskimos have one mate, but the chief hunter of the tribe and the leading shaman, or medicine man, usually have three or four.

One day in January Mr. Shields telephoned and asked me to go to the Lutheran Mission on Golovin Bay and look over the reindeer herd there. I took four or five Eskimos with me for company, youngsters who wanted some adventure.

The mission was a large one. We arrived in the afternoon. I examined the herd, took notes for Shields, and went inside. We were invited to dine with the mission children. We all sat at long tables, bowed our heads while the Reverend Mr. Ost made a lengthy prayer, then fell to on ptarmigan soup. After dinner we sat around in the big living room and talked.

I urged the Eskimos to dance. I wanted especially to see what they would do with the *poi-ler-uk*, a solo dance in which each participant acts out his individual emotions. When the first dancer warmed to his task, Mr. Ost, looking very stern, came in from the kitchen and stopped him.

"What's the matter?" I called out.

"Mr. Snow, this is a Christian mission and we do not allow those pagan dances to be performed here."

The way he said the word "pagan" made me shudder. I was roused to indignation. To think that the Eskimo youngsters were being deprived of one of their greatest emotional outlets filled me with horror. Ost, straight-laced and Puritanical, did not realize what he was doing to one of the most cheerful and happiest peoples on earth. My disgust mounted and I resolved not to stay an hour longer at the mission. I told the children to put on their parkas and get ready to leave. I did not even say good-bye to Mr. and Mrs. Ost.

It was a lovely night. The stars up north look bigger than they do in the States. The air was pure and the temperature was about 20 or 25 above. On the sled I was seated next to a smiling Eskimo girl of seventeen. I was so wrought up emotionally that I embraced her and kissed her. I learned that night that an Eskimo girl has an exceedingly small round thread of powerful muscle around the edges of her lips which white girls do not have, and that when one kisses her, he is trapped as in a herring net with a purse string drawn up at its top. In this way I learned why so many white men got caught for keeps by these "Kobuk maidens." I learned also why so much of the kissing of Eskimos consists merely of the rubbing of noses together. That form of kissing is a much needed safety measure.

Long, long after midnight we reached John Dexter's Golovin Bay Roadhouse.

The white married couples carried on an active social life. Card parties, dances, and constant visiting filled the days. At Nome on Washington's Birthday there was a big *bal masqué* to which I was invited. It was held in the Arctic Brotherhood Hall. As earlier at Council, the punch bowl was a mammoth ice cube hollowed out and filled with champagne. This drink was a fairy wand that changed common men to kings! The costumes called for ingenuity as the materials were limited. The men dressed as Eskimos or miners, while some put on women's clothes to make up for the scarcity of dancing partners (there was one woman to thirteen men in Nome). I danced all night and no one rose from his bed to open school the next day!

At Council we had a "potlatch" (stag party) which lasted three days. The men ate and drank, sang and talked, discussing everything from the weather to the future of Alaska. The party ended with a banquet at which I was one of the speakers. I took my cue from Shakespear's "Seven Ages of Man," substituting seven leading citizens and the seven varieties of drink each was known to prefer. Each name I called out was greeted with an outburst of cheers and laughter. Old man Morrison told me that John Dexter paid the liquor bill for this party to the tune of $2000.

Ewen MacLellan was always a leader in the social activities. He loved drama and put on a few one-act plays of his own invention for our amusement. They were hastily written, and I recall now only one scene in one play. The scene shows a Negro looking for a place to sleep in a roadhouse. The manager takes him to a bunk and says, "This is the only bed I have left. Nobody wants to sleep in it because the last man who slept here was murdered. His throat was cut from ear to ear." At this point the Negro was supposed to roll his eyes and cry, "O Lordy, Lordy! I can't sleep here!" The man who played this part was a Swede. His make-up was excellent—Mrs. Welch, who had once been in Modjeska's company, had done a first-rate job on him—and he looked the part. But when the manager led him to the bunk, told him of the murder, and dramatically illustrated the throat-cutting, the Swede got excited, forgot his blackface role, and shouted, "*Holy Yesus!*" The audience exploded, his lines were never finished, the play was over!

One night after a long talk Mac said, "Let's write up the story of a winter in a mining camp." "All right," I said, "Let's do it in verse. You write half a dozen and I'll do the same." We wrote rhymed jingles about the people, calling them by name, and recorded all our social activities. It was journalistic verse and I was never proud of my part. But the people in Council thought the "poems" were just great and wanted them printed. So I took the manuscript home to Maine the following summer, wrote a short introduction, and got the book published by the Rockland newspaper, the *Courier Gazette*. The editor, unknown to me, had it copyrighted. One hundred copies were printed. I kept three and sent the rest to my old friends in Council. The cost was $165; they sent me $175, giving me an unhooked-for profit of $10, more than adequate to pay for such verses!

Mac gave me the feeling of being a pioneer. To him it was a thrill to look upon mountains and sail on waters yet unnamed, to be a trailbreaker in a new, fresh, unspoiled country. But he had one failing. When he went on a drinking bout, he could not stop until he was down and out with delirium tremens. A few years later, after I returned to the States, a letter from my old sourdough friend Paul Schwarz brought the sad news that he had drunk himself to death on the boat from Nome to Outside.

An unforgettable event came late in the spring when I was inducted into the Sourdough Club. (A sourdough in 1911 was a man who had lived in Alaska long enough to see a freeze-up and a break-up.) The ritual was a good deal like a fraternity initiation, only rougher. At one point I was taken upstairs in the A. B. Hall, rolled up in canvas, and shot down from a second-story window into a bank of snow. This rite was called "Going over the Chilkoot Pass." When I landed in the snow a man called out, "Another brother has made it! Let's give him a good slug of hootch!" Thereupon they put to my lips a cup containing the most repulsive mixture of bitter drugs ever concocted by witch or wizard. While I was choking on it, they gave me an electric shock from a battery that almost killed me. When this was over I felt that I had really been over the Chilkoot Pass. Back in the A. B. Hall I was put under oath to uphold the principles of the Brotherhood, which included a promise never to mix my blood with that of an Eskimo. (Here was racism rearing its head. The white man considered the Eskimo an inferior person. Yet this warning to keep his race pure had not been observed—witness the proportion of half-breeds in the "white" school, mentioned earlier. This much can be said for Alaska: whereas in the South at that time a child with one-sixteenth Negro blood went to the school for Negroes, in Alaska a child with one-half Eskimo blood went to school with the whites. But no Eskimo was admitted to the Arctic Brotherhood.)

As a concluding ritual, I had to sit and listen to the reading of my "Sourdough Papers." This was no simple certificate of membership in the Brotherhood; the occasion called for an oration, no less. To be chosen to perform this office at the climax of the ceremony was considered a high honor. In my case the address was composed and delivered by Dr. Ramsay, who used Johnsonian English with long periodic sentences and sesquipedalian words. It was impressive to say the least.

The story of the reindeer in Alaska is a sad one—a worthy experiment gone wrong through bureaucratic inefficiency and other people's greed.

The program was launched in 1892, as the wild caribou herds on which the Eskimos depended for meat and skins were beginning to dwindle, shot down ruthlessly by white men. Domesticated reindeer, it was believed, would make up for the loss; besides, they could be used for transportation. Under Department of the Interior direction, 1280 deer had been imported by 1902, and distributed in herds of about 100 head among the Alaskan missions. Herders from Lapland were also brought in under contract to teach the Eskimos the breeding and training of the animals; and if they remained in government employ for a certain length of time, each Lapp would be given a herd of his own at the end of his term of service. Apart from this, there was a Department directive that no female deer should be sold or transferred to anyone except an Eskimo.

At first the program flourished. The natives entered into it with zeal, and many of the better and brighter young men soon became as proficient as their Lapp instructors. By the time I arrived in the fall of 1911, there were 38,000 reindeer in the country. I figured that there would be a 20 per cent increase each year, so that by the mid-1930's there would be 3,000,000 of these valuable creatures in Alaska. Like Walter Shields, I expected that the reindeer industry would surpass salmon or fur or gold. More than that, it would bring economic security to a people I was learning to live with.

But alas, something—a lot of things—went wrong. The Lapp herders, as they became entitled to herds of their own, made off with the finest animals, in particular the Tunguz strain, larger of body and longer of limb than the ordinary deer. Then some of the Lapps caught the gold fever and sold out to white men. Other whites married Eskimo women just to get hold of their share of deer. Still others—for example the Lomen brothers, whom I have already mentioned—went out with cash and bought up the mission herds. The Superintendent of the Northwest District protested strongly against these sales, but there was no way he could stop them, for the Interior Department directive under which he operated did not have the force of a congressional law. The Lomens then built slaughterhouses and began shipping reindeer meat to the States, as steaks for men and food for dogs. (The meat is delicious, resembling a cross between beef and mutton but more tender and tasty than either.) The Ekimos, faced by this high-powered competition and feeling that the white man was taking over, began to lose interest in reindeer.

That was the beginning of the end. Finally, in 1937, Congress enacted a law stating that none but Eskimos could own reindeer, but not until two years later did they appropriate any funds to buy the herds owned by whites. By that time the industry had sunk to a position from which it never recovered. In 1968, if the *Britannica* is correct, there were only 35,000 reindeer in all Alaska—3000 less than there had been in 1911. There should have been two million.

My own duties with respect to reindeer were simple enough. I was to visit all the herds in the district periodically, inspect them, check on their condition and increase, see that the calves were earmarked, and report my findings to Mr. Shields. Then in the summer of 1912 I was directed to visit all the Lapp herders still operating and to buy their fine herds for the government. That mission was a dismal failure; not one of them would sell. But at least I saw many beautiful deer, and the finest displays of wildflowers I have ever seen. In the sudden northern springtime, the whole tundra was a paradise of Alpine flowers, lupine, firewood, yellow poppies, and dozens of other blossoming plants whose names were unknown to me.

During this summer of 1912 I was faced with an urgent decision. Should I remain another year in the North? I was pulled both ways.

A powerful temptation to stay came from the government, offering me money, materials, and manpower to build a model Eskimo village on the Neukluk River. I all but rose to this challenge. In addition, the *Nome Nugget*, the lending newspaper in the region, offered me a job as reporter and columnist. And John Dexter told me that he would pay me full salary if I would stick around his roadhouse and be handy for conversation!

Most of all, the North itself was exerting a strong influence. I loved the States, but I also loved Alaska, and I had learned to love the Eskimo too. It was he who first owned the land by the right of quiet possession. He trained the dogs that make travel in the North possible. He invented the mukluk and the parka, the two articles of clothing that make living in the North comfortable. He kept Dr. Cook alive during eighteen months of wandering on the Polar Sea—perhaps a greater feat, to anyone who has wintered under the Arctic Circle, than Peary's dash to the Pole, which again the Eskimo made possible. He had been the successful though silent partner in all the great relief expeditions; and even today he can mush over the tundra and bays of Alaska when the spring break-up forces the white man to turn back.

I had learned to live with the natives. They had taught me to drive a reindeer and to maneuver a kayak. I had traveled with them and eaten with them for days on end. They were the happiest people in the world, and being with them, I caught their joy in living.

But strong influences were drawing me home. After the spring break-up, boats from the States arrived every three or four weeks. Our mail was still a month late, but news of the coming Presidential election was reaching us. I began to get steamed up over the nomination of Woodrow Wilson. He represented to me a new and needed voice in American politics, and I wanted to go home and work for his election. I might still have remained had it not been for sad letters from my sister Cora, begging me to come home.

Cora was only thirteen when our mother died, and I had taken her under my wing. I believed that she had real talent in music and, if she had the necessary training, would make a name for herself as a singer. Each month of that Alaska winter I had sent her $50 to pay for her vocal lessons and her living expenses in Boston. (She had piano lessons free of charge from my friend Harris Shaw.) She started out with great enthusiasm; but alone among strangers, with nothing to do but practice her music, she soon became bored and lonely. By spring she was writing pitiful letters begging me to come home. This decided me.

On May 10 in 1912, on one of my trips across the tundra attempting to purchase Laplanders' herds for the Government, I sat down and wrote the following verse. It is verse rather than poetry, but it expresses better than anything I can write or say how I felt about leaving Alaska. So let it be the concluding words of this chapter:

MY ALASKA

Many others have sung of Alaska
Her half-frozen men on the trail,
Others have damned the mosquitoes
That sting worse than ice in a gale;
I will sing the pink glow on white ranges,
The Eden-like midsummer days,
The unburdening spirit of freedom
That smiles on her mountains and bays.

Could I paint only one of her sunsets
On the banks of a spruce-bordered river
Whose countenance blushes to crimson
Like a maiden first touched by love's quiver,
I would blazon the sky in the background
From crimson to mother-of-pearl,
And out of each spruce tall and stately
The bird notes of springtime unfurl.

Could I paint only one of her valleys
When winter has held nature's breath
To add to her beauty a silence
Like the strange, silent beauty of death,
I would paint alpine glow in the morning
And moonbeams on trees through long nights,
Hang stars with intensified stillness
On the blazingly weird Northern Lights.

Could I tell all the joys of a dog-ride
In the trail's early morning embrace,
When the Ptarmigan fly from the willows,
And the Malemutes double their pace,—
I would open a pure panorama
On hills of immaculate snow
And open new joys to the body
That thrills to the keen Arctic glow.

Could I tell pent-up people in cities
What it means down these rivers to glide,
Sleeping out under cottonwood branches,
Eating salmon or goose crisply fried
On the spit of a crackling wood fire
Whose odor alone is a joy,
I could bring them once more the adventure
That sweetens the life of a boy.

Could I plead with the souls that are mired
In custom, convention, and fraud,
Partners in social delusion,
Indifferent even to God,—
I would urge them to gaze on these spaces,
And hark to this silence that speaks,
Till the shackles that bind, drop and leave them behind,
Adrift on these valleys and peaks.

O Freedom that dwells on these mountains,
Blest freedom that swells on these shores,
You are more than the coal, seal and salmon,
You are more than the rich, golden ores
That lured men to brave darkest dangers
For the streams by the bleak Behring Sea,—
They sought only grubstakes and homestakes,
But found what it is to be free.

When the Eskimos heard I was leaving, they gathered round and
told me how sorry they were that I had to leave their beautiful land
for the dark and dismal Outside. Their love for their country overwhelmed me—and indeed, I had nearly succumbed to it myself.

The day came when I stepped aboard the *Portland* on her last
trip out.

CHAPTER 10

Home From Alaska

THE boat I boarded at Nome was the *Portland*, commanded by Captain Scoby, the same captain who had brought me north. On this ship there was no first, second, or third class; everybody mixed and talked with everybody else. The weather helped out; the sea was calm, the sun bright and warm. I had eight pleasant days aboard, saw the usual number of whales (three at one time), played poker and checkers, and told stories that I had told a hundred times before.

When I stepped off the boat in Seattle after more than a year in the Arctic, I felt as if I were at that moment the happiest person on the top of God's green earth. I went to the Arctic Club and settled down for three days. My first breakfast was one of the events of my life. The fresh eggs, the fresh milk, the clean tablecloth, the napkins, the ice tumbling into a clean glass of water, the silver, and the decorated walls of the dining room—I didn't want heaven to be better.

In the club lounge I read John Masefield's *The Everlasting Mercy* in a magazine edited by Ford Madox Ford and was so impressed I resolved then and there that if I ever got back to teaching I would initiate a course in modern American and English poetry, from Whitman to Yeats and the present day.

After three days I took a train for Portland, to visit the William T. Foster family and get a look at the newly established Reed College. Foster's wife had had another baby—this one a girl who was now four months old. I thought she was the most beautiful child I had ever seen, fell in love with her, and gave her a unique place in my heart which she still retains.

From there I traveled to San Francisco at the urgent recommendation of Dr. Welch, who insisted that it was America's finest city. Its location on steep hills, its Chinese quarter, and its art life delighted me. Before I knew it, I had spent most of my money and was still three thousand miles away from home.

I decided to travel hobo style to Chicago. I knew that the railroad fare from there to New York was $18, so I put $20 in the bottom of one of my stockings and set out. I also knew that once in New York, I could make contact with Bowdoin classmates and Columbia friends who would lend me money to get the rest of the way home.

Nothing eventful happened on my tramping experience. I spent most of the trip in the corner of an empty box car. I was thrown out only once by a "bull," and had to walk across Iowa before I was able to slip aboard another empty car. On that walk I slept under bridges and was astonished at the cozy spots the hoboes had made for themselves at these locations. There were fireplaces, cans for water, and great wads of hay and grass and newspapers for sleeping comfort. The intelligent men among these tramps were disgusted with the routine required of a laboring man working nine hours a day in a mine or a factory. "It was too monotonous," they said, "to keep a man's soul alive." One with a deep voice sang over and over, "I'd rather be a slave and be buried in my grave / Than to work in a factory, mine or mill." This was his version of a well-known Negro slave ballad.

One red-haired Irishman told me about his technique as a panhandler. He would go up to a house, knock at the door, and when a man opened it this hobo would say, "Are you crazy, too?" The man would look at him and say either, "Get to hell out of here!" or, "I suppose so, come on in." The method worked with people who had a sense of humor and not only gave him access to coffee and food, but to some good talk.

Another bearded character on that trip thought the whole world was going straight to hell. As a young man he had come over from Wales with high hopes, got a job working on the railroad, married a boardinghouse chambermaid, and started really living. Inside of six months his wife had become the boss's mistress. "That's America for you," he said with great bitterness. His one great adventure had been tramping across the country with Coxey's Army. "But even that got us nowhere," he said. "Everything in the capitalistic system is wrong."

The philosophy of tramps was not much different from that of the "hippies" of today, except that these men definitely did not believe that women furnished the answer. Several of them had been married and had had enough of the "women and the flowers" as a solution to the troubles afflicting mankind. They felt about the capitalistic system the way Bernard Shaw felt after he had given up a job in the Edison Telephone Company: "I would not sin against my nature by attempting to make an honest living."

On this trip I saw only one case of degeneracy—a man of about sixty, who apparently had an income, dragging in tow a weak-chinned pale youth of about eighteen. To me they were a sickening sight.

Fresh out of Alaska, I had many stories about that country to tell the hoboes and on two nights when I had an attentive audience urged them to spend a year up there. Some of them thought they might give it a try.

At Chicago, I paid my $18 for a train ticket to New York. With the $2 left I bought a few grapes and a sandwich, and these lasted me to Grand Central Station.

Arriving in New York, I suddenly remembered that I carried a miner's leather pouch in my pocket and in it a few small gold nuggets that I had planned to give my sisters. So instead of going to my friends as a beggar, I went to Tiffany's and asked if they would buy a nugget or two. They readily agreed and offered me $35 an ounce. That was exactly double the price of an ounce in Nome. With this $35 I felt like a rich man. I went to an art exhibit on 57th Street, took in a matinee of *Milestones* by Arnold Bennett, and at midnight boarded a train for Rockland, Maine. From there a streetcar carried me to South Thomaston, leaving a walk of four miles to Spruce Head and home. (I later recorded that walk in a poem entitled "The Return.") I was in a happy nostaligc mood and received a warm welcome from my father and his wife, my stepmother, when I finally reached home.

I did not immediately look for a job. For the last few years I had been having a great deal of trouble with my stomach. Dr. Welch had suspected an ulcer. Seal meat, ptarmigan, and salmon caused me no trouble, but the basic foods in the white man's diet—canned beans, canned salmon, and canned corned beef—had given me many sleepless, painful nights. My father saw that I was not well and did not urge me to go to work. I helped out the family larder as much as I could by digging clams, fishing for haddock, and hunting rabbits. I was happy to roam the woods and the shore, living over again my boyhood days.

Nostalgic moods are not healthy if long continued, and within a few days I went to Democratic headquarters in Rockland and volunteered my service in the campaign for Woodrow Wilson. I was welcomed by Obediah Gardiner, United States Senator from Maine. He said he would help me make the contacts I needed to stump the state. A Rockland man, a young, enthusiastic, idealistic lawyer named Henry L. Withee, had the same ambition for Wilson's election that I had. We struck up a great friendship and visited towns together up and down the coastal region, making speeches and answering questions.

There were two major issues in this election. One was the lowering of the tariff; the other, what to do about the great monopolies and trusts that were taking over the country's industries. I was disappointed to find that my Thomaston friend Dr. George L. Crockett had left the Democratic Party and was working for Teddy Roosevelt's "Bull Moose."

The village of Vinalhaven out on Penobscot Bay gave Withee and me a large and friendly audience; and I had a fine reception, too, at the town of Appleton. Political speakers in those days drew large crowds, for there were few other forms of entertainment—no radio, TV, or movies. Stump speaking had a real value too, as it helped people to think and decide on the issues and the candidates.

When the election came, the Democrats turned out to be the winners. The State of Maine went 52,000 for Woodrow Wilson, 48,000 for Teddy Roosevelt, and 13,000 for William Howard Taft. Women had not yet acquired the right to vote. This result early in September was believed to point the way the nation would go in November. At the time I was interested only in the over-all vote, but later I found out that in Appleton the count was 80 for Wilson, 66 for Roosevelt, and 59 for Taft; while Vinalhaven gave 261 to Wilson, 109 to Roosevelt, and 59 to Taft. I flattered myself, and claimed some of the credit for turning these Republican towns upside down.

When the election was over, I was completely exhausted. Dr. Crockett diagnosed my trouble as a duodenal ulcer. As I grew worse and worse, he advised an operation, but I had no money. If I could have stopped eating, I would gladly have done so. My diet had to be milk and toast and mild soups in small quantities. At times I was driven to bed—a sorry experience for a restless man.

My freshman roommate at Bowdoin, Ensign Otis, and his wife Betty opened their home and their hearts to me and helped to make the winter endurable. In their library, I met with and devoured Tolstoi. Reading his *War and Peace*, I sensed his driving energy and greatness. His conversion to Christianity fascinated me; his doctrine of nonresistance puzzled me; and his essay, "What Is Art," repelled me. I felt that he had more intensity than balance. His desire to live the life of a peasant met with my approval. I was inclined to agree with him that the poor people of earth are the only ones who have learned how to live. He was a one-sided genius. But how I envied him his all-out intensity!

I decided to give lectures on Alaska and had a small brochure printed, announcing a talk entitled "On Alaskan Trails." I had no agent, no newspaper advertising, and I was shy and inexperienced in ways of circulating my brochure successfully. Once in a while, though, I did get a call for the lecture. The usual fee was $5; sometimes a collection was taken which netted about $3. I carried a life insurance policy for $1000—on which I had already borrowed $800, the limit on that policy. I was stone broke.

At this time, too, I put together the verses that Ewen MacLellan and I had written the previous winter in Council City, and got them printed under the title *Songs of the Neukluk*—at an unforeseen profit to myself of $10, as earlier described. The book sank into well-deserved oblivion until 1944, when my Wesleyan colleague Fred B. Millett found a copy in the Library of Congress, where the printer had sent it for copyright purposes. Recently one copy was sold as a collector's item for nearly double the cost of the whole edition.

During that winter, on days when I felt well, I went to Chickawaukee Pond with a few congenial souls, spent many hours skating—which is still my favorite sport—and sailed an iceboat whose wealthy owner was generous enough to let us all make use of it. This was an exhilarating experience. With a beam wind I could sail the half-mile from one end of Chickawaukee Pond to the other in less than a minute. This was incredible speed, unknown to me in any other vehicle on land or sea. The joy of flying over the ice was breathtaking. Beating back against the wind was another matter and sometimes took nearly half an hour, but the experience was new and exciting. That winter I often found myself standing in line at the head of the pond, awaiting my turn for the joyous sensation of another trip.

In spite of this thrilling activity, I had days of unmitigated gloom which I attributed to my ulcer. It was the winter of my discontent. How I managed to live through it, without money and broken in health, I will never know. When I felt up to the task, I worked at my verse. Few realize it, but writing poetry is hard work. I went over and tried to make something out of my long Gethsemane poem. I sold a child poem named "Her Dreams" for $5 to a magazine in Boston called *The Beacon*, and was pleased to see it printed on the outside of the front cover. I also sold a sonnet on "Alaskan Trails" to *Zion's Herald* for $1 —the lowest stipend I ever received for a piece of writing. I cashed the check in Rockland rather than at the village store because I didn't want to give Aunt Fronie the chance to spread the news of my small pittance around the village. I knew well enough that people were saying, "Why does he hang round here doing nothing—him with a college education—living on his poor father."

Spring in Maine came late, but it came with a rush, and that rush more than made up for its lateness. With spring also came a letter offering me $1500 if I would come to the University of Utah for a year and teach English and debating. My senior roommate and close friend at Bowdoin, Ami Roberts, who was teaching debating at Utah, had received a call to Reed College, and it was undoubtedly he who recommended me for the job. Sick as I was, I accepted the offer and made plans for another jaunt West.

That summer my favorite cousin and fraternity brother, William J. Norton, spent a few days at Spruce Head visiting his relatives. We had many delightful hours together. During his visit a neat sailing yacht named the *Bluff Wind* anchored in the harbor. The owner, a man named Ayres, received a telephone call to come back to Boston at once, and he had to return immediately by train. What to do with his yacht was the problem. He offered $75 to anyone who would sail her to Boston. I was the only one who accepted. My father warned Mr. Ayres that I did not know enough about navigation to sail that yacht. I allowed I did, and in desperation Ayres gave me the key to the hatch and took a train out of Rockland. Bill Norton was excited over the prospect, and offered to go as cook, mate, and deck hand.

I bought a set of Eldridge charts in which, unlike government charts at that time, red buoys were marked *red* and black buoys *black*, and off we went—leaving my father with a sad, anxious look on his face. He himself as a youth had learned how to handle a quadrant and a sextant and was able to find where he was at any time on the high seas. I had none of this knowledge. I did know how to sail small boats. I merely trusted that we would have no fog, a fair wind, and good weather, which we did.

Just before we began our walk to the wharf that morning, I dropped into the post office. There was one letter, from my former teacher and later colleague at Bowdoin, Professor Charles T. Burnett, and in it there was a check for $75. He was traveling in the Holy Land, and when he came to the Garden of Gethsemane, he remembered the struggle I had had writing a four-hundred-line poem on the subject. He added that he had just received news that I was ill and out of a job and hoped the check might give me a bit of cheer. Talk about "Manna from Heaven"! This was it. Words are utterly inadequate to describe the joy I felt that morning.

We hoisted the two sails and one jib of the *Bluff Wind*, and a brisk northwest breeze carried us out beyond White Head Light onto the bosom of the Atlantic. On the deck in front of the wheel, I placed an Eldridge chart and weighted it down with pieces of iron to keep it from blowing away. It was a wonderful day for sailing. This trip with all its potential hazards made me more convinced than ever that nothing on the high seas can quite compare with a sailboat scudding over the water with a fair breeze. A short time after this trip I started a poem on a sailboat, letting the boat speak of the experience. One strophe reads:

> But when the air springs up and tells the shrouds
> In scarce-felt whispers from the purple tide
> The coming of a spanking southwest breeze,
> My master spreads completely every stitch
> Of canvas, takes the helm, away I spin
> Along the slapping waves, my sails bulged out
> In rounded fullness gloriously white;
> The foam crest, boiling, bubbling at my bow,
> Sings sailor chanteys to my pilot's ear,
> And I am free and happy as the wind
> That drives me as it drives the happy birds
> Along the lime-green gullies of the sea.

At sundown, we anchored at Peak's Island off Portland, where Bill Norton with his wife and children were vacationing for the summer. We went ashore and Effie, Bill's wife, treated us to a sumptuous dinner. We had eaten sparingly on the yacht, and the meal climaxed a great day of sailing.

The next day we were favored once more with a northwest breeze. We changed to another Eldridge chart and anchored it on deck as before. We kept well off shore, sailed past the Isles of Shoals, skirted the New Hampshire coast, and made Gloucester breakwater as the light of day was fading. The wind died down and we just barely glided by the end of the breakwater and into the harbor when darkness overtook us. We had no lights on and anchored with all speed. That night we slept on board and congratulated ourselves on our good luck.

It was a short run from Gloucester to Boston the next morning. I tried twice to engage in impromptu races with two other craft but neither of them accepted the invitation. (The *Bluff Wind* was an uncommonly fast sailer and had won races at Marblehead.) Mr. Ayres was on the wharf when we arrived. He handed me $75 in crisp bills, jumped into the *Bluff Wind,* and took her out to her anchorage.

I went to the North Station with my cousin, thanked him for all he had done, and bade him good-by. I then headed for Huntington Avenue where my friend Harris Shaw had a studio. I slept on an army cot he kept for old friends dropping in.

The next day I called on a Bowdoin classmate named Chandler, a general practitioner, and told him the story of my illness. He sent me at once to an internal medicine specialist named Preble, another Bowdoin man, who had had a struggle getting through college and had taught high school between college and medical school. We had much in common.

Late in the afternoon he gave me a thorough examination and after much probing and questioning told me that I ought to undergo a gastroenterostomy. He said Boston had a surgeon who could do this operation, a man who was, in his words, "as good as any man at Mayo's." I cringed at the word "operation," for I could not wholly shake off the fear engendered in my boyhood in a village where surgery was spoken of as "going under the knife," a gruesome experience. I told Dr. Preble about my engagement to teach at the University of Utah in a few weeks, at which he laughed heartily, saying that at least I had courage to take on such a tough assignment in my condition.

He procured me a bed in the Boothby Surgical Hospital and told Dr. Fred B. Lund that I needed an operation. The surgeon called on me and we became friends at once. He loved Latin, he told me, more than any other subject. His engaging personality drove away all my fears, and when he casually announced that he would meet me in the operating room at nine the next morning, he gave the impression he might just as well have said, "We'll have a round of golf at nine tomorrow."

That evening the nurses went quietly through their ritual of preparing me for the operation. After that I lay awake a long time thinking, "Only Harris Shaw of all my friends and relatives knows where I am and what is going to happen to me. I should at least have telegraphed my father my safe arrival in Boston. I'll do that tomorrow. Tomorrow? Anything can happen tomorrow! Oh well, I'm in for it now."

The next morning they took me upstairs to the operating room. The anesthetist told me to breathe deeply and not resist going under, and after a few breaths it was all over. The next thing I knew I was in the recovery room with an intern sitting beside me. They took me back to my cot, tucked me in, and told me that I would be all right in a few days. The exhaustion of exhaustions took charge of me, and I sank into the pit of complete forgetfulness.

When I awoke the gas pains had already arrived, and my abdominal region was yelling out loud at all the rest of my body. Within an hour my mind asserted itself and I asked to see a daily paper. The head nurse called on me, told me that my operation was a success and that the doctors had found nothing malignant. I immediately wrote out a telegram to my father and told him what had occurred, adding that all was well.

The surgeon and I had long talks together. He confided to me that he occasionally made contributions to the *Classical Journal*. The nurses were proud of him. They told me he was the best surgeon in Boston. This I could easily believe. There was a sense of power and a nobility about him which I admired. At the end of ten days he said, "You have been such a good patient. What can I do for you?" I replied, "You can do just one thing: let me see you operate." He was taken aback by this, but he said, "All right. I'll tell the girls to take you to the operating room tomorrow morning. But you'll probably faint and will have to be dragged out. You are still weak after that operation."

The next morning two nurses, "one extremely attractive," put me on an elevator and took me to the operating room. One stood holding my right arm, the other my left. There was only one operation on the docket and that was a Caesarian section. I watched Dr. Lund perform and was so aroused mentally that I forgot my bodily fatigue. When the baby came out she was one of the most adorable creatures I have ever seen. And Dr. Lund seemed to be as pleased with the child as the rest of us. I felt that I had seen a great artist in action.

On the eleventh day I was discharged. I told Dr. Lund what money I had. Together we figured that I had enough to pay the hospital and get myself out to Utah. "You can pay me when you are on salary," he said. I thanked him, took a train for Middleboro, stayed with my sister Agnes all night, and the next day headed for Salt Lake City and the University of Utah.

This hectic year brought a change in my life. I realized that I was obsessed by activity—physical and mental. I resolved to live a more passive existence. A copy of the sayings of the Tao became my Bible. Observations such as "A muddy brook will clarify itself if let alone for a while" affected me profoundly. Such scripture passages as "Come into the desert and rest a while" and "Be still and know that I am God" gave me comfort.

Emerson's "Why so hot, little man" and his "I don't know of any music there is in a rest, but a rest seems to be an indispensible part of a musical composition" hit home. Wordsworth, whose poetry I loved, was full of such material. I sensed that Americans were so busy playing the game of life that they had no time to contemplate its aims. An Oriental streak in me asserted itself. I decided to stop worrying. I would simply drift across the cove of life, look down, and take careful note of what was on the bottom. It was difficult for me to carry out such resolutions, but a recognition of the wisdom of "a wise passiveness" changed the direction of my thinking and my life.

So it was that I rolled westward over the prairies, this time in a comfortable seat. I carried with me a fresh outlook on life, a renewed ambition to be a poet as well as a good teacher, and, very important, a fair promise of good health.

CHAPTER 11

Utah

WHEN I stepped off the train at Salt Lake City in the early morning sunshine, the air was clear and exhilarating. Taking a deep breath, I looked up and saw snow-topped mountains towering over the city on one side. On the other, a plain strewn with wildflowers sloped down to the Jordan River. A brilliant sky arched over all. I could understand why Brigham Young, when he first arrived in the valley, declared, "This is the place!"

As I walked along I could see that the city had not just grown; it was carefully laid out with tree-lined streets crossing at right angles, like a checkerboard. Brigham Young's Beehive house and other Mormon headquarters occupied the center of the city, with business buildings crowding around. The Mormon Temple, an immense granite box with three square towers at each end, struck me as an architectural monstrosity, but the Tabernacle was a work of art. Its dome has been likened to the shell of a turtle, and its acoustics are said to be the best in the world. Non-Mormons are not allowed in the Temple, but I sat for an hour in the Tabernacle, trying to get the "feel" of my new environment. Outside, the city like many American urban centers seemed given over to commercial materialism. Here in this vast room, its walls in muted colors, I sensed the peace of religious faith.

At the University I reported to Professor Frederick Reynolds of the English Department. He was well dressed, of pleasing appearance, a man reaching out to be agreeable to those around him. He told me he had done graduate work at Harvard, which with its immense library and distinguished body of professors he thought unique among American educational institutions. He told me I was to teach three sections of English 1, give a course in argumentation, and coach all the debating teams. In addition to this he wanted me on week ends to teach an extension course in American literature at Provo, a city about fifty miles south. This was to be merely a lecture course. I told him that he was giving me a larger assignment than I had been accustomed to elsewhere. He said he thought I could handle it, and gave me a folder telling when and where all these classes would meet.

In English 1 there were about thirty students in each section. I told them they were to write three themes a week. That meant 270 themes each week for me to correct. At the end of a month I found myslf correcting commas and semicolons in my dreams. After that, on Reynolds' advice, I cut the assignment to one theme a week.

From the first I was anxious to learn as much as possible about the Mormon way of life. I had read in Mark Twain how uncommonly plain were the women who followed Brigham Young to Utah, so I was surprised to see how good-looking the Mormon girls were. One handsome young lady who was getting low grades came to a theme conference with a bunch of violets on her breast, and dropped her hand down on mine as we talked. She wanted a grade higher than C and intimated that she was willing to do me a special favor if I would give her an A or at least a B.

I was greatly surprised by another girl who asked me if I would put in her middle name when I called the class roll. "Don't say Mary Smith, say Mary Miles Smith. I was a daughter by the first wife, and I want people to know it." This incident led me to discover that sororities in the university at that time did not want to take in any girls who were not daughters by the first wife.

The student who interested me most was Bernard DeVoto, whose every theme was a damnation of the Mormon hierarchy, what we would now call "The Establishment." His father was a Catholic, a graduate of Notre Dame, and his mother was an apostate from the Mormon Church. One day I read the class some Masefield, Robinson, and Santayana, and DeVoto stayed for an hour to talk it over. He hated the Mormon Establishment so much that I urged him to go elsewhere after finishing his freshman year. He entered Harvard the next fall, and went on to become a distinguished man of letters. His life of Mark Twain and his books on the winning of the West are major contributions to Americana.

An offset to DeVoto was an attractive girl from southern Utah named Marian Redd. She was disturbed by the challenging essays in the textbook I was using—works of Emerson, Thoreau, and other daring spirits. Such heretical writings were undermining her religious faith. I tried to reason with her, assuring her that light had to come out of darkness, that every thinking college boy or girl had to go through a period of religious doubt. She said she didn't want to go through it. She wanted to remain happy in her beliefs. There were tears in her eyes as she listened to me, but her mind was made up. She was leaving the University and going back to San Juan County, where she could be happy as she was before coming to college.

Another girl in that class interested me. I had asked the group to retell in their own way a Bible story after reading it carefully in the King James version of 1611. I wanted to see how many of them could recognize the excellence of that remarkable translation. The next week a girl from Idaho with an expansive, breezy way about her asked me if I would let her write another Bible story instead of the subject I had assigned. I said, "All right, go ahead." When she asked me the third week if I would let her do another Bible story, I began to wonder. I said, "What is the matter? Why do you want to write nothing but Bible stories?" She said, "My father's a follower of Robert Ingersoll. He will not allow a Bible in the house. He will not let me go to church or Sunday School. I think the Bible is just wonderful." "All right," I said. "If you will stick to the King James version I will let you write themes on the Bible throughout the semester"—which she did.

I took some of my debaters over to the Capitol where lobbyist friends of mine had been working on a minimum wage bill for the state. It made them see the reality of what we were debating. Girls working in the candy stores and the laundries were getting $3.00, $3.50, and $3.75 a week. They could not get along on such small wages. This 1913 bill set the exact minimum pay per week. It did not allow for future increases in the cost of living, but for a time it did help the terribly underpaid girls.

My debating class was held downtown. In it were some of the liveliest minds of the university—boys who were looking forward to law and public life. Like myself, they were interested in the minimum wage bill. Many of them were absorbing the fresh new spirit in American politics that Woodrow Wilson was engendering. One of these boys, Herbert Maw, later became governor of the state. Another, Milton H. Sevy, had one of the keenest minds I have ever encountered. I was grieved to hear later of his early death.

Another boy in that class, named Doyle, was summoned to Church headquarters and told he had been selected to go overseas on a missionary tour. He was getting ready to go into law and I felt that his career should not be interrupted. So I went to the Beehive house (a completely irregular and heretical thing to do) and protested. I told the elder in charge of missions that this boy's interest was law and public life, and in my opinion he should go on with his studies. During our talk I blurted out, "Whom do you expect these boys to convert?" "Themselves," was the answer, which came to me as a decided shock. I came to realize that these fine boys were chosen with the idea that, if they punished themselves and made sacrifices for the cause of the Church, they would come back deeply loyal and become the leaders of the Establishment. Psychologically it was thoroughly sound, and I was rapidly becoming educated in Mormon procedure.

Long journeys on railroad trains by the debating teams were common. Our boys traveled eight hundred miles to Boulder and back to debate the University of Colorado. Such long jaunts would be unthinkable in the East. On one occasion after a trip to Montana one of the boys sent me a telegram which read, "We won the debate but lost the decision." Such an outcome often happens in the debating world. Judges of debates find it difficult to be neutral, although a minority lean over backward in favor of the visitors.

There was a congenial group of young men on the faculty. One of these, Frank Holman, dean of the Law School, was a Rhodes scholar who loved to regale us with his Oxford experiences. Another, George Hedger, the assistant dean, came from a Mormon family and gave us background knowledge of earlier days. His widowed mother interested me. She had come west by ox cart, and her account of that experience made one feel all the fresh beauty and space of the high prairies, with their meadowlarks and wildflowers, before the railroads were built. She had also known Brigham Young, and had vetoed his suggestion that her husband take a second wife. "A great man and a practical man," she said, "but he didn't seem to me to be very spiritual."

A kindred soul in my department was Phil Bing, a wit, a delightful table companion, a fine critic, and an excellent teacher. He loved puns as much as Shakespeare. He once explained to a group of us that the Angel Moroni, whose bronze statue caps the central tower of the Mormon Temple, was the father of all the morons! This pun later led to his dismissal.

Two of our number, Elbert Thomas and Leo Marshall, although they were members of the Church of Jesus Christ of Latter-Day Saints (to give it its full name), enjoyed with us at the Louve (pronounced "Louver") Café the beer and coffee denied to Mormons but drew the line at our criticisms of the hierarchy. Thomas later became a United States Senator. He was a plodding upright man, good-natured but humorless, lacking spark and enthusiasm. Those qualities were reserved in his family for his sister Kate, who added much to our campus life and activities. She introduced me to the Mormon publications, and I sold to *The Young Woman's Journal* a number of verses, including revised versions of "Sailor Song" and "Life" which I had written for the Bowdoin *Quill* in my undergraduate days.

Dr. George Marshall, chairman of the English Department, was a gentleman who had been at the University for twenty-three years. He was an Episcopalian who admired the Book of Common Prayer and detested the long, extemporaneous prayers of the Mormon preachers. The fact that he was married to one of Brigham Young's daughters may have given him courage, but at any rate he spoke out fearlessly against the rigid Mormon hierarchy whenever the subject arose. He also insisted on recruiting Gentile instructors from Eastern colleges and universities. He told me that the account of the Mormon totalitarian government as depicted in the eleventh edition of the *Encyclopaedia Britannica* was the correct one. He was not altogether happy with his life in Utah, but his wife was a Mormon, he had two daughters to educate, was getting on in years, and had no idea of fighting the Establishment. He told me he had tried to read the Book of Mormon but could not get very far.

I had already resolved to read the Book in order to understand the thinking of my students. I plunged into it and found the going tough. It was like walking through a mud cove in which one bogged down knee-deep at every step—"chloroform in print," as Mark Twain had called it. After reading it I felt exhausted and bewildered, but I soon found that the students themselves paid little or no attention to it.

Few of my Mormon friends had ever read the Book. One of them said to me, "Don't bother with that. We gave it up years ago." But many of these very people had a good working knowledge of the Bible. One man I knew had just come back from Vermont, where he had taken down the names of his ancestors from gravestones, brought them back to Salt Lake, and had "Temple work" done over them. "Temple work" is a ceremony for baptizing into the Mormon Church those who died in their sins or in other faiths.

One day I asked this man, "Where do you get your authority for Temple work?" "Why, in your Bible," he replied, and rattled off from memory the words of the First Epistle of Peter, 4: 6:

> For this cause was the gospel preached also to them that are dead, that they might be judged according to man in the flesh, but live according to God in the spirit.

He had me licked. I felt doubly humiliated, for I prided myself on a close familiarity with the Bible but had missed this passage completely. I suspect this manner of thinking must have been very active in the minds of the Christians of the first century, whose parents and grandparents had died as pagans.

I made it a point to attend Mormon Tabernacle services, hear their famous choir, and listen to the preachers, some of whom were eloquent in their defense of orthodoxy. And of course I heard many times the well-known story of the sea gulls—how in the first summer of settlement swarms of locusts appeared and set about devouring the young shoots of grain on which the settlers' lives depended; how as if by a miracle huge flocks of sea gulls arrived, gorged themselves on the locusts, and saved the crops. This tale is included in their Sunday School books as an example of God's special mercy toward the Latter-Day Saints.

After I had been in the city for about five months, I was asked to join a group known as "The Saturday Night Club." The membership was made up mostly of professional men and their wives, all Gentiles. Two of the wives were aspiring writers. One wrote children's books, the other short stories and novels. They knew I was writing and selling verse, and booked me at once for a talk on John Masefield, whose *Everlasting Mercy* was then almost a best-seller and whose short lyric "Sea Fever" had caught the attention of the reading public. The people in this club were intelligent, the discussion excellent, and I resolved to be present at every meeting.

In the Club there was an Episcopal bishop named Spaulding, a liberal in politics, a great reader, a man with a generous sense of humor, an ornament to the community. One evening he was struck and killed by a car driven by one of my students, Adrienne King. My next theme conference with her was a distressing affair. She was very beautiful and very sad. I longed to take her in my arms and comfort her, but I checked that impulse. I hope she saw in my eyes the sympathy I had for her. The tragedy was considered accidental and Adrienne was never brought to trial.

Two months later an Armenian joined the Club. He was the answer to a woman's prayer—young, slender, with flashing black eyes and an olive complexion. He had come to Salt Lake as an assistant manager in one of the Bingham Copper enterprises. The ladies urged him to give a paper. He insisted that he was not a writer, but they broke down his resistance with cajolery and flattery, and the poor boy finally agreed to give a paper on Armenia. He went to the *Britannica*, found a long article on his native land, and got the girls in his office to copy this material, triple spaced. It added up to about seventy-five pages. Lying on the lectern it looked formidable. One glance at the pile of manuscript and I slipped into a back seat. Two or three other men did the same. The meeting opened, the speaker was introduced and started reading. At the end of the first long hour I got up and walked out onto a veranda. Pretty soon a member named Critchlow joined me, saying, "Snow, for the first time in my life I have been able to understand the Armenian Massacres!"

All the while my ambition to write kept my pen moving over sheets of clean white paper. To the *Salt Lake Tribune*, the Gentile newspaper, I sold the story of an interview I had on my trip west with Mayor Hunt of Cincinnati, a political figure who was receiving much attention and was heralded by some as a man of increasing stature in the national Democratic Party. This gave me an introduction to the editors of the paper, and I had many good visits with them.

I happened to be in an editor's office one morning when there was a big cattlemen's convention in town. A very young cub reporter was sent out for an interview with one of the richest of these tycoons—a millionaire named Eccles. An hour later the boy, all out of breath, came running back with a sheaf of notes in his hand. "Guess where I found him? I went to the Salt Lake Hotel and he wasn't there. I went to the Morrison Hotel and he wasn't there. Then I went to a lot of rooming houses and finally there he was, stashed away in a dingy room *like poets die in!*" His use of the word "like," which I heard then for the first time, offended my New England ears, but I recognized in him a true American boy. He knew that poets, as persons of no consequence, must expect a sad end, but any self-respecting millionaire was duty bound to make an exhibition of his wealth!

Seeing how interested I was in the "Mormon question," Frank Holman took me downtown one evening to meet a Mr. Baskin, a lawyer with a judicial mind who had spent the best years of his life fighting

Brigham Young's dictatorial government and the institution of polygamy. He believed that no Oriental despot ever ruled a territory with a crueler hand. He spoke of the group of men known as "Avenging Angels" or Danites, who put out of the way anyone who interfered with Young's program. One of these, Bill Hickman, "confessed to me that he personally knew of thirteen persons having been murdered, some of them by him, and others by various Danites; that at one time he murdered a man by the name of Buck at the personal request of Brigham Young." The quotation is from Baskin's *Reminiscences of Early Utah,* a book he was forced to print at his own expense since no publisher would touch it.

Baskin had come to Utah in 1884, entered at once into a war against polygamy, and ultimately became chief justice of the state's Supreme Court. He was small in stature, had penetrating blue eyes, was an excellent scrapper and an alert, interesting man to talk with even in his old age. He confirmed my opinion that it is the fighters who live long if they don't get ambushed early in life. On one occasion he said to me, "I am not a prophet or the son of a prophet, but I don't believe you are going to last very long here."

My first year at Utah was a busy one and the bracing air of Salt Lake City, nearly a mile above sea level, was an incentive to work. I found many of the students good company. The sorority girls invited me to tea, although they were not permitted to drink either tea or coffee. They served cocoa or chocolate invariably, and I wondered why many of them did not come down with jaundice. A few undergraduates with linguistic curiosity were fascinated with my Maine accent—especially the words that put in an "r" where it should not be and leave it out where it should be. They took me downtown to dinner and begged me to repeat over and over such words as "EmmarEames," and "Indiarink," and such sentences as "They've got betta butta in that otha stowa ova theah." I felt exactly like little Tommy Tuckah singing for his suppah.

In the spring a number of us took a trip up Timpanogus, the highest mountain in the Wasatch range. We had been told that old miners prospecting for copper or gold were a common sight in the hills. Sure enough, halfway up the mountain we came across two white-haired men excitedly picking away at the wall of a small cave they had dug in the hillside. "Keep away! Keep away!" they shouted at us, wild-eyed. "We're mighty close to a strike! Just a little more . . ." and they dug on, laughing and shouting, "Just a little further in!" We felt sure they were crazy, deranged by a lifetime of frustration and disappointment.

The last thousand feet of our climb were extremely dangerous. We had to pass over a glacier, full of unexpected crevasses. We roped ourselves together and crept cautiously along. Even so, George Hedger fell into a crevass, but roped as we were, we were able to pull him out. Reaching the summit, we sat down and enjoyed the wide view, so endlessly lovely it was worth all the hard climbing and the danger.

I went home to Maine for the summer, planning to return to Utah in September. Then out of the blue came a letter from Professor Reynolds, which gave me a shock. He wrote in longhand advising me not to come back. He said that I was out of favor with the Mormon leaders who watched over the well-being of the state, that I had a brashness which offended some of them. He added that I was accused of having had illicit relations with a girl who lived in the University apartments, and that if I did come back I would have to face charges of immorality.

The letter aroused my anger. I sent it to Frank Holman and asked him to read it to the inner circle of our friends, one of whom was engaged to the girl named as my partner in sin. The charge was completely false. My Irish blood was aroused and I was ready for a fight.

Arriving at Salt Lake, I went first to see Holman. He questioned me sharply and became convinced of my innocence. I then went to President Kingsbury's office. He said he wanted me to go with him to face my accuser. Together we walked to the University apartments (about a quarter of a mile away) and met the "lady" in charge of the rooms. Instead of conducting myself as a gentleman should, I looked the woman in the face and told her she was a liar. I told her that this girl was clean and straight and that she had no right to call her a *tramp*. I further told her that the girl was one of the finest young ladies I had ever known, and it was a sin to tear down and ruin her reputation. My anger was almost uncontrollable. I felt I was fighting for this girl's life, and I wanted the landlady to realize what she was doing. She mumbled something about hearing loud laughter coming out of the girl's room on Sunday mornings and then dropped into silence. Not another word would she speak to either of us. The President and I walked back to the main university building. As we went up the steps he said, "You need not come to my office. You may go on with your work."

I went back to Holman's office and told him what had happened. Frank said, "You did just right." The girl in the meantime had heard all about the story from her fiancé and was so nervously upset that she became ill and spent several days in the hospital. The couple were married and showed up years later, with two attractive children, at my camp on the Maine coast.

That year (1914) Reed Smoot, Senator for Utah and one of the twelve apostles of the Mormon Church, came up for re-election. I decided to do what I could to defeat him. Still full of Wilson enthusiasm, I thought a high protective tariff was a form of selfishness designed to enrich a few. To me, Smoot and a high protective tariff were synonymous. His special interest was beet sugar, an important crop in Utah, and he wanted to prevent cane sugar from coming in duty-free from Cuba and other Latin American countries.

Running against him was a man by the name of A. J. Moyle, nominated on a fusion ticket formed by the Democrats and what was left of the expiring Bull Moose party. I made speeches in several Utah towns in favor of Moyle and against Smoot. President Kingsbury called me into his office and warned me that it was the wrong thing to do. He said that the University was dependent for its money on the legislators, and it was wise for people in the University to keep out of politics. I replied that I had as much right as a bootblack to express my opinion on public questions. He answered, "I'm only giving you a warning and hope you will desist." I did not desist, and on the following March 17 I was told that, come June, I would no longer be needed at the University. I was not surprised. I had been warned and had only my dogged independence to blame.

That evening I heard Phil Bing had received a similar dismissal because of his famous pun about the Angel Moroni, a blasphemy the Church could not forgive. I went over to see Bing and said, "You and I have been buried in the same graveyard!"

"Bill," he cried, "you haven't heard the half of it! Not only you and I (we're small potatoes), but two of the best men here, and they're associate professors, have been given the sack, Knowlton and Wise!"

"Knowlton and Wise! Are you sure? How could that be? Why?"

"Yes, *why*. That's what people are asking."

The next day the whole University and the city of Salt Lake were in an uproar. News spread rapidly that not only two instructors and two highly respected associate professors had been purged, but also Professor Marshall, head of the English Department for twenty years, had been demoted although not dismissed. The story leaped into the headlines. Under pressure, President Kingsbury gave his reasons for dismissing the men of professorial rank. Knowlton was accused of working against the administration and speaking disrespectfully of the chairman of the Board of Regents. Wise was dismissed because, it was alleged, he had spoken in a deprecatory way of the University before his classes. Marshall was accused of inefficiency as a teacher though praised as an administrator.

The true story of Knowlton and the chairman of the Board is as follows. After the Christmas holidays there was a reception in which the faculty lined up and shook hands with the Regents. When Knowlton got to the head of the line the chairman reached out his hand, saying, "And what is your department, Professor Knowlton?" "Physics," was the reply. "Ah yes, doctor. How *is* the Medical School getting on these days?"

Knowlton said to a few intimates that evening, "What do you think of a chairman of the Board who doesn't know the difference between physic and physics?" His remark leaked out and deeply embarrassed the chairman. President Kingsbury, his close friend, called Knowlton to his office and told him his services would not be needed after June.

It was true that Wise had spoken highly of some Eastern institutions and had pointed out some weaknesses in the University, but solely for the purpose of rousing his students to make Utah the equal of any school in the country.

As for Marshall, the excuses for his demotion were transparently just that—excuses. He was to be replaced as department head by one O. J. P. Witsoe, an English teacher from a Latter-Day Saints high school in Logan and author of a volume of Mormon apologetics titled *The Restoration of the Gospel*. As chairman, he would be able to pick instructors who were rooted in the Mormon faith rather than irreverent questioners like Bing and Snow.

The students were greatly upset by these events, particularly what had happened to the popular Marshall. They sprang to his defense in a long editorial in the *Chronicle*, the campus newspaper. And they got up a petition to the Regents, signed with 750 names, which stated their disapproval of the President's actions and asked the Board to "investigate the reasons and motives for the removal of these men and make public the results of the investigation."

The faculty was still more deeply disturbed. Twenty-two members signed a resolution calling on the Regents to assure a hearing for each man affected, the results of the hearings to be published—a resolution which the Regents promptly rejected. Then there was a wave of resignations—nineteen within a month—in protest against the purge. Dean Holman, with his Rhodes scholar's admiration for English university freedoms, was the leader of this group. Utah was his alma mater, and he feared it would never become a great university while under the dictatorial domination of the Mormon Church.

At the college cafeteria there was only one subject of conversation. In restaurants downtown it was the same. The whole city was in turmoil, and the excitement reached every corner of the state and spilled over into other states too.

One result was a mass meeting on March 25 at the Salt Lake Theatre, held under the auspices of several women's clubs and attended by more than a thousand people. It was presided over by George H. Dern, then a state senator, later governor, and later still Secretary of War in F.D.R.'s first Cabinet. Several weeks earlier he had introduced a Senate resolution calling for a committee to investigate conditions at the University, and he accused President Kingsbury of lobbying for its defeat. Then Professor Harold Stephens, who later became a judge of the United States Court of Appeals in Washington, made one of the finest speeches I have ever heard in defense of academic freedom—freedom in teaching, freedom in personal and professional life, freedom from church domination. These freedoms were denied us. We noted that the four who were kicked out and the nineteen who resigned were all non-Mormons. The twenty-three who were brought in to replace them were all Mormons.

Ten days later there was a stormy meeting of alumni. After much lengthy, acrimonious debate, they rather narrowly adopted a resolution calling for an investigation of the dismissals, demotions, and resignations. They also named a committee of twenty-five alumni—Holman among them—to meet with the Board of Regents.

At this meeting a resolution was passed reminding Governor Spry that the terms of seven Regents expired in June, and requesting that he discuss their replacements with the committee. To this request the Governor agreed.

In spite of this promise, within three days Spry reappointed the same seven Regents whose terms were running out. Ten years later—when both of them were long gone from Utah—he admitted to Holman that he had done this at the express "wish and desire" (meaning command) of Joseph F. Smith, then president of the Latter-Day Saints—

an order that Spry, as a good Mormon, could neither ignore nor disobey. But at the time it occurred, Spry's turnabout was both amazing and disturbing.

So much publicity was given to our struggle across the country that the American Association of University Professors (AAUP), organized to protect the rights and advance the interests of college teachers, sent a committee to investigate and make a report. It consisted of some of the finest scholars and administrators in America: such men as Edwin R. A. Seligman, John Dewey, Dean Roscoe Pound of the Harvard Law School, Arthur O. Lovejoy of Johns Hopkins, Frank A. Fetter and Howard C. Warren of Princeton, and James P. Lichtenberger of Pennsylvania. Lovejoy arrived in April and set to work. Questionnaires were sent out to faculty and alumni; hundreds of interviews were carried out; meetings were held, depositions taken.

The whole thing boiled down to a question of the right of the President and the Board of Regents to dismiss anyone in disagreement with them. The Regents insisted that for the sake of unity and the smooth running of the University, when "serious friction arises between university officials and teachers the governing body . . . should not consider the question 'who is right and who is wrong in the disagreement.' The functionary of superior value should be retained, the others removed." The Committee found this principle to be wholly inadmissible.

In the course of the investigation, the 1914 commencement speech of my former student Milton H. Sevy was examined. Like others, he had caught the idealism of Woodrow Wilson's leadership and was anxious to do something to improve the country. His address enumerated some of the shortcomings of the University and proposed an overhauling of its values, a cleaning out of the Augean stables. He called for larger appropriations for the University and rebuked the legislators for spending more on the housing of cattle at the state fair than on girls' dormitories. I was suspected of having written the speech. A Professor Lyman, one of Kingsbury's men, put me through a third degree. Had I had any part in writing the speech? I said I had not; I had only gone over it with Sevy for the sole purpose of aiding him in rhetoric and delivery. (Lovejoy had me make a deposition stating that I did not write the speech, for inclusion in the report of the AAUP Committee.) Dean Byron Cummings told me that he too had been pressed to acknowledge that Sevy had read the speech to him before delivering it, which in fact was the case.

We wondered why this speech was being given so much attention.

It all came out in the AAUP report. The Governor, present at the 1914 commencement, had taken umbrage at the speech. He wanted no criticism of state institutions and no requests for larger appropriations. He demanded the University seek out and punish by dismissal the teachers who had allowed the address to be delivered. He repeated his demands in the winter, when the appropriation bills were before the legislators. The axe did not fall on the head of the venerable dean, but it did fall sharply on mine.

Nonetheless Byron Cummings was one of the first to resign. He could not retain his self-respect if he kept on at the University, though he had much to lose in this upheaval. As a childless professor of classics, he and his wife had helped many a poor student through a financial crisis; and he had stirred several of his best students, like Frank Holman, to seek Rhodes scholarships and to aim for high honors.

More than that, Cummings was an archeologist of distinction. Each summer he took a carefully selected group of students into southern Utah to dig for Indian artifacts. They collected a considerable amount of material—mummies, vases, and bowls that were works of art—enough to establish a small museum on one floor of the main University building. All this he would have to leave behind him.

It is pleasant to report that Cummings was able to continue this work at the University of Arizona, which immediately offered him a professorship. There the Federal government erected a splendid museum for his new collection. But when he wished to bring his Utah materials there, the Regents said a firm No. And later, when George Dern —by that time a Cabinet member—repeated the request, the Regents said No again.

During this time there was one incident in my life about which I still wonder. Along in April I received a letter from a girl who signed herself Mary Gray. She said she had noticed me on the campus and in downtown restaurants, had read my poems in *The Young Woman's Journal*, and would like to get acquainted with me. She too wrote poems and wanted to discuss her work with me. I knew of no Mary Gray, and let the letter lie unanswered. Two days later a second note appeared. Mary Gray hoped her first letter had not offended me; she really admired me and my poetry very much; and would I meet her at a certain restaurant downtown?

This puzzled me. She had touched me on a weak spot, my poetry, but the flattery was a little overdone. I took the letters to Frank Holman.

As I came into his room, he laid aside a lawbook he had been reading and said, half to himself and half to me, "It's hard to believe, but there it is, in the report of the Grand Jury of the Third Judicial District of the Territory of Utah of December, 1885. It must be true."

"What is it?" I asked.

"This story of the conspiracy of a group of Mormons against the Federal officials of the Territory, who were trying to stamp out polygamy." And he went on to explain the plot: how de luxe houses of ill fame were set up, so arranged that hidden spies (who included every Salt Lake City policeman except one) could see all that went on; how women were hired to lure Federal officials into these dens, with the purpose of entrapping them *in flagrante delictu* and thus discrediting them completely. One woman had been offered $1000 if she could snare the governor of the Territory. But there were leaks; the matter came to the attention of the Grand Jury, which examined witnesses and issued a number of indictments.

"What a story!" said Frank. "Can you believe it?"

We then turned to my errand. Frank read the Mary Gray letters and immediately felt that they were meant to entrap me—another Mormon conspiracy. I sensed that the girl was intelligent; she had ideas about life; she wrote with excellent style. I really wanted to see her and talk with her. But Holman said No. "Wait and see if there are any more letters." They kept coming, almost one every day, each more loving than the one before. I was sorely tempted; but Frank became wholly convinced that they were a trick to catch me and blacken my reputation. So I answered none, though I read them and loved them all.

I have thought about Mary Gray for years. Every summer at my camp on the Maine coast I choose a young gull and give her the name of Mary Gray. I entice her to my ledges with all the stale bread I can get my wife to save for her. Although they do not know the story, the grandchildren join in and we all feed Mary Gray. I still think Frank was overly suspicious, and I still regret that I never looked the original Mary Gray in the eye.

At the conclusion of the AAUP investigation, a report was issued and the charges against the dismissed men were not proven. But the Regents refused to reconsider their cases. However, some good came out of this experience. The Regents agreed to the setting up of an administrative council, with members from both administration and faculty, which in the future would handle all appointments, renewals, or changes in rank of the teaching force. That at least was the beginning of the movement to make Utah a free university. Moreover, all the men who were dismissed or resigned found positions in other institutions for the following September—with one exception, myself.

My teaching went on until June. On my birthday, April 6, my students together with a number of others who were not in my classes gave me a banquet. My activities had extended beyond my courses. I had written criticisms of student plays; I had contributed to their literary magazine; and to my everlasting shame be it said, I had reviewed a student performance of *Pagliacci* even though I knew nothing at all about the technical aspects of music and—worse yet—was at that time dating Edna Evans, who sang the role of Nedda in that production. All I could do was tell the story of the opera, say something about the composer and the performers, and keep still in seven languages about the music. At the banquet, the boys who knew music gave me a hard time. They also discussed with much irony my successor, who had announced that he was going to introduce no-decision debates the next year. Debating students like to win or lose, and they took a dim view of this plan.

My own debating work ended with a flourish. In mid-May my three star speakers, Bateman, Anderson, and Ferguson, traveled to Boulder and won a very exciting debate. The *Utah Chronicle* for May 14 featured a front-page photo of the victors and a long write-up of their achievement. "For the first time since 1905 the Colorado school had been defeated. Credit for the victory is due in large part to Coach C. W. Snow who concluded his debating work at Utah with this winning contest." Several of my colleagues told me I was crazy to spend so much time with these students after my summary dismissal. "Why bother with the brats? Sit on your hands the rest of the time!" But this debating group was one of the bright spots in my life in Utah and, dismissed or not, I gave them the best I had.

Indeed, I had nothing but admiration for the students, their independence, their willingness to speak out. There had been vigorous editorials in the *Chronicle*, upholding the English Department as Reynolds and the rest of us had tried to shape it, and openly attacking the new direction to be expected from the incoming Mr. Witsoe. Now the leaders of the graduating class of 1915 proposed that, in this commencement week, the usual Class Day rites and ceremonies be abolished to demonstrate their disapproval of the administration. This was carried out by the entire class. Even after fifty years I have kept in touch with some of its members.

In that year's issue of the *Utonian*, the yearbook of the University, the student editors filled a page with brief humorous assessments of the faculty. One entry reads as follows:

> CHARLES WILBERT SNOW . . . Inciter of Young Utah. Agitated Interest in Debate, 1913–1914; Temporarily Dismissed, September, 1914; Summarily Dismissed, March, 1915.

In June my work was done. I was getting ready to leave for Maine when a student of mine named Ambrose McGarry told me he was going to southern Utah with a group of archeologists from the Smithsonian Institution to hunt for Indian graves and artifacts. I had long wanted to see that part of the state (near the present Zion National Park) and to go over the trail of the emigrants who were massacred at Mountain Meadows in 1857. This bloody massacre is the most dramatic and horrible event in Utah history. Anyone who lives in the state even for a short time is intrigued by it. I wanted to talk to the old men who knew at first hand the details of the episode, and form my own conclusions.

Of course I should have gone home and spent the summer lining up a job for the fall. But I recalled John Burroughs' lines "Nor time nor space, nor deep, nor high / Can keep my own away from me." I decided not to worry about a job, and when a letter came from Neil Judd, leader of the Smithsonian expedition, accepting me as a paying guest, I said to myself, *"This is my own."* I was told to provide myself with a horse and money enough to pay my share of the grub. I arranged to join the expedition at Beaver, McGarry's home town.

My train left Salt Lake City at five in the afternoon of June 3. Fortified with a pair of high hobnailed boots, a hunter's knife, a raincoat (little did I understand the climate!), thick army shirts, heavy woolen stockings, towels, candles, tobacco, and soap, I felt well equipped for the summer's work. A man on the observation platform asked me if I were going to work for a movie outfit! The train rolled into Milford, two hundred miles to the south, late that evening. It was raining—for the first, last, and only time that summer.

Next morning I took a rickety bus for Beaver, thirty miles east. There I found Ambrose, who took me home to meet his mother. She told me her husband had served in two wars; the Civil War, in which he was an officer, and the war against polygamy in southern Utah. She had many stories of the "co-habs," as the people of that region called them, who took their plural wives and hid from the law in the fastnesses of this wild and little-explored country. It was odd, she said, that her son had turned Mormon after the vigorous fight against Mormonism his father had made. Ambrose defended himself in a most practical fashion. The Mormons had given up polygamy, he argued, and were fully as respectable as any other Protestant church. His girl was a Mormon, and he would stand a better chance of winning her if he joined her church. Beyond this, no young man who did not affiliate with the Saints could expect to get very far, socially or politically, in the state —and he could not bring himself to live anywhere else for long. So it behooved him to "belong."

The world of archeology was new to me, and I found it absorbing. We first dug up an Indian who had been buried near the McGarry home hundreds of years earlier. The skeleton proved to be that of a large man. Beside him was buried a child, apparently chosen to accompany him to the Happy Hunting Ground. Every item of the burial was meticulously recorded by our scribe: the position of the body with head toward the east; the exact position of the child alongside the man's hips and shoulders; the fragments of pottery buried with him—all was measured and carefully set down in Judd's notebook.

At our next stop near Parowan we discovered a great deal of pottery. Most of it was broken, but Judd told us that many of the pieces could be put together so well that a layman would need a magnifying glass to see the seams. Farther south we unearthed the adobe walls of a dwelling which contained a number of rooms—probably the home of a large patriarchal family. When I saw the outlines of this huge dwelling, I wondered why this lodging place was so superior to the tepees the Utes, Paiutes, and Apaches lived in today. When and why did the degeneration set in? Pondering over the buried homes of vanished tribes, I wrote the following sonnet in my journal:

CLIFF-DWELLER REGION OF SOUTHERN UTAH

These potsherds, skeletons, and arrow heads,
Kernels of Indian corn, beads, vases, walls
Of firm adobe whose rich browns and reds
Bespeak a love of Beauty's coronals;
These relics of a folk who roamed the plains,
And scaled the peaks a thousand years ago,
Who lived and died and left these few remains,
Remind us with what speed tribes come and go.

The glory of all races fades away
From Babylon to Utah's hills and vales,

The giant races hold their giant sway,
Then sleep till excavators tell their tales;
The tribe whose art best limns its crowning hour
Best holds at bay Time's devastating power.

Later, at a cliff-dweller location, I helped discover a kiva, a round hole in which the medicine man or shaman stood when he preached to the people under the overhanging cliff. In the bottom of this hole we discovered a pouch holding a kernel of corn. Judd said the kernel was a symbol of immortality; if we should plant it even now after a thousand years, it would probably spring up and bear Indian corn.

Roaming these hills on horseback was itself a rewarding experience —one which the Indians knew and enjoyed as much as we did. At times the country was too hot, exhausting to move through. One day when the thermometer was over 100 degrees Fahrenheit we just sat all day under a sycamore tree and waited for the sun to go down. The water we had to drink tasted like Epsom salts. Our horses, I noticed, could take that water better than we could.

One day as we were eating supper on the desert a cowboy came up on horseback and spent the evening with us. He had been drinking, was in a cantankerous mood, and complained that people were beginning to fence off areas of this land with barbed wire. I recorded his visit in this verse:

DESERT COWBOY

One night as we camped on the desert
There came through the blue-lemon glow
Of twilight a weather-worn cowboy
On a weather-worn nag—friend or foe
Our tenderfoot company knew not,
We knew we were thrilled as we saw
A *Remington* freed from its canvas
At a moment of stillness and awe.
He hobbled his pony, walked over
And sat by our fire; one eye
He had lost in a barroom, he told us,
In a fight with "a cheap barroom fly."
We poured him the dregs of our coffee,
Though his breath marked him fully sustained
By a headier liquid. He sobered,
And sobering, cursed and complained
Of barb-wire fences erected
On trails over which he had reined
For forty-one years. The barbed wires

Put barbs in his voice as he reached
In his pocket and pulled out his pliers:
"My answer," he snarled, almost screeched,
"To all Eastern bums and sheepherders
Who would fence off this cowpunchers' land,
Is *this*, and, boy, do I use it."
We felt we had seen the last stand
Of the Old West in that trembling right hand.

The most vivid of all experiences that summer was watching a mother eagle teaching her young ones how to fly. She would drop them one by one from the top of a high cliff, then swoop down and catch them on her back before they crashed. She worked on them one at a time as a good teacher should.

Interesting as I discovered the world of archeology to be, it became increasingly clear to me that I was on the trail not of Indian burial mounds, but of the truth of the Mountain Meadows Massacre, one of the most hideous events in the annals of America. From the first Indian burial we uncovered to the end of the journey, in all the towns I listened to the old folks who were willing to talk and give me glimpses of that great catastrophe, even though friends in Salt Lake City had warned me that it might not be safe to show too much curiosity. Some of those old co-habs were thoroughly suspicious of strangers—and possibly dangerous.

My trail started at Beaver, in whose courthouse (later burned with all its records) had taken place the two trials of John D. Lee for his leadership in the affair. Then as our expedition jogged along through Paragonah, Parowan, and Enoch to Cedar, I gathered information from many sources. People talked freely, Mormon and Gentile alike, save only John Lee Jones. This venerable Mormon, who looked like a biblical patriarch, welcomed us to Parowan, and spoke of "the truth of the Mormon gospel" and of the Temple work he had had performed on behalf of a hundred relatives who had died in ignorance of the true faith (it had cost him a dollar each). He said with pride that he had served time in the pen for the gospel's sake—that is, as a co-hab, "if that is the name you want to give to an institution sanctioned by the Scriptures." But of the Massacre he told me point-blank, and rather angrily, not to ask him any questions. I have since wondered what part, if any, he took in that affair.

One way or another, then, I patched together the story. In the summer of 1857, an emigrant wagon train was making its slow way through this territory to California. As such trains went, it was a large and rather prosperous one—18 wagons; 120 men, women, and children; 820 head of cattle; household goods in quantity; besides money estimated at $80,000 to $90,000. These people were largely from Arkansas, with others from Missouri and Illinois—all states in which the early followers of Joseph Smith had been harshly used.

By local accounts, these emigrants were a rough lot. They were said to have boasted of killing "old Joe Smith" in Illinois and Parley Pratt in Arkansas. There were other stories too. They had poisoned an ox; Indians ate of the carcass, and several of them died. They had poisoned a spring, from which more Indians drank and died. Worst of all, some of their draft oxen were named for the twelve apostles of the Mormon Church; so it was "Get up there, Brigham, you old son-of-a-bitch!" or "Haw there, Heber, you old bastard!'" This was sacrilege indeed.

It must be remembered that that was an especially tense time in Mormon affairs. Utah, when they settled it, was Mexican territory; now it was part of the United States. The Mormon settlements had sought admittance to the Union as the "State of Deseret," with Brigham Young as governor; the Federal government had instead organized the area as the Territory of Utah, with a governor appointed in Washington. A dangerous power struggle was shaping up between the Saints on the one hand and Federal authorities on the other. These were the days when the Danites flourished; Federal troops were being sent in, and there was talk of reviving the Nauvoo Legion to oppose them. "Blood atonement" was openly advocated by Mormon leaders. Moreover, a number of lukewarm Saints had abandoned the Church to go with emigrant trains to the goldfields. This background of exacerbation undoubtedly had a large role in what happened next.

What happened next was that one of Young's leading henchmen came down from Salt Lake and instructed the people to do no trading with these emigrants, who had now reached the vicinity of Cedar. This was a devastating blow, both to the farmers who wanted to sell their crops and to the emigrants who desperately needed to buy food for themselves and their livestock. It was also a clear signal to the faithful that this train was to be offered no help or protection.

Bishop Haight was head of the Church in southern Utah, and John D. Lee was his right-hand man. Lee was an old-line Mormon, sometime bodyguard to Joseph Smith (whom he regarded to his dying day as divine), adopted son of Brigham Young, husband of twelve wives, and by his own confession "deeply steeped in fanaticism." He had lived among the Indians, could speak their language fluently, and had their trust. Acting (he claimed) under Haight's direction, he became the ringleader in a desperate plan, which involved both Indians and Saints.

One Sunday evening the emigrants, seeking water and pasturage, made their camp at Mountain Meadows. On Monday morning the Indians, excited over the alleged poisoning of the ox and the spring and egged on by Lee, began to fire on them. Some fifteen were killed. The remainder drew their wagons into a circle, filled the spaces underneath and between with earth, and thus constructed a fort. They successfully repulsed the Indians for four days.

On the fifth day Lee and some others approached the corral bearing a white flag. The emigrants accepted this signal of truce and let Lee and his party come in. Their case was hopeless; their water casks were empty, food was short, they had wounded to care for. Lee persuaded them that, if they would lay down their arms and abandon their property, he and his men would lead them to safety at Cedar; otherwise the Indians were sure to wipe them out. Trusting his honor and sincerity, they agreed to these terms. The wounded and small children were put into wagons and sent on a little ahead. Then marched the women and older children. Last came the men of the train, each one accompanied by an armed Mormon "to protect the emigrant." About a mile down the road a signal was given. Each Mormon turned and with knife or gun slaughtered the man in his care. At the same time Indians sprang out of ambush and murdered the wounded, the women, the older children. Only seventeen young boys and girls were spared. All of these—some too young to know even their names—were sheltered in Mormon homes round about. Eventually they were gathered up by Federal officials and returned to relatives or friends back home. The Mormons later tried to collect $7000 from the government for taking care of them! As for the emigrants' property and money, it gravitated to Bishop Haight, Lee, and other leading dignitaries of the Mormon Church in that area.

Such was the Mountain Meadows Massacre; but there was a sequel. Brigham Young well knew what would be the effect of such an event on the outside world, and I was told that, when he learned of the plan, he dispatched a courier with orders to stop it. The man in his haste rode three horses to death, but he arrived too late; when he drew up at the Cedar post office, the deed had already been done. Months and years dragged by; there were self-serving reports by Lee to Young and by Young to Washington; there was widespread use of the incident by anti-Mormons on the lecture platform and in books; there were government investigations. Young must have been really worried, for it is said that he had no children by any of his wives during the year following the massacre. The uproar continued for years, and finally Young broke with Lee—ordered him excommunicated in 1871; brought him to an abortive trial in 1875; had him tried again in 1878. This time Lee was found guilty and was executed—at Mountain Meadows—by a firing squad.

There is, it seems to me, something very American indeed about this crime—or more precisely, about the mixture of religious and economic motives that lay behind it. This is perhaps the one thing that has characterized us as a nation more than any other. Thus we read in Challon's *Voyage* (1606) that the purpose of the first colonists was "both to seek to convert the savages, and also to seek out what benefits of commodities might be had in these parts." That double purpose has motivated us ever since.

Returning from southern Utah in September, I had only two days in Salt Lake City in which to say good-bye to the Holmans and other friends, pack my books and belongings, and take a train for home. No job, no prospects, no Ph.D., and no desire to get one—I was not even in the mood for further teaching.

As I sat on the train ruminating over my two years in Utah, I remembered my last conversation with my mother just before she died. I had been telling her a great deal about Bowdoin. She said, "When I was carrying you, Wilbert, I felt calm and at peace. I hope you will go on with your education and become a college teacher. In a college you can spend your life calmly and peacefully."

"No," I said, "I want hard things to do. I want to be out in the storm."

Her ambition for my vocation had been realized, but mine too had come to pass, with Utah its Walpurgis night! Now I was facing the winter without work. I knew the Spruce Head neighbors would say, "There's Wilbert back again, living on his father. What's the matter with him?"

At my father's house, however, it was "Welcome home" and no

questions asked. My stepmother seemed truly pleased to have another man to praise her excellent cooking.

I had not been home many hours before I realized what I had been missing. It was the sea. The rote on Brown's Island ledges, which I had loved from boyhood, now sounded more mysterious and seductive than ever. That night, before blowing out my lamp, I sat down and wrote a sonnet which I entitled "Groundswell":

> Often at midnight I have left my bed,
> Opened the kitchen door, not knowing why,
> Stepped out into the yard whose silence shed
> No balm on my unrest; turned to the sky,
> Star-poised, in quiet league with elm and oak,
> Whose overshadowing calm confounded me;
> Slowly the reason for my coming broke—
> I heard far off the groundswell of the sea.
>
> Dead the whole belt of calms; my spirit craved
> In those volcanic crises vastly more;
> The rote on distant shoals, resounding, saved,
> When harbors muffled by an inland shore
> Were mockeries; deep registered to deep,
> Filling a need beyond all need of sleep.

CHAPTER 12

Home—and on to Indiana

In September I left the beautiful intermountain country and went back to Maine and home. I had no job, so I spent the time pondering over the vicissitudes of life. My dip into Tao and other Oriental thinkers helped. The individuality of the people of Spruce Head village struck me with a new force. I suddenly rediscovered the region I was brought up in. The men here had learned something about passivity without the help of Oriental philosophers. One night, thinking it over, I said to myself, "This, too, is life." These four words, commonplace as they are, burned themselves into my mind, and I decided to record what this place and these people meant to me. "Men and women are born, marry, and die here," I thought, "and no record remains." I had recently read George Crabbe's *The Village* and it had made a deep impression. He saw only the dark side of village life which he recorded in unforgettable verse. As E. A. Robinson says of him:

> Whether or not we read him, we can feel
> From time to time the vigor of his name
> Against us like a finger for the shame
> And emptiness of what our souls reveal
> In books that are as altars where we kneel
> To consecrate the flicker, not the flame.

I wanted to portray more than the flicker. I knew the sorrows and failings of these people, knew also their deep emotions of joy born of courageous triumph over a harsh environment. Could I express all this in poetry?

One night I started to write about a paving quarry. As a child I had watched men plug-drilling and trimming paving blocks which were carried off in sailing schooners to pave the streets of American cities; I had even had a short spell of quarrying myself. Now all these quarries or "motions," as we called them, were abandoned. Asphalt had taken

the place of granite. I was so stirred emotionally by the subject that I
didn't notice whether the poem was turning out to be free, rhymed, or
blank verse. The next morning I saw that most of it was blank verse, a
result, I think, of my teaching English poetry. So I rearranged the ragged lines to fit the iambic pentameter pattern. I could not be as grim
as George Crabbe. There is nostalgia in the poem, but no tears, no
weakness. It became the lead poem in my first book.

THE PAVING QUARRY

Our pathway led through birches shoulder-high
'Twas autumn, and the little yellow leaves,
So slender were their stems, seemed poised in air,
And gaily did they flutter in the wind.
The huckleberry leaves shone brilliant red,
And bayberry scattered incense on our way,
As now we walked through plots of velvet moss,
And now on granite ledges gray and hard.
Abruptly came our journey to a stop,
And there in ragged grayness lay the quarry.

"This pavin' motion," my companion said,
"Was goin' to make me rich, and made me poor.
'Twas in the *'eighties* I began work here,
When all great cities paved their streets with blocks.
A nickel apiece they were, and I could reel
Two hundred blocks or more each blessed day.
The reelin' wasn't much like the reelin' now:
'Most anything would do. Along this hump
Were fifty motions clickin' every day.
Beside that barrel there filled up with chips
I reeled, the happiest hours of my life,
I wouldn't say how many thousand blocks,
While Fred, my butty, plug-drilled and broke stone.
I somehow liked the music of the sound,
The click-clack-clickin' of a hundred drills
From all these motions in among the trees.
How different now, when all you ever hear
Is chickadees, or crickets, or the frogs!
I sometimes think they liked the noises, too,
Of hammers clickin', and the rattlin' wheels
Of wagons, or the creakin' of the hames
In horses' collars on these rocky roads.
For we were prosp'rous then; at half'past four
'Most any night but Friday you could smell

Beefsteak a-fryin' anywhere in town,
And hear the snap and sizzle in the spider.
(We can't afford to eat beefsteak today.)
'Twas fun at night to see the youngsters bolt
To met their daddies, grab the dinner pail,
And find a cookie or a piece of cake
Left there like toll-bait to be sure they came.
'Twas fun just after supper to drop 'round
To Em'ry's store, and hear the boys run on.
They'd smoke, and fight John L.'s big mills again,
With Paddy Ryan, Mitchell, Jack Kilrain—
They never loved another like John L.
And sometimes, when the bottle went around,
The boys would sing. I wish you could'a'heard
Mike Flemin' sing 'The Wind That Blew Across
The Wild Moor'; somethin' in his Irish voice
Would make you think o' lonely winds at night,
And cryin' children strayin' on the moor.
And then on Saturdays we'd have a dance,
And start it with a breakdown in the store.
I always liked the breakdown best; the boys
Were keyed just right, the jew's-harp twanged and twanged,
The harmonica began with 'Home Sweet Home,'
And Cowin', wounded at Bull Run, would clog,
And dance the 'buck and wing' in perfect time.
Then all would leave to join the 'march and circle'
Except the old men who would set and smoke.
Ah, them were jolly days; I never thought
They'd leave us as they did; the price went down,
And cities paved with asphalt room o' blocks;
The young folks moved away, but we were old,
Too old to think of other towns as home—
And there we were without a place to farm,
Who might 'a'had ten acres turned to field.
Perhaps it's just as well. A hundred hens,
A little garden truck, a chance to fish,
And time to talk of pranks we did as boys—
One way of life's as good's another I guess,
If we just take it right—that's all that counts."

He gazed along the west; the golden sun
Was streaming through a clump of tall spruce trees.
The dead, low limbs, transfigured in the light,
Had brought the sunset near; the background stood
In lemon-colored glory; back we turned
Without a word, and down a birch-fringed path
We found the road that led our footsteps home.

Writing that poem was a major event in my life, and I decided I would record the whole village. I wrote the story of a Swedish lobster catcher and herring-weir fisherman, named "Olaf," one called "Mail Time," and a long one on the life of a lobster catcher. One half of my nature was full of Irish romantic imagination, while the American religion of pioneer optimism had a three-hundred-year-old root in the other half. I varied these narratives and character sketches with sonnets and lyrics which demanded to be written every now and then.

In October I took a trip to New York and made a visit to Carl and Irita Van Doren. Carl was then the literary editor of the *Nation*, and his first question was, "What have you been writing lately?" I showed a lyric and a sonnet. He said, "Is that all?" "No, I have been writing up the village of Spruce Head, but I doubt whether it would have any publication value or would interest editors at all." He said, "Let's see some of it." I brought out "Olaf" and "The Paving Quarry," the only two I had with me. He read them slowly, got excited, and said, "My God, Bill, these are ten times better than the lyrics and sonnets you have been writing. Let me have some of it for the *Nation*." He pubblished "Olaf" at once and "The Paving Quarry" later. Van Doren gave me courage, made me feel that I had hit my gait, and urged me to go ahead and write an entire book of these village characters, their stories, and some local genre pictures of the coast.

I had no intention of making fun of these people; hence I decided to avoid using so-called Yankee dialect. I sensed that when a writer uses dialect he is in danger of turning character to caricature. After all, these were my people. Their life was my life; I had spent three years in what during my childhood days was regarded as the lowliest of their occupations—lobster catching. So this was not to be a "Cape Cod Folks" or anything of that ilk. It was to be the plain story of a village exactly as it impressed itself in my mind and my imagination.

When I told my friends the Otises my project, Betty put in my hands a book by one Robert Frost entitled *North of Boston*. It is not easy to describe the impact that remarkable volume had on me. He had done for a farming village what I had planned to do for a coastal fishing village, and he had done it so perfectly that I felt myself awed. Poems like "The Fear," "After Apple Picking, " "Home Burial," seemed to me to be nothing short of masterpieces. *North of Boston* struck me as a permanent contribution to American poetry. Still the coast and the islands that were mine bred people somewhat different from the introvert hill folk Frost knew, and I cherished the comment of Longfellow in his Journal in September, 1846:

> Went to town and over the ferry to East Boston. Delighted to behold the lovely sea again. Ah, why did we not pass the summer on its shores, instead of putting ourselves into the close custody of the imprisoning mountains? I prefer the seaside to the country. The idea of liberty is stronger there.

Before I had got very far in my project, I was called upon by Professor Harry Baker of Rockland. He was home on vacation from Indiana University, and was looking for someone to teach his English courses the second semester. He had received a call from the University of Illinois and wanted very much to accept it at once so that he could work under Stuart P. Sherman, head of the English Department there, a man of national reputation whom he greatly admired. If he could get a satisfactory replacement he could go to Illinois in February, otherwise he would have to remain at Indiana until June. He was confident that I could carry his five courses. There would be two theme courses in English, a course in American literature, and a survey course in English literature from Caedmon to Kipling. There would also be an extension course in Indianapolis at the end of each week.

It was already Christmas and I would have to be in Bloomington, Indiana, the first week in February, so I didn't have much time for writing my book after all. The "social expectation of the village" was beginning to weigh heavily upon me. The neighbors were asking one another why I had no job, why I was home again living on my father. So, instead of continuing work on my first book, I said yes to Baker and prepared to enter the academic lists once more.

Bloomington looked relaxed when I first saw it. There was a touch of the Old South in its school population. The girls had the unusual attractiveness of their sisters in Dixie. A few of the professors retained the pioneering Daniel Boone look. One wore a coonskin cap and refused to dress in academic regalia in faculty processions. The beech trees on the campus were endlessly beautiful. Downtown, lean horses were tied to iron rails on the courthouse square. The shops in the center of town had a shoddy look. Ditch diggers were not foreign imports but descendants of old English pioneer stock. Theodore Dreiser, who attended the University for a year or two, described the town in his *Hoosier Holiday* as a crude, grubby, untidy place, and although the natives I talked with resented the grimness of his portrayal, I felt it was realistic, true description. I took walks into the country nearby, and the rural people I saw there were toothless and sallow. They looked as if they had somehow escaped the efficient, driving, ambitious way of life that characterized their pioneer brothers in other Northern states.

I had no more than got started on my work when I received a letter from President Hyde, which read:

> Hearty congratulations to Indiana and yourself. I am delighted that you are back again where you belong, and trust the political lightning will not strike you again.

Here I was nine years out of college, and Hyde still remembered me and decided to warn me against politics. Why had he followed me all these years? He was a busy man. Did he have a guilty conscience about me? Years earlier there was a vacancy in Bowdoin, and he had a chance to settle me there but refused. My radicalism, he said, might offend some of the trustees. Yet Hyde was hardly the man to let the trustees dictate his choice of faculty. He did help me get calls to Williams and Miami University.

For the first time in my career I was not teaching argumentation or coaching the debating squad of the University, although the chairman of the English Department slated me for three courses in debating and public speaking in the forthcoming summer school. My courses in American and English literature were altogether too large—about forty in a class—but at the end of every lecture I allotted time for discussion and questions, and these ten-minute dialogues helped me to get to know the Hoosiers. The students were a relaxed group. The girls came to find husbands, and the boys came to have a good time, to think over what they wanted to do as a lifework—law, medicine, business—and to get well acquainted with other young men they would be dealing with later on.

It was an ideal place for lovers, and there was much lovemaking going on in the spring of 1916. The campus, with its magnificent beech trees, its gentle climate, and its colorful cardinal birds, was a perfect spot to make "a young man's fancy lightly turn to thoughts of love." I pondered over the difference between this spot and the all-male Bowdoin campus, where a man was lucky if he caught a glimpse of a beautiful girl once in three weeks.

The glories of Monroe County have never been sung as they deserved. It is a spot of little hills and valleys, a land of trees in which the beech predominates, where the scarlet tanager, the cardinal, and the blue jay add color. In my many walks around the countryside I would come upon couples loitering in the ravines and enjoying the lovely landscape. At the University there were a few ambitious students digging for A's in their courses, but the great majority were there for four years in which to have a good time. A gentleman's grade was still C, and those who reached no higher were fully respected. Social life was carried on largely by the fraternities and sororities, and there were dances and parties. No institution for the mating of boys and girls in their teens could improve upon the great state universities of the Middle West. Indiana University was perhaps the finest example, for here was an atmosphere of leisure which enhanced its charm. To support this idea of a mating ground was a much read article by David Starr Jordan, former president of Indiana. In it he showed that the chances of divorce for a couple married out of the great coeducational institutions were only about one-fourth of those who went to exclusively men's or women's colleges.

A senior girl confirmed Jordan's thesis when she told me how it was accomplished. She said, "We have a date during our freshman year, another when we are sophomores, a third when we are juniors, and by the time we are seniors we latch onto a fellow we know we can live with for forty years." I felt a bit shocked at her frankness, but it had a pragmatic ring that President Jordan himself would have liked. I was amused when I found a boy taking a course just because the girl he was keeping company with at the time elected it.

The center of our social life was a place called the "Book-Nook." There the students went between classes to talk over the affairs of the day while drinking coffee or Coke, and every day I went along as one of them. The literary-inclined boys flocked around me, for I was beginning to sell poetry to magazines in New York. These students were proud of Indiana's literary accomplishment. The best of them knew Edward Eggleston's *The Hoosier Schoolmaster*; more of them knew Lew Wallace's *Ben Hur*, Maurice Thompson's *Alice of Old Vincennes*, and Meredith Nicholson's *House of a Thousand Candles*. All of them knew James Whitcomb Riley and could recite his poems by heart.

The night Riley died in the summer of 1916 three of these boys came to the house where I was rooming, woke me out of a sound sleep, and told me of his death. They wanted me to write a tribute to be published the next morning in *The Indiana Daily Student*, their college paper. Under the guise of a tribute to Riley my poem was in reality a tribute to them, although I did recognize that Riley had an exquisite ear and based my approach on that.

JAMES WHITCOMB RILEY

A thousand valley-lilies, golden-belled,
Stirred by a mild west wind, would charm the ear
No truer than the lyric notes that welled
From Riley's heart, our common life to cheer;
A thousand souls who never glimpsed the peaks
Adventurous bards attained on wings of song,
Have found deep solace through the weary weeks
Among the meadows that to him belong.

He knew the music of the leaves in spring,
He knew the clear fresh bloom of childhood's hour,
He knew the poetry that love could wring
From unresponsive hearts, and through love's power
He showed a listening world how homely grace
Could make this earth a sweeter, holier place.

These few names that I have mentioned show that Indiana was proud of her literary heritage. It seemed as if there were something in the soil that bred literary talent. There was a story in vogue at the time about a famous Bostonian author who was lecturing on New England writers in a small Indiana town. Before delivering his address he said, "Ladies and gentlemen, I make it a custom to ask people in the audience who are authors to come up and sit with me on the stage." At this call people rose and rushed forward. All but one came up on the stage. The speaker looked at this forlorn character and said, "Young man, why are you not in this procession?" The young man answered, "I am now only reading the galley proof of my first book."

The students of my time had other literary heroes, including Booth Tarkington whose novel *The Gentleman from Indiana* had sharpened the pride of every literate Hoosier. There was also George Ade, whose *Fables in Slang* had a wide national vogue and whose popular plays such as *The County Chairman* took good-natured shots at the American political animal and the American way of life. Abe Martin was another of their favorites, but most of them saw only his humor and missed his devastating assaults on American dullness and stupidity.

Will Howe, a short, light-haired Hoosier, who always greeted a visitor with a smile, was the only faculty man I met who relished these Indiana authors. He was the head of the English Department.

Savage realism and naturalism such as those of Theodore Dreiser were offensive to him. He was a gentle soul who had a charming wife and two delightful daughters. Along with his genial manner there was a driving ambition in his nature that seemed to contradict the rest of him. He told me his real wish was to go to New York and help start a publishing house that would pay attention to native American writers. This ambition he later realized, but when a brilliant American novel was submitted to the firm (Harcourt, Brace & Howe), namely, Sinclair Lewis's *Main Street*, he voted to reject it. (His idea of native writers was clearly novelists like Booth Tarkington and Meredith Nicholson. Oddly enough, Howe's secretary, Ellen Knowles Eayrs, whom he had brought from Bloomington to New York, was the loudest voice in favor of publishing the book.) Looking for quieter waters, Howe left Harcourt Brace and ended his career with the Scribner firm.

Another member of the English Department was Henry Thew Stephenson, whose brother Nat was the first Southerner to write a book extoling the greatness of Abraham Lincoln. Stephenson had done work on Shakespeare's London in graduate school, and he loved to lecture and show pictures on the subject. His major interest, however, was photography. He specialized in trees, insisting emphatically that trees in winter were more attractive than they were in summer. He had hundreds of examples to prove it. I told him that trees in winter were like people in the nude—the shapely look more shapely undressed, but the others needed clothes to make an acceptable appearance. He didn't like my analogy and gruffly told me so.

A faculty friend of a different sort was Paul McNutt, sometime Indiana undergraduate, graduate of Harvard Law School, and a man filled with political ambition. I met him often at the Beta Theta Pi house, his fraternity as well as mine, and we discussed the state of the nation, the state of the world, and the state of Indiana over and over. He married a charming wife and I ate many fine meals at their home during the honeymoon period. At the time he was an instructor in the Law School. He wanted to be dean of the Law School, governor of Indiana, and President of the United States. He achieved the first two, but by the time he was ripe for the Presidency, the towering figure of F. D. R. blocked his way. He ended his political career as U.S. High Commissioner to the Philippines.

I spent a great deal of time on the tennis court and in his room with a young English instructor named Horace O'Connor. An excellent teacher and a delightful colleague, he had acquired a good prose style and was a resourceful talker. He purchased and read many books on birds. He wrote and sold to a magazine an essay "In Behalf of the Bluejay." In it he found more good things to say about this lazy scavenger of the woods than I ever believed possible. One day he told me he was sick and tired of living on twelve or thirteen hundred dollars a year, pulled up stakes, and moved to Chicago, where he joined an advertising agency and became eminently successful. He was an excellent example of a man born to be a teacher who could not bear to spend his life on a semistarvation salary.

Our English offices and classrooms were on the second floor of the Biological Building. The top floor was ruled over by a crusty old German scholar named Eigenmann. He repeated commonplaces with an energy that lifted them above the commonplace. His hero was David Starr Jordan, an ichthyologist of world distinction and something of a poet, who was now the first president of Leland Stanford University in California. It was Jordan who had inspired the erection of the big building we were occupying, and it was Jordan who had gotten Eigenmann interested in ichthyology. Eigenmann let me know that he was the world's leading authority on South American fishes, and each summer he took a group of Indiana boys to some country there so that they could study the fishes of the region. He was very proud of a letter in longhand from Theodore Roosevelt on the subject; he read it aloud and then handed it over to me. He also had a letter on his work from Kaiser Wilhelm, which was not in longhand. All this scholarly enthusiasm fascinated me.

In the spring of 1916 the college put on a pageant celebrating the hundredth anniversary of Indiana, both the state and the University. The pageant master was William Chauncy Langdon, who specialized in such performances. He struck me as a man who wanted to write dramas for Broadway but could not make the grade. He had a good feeling for showmanship but almost none at all for a telling phrase. His sentences were mouldy and bearded, and as I was one of the performers I had to learn long passages by heart.

The play, which was entitled *Pageant of Bloomington and Indiana University*, consisted of nine episodes, each of which depicted one of the highlights in the state's or the University's history. The master of the revels ingeniously succeeded in bringing everybody into the acts. Perhaps that was the best part of it, for everyone thinks he is something

of an actor. My part in Episode 4 was that of an Eastern man who
had come West and was making a plea for taxing the state to defray
the expenses of education. My eloquence was in vain, for at the end
of the episode the people voted an overwhelming *No*. On the same day,
however, I was chosen by a overwhelming majority to go to the
capital and help build a constitution for the new state of Indiana. The
two votes seemed to me to be incompatible, but that is politics. (It may
be out of place here, but forty-nine years later I was actually chosen
as a delegate to help build a new constitution for Connecticut.)

Mr. Langdon insisted that the pageant was a real art form and
ought to be regarded as such. To my thinking, pageants belong with
such performances as the Chester Plays of the 1590's or the York Cycles
of the sixteenth century. They have a certain historical value. They
bring the whole town or the whole guild into the world of drama, but
they rarely rise to the level of real dramatic art. A number of pageants
like the York, Wakefield, and Coventry cycles covered church history
from the Creation to the Day of Judgment. Ours did not take in quite
so much territory, but we did cover a hundred years of Indiana history.

The pageant master did have a good feeling for ballads and folklore, and that drew me to him. He told me he was present the year
before when Cecil Sharp, the famous English ballad authority, had his
first meeting with Olive Dame Campbell, the woman who collected
the ballads of the Southern Appalachians. He said Sharp flipped over
the pages of her collection, expecting to find nothing memorable or
noteworthy. He hadn't got far into the sheaf when he stopped short
and stared at a ballad which had been lost in England but was still
being sung by the folk of North Carolina. Sharp's attitude suddenly
changed. He discovered what a remarkable collection Mrs. Campbell
had gathered, was especially pleased with the way she had recorded
the music, and offered then and there to help her get the ballads
published. The book, which was a landmark in American balladry, was
brought out by Putnam's in 1917.

All this fascinated me as much as it did Langdon, for my introduction to poetry came through folk songs, folk sayings, and ballads, and
I hoped one day to put together my favorites in a book with an
introduction of my own.

Throughout 1916 the more serious boys at the University discussed
the world situation and the part their country should play. Several of
them felt with Lord Grey that the "lights were going out all over

Europe." A year earlier the *Lusitania* had been sunk without warning by a German submarine off the southern coast of Ireland and 124 Americans were lost. Many of the students felt that we had stayed out of the war long enough. Talk about the *Lusitania* continued all winter, and shortly after the close of the spring recess a number of the boys in my classes signed up for the Plattsburg Naval Cruise, officially designated the "Naval Training Cruise for Civilians." I too signed up, and spent four weeks that summer aboard the battleship *Kearsarge* as a common sailor or "deck ape." This ship had been the flagship of the so-called "Great White Fleet," which Teddy Roosevelt had despatched on a world cruise as an exhibit of America's naval might eight years earlier.

On its present training mission, beginning August 16, 1916, the *Kearsarge* carried about three hundred of us civilian trainees, along with an equal number of Navy regulars—commissioned officers, petty officers, and enlisted men. We slept in hammocks, ate huge seagoing meals, swabbed and holystoned decks, studied the manual of arms, stood watches, learned battle stations, practiced firing the ship's three-inch and five-inch guns—several days of this while cruising the waters off Block Island and Nantucket. We even had twenty-four hours' shore leave at Newport, then as later both a socialite center and a sailors' town. This gave me the opportunity to hear a fine orchestral concert on Saturday evening and to see an exhibition of paintings on Sunday morning.

Next we made rendezvous at Block Island with the Blue Fleet—eight other battleships, a score of supporting craft, airplanes, and so on—to take part in the forthcoming war games which were the point of the entire program. It was our job to defend the northeast coast against the hostile Red Fleet, which along with its transports was to attack somewhere between Eastport and Hatteras and establish a base from which the "enemy" could take over our country. We made contact with the invaders near Nantucket and fought a a day-long running battle, which was disastrous for our side. We Blues were well-nigh annihilated, and the Reds landed a large force at Rockaway Beach. This outcome had been planned from the beginning, in order to arouse the nation to the need for preparedness.

After that, more training exercises and cruising, which took us as far down the coast as Hampton Roads and Old Point Comfort. We were through with it all and mustered out on September 9.

The civilian trainees I thought a fine type of American—idealistic and adventurous, mostly young but some approaching middle age and belonging to the Back Bay set. The commissioned officers too—especially the younger ones recently out of Annapolis—struck me as well-educated and companionable. I was particularly impressed by Captain (later Admiral) William S. Sims, who on one of the first days out had given us a stirring address on loyalty and initiative, illustrated with some capital yarns. Intelligent, widely read, and endowed with a fine sense of humor, he was an officer the country could be proud of. Nonetheless I spent much time with the enlisted men of the regular crew—some colorful old-timers, but on the whole a sorry lot, who worked well enough abroad ship but would then go ashore and blow every cent they had on trivial knickknacks, tattoos, and dissipation.

In the end, we trainees had gained an idea of the needs of the Navy. We felt the cruise was an argument in favor of universal military training. We had saluted the flag so often that we acquired a reverence for it. We agreed with H. G. Wells that ours is the most beautiful of all national flags—something which, Captain Sims said, "had got into the backbone."

In the fall I came back to the University with a good sea tan on my face and a congenial group of courses in modern American literature to teach. In those days we were all expected to teach five classes. Two teachers of English from New England, Richard Rice and Robert Withington, and I soon grew tired of the food served at the University cafeteria. We rented a house on South Street, hired a Negro cook named Katie, and set up housekeeping on our own. Katie came about ten, washed the breakfast dishes, and served us our luncheons and dinners. At table, Rice had a habit of throwing out well-known lines of poetry and demanding the name of the author. He would burst out with a line such as "Woodman, spare that tree" or "Why should the spirit of mortal be proud" and call for the author. It was a revealing game, for we didn't even know the author of "Mary had a little lamb." One night Rice came out with " 'We are lost,' the captain shouted, / As he staggered down the stairs . . ." "Who wrote that, Bob?" he asked of Withington. "I don't know." "Snow, can you say the name of the author?" While I was trying to puzzle out the answer, I noticed that Katie's eyes expanded and her body wriggled. So I said, "I can't tell you, but I believe Katie here can." "How about it, Katie?" said Rice.

"The poem is entitled 'The Tempest' and the author is James T. Fields,"
was her immediate reply!

Some of the girls in my courses did excellent work. Every once
in a while they would leave teasing notes on my desk. One of them
read, "When you lean forward and clasp the edges of your desk with
your long artistic fingers, don't you ever think you ought to be clasping
them around the neck and shoulders of some good looking girl?" I was
pleased with these anonymous notes, but threw most of them into the
wastebasket. One blonde in a literature class attracted me immensely,
but I had no desire to marry and settle down on $1400 a year—so I
kept the desk solidly between me and the girls. The day of the pill
and female permissiveness had not yet arrived, and I comforted myself with a poem of Kipling which declares that a man travels fastest
and farthest who travels alone. One poem left on my desk by a girl in
that class, like the letters of Mary Gray in Utah, lifted my spirit out of
its loneliness and gave me immense cheer. I have kept it all my life.
Addressing me as "O flaming spirit!" it ends:

> And yet . . . I hold you in my arms . . .
> When but to hear you speak is worship,
> To touch your lips a sacrament!

That last item means that I had held her in my arms on the ballroom floor. I loved dancing and appeared at a sorority or fraternity
dance about twice a week. Praise like hers makes one born and reared
in northern New England embarrassed and uneasy. It seems an efful-
gent extravagance. Down South—and this university had many of the
characteristics of the colleges of the Old South—praise and flattery
are part of peoples' way of life; girls take flattery in their stride and
thrive on it. Reticence and restraint unfit a boy to mingle easily with
them. I enjoyed their delightful surface affection but was not at ease
in its atmosphere. I did feel perfectly at home with the young men
at the university and kept up a correspondence with a few of them for
years.

The war spirit was growing rapidly among the boys in my classes.
War was declared on April 6, 1917, my birthday, and news circulated
around the campus that boys who volunteered would get a better break
than those who waited to be drafted. The Zimmerman note, promising that a Germany victorious over the whole world would give
back to Mexico the states of Nevada, New Mexico, Arizona, and
southern California, lifted the war spirit of America to the boiling

point. Professors at the college smashed dozens of beautiful German musical records in the excess of their patriotism. Courses in the German language and literature were flagrantly scuttled. Some of the finest German teachers found themselves without a job, and I personally witnessed some of the suffering in one of these families. One by one the boys in my classes dropped out and flung themselves into the fray. It affected me so deeply that I myself decided to join them.

I recorded my feeling in a sonnet:

THE YOUNG INSTRUCTOR DECIDES
(World War I)

He never knew how much the boys had meant
To him till one by one they came and said
Good-bye in tones that made him bow his head
And pray that Heaven's strictest watch be sent
To guard these men with zeal so overpent,
So quick to suffer in the global flame,
So eager to keep clean their country's name
That Freedom might look twice, and then relent.

Yes, his they were, he loved them as his own,
Their spirits kept his own in tune with mirth
And since they left him everything seemed grown
As stale as burned out slag on desert earth;
He could no longer bear the strain, his chance
Like theirs he chose to risk on the fields of France.

So I was off as a volunteer to join what one writer called "The Great War."

CHAPTER 13

World War I

I had signed up as an officer candidate, and was sent to Camp Benjamin Harrison, outside Indianapolis, for my induction into the armed forces. What a bleak and ugly place it was! A flat plain with rectangular barracks scattered all over, the spaces between paved with thick layers of gray cinders to keep our feet from being stuck in the mud. No trees, no shrubs, no flowers, just a dismal waste of gray flatness. That was to be my home for six long months.

In each of these barracks there were sixty army cots, thirty on each side of the room. There were no chairs. When we were not sleeping we sat on the cots, read, smoked, and talked. The latrine was in another building about two hundreds yards away. We went there each morning at five to shave, shower, and gossip. "Latrine rumors" were our substitute for the morning newspaper. Bits like "We are going to have a new commanding officer—a strict West Point colonel," or "Hibben is going to leave us and go with the Intelligence," or "Lieutenant Fisk went on a big binge last night and will be ugly this morning."

During our first three months we were trained as infantry. Our days were filled with shouts of "Squads right," "Pee-rade rest," "Arch" (for *march*), and "Company . . . halt" in the universal sergeant lingo. We learned how to shoot a heavy .45 caliber pistol. Each Thursday, loaded down with full battle equipment, we marched through the streets of Indianapolis, flags flying and band playing. This was a pleasure, for the townspeople turned out to watch us. The children were excited and joyful, even worshipful! Pretty young maidens were much in evidence, and after the march when we were all dismissed and given a night out, a number of our brothers went searching for girls. On these Thursday nights I had a haven of refuge, a standing invitation to dinner from a college classmate of mine, Dr. Lester Adams, and his wife. Dinner was followed frequently by a trip to the theatre. Reveille the next morning at five came all too soon.

Twice a week we were marched into an open field for drill in calisthenics. Every third day we marched onto the same field to sing Army songs—morale builders. Who remembers "Over There," "Smiles," and "Tipperary"? The music was of the Tin Pan Alley variety and the words could not classify as poetry, but their hearty rendering by a large group of men was impressive.

Our pay was thirty dollars a month. Out of this sum the paymaster held back six for insurance, in case we should suffer that which was "common in the life of man," as Cicero puts it. He also took six more as an allotment for our nearest of kin; and six more for laundry. Very likely borrowing had to be paid. So out of thirty dollars we would have six or seven left. That evening, on the floor of the latrine, we put on a big crap game. One or two boys pocketed all of the money. When desperate for cash during the following thirty days, we knew where to go to borrow.

I learned that the gambling table was a good place to discover character. Most of these boys were happy-go-lucky in their attitude. With money it was easy-come and easy-go. The winner knew he would be besieged for a month, and he smilingly made the best of it. A few would have nothing to do with either cards or dice. They were the "tightwads." A few stayed out for religious reasons.

When I tried to discuss the issues of the war, I found myself up against a stone wall. Most of the men didn't know or care. One Dane in our group named Nielson-Lange did care, and he and I discussed Wilson, the Kaiser, and all the others in power over and over. He knew a great deal about the Balkan wars, the Austro-Hungarian monarchy, the aspirations of Germany, the desire of Russia for a "window on the Baltic," and the weakness of France which had never completely recovered from the War of 1870. Much of this was new to me, and made me understand better Wilson's reluctance to involve our country in European squabbles.

What really interested the boys in our barracks was the Sam Browne belt. This wide brown leather belt around the waist and over one shoulder was to be worn only by officers overseas. Some of our group argued they should wear one just as soon as they were commissioned. I was amused by their earnestness over this trivial question.

The last half of the course was a training in artillery problems, some of which reminded me of the "originals" in plane geometry—things that racked my brain in high school and racked it still more here. Our lights were out at nine, and some of us repaired to the latrine (where the lights were on all night) and wrestled with these problems until midnight and beyond as Jacob wrestled with the angel. The course was intensive and exacting.

One rainy night I volunteered to give a poetry reading, and most of the men remained at the tables after supper to hear me. I knew many of Kipling's *Barrack-Room Ballads* by heart and gave them "Tommy Atkins," "Mandalay," and a few others like "L'Envoi." The West Point officers in charge of our group came up to my table and thanked me after the performance. One of them said, "I'm going into town tomorrow and buy a copy of Kipling's poems. I thought he was just a short-story writer." These officers for the most part were haughty and proud, and impressed us with their superiority whenever possible. They called us "Sears-Roebuck officers." We were trying to crowd into a few weeks what had taken them four college years to learn.

I often feared I would never pass my final examination, but I squeaked through and with the others was lined up and given a commission as second lieutenant.

Most of us were scheduled to go to Camp Custer at Battle Creek, Michigan, where we were supposed to put an entire division in readiness for service overseas. I was assigned to the 329th Artillery Battalion, which was horse-drawn. For that I have never ceased to be thankful. I loved horses. I had worked in a livery stable as a boy. And from now on I was going to be on horseback almost every day. My own horse, a roan with white stockings, was named Fritz. I saw to it that he had some special lumps of sugar each morning—even though sugar was rationed at the time. It is difficult to make personal rapport with a machine. It is easy and satisfying to make friends with a horse. Fritz and I understood each other well.

There was not enough artillery work to keep us "shavetails" busy during our first two months at Custer, consequently orders came from higher up to put us to work inducting a few thousand new recruits who had just arrived at the camp from the deep South. My own assignment was a motley group of Negroes from Alabama. They were told to stand in line, approach the desk one at a time, and give name, home address, married status, and dependents. It was a hot afternoon.

The line was long and moved slowly. Each man had to let us send a part of his salary to his wife or mother monthly. One said, "I don't want to send nothing to my wife. She's a low-down, good-for-nothing, no-account nigger and I don't want to send her nothing." I said, "This is Army regulations and you must do it." "Who makes them Army regulations, Lieutenant?" I said, "Uncle Sam." He replied, "He's no uncle to me, and I want all my Army money myself."

Later another man, a six-foot-five giant, a fine-featured man who had been standing in line for a long time, began telling me about his misery. "My feet are killing me. My shoes don't fit and make sores on my feet." I looked down and saw that he would need a number 14 or 15 shoe. We had none that large in camp. He painfully pulled off one shoe and showed me raw red sores. I learned later that headquarters held a "summit conference" on his case to decide whether to have a special pair of shoes made for him or send him back home. They sent him home.

When I had finished this task I discovered that Air Force officers from Fort Sill, Oklahoma, were looking for recruits. I went to their temporary headquarters for flying tests. The man in charge put me on a revolving chair and spun me around and around, then watched to see how I would fall. I fell the wrong way. This was a great disappointment to me, for the Air Force men in World War I were a favored group. They were treated like knights of the Middle Ages. The officers had a cigarette with me, politely rejected me as an air candidate, and wished me luck in the artillery. Disheartened, I returned to my barracks and picked up again my Field Artillery Manual.

The cold kept us indoors whenever we were not out on the range. At the officers' lounge poker was the favorite game, and the older officers took delight in fleecing us shavetails. On my first pay day I was given a special invitation to play poker with the more seasoned officers. The game started conservatively. One could open only if he had a pair of jacks or better. Once I drew three kings and I looked forward to a cleanup. But alas! I had never learned how to turn on that flat, dead-pan expression such as one finds in Cézanne's famous picture "The Card Players." They could tell by looking at me that I had a good hand. Nobody would bet. So I had to be content with the kitty. In the midst of the game one officer said, "This is too tame. Let's play deuces wild." The betting grew fast and furious. Within an hour all of my pay-day money was cleaned out. I later discovered that fleecing a new arrival was an old Army game, and that my treatment that night was par for the course.

My most vivid memory of the experience in Michigan is the cold. The winter of 1917 was the toughest I ever lived through. It was so cold that when I opened the breech-block mechanism of one of my four guns, a piece of my flesh would be torn off my fingers.

Once during the winter we had a big dance. Women and girls were brought into camp from the surrounding region—enough to provide for the artillery and machine gun battalion personnel. It was a "blind date affair," and as my ill luck would have it, I drew an Amazon from Kalamazoo. She was tall with a large frame and large feet, and had a bold noisy manner. We had nothing in common except that we were two human animals. She was not a bad dancer, and if she had captured a whale of a man that night she probably would have had a whale of a time. She should have had a big hearty fellow who would kid her along, hug her up, even pinch her bottom a few times. Instead she drew a college professor. So for us both it was a "long day's journey into night."

I spent many week-end hours in the breakfast-food town of Battle Creek near our camp, where Dr. J. H. Kellogg had an elaborate vegetarian hotel, sanatorium, and restaurant. On the menu with each article of food was printed the number of calories involved. Kellogg, dressed in white like Mark Twain, moved about in the restaurant like the lord of a manor. One Saturday I told a companion, a Battle Creek dentist, that I would like to talk with the maestro. He said, "Go ahead and introduce yourself, but don't mention anything about bringing up children." I said, "Why not?" "Well," he said, "years ago Kellogg embarked on a plan to prove to the world that everything in the development of a child depended on environment. To him heredity had no value. So he went down in the slums and adopted twenty or thirty children to prove his point. Half of the children turned out bad. So it's a touchy subject. Lay off."

I did meet and talk with Kellogg and found him a good deal of a crank. He was proud of the V.I.P.'s who came to his sanatorium— such as S. S. McClure and Ida Tarbell, who were there at the time— and he felt he knew the cure for nervous afflictions. "It's all a matter of hot and cold," he said. "My patients here have to go under a shower where my assistant first turns on hot water, then cold, then hot again, and again the cold. It's a strenuous treatment, many of my patients rebel at it, but it gets RE-SULTS."

On Memorial Day we took part in a military parade in Detroit. On the reviewing stand were the mayor of the city and a number of dignitaries who were to judge the outfits and award prizes. So we groomed our horses especially well, dressed with all the spit and polish we could muster, and put our men and horses, guns and caissons in perfect order. As we approached the reviewing stand our band struck up "When the Caissons Go Rolling Along," to my mind the best of all military tunes. Fritz seemed to sense the necessities of the occasion and behaved beautifully. When all the outfits had passed the reviewing stand, we were told we could have the day off. Just as the battalions were breaking up word came that Battery B, our battery, of the 329th Field Artillery had won first place in the votes of the judges. Pandemonium broke loose. We cheered our men, slapped each other on the backs, and told ourselves that the 329th was going to do big things in the fight overseas. I never before realized that there could be so much fun in the army.

The following week we were ordered to go to Camp Stonewall Jackson, Columbia, South Carolina, for intense artillery training before embarking for overseas. After enduring the most cruel winter it ever knew, Michigan was enjoying a delightful spring and we felt we had earned its joys. But no! We had to plunge into the muggy heat of a South Carolina summer. It somehow seemed unreasonable and unfair. But that was the Army!

Columbia, like most Southern cities, was small. In front of the statehouse there was a statue of George Washington holding an outstretched sword. The tip of its blade had been shot off by Federal troops, a guide was quick to tell me. In his voice I heard Southern anger still very much alive over Sherman's occupation of the town in February, 1865, when many of its finest homes were burned.

General Wade Hampton was still regarded as the great man of the region and his statue occupied the place of honor in the city square. I was told that his daughter still lived in town and went to call on her. She was a widow living with two beautiful daughters and a Negro servant who wore clothes that certainly dated back to the Civil War. As he waited on table his black suit showed streaks of green that betrayed its age. I engaged a cab and with Mrs. Hamilton, one of Wade Hampton's granddaughters, as guide drove slowly through the city. She pointed out to me where her grandfather's magnificent home had stood. The only part visible now was the wine cellar; the rest was an ash heap. She pointed out the spots where other fine homes once stood, named the families that owned them, and insisted that Sherman's army treated her city worse than it treated Atlanta. She was glad to get out and ride through the city on a Sunday afternoon, but my pleasure was spoiled when I realized that to her it was a journey of sorrow.

At the end of our first week we were assembled on a large field to hear a lecture on artillery. The speaker was an earnest officer who waxed eloquent on his favorite subject for nearly an hour. He said, "Artillery is the most important arm of the service. See what has happened in Europe. What was it that laid low the great fortress at Liège? What conquered Namur and Antwerp? It was the German howitzers. And it is up to us to match them. Get acquainted with your guns. Know them intimately. Be accurate first. When you have conquered accuracy, add speed. America can match the Germans. It is up to us in the artillery to go over there and win this war." My admiration for this colonel's zeal was unbounded. But I knew I could never match his personal enthusiasm for an impersonal machine like the howitzer.

The following Saturday we were invited to attend a dance at the Columbia Country Club. The Ladies' Auxiliary had rounded up a large group of girls from the best families to be our partners. We had a chance to look on and admire the finest sight the South had to offer—a group of beautiful teen-agers. Among our officers was a grandson of William T. Sherman. Throughout the evening I saw one girl after another pointing him out to friends and saying, "Why, he looks like any other boy." Were they expecting him to look like Frankenstein's monster or an anthropoid ape?

Two days later we were called together to receive a tongue-lashing from Colonel Campbell. He said, "American officers are supposed to be gentlemen, but the leading citizens of this city have told me that some of you at that dance behaved like dogs. Some of you treated these girls as if they were women of the streets. We may never have an invitation like that one again, but if we do I want every mother's son of you to behave like an officer and a gentleman." During our stay there we were never invited to such a grand party again. Our welcome was worn out in one brief evening.

At Columbia I often left the camp and went downtown for supper. One evening at the Jefferson Hotel whom should I see among the throng but John Masefield! I went up and introduced myself and told him how much I liked his long narrative poem, *The Everlasting Mercy*. He said people didn't usually recognize him in a crowd and it surprised him that I could pick him out. He was tall and slightly stooped. He had a chunky face, broad rather than elongated, sharp brown eyes, and dark brown hair. His face was tanned and weather-beaten, probably from his early life at sea. He told me he was here on a speaking tour to counteract German propaganda about his people, especially such statements as "England will fight until the last Canadian (or New Zealander or Australian) is dead." He had statistics showing that the deaths of English soldiers outnumbered proportionately those of any one of her dominions, and he rattled them off for me as we sat in the Jefferson lobby. All the time he was talking I sensed that he hated his assignment. He was not an accomplished lecturer and knew it. But he loved England and would do anything he could to help her win this war.

He brightened up when the talk turned toward poetry. He praised highly the American poet E. A. Robinson. When I asked him what young poets in England were worth while, he said, "Keep your eye on Robert Graves and Robert Nichols—those are the two most promising of our younger poets." Robert Nichols I knew had written enjoyable verse, but he had poured his passion into his anti-war essays. No one in the world hated war as this man did. His hatred was so deep that he deplored the English habit of extracting humor out of its misery. He said the humorous sallies were vicious and must be eliminated so that we may get on with the serious business of abolishing man's most horrible and devastating activity. In this crusade he became an extremist, lost his balance and his sense of proportion, and wrote little more poetry.

Robert Graves first published a modest volume entitled *Over the Brazier* and then went on improving his art until he became one of the foremost poets of Great Britain. In his old age he is still turning out good poems. So Masefield's prophecy of the two men was 50 per cent correct, and that is a high record in this most baffling and fascinating literary gamble.

Our camp was visited by poets, singers, lecturers, humorists, and other people of the entertainment world. Most of them were poor performers. One Southern girl who tried to tell us funny stories about New England rustics invented a New England dialect which was closer to Choctaw than to the Yankee vernacular.

There was one notable exception. The concert given by Madame Schumann-Heink was an event in my life. She was not only a great singer but a great woman. She sang a few arias from operas but for the most part sang well-known songs such as *Silent Night* in German and *The Rosary* in English. It was the most moving concert I ever attended. When she finished we refused to leave. We just sat there and clapped. She made us feel her genuine love of America. She told us she had one son, her oldest, fighting in the German navy, and three other sons fighting with the Americans. Against a thousand odds in her career, including the bearing of eight children, she managed to make herself one of the greatest opera singers of the world.

One week end three of us hired a car and drove to Charleston—about 140 miles through groves of live oaks covered with Spanish moss, on narrow dirt roads which in places were blocked by fallen trees that we had to cut away with an axe. It took us most of the day to reach the city. While walking the streets and viewing the sights we were approached by a well-dressed businessman and invited to his home for dinner. We accepted with alacrity. While waiting for dinner our host brought out wine and whiskey for an appetizer. (It was the prohibition era in South Carolina, but the liquor law had not yet reached Charleston.) We ate a dinner of roast chicken and rice prepared as only a good Southern Negro cook knew how. After dinner we sat out on the veranda overlooking Charleston harbor in the moonlight. I didn't dare tell an ancedote of Oscar Wilde's. When Wilde was a guest in a similar home many years before, he remarked that he had never seen a view that would match the rising moon over the waters of Charleston harbor. His host, with ancestors in the Confederate Army, replied, "But you should have seen it before the War."

At the table there was one beautiful girl, the daughter of our host. But she disappeared after dinner. Her father must have heard about our carryings on at the Columbia Country Club dance.

Such spontaneous hospitality was typical of what was happening all over the country to men in uniform. People went out of their way to be kind to us, to drive us when we were walking, to supply directions, to invite us to their homes. The war somehow drew North and South together in a way never known before. It seemed to be the only thing that could unify the nation. I fear we can never end war until we can devise substitutes that will challenge young men and satisfy their deep need of adventure.

While still in Columbia I took time out to visit a Negro school on the outskirts of the city. I knocked at the door and asked if I could come in. The surprised teacher was a woman approaching middle age. She looked at me doubtfully at first, thinking I might be some kind of spy. I told her I was a boy from the North and had taught a country school for six dollars a week. She said, "I'm getting seven dollars." I asked her how many grades she had. She said eight. "And do they go from here to high school?" I asked. "Most of them don't go to high school. They go to work." The floor of the room was covered with litter, so deep that one could not sweep it with a broom. One would have to use a shovel. Window panes were broken out, and the stairs leading down to the street from the front door were so rickety that I had to watch my step every second. I thought of the phrase "separate but equal" decreed by the Supreme Court. In South Carolina it meant "separate and unequal," for no white child would ever go to school in such a filthy room.

There was much talk in the camp about a new military center that was being established in Camp Zachary Taylor, outside Louisville, Kentucky. It was to be the biggest artillery center in the country, made up of two units: one, a Field Artillery Central Officers Training School; the other, a Field Artillery Replacement Depot—the F.A.R.D. When my 329th Battalion was getting ready to embark for overseas and every man was keyed up with an intense desire to go to France, the Colonel called me in and told me he wanted me to go to Louisville and help organize the F.A.R.D. I was deeply disappointed. I protested that I thought it unfair to send my battalion to Europe without me. He replied, "We can't let all of our second lieutenants go across. You are one of the older and more mature officers and we need you to help get the F.A.R.D. on its feet." Orders are orders, so I said a grim good-bye to my friends of the 329th and headed for Louisville.

At Camp Taylor I was promoted to first lieutenant and given charge of Battery B, Field Artillery, Replacement Depot. Although I would be out on the range occasionally, my work would be largely administrative. Mine would still be a horse-drawn outfit. At the officers' table I made one good friend. Frank Abbott. He and I took long walks and horseback rides together. He soon became the first supply officer of the Camp Taylor artillery contingent and did an excellent job. On week ends we went into the city for a play, a concert, or just relaxation. Our headquarters was the Hotel Seelbach. Usually some businessman at the hotel would give us the keys to his room, tell us we would find some good liquor there, and say, "Go ahead and try it." It was still the day of prohibition in Kentucky, but these business-men always managed to find a supply of the forbidden article.

In a replacement depot the enlisted men are constantly changing but the officers in charge stay on. I had a sergeant and a mess sergeant who were old army men, skilled in all the details of how a battery should be run. I picked out an intelligent-looking young corporal to do the paper work, the endless reports in quadruplicate demanded by the Army, and he exceeded all my expectations. We drilled the men in pistol firing on the range, and taught them how to harness the horses and move a battery over rough terrain on a dark night.

One of my new recruits was a conscientious objector, a "House of David" character with a long dark beard. Battery commanders as a rule had no time to waste on these "jerks" and sent them at once to Leavenworth. But I decided that, before taking such a step, I would send for the man for a talk. He carried a black leather-bound Bible and quoted to me the passages on which he based his stand against war and killing. He was sincere and intelligent, and while I could (and did) argue the contrary, I wanted to save him from prison if I could. It took a bit of maneuvering, and patience on both sides. But in the end, when his contingent went overseas, I saw to it that he re-mained in the States with a custodial job on a sand pile, so that he would never have to break the Sixth Commandment.

On the second Saturday in May I had my first introduction to the Kentucky Derby. My interest was more than normal because I had been living with horses ever since I entered the army. The three-year-olds on view at Churchill Downs were something special—the finest exhibit of horseflesh in the country. My partner on this occasion was a lovely Southern miss named Amelia, who worked at the U.S.O. at our encampment. She was good-looking, possessed a sense of humor, and claimed to be a good judge of horses. We watched the three-year-olds warming up and Amelia picked a horse to bet on. She chose a filly. I told her that fillies rarely won the Derby, but she insisted, and we both put up all the money we had on her choice. We lost every-thing and had to walk back to Louisville, a distance of two and a half miles, as dead broke as hoboes.

In the summer of 1918 when all was going smoothly, our camp

was stricken with the most virulent disease imaginable—a deadly form of influenza. It came on with chills and fever. It hit first in the throat, then passed into the lungs. In a day or two the lungs filled up and the patient died. It hit the strong, active members of the camp even more drastically than the weaker boys. Our hospital unit soon became overcrowded, and we had to use barracks as temporary hospitals. As soon as a boy was stricken we telegraphed his family, and in many instances his mother appeared. Some of the mothers tried frantically to get more done for their sons. Others accepted the outcome with sorrowful stoicism that was appealing and saddening. I called on the sick boys of my own battery every day and caught the disease. Instead of my lungs it attacked my nose and I had an almost continual nosebleed for five days which weakened me and put me to bed, but I soon recovered.

Boys were dying all around us. Two of the nurses we loved and admired were stricken and died. The undertakers ran out of coffins. We buried many of the boys in mass graves. Each night one of the officers of the camp had to take charge of these mass burials. One night it was my turn. I invited a Catholic priest, a Jewish rabbi, and a Protestant minister to come out and say prayers over the grave. I ordered the boys to take pliers and remove the identification tags, known as dog tags, from each one of the victims' wrists. During this part of the ceremony one of the boys went insane right before my eyes and was taken to the psychiatric clinic. This burial had a gruesome effect on all of us.

The redeeming feature was the heroism displayed. The nurses working eighteen hours a day. The doctors, frustrated because there was no specific vaccine for influenza virus infection at the time, and the boys themselves dying such unheroic deaths—all this was one of the darkest experiences I ever endured. As I was going through her ward one day a nurse told me something I could never forget. She said, "One of your men rose up and said, 'I shall have to let one of you boys be the fellow that picks off the Kaiser,' and then fell back on his cot dead."

Such wonderful boys going out like so many flies overwhelmed us, and we sought relief however we could. One way was rather ghoulish. Every night at the officers' mess each one of us would put a quarter in the pot and guess the number of deaths that would occur that night. The man who came the nearest would take all the money at breakfast the next morning. We were walking daily through the "valley of the shadow of death," and this gambling was a grim American way of relieving our feelings.

For the first time in our history the number of battle deaths was equal to deaths from disease—50,510 on the battlefield of France in 1918, and 51,477 at home from the flu. The deaths in Fort Devens, Massachusetts, exceeded ours at Camp Taylor. The disease went all over the country. People wore masks over their faces when they mixed with a crowd or went shopping downtown. But with the coming of frost in the fall the disease left us as suddenly and as mysteriously as it had come.

Our depot was busy sending replacements overseas. At times we added a group of officers. On one occasion I added to the list the name of Lieutenant North, an upstanding man and an excellent officer. Immediately I was called to the Colonel's office where I received a rebuke. "North is too good a man to lose. He is resourceful and has made many good suggestions for improving this depot. I simply can't spare him." I went back and took North's name off the list. This is a side of the Army that is never made public. If it were, it would add trouble all around, for John Q. Citizen thinks that in a time of national emergency the best men should be on the firing line and no favoritism should be shown.

Things were going well overseas, although the boys who went over were disillusioned. One pink slip that came to my desk was a copy of an official order in the European theatre of war forbidding the singing of a song which went "Oh, my / I'm too young to die / I want to go home!" This song did not reach outside and made no smash hit like "Over There," but it told more about the private in the rear ranks than that popular favorite.

When November came around there was a feeling that the war would soon be over. On November 9 the rumor of an armistice reached us. The civilian population went wild over the tidings, but the Army, lacking any official report, took no part in the celebration. Two days later, however, the report was officially communicated to us, and we reacted in different ways. I went on a long walk alone. It was humiliating to have been in the war and not to have been across the Atlantic. I could not keep back the tears. Behind headquarters I saw Brigadier General Austin walking alone looking very sad. I went up and saluted him, and we talked about the one and only subject in all minds that day. He said, "It means little to you, for your career is in civilian life.

It means everything to me, for the military is my career and my life."

I now determined to get out of the Army at the earliest possible moment. I wrote to friends all over the country to help me. An answer came from President Foster of Reed College. He wrote, "Professor Coleman of my English Department is going overseas to entertain the stranded troops, and I would like you to come and take his courses in English for the remainder of the school year. The job pays $2500 a year." That was twice as much salary as I had ever made before, so I accepted in a hurry.

I went to headquarters and showed the top sergeant my letter. He handed it over to a colonel, who said, "Well, you're in trouble. As acting captain you cannot leave until you have made an inventory of everything connected with your battery. And before you are discharged you will have to pay for everything missing."

I went back and repeated this order to my mess sergeant. He said, "I have been through this before and can help you out." I asked how. He said, "By stealing temporarily from other batteries the things that are missing." He added, "I hate to have you go," which pleased me more than anything that happened that day.

There were horses, harnesses, bridles, halters, axes, hammers, chairs, cots, spittoons, and many other things that I didn't know belonged to my battery.

The accountant was a square-jawed, unhumorous, middle-aged man who moved about with a list as long as a Connecticut clothesline. He was a certified public accountant in civilian life. When he discovered that the mess sergeant in his zeal had collected five more spittoons than my battery was supposed to possess, he did not even smile. I feared that I was in for trouble. And I was. He showed me a list of everything, four long foolscap pages of items, and said, "You owe the Army $134.27." I looked at him and gasped. I saw that he was no man to argue with, and made a note of the amount.

Going through the door, he turned to me and said, "For all the months you have been doing the work of a captain on lieutenant's pay, you can apply for a reimbursement to make up for the difference. The application will have to be made out in quintuplicate and you will have to wait several months before the money comes through." I said, "To hell with it," and never applied.

On November 21, 1918, all the red tape was in order, and I left the U.S. Army a free man.

CHAPTER 14

Reed College

LEAVING the Army was not sweet sorrow, it was an emancipation. I did leave behind a few friends, but most of them, such as Frank Abbott, were civilians like myself. A number of those at our officers' mess were sorry to hear the news of the Armistice. They would never be so important again, and they knew it. They would go back to the industrial world of America and get lost in it. I could not tolerate their attitude.

Some of the soldiers in the ranks deserved a chance to go on for more education. A corporal at my headquarters had an excellent mind but was merely a high school graduate. He would go back to the Gruen Watch Company's office and spend his life there in a subordinate capacity. There was no G.I. Bill for veterans of World War I.

When war heroes go back to civilian life their deeds of valor are soon forgotten. A few young American officers in France, realizing this, organized the American Legion. It spread rapidly over the United States and exercised considerable political power. I joined it at the first opportunity. It established a good lobby in Washington, got laws passed to help disabled service men, and persuaded Congress to award a cash bonus to all veterans. Later the Legion developed into a strong right-wing organization, though chapters like the Willard Straight in New York, full of liberal ideas and programs, were noticeable exceptions. Today the Legion is held in contempt by liberal left-wing groups who do not appreciate the needed legislation it sponsored, and still sponsors, in behalf of our neglected soldiers and saliors.

I took a roundabout train journey to reach my destination, going first to the University of Minnesota to visit Phil Bing, who enjoyed talking about the excitment of the great upheaval at Utah. He was holding a fine position in the English Department of Minnesota and had

234

written a book entitled *The Country Newspaper*, full of wit and humor as well as sound scholarship. His wife Peggy received me with open arms. During my two days there we talked incessantly about the people and issues involved in our stirring days among the Mormons. Shortly after my visit Phil came down with the flu and died. In his death I had lost a delightful companion and a great friend.

I arrived at Reed College in Portland, Oregon, on Christmas Eve. President and Mrs. Foster had been planning for weeks to make this holiday an unforgettable one. It seemed to me the right spot for a Christmas celebration, for the finest holly I had ever seen was growing all over the campus. There were a Christmas dance, a carol sing, and a turkey dinner for every member of the student body and for all those neglected workers who kept the campus clean and the buildings redded up and in order.

Reed College was then in its formative years, and the President was determined to make it a unique institution. The college was hampered by no traditions; these would develop with the years. The faculty were mostly young people. Foster believed with President Eliot that there were two kinds of people who make good teachers, "those who are young and those who don't grow old." At the end of each semester the grading system was put on a scale which I disliked. The teachers in each class had to give a fixed percent of A's and B's, of C's, D's, and E's. I wanted to use my own judgment in grading. I complained to the President about this, and he said, "Never mind the scale, go ahead and grade them as you like!" I fear I erred on the side of generosity.

At Reed there were no varsity sports teams and no fraternities. Whatever athletics the college had were intramural, and whatever rivalry there was with other colleges was intellectual, such as debating. In this field I coached a team that defeated the University of Washington. On the Washington team there was a bright senior who later became a distinguished United States Senator, Warren G. Magnuson; and on our team there was a man who later became president of the University of Maine, Arthur Hauck. I was feeling rather savage about my own country and proposed questions that were later taken up by the New Deal—questions like collective bargaining, minimum wages, guarantee of bank deposits, and medicare. The bright undergraduates were as excited as I was about these new questions, and the college was too young to have an alumni group to restrain us. A new college can be a great place for the discussion of "lost causes," and Reed's major effort was the creation of a lively intellectual atmosphere. In such a college there was little room for the "rah rah" boys. Foster set his mark upon the college from the very beginning, and as a result of his effort Reed, when evaluated by intellectual standards, grew to be the premier small college of America. It was a pleasure to be in on the ground floor of such a college.

It was now three months since the Armistice, and a few Reed service men had already returned from Europe. One of these came back with a face disfigured by a burst of German shrapnel. The President's wife told me that before the accident he was one of the most attractive boys on campus. Now his features were twisted and scarred; one could not bear to look at him. He remained at the college three days and then disappeared. I had always accepted war as a regrettable but normal fact of life, bound to recur as nations disagreed, but the sight of this boy stirred me to hate war and to question its value as a means of settling disputes.

Another returned veteran, Ned Larrabee, had been in a German prison camp. Flying over enemy territory, his plane was shot down by snipers. When he hit the ground he was badly shaken up and bruised. The German medical men injected shots under his arms. Ned feared that they were designed to kill him but they were really tetanus shots. (In the air corps of World War I there was a feeling of comradeship among fliers that extended across enemy lines.) In the prison camp he was treated like a hero. His parents sent him each week a box of good things to eat and they all got through the German army post on time. He shared the food with the officers in charge of the camp.

As a homecoming present his father bought him a Stutz Bearcat, and in this machine three of us—Ned, myself, and another student—rode all over western Oregon at high speed. On our trips I got a good look at the state. The ride up the Columbia Highway with the lordly river on one side and surprises like Multnomah Falls on the other was one to remember. The sea coast at Neahkanie Beach, with its perpetually agitated waves; the rose gardens in everybody's front yard on the streets of Portland; the rapid way the landscape had of drying suddenly after a shower; the challenge and benediction of Mount Hood with its snow-covered summit; the gracious cordiality of the people—all these endeared the state to me and made me regret that I was going to have only six months in which to enjoy it.

In addition to debating, I gave a course in modern English and American poetry. So many of the returned soldiers took this course that it was nicknamed "The War Veterans' Poetry Course." Up to this time poetry courses west of the Alleghenies were generally elected by girls only. Boys thought such courses were designed for "sissies." A professor at Knox College in Galesburg, Illinois, told me that the attitude was so deep-rooted there that he offered a course in modern poetry "Open to Men Only"; that was the only way he could induce boys to read poetry.

The men who returned from France after World War I had discovered the importance of the arts, and at Reed and elsewhere did not hesitate to take courses in poetry, painting, and music. The French experience made many soldiers aware of the shabby treatment given to the arts in the U.S.A. A few misguided souls felt this neglect so profoundly that they started an exodus of poets, novelists, and artists, heading mostly for Paris. There they wrote their poems and novels, painted their pictures, and made visits to the salon of Gertrude Stein. One of them, Ernest Hemingway, succeeded in making himself a distinguished novelist. The others did some second- and third-rate work, lived a delightful Bohemian existence, and came home to live on memories of Paris. They were, in my opinion, on the wrong track. American art must spring up out of American soil. It doesn't belong in the import category. I was still a bachelor free from marital obligations, but I definitely refused to join the exodus.

Our country's first reaction to the war was a mood of isolation. The words "no entangling alliances" were heard everywhere. The boys were saying, "Next time let them settle their troubles themselves. We'll not go over again." To negotiate a peace settlement President Wilson made some disastrous appointments. His heart was set on putting the League of Nations into the treaty itself, and everything else was subordinated to that one aim. More than anyone else in power, he had a vision of the world's major need, but he lacked the grass-roots political know-how to accomplish his ambition. And the mood of his country was militantly national. The Ku Klux Klan was spreading all over the land and isolation was uppermost in men's minds.

I lived at the President's house while at Reed and found it, in contrast to barracks life, a Paradise. I had already lived with Mrs. Foster at Bowdoin while her husband was off at Columbia securing a Ph.D. in education. Measured by any standards, Bess was a beautiful woman. We both had a New England Puritanical upbringing and were taught that life's major virtue was restraint. We liked each other immensely and found a Platonic relationship difficult to maintain. But we did manage to achieve an unemotional friendship that was enduring if not altogether satisfying. At Brunswick she had two small boys. The third child, born in Oregon, now five years old, became the joy of my life. She made me dream of the day when I would have a girl of my own, a dream that was never to come true.

Bess Foster was a born matchmaker and was determined that I should get married. She would often invite a girl to drop in and get a book she wanted her to read. After the girl had settled down on the living room couch, Bess would excuse herself and go out, leaving us alone. She brought in some lovely young females (Reed had more than its share of attractive girls), but her program never worked out. I was still in uniform. The U.S.A. was my girl at the time and I didn't like the way she was behaving.

The subjects I had been debating like collective bargaining, minimum wages, medicare, and a more equitable distribution of wealth in America haunted me continually. I looked around to find someone who was trying to make democratic dreams a reality and hit upon Big Bill Haywood. He had proved himself to be a great leader. More than anybody else he helped to establish the eight-hour day. He had the main role in establishing the Western Federation of Miners, and he was the leader in the formation of the Industrial Workers of the World, the I.W.W. He had the gift of trenchant phrase-making, and he was desperately in earnest. So I joined the I.W.W. chapter in Portland and paid my fifty cents for dues at each weekly meeting. Another Reed College professor went along with me.

At these meetings the men sang I.W.W. songs, revolutionary words set to favorite revival-hymn tunes. The poet of the movement was Joe Hill, a Swedish immigrant, whose song "God's going to set this world on fire one of these days" can be found in many ballad books. The hymnal this congregation used was called *The Little Red Song Book*. It contained many of Hill's parodies which became more or less widely known, such as "Hallelujah, I'm a bum, bum" and "Onward Christian soldiers, blighting all you meet,/Trampling human freedoms under pious feet . . . ." The one best remembered today had a chorus which went:

> You will eat bye and bye,
> In that glorious land above the sky (way up high);

> Work and pray, live on hay,
> You'll get pie in the sky when you die (that's no lie)!

The hearty singing of these songs by rough workmen was so convincing that for the moment I was less critical of the ideology of the various speakers.

At my fourth meeting the presiding officer asked me if I would like to say a few words. I went forward and told them I had not too much sympathy with their program of putting the Ins out and the Outs in. I wanted to see the whole body of American economic life raised to a higher level. I wanted to see Longfellow's "A land where the richest are poor,/And the poorest live in abundance" become a reality. I had not got very far when two men grabbed my legs and two more grabbed my arms and dragged me toward the exit in the rear of the hall. (I found out later that they were going to give me the "water cure.") When they were dragging me through the rear door the head man on the stage arose and said, "Bring him back! There is something in what he says." I shook hands and thanked the presiding officer, and assured him that like himself I wanted to help build a better America but I was not in favor of extreme methods.

That was the last time I attended an I.W.W. meeting, but I made a more careful study of Haywood during the next few weeks. Looking into his speeches, I discovered that he was an out-and-out extremist. He spoke disparagingly of other American labor leaders like Samuel Gompers because they were too moderate in their demands and wanted to unionize only skilled workers. He even criticized Eugene Debs, who for a long time was the standard-bearer of the Socialists in America. He advocated an organization "formed, based and formulated on the class struggle, having in view no compromise and no surrender, and but one object and one purpose, and that is to bring the workers of this country into the possession of the full value of the product of their toil." He saw no chance of cooperation between the working class and the employing class, and looked forward to the day when the workers would "confiscate the factories and drive out the owners."

When World War I broke out and America entered it he was just as uncompromising. He was doing propaganda work for his I.W.W., posting up stickers which read, "Don't be a soldier, be a man." He was accused of conspiring against the state and like Eugene Debs was thrown into prison. Released on bail, he absconded and escaped into Communist Russia, where he expected to find the

Promised Land. They put him in charge of a large mining project beyond the Urals. There he learned the bitter truth: that Russia had exchanged the Czar for the commissar, one form of authoritarian government for another. (Here is one more example of the fact that there is more continuity than change in human history.) Fred E. Beal, who visited Haywood in his Soviet exile, reported in *Proletarian Journey* that he died hating Russia.

Looking back on Bill Haywood and the I.W.W., his shadow, I am amazed to see how completely he prefigured the violent attitudes of the Weathermen contingent of the Students for a Democratic Society. Unlike the other Socialist leaders, Haywood wanted a complete overthrow of our nation's government. The others believed, as I did, that the machinery of our Constitution and its amendment possibilities would be sufficient. Under it, we felt we could achieve any welfare or industrial reforms we wanted. Wilson and later F.D.R. proved that we were right.

Planning to leave Oregon and return to my job in Indiana, I decided to get a glimpse of the Canadian Rockies on the way, where the scenery was said to be finer than anywhere else in America. George Henney, one of my students, volunteered to go along with me, and I counted myself lucky. He was a real outdoorsman—mountain climber, hunter, fisherman, camper—who knew how to live off the land. We packed our knapsacks with the irreducible minimum—two blankets, cooking utensils, two cups, three tin plates—added fishing tackle, my Army Colt .45, and some staple foods including a Virginia ham, and went by train to Lake Louise.

We couldn't afford to register at the Chateau at Lake Louise, but we sat on the veranda and admired the scenery. The blue lake below us; the mountan ranges in the distance; the gaps between the peaks; the crystalline unpolluted air; the glorious silence of the mountains—all this took our breath away. Then, in a shed behind the hotel, we found a remarkable old Swiss cobbler who fitted our shoes for mountain work by adding clips and hobnails, at $1.50 a pair. We told him we'd be climbing for the next ten days, and he said, "You are going to find it cold nights."

Never were truer words spoken. In those high regions, the temperature plummeted at nightfall, and it stayed down until mid-morning, when the sun finally climbed over whatever snow-capped peak lay

to the east. We developed a regular procedure. Each evening we lit
a fire, and one of us slept while the other fed the blaze until two in
the morning. At that point we huddled together under our two blankets
and tried to keep warm—with little success. Toward six the most miserable one got up and rebuilt the fire, and we waited for the sun to appear.

So it went for ten days of hiking, climbing, fishing, and half-
freezing in the most breathtaking scenery I have ever seen. We had
some small adventures along the way. Occasionally we had to jump
aside when a boulder, loosened from its snow bed by the sun, came
bounding down a mountainside. One night a bear entered our camp
and made off with the Virginia ham; I wanted to take a shot at him
but George said No: "If you shoot and only wound him, he'll kill us
both." Another night a marmot made a strange meal off one of my
woolen Army shirts, biting it full of small holes. Then, at Lake Moraine
in the Valley of Ten Peaks, we discovered a tearoom kept in this
wilderness by two middle-aged English ladies with strong Yorkshire
accents. I managed to cure their sick dog with hot water, orange
juice, and a brisk walk, and they treated us to a fine cup of tea (for
which their ordinary charge was a dollar). They also let us have a
slab of bacon in exchange for two large rainbow trout. These women
—bright-eyed, intelligent, up on current events—were entering middle
age without husbands, seeking an adventure together.

They had chosen one of the most glorious spots on earth in which
to have it. The beauty of this area is beyond any descriptive power
of mine. If you can afford to visit only one scenic spot on this con-
tinent, then the Lake Louise region is the place. But be sure to take
a warm sleeping bag as well as blankets! The nighttime chill in these
mountains is penetrating indeed.

When our ten days were over, Henney went home to Portland,
while I took a train to Quebec and the Maine coast. At home I rested,
sailed my father's sloop-boat, caught a few cod and haddock out in
the bay, and visited friends. I spent long hours talking with my father
about the war, ate the excellent meals prepared by my stepmother,
and chatted with my Aunt Aggie who lived next door. She was caring
for my sister Cora's little boy, my namesake Charles Wilbert Murphy,
while his mother worked. For a time I took over the role of father,
playing with the child and telling him stories of Alaska and the West.
He was intrigued by my marmot-bitten shirt and insisted on having

one just like it, holes and all—which caused my aunt much annoyance. She loved the boy so much that she probably humored him—I don't remember.

Within a few weeks I was back at Indiana preparing for another round of studies.

CHAPTER 15

Return to Indiana

WHEN I returned to Bloomington in September, 1919, I discovered that my two housemates, Dick Rice and Bob Withington, had moved on to Smith College, so I secured a room at the Gentry home on University Street. This family made Bloomington their winter quarters; in the summers they traveled over the country with the Gentry Dog and Pony Show, a kind of circus that assured them a comfortable living. They were a group of extroverts who loved to tell about their experiences. Besides money, their major reward was the joy of the children who loved dogs and ponies. Whenever they described a hazardous dog trick they always added, "And you should have seen the smiles on the faces of the children."

In the Gentry home there was an oversized bathroom which was heated by a gas burner attached to a side wall. One had to light it with a match and within a few minutes the room would be sufficiently warm. In my second week there I lighted the burner, shut its door, and began to undress. Suddenly the burner exploded, broke away from the wall, and flew across the room, missing my head by about three inches.

The next day in the Library I described graphically my bathroom adventure to the librarian, Mr. Jenkins, and Professor Amos Hershey, who taught international law. Hershey said, "Why don't you come over with me? I have plenty of space." I grabbed the offer and moved over at once. Hershey, with his bluestocking wife and charming teen-age daughter Frieda, lived in a large two-and-a-half-story brick house that was originally the University president's home. I had a large room on the second floor. The autumn leaves on the trees just outside my window made the room doubly attractive. Within a few days the Hersheys were treating me as one of the family.

Hershey, a rather short, stout man with blue eyes, a ruddy complexion, and a cheerful countenance, belonged to the wealthy Pennsylvania family that produced Hershey chocolate bars. Making money did not interest him. He had been educated at Harvard, London, and Heidelberg, and his happiness came from exploring the political condition and needs of the world. He was the author of an excellent scholarly book entitled *The Foundations of International Law*.

Along with three other scholars in his field, Hershey had gone to the Peace Conference on the steamship *George Washington* with Woodrow Wilson, and he told me much about that trip. Inasmuch as Wilson was my hero, I listened to his account with avid interest and drew out of him every scrap I could gather. "On the way over," he said, "Wilson asked the four of us to write a brief diplomatic history of the world since 1870—including peace treaties, agreements, spheres of influence, and understandings between nations during that period. He wanted it written down as briefly and succinctly as we could make it. He didn't realize what a large order he was giving us, but we kept at it all the way across the Atlantic."

Hershey said that the American delegation at the Peace Conference was a glum, unhumorous group of men who didn't know how to have a good time. One night at the Hotel Crillon in Paris one of the members of the group burst into the room and said, "What do you know; Balfour is out there in the ballroom dancing with his secretary!" The Americans at that conference wouldn't think of doing such a thing. "In the world of diplomacy," Hershey said, "the Americans had not yet learned how to enjoy life." They were all as sober as the old Presbyterian himself.

Mrs. Hershey was a "women's rights" advocate and had written many articles on the subject for the *Independent* and other magazines. When Mrs. Emmeline Pankhurst visited the University that winter, she and her daughter stayed at the Hershey home. One evening the family put on a sumptuous dinner for the two, to which I was lucky enough to be invited. Mrs. Pankhurst told us how the women chained themselves to the lampposts, poured tar into the mailboxes of England, were arrested and underwent great suffering to get the right to vote. Under the urge of my Spruce Head upbringing, I suggested that those brave women ought to have been home taking care of their children, whereupon the great reformer rebuked me with a tirade that was the high point of the evening. "Young man," she said, "you don't realize that our

Western democracy is on the edge of a disaster," and launched out into a fiery speech in behalf of women's rights. I was reduced to silence. I got what I deserved; but I also got a glimpse of Mrs. Pankhurst as a powerful, strong-willed woman untroubled by a sense of humor, a forceful driving human being with a one-track mind. English tradition had to stand aside at her bidding and give the women the vote.

While I was away at war a man had joined the English Department who was going to have a major influence on my life. His name was Homer Woodbridge. He was a graduate of Williams, and he knew many of the people I had met and enjoyed during my year in Williamstown. He had published in *McClure's Magazine* a poem that I knew by heart: "Dark are the hills, my sweetheart, / They dream of the dawn and thee . . ." His major interest was dramatic criticism. He had written critical articles for *The Nation*, the *Yale Review*, and many other periodicals. His essay on Eugene O'Neill was the best brief critical article on the playwright I ever read. I had shown him two of my poems, "Olaf" and "The Paving Quarry," which were going to come out in *The Nation*, and he said good things about them.

Woodbridge had a wife and three children, and when they ate luncheon at the University cafeteria the children insisted on carrying their own trays. The two youngest were so small and the trays were so large that they put on a good show every time they went through the line. He was a great walker and would corral a few members of the department to go with him almost every day after four o'clock. I went on a few of these jaunts, but I had acquired a golf outfit and preferred nine holes of golf as my outdoor daily exercise.

At this time I was on a ballad binge. I carried around in my pocket the book on the ballads of the southern Appalachians by Olive Dame Campbell and Cecil Sharp and gave unscheduled readings whenever a group of students would listen. At one of these impromptu lectures my most interested listener was Hoagy Carmichael, who later became famous as the composer of "Stardust." I urged all my students to bring me some ballads when they came back to college after the Christmas and Easter vacations. The results exceeded all expectations. I had already gathered ballads in southern Utah that were unknown to other parts of the country. I also had such Alaskan ballads as "The Kobuk Maiden" and "Life Along the Yukon." Before I got them in order for publication, I had moved on to Wesleyan University. There they were all burned up in the East Hall fire, and I was left desolate.

The people of southern Indiana were much like the people of the mountain region of Kentucky and the Carolinas. They sang ballads imported from England which they had revised to suit their own locale. Many of my students became greatly interested in these old ballads and one of them, William Jensen, became a specialist in the field. I generated so much interest in the ballads of our country that when I left the chairman of the Department told me he was going to get a professional ballad scholar to fill my place. This he proceeded to do when he secured Professor Stith Thompson as my replacement.

I learned that Carl Sandburg was beginning his ballad collection, and I persuaded the chairman of the Department to secure money for a Sandburg appearance at one of our assemblies. Carl thrumbed his guitar and sang the ballads of Jesse James, Sam Hall, Frankie and Johnny, Stacker Lee, and other old favorites, holding the audience spellbound. At the end of each ballad the crowded auditorium applauded him with great enthusiasm. He concluded his program with four or five poems of his own. To these the students responded politely but coolly. The difference in the reception of the two parts of his program disturbed Carl greatly. On the way back to my lodgings he asked why there was such a difference. I replied that a single individual shouldn't expect to compete with the race. "What do you mean?" he asked. "The ballads," I said, "appeal to highbrow and lowbrow alike because they come out of the hearts of the people. Other poems are done by lone individuals like yourself, and lone individuals should not expect their wares to appeal to everybody as ballads do." He was grouchy and still not satisfied when I walked him down to the station to catch his train. That meeting was the beginning of a long friendship which lasted until his death.

After the Sandburg visit had proved to be such a great success (to get a bit ahead of my story), I resolved to get Vachel Lindsay to come and wrote him a warm invitation. His response was much delayed—it turned out he had been in England—but after some letters back and forth, he arrived in Bloomington on April 5, 1921. I met him at the station and we liked each other at once. I suggested a cab but he said, "No. Let's walk."

He proved to be the most exciting and outgoing poet I had ever met. In appearance he looked like a Swedish immigrant who had recently arrived on our shores and was already in love with his adopted country. He had golden-yellow hair, violet-blue eyes, broad square shoulders, and an expression of expectation on his face. It was nearly noon when he arrived, and I took him at once to the University cafeteria. On his way along the line he burst out singing, "Chain them lions down!" The students looked at him with astonishment, but he didn't seem to mind at all. To bring him back to conversation, I asked him were he got that poem. "In the deep South," he replied. When he was taking a long tramping trip through the South, he often slept on the floor in a Negro cabin. The Negroes were the only ones who would take him in. One morning, when the floor seemed harder than usual, he awoke early and wandered over to a big barn that was rigged up inside for basketball. There, all alone, was a tall black boy practicing. As he threw the ball into the net, which he was doing with great accuracy, the boy would sing out, "Chain dem lions down." "Out of that incident," Lindsay said, "I wrote my poem." He told me that these long walking trips—one to the South and one to the West—shook the cobwebs out of his brain as nothing else in the world could do.

At two o'clock the president of the student body introduced Lindsay to a large assembly of the undergraduates and faculty. He began with two of my favorites, "The Congo" and "General William Booth Enters into Heaven." When he read the "Sea Serpent Chantey" and "Simon Legree," Mrs. Hershey, who was sitting beside me, turned and said, "That man's crazy." I replied, "Yes, I suppose so in the sense that William Blake was crazy and the man who wrote the Book of Revelations was crazy."

Lindsay stuck around for two days. On one of these days I arranged to have him recite his poetry to four English classes. Without looking at a book he read to four separate classes and only once repeated a poem—"The Congo." He apparently knew by heart every poem he had ever written.

With four students, we took a ten-mile walk through Brown County, east of Bloomington. Our objective halfway out was the home of an artist named Theodore Steele, whom I had met and enjoyed in my first period at Indiana. During the early part of the walk Lindsay sauntered along leisurely, now and then stopping to scoop up berries off bushes. Toward the end he hauled himself together, drove ahead like a professional, and outstripped us all.

Brown County fascinated me. Some of the old settlers' homes were log cabins with dirt floors similar to the cabin Abraham Lincoln was born in. At one of these the woman of the house had built a glorious flower garden. Artists came clear from Chicago to paint her garden against the background of that old cabin. I talked with the woman several times and finally learned her story, which I wrote in the form of narrative verse. I called it *An Indiana Pioneer*. Some years later a disk jockey named Tony Wons saw the poem and used it on his program; he then published it in a pamphlet called "Tony Wons' Book." He gave me no credit, nor did he consult my publishers. Several people who knew it was my poem wrote me about it. At long last I sent him a chastising letter. He replied by saying that he was a cousin of mine—his real name was Anthony Snow (read it backwards)—and he didn't think I'd mind his using the poem without paying for it.

I brought together those students who were deeply interested in poetry and ballads, and with them started a literary magazine called *The Hoosier*. The editor was J. Harold Schuler, one of the most engaging young men at the University, intelligent, witty, and resourceful. Within a few weeks he was stricken with peritonitis, underwent an operation, and died—a stunning blow to us all. His assistant, Mary Mack, took over the editorship. She was a junior, an extremely attractive brunette with curly hair, a ruddy complexion, and a shapely form. Rather to my surprise, she did a magnificent job, and I marveled at her ability as a woman to run a magazine.

Our intention was to put out a journal that would be more realistic, more autochthonous, more honest than the popular products of the state. We planned many trips that would get us acquainted with Indiana, and took long walks together—for instance to Spencer where William Vaughn Moody was born, and to Robert Owen's nineteenth-century cooperative community at New Harmony. On this last trip I wrote a poem which I titled "Southern Indiana":

> A purple haze against a pale blue sky,
> As full of changes as the purple seas,
> Rounds out the hills' sharp lines to soothe the eye,
> And drapes mantillas over tops of trees.
>
> The penetrating tenderness of night
> In this brown soil instills a patient mood,
> An Oriental calm, an inner light
> As haunting as the stillness of the wood.
>
> I like to think these quiet nights and days
> Pervaded Lincoln's heart as through his youth
> Alone he walked these hills and made delays
> To find the path that led his land to Truth.

I like to think the mystic chords he felt
From earth's huge silences released their bars
On his great heart while in this land he dwelt
Beneath the silent beauty of the stars.

O land of Owen's dream, Abe Lincoln's land,
Soft haze by day and gentle breeze at night,
The mystic's heart is yours, the artist's hand,
And yours the prairie's wide-horizoned light.

Meanwhile I was teaching four courses at the University plus an extension course in Indianapolis each Saturday afternoon. This meant a visit to the capital and a chance to see some good shows each Saturday night. It also gave me a chance to visit the Heron Art Building and the bookstores of the city. In one of these shops I met Frederic Melcher, who knew books, loved poetry, and pushed the sales of Robert Frost. He and I had many good talks. He subsequently went to New York and joined the R. R. Bowker Company, where as editor of *Publishers Weekly* he became, in a quiet, behind-the-scenes way, one of the most influential men in the world of books.

I was carrying too heavy a schedule. I was working about seventeen hours a day and was heading for a breakdown. In the winter of 1920 I was taken ill and went to see the University doctor. He thought I had rheumatic fever and urged me to go to a hospital in Martinsville, where they cured people with mud baths. I found Martinsville to be a place of almost five thousand people, whose main business seemed to be the care and cure of rheumatic patients. Years before, men digging a ditch for gas-pipe lines struck a spring of mineral water. It was gushing like an artesian well. According to the town's most famous story, the curative properties of the water were discovered by a broken-down racehorse which was put out to pasture in a field through which this water ran. The old nag drank the water and became rejuvenated. He was put back in service and won many notable races for his owner. Now there were several sanatoria for the rejuvenation of men and women, and at one of these I was a patient for three weeks. The doctors examined me and told me I did not have rheumatic fever; I was simply overworked and needed a rest.

News of my father's death reached me in the hospital and drove me into a gloom bordering on despair. He was built for endurance, and I had felt sure that he would be with us twenty years more. His physical strength had amazed me. He could turn a handspring at forty-five without the least difficulty. He enjoyed playing baseball during his middle years. He could build a boat that would survive in a hurricane —and did, as I showed in my poem entitled "Vigil." I found it hard to accept the fact that he was dead before his sixty-third birthday. I was unable to go to the Spruce Head funeral, sat in the dark corners of the sanatorium and brooded.

One tall, angular fellow-patient caught my attention. He was really rheumatic and was taking the mud baths. His name, I discovered, was Kenesaw Mountain Landis. I had read about his trust-busting decisions as a Federal district judge during Teddy Roosevelt's second term; when he fined the Standard Oil Company $29,000,000 in a rebate case, he made headline news. He told me that the wealth of the U. S. A. was built up with small farms and small businesses. His hatred of bigness in both farms and corporations was intense, so intense that it drew me to him. We both loved the game of baseball and talked about it daily. I was not surprised when after the "Black Sox" scandal he was made National Commissioner of Baseball and did much to clean out the corruption which had crept in to degrade the game. I was loath to say good-bye to him when I left the sanatorium. But my work at the college was piling up.

Back at the college I brooded over my father's death and wondered what I could do to get back in a cheerful mood. I fell back as usual on Benjamin Franklin to help me out. A pamphlet he published (but did not himself write) entitled "Reflections on Courtship and Marriage" urges a young man who is not yet financially able to start a home and family to cultivate the acquaintance of a young widow. The devastating flu that swept the nation in the summer of 1918 left too many widows in every college town in the country. On one street in Bloomington there were three, and one of these was a charmer. She was small-boned, with delicate facial features, light brown hair, hazel eyes, and a gay manner. I met her first on a moonlit night at the home of a professor whose wife was her friend. She loved dancing as much as I did. We danced many evenings together. She was rather innocent of books and read only the advertisements and women's section of the daily paper. She had an attractive son about five years old who began to call me "Daddy." This was "the winter of my discontent" and Anna did much to help me through it. I was relieved to know that she had another suitor seeking her favors, for I had no intention of starting a home on $1400 a year. But through her I discovered that mating was a thing of the mind as well as the body. The opening lines of Shakespeare's great sonnet on marriage—"Let me not to the marriage of true minds / Admit impediment"—hit me harder·than ever. The master knew that marriage was primarily a matter of the mind. After my confrontation with Mrs. Pankhurst, I decided I wanted nothing to do with reformers or career women. This young non-intellectual woman made me realize that I wanted a wife with a head as well as a heart. The affair was over at the end of two months and a half.

This episode taught me that I was living too monkish a life. It began in college where most of my social existence was with men. There we held long midnight bull-sessions, discussing the problems of philosophy, religion, and life. It continued in college teaching, where most of the young professors were males. In the midst of my acquaintance with the widow, I found myself now and then casting a "longing, lingering" look behind! I had conditioned myself to long night sessions with congenial male companions. And this conditioning had become one of my chief delights. I knew full well what Milton meant when he burst out in *Comus*: "How charming is divine philosophy!" Nor was I "unmindful of the crown that virtue gives." Virtue had rescued me in my Utah days from one of the major crises of my life.

After a six-weeks summer session at Winona Lake in the midwest heat of northern Indiana, I fled to the Maine coast to cool off. My father was not there to greet me, but his widow gave me a genuine welcome and made me feel completely at home. She told me all the news of the village and dwelt at length on my father's last days, which I wanted most to hear about. For three weeks I dug clams, caught fish, worked on my verse, and took long walks in the woods and along the shore.

Toward the end of my vacation I read one day in the local paper that Mrs. Charles Dana Gibson was going to give a talk on the League of Nations in Thomaston. Thomaston was my high school town; I had many friends there; and I was still eager to see our country a part of the League. I decided to go.

The hall was full but the speaker failed to show up. The engine of her cabin cruiser had broken down on the way from Isle au Haut to the mainland. A message had been signaled to Kitty Creighton, Democratic National Chairwoman from Maine. Kitty, a dear friend of mine, called me out of the audience, told me of her predicament, and said, "Wilbert, you must go on and make the talk yourself. I know you are full of the subject." Which I was, but I had just been in the mud flats clamming, my trousers were not pressed, I had no necktie, I needed a shave; in short I was not properly dressed for the occasion. My zeal for the League and my love for Kitty Creighton, however, overcame all obstacles, so I went to the rostrum and faced the assembled crowd. My first words were, "I have appeared impromptu and unprepared before audiences on many occasions, but this is the first time that I ever was a stand-in for a Gibson girl." This brought down the house, and I had no trouble thereafter. I told them that the one and only thing worth salvaging out of the Versailles Treaty was the League of Nations, and if that were not salvaged, then thousands of American boys had died in vain.

After my speech, cakes and coffee were served in a side room to a few people who were especially interested in the fate of the League. Among this group I spied a tall and stately girl with bronze-gold hair, blue-gray eyes, shoulders wide and erect, and a captivating smile. Her presence blotted out everything else in the room. I felt like Dante when he got his first glimpse of Beatrice on the Trinity Bridge of the Arno, like Abélard when he first saw Héloise. I had heard of "love at first sight"; I now experienced it.

Returning to Rockland with Betty and Ensign Otis, I told them of the girl I saw at the reception, described her in detail. They guessed correctly who she was and told me her name. She was a social worker whose father had been killed in an automobile accident and who was now at home with her widowed mother, teaching in the Rockland high school and presiding over the needs of the city poor. Betty offered to arrange a meeting, but I was leaving for Indiana within three days and that was too short notice. Also the lecture I gave stirred me up on the subject of the League of Nations and I resolved to be active in the fall campaign. Woodrow Wilson's dream of a League that would put an end to war haunted me.

Back again in Bloomington, I went down to Democratic headquarters and offered my services. The place had not yet been cleaned up to adjust to women, although they now had the right to vote. The floor had not been washed or swept for months. Spittoons stained with tobacco juice were prominent in all four corners of the big room. The woodwork was covered with dust and cobwebs. It was a smoke-filled room to end all smoke-filled rooms. Nobody but Dreiser, whom we had persuaded to let us copy the Bloomington section of his *Hoosier Holi-*

day in our new magazine, could do justice to these Democratic headquarters.

But an election was coming up, the League of Nations was going to be the paramount issue, and I wanted to be part of it. So I said, "Put me to work." I visited small towns under the auspices of the party, recounting the things Woodrow Wilson had done to improve the country in his first administration—the income tax, an effective Seaman's Act, a Parcel Post Act, rural free delivery, much important labor legislation. The Federal Trade Commission Act had removed our tight bond-secured currency and gave the country an elastic currency for the first time in our history. This one law enabled our country to stand the strain of a great war and made us the greatest creditor nation of the world. After reciting all these accomplishments I launched into a defense of the League. I found the people hostile. The Middle West—always more isolationist than the East—was now more isolationist than ever.

When the James Cox train came through the state I went aboard and offered my services. The committee in charge put me to haranguing the crowd while the people were gathering and the trains were shuttling about. I was lecturing against screeching train brakes, moving cars, and yelling crowds. When all these raucous noises ceased, the candidate himself would step out to the rear platform and expound the different sections of the League covenant and defend the controversial Article X. I went all over southern Indiana, made speeches at whistle-stop towns and villages, and prepared the crowd for the candidate.

In November our party went down to defeat by an overwhelming majority, and Warren Gamaliel Harding, "the only man, woman or child who could make seven grammatical errors in one declarative sentence" according to E. E. Cummings, was elected President. I was downhearted at this defeat, but I continued to agitate for a world organization that would change international chaos into international order. Oherwise I felt that all our efforts and sacrifices had been in vain.

In spite of my political activities, I still had my academic work to do, of course. I missed Homer Woodbridge, who had accepted a call to Wesleyan University in Connecticut. He and I had become good friends and I felt a bit lost without him. I spent many hours with a French instructor, Henri Bourdin, who had been an interpreter for the Marines in World War I. My course in American literature interested him immensely, and he actually took it by reading every item in the textbook I was using. He became especially interested in St. John de Crèvecoeur's *Letters from an American Farmer*, and not satisfied with the excerpt in our text, went to the college library and took out everything on Crèvecoeur he could find. I knew that Crèvecoeur had written much that never got into print, for his English publisher had promised a second volume if the first succeeded; and I suspected that Bourdin would probably find it in the Crèvecoeur home in northern France. Acting on my suggestion and encouraged by my colleague Frank Senour, he went to France, visited the Crèvecoeur home, and uncovered valuable material which the Yale University Press published in a volume entitled *Sketches of Eighteenth Century America*. He offered to give me credit for my part in his discovery, but I said, "No. A hunch is not sufficient justification for giving credit."

During the second semester I canceled my weekly trip to Indianapolis and concentrated on my poetry. Some of my colleagues thought I had discovered a new girl. I had, but she was a thousand miles away in Rockland, Maine, and was invading my dreams almost every night. She often stood between me and the typewriter, her thick bronze hair in two curls down her back, her gray-blue eyes smiling, and her cheeks tanned by Maine sun.

In March I had a call to Wesleyan University as assistant professor of English and debating at $2500 a year. It had been maneuvered by my friend Homer Woodbridge, who had been asked to look around and find an English teacher to take complete charge of the debating work, teach a course in argumentation, and handle three sections of freshman English. It was a formidable assignment, but I accepted it with alacrity. When President Bryan heard I was about to leave Indiana, he sent me a letter offering me $2100 if I would stay—a $300 increase over the $1800 a year I was receiving. He did not know I was already offered $2500 by Wesleyan.

William Lowe Bryan was one of the most interesting men on the campus. He was a philosopher and a wide reader in Americana. He read and admired the novels of William Dean Howells, and like Howells and many other Americans loved the writings of Emanuel Swedenborg. He did not object to my advocacy of the League of Nations; he himself favored it. He was at his best at commencements. I saw him at four of these. He would prepare a three- or four-minute speech on a single aspect of education and deliver it at the close of the ceremony. It was evident that Lincoln's brief Gettysburg Address was his model and that he worked over the phrasing of these statements assiduously.

No matter what national character came to speak at Bloomington, it was always Bryan who stole the show. His moral principles had a sharp Puritanical quality. To him the decalogue was sacred. When a distinguished professor of history divorced his wife and married one of his students, Bryan was so greatly outraged that he dismissed the man from his faculty. When a man in my department snipped pieces out of the *Encyclopedia Britannica* and other reference books and pasted them in a textbook he was preparing on Southern American literature, Bryan threw him off the faculty immediately and would not let him finish out the year.

I continued to do what I could to keep the League of Nations issue alive, but in one instance met with a stunning—and as it turned out, potentially dangerous—rebuke. The occasion was a Memorial Day program sponsored by the American Legion in the small town of Orleans, where I was the principal speaker. After showing that all our wars had been fought on behalf of human liberties, I spoke of the national ideals as set forth in the Declaration of Independence, the Monroe Doctrine, the Gettysburg Address, and Wilson's vision of a world made safe for democracy. I deplored our rejection of the League and said I saw no other way to avoid the utter overthrow of civilization by another great war. For this I was roundly lambasted by the local *Progress-Examiner*, which accused me of making a partisan political speech on a nonpartisan occasion, and suggested that I wasn't a fit person to "guide the youth of America in these troubled times." The *Republican* in nearby Corydon, under the headline "Snow Is a Nut," went on to call me a "mental misfit," and found it an imposition on the taxpayers that I should "receive their money for inculcating nonsense in the minds of their children."

That last item almost lost me my job at Wesleyan before it began. Someone (who?) wrote Wesleyan President William Arnold Shanklin that I was a poor risk, that I had a habit of rocking the boat wherever I went, and that my thinking about America was too far to the left of center for a good college teacher. I thought everything about the job had been settled, but out of the blue came a telegram from Shanklin:

> Although you have tentatively accepted a position at Wesleyan we make it a custom to have the candidate come on and have a good look at us while we are having a good look at him before matters are finally settled. So please come on at once at our expense and let us talk things over.

This telegram came to me as a shock. I had sent in my resignation at

Indiana and was making all preparations for my new job. I showed
the wire to my friends at the Faculty Club. They said, "What kind of
a college is this? Didn't they throw out Willard Fisher a year or so
ago? And wasn't it Upton Sinclair who said that the day Willard Fisher
was kicked out of Wesleyan University, that college was reduced to the
level of the Garrett Biblical Institute? You'd better stay with us."

But no, I wanted to go back to New England. Wearing a necktie,
an American Legion button in the lapel of my coat, I called at President
Shanklin's office. He turned me over to Dean Nicholson and two
others for questioning. They asked me if I were a Communist. How did
I feel about the League of Nations? I frankly said I still believed in it,
still believed that it would be better than the "balance of power" under
which Europe had been operating. One of my questioners asked why
a teacher of English should be so much interested in politics. My answer was that I had taught argumentation in three colleges, and this
forced on me an acquaintance with public questions. My war experience also had a tendency to make me think long and hard about national affairs, and I hoped that the boys who died in service had not
died in vain. After an hour they let me go, and I made a visit to the
Woodbridges. While I was there Homer received a telephone call from
the Dean, saying that I had survived the interrogation and was satisfactory to the administration.

So I returned to Bloomington, somewhat subdued, and finished
out the semester. Some students begged me not to leave Indiana but I
had already made my decision. I hated to leave the good friends I had
made on the faculty. Going to a straight boys' college, I would miss the
beautiful southern Indiana girls who brightened my classes. I would
miss the Indiana countryside, too, which I had grown to love. The
beech trees, the magnolias, the redbirds, the soft gentle climate, and
the unspoiled hills and valleys—all these made me wonder why I had
accepted a call to the bleak, cold country of New England. But the
relation of a man to the soil on which he was born is a powerful reality,
and the homing instinct is one of the strongest in human nature. So I
reluctantly said good-bye to the many friends I had made and headed
East.

CHAPTER 16

Early Married Days and Honeymoon in France

Now the best vacation of my life was opening to me. Armed with a sharp increase in salary, I had one purpose—to woo and win Jeannette Simmons. My friends the Otises arranged a meeting at their home and the siege began. Her mother's coolness did not deter me from bombarding Jeannette with calls and dates to keep, morning through evening. I found that Jeannette had warm blood in her veins and was not unwilling to give a little boost to my project. One morning on Main Street when I was engaged in a long talk with a Bowdoin classmate, I saw her crossing over to our side of the street. In another minute she would pass close by. Why did she cross to the eastern side of the street when her home was on the western? Ask *her!* I have never stopped teasing the bold hussy about this crossing.

I escorted her home where I met and talked with her mother. Mrs. Simmons was a thoroughbred who had little use for people who were less than thoroughbred. Her definition of this word included neat appearance, good family, an interest in books and reading, an admiration for success in business, and an unswerving devotion to the Republican Party. She thought the Democratic Party was made up of drunks, wastrels, and shanty Irish. They didn't belong in her world. (I once found her listening to a radio speech by Al Smith. She blushed as if I had caught her with nothing on but her petticoats.) She was uncommonly good-looking for a middle-aged woman and gave fastidious attention to her grooming. She was as unlike most of the women I knew at Spruce Head as Queen Victoria was unlike her Hottentot subjects in Africa. I plainly saw that I was unsuitable as a son-in-law.

Later in August Jeannette came to stay at the Inn on Spruce Head Island. She was the city overseer of the poor in Rockland and was tired from taking care of the indigent, the ill, and the wayward. She needed a real rest.

I fear Jeannette got little rest on this vacation. I wanted to be with her morning, noon, and night. At first she slowed me down by asking me not to come until after lunch. Later she suggested that I should be working on my new book and I might call in the afternoon or evening, but not both. I could not keep to any such rigid schedule and turned up at odd hours, always armed with an excuse. Even so, I was not seeing her often enough to suit me. To show her how I felt, I wrote and sent her this verse:

> To let this moonlit night slip by
> With never a glimpse of you, dear heart,
> Is sin against the night itself,
> The sin that tears me wide apart.
>
> If there be sins more deadly yet
> I know them not—I only know
> The surge of Love that sweeps me through
> The gates that guard you—and I go!

We found time to go rowing in an old thirteen-foot dory and visit White Head Island, where I was born. We went swimming, took long walks through the woods along the shore, and had long talks together.

One evening when leaving for home I demanded a long kiss. She was willing and performed so nobly that I was set on fire. But when I began nudging her toward the sofa she broke away and ran upstairs. She did not know what to make of such an aggressive suitor. I saw I was scaring her off, and I went home to Spruce Head to think it over. The next time I went to the Inn I apologized to her for my rough treatment and promised that if—no, *when*—we were married she would find me more affectionate than passionate. I really believed that—I did, and I was so humble and sincere that Jeannette believed it too. So on September 9, 1921, as we were walking through a spruce grove we became engaged.

I wanted to get married at once but her mother said, "No, one must wait a proper length of time after an engagement." "How long?" said I. "Until June." I said I could not wait that long. I suggested Christmas, and she said that would be too soon. We compromised and settled on Washington's Birthday, Thursday, February 22. We planned a simple home wedding.

A superstitious person reviewing our wedding day would have prophesied a divorce within six months, for all the signs and portents pointed to doom.

First of all, the date had to be changed. I had assumed that Washington's Birthday would be a holiday at the college and a man's marriage would be considered important enough to warrant another free day. Not at all. President Shanklin was displeased with my request to leave town with college in full session. He said I would have to find substitutes for all my Thursday and Friday classes. Other members of the English Department graciously helped me out, but even so, I could not reach Rockland by noon on Thursday. I telephoned Jeannette and we agreed on Friday, the twenty-third. Postponement of the wedding was a bad sign.

The second misfortune was the illness of the five-year-old nephew who was to be the ring-bearer. On the train from New Jersey he developed a case of chicken pox. So we moved the wedding—flowers, collation, and all—from Jeannette's home to a friend's house two doors down the street. This change was undeniably a portent of calamity.

Not exactly a sign but an unpleasant incident was Mrs. Simmons' refusal to invite Dr. Crockett, a friend of mine but a convicted abortionist, of whom I wrote in an earlier chapter. Jeannette was on my side in this argument, but since she was hurting her mother by consigning her to live alone the rest of her life, she could not press the point.

Another mishap! We forgot to send a cab for the minister, who had to walk a half-mile in a snowfall.

In spite of all these untoward circumstances, the wedding was a happy one. About forty friends and relatives were "gathered together to seek the Lord's blessing" upon us. Even Mrs. Simmons went through the final leave-taking without a tear. One of her most trusted friends, instead of commiserating with her, had said firmly, "Annie, you have had your life; now let Jeannette have hers." This had made an impression on Jeannette's mother and did away with most of her self-pity.

I was pleased to hear my Aunt Agnes whisper to a cousin, "I'm glad Wilbert didn't get a *poultice!*" "Poultice" was the standard word for most of the unlovely brides brought home by Spruce Head boys. And William O. Fuller, the editor of the local newspaper, said to me, "Wilbert, however high you go in your career, you have a wife who can go along with you!"

The part of that day I remember with deep pleasure was the drive to the train. Large flakes of snow were floating gently all around us. Since my wife's great-grandfather was Elisha Snow, a Snow had on this day married a Snow, and the gentle fall of flakes seemed like a blessing from Heaven descending upon us.

Jeannette's mother wanted our first night to be at Young's Hotel in Boston, where she had spent her first night of marriage. This was an establishment that had seen better days. It was run down and shabby. The clerk saw the rice on our coats and assigned us to a room that had only a single bed. We made no complaint. Luxurious surroundings were not necessary. We simply wanted to be near each other and that was happiness enough.

We spent Saturday and Sunday in Boston visiting the art museum, taking in a show, walking around Boston Common, and talking about our future. We decided to spend the summer in France. This would be our real honeymoon. Financing the trip would be a problem, but since we were going to share a house and its expenses with Professor William Gerrish and his wife Grace, from whom I had been renting a room, we were confident of piling up savings the rest of the academic year. Also I had a life insurance policy on which we could borrow money. I was sure we could manage.

We reached the Gerrish house in the late afternoon of Sunday, to find that Grace had invited a few friends to welcome us and, I suspected, to get the first look at my bride. I could see that Jeannette was passing the test and I felt very proud.

Two women under one roof, the Chinese symbol for war, did not apply in this case. The girls got on very well. There were a few rough spots. Grace was a trained nurse and a stickler for cleanliness and order. My mother had failed to teach me to fold a towel and hang it smoothly on the bar. My towel was often on the floor or at best bunched up and thrust over a corner of the bar. If Grace found it this way before Jeannette had time to retrieve it, she was troubled. One day my wife was beating icing for a cake in a pan resting on a newspaper. Grace was horrified. "No, please," she said. "Newsprint is poisonous and that pan will go into the dishpan with other dishes!"

Bill Gerrish was a man of very refined sensibilities. He could speak of a limb but never a leg. On the dining room wall we drew up an imaginary list of unpleasant subjects taboo at the dinner table. If I carelessly strayed onto one of these subjects, Gerrish would shift in his chair and stare at the blank wall. That was enough! With a laugh, I steered the conversation into safer channels.

In the spring of the year Jeannette became pregnant and for some reason that I could not fathom did not want Mrs. Gerrish to know that she was already "on the road to Boston," as the Spruce Head people used to say. Jeannette went to the breakfast table day after day when her stomach was upset and she shouldn't have gone downstairs. But, in an old-fashioned way, she wanted her secret to be completely her own.

On the whole, we were a happy family of four. Laughter prevailed. Grace taught Jeannette a good deal about cooking, also how to press a man's pants and iron his shirt.

These early days of married life were the happiest I had ever known. There was a strong urge in me to express how I felt by writing verse. Like Pope, "I lisped in numbers, for the numbers came." Some of the verses I dropped into the wastebasket. Some I sold to magazines like *Snappy Stories* under an assumed name. And a few I kept. One of these was titled "Abélard to Héloise"; its first stanza reads:

> I love you when you loose your chains,
> Let passion gallop through;
> When not a single check restrains
> Your smiling disregard for reins
> I lose myself in you.

Our plans for a trip to France were taking shape. I borrowed on my insurance policy and with what we had saved, we faced the summer with $800. (Sober members of the English Department told us we should be spending our money on furniture, for we had none. Of course they were right, but we were full of adventure and both wanted desperately to spend the summer in France.) Then, the morning we left home, a check for $50 came from *Scribner's Magazine* for a poem entitled "Country Funeral." That was like manna from Heaven. I thought of another morning in my life when the mail brought me a desperately needed check for $75 from Professor Charles T. Burnett of Bowdoin. I concluded that some ministering angel must have been keeping watch over me, conscious of my hours of great need.

We now had $850 for the summer, and our third-class round-trip fares would account for about half of it. As we were going to France, we picked a French ship for the outward voyage: the *Paris*, fastest liner of the Compagnie Générale Transatlantique, for we had heard monstrous tales of steerage conditions and wanted to make the ordeal as short as possible. We reserved by mail a two-berth cabin at $100 apiece, the tickets to be picked up and paid for the day before sailing—as it turned out, in a dreary basement room below the glittering offices of

EARLY MARRIAGE SONG

Your hair is a sun-caressed garden
Through which I leisurely stroll
Breathing the musk of roses.

Your eyes are quiet coves
Into whose waters white birch limbs
Cast dappled reflections.

The curve of your neck
Is a delicate new moon
Over sycamore trees
In early April twilight.

Your warm pink cheeks
Are tea-rose petals,
Curls linger above them
Like honey-laden bees.

The breath of your nostrils
When fragrant with passion
Is a New England hillside
Fragrant with trailing arbutus
At the first melting onrush of spring.

The soles of your feet
Are water-lily pads
Stirred by evening breezes.

the French Line. We also had a passport to be visaed, at a charge of $5—but only one, for in those days man and wife could travel together on a single passport.

We went to New York by train, took care of the preliminaries, and on sailing day carried our luggage to the pier—Jeannette with two handbags, I with two heavy suitcases. Following the crowd through the delightful turmoil of a sailing day—flowers everywhere, pretty girls and laughing boys shouting farewells and wisecracks across the rail, porters manhandling luggage, and so on—we were brought by a movable stairway to the ship's upper deck. Once there, we were politely told this was not our place; the steerage entrance was toward the stern, nearly the vessel's full length away. So back we went, too happy to feel

Your breasts are ripe pomegranates
Shining through green leaves at dawn
In the Virgin River valley of Utah.

When you stand at the mirror
Disrobing at night,
You are Arethusa,
And the green shimmering robe
Your rippling fountain.

Two dreams that were with me in youth
Took shape at my first glimpse of you:

The first, sunny hours of love
On a long sloping hillside in June,
Green and gray moss underneath,
Evergreen branches above,
And a startling prevision of you.

Then a world out of ugliness moved
Into Danaan beauty—men free

As they dream everywhere to be free—
A world in which Love holds the reins

And rides over Death and Despair;
Such a world I prophetically saw,
Still see emanating from you.

humiliated (though the suitcases had suddenly doubled their weight), to begin our trip all over again by way of a gangplank leading to the lower decks.

Here flowers were noticeably absent, and as for baggage, everyone rolled his own. We found ourselves in a truly international group: Medes, Parthians, Elamites, and dwellers in Mesopotamia—they were all there and all cheerful. A white-coated cabin boy named Jean took us in hand with true French courtesy, found us a couple of canvas deck chairs, and led us to our cabin. More accurately, our cubicle; it was clean but dark and Spartan, measuring about four by seven feet. The metal partitions were open a foot at the bottom and more than that at the top; the springless bunks, one above the other, had straw mattresses, feather pillows, coarse linen, and rough wool blankets. There was a white porcelain washbowl for running water, with a good mirror and an electric bulb, and there was a small rug on the cement floor. Any fresh air came through a porthole at the far end of the passageway. When Jeannette complained of the hard mattress, Jean found her a better one, plus additional pillows and a second rug for the floor. He also let us keep the cabin key, which was against the ship's rules. (A ten-franc tip at our first meeting probably played some part in these favors.) He then led us up three flights to the open foredeck reserved for steerage passengers, and placed our deck chairs for us. At this point the bell rang for *déjeuner*, our first meal aboard.

The way to the dining saloons led past the engine room and the galley. The combined odors of their hot steam, oily cotton waste, and cabbage soup became a thrice-daily ordeal and proved to be almost the only unavoidable hardship of steerage travel.

But no! I must add my wife's experience of the women's "john." She followed directions, opened the right door, and found herself in a long narrow room. Along one side was a metal trench through which water rushed noisily; and over it, the length of the room, was a pipe three or four inches in diameter. Here sat a woman with her buttocks thrust back over the water—no partitions, no curtains, no privacy. My wife was shocked. She ducked out fast, waited until the woman had left and the coast was clear, then went in and came out as quickly as possible, doubly thankful that this was the swiftest ship of the line! (The counterpart for men was similar, but after a couple of years in the Army I could put up with almost anything.)

That first *déjeuner* gave us a good look at our fellow passengers, a motley crowd. There were a few quasi-intellectual young ladies, akin to Don Marquis' Hermione, who were out for a lark among the lower classes ("Steerage would be just wonderful, don't you know"); but one look at the rest of us and they weakened on the spot and had themselves transferred to second class. For the rest, there were a group of Italians at the table next to ours; twenty jolly Frenchmen with war decorations behind us; five American doughboys returning for a drink of wine and a kiss to a land they had once cursed extravagantly; a score of Yugoslavs, Poles, and Lithuanians going back to help rebuild their newly liberated countries; two elderly and uncertain American mothers on a pilgrimage to the graves of their soldier sons; several college undergraduates out for adventure and experience; two old Alsatians returning to their native land after fifty-five years away—one of them a religious fanatic who spoke constantly of the Second Coming, the other a hardened agnostic who advised the boys to drink wine and improve their blood. There was also a Syrian with an olive-green complexion and disgusting table manners, who at every meal ate three or four times as much as anyone else.

As for the food, every day there was onion soup for breakfast. Other meals always brought cabbage soup and *vin rouge*. For the main dish, it was *boeuf à la Bourguignon, sauté de mouton printanier, civet de mouton*, and so on—which sounded very grand but turned out to be soups and stews, soups and stews, soups and stews. These were served at well-scrubbed tables, without linen, on dishes of the "inch-thick" variety. (If one did not relish this fare, one could—and an undergraduate from Pennsylvania regularly did—get enough to eat from the ship's canteen: apples and oranges at a nickel each, sweet biscuits and candy at Park & Tilford prices.) But our last dinner afloat, on the run from Plymouth to Le Havre, made up for all. That evening we coped with a banquet of bouillon, roast chicken, mashed potatoes, romaine salad, and cherry ice cream. With that meal, the hour for *pourboires* had come, and nobly did we respond. I had intended to tip the *garçon* five francs in orderly third-class fashion, but this one meal was so good that I doubled it.

There is not much for passengers to do on a ship, and we all spent a lot of time on deck. The section for steerage passengers, at the bows, was decidely a choice spot in good weather. To see the lime-green water curl up and break as the liner butted her way along, and to loaf within easy hearing of the tumbling waves, was the best part of ocean travel. On our first evening we were accompanied by a shoal of porpoises racing through the waves and playing leapfrog like children about to be sent to bed, thoroughly conscious of the fact that they were giving us a good show. On the next day there was more wind blowing and the water had changed from green to blue-black; we were now in the Gulf Stream, with floating rafts of Sargasso weed and an occasional Portuguese man-o'-war or ocean sunfish. Beyond the Gulf Stream, the North Atlantic was a gray and rather unattractive ocean, with few sights of interest until we raised the Scilly Isles and their lighthouse after five days at sea.

We did, to be sure, have one bad day—the third, when a big wind kicked up choppiness in the sea and in the stomachs of the passengers.

Only good sailors—and not all of them (witness my wife)—escaped the deathlike feeling. Even Mothersill's remedy was of little help and came in for a large share of curses. So much seasickness kept the cabin boys busy with mop and pail, and the stench was more than we could bear. So we climbed the long companionways to the open deck, but wind, rain, and waves forced us to take refuge in a little forward deckhouse. Jeannette sat in the only open doorway, that to leeward, where she was an obstruction to sailors going about their work, yet the courteous Frenchmen never once asked her to move.

Over the days a marked change took place in the relations among the passengers. At first we had been so many individuals, keeping much to ourselves, but on the second evening the steerage began to sing, helped along by the heavy patronage accorded the bar (Bacchus is still the god of song). The Yugoslavs started it, led by a charming egotist with a big broad face and a mouthful of gold fillings. Another night it was a merry crowd of Frenchmen, with mandolin and guitar. One of their Paris street songs stood out above all others, and became in effect the "theme song" of our voyage:

> Sous les ponts de Paris
> Lorsque descend la nuit,
> Toutes sortes de queux se faufillent en cachette,
> Dans l'espoir de trouver une couchette;
> Hôtel du Courant Air,
> Ou l'on ne paye pas cher,
> Julot partage les baisers de Mimi
> Sous les ponts de Paris.

We learned the words of that song from Madame G., the largest-souled, most generous-natured woman among us. She was fat, slightly gray, wore bedroom slippers over white stockings on deck, and had a jollity that was contagious. When she laughed, she rippled in such a magnetic, wholehearted way that everyone was hypnotized into laughing with her. When she sat down to table, she raised her glass of *vin rouge* and toasted anyone or anything that caught her eye. Yet Madame G. had seen some grim times. All her sons, she told us, were resting in the fields of Artois. When the Germans occupied Lille, she and her husband had refugeed to Pittsburgh, where their daughter joined them later. Now the three were going home to manage a *pension* and cater to rich American tourists. Not even such events, it seemed, could dampen her *joie de vivre*. She sang so lustily that everybody nearby wanted to join in, whether they could sing or not.

Folk songs are appealing even when one cannot make out the foreign words, and I felt more strongly than ever that a ballad lover ought to be a linguist with a memory like an elephant's. By the third day all the passengers felt better acquainted, trusted each other with confidences, and talked as if they were comrades. As the barriers fell, argument followed argument all over the steerage deck.

The main topic was America. "America no good any more. No pleasure. All prohibition, that foolishness. Home brew bad. Moonshine no good. A few men spoil America. A few men treat, treat everybody in the room. Then all must treat. Then go home dead broke Saturday night. Wife hungry, children hungry. These few men spoil America." That, as Carl Sandburg might have said, was one song of the steerage. Others insisted that prohibition was merely one factor in their dissatisfaction. America's rush—"money-making madness," they called it—caused all the trouble. In the old country they could have more fun, more life, on much less money. The people who spoke thus were of course the disappointed ones, the disgruntled. They had come as to a Promised Land, expecting to get rich in a few years. They had found an ugly place of mills, mines, and factories; they had made good wages but costs were exorbitantly high and the way of living strange, and they were almost as poor as ever. Now they were returning to their homelands, and if these did not measure up—well, there was Russia.

Strangely enough, America also found her most vigorous champions among these people. Many of them had tried a dozen countries, and they avowed that America was best for the workingman. Nearly all agreed that they would advocate American hygiene and sanitation—cleanliness in general, bathtubs and toilets in particular. America's real contribution to the world, they insisted, was a porcelain bathtub for the poor as well as for the capitalists.

One old Italian who had sailed into all the ports of the world defended the States more stoutly than any other. He remembered when some of these very people had come in through Ellis Island—that Malebolge of immigrants—with one shirt, no collar, and their few personal effects tied up in a red bandanna. Now, he pointed out, they had a collar on the shirt, additional shirts in their traveling bags, two or even three suits of clothes, and a pocket full of money.

From America the discussion drifted into world politics, and at times grew so animated that I thought the master at arms would have to be summoned. Our college boys, who had hitherto looked upon these immigrants as illiterate nobodies, began to show a wide-eyed wonder at their political and economic acumen. It was a delight to see the transformed respect of these boys when it dawned on them that an immigrant could have a mind as keen as a razor and an extensive knowledge of world affairs. The boundary dispute over Lithuania; the articles of the League of Nations Covenant; the state papers of Tchicherin; the Arms Conference; the Turkish situation—these were some of the topics which gave the steerage intelligentsia a chance to show how much they knew.

On June 20 we made Plymouth at four in the afternoon. All hands were on deck for this first near sight of land, and first-class passengers threw down boxes of candy for third-class children as a thank offering for their deliverance from the terrors of the Atlantic. Two lay missionaries, well-dressed women of about thirty, felt this joy so keenly that they came down from the first-class deck and began to preach about the wonderful message of the Son of God. One of our college boys asked whether they thought Christ would go first class or steerage if He were traveling the Atlantic today. The question disconcerted them, and the boy was chivalrous enough not to press his advantage.

These missionaries were the vanguard of an inspection tour of the whole ship, open to first- and second-class passengers. Thirty or forty of them, mostly women, came to see how we poor immigrants fared. They were shown our berths, our recreation quarters, our *salles à manger*, and most interesting of all, ourselves. Their cameras were busy taking our pictures, and we retaliated by taking theirs. The expression of self-conscious superiority on some of their faces was an interesting study. The steerage people deeply resented this tour, which robbed them of the respect their pride demanded.

At Plymouth we sent ashore, by launch, three or four hundred bags of mail and some seventy-five passengers. Then we weighed anchor for France, with our gala final dinner en route. We tied up at Le Havre at five the next morning, June 21. They routed us out at five-thirty—no breakfast, nothing to eat or drink—and herded us into the dining rooms to wait. After three hours we were marched around to have our passports examined, and were handed our little blue landing tickets. Then back to our *salles* again—this time for an hour and fifty minutes—until our patience was exhausted and, without waiting for directions, we went up the gangplank and stepped ashore. For all any of us knew, we might have done this an hour or more earlier.

From Le Havre we took a train for Paris. The landscape of Normandy so fascinated me that I stood up and gazed almost all the way.

The poppies in the fields, the kitchen gardens with flowers around the edges, the stone cottages in which generations of families must have lived, strange birds and strange trees—all these were intriguing to American eyes. I was so wrapped up in what I was seeing that when I got off at Rouen to buy Jeannette a sandwich—remember, we had had no breakfast—I forgot to buy one for myself. But I did not forget that Rouen was the city in which my favorite woman in history, Joan of Arc, was burned at the stake.

Arriving in Paris, we climbed into a horse-drawn cab and were driven to the Hôtel de Nice on the Rue des Beaux-Arts, where we engaged for a month a sixth-floor room overlooking the street. There was no elevator, so we had to walk that dreary distance—a severe hardship on Jeannette, who made it only once a day. Our *café au lait* and *croissants* were brought up by a maid each morning at eight. Jeannette remained in bed while I worked on my poetry. But often I went out alone and explored the city. I did not go to famous places—the streets of Paris were sufficient for me. The tradesmen with horses and carts singing their wares as they walked slowly along were something I never tired of. They could, for example, make a song by intoning the word *haricot*—"Ha-ri-co-ooo." The flower girls arranging their stands for the day; a lone artist painting a long Paris street after the style of Utrillo; a cabbie currying his horse and standing off to admire his handiwork; a boulevardier stumbling back to his lodgings after a night on the town; all these morning sights interested me. On one of these walks I bought a small watercolor from an impoverished artist whose dungaree trousers were unraveled around the edges (not the style in 1922!), bought it for six francs, and carried it home to Jeannette. I don't think I ever did a thing in my life that pleased her more.

On days when I was not exploring I worked on my first book, *Maine Coast*. It had already been accepted by Harcourt, Brace & Company, and I was trying to smooth out the rough spots in the lines. (I am almost never satisfied with a poem. I revise it, work it over, even after it is published in book form.) This chore was endless but it was one I enjoyed.

At noontime Jeannette dressed and we went in search of a cheap restaurant for our déjeuner. We looked in at the famous places such as the Café de la Paix and Maxime's, read the bills of fare pasted up in the windows, and shuddered at the prices. On any side street in the Latin Quarter we could get a good meal for about five francs (the franc was then eleven for a dollar). We talked in French with the people eating at these restaurants, found out what they were doing, found out also the slave wages some of them were receiving, and got far better acquainted with Paris than we would have done if we had gone to the usual tourist spots. At these cheap restaurants the food was often very good and the conversation was better. Two girls who made a living coloring picture post cards were very friendly with us. After we had eaten with them three or four times, I asked them if I could come to their shop and see them in action. They consulted their boss and he said No. I later found out that their shop was so shabby, cribbed, and confined that he did not want us to see its poverty.

On the advice of Henry Bourdin we ate one day at the Café Petite Chaumière, where he said we would see impoverished students and artists with their models gathered for lunch. We found the place, sat down, and enjoyed listening to the young people. Now and then a young man near us would lift the top of his girl's dress and peek in at her bare breasts. At this the boys and girls all around broke into laughter. Although the restaurant was anything but first class, these kids were having a first-class time.

We visited the Louvre for thirteen straight days. The paintings pleased me most, and I literally lived with them for two weeks. One day I was so much taken with da Vinci's "La Belle Ferronière" that I wrote a sonnet to her.

My fourteenth trip to the Louvre was made with Roscoe Hupper, a Bowdoin classmate and dear friend who was touring Europe first class. We spent all the afternoon in the top story viewing models of watercraft—everything from the crudest early rafts to the magnificent transatlantic liners of the twentieth century, arranged in chronological order. Roscoe was an admiralty lawyer, and this display of shipping carriers interested him more than the priceless pictures on the lower floors. He knew our financial limitations and took us to a first-class hotel for a sumptuous dinner. We had an interesting glimpse of the Paris wealthy tourists know, but we were fish out of water!

One day we came across the restaurant named the Dôme, at the crossing of the boulevards Montparnasse and Raspail, in which Lenin and Trotsky formulated the plans for the Bolshevik Revolution. We did not eat there, but I stood and looked at the corner in which the two Russians talked and planned, and felt the fragility of the episodes that go into the making of history. These two human beings, steeped and saturated in Karl Marx's *Das Capital*—their Bible—sat in the corner of this restaurant, drank coffee, and made plans to shape a new world. Alas for their dreams! They merely succeeded in replacing one authoritarian dictatorship with another of their own.

We were rigidly holding our expenses down to thirty-five francs a day. If we bought a book on any given day, we were not able to have a restaurant lunch. On such days we bought a loaf of French bread and some cheese and ate on a bench in Luxembourg Gardens. One day we noticed an old man hungrily watching us eat. We left some of the food on the bench, walked off, then glanced behind. He had dropped over to the bench and his face was buried in the paper wrappings of our cheese. There were people in Paris who were poorer than we were.

The Luxembourg Gardens made a restful, inspiring spot of shade that I couldn't get enough of. I thought, as I sat there, of Vachel Lindsay's lines, "We should build parks that students from afar / Would choose to starve in rather than go home." We both knew a girl who did just that. She was having a summer in Paris with her husband, and when the time came for them to take a boat home, she announced that she wasn't going. She had planned, like Ezra Pound, to live in Paris on fifteen or twenty francs a day and spend her time in the parks she loved like this one.

At the Trocadéro, arranged in chronological order, were examples of French architecture from the twelfth century on. This visit was an education in itself. The care for technical exactitude struck me as a particularly French trait. I had noticed it most in French poetry, where every individual syllable counts. With a few exceptions such as the work of Victor Hugo, Jules Laforgue, and Paul Fort, French poetry had seemed to me always too much hemmed in and cramped by its overattention to technique. In some cases—as with Racine, for example—the devout attention to technique was an asset; but over all, I felt that French poetry lacked the superb sweep and gusto of English poetry, where the stress is on the natural accent and is not hampered by an accounting for every individual syllable. Matthew Arnold's pronouncement that "France was superior in everything but supreme in nothing" had its chain and anchor right here. He meant that France had never produced a supreme poet like Dante or Shakespeare or possibly Goethe.

One Saturday morning I ran unexpectedly into a young lady whom I had met at the Harvard Summer School in 1910. She was Grace Guest, whose occupation was research in the history of art for the Freer Museum in Washington. She told me she was going the next day to Rheims to get a good look at the cathedral. I said, "Let's go together." So the next morning the three of us took a train out of the Gare d' Est. On the way Grace shocked us by telling about her landlady in Paris, who said she would work her knees to the bone to give her son money enough to keep a mistress. That opened a new world to all three of us innocent New Englanders.

Arrived at Rheims, I looked over the damage inflicted on the city by the German artillery. As an artilleryman in World War I, I could see that the gunners had sought to avoid hitting the Cathedral. Buildings all around it were struck and reduced to ashes or cellar holes, in many of which families were now living. A few shots did hit the Cathedral and set fire to the roof, but anyone who has directed batteries knows that some shots will fall over or fall short in spite of any precaution one may take. I tried to argue this point with some French natives but they said No. They insisted that the Huns deliberately tried to wreck their famous and beloved Cathedral, which was still intact enough for services.

We attended Mass in the Cathedral, then found a good restaurant in a building that had partially escaped the bombardment. I ordered a bottle of Beaujolais to start off with. We had no more than begun with the wine when a big Alaskan dog came in the door and ran across the room. I was excited, stood up, and said, "My heavens! That looks like a real Alaskan malemute!" At that the manager, who had been watching us from a corner, came to our table and said, "Do you know anything about Alaskan malemutes?" I said, "Yes, I lived on the Seward Peninsula in 1911 and 1912." He said, "Did you know Scotty Allen?" I said, "Yes." "Did you know Fox Ramsey?" "Yes, he was a remittance man and a great fellow for dog racing." He then yelled out, "Waiter, come here! Take that Beaujolais off the table, go down cellar, and bring a bottle of that ——." I did not catch the name. but the waiter did as ordered and brought up a bottle of ancient vintage covered with cobwebs. The manager himself opened it and poured into our glasses the finest wine I had ever tasted. We drank to the manager's health, to Alaska, to Scotty Allen (who had brought these dogs over to France to help in the winning of World War I,) and to the France we all loved. The manager's English was good, and we argued once more about the German bombardment of Rheims, I insisting that the artillery shells which struck the cathedral were not intentional, and he arguing that they were.

The Cathedral itself meant first of all to me the place where Joan of Arc had crowned Charles VII king, and I wrote a sonnet describing my feelings:

RHEIMS CATHEDRAL (1922)

The psalm-like music of the centuries
This tall and stately bride of Christ has sung,
Inspiring pilgrim souls, now lifts a tongue
Of broken accents, void of harmonies,
To frayed, indignant minds,—imploring these,
The remnant who have heard her glad chimes rung,
To stay the crushed and broken doors among,
And bear new sorrows with her Prince of Peace.

Forgive me, Rheims! but my heart twines about
The Maid who stood here centuries ago
And crowned a puppet King: never so stout,
So pure a heart was France again to know;
Like Christ, her Lord, she faltered, then went out
In flames that still light Heaven with their glow.

Wandering around Paris, we often sat and rested in one of the many churches scattered about and studied the pale women in deep mourning who were praying there, seeking the comfort the Christian religion could give them. Some of their faces were beautiful; others, not beautiful, showed a wistfully quiescent resignation. Some time later I tried to capture the moment in a sonnet titled "In a Paris Church."

We visited the tomb of Napoleon, that "magnificent mausoleum of gilt and gold fit only for a dead Deity," as Robert Ingersoll phrased it. I felt half-ashamed of being in that rotunda looking down on the tomb and thinking of the sorrows its occupant had brought on the people of France. I thought of the half-million soldiers who had gone with him to Russia and the pitiful 35,000 that came back. As a boy I had learned by heart Ingersoll's brief piece of grand rhetoric on this subject, and I repeated it to Jeannette while other visitors looked at me with curiosity. The last sentence of that speech, in which he calls Napoleon "that imperial impersonation of force and murder," echoed how I felt about war; for we had failed to ratify the treaty containing the League of Nations, and the boys who had died in my own regiment had nothing to show for their sacrifices.

Before leaving Paris we made a day trip to Amiens. Jeannette was so weak and shivery with a cold that she would not enter the chilly, dark, damp cathedral. Sitting outside in the warm sunshine was the only comfort she could find. So I had to go in alone. Outside the door a very attractive French girl tried to sell me an engraving of "The Smiling Virgin." When I looked over the various reproductions of this famous feature of Amiens, I found not one of them satisfactory, and refused to buy; she cried out, "Je suis désolée." I thought how well that cry fitted Jeannette's condition, and went back to comfort her. She insisted that I go in and examine the interior, which I did. But I was not aware of much of anything except Jeannette's illness. The cry of that salesgirl matched my mood.

The month in Paris came to an end. We planned to go south to see two of France's finest cathedrals, Chartres and Bourges, then west down the Loire to Saint-Nazaire. From there we would follow the coast around Brittany to Mont-Saint-Michel and on to Cherbourg, where we were to take ship for home.

As we packed up our garments, shoes, and books, I suggested that we forward the heaviest of the luggage to Cherbourg, travel light, and make a few more side trips. I asked the American Express agent to send two heavy bags on ahead to meet the boat. The agent called a taxi, whose driver refused to handle third-class matter. The dialogue between the two was spirited and lengthy, but he finally yielded when the agent told him we were Americans. That seemed to make it O. K. for him to handle third-class baggage!

Our first stop was at Chartres. We checked our bags at the railroad station and walked through the streets of the town looking for a sign in a window, "Chambre à louer." We soon found one in the window of a restaurant in the central square. It was a neat second-floor room for six francs a night, and the people were very friendly. The toilet, however, outdid the one on the *paquebot Paris*. It was a small, windowless room with a concrete floor that sloped from all sides to a hole about eight inches in diameter. One had to stand or scootch over this hole and try not to breathe in the horrible stench that rose from below.

It was my misfortune to take my turn having a cold here—with chills, then fever, then chills, and so on. In spite of my wretchedness, I couldn't keep away from the cathedral. We lingered there, day following day, to give me time to recover. Every afternoon I got out of bed and walked to the cathedral. To me it was a revelation. I had never believed that an edifice could move me emotionally as a great well-rendered symphony does, but here I stood with tears blurring my eyesight. The twelfth-century tower, the nave, the great rose window, the Tree-of-Jesse window, the side chapels splashed with the matchless deep red and blue of the glass wherever the sun could get through, all these stirred me to the depths of my being. Nothing made by the toil of human hands had ever affected me like this. Here for once was a revelation that I could not bring myself to record in poetry, for I knew the verse would be inadequate.

My first impression of Bourges was unsatisfactory. Neither of the two towers has a spire. The towers seem too short for the building and the façade seems built on too large a scale. The façade is crowded with five portals instead of the usual three. However, a close view of the sculpture in the central portal made me forget all criticism. It depicts the Last Judgment, with the righteous coming up out of their graves, and the unrighteous chased by imps, bitten by wasps, and beaten by devils. The interior has a spaciousness and solidity that is strengthened by the absence of transepts, "a tranquil largeness," as Henry James wrote, that "soothes and purifies the spirit . . . illuminates the mind."

The five cathedrals we visited gave the lie to Matthew Arnold's pronunciamento that France was supreme in nothing. The vastness and beauty of these edifices, from façade to crypt, lifted our spirits as would a sunrise on Penobscot Bay.

In the course of time we came to Concarneau, a fishing town on the coast of Brittany. Tourism had not spoiled it. The men were real fishermen, every day out in their boats with their orange and deep blue sails. They paid no attention to strangers strolling about the town. The women wore lovely starched white bonnets whether they were going to church or were on their knees scrubbing a floor.

Late one afternoon, while I was writing, Jeannette walked down to the beach to see the fishing boats come sailing home. Not ten minutes later she came into our room and fell across the bed, very pale and seemingly quite exhausted. "What is the matter?" I asked. Half-crying, she told me, "I slipped on the seaweed and fell down on my back with a crash." I went over and put my arms around her. "Are you hurt?" "I haven't broken any bones, but I was so afraid for the baby that I just lay there a few minutes without moving. Then I turned over, got up on my knees, and struggled to my feet. Oh Bill, losing this baby would be more than I could bear!" "It would certainly ruin this trip," I thought to myself. I put her to bed and had supper sent up. In the morning she was as strong as ever. Already the baby must have had a firm grip on life and didn't want to be lost!

On our first afternoon at Mont-Saint-Michel we took a long walk out on the sand, which almost proved disastrous. The coast reminded me a little of the Maine coast, but I did not realize that when the tide began to flood it came with a rush and overwhelmed everything before it. A quarter of a mile from the Mount we saw it coming and turned hurriedly back. We could hear the water creeping up behind us and felt a terrible fear. As we got near the Mount and our feet were ankle deep in water, Jeannette became almost too tired and weak to go on. I had to drag her across brooklike ravines as we neared the end of our journey in water up to our knees. We finally made it. Jeannette went to bed and stayed there. She couldn't come down for supper, though we had planned to indulge in the famous omelets of Madame Poulard. She fell asleep and I went out to walk around the island once more. I could share a little of Henry Adams' enthusiasm for the monastery up on the Mount, but I had none of the architectural or historical background that he had and remained uninspired by the architecture which he describes so minutely and so lovingly.

Two priests walking out on the sand later that night (the tide had turned) caught my attention. They were deep in discussion—so deep that they did not notice tourists who passed them and wondered what they were saying. I watched them for a long time, went to our room and wrote the first draft of the following sonnet:

AT MONT-SAINT-MICHEL

Down from Mont-Saint-Michel when sunset traced
The Abbey window panes with green and gold,
Two sable-suited monks devoutly paced
Far out upon the desert sand to hold
Converse of things eternal: one, a youth,
The Emmaus-journey marvel in his eyes;
The other ancient, steadfast in the Truth
Preached on the Mount for fifteen centuries.
High on the Rock in vision reappears,
Through dusk inpouring like a great spring tide,
A line of kings spanning a thousand years,
To view the station of their former pride;
Their pomp is gone, but sons of Saint Aubert
Still walk the self-same sands and speak his prayer.

At Cherbourg we were ferried out to the *James K. Polk* of the American Presidents Line. We two were given a cabin with bunks for four, giving us room to spread out. All I could think of for a while was the contrast between third-class accommodations on this American ship and steerage on the *Paris*. Our tickets were labeled "Tourist Third Class"; the word "steerage" had seemingly passed out of the American language. Our quarters were almost as fine as second-class quarters on the *Paris*. We had clean sheets, comfortable mattresses, a porthole of our own, and decent toilets around the corner. The dining room with silverware and white linen was immaculate enough to make "good digestion wait on appetite and health on both."

The most dramatic moment on the way across occurred in Cork Harbor. There the *Polk* took on a large contingent of Irishmen who were fleeing the civil war raging there. The Irish Free State had been established, but the Sinn Fein was split into two factions, one for the ratification of the treaty with Great Britain, the other for complete separation from everything English. Eamon De Valera led the left-wing faction. At this moment in 1922 he was hiding among the hills of western Ireland. The Free State army was out to capture him.

I was standing on the deck looking out on the deep unbroken green of the Irish landscape when I found myself surrounded by a squad of soldiers, armed and wearing uniforms like those of our boys in World War I, but with patches of green on the shoulders. The leader of the squad informed me that I was De Valera and that they were going to take me ashore and put me in jail. I asked what the jail was like. "You should know!" they said. My wife clung to my arm and said, "If you go to jail I am going with you." The purser of the ship arrived and convinced the leader that I was not De Valera. Taking his solemn word for it, they let me go.

I mingled a great deal with the Irish contingent and will never forget the grief on their faces when word reached us in mid-Atlantic that Michael Collins, leader of the Free State army, had been ambushed and assassinated. Our Irish aboard ship had a memorial service for him on the same afternoon that the news reached us. Volunteer speakers eloquently recalled his bravery, extolled his leadership, and ended the service by singing together the ballad of Kevin Barry.

Whatever social contacts we made on this trip were tame compared with steerage friends we learned to love and admire on the way over. One morning some of the women warned my wife, "Don't get too near to Mrs. Gilley. Her hair is full of lice." Jeannette's curiosity led her to sit near enough to Mrs. Gilley to see the black lice crawling across her forehead along the hair line. One of the women reported to the stewardess, who said, "Never mind now. That will be taken care of."

Two days before we were due in New York, the stewardess came to us and asked us if we would like to have a bath. She had arranged for us to have the use of the infirmary bathrooms on the floor above. We thanked her for her kindness as she showed the way. She suggested that we might like to shampoo our hair at the same time. She helped my wife undo the braids that she wore around her head.

This courtesy was extended to all the other passengers, and most of them were glad enough to bathe in the water of the Gulf Stream we were passing through at the time. A few demurred, saying they might take cold and would rather wait until they got home. These were persuaded to join in the general washup. When Mrs. Gilley flatly refused, the truth came out: the U. S. Department of Health had a rigid rule that all third-class passengers must be bathed and deloused if necessary before they could land. Poor Mrs. Gilley! She had to yield. The nurses worked over her for two days. My wife and I laughed to think that the stewardess had helped with our hair in order to see if we needed the same treatment as Mrs. Gilley!

We arrived in New York City a little after the noon hour. I had $1.35 in my pocket, and that was all. Luckily I did have a key to Roscoe Hupper's bachelor apartment (he was still abroad). So after enjoying the sights and smells of New York we ate a slender bite at a drugstore and went to Roscoe's lodgings. We found beds but no sheets or blankets, only mattress covers and counterpanes. But the night was warm and we were thankful to have four walls and a roof. We could not afford to go to any place of entertainment, so we went to bed early. The next morning I borrowed $35 from my publisher, Alfred Harcourt, left him the manuscript of my first book, and took the train for Middletown.

CHAPTER 17

Rough Days at Wesleyan

Our first business was finding a place to live. It had to be fully furnished for we had not a bed, table, or chair of our own. We stopped at Middletown and quite readily found a house on the corner of Church and Broad streets. It had a hot-air furnace with an enormous coal box, a kitchen that used gas, and more rooms than we needed—all for $50 a month. We went happily off to Maine for a brief visit home, not knowing the troubles we were going to have in that house. It was the year when the coal miners across the country were on strike. Shipload after shipload of fuel came over from Wales, but it was never enough. The dealers looked after their old customers. We could not get more than one quarter of a ton at a time. For the most part we lived in the kitchen, and on bitter nights we sat by the gas stove with our feet in the open doorway of the oven. In spite of this discomfort, we took our place in the academic and social life of the college community.

The Wesleyan we knew in those early '20's was a small college with an excellent reputation in the academic world. The faculty of 49 men were for the most part serious, dedicated teachers. The student body, numbering about 550, was made up largely of businessmen's sons who believed that C was a gentleman's grade. They wanted to have a good time, make friendly contacts, and delightfully prolong the days of their "infancy." A few, sons of ministers, teachers, and missionaries, had academic aspirations. These were a distinct minority. Now and then there was a boy who wanted to become a writer. They were a still smaller minority.

One of these, James Warner Bellah, whom I met at the Short Story Club, showed genuine creative ability in the stories he read before that small group. Bellah spent a whole summer studying the technique of stories published in the *Saturday Evening Post*, and when he was ready to submit his manuscripts to that magazine they were ready to

279

pay him top prices. His first book, *A Cadet of Gascony*, drew heavily upon life at Wesleyan as Hawthorne's first book *Fanshawe* drew its material from life at Bowdoin. A free-thinking Southerner, he depicted Wesleyan as a socially narrow, puritanical, sombre, God-fearing community. My wife and I found it a very agreeable place!

Many of our colleagues could remember when dancing was not permitted at the college, but that was happily in the past. The young Faculty Club put on dances which we attended regularly, for we both loved to dance. On one of these occasions the men lined up along one side of the hall and the women along the other. Each girl took off a shoe and tossed it across the room. The man who picked it up claimed its owner for the next dance, a breathtaking, double-quick waltz. The students were amused when they heard reports of this display of youthful spirits and the next issue of the *Argus*, the college paper, carried the story under the headline: JOHN WESLEY BLUSHES.

For the most part, Wesleyan in the '20's unduly respected the forms of social behaviour. Professors and their wives devoted Sunday afternoons to making formal calls of fifteen minutes (no more!) on friends and on newcomers in particular, leaving the correct number of calling cards on a plate by the door as they went out. The Faculty Club once a year opened its meeting to the ladies, who at other times were relegated to the kitchen, preparing refreshments, unless they were bold enough to sit out of sight on the front stairway and listen to the learned paper being delivered in the next room.

The Monday Club, made up of faculty wives, gave a full-dress party each spring. At one of these gala events the wives of Professor George Dutcher and Professor George Humphrey took out cigarettes and in full view, calmly, without embarrassment, smoked them. The effect on the assembly was electric. One woman whispered to another, "See how she handles it! This can't be the first time!" Some felt that the act indicated the passing of the old Wesleyan, whose Methodism had condemned "softness and self-indulgence" in its ritual of discipline.

My wife played a small part in the struggle for social change. She had her calling cards engraved "Mrs. Jeannette Snow." When they went into circulation I was stopped by the dean's wife, who demanded, "Why doesn't your wife use your name on her calling cards?" "Well, perhaps she wants to preserve a little individuality." "But she is here as your wife!"

When Jeannette found in vogue at the college the English custom of allowing the men at dinner parties to linger at the table for conversation and coffee, joining the ladies later, she was outraged. She enlisted my support and with the Gerrishes planned a new procedure for our next dinner party. After dessert I rose and suggested that we *all* find more comfortable chairs in the living room. "I believe that coffee is waiting for us there." My wife does not claim the credit, but after a while the custom of "joining the ladies later" disappeared from the campus.

These attempts at reform proved to be the least of our troubles. President Shanklin had been given a terminal leave of absence. Until his successor could be found, a charming gentleman named Stephen Olin, son of Wesleyan's second president, filled in as acting president. He loved the college campus where he had played in his childhood. This year as acting president he was singing his swan song, for he died the following year. With his own funds he brought to the college a famous art critic, Royal Cortissoz, to give a series of lectures on art. Those invited were expected to appear in tuxedos and their wives in evening dress. It was an attempt to do something for the arts at Wesleyan, an activity in which this college was lagging far behind others of its kind in New England. The lectures consisted of a defense of tradition and a scorn for the new. The thing the group most enjoyed and remembered was Cortissoz's pronunciation of the word "accessories," which he used frequently, calling it *ac"-cess-o'-ries*, with a heavy accent on the first syllable, a lighter one on the third.

In November I easily persuaded President Olin to offer Sandburg an honorariam and bring him to the campus once again. His first visit had been made in February, 1922. The advance notices had described him as a poet and ballad singer. Posters showing photographs of Carl with his guitar attracted the students. The gym was crowded and the freshmen had to sit on the floor. It was a rousing evening.

Somewhere in his remarks Carl had mentioned Professor Caleb T. Winchester's *Some Principles of Literary Criticism* as the only book on criticism that had ever made sense to him. I took him the next day to call on Mrs. Winchester, and she presented him with some of her husband's favorite books with his priceless comments on the margins. Up to this time Sandburg had not known that the *Methodist Review* in the fall of 1920 had as its first article an essay by Professor Winchester on modern American poets, giving the major honors to Sandburg.

The students had shown such keen interest in ballads I decided that we could have an evening of ballads on our own. So at the Psi Upsilon house I gave a lecture on American ballads followed by ballad singing the rest of the evening. This was a carry-over of my ballad collecting at Indiana University. Two undergraduates, Arthur Sutherland and G. L. Straub, helped mightily with the piano and the guitar. The *Argus* called the evening a "huge success." If so, it was because so much of it had been done by the students themselves.

On Sandburg's second appearance at Wesleyan, he faced another full house. At that time he was putting together his book called *The American Songbag*. Before he took up his guitar he spoke of ballad collecting as an extremely worth-while and enjoyable hobby. Arthur Sutherland confessed that he had taken a tramping trip through the South during the summer vacation and had picked up a number of songs—taking down both the words and the music. One of these, called "Alice B.," fascinated Sandburg and he wanted it for his book. Just under the title Carl placed this amusing story of the source of the ballad:

> This is arranged from the ballad as sung by Arthur Sutherland and the Buccaneers of the Eclectic Club of Wesleyan University. Sutherland, who is the son of a lawyer in Rochester, New York, first heard of Alice B. when he was with the American Relief Expedition in Armenia, riding on top of a box car to Constantinople with a friend who came from New Orleans, Louisiana, and who in that gulf port one day paid $1.50 to a hobo to sing Alice B. as he, the hobo, had just heard it a few days previously in Memphis from a Negro just arriving from Galveston, Texas. This is as far back as we have traced the Alice B. ballad. Though the verses have wicked and violent events for a theme, they point a moral and adorn a tale in their conclusion. In a sense the ballad is propaganda in favor of the Volstead act.

Sandburg often spent the night with me when he was performing in nearby New Haven or Hartford and he always asked about Sutherland, long since graduated. When I told him that Art had become a professor of law at Harvard Law School he said: "Another good vagabond and troubadour gone to hell!"

Early in December of 1922 I received a summons to Vice-President LeRoy Howland's office. I knew he was handling dismissals, for Olin did not wish to take any part in this unpleasant job. I was worried, not for myself for I had weathered many dismissals, but for my pregnant wife. As I approached Howland's office I met a French professor coming out weeping. To Americans a man crying is an unpleasant sight, and this contorted face of a friend whose office in East Hall was next door to my own disturbed and saddened me. Inside, the Vice-President laid out my case. First, I was reported swearing on the tennis courts, an offense which was especially obnoxious to Dr. Fauver, the man in charge of athletics. Secondly, I had used profanity in a debating class when the boys came unprepared and tried to bluff their way through an argument. In the third place, I was reminded that I did not have a Ph.D., a degree which Wesleyan apparently cherished. My lack of a doctorate was the Damoclean sword forever hanging above my head. "For these reasons," said Dr. Howland, "I am sorry to tell you that the college will not need you after the close of the next semester."

"Mr. Howland," I replied, "you need not be sorry, for I have heard this story many times before." Howland was so surprised by my cool response that he reached for a jar and offered me a cigarette. I had a smoke with him and he became my friend and supporter from then on.

I had been calm and unruffled in Howland's presence, but on the way home I was deeply troubled. At the time of my other dismissals I had been a bachelor with only myself to consider. Now I had a wife. She had put her trust in me. When a year and a half married, I would be out of a job. I had given of my best to Wesleyan. I had written careful appraisals of hundreds of freshman themes and spent countless hours on individual conferences with students. My debating teams had been remarkably successful. We always had two teams working, one on the negative and one on the affirmative side of the question. Many times both teams had won in debates with other colleges. I was in the midst of a free course of lectures on modern poetry. Then, too, there were the evenings I was spending coaching a play. What more did the administration want? Could a few "damns" and "hells" cancel out all this?

To the criticism that I lacked a Ph.D. I had no answer. Homer Woodbridge had urged me to go to Yale and get the necessary degree. I felt that to spend the next few years in research on some literary problem and then write in prose a book-length dissertation would kill my poetry. Poetry was my breath of life. What would Jeannette say?

Reaching home, I told her of my dismissal. Her reaction was magnificent. She said, "Never mind. You will find another place. Let's take a walk." That afternoon there was a gentle snowfall with big flakes slowly descending. On that walk I learned that when a woman is going to have a baby all the normal struggles of this world are insignificant. She is a creator, living on a plane above the ordinary affairs of life. She is at her best and she knows it. This attitude of hers was so surprising to me that I forgot everything else that had happened that day. With her I was moving in a world above troubles.

At midyear in this, my second year at Wesleyan, my work load was lightened a bit. Professor Hench of the English Department resigned. His father had been taken ill and he felt he must go home and take charge of the family business. I was relieved of one of my three courses in freshman composition with all its papers and conferences, and given instead one of Hench's divisions in the sophomore literature course, "A Survey of English Literature," which extended from Beowulf to Virginia Woolf, as one wag put it. To change from composition to literature was definitely a step up. I would have felt very happy had not my dismissal, come June, been gnawing at the back of my mind. I should have been sending out letters hither and yon, seeking a job for the fall, but I had no time for that. A faint but steady hope that I might stay at Wesleyan was nourished by a report along the grapevine that I was to remain. But nothing official came from headquarters. When I announced the extracurricular course, my friends had said, "Why do you work so hard? You are knocking yourself out for a college that has given you a kick in the pants!" No matter. I loved the boys and enjoyed the work. I could not be wholly cast down, for my first book of poems, *Maine Coast*, was going through the press. I was busy reading galley and page proofs. Alfred Harcourt was enthusiastic about my book and thought it ought to cancel my dismissal.

Our long wait for the baby came to an end in February. Our first boy was born and we looked upon him as the finest, fairest child that ever came into this world. Other babies, of course, may have been born, but this was something special! He was an exceptionally good-natured baby. He looked upon the whole world as a place of joy and happiness. He took over my name as his own—a mistake, I think now. Every child deserves a name altogether and uniquely his own. The day he was born I sent Jeannette a bouquet of roses with the following verse:

> Twelve white roses I bring,
> One for each month since my joy
> Blossomed with you, my white bride.
>
> Unopened buds round them cling,
> The first for the roseate boy
> Who stretches and yawns at your side.
>
> We count every finger and toe,

Miraculous tendrils that grew
From one more love born of sea foam;

And now, joyous parents, we know
It takes at least three to make two
In the higher mathematics of home.

My book was finished and put on the market in March. Mrs. James, wife of our librarian, had expressed her opinion: "Mr. Snow's book, when it comes out, won't be fit for the students to read." I had heard of this and waited apprehensively for the reception of my book by the Wesleyan family. I sent the first of my own ten copies to President Olin. He was apparently charmed by the volume and wrote me a gracious letter. He also showed the book to several trustees and spoke in my favor. "The man who wrote these poems," he said, "cannot be evil."

Among the alumni and trustees my most loyal defender was "Mike" Berrien, an official in the Hanover National Bank. His letters in my behalf started when I gave some slight assistance to his son Stephen. At a sophomore banquet to which I was invited as the faculty guest, Stephen drank some vile prohibition liquor and threw up on the floor. I told him he would be reported and urged him to go see the President himself the first thing in the morning and apologize. Steve did this and was not kicked out. His father came to thank me and we became fast friends. He made many visits to our home. We had delightful talks and he presented us with many gifts.

As a result of my book, I was invited to be a guest at the New York Wesleyan Alumni dinner. Did they know I was on my way out? I was seated at the head table beside Dr. David Downey, president of the Board of Trustees and head of the Methodist Book Concern. He asked me if I had ever written any religious poetry. I said, "Yes, I once wrote a long poem on 'The Agony in the Garden,' with a new interpretation of my own." He said, "Send it to me and I'll publish it." At home I looked it over and decided it was not worth publishing, so I didn't send it.

At another alumni meeting, this one put on by the Bowdoin men of New York City, I met a graduate of the college named George Stover, a delicately featured, handsome New York lawyer. When he told me his name, I up and recited the first two lines of his senior class poem: "The road was long and all the cavalcade / Longed for the water and the cooling shade." The poem had been published in the Bowdoin

Orient when I was a freshman in Thomaston High School, reading everything I could get my hands on. "What a memory!" he exclaimed.

He was so deeply impressed by my recital of his lines he loosened up and confided in me, "I should not be in the law. I would be much happier if I had gone into writing as a career." I was destined to hear this story many times. Another alumnus put it this way: "The day I graduated I was offered an instructorship in English at the University of Maine. I should have taken it. I wish I had had a life like yours, with boys and books." Were they sincere, or was it a case of another man's pasture appearing greener than our own? Is it a part of man's general restlessness? Women are natural creators. The nearest a man can come to that is to produce something original in the arts or sciences. For my part, I just could not stop writing poetry, filling folders, getting ready for a second volume.

The weeks slipped along into spring. We could forget the cold winter and eat our supper in the rose garden under a warm sun. We still had no plans for the fall and could not accept an attractive offer of four rooms and a bath in the Losey mansion on High Street. The spring number of the *Alumni Quarterly* carried an article of mine on modern poets. It was reported to me that Professor Farley, head of the English Department, on reading the article, had said to Professor Woodbridge, "This is not the work of a wild man. It's level-headed scholarship." Moreover, my book was receiving some very favorable reviews, along with others that pointed out faults as well as virtues. I was glad to see it reviewed by responsible critics in important magazines. I kept hoping that the trustees in their mid-June meeting would reconsider my dismissal. But they came to the college, held their meeting, and went away. The college closed down for the summer and left me there with a wife and baby and barely money enough to get through the next two months. The sun may have been shining, but not for me. Then on June 20 I received this letter from Acting President Howland:

> I take pleasure in informing you that you have been reappointed by the Trustees of Wesleyan University, Assistant Professor of English for one year, at a salary of $2700.00.

What rejoicing! The sun came out in a burst of glory! Tears streamed down my wife's smiling face, which showed that she had been under more tension than she had let me believe. We hastened to accept the four rooms at the Losey home and spent the summer raiding the attics of our Maine relatives for furniture, which we scraped, polished, painted, and delivered to the freight office.

At the end of the summer we went to Rockland to spend the September weeks of our vacation with Jeannette's mother. Living with her was her mother, Grandmother Packard, who was ninety and feeble and who spent long days alone in her room. Annie was never unkind to her mother, but there was a lack of warmth in their relationship, a doing from a sense of duty on the part of the daughter.

When we arrived at the house Jeannette went in and gave her grandmother a kiss.

"Thank you, dear. No one but you ever kisses my wrinkled face."

A little later she asked, "How long can you stay?"

"Two weeks," Jeannette replied.

When the two weeks were over, her funeral was over. She had decided that it was time for her to go. When we reported to the doctor that she was refusing food and losing strength, he said, "Don't force her. Don't trouble her. Let her go her own way." The funeral was held in Annie's parlor. When I saw the few friends, mostly Annie's, gathered there I was moved to write a poem about it. The title was "Aged Ninety Years," and it appeared three years later in my second poetry collection.

Years later Robert Frost told me that he never read the reviews of his books. Once he had dropped a manuscript into the lap of a publisher, he forgot it and let his mind dwell on new poems for a new book. But sometimes, by mentioning the name of a reviewer or speaking disparagingly of a magazine that had dealt roughly with him, he would show that he had seen the comments. I admit quite without shame that, since the publication of my book in March, 1923, I have watched eagerly for the reviews.

At least I was not ignored, a disappointing experience a man may expect for his first book. The reviews ranged all the way from "Could never have written without Mr. Frost's hand to guide his pen" (J. G. Fletcher) to extravagant praise in the Baltimore *Sun* ("This book is an event in American poetry—this man is America": Maurice Hanline). Most reviewers expressed adverse as well as favorable comment. Typical of these plus and minus reviews is one in the *Dial*, the magazine young aspiring American writers of the '20's admired most. It read:

> The poetry inherent in the sea and the dwellers next to it saturates this book, the author's first. Verse forms are sometimes rather crudely

handled, and occasionally the poetry remains a little outside the net cast for it, but there is vision in this verse and some fine interpretation of character. It has much the quality of Sarah Orne Jewett's tales, though it gives a more intimate presentation of the foibles and philosophy of an isolated community of fishermen and sailors.

I studied the weaknesses pointed out, to learn how I might improve my next book. I confess that the praise delighted me no end. A poet with his first book is like a four-year-old boy who has landed his first fish. "See, mommy! See, daddy! I have caught a fish!" Both Harriet Monroe in *Poetry* and John Gould Fletcher in the *Freeman* scolded me for leaning too heavily on Robert Frost, although Miss Monroe ended her long review with this sentence: "Mr. Snow may be in the [Frost's] school, but he has his own eye and mind and voice and he is telling his own story." Fletcher, it seems, did not know that a good share of my early poems were written before I had ever heard of Frost.

Homer Woodbridge in his review in the *Argus* pointed out the difference between Frost and me:

A strain of Celtic blood has sharpened his [Snow's] sensitiveness to beauty, and at the same time has freed him from the bonds of New England reserve and constraint in the presence of emotion. If I had space to make it, a comparison with the poems of Robert Frost would bring out this point. Mr. Frost is more reserved and subtler in his analysis of mood; he has more of the Yankee shrewdness and "cuteness"; and he has a surer mastery of verse-form. But he always seems a little afraid of beauty, or of strong emotion. . . .

Mr. Snow's point of view also distinguishes his work from that of other writers of New England verse. It is that of the returned wanderer —the Yankee who has traveled far, and lived all over the west and loved it,

> And yet the soil,
> The harsh New England soil, was calling him,
> And would not give him peace.

"The Return," the poem from which these lines are quoted, is really central in the volume. The wanderer, come home, sees . . . things in the light of early recollections and associations; and this gives a slightly wistful or elegiac quality to his description of them. The reality is always falling short of the picture which imagination has colored in his memory. This is the experience described in "The Return"; here, in some of the most stirring lines in the book, the sound of the sea wakes the disillusioned man's will to accept reality:

> The vigorous, far-off music of the sea—
> 'Twas not for child's play that majestic sound
> Had thundered on his inner ear at birth,

Or been the tuning-fork his ancestry
For countless generations had obeyed
To pitch their song of life to, when in need.
He caught the dauntless note its iron voice
Forever sings to lift the hearts of men
To face life's great defeat unfalteringly.

These fine lines represent Mr. Snow's blank verse at its best. It has, of course, its faults—occasionally monotony and trailing syntax; but at its best it reaches a level of high distinction.

I cannot resist sharing a letter from Carl Van Doren sent to me in early April:

I have just read your poems from cover to cover. You have done a good job and begun, I think, a sound career. The most "poetical" and haunting poem is "Haunted"; the most elevated and flawless is "The Eagle"; "Olaf" is the best character work; "Autumn's Country" is your best argument. Do you agree at any of these points?

Bill, Bill, what a march toward Parnassus I have seen you trudge through. When my account with literature is made up I want it to appear to my credit that I always thought you had the stuff, and that I had published more of you in *The Nation* before your first book than any other editor had published anywhere else. Go on and prosper.

The Y.M.C.A. at the college asked me to address one of their weekly meetings on any subject I wished. I chose my old theme, "The world's need of a League of Nations." I still smarted over America's rejection of the Covenant and accused the U.S. Senate of selling out for "thirty pieces of silver." A devout retired professor named William North Rice attended the meeting. At its close he asked me to call on him at his home the following afternoon at four. What did this mean? Did he like what I had said, or had I offended him?

I made the call and he took me up to his room on the third floor and asked me to kneel. I pretended not to hear him, and settled myself in a rocking chair. He knelt down and made a long prayer over me. I didn't know what to do or what to say. I was discomfited beyond anything that I had ever experienced. The man was entirely sincere. I looked at his gray hair as he was praying, and I was disturbed over his concern for me. He was dealing with an Indianlike stoic who didn't like being prayed over. I thought of creeping quietly out of the room, but that would have offended him.

After the prayer he talked about the Christian religion. He asked me if I belonged to any church and I said, "No." I spoke of the Union Chapel at Spruce Head where I was brought up. I was not affiliated

with any one church. It was next door to our own home and I went to
Sunday School and prayer meetings there constantly at my father's in-
sistence, and found them all dull. Sunday was the dullest day in every
week. He smiled for the first time that afternoon and I felt better. He
then asked me if I knew the Bible. I told him yes, I had read it through
once a year (three chapters a day and five on Sunday) for two or three
years. He told me that was not the right way to read it, and I assured
him I had found that out. The book should be read one book at a time
except in the case of the Psalms and Proverbs, which need slower reading to allow for meditation on the truths expressed there. He emphasized at length the responsibility of teachers to guide students into the
paths of righteousness. The faculty must lead lives of purity and show
the boys an example of Christian love. With that he dismissed me. I
went home shaken and exhausted. I recall the whole experience now
with a shudder. A man's religion is too sacred a thing to be invaded by
an outsider, even if the outsider is a splended human being like this
one. Professor Rice spent the days of his retirement lecturing and writing on the compatibility of science and religion.

In the spring of '24 I was given another one-year appointment. I
sensed that I was not wholly acceptable at Wesleyan, for in spite of
my success with the debating teams the college was bringing in a new
man, one Walter Edwin Peck, to take over the debating. If he were
successful with it, there would be no need to keep me on. In other
words, he was brought in to ease me out. I was supposed to be relieved
from this coaching job but the old debaters I had trained still called
on me almost every day as a secondary coach, and I continued to
help them.

Peck was an unusual man. He was writing a life of Shelley, following the pattern Amy Lowell had used in her life of Keats, a pattern
which involved a day-by-day account of her subject's mundane activities. He also started an addition to the college bookstore by putting in
first editions and rare editions of famous books. Knowing I was a lover
of George Crabbe, he gave me an eight-volume edition of Crabbe as a
present. The next day he charged me $5.00 for a $1.50 copy of Byron's
poems. That illustrates the kind of person he was. He also bought a
house in Portland across the river and had it made over at enormous
expense to suit his whims. He had a wife and two attractive children.
He loved night life and often visited the "Bow and Arrow," a restaurant
where girls of easy virtue were available on week ends for sex-starved

students and other males in the region. He was at heart a John Everel-down who "followed the women whenever they called." He took several students in his public speaking class to visit the "Bow and Arrow" and in June gave each one of them a grade of A. He was unable to pay the bills for fixing over his house and left the college in 1926 for a position at the University of Washington.

Peck's subsequent career, as reports of it filtered back to us, was both scandalous and sad. At Washington he seduced a faculty wife and was summarily dismissed at the year's end. He taught for a time at Hunter College; instituted divorce proceedings; married a freshman student who had fallen into some money; drifted to England where he pursued his research at the British Museum; and eventually gravitated toward "Skid Row" in New York, where he cadged drinks by reciting Shelley's "Ozymandias" to anyone who would stand treat. There, one bitter zero night, he leaned up against a building and froze to death. Yet he had managed to complete and publish his two-volume *Life of Shelley*, a somewhat erratic work that nonetheless contained invaluable material. He was, in all, a potentially brilliant scholar who had lost the ability to co-endure with his own existence.

While visiting my publisher in New York City, I went to the theatre as often as possible. Alfred Harcourt was unusually kind to me. He took me to the Algonquin for luncheons and often gave me tickets to Broadway shows. Returning to Wesleyan after these trips I gave the *Argus* a list of plays the boys ought to see when in New York. The list carried the headline, "Professor Snow Recommends." As a result of this interest in the theatre, the Wesleyan Paint and Powder Club asked me if I would help Mrs. Howland put on a play. At this time there was no drama department at Wesleyan. In a weak hour I consented, and Mrs. Howland and I announced tryouts for Arthur Wing Pinero's *The Magistrate*, a domestic comedy that was very popular at the turn of the century but now is entirely forgotten. We spent hours working with the boys, and gathering stage properties and costumes for the different acts. All in all it was a task ten times larger than I thought it would be—a long, hard struggle. We started in November and the play was produced February 10. We played to a full house and the *Argus* praised us extravagantly for the performance.

In the following spring when baby Billy was fourteen months old, our second child was born. When Jeannette was admitted to the delivery room at the hospital I was sent to the lounge on the floor below waiting to hear that I was the father of a little girl. Dr. Chedel knew how much I wanted a daughter. When he came into the lounge I jumped up to hear the report. He said, "Have you heard the bad news?" My heart seemed to stop beating. I lost all my strength and fell back into my chair. "Is Jeannette . . .?" The doctor saw what had happened and cried out, "You have another fine boy!" He then apologized, and assured me that Jeannette was in excellent form. I called up Mrs. Olin at six o'clock in the morning, feeling sure she would not want to sleep another minute with such wonderful news waiting for her! Perfect lady that she was, she responded most graciously.

In the fall of 1924 I decided to support Robert LaFollette for President. I was a Wilson Democrat and hated to desert the party. But John W. Davis, the candidate of the Democratic Party, was so conservative that when he was the president of the American Bar Association in 1922 he came out for the suppression of the minority opinions of the American Supreme Court. I had won many college debates with minority opinions and was destined to win many more; hence I couldn't support Davis even though I was a registered Democrat. This decision on my part came near ending my career at Wesleyan a second time.

At the height of the campaign we had a big three-way debate in the Gymnasium. Professor George Matthew Dutcher was to present the case for Coolidge, Professor Kossuth Williamson the case for John W. Davis, while I supported Robert LaFollette. The students came out in large numbers and filled the Gymnasium. Some were sitting on the floor. It was the first time at Wesleyan that I had seen undergraduates really interested in an election, and I was delighted.

I went all over the state stumping for LaFollette with Edna Purtell, whose brother later became a Republican United States Senator. Edna helped greatly to prepare rallies and other activities. After a speech on the New Haven Green the Communists took hold of me and led me to their cell. They thought I was one who could be easily won over to Communism. They talked Karl Marx to me. One of them explained to me the meaning of "dialectical materialism" and other jargon of the party. Another member filled my ears with the glories of "free love," but if ever seed fell on unsatisfactory ground this was the prime case. A pragmatic thinker like myself could not possibly feel at home in such a company as this, but I was glad to discover what was meant by a "Communist cell."

At Waterbury I spoke in front of the Elton Hotel. The crowd was noisy and riotous. I tried to explain some of LaFollette's progressive ideas, which the crowd took for leftist doctrine and yelled, "You're a Communist! Go back to Russia." So many shouted "Go back to Russia" that I couldn't make myself heard. They grew so violent in their anger that a policeman said to me, "We'd better stop this. To satisfy the crowd I'll take you into protective custody," and he walked me toward the police station. Mr. Elton, thinking I was being arrested, followed us and rescued me. This man had bought a copy of my book, *Maine Coast,* and was already a fan of mine.

LaFollette did not win the election but he did receive nearly five million votes of the twenty-nine million cast—the record number for any third-party candidate up to that time. When the campaign was at its height George W. Davison, chairman of the Board of Trustees, came to the college and told President McConaughy that if Snow were not dismissed he would resign as a member of the Board. This was a frightening threat, for Davison was the greatest benefactor the college had ever known. Luckily for me, President McConaughy wanted me to stay. He was pleased with the work I had been doing in the field of debating and poetry. So he and his wife arranged a dinner for six—Mr. and Mrs. Davison, Mr. and Mrs. McConaughy, Jeannette and myself. The dinner was a long one, the food was excellent, and the discussion extensive. Jeannette sat beside Mr. Davison, and I am certain she made a fine impression on him. I myself convinced him that I was just a simple, plain, New England country boy who was interested in ideas.

Another trustee, Addison Green, owner of the Holyoke Mills, had also notified the President that he would resign from the Board if Snow were not dismissed from the faculty. Green told McConaughy that he had heard me speak on the New Haven Green and that I impressed him as a dangerous radical. A few weeks later McConaughy had a long talk with Green. During the interview Green told the President that he was pestered by many social obligations, didn't want to make calls on people, and wondered how he could get out of it. McConaughy suggested that he invite all these neighbors to a big dinner and have Snow come and read some of his *Maine Coast* poetry. The suggestion hit Green as a good way out.

Several days later McConaughy drove me to the Green home in Holyoke. It was a tremendous house set back from the road with trees and gardens, flowers and servants all over the place. I was not at home in such luxury, but I went to my room and picked out carefully the

poems I should read. The supper bell rang and I went down to the dining room. The men wore tuxedos and the women wore beautiful
dresses. There were bouquets of roses on the table. I was the only one
there not feeling at home, for I wore only a plain business suit. I felt
like little Tommy Tucker singing for his supper, but I had far more at
stake than Tommy ever did. My job at the college hung in the balance.
I was at the head of the table with the President on one side of me
and Addison Green on the other. After the dessert Mr. Green arose and
said, "I have a surprise for you tonight in the person of a new American
poet, a professor at Wesleyan who will now give you a reading from
his first book."

I arose and said something about the American male's suspicion of
poetry, and his success in passing off poetry readings to his wife. This
occasioned a laugh, and I read four or five poems interspersed with
comment. My efforts lasted about forty or fifty minutes. The party broke
up and I headed for my bedroom.

In the middle of the night someone broke into my room. He was
breathing heavily. I jumped up, put my arms around him in the dark,
and started to wrestle with him. He was a Negro. He said, "Mister, I
don't want any trouble with you—I just want your shoes." "My shoes!"
I said. "What do you want of my shoes?" "I just wants to blacken them.
That's all."

It seems that Mr. Green rented a great estate in Scotland each year
for grouse shooting, and while in the British Isles he had acquired the
habit of putting one's shoes outside the door at night for the servants
to shine. I knew absolutely nothing about the custom. At the breakfast
table the next morning there was no subject in the Green family that
could compare with this struggle for my shoes. There was laughter all
over the place, and I am convinced this episode was mainly responsible
for Mr. Green's withdrawing his opposition to me.

After the favorable reaction to me by Davison and Green, the
President's wife Elizabeth took Jeannette and me to a "sugaring off"
party in northwest Connecticut and told us privately that I was not
going to be dismissed from the college. She was a charming hostess, a
lover of poetry and good talk, and a writer of short stories that found
an enthusiastic reception in the pages of the *New Yorker* magazine.
This was a red-letter day in our lives, and we never forgot her kindness.

A short time later the President himself called me to his office and
told me officially that I was going to stay. He added that I should make

up my mind that I would never be a full professor because I was not a conformist and did not have a doctor's degree.

In January 1925 Bowdoin College announced the offer of $100 for the best poem to celebrate the hundredth anniversary of its famous class of 1825, the class of Longfellow and Hawthorne. The author was at liberty to choose his own subject. I entered the contest, and my theme was a New England Thanksgiving celebration as I knew it in my childhood. The judges were Robert Frost, Henry Seidel Canby, and Professor George Roe Eliot. My poem, titled "Thanksgiving," won the contest and was later included in my book *Inner Harbor*.

I was asked to read it at the Bowdoin Commencement in June. My wife decided that she wanted to go with me to Brunswick. She already had received an invitation to stay with the Burnetts, longtime friends of ours, during the exciting days of the Commencement. So for $200 I bought my first car, an old second-hand Overland that should have been relegated to the dump heap long before. I belonged to the horse-and-buggy generation, knew nothing about driving a car, and had only a week to learn. The Wesleyan boys took me in hand. First one would take me for an hour, then another would relieve him. We practiced in the back woods where there was little or no traffic. My most patient and devoted teacher was Gurnee Gallion; what a name, and what a boy! He stood by me and to his credit I passed the test for a license. I was ready for the ordeal. It took us three days to make the trip that we now make in five hours. The first day we got as far as a suburb of Worcester where we found a cheap hotel; the second day we reached Biddeford Pool, Maine, where my brother lived. He was not at home but the children found the door of an empty chicken house open. It was late, we were tired out; we had no choice. We set up our cots among the hen droppings and tried to forget the odor. The third day we reached Brunswick. We had planned a camping trip into Canada and our running board was loaded down with pots, pans, kettles, and blankets—so completely loaded down that the right front door could not be opened. Jeannette had to crawl out over the top of this miscellaneous luggage to get out of the car.

We pulled into the Burnetts' back yard in the early evening—a dishevelled, unwashed pair of travelers with two tired little boys in the back seat. Our car with its baggage was the most disreputable contraption to reach Bowdoin at that Commencement, but Professor Burnett and his wife Sue greeted us as if we had arrived in a Rolls-Royce.

We cleaned up and went late to a dinner party at the home of a Greek professor next door. I learned that Edwin Arlington Robinson was going to receive the next morning a Litt.D. from Bowdoin and I an honorary M.A. Later that evening I sneaked over to the home of Mrs. Henry Johnson where Robinson was staying, introduced myself, and talked poetry with him until after midnight. He told me he never had a decent check for his poetry until his *Collected Poems* came out in 1920. He was then fifty-one years old. He was tall, with a slight stoop which made him seem a bit shorter than he really was. His eyes were dark brown, and when he warmed to a subject they took on an intense black tinge. He had the habit of saying nice things about the verses of younger Americans. He could be ironical or satirical about older poets, but he rarely showed this side of his nature in conversation. When one of his biographers, Chard Powers Smith, told him he had decided to leave poetry and write a novel, Robinson replied, "I don't see any reason why you shouldn't write a good novel." I can sense just how bored Robinson must have been at that moment. But on the whole his attitude toward his contemporaries was gracious, affirmative, and kindly. He said more nice things about his contemporaries in that hour than Frost said in praise of them in two weeks.

I told him how my cousin and I had discovered him in 1905 on this very campus and spent most of the night reading and discussing his *Captain Craig*. He said, "Houghton Mifflin would not publish *Captain Craig* until a few well-to-do people offered to pay the expenses of publication." I said that Hawthorne had the same experience with his *Twice Told Tales*. I added, "But you and Hawthorne have much more than that in common." When I said this his eyes sparkled but he was too modest to ask for my meaning. Both of these men were well acquainted with the darker angels of their natures and both were superb craftsmen. I asked him to come to Wesleyan and give a reading. He said, "No, I can't do that. Frost and Lindsay can do that thing well, but if I spoke from a platform, I would only mumble in my beard."

He was a shy man but a delightful person to meet—especially if one cared to talk about poetry and philosophy. Not more than a month later I received an invitation to come to the Peterborough Colony and work on a book. He was the grand old man of that institution and I know he was responsible for the invitation. He was the kind of man that would shy away when he first met you, but after you were better acquainted would give you the shirt off his back. I did not accept the

Peterborough invitation, for I wanted to be near the ocean when I worked on my next book.

Before leaving Middletown for the trip to Bowdoin, we had decided to move. With two babies, we needed more room. I was still receiving only one-year appointments from Wesleyan, but I felt a little more secure, enough so to accept my lawyer's advice and take a three-year lease on a house we found out at Gildersleeve Corners, five miles from the college. It was an old Colonial, set behind a white picket fence where lilacs bloomed in April. Since the heat came only from two large baronial fireplaces and the toilet was a small shack in the back yard, the rent was only $20 a month. We lived there one year with the existing facilities plus a coal-burning cook stove which we bought for the kitchen. Each morning in the bitter cold I got up, built fires, and warmed the rooms before I allowed the family to get out of bed. After that rough and chilly winter we made a deal with the owner, Mrs. Goodrich. (Among ourselves we called her Goobitch, the children's version.) We paid for a furnace and a bathroom, with the understanding that if we did not buy the house she would reimburse us for the improvements. The rent remained at $20.

After I had survived two dismissals and had seen a class through its entire four years, I began to feel myself a member of the Wesleyan community. The people who were the most hostile became my best friends. The Wesleyan family accepted me the way England accepted Bernard Shaw, as a sort of devil's advocate. When the students of the college joined with students all over the country to question our prohibition laws, I was chosen to champion the repeal of the Eighteenth Amendment as naturally as Dr. Fauver was chosen to defend it. It was a lively evening and the students turned out in record numbers to hear the matter discussed. Modestly enough, I merely called for the legalizing of wine and beer. But the good doctor urged stricter enforcement, a closing of all "speakeasies," and a completely dry U.S.A.—as dry as Kansas. My reappointments were always for short terms but even at that I felt settled. My second book had been accepted at Harcourt, Brace & Company. Harrison Smith rather than Harcourt guided me through the galleys, the page proof, and all the other details of publication. My lecture classes were large, and my third child was on his way to earth.

CHAPTER 18

Outdoors With a Carload of Kids

THE 1925 trip to Canada was the first of four camping trips we made into that northern region. We had determined to spend our summers out of doors. So much of my early life had been spent in the woods and on the sea that I felt "cabined, cribbed, and confined" in classrooms, and wanted our children to be brought up, as far as possible, by the sea, and among wooded hills and mountains. For many years our summer abode was a canvas tent. We learned to live in it on rainy as well as sunny days.

On one occasion we set up our tent in the rain in a Vermont field. The next day at ten o'clock I had an engagement to read my poetry before a group of Genevieve Taggard's students at Bennington College. Early that morning we packed the boys into the car. They ate sandwiches while we broke tent in the rain. Our shoes were soon filled with water, our coats soaked through. Since all four of the children were afflicted with whooping cough, we could not go into any building. There was no time to get dry. Ten o'clock was catching up with me. So Jeannette drove the children around town until the sun came out and she found a warm sand pile by the side of the road. The boys happily played there and waited for me.

I went into Mrs. Taggard's class and gave my reading. The fifty or sixty girls in the room were shocked and also delighted with my water-soaked appearance, which they seemed to think was purposely designed for the occasion. I could have annihilated every smiling face. They looked so dry and I felt so wet that I had some difficulty getting started. By the time I read the second poem I had forgotten all about my soggy condition. They must have forgotten about it also, for at the close of the hour they asked me some of the most intelligent and far-reaching questions about poetry I ever had put to me.

A few weeks later we camped near a little town west of Quebec. Our children had recovered from the whooping cough, the weather was excellent, and we were feeling great. One other family camped there that night. At about six o'clock the girl next door, an attractive blonde, was grilling a chicken and other delicious-smelling things over a wood fire. Her husband, obviously drunk, came to the door of their tent and demanded that she "come in unto him." She pled, "Not now, dinner is ready." He came out to the grill, drew back his right foot, and kicked everything into the dust. The overturned coffee sizzled and steamed in the fire and the chicken was scattered all over the ground. The girl ran into our tent and began to cry. The man stumbled and fell to the ground, too far gone even to brush away the mosquitoes that soon surrounded him. The girl said this was the climax of a very unhappy camping honeymoon, for he had been drunk since their wedding day. She had looked forward to this trip as the finest vacation of her life, and now the marriage as well as the chicken was lying in ashes. We offered to take her in for the night, but she said No. She would go back to Detroit with him and return to her own home. I have wondered about her many times since, grieved for her, and remembered her beauty.

On one of these trips we camped at dusk near the little village of Massey, Ontario, in a grove of pines on a bluff forty feet above the Spanish River. Here the river sprawled beside a white sandy beach, but a few rods upstream there was a deep rocky gorge where a waterfall sparkled, and beyond that both the stone arch of a highway bridge and a delicate iron railroad trestle.

It was sunset when we made camp, and the beach looked so alluring we decided to go down and have a swim. Our supper was delayed; we had to wash the pots and pans by the light of the campfire. Before everything had been stowed away for the night, we heard voices coming up from the river and caught the notes of a violin rising above the heavy twang of a guitar. I crept to the edge of the embankment and looked down. There on the sand a dozen young people were circled around a fire. The effect from above was theatrical; the fire blazing brightly, the tall violinist facing the flames, the others seated on the sand singing ballads.

One would not have to be a professional ballad collector to realize that here was the setting for a new find, and I was off down the bank in a hurry. Unnoticed in the darkness, I crept up to the circle and listened. An old English version of "Barbara Allen" and the mournful log-jam tragedy of "Young Monroe" were mingled indiscriminately with the recent radio offerings of Frank Crumit and Julia Sanderson. I was soon discovered, and the violinist asked me rather bluntly what I wanted. I asked if the group would be kind enough to sing again a ballad that was new to me. This they willingly did, and I invited them up to the grove for a snack. There my wife—who knows all the little tricks of ballad collecting—put on the fire a generous amount of fudge material which soon began to boil and pour out its fragrance. By this time the moon had come up and added its share to the enjoyment of the evening. Two of my youngsters stirred out of their beds and listened with eager ears as the ballad singing went on. While the fudge, spread thickly on Uneeda biscuits, was passed around, I sat in the car with a few of the singers while they repeated songs and my wife copied down the tunes of their versions of several ballads. We succeeded in securing two ballads unfamiliar to us, and new words to three old ballads.

While the singing was at its height another automobile wheeled into our camping ground among the pines and came to a stop not more than fifty yards away. A few of the young blades went over to the new arrivals and helped set up their tent, hoping perhaps for a small handout. The tent was large and new, and the owner kept repeating, "I don't know much about this thing," as the boys showed him the uses of guy ropes, pegs, and steel supports. The boys came back and told us what a luxurious three-room tent the newcomers had and how green the man seemed to be. We thought no more about it, said good night and thank you to the ballad singers, and made ready for bed.

The moon by this time was high in the heavens. The peace of the night had taken full possession of me, and I was loath to go in under cover. I went off a few yards, stretched out on a bed of pine needles, and gazed up through the trees at the luminous sky. I wondered how a world that offered such profundities of peace had been riddled by the military forces of many nations. I resolved then and there to keep my four boys away from the strife and tension of modern cities and transplant them into wide open spaces. These thoughts had taken possession of me when I heard the shrill voices of two women, one young, one older, emerging from the neighboring tent.

"I know what you told me," said the younger of the two.

"I told you, you give my children their supper."

"You told me no such thing. You said it was late and that I should put them right to bed."

The argument went on, louder and angrier—"I did not," "You did so," peppered with words like "liar," "slut," and "bitch." In the midst of it a young girl rushed out of the tent, followed by the slow steps of a heavily built older woman, who was saying:

"You are my servant, and I want no servant of mine to talk to me like that."

"Then why do you tell lies about me?"

"Because you're just a lying bitch. Why did you come with us anyhow?"

"You know why I came. I wanted to get away from Ernie."

"Oh, Ernie, is it? I thought you wanted to be near some other man."

"What other man?"

"No matter. You're just a lying slut and a bad servant."

"I won't stand no such talk from nobody. I'm going back to the Soo."

"Well, go then, I've no use around here for your lying saucy tongue."

The girl stepped into the tent for a short time, then emerged into the moonlight with a coat on and a suitcase in her hand. I became excited and stepped into our own tent, where I found my wife awake and listening. My sympathies were all for the young girl, who was facing a hundred-mile walk to Sault Ste. Marie through the wilds of Ontario in the middle of the night. I wanted to do something to help her. But my wife had already decided that the girl's tongue was nearly as filthy as that of her mistress, and poured cold water on my Good Samaritan resolves. In the meantime the girl had walked out of the campground onto the highway. Once there, instead of turning west toward the Soo, she turned east and headed for the high bridge. The man in the tent, who up to this time had not interposed a word, now came to life and set out after the girl, calling out words which I could not distinguish. I did hear her say that she was going to throw herself off the bridge.

As she reached the middle of the bridge, the man yelled sharply for her to stop, and in a moment his arm was about her waist holding her fast. I could hear her saying over and over, "It's no use; I hate her and she hates me." While the two were arguing, the man's wife was crying out, "Leave her alone, let her do what she wants to! You are making a fool of yourself! Turn her over to the police!" The husband paid her no attention. He partly dragged, partly led the girl across the bridge and onto a point of land nearer to me, so that I could catch a phrase of their talk every now and then. He made her promises—one was plainly a raise in her weekly wages. He excused his wife's unreasoning outbreak on the grounds of fatigue, reminded the girl that this was their first day out, and promised that things would go better after they had become accustomed to camping. He painted the attractions of Montreal and Quebec, cities he was apparently well acquainted with, and finally calmed her down.

The wife in the meantime was standing in the door of her tent still calling out, "Turn her over to the police! Turn her over to the police!" Her cries died down and she stood there rigid, dark in the moonlight like a broken obelisk.

The husband now felt it was safe to lead the girl back across the bridge. When they were within a hundred yards or less of the tent, the wife let out an eerie cry, enough to make the night shudder, and fell back into the folds of the canvas. She was a large woman, and I could feel the turf stir beneath me as she went down. The tremor had hardly ceased when a boy about ten years old ran out of the tent shrieking, "Mother's dead! Mother's dead!" The terror in his voice wakened everyone within the campground. I ran over to him, filled with no little terror myself. Two smaller children rose up out of a bed in the back of their station wagon and repeated their brother's shrill cry, "Mother's dead! Mother's dead!"

I ran to the prostrate woman on the ground and felt her pulse. I asked the boy if he had any ammonia. He said, "I don't know. What is it?" I said, "Bring some water quickly," and called to Jeannette, who hurried over with ammonia. Sweat was pouring down the woman's face, and the lower part of her body seemed strangely rigid. She had apparently become psychologically blocked, having arrived at the end of her meager mental resources. I suspected she knew she was in the wrong, for the young girl had in all likelihood carried out her orders concerning the children. She dared not face the girl. There was but one thing left for her to do and that was to fold up. I rubbed her large legs trying to restore her circulation. I tried to lift her onto an army cot that was there, but found her too heavy to move.

The husband and the girl ran up and I got my first good look at her. She had light, coarse, Saxon hair and steel-blue eyes. Her skin was rough, so rough that it minimized whatever beauty she might have possessed. She was young and curvaceous, and carried an air of self-reliance in every move she made. She was burdened with that brand of independence which puts up a sign "No advice wanted," yet fails to distinguish between essentials and nonessentials. I pitied her, not so much because of what had happened that night but because of the temperamental handicap that would dog her through life.

Benumbed and bewildered, the husband looked at me with eyes full of apology. He bent over his wife to make sure she was alive. I told him that she had merely fainted and would be all right after a little rest. Together we lifted her onto a cot. He thanked me sincerely for what I had done.

I sized him up as a successful businessman who was entering middle life without much enthusiasm, as one tired of the "rat race." His new Auburn car and his luxurious camping equipment showed that he was not the ordinary tent camper who seeks an adventurous vacation in spite of limited resources. His was a more deliberate mood—the mood of one who has lost his zest for business without finding new incentives for living. The present-day world is dotted with too many such men. Having cultivated no other interests, this man had apparently turned to the great outdoors for healing and compensation. I bade him good night and went back to my own tent. I had forgotten all about the peace of the Northern night, forgotten even the jolly ballad-singing party we had had only a few hours earlier. My thoughts were entirely on this bewildered man. Sleep would not visit me for a long time; and the sun was high when we made our morning meal by the campfire.

We were in no hurry to break camp that day. My wife humored me by letting me stay around to watch the outcome—or at least to watch the play of character on character that would be sure to reveal itself.

The woman sat in the sunlight all morning in a large-sized camp chair, saying hardly a word. She was a stolid creature with dark eyes and an olive complexion. There was a grimness in her expression that bespoke a life of early hardship and struggle. Her chin was both long and wide, indicating a nature of determination and resolve. The lines in her face this morning were deep, and her haggard appearance at this hour was probably absent at other times. Very likely she had come up from a servant in a miners' boarding house, or something similar, had married a clever man who was bound to get on, and had accomplished her ambition to be mistress of a good home with servants, children, and considerable wealth. This camping trip was undoubtedly her husband's idea, for one could see at a glance that little or nothing in the great open spaces really interested her. She sat there like a disappointed Sphinx, and let the maid brush by her several times without once speaking or raising her eyes in greeting. The maid got the breakfast alone and found bathing suits for the youngsters, who were soon off swimming in the Spanish River, where my own children joined them.

The husband lingered long over his coffee, tried a few pleasantries on his wife which met with no response, and looked around for something to do. He went into the tent and brought out a large blue book which he began reading. His wife glanced at the book and said, "I wish, Arthur, that you wouldn't read such books. I fear God will take vengeance upon us." He put down the book and began fumbling with a fishing rod and reel, and with these, which were as new and expensive as the rest of his outfit, he soon demonstrated that he was as innocent of fishing technique as he was of all other accomplishments that make up a camper's life. I was eager to find out what his book might be. After he left I sidled over and caught a glimpse of it—Tom Paine's *Age of Reason*. I realized at once that the man was searching for something more than the conventional routine of the business world. He was trying to find his place among the eternities. He had come to the wilds of the north woods to take an account of stock, and his first night out had proved to be a nightmare. The outcome of his venture I would never know. I could only hope that the peace and the beauty of the virgin country would impart to him some of the joy that could be seen in his children shouting and splashing each other in the Spanish River that morning.

On one of these Canadian trips a strange thing occurred. We were camped on the side of Lake Nippissing in Ontario and enjoying it so much that we decided to stay over for a few days. Our boys and the children of ten or fifteen other campers around us were having a glorious time playing together. One afternoon I stuck my head out of the tent and called to my wife, "Aunt Jean, please come!" Within an hour all the other children were together at the far end of the campground. Our boys came into the tent and said, "Daddy, what's the matter? These children won't play with us any more. Why?"

Before she married, Jeannette had given many of her best hours to her sister's two children. When they called, "Aunt Jean," she was right there to help them. She responded so quickly to this name that I too, when I wanted an instant answer, would call out, "Aunt Jean!"

But the people at Nippissing Lake did not know this. They whispered together and evidently concluded that I was camping to be far from home and living in sin with my wife's sister! It was no use for us to explain and do battle with Mrs. Grundy. So we packed up and headed west.

Our destination was Basswood Lake near Thessalon, Ontario, where my cousin Bill Norton had a summer camp. We pitched our tent on the far side of the cove in a small cleared space backed by dense forest. There was no road, not even a path through the woods. We rowed back and forth to Bill's camp in one of his small boats. We had a grand three weeks with the Norton gang, fifteen strong.

Bill wanted to show me some real fishing, so he and I took my canoe and left our families for a long week end. My Airedale was assigned the job of protecting my wife and children from wild animals out prowling for food in the night. Leaving the dog was a serious mistake. He slept across the doorsill of the tent and every few minutes stirred and growled, keeping my wife awake and apprehensive. His sharp ears caught noises she would not have noticed—the flight of an owl, the hop of a rabbit. Three nights in a row she slept very little. Bill and I fished five lakes in the region where the famous quintuplets were born, and we slept out in the open. We lived on trout and bass, and at the end of our holiday brought back eighteen fine bass for a reunion dinner.

Our last Canadian trip came when three of our boys were off to World War II and only Gregory, the youngest, was at home to go with us. An old student of mine, Spencer Reeder, had invited us to spend a week with him at his camp on Cache Lake, in the Algonquin Provincial Park country.

Clad in overalls and sweaters, and equipped with one small tent, one sleeping bag, a few blankets, and an Old Town canoe, we started from our own camp on the Maine coast at ten o'clock one Sunday morning. We drove straight across Maine and New Hampshire, crossed the Canadian border at Derby Line, Vermont, and long after dark bedded down beside a narrow dirt road forty miles east of Montreal. All night long a gale of wind battered our tent, keeping Jeannette and me awake; but Gregory arranged his sleeping bag at the bottom of a dry ditch and slept soundly as only a healthy boy can. Another day's drive carried us well beyond Ottawa. Although the country was sparsely settled, it was not easy to find a good camping place with a decent water supply. Finally we pitched our tent in a grove of pines near a gasoline station, where three children kept up a running chatter in French as they watched us get supper and put our tent in order.

The next morning, refreshed, we headed west and in an hour passed through the gates of Algonquin Park. At noon we cooked our dinner at the Camp of the Two Rivers, where the fireplaces were excellent, the wood plentiful, and the landscape restful. An hour later we reached our destination, Cache Lake. It was a joy to park our car and realize that there would be no more auto travel for a week.

Our host, Spencer Reeder, an intrepid hunter and fisherman as well as a good lawyer, met us at the dock, helped us to launch our canoe, and with his own aluminum canoe guided us to his camp. The camp, a log cabin on the shore of the lake, proved a restful and fragrant spot. Our host's wife and three daughters gave us a heartwarming welcome. We soon washed off the dust and fuzz with a dip in the lake. At five o'clock Spencer, Gregory, and I put out for our first fishing. Before my line was ten feet under I got a bite and hauled in. I had a small bass, well below Canada's legal limit of ten inches, so I had to throw it back. I then landed a pickerel, a bullhead, and another small bass before darkness came in. We took the bullhead home and had it for breakfast. Here at last was a fresh-water lake in which a man could go fishing and get results!

Reeder's plan for a trip around several lakes had to be abandoned. All Canada was the victim of a long drought. Fires were raging in the Park, particularly in the vicinity of Lake Proulx and Lake Lavielle. The latter was full of fish and was the lake to which I had looked forward as the central point of our trip. But alas! There would have to be three days of rain before the ban on travel through the woods from portage to portage could be lifted; and in Canada a ban is a ban. We were happy to go fishing on our own Cache Lake.

Our days developed into a ritual. Each morning early, leaving the others asleep, my wife and I would paddle to the head of the lake, cross illegally through the woods to a small river, bait our minnow trap with breadcrumbs, and wait for results. On the way to the river, and while waiting for the trap to fill, we met with deer, porcupines, beaver, and other wildlife. One day while we were there a neighbor ran into a bear on this portage, but we encountered no bears. With a pail full of minnows we paddled back to camp and ate a belated breakfast with the family.

Every day in the early afternoon we paddled to "Headquarters," where the railway and the highway touch the north shore of Cache Lake, learned the latest news about the Park fires, bought souvenirs, mailed our letters and postal cards, looked at our automobile, and then paddled back to camp in time to go fishing. Gregory and Spencer went trolling for bass. My wife and I anchored over one especially deep spot and fished for trout. We always came home with trout—sometimes only one. And our bass fishermen always came home with bass.

Cleaning our fish on the dock in the long summer twilight was not an unpleasant job. In order to retain their juices we rolled our fish in aluminum foil and set them on the red coals in the baronial fireplace. With all this cleaning and cooking and washing up (which often included a dip in the lake), it was ten o'clock before we sat down to the chief meal of the day. The out-of-doors air, the canoeing, and the fishing produced enormous hungers. After the meal we gathered around the fireplace, told stories, read poetry, sang songs, and discussed national and international politics.

The day before our week was over, the fire ban was lifted. We were free to go anywhere in the Park. We packed up in the early forenoon, made sandwiches, and started off in our canoes. First we paddled to the head of Cache Lake. From there we dragged our canoes over a short portage to Beaver Pond, a body of water full of fragrant lilies, white and yellow. From here we carried the canoes over a quarter-mile portage to Little Island Lake. We fished for a time with little success, went ashore on Little Island, started a fire, and ate a hearty meal. Darkness came on suddenly, and we all felt an uneasy desire to get back to camp.

The night was really dark. The only reasonable thing to do was to halt and camp down by the portage with a good fire, but we had no blankets and no other provisions for a stopover. So we paddled across the lake and tried to find the portage back to Beaver Pond.

In the Park finding a portage is a must. Aside from this narrow path, everything is impenetrable jungle. Alas for us, the portage failed to reveal itself. We paddled up and down the lake, over and over again. Our one flashlight grew weaker and weaker. Its usefulness was about finished when, at the end of what seemed like difficult hours, we found the landing. One of us then went ahead striking matches to guide the others. Two trips were necessary to carry the two canoes. When they were afloat again in Cache Lake, I discovered that in the darkness I had left my beloved rod and reel behind. To go back was impossible. The paddle home took until well after midnight, and we were all hungry as well as tired.

Next morning we said good-bye to our hosts, thanking them for one of the best weeks we had ever known. I had one regret: I hated to leave that fine rod and reel in Canada.

A few days after arriving home we had a letter from Spencer. The morning we left he had gone to Little Island Lake for the express purpose of retrieving my rod. He wrote, in language that smacks of the lawyer:

> Two men had just arrived by canoe from the opposite direction and were engaged in a spirited argument as to whether or not the equipment had been left there with intent to abandon or whether it had just been mislaid. I settled this argument by seizing the property and making off with it.

So the one casualty of the trip was averted!

I have wondered since then how it is that a week in Algonquin Park is so very restful. It must be the Canadian air, uncontaminated by industrial smoke. Getting away from the automobile with its tension and its continual demands counts as a second factor. The canoe is a heavenly substitute for the car. All our work and play centered around the canoe. And the daily paddling gave us just the right amount of exercise. For people who say they "want to get away from it all" and really mean it, I know of nothing more exhilarating, more wholesomely satisfying, than a canoe trip among the lakes of Algonquin Park.

The wildest and most extensive of our journeys with the children was a trailer excursion around the United States in 1937. I had a sabbatical leave coming up—either a half-year at full pay or a full year at half-pay. I also had an offer from Joe Beach, a Wesleyan missionary and educator in China, to give lectures on American life and literature at West China Union University in Chungking, which I was eager to accept. But my family insisted on going too. I really didn't want to leave them behind, and neither I nor West China Union could afford the $5000 or so needed for their travel expenses. So with great reluctance I wrote and refused the offer. This episode made me keenly aware of how closely knit our family was.

Now what should we do with our semester off? Jeannette suggested that we buy a house trailer and make a slow-boat-to-China excursion around the four sides of the U.S.A. "A great idea!" by unanimous vote. After an intensive study of different trailers, we settled on a Schult, made in Elkhart, Indiana, which cost $800. A local bank made me a loan, and after several delays the trailer was driven to our door. House trailers were fairly new at the time, and friends and neighbors came to look and comment. Isabel Woodbridge examined the thing and remarked, "I have been sending money out to the Indiana Flood Relief to keep people from living in quarters like these." It was a bit cramped, we could not deny. There were beds for four; we were seven plus a large dog. But Jeannette built an upper berth for two, which could be tucked behind the sofa during the day. For Gregory there was a small folding cot that in daytime could be slipped under the sofa. The dog would sleep in the car guarding our baggage, which had to be removed from the trailer to make room for us.

Getting a license for the trailer turned out to be another worrisome thing. There was so much red tape, so many delays, that I appealed to Governor Cross' son, who was in the State Motor Vehicles Department. He promised that the license would be in the afternoon mail at the college post office on February 12, the day of our planned departure—and it was. What a relief! for we were all packed and ready to go.

Included in our packages were two pairs of boxing gloves presented and autographed by Gene Tunney, a gift that proved to be a godsend. When the noise in the back seat grew too rambunctious, I would draw off to the side of the road and demand that the two older boys should box three one-minute rounds. I was both referee and timekeeper of these bouts. This exercise relieved the tension and we would continue our journey.

We moved cautiously along High Street. Students waved and shouted "Good luck!" "Bring 'em back alive!" "All the way!" Cameras clicked and reporters made notes. Friends saved for me the press notices—a somewhat embellished account in the Hartford *Courant*, a mock-solemn "tribute to the greatest American since Daniel Boone" by an undergraduate humorist in the Wesleyan *Argus*, which still adorn my scrapbooks.

Driving with a trailer behind was a new experience, and I cannot honestly say I liked it. The connecting rod was too long, and the trailer swayed from side to side as we rode along. We were driven off the Hutchinson River Parkway by two policemen who said, "Trailers not allowed on this road." Driving in traffic with the lights of New York and New Jersey in my eyes was a trying experience. We finally reached the home of Jeannette's sister Mildred, in Plainfield, at 9:30 P.M. We were worn out and hungry. A good supper was ready for us, but we were too tired to do it justice.

In Washington we camped in a small parking area with lovely trees and a lake—a spot now occupied by the Jefferson Memorial. The next day we looked over the city with its beautiful but largely Graeco-Roman architecture. Why, I wondered, could not architect Henry Bacon have made the Lincoln Memorial a glorified replica of a Midwestern log cabin? I felt sure Praxiteles would have done that if he had had the assignment. Didn't he use the Greek peasant's hut as his model for the Parthenon? But why be critical? Washington is a beautiful city.

The older boys wanted to climb to the top of the Washington Monument. I rested at the bottom while they went up. My desire was to go alone to Rock Creek Cemetery and take a look at Saint-Gaudens' "Peace" over the grave of Henry Adams' wife. But the family insisted on going along. We had a hard time locating the grave. Finally one of the boys discovered it and called us to come and see. The bronze head had an Oriental look, relaxed, peaceful, penetrating, haunting. It was so absorbing that I found it difficult to take my eyes away. To me it is Saint-Gaudens' masterpiece.

We were also visited by our Congressman Bill Citron, who gave us a letter to the White House. The children wanted to go to the National Zoological Park instead, so we had to give up the White House visit.

Our way of travel, at the rate of about 150 miles a day, soon settled into a routine. At night we would find a trailer camp or a gasoline station's back yard, pay fifty cents or a dollar for the privilege of plugging into a power line. Then we would take all our extra baggage out of the trailer and put it in the open car. Pal, our dog, guarded the bags with a sepulchral growl that would drive any intruder away. We pulled out our beds and sank into a deep sleep. We usually had breakfast and supper in the trailer. Our noonday meal we ate at a restaurant, hotel, or coffee shop. Jeannette would enter the place alone, smell it, look it over, and decide whether it was sufficiently clean. She also scanned the menu to find food suitable for the children. If she gave us the come-along sign, we would enter and search the menu for an inexpensive meal. Our independent youngsters soon grew tired of our choice of food, took thirty-five cents each, and trotted off to another restaurant, often the lunch counter in Woolworth's for pizza pie, hot dogs, and other food that I eyed with suspicion. They enjoyed being off on their own and learned to keep within their allotment. The scheme worked out all right, for they were poisoned by food only once, and that was on the Mexican border.

We had only $10 a day to spend for gas, oil, tires, food, clothing, and all the rest. Wesleyan mailed $300 to planned locations the first of each month. The rest of my salary was left at the Middletown bank to cover continuing expenses at home such as taxes and insurance. To keep our outgo under $10 a day took some austere maneuvering, but with 1937 prices and young boys who were not fussy about what they wore, it was possible.

Along the way there were many high points and many small, revealing local incidents, for I wanted to see how people felt as they pulled out of the great depression. In one little Southern town I was astonished to find that the wage for gathering pecans was a dollar a day. I said to one worker, "Isn't that a terribly small wage?" He replied, "I suppose so, but it seems pretty good when you realize the others [i.e., the blacks] get only fifty cents." In the grocery store where I was having this conversation, I began to feel out of place. The people, noticing my Northern accent, looked at me coldly, and gave me to understand that they did not welcome foreigners. The atmosphere grew so cool that I went back to the trailer.

In Atlanta I had a lecture engagement at Spelman College, where President Florence Reed gave us a warm welcome. I had known "Floppy" when she was a secretary to President Foster at Reed College, and she was now filling her bigger job with distinction. She took me at once to meet William Stanley Braithwaite, formerly the distinguished poetry editor of the Boston *Transcript*, now teaching English at Spelman. In the *Transcript* he had pirated some of my poems, so knew who I was. He told me he thought Robinson was America's greatest poet; and since we both knew his work intimately, we "had a ball" discussing his achievements. Braithwaite had been one of the three judges who had refused to give first place to Edna St. Vincent Millay in the famous contest in which her "Renascence" was the outstanding entry. He said, with some bitterness, "Mitchell Kennerly, the publisher, who ignored the judges, made himself the judge. He magnified the merits of Millay's poem. The quality of the poetry had nothing to do with his decision. With Kennerly it was a search for power and his recognition as a critic." I saw that this was a touchy subject and laid off it. Of course I did not dare mention Orrick Johns and his poem "Second Avenue," to which the judges gave first place. Johns, recognizing the superior merit of Edna's poem, turned down the prize and refused to attend the presentation dinner! Edna told me that the fiasco gave her $10,000 worth of publicity.

The next morning I gave a poetry reading at Sisters Chapel before an appreciative audience of bright-eyed, ambitious Negro girls. In the afternoon Miss Reed's chauffeur drove the boys to a movie house in downtown Atlanta. My boys, who had grown to like the man, were flabbergasted to find that he could not enter the front door of the movie house with them, but had to go around to a side door and climb to a balcony reserved for Negroes. Negro boys had been coming daily to our house in Middletown, where color was of no concern.

At Jacksonville we spent three days at the home of my Bowdoin classmate Lorenzo Baldwin, talking of old days and old friends—among others, Carl and Irita Van Doren, whom we had both known as graduate students at Columbia. I learned that Irita came from Tallahassee; that her grandfather Bradford had been a generous and popular governor of Florida just after the Civil War; and that her father had been murdered brutally by two unscrupulous and clever landlords—a shocking fact I had not known anything about.

One evening, at the Baldwins' table, I sat next to a very lovely woman who was one of General Kirby Smith's six daughters, and a charming unreconstructed rebel she proved to be. She assured me the South would have won the war if Jackson had lived, and she didn't know or care about the date of Lincoln's birth. I won her over, however, by knowing that Robert E. Lee was born on January 19, 1807 (a fact I had only recently learned by reading Gamaliel Bradford). I was rewarded with a hug and a request for a ride in our trailer the next morning; so we had her as a passenger for the first twenty-five miles of our push toward Miami.

At that resort city we spent a week swimming, loafing, and taking in the "acts" that came nightly to our trailer camp—a comedian, a sleight-of-hand artist, a fellow who wrestled with a bear. One evening a man brought some baby alligators for sale; I bought one and had it shipped to the Wesleyan Beta house—to the mingled delight and consternation of my undergraduate fraternity brothers, as I learned later.

So it went—a band of Seminoles seen in the Everglades, the Ringling Circus winter quarters at Sarasota, the superb and little visited coastline between Panama City and Pensacola, the vicious undertow at Pensacola Beach, which seized our son Stephen so strongly that I was barely able to pull him from the water. Only afterward did I see the sign: "No swimming allowed. Dangerous undertow."

Mobile brought troubles of a different sort. We made several false landings before we found a trailer camp at which we cared to stay, and maneuvering car and trailer through the narrow, winding streets was not easy. And we were running out of money. A check from Middletown should have been awaiting us but it was not. Every day we went twice to the post office; every day there was nothing for us. I grew more and more worried, for we were down to our last $10. I said to the boys, "We'll have to go fishing in earnest if the money doesn't come on Monday."

Even so, we spent Sunday seeing the sights. There was the Duffy Oak, a truly marvelous tree with a spread of 115 feet. We saw the ruins of the house where Augusta Evans Wilson wrote *St. Elmo*, that fearfully sentimental and melodramatic best-seller of 1866 (I tried to read it but couldn't get beyond Chapter I). We saw the statue of Raphael Semmes, commander of the Confederate raider *Alabama* which destroyed many Northern merchant ships. The inscription on his monument calls him a soldier, patriot, and Christian gentleman; but up in Spruce Head, where some of our families had suffered heavily from his raids, we had thought him no better than a pirate.

On Monday our money did show up—not at the post office, but at a bank where it had been awaiting us for a week. And then our dog Pal was missing! Search as we might, we could not find him, even with the help of the police. What to do? We decided to wait one more night; and during that night he found his way back to the trailer, just in time for my birthday on Tuesday, which brought me a new rod and reel, line, lures, flies—and a flashlight from Nick, who spent his whole week's allowance of seventy-five cents on it.

So, through the fine yellow dust of Mississippi's dirt roads, we set out for New Orleans. We inspected the schools in the small town of Spring Hill—a frame bungalow for the village's eight white pupils, and a much larger-two story building for the Negroes. The latter was already closed for the year (only seven months' schooling for blacks) and was in frightful state of neglect—windows broken, floors deep in dirt, sills gone.

Natchez was a strange town: proud old antebellum houses atop the bluffs, yet its waterfront on the Mississippi was still Old-Natchez-under-the-Hill, as squalid and piratical-looking as a hundred years earlier. It was a relief to get onto Louisiana's fine new roads and bridges, to see and climb to the top of the skyscraper state capitol at Baton Rouge, to think of the free textbooks for every schoolchild in the state. These were three great accomplishments of Huey Long—who had been a dictator in his own state and had wanted, I think, to be a dictator over all America. For me, all his achievements were blotted out by his undemocratic threat to a democratic nation. I had feared him as some Italians I knew feared Mussolini. Neither of these men had truly trusted the people.

At New Orleans I felt I was in a new world. The French influence was everywhere. The wrought-iron grillwork on shops and houses was probably the finest in America. We drew up at the famous Antoine's Restaurant, where a courteous, kindly headwaiter assured my questioning wife that lunch for seven "would not be inexpensive; it *would* run into money." At the Court of the Two Sisters we found an excellent lunch, served at outdoor tables among trees and flowerbeds, for only sixty cents.

We went on through St. Martinville, the home of Longfellow's Evangeline, and entered upon our longest hitch—the entire width of Texas. We hadn't gone far into the state when we saw two young men on horseback driving a herd of cattle along the road. Our boys were excited as we halted to watch them go by. There were about two hundred cattle and thirty or forty calves in the herd. The cowboys urged the animals along and kept galloping out to retrieve strays and runaways until the herd was out of sight. These were no drugstore cowboys dressed up for tourists. What our boys had seen and admired in Western movies and Tom Mix pamphlets had become a reality.

My first impression of Texas was that it had not been hit by the depression like the other states we had seen. The villages looked clean and neat, and the wide fields were covered with bluebonnets. We saw posters along the highway urging us to come to Trailer Haven in San Antonio, so that was to be our next stop. It did not live up to its billing—no grass anywhere, and since it had rained for a day, everything was deep in mud. Keeping ourselves and the trailer clean was a problem. The next morning we "remembered the Alamo" and saw the relics of Crockett and Travis and the rest who had died there. We also saw the annual "Feast of Roses," a fiesta parade whose lavish floats carried some of the loveliest young women imaginable, the stuff of which men's dreams are made! Our boys were particularly fascinated by a group of square dancers on one float, a blacksmith's shop set up on another, and several old covered wagons drawn by oxen.

But oddly, they were not much interested in the Billy the Kid Museum some twenty miles west; and I, who knew the story of Judge Roy Bean—"Law west of the Pecos"—and his admiration for the actress Lillian Langtry, was more intrigued by the town of Langtry than they were. We did not linger very long, for we were all looking forward to the Carlsbad Caverns in New Mexico.

These great caves were not disappointing. We had seen other caverns, such as the Howe Caverns in New York State with its stalagmites and stalactites; but Carlsbad was much bigger and deeper than all we had seen before. The Big Room there was 6000 feet long and 485 feet wide. Guides took us through the portions which were then open, and ended their tour by turning out the lights and singing, "Rock of Ages, cleft for me, / Let me hide myself in thee . . ." To some people it was a fitting close, but to me it was a sacrilege. I expressed how I felt about it in the following lines:

> A sanctimonious guide
> In the Big Room of Carlsbad Caverns
> Where Nature's hidden beauty,
> Crystallized and distilled,
> Needs no additional utterance
> To hymn the glory of God,
> Gathers the tourists around him,
> Turns out a long row of lights,

Compels them to sit down and listen
To a quartette of amateur rangers
Droning the dolorous hymn
"Rock of Ages, cleft for me,"
As if they resented the order.

But neither bad singing nor anything else devised by man can ruin this cavern. It is one of the most impressive sights in the country.

We parked for a week at the Grand Canyon, where every night the Forest Rangers put on a free "entertainment" in the lobby of one of the hotels. This consisted of corny jokes interpersed with Western songs like "Bury me not on the Lone Prairie" and popular sentimental ballads. Two of the instruments in their band were an old-fashioned washboard and a saw, which gave the performance an "old settler" flavor. The men themselves sat on the stage in ten-gallon hats and red bandannas. One of them told me that if he should go back home to Montana in that costume, the boys there would shoot him. But to our sons, who had been thoroughly indoctrinated in the exploits of Tom Mix, these young men were merely extensions of that fabulous hero. More interesting to me were the Navaho dancers, who performed once a day in full tribal regalia. Their voices, their dress, their drums, and their dances made an unforgettable spectacle. (A few evenings later, out on the Painted Desert, two-year-old Gregory did a Navaho dance for us; his slow steps, hunched shoulders, and constant turning round and round made his performance truly Indian.)

During these days at the Canyon we spent no money on gas and oil, and so we accumulated enough to go on muleback down to the Colorado River, at the bottom of the mile-deep cleft. This is one of the most precarious rides ever dreamed up for tourists. Visitors go down in groups of eight, each attended by a "cowboy," who guides them down a narrow zigzag trail on the face of the rugged cliffs.

We looked forward to this trip as a high point of our Western adventure. Gregory of course was too small to go; we had to leave him at the infirmary. While Jeannette and I were arranging this, our four impatient older sons joined an earlier group and were on their way to the bottom.

Jeannette's mule was a large white creature called Marble. I rode immediately behind her and saw her badly frightened for the first time in my life. Marble stopped suddenly, reached his long head down over the outer edge of the trail, and tried to pluck a patch of

(above left) The newlyweds in their passport photo, 1922; (above right) The young father with his first-born son, 1924; (below) The Wesleyan professor at work over coffee and Cokes, ca. 1927 (photo by Hartford *Courant*)

(above) Coffee time in a North Country camp, early 1930's; (below) The trailer on a South Dakota road, 1937

grass. This left Jeannette high in the air. She leaned as close as she could to the canyon wall, for she knew that one false step would plunge her and Marble to their deaths.

Fear would have seized us both if we had gone down in the earlier group with our boys, for Nick's mule did stumble and fall flat on his belly. He scrambled quickly to his feet; Nick kept his seat unruffled, and no harm was done. Pretty good, we thought, for a ten-year-old on his first-ever horse or muleback ride!

On the way down into the canyon we went through several zones of climate, several ages of creation. The scenery around us defied description. The changes of light and shade were so stunning and so frequent that they would drive a painter crazy. In spite of these bewildering changes, the dominant atmosphere was one of peace almost impossible to describe. Priestley made a brave attempt at it in his book *Midnight on the Desert*, but even he was not entirely successful. He did, however, say something I have never forgotten: "If I were an American, I should make my remembrance of it the final test of men, art and policies; I should ask myself: Is this good enough to exist in the same country as the Canyon?"

For my part, I believe that if the Canyon is ever depicted correctly, it will be in poetry and by someone who was born and has lived there. My own reaction came out in a sonnet which reads:

> Great scenery has been my meat and drink
> Since waves first leaped with me on cliffs of Maine.
> But not until I reached Grand Canyon's brink
> Did I know the view that makes all language vain;
> I wondered then what star above this spot
> Wore on its breast a jewel half so fair,
> And envied constellations whose fixed lot
> Would let them nightly gaze and worship there.
>
> The ages of the world are in this gorge,
> Illimitable mystery haunts its haze;
> The hammer and the anvil that can forge
> So many miracles of stones and clays,
> Pre-eminently here have shaped and riven
> Fit buttresses for naves and vaults of Heaven.

On the way to Zion Canyon we drove across the Painted Desert, where red and yellow sands stretched in all directions. Ours was the only vehicle on the road; and the silent, peaceful desert made us feel that we were the only living humans in that part of the world. Late in the morning the boys spotted a large herd of wild buffalo a quarter of a mile off the road. We stopped and tried to photograph them, but for every yard we walked toward them, they pulled back the same distance. Weeks later a rancher told us that if we had stood perfectly still, the herd, full of curiosity, would have moved slowly toward us.

Zion was deep, narrow, and in spots vertically walled, with the Virgin River cutting ever deeper into its floor. We camped near some other tenters in a grove of cottonwoods whose falling "cotton" lay like a veil over the red earth. Deer came to the river to drink and did not seem frightened when they raised their heads and saw us. Singing birds woke us in the morning. The tall cliffs soared upward around us, splashed with what one writer has called the colors of a million rainbows.

Late in the evening, after a day of climbing to a high waterfall and replenishing our larder at the park store, we finally got the children to bed. Jeannette was dead tired, but I insisted that we walk down the road and see the canyon in the moonlight. It was surpassingly lovely. It made me tender, "This place," I said, "is a perfect setting for a honeymoon." But Jeannette was lifted beyond human emotion into the clear cold passionless Infinite. Those canyon walls in the chill night air, rising stark and ageless, spoke to her not of warm human relationships but of cool abstractions: Destiny, Space, Life in Death. The result, of course, was a difficult situation!

Weeks later I wrote a sonnet in which I tried to express the sublimity of these soaring walls of rock:

ZION CANYON IN MOONLIGHT

Cathedrals were inspired by scenes like this;
But Chartres' long nave itself cannot compare
With Zion Canyon in the moonlit air
Of Southern Utah spring. The mood of bliss
Stirring within the noblest edifice
The Middle Ages left in Mary's care
Moves me no more toward reverence and prayer
Than does this Intermountain Oasis,—

This masterpiece of Time on which are spread
Brown, gray, and ruby walls, the Great White Throne,

The Virgin River singing in its bed,
The fragrance of the sage like hyssop blown
Down tessellated floors, while stars on high
Sprinkle the dome as they wheel slowly by.

We loved Zion and were sorry to leave it as we headed northeast for Bryce, the most arresting of all the canyons. It is a "box" canyon. Such a dazzle of red, pink, and cream, and such a variety of formations like castles, temples, and thrones, are enough to make a jaded sour man forget his doom and rejoice. For a while we just stood and looked at the stupendous spectacle. It was a perfect day. The white clouds and deep blue sky intensified the beauty of the canyon. As before, I tried to express my emotions in verse:

IN BRYCE CANYON

Vermilion vistas halt the traveler here!
Domes, minarets, and spires, row on row.
Temples too gaudy for devotion show
Bright pink and coral shades the sun holds dear,
Gleaming as though in some lost glacial year
This region were a cavern, and the ice
Through alchemy unknown outside of Bryce
Ripped off the crust and let the gold appear.

And Oh! what gold it showers at set of sun!
The pinnacles are spaced and toned like strings
Of some celestial harp; bright colors run
Like notes along the canyon—offerings
That yield the eye a visual overture
Sweeter than mortal hearing could endure.

From Bryce we drove to St. George, bought groceries, and headed westward across the Nevada desert, for I was due in Pasadena on May 27 to meet the Wesleyan Alumni of Southern California and give a report on the college. Somewhere on the desert we lost track of time. Was today tomorrow, or yesterday today? With luck, and despite a delay of many hours when two tires failed simultaneously, we reached Pasadena on the right afternoon, only to find a disturbing roadside sign: No HOUSE TRAILERS ALLOWED WITHIN THE CITY LIMITS. But there was a trailer camp just a few blocks away, still outside the city proper. We checked in and hustled—to feed the children, make the beds, clean up and dress, find my notes—all by seven-thirty. At the close of the meeting an alumnus named Jack Little invited us to camp in his back yard at La Canada. Which we did, until Jeannette, sensing that our rambunctious boys were something of a trial to Mrs. Little, suggested that we move on to Santa Monica. Jeannette believed in this rule: Never take more than two children visiting, and never stay more than two nights. We had planned to spend one of our evenings with the Littles at the observatory on Mount Wilson, viewing the stars through the world's largest telescope, but a heavy fog ended that trip before it began.

For the next few days our plans to go farther north were shattered by two of my former students: Allie Wrubel, now a successful songwriter, and Barton MacLane, who had become a firmly established film actor in character and leading roles. They took us in hand and showed us Hollywood. One lunchtime at the Country Club Barton introduced us to Bing Crosby. He looked at our five children and asked, "Are they all boys?" "Yes." "Well," he said, "this is no place for me. My wife is going to have a third, and if she doesn't present me with a girl, she is going to hear from me." Many weeks later I read a news report that a third son, Michael, had been born to Mr. and Mrs. Bing Crosby. I knew exactly how he felt, for when my third was born, I wept because he wasn't a girl. After that I gave up and cheerfully accepted whatever was sent.

Barton took us also to a studio to watch the filming of a scene from *The College Swing*, with Dick Powell. There I met Ed Wynn, who told me he never got beyond the eighth grade in school but was forever being cast as a teacher or college professor or minister. Barton, with a lead-bladed jackknife, showed our Billy how a man is stabbed by a movie villain; the lead blade simply crumples against his body. This fake villainy was fascinating to the boys. But in that studio I was far more interested in the girls who had come seeking Hollywood stardom and had failed to achieve it. Instead, they hung around the fringes of the sets, hoping to fill in in a mob scene, carry a tray for a duchess, or do some other bit part. There they were, at least a dozen of them that morning, looking forlorn and trying hard to smile, living and yet not-living in Hollywood.

Out in the sunshine I felt more cheerful and said I would like to visit the Huntington Library and Art Museum. At the Library I asked to see the correspondence between Edgar Allen Poe—one of my favorite poets—and Thomas Holley Chivers. The latter, also something of a poet, had lived for many years in Middletown, where he had written violent articles to the *Penny Press* against the use of tobacco; he had also challenged a man named Bacon to a fight during an argumentative town meeting. Alas for me! Someone else had drawn out the correspondence that very day and was dissecting it off in a room by himself. The Art Museum, however, made up for the disappointment. The paintings included Gainsborough's *Blue Boy*—far finer than any reproduction could possibly be—and works by Sir Joshua Reynolds, Romney, Lawrence, Hogarth, Hoppner, Raeburn, and others of that era. I went away fully satisfied.

On the way to San Francisco we had a scary encounter with a holdup man north of Bakersfield—a short, dark, saturnine, bearded fellow who stood by the roadside, pistol in hand. We got out of that one when the boys in the back seat, who had not seen this man, threw little Gregory bodily into the front seat, amid loud laughter; whereupon the holdup man slipped his gun back into his coat pocket.

We took in a rodeo at Visalia. First there was a parade of mounted cowboys led by a beauteous Queen of the Rodeo, tall and at ease in the saddle, as lovely to look at as any of those beauties who had decorated the San Antonio Feast of Roses. Then came the usual events—calf-roping, riding bucking bronchos, bulldogging steers. There were many injuries—broken arms, splintered ribs, crushed legs. I did not relish this sort of Roman-holiday spectacle, but the effect on the boys was exactly the opposite. They were impatient to learn to ride like these cowboys—eager to grow up, so that they too might become professional rodeo riders.

At Sequoia National Park the giant trees surpassed description. Many were over three hundred feet tall and were said to be three to four thousand years old. The inevitable and irrespressible poem was this:

TO A GIANT SEQUOIA

You who have known the world three thousand years,
Enduring earthquake, hurricane, and fire
While empires fell, and Israel saw expire
Jesus upon the Cross in blood and tears, —
How have you risen above the myriad fears
That hound men's lives, and from a lofty spire
Retained full faith in life? Is your desire
Conquest of Death whose drums reach other ears?

Instruct us how the fires that lay us low
Can save, like yours, our sinews from decay;
Your imperturbability bestow
Full-branched upon our race; teach us your way
Of growing old in redwood fortitude,
That we with your own strength may be imbued.

At Yosemite the bears put on their usual evening show, and the nine o'clock "firefall" (still a nightly feature in 1937) was surely spectacular. It was caused by rangers lighting a huge bonfire on the heights, then pushing the whole blazing mass into the canyon. The waterfalls were not at their best, for in June the streams run low.

San Francisco meant a reunion with two of my dearest Alaska friends, Curt and Lou Welch. His health had failed and he was confined to a chair most of the time. But he still loved word puzzles, rebuses, and difficult literary and philosophical questions; and still wanted the answers to be cushioned by a modest bet. So a little money-passing enlivened this game. Lou seemed in excellent health and told us she would visit us in Connecticut the following summer—which she did.

We talked much of our days together in Alaska, and they told me what had happened to many of the folk we had known in Council City. One of the saddest of their stories was about two people I loved: Fred Ayer and his wife Elsie. It came out that Fred, while he was managing the Blue Goose mine, had been sending money Outside to help his nephew get through medical school. Then, when Fred and Elsie left Alaska themselves, they found the nephew had become not only a doctor but also a drug addict. Elsie determined to cure him. She went with him to call on patients and sat in the car until he returned. She served him the finest meals she could prepare, and she was an excellent cook. She left poor Fred day after day to provide for himself as best he could; she was obsessed and could think only of the boy. Fred, one of the most gentle souls I have ever known, finally forced a showdown. "It's either me or that boy. You choose." Elsie replied, "I don't believe he's hopeless. I cannot give him up." But her effort was wasted; the boy was incurably addicted, and Elsie ended her days in a Santa Barbara rooming house. As for Fred, a little Jewish girl got her eye on him and went back with him to Alaska.

After this visit we moved north through the redwood forest and regretted to see these magnificent trees being cut down and sawed into lumber. Here the landscape grew to look more like New England, though the valleys were deeper and the hills higher—a sort of New England, one could say, with less coziness but greater grandeur. Farther along I found myself gravitating toward the seacoast, which drew me more and more. I could not resist the unspoiled beaches and blue sky, and often stopped to gaze out over the Pacific. I finally took out my notebook and wrote:

CALIFORNIA COAST

The California coast for many a mile
Sings to the world an oratorio
Whose major strains through salty breezes blow
Strength and good cheer enough to wipe all vile
Contagion from the land. Here the grand style
In Music's offering rings fortissimo;
Here flowers that fringe the rolling sand dunes glow
Deeper than inland blooms. Here single file
The urge to Freedom lives in militant waves
That break themselves upon the indifferent sand.
What music in the effort! How each braves
Impossible hazards rushing toward the land
In thunder tones as up the gradual stair
It crashes on the keyboard of the air!

In Oregon the roads were already familiar; years earlier I had traveled them at breakneck speed with Ned Larrabee in his Stutz. Now, seen at a more leisurely pace, Mount Hood and the Columbia and Multnomah Falls had, if anything, gained in their appeal. It was good to see Reed College again and receive a warm welcome from Professor Knowlton, my sometime colleague at Utah (kicked out at the same time I was), who was extremely happy in his new post here.

Seattle meant a four-day visit with other good friends of Utah days—Frank Holman and his wife Carol. Frank had been the acknowledged leader of the great anti-Mormon rebellion. Now he was among the most respected lawyers in the Northwest. He was later elected president of the American Bar Association, and still later was the man behind the Bricker Amendment to the Constitution, which would have limited the President's treaty-making powers (it was defeated). Frank was an old-fashioned patriot to whom alliances meant "entanglements," and he feared that international treaties would take precedence over our own Constitution. I on the other hand felt that the only future for this planet lay in international understandings and agreements. Frank and I still differed and still argued, but remained fast friends.

We said good-bye to the Holmans and turned homeward. A traveling New Englander is at his best when he is heading home, and we were no exceptions. I was ready to agree with Emerson that "Travel is a fool's Paradise." But we still had miles to go, wonderful things to see, and experiences we would never forget.

The first of these was Mount Rainier, which we found an inspiration when initially seen in the distance. It is not as tall as Mount McKinley or Mount Whitney, but it seems much taller because it rises out of a plain. With no nearby foothills to nudge its shoulders, it stands alone in naked glory. The Indians had called it "the mountain that was God." Taking this as my cue, I wrote:

MOUNT RAINIER

"The Mountain that was God," the Indian said,
Rainier, whose glorious Fujiyama cone
Entered his breast and clarified his head,
And led him to a hitherto unknown
And loftier Hunting Ground. The white man felt
His spirits drinking from a purer fountain
Sighing, like Bunyan's pilgrim, who had dwelt
Too long away from his Delectable Mountain.

Rainier's white breast looms as a Comforter
To restless men who roam the world for peace;
Its majesty invokes an inner stir,
A Hermon dew, a breath of ancient Greece;
Its glistening slope, in glacial glory shod,
Holds nooks where Moses might have talked with God.

On we went to Yellowstone, pausing en route to gaze at the Grand Coulee dam — not then completed, but still an engineering project of staggering proportions. At Yellowstone we camped and waited for our June 30 money to arrive. By July 5 it had not come and we were desperate — no milk, no bread, no sugar, and no funds. There was only one thing to do: try to cash a personal check somewhere. Could I do that wearing the scraggly beard I had been growing since Seattle? Jeannette was sure I could not; so the beard had to go. Freshly shaved and with curly-haired little Gregory in my arms, I went to the Old Faithful Inn with Jeannette beside me. Despite a sign reading "No personal checks cashed here," the manager finally relented when I offered my watch as security. "All right," he said, "how much do you want?" "Fifteen dollars." He took a good look at Gregory and said, "Here! Keep your watch" – and handed it back to me along with three beautiful five-dollar bills.

One of my friends has called Yellowstone "a tourist-ridden bore," but we did not find it so. The park was much bigger than I had realized, three-fourths the size of Connecticut. The fishing was good, the bears always interesting (though the occasional bear that goes berserk – and one of these raced by within a few yards of us – can be a real danger). Old Faithful was fascinating as it shot into the sky. I put my watch on it and was surprised and pleased by its irregularity. It is said to go every hour on the hour, but not so. Old Faithful was a poet that knew the rhythmical value of regular irregularity. After watching it a long time Jeannette took two movie shots of it; the one in color was magnificent—sparkling water against a deep blue sky.

Going out of the park, we met with the most terrifying hour of our entire trip. We were rolling rapidly downhill on a single-track mountain road that had turnouts here and there to let cars pass in the opposite direction. When I tried to slow down, I found the electric brakes on the trailer wheels were not working. The enormous weight of the trailer plunging faster and faster downhill was too much for the car brakes to handle alone. All I could do was keep going down and pray that we met no car coming up. Those two miles seemed like three hundred. But our guardian spirit was with us. We made the bottom safely, and I quickly replugged the trailer brake connector and wound it with tape so that such a thing could not happen again.

Crossing Wyoming, we had one close call as we drove eastward on a sunken road from which we could not turn without upsetting. Night had already fallen, there was a torrential thunderstorm, and the gas gauge read "Empty." We could only hope to find a turn-off before we stalled in the middle of the road. Finally a lightning flash revealed gas pumps and a dark building ahead; we gratefully pulled in and spent the night there. Next morning, when the red-headed young owner appeared, we found our tank was bone dry; I couldn't even start the engine until I had poured a gallon of gas into it. This place had a sign reading "Wild Cat," and in fact there was a big yellow wildcat caged on the other side of the pumps.

Every now and then we were reminded by historical markers of the wars with the Indians. I told the boys the story of General George Custer and his rash attack on the Sioux at the Little Big Horn, where he and his entire brigade were wiped out. Instead of mourning the loss of these brave men, the boys asked, "Why weren't we born in those days? We could have loaded our muskets and fought the Indians." I had already learned that pacifism receives its first defeat in the nursery — with boys wanting pistols, guns, bows and arrows, military uniforms, and all the rest. Having nothing but sons, I found myself living in a bloodthirsty world. There was nothing to be done about it. Not Utopia but a battlefield is a boy's wish. Even the church gets drawn into the military picture. The children said if they had lived in Pilgrim days, they would have chosen to be guards standing before the church, muskets loaded, watching for Indians. Their dreams of riding horseback and shooting redskins made me think of Mark Twain's prayer to God to help him grow up and become a pirate.

Then it was a horseback ride up Mount Kearney, on through the well-named Badlands of South Dakota, and so to Lincoln, Nebraska — with a few bad hours when we were stuck in the gumbo mud of a narrow uphill detour just west of Murdo. We couldn't pull off the road because of deep ditches on each side, the rain fell in torrents, and we couldn't move more than a few feet without stalling the engine. Finally we gave up and just sat there. Jeannette counted thirty-five cars stopped behind us, and many more as far up the hill as we could see. At length the rain stopped, and a dozen men pushed our trailer to a level spot at the hilltop, where we could move aside and leave room for their passage.

At Lincoln I headed straight for the University of Nebraska, where Lane Lancaster, a former colleague at Wesleyan, was now teaching. We had a fine reunion; but the person I most wanted to see there (aside from the Lancaster family) was Professor Louise Pound, who had done such important work in the field of American ballads. It was she who, with only a few English teachers to back her, had taken hold of balladry and made it an integral part of the programs at the annual meetings of the Modern Language Association. Lancaster arranged a luncheon at which I could sit beside Louise, talk ballads, and thank her for what she had done. She was one prophet honored in her own country; her brother Roscoe, famous dean of the Harvard Law School and a pioneer in social jurisprudence, once told me, "When I go back home to Nebraska, I find I am identified as Louise Pound's brother."

From there on it was plain sailing, with only a stop at Elkhart, Indiana, to have some punctured spots in our trailer's sides repaired. New England had lost none of its charm, and the day we reached our Spruce Head cottage was one of the happiest of my life. That same evening I went over to my writing desk and wrote a poem entitled "Leaves," which apparently has no direct connection with the trailer trip but is a commmentary on people:

LEAVES

Some leaves are plucked by whirlwind,
Some by frost;
And some high oak leaves cling
However tossed
By hurricane or numbed
By rain and chill—
Cling and hang on throughout
The seasons till
Spring dances round again.
Her gay allure
So little counts with those
That could endure
The perilous time, they strive
No more to stay,
And drop contented in
Untired clay.

P.S.   Back in Connecticut we were called upon by church groups, service clubs, schools, colleges, and other organizations to retell the story of our trip. Jeannette ran the 16-mm. movie projector and I made the comments. Some of these were paid engagements; some were not. One salesman in East Hartford told us he had sold so many trailers as a result of our story that he ought to make us a present of a new, up-to-date model. But he never did.

P.S. 2.   We had paid $800 for the trailer. We sold it for $500. Since we had held expenditures to the amount we would have spent living at home, we figured that the entire five-months trip for seven people (and a dog) set us back the magnificent sum of $300!

CHAPTER 19

Works and Days, and Some Students

In telling of camping trips with our children I threw chronology to the winds and covered a space of twenty years or more at one sitting. Now I would like to go back and set down some high lights of those same years.

My second volume of verse, *The Inner Harbor*, came out in 1926 and was well received by the critics. I enjoyed most the review by Katherine Lee Bates, whom I respected as the author of "America the Beautiful," a song I had hoped would displace "The Star-Spangled Banner" as our national anthem. In her review, after quoting approvingly nine lines from my poem "Advice to a Clam-Digger," she went on to say:

> This second book of "Maine Coast Poems," more varied and more vivid than the first, is intimate not only with the sea in calm and storm, "limitless, fog-curtained," or "infuriated," "The breakers boiling high," but with the seashore dwellers—clam-diggers, driftwood-gatherers, lobster-trappers, fishermen, sailors, surfmen, all who tread "the windy wave-battered beach," bringing home their spoils by "A dappled path through evergreens and birches."

The Inner Harbor brought me many invitations to give readings at schools and colleges, and one opportunity to sign with a lecture bureau and scoop up a pile of money. I decided against the bureau. I needed the money, to be sure, but I took a jaundiced view of poets spreading themselves over the landscape. Deep in my heart I felt that platform contacts were injurious to creative work. I saw what had happened to Vachel Lindsay and didn't like what I saw. I accepted a few requests to read my poetry at neighboring schools and enjoyed the young people immensely. But I was always haunted by doubts about how much time I could give to lecturing, how much to students, and how much to solitude and poetry. I kept to my classes where, Heaven knows, I had challenges enough. I lived with my students, shared their victories and defeats, and knew many of the problems of their personal lives. There were no barriers between us.

At these coffee sessions the boys would often tell me of their escapades. I recall one in which three of the boys were spending a Saturday afternoon in a nearby town with three girls of the giggling, wiggling variety, and in an unfortunate moment one of the boys invited the girls to come over and visit them at their fraternity house. Sure enough, the girls showed up the following afternoon and were ushered into the living room. After saying what a fine day it was, there didn't seem to be much else to talk about. They were like Wordsworth's "Party in a parlor,—all silent and all damned." The boys became nervous and feared that someone would notify Dean Chanter (a strict moralist) of this innocent but unaccustomed visitation. "We've got to do something to get rid of these creatures." But how? They finally decided on a plan. One of the boys, named Studwell, went upstairs and dressed up in a cap, hood, and gown. Studwell was on the football team and weighed well over two hundred. He had an impressive physique in civilian clothes, but in hood, cap, and gown he was really magnificent. He descended the stairs slowly and with great dignity entered the room, looked over the girls, and said, "Young men, don't you realize that you have an examination in my course tomorrow morning?" He proved himself a successful actor, for the girls thought that they ought to be going. Studwell scowled at them as they went out, and before they had gone two hundred yards the boys all burst out into the one and only laugh they had had all afternoon.

Once when Robert and Elinor Frost were visiting at our home, a student entered by the side door and went up to my study. Elinor looked at Jeannette with astonishment and said, "Do you allow that? I wouldn't think of letting a boy come into my house and run upstairs to see Robert. I'd shoo him away in a hurry. And only God knows what Robert would do to him."

I not only knew the boys in my classes but I got well acquainted with other groups at the Wesleyan store over daily Cokes and coffee. We talked literature, sports, and social problems in America. Many of them have since told me that it was there I did my best work—a rather doubtful compliment.

In debating work a professor cannot hide himself. In a sense he is like Henry the Eighth wrestling with his courtiers. He is compelled to show what he knows and how he stands on any current public question. This was doubly true in my case, for I paid little or no attention to the tricks of stage oratory. I put all my stress upon the subject matter of both sides of the question. In this way I unconsciously prepared myself for a fling at public life later on.

Even though I needed money desperately, I refused offers of summer-school work. Each summer I went back to Maine to write. Henry Ingraham, the treasurer of the Board of Trustees, became interested in my poetry and arranged the payment of my salary so that I would have three months due in June to last me through the summer.

In 1927 I bought a hundred feet of shoreline property at Spruce Head Island for $3 a foot. That summer I had no money to pay for the rent of a cottage. We lived in a canvas tent with our three children. With rain and fog and storm, it was the most unpleasant summer I ever knew. Each morning for forty days I built a fire in front of our tent in the dampness, and each morning Jeannette went out with a topcoat over her head and cooked the cereal for breakfast. The only thing that saved us was an extra tent for the storage of games and reading, which Robert Frost gave us on our way to Maine. It was a grim summer. On September 1 the sun repented and came out "with all his beams full dazzling"! And those fourteen first days of September, their light enhanced all the more because of the misery we had been through, were red-letter days in our lives.

The following year we bought for $338.25 an 18 x 18 garage, prebuilt in sections including a fir floor, and set it up on our property. Later we built on a 6 x 10 kitchen, and a year later an 11 x 18 screened-in sleeping porch. Still later we built a spacious fireplace in the living room which cost us $200. The village neighbors laughed at this expenditure, and thought that the money should have been used for an interior toilet. But no. We put first things first, and did not change our cottage from the eighteenth century to the twentieth century until ten years later. I did spend another $200 for a "writing shack" about three hundred feet from the camp. There I could be alone to "meditate the thankless Muse." Jeannette did me a great service by keeping the children away, at least during the morning—a service she was unable and unwilling to render when grandchildren swarmed all over the property. With a few hundred dollars bequeathed to Jeannette by her mother we purchased more land along the shore. We also bought a wherry with a 3½ horsepower make-and-break Mianus engine. With this we made many trips into the bay fishing and many excursions to Mussel Ridge Islands.

In 1926 my third child was born. I wanted a girl. I had observed what comfort other daughters had been to their fathers, and felt left out. When my third turned out to be a son, I went home and shed a few tears. When I got him into my arms, of course, he was a joy like the other two. I decided then that I could never have a daughter of my own, but I knew what I was missing as these lines testify:

DADDY

When a little girl says, "Daddy,"
I sense there is something more
Than there is when a boy says, "Daddy."
I try to open the door.

And view the delicate difference,
I dig to uncover the gist
Of the little daughter's "Daddy"
Which no sane man can resist.

Is it not the mystique of woman
That rouses the maleness in Dad
And makes him the blob of putty
That Eve made of Adam unclad?

We fathers who have no daughters
Are the first to decipher the tone
That never on earth will be ours,
A joy we can call our own.

In 1927 I was raised to associate professor, but I was given to understand by the President that it was for one year only and did not guarantee me tenure. Some of the trustees still regarded me as a wild man, and some of the fathers asked their sons not to take any courses with me. A few of the sons told me this over coffee. I assured them that I was just a plain old-fashioned American who would like to see in this country a more equitable distribution of wealth. In these days at Wesleyan we were not distracted by coeducation, and spent long hours arguing about the state of the nation and the world—something we could not have done if the alluring charm of the fairer sex had been seducing us.

In 1925 I joined a group of undergraduates in an effort to write and publish a literary magazine. In it we wanted stories, essays, poems, and criticism. The college gave us no financial help for the first two years. We had to scrounge around at laundries, drugstores, bookstores, and other such places selling advertisements. I did some of the begging myself, but George Reynolds, the business manager, saved the pamphlet from going under in the middle of the second year.

We named our magazine the *Cardinal*. At the beginning of the third year the college stepped in and to our great relief helped us finance our venture. The magazine endured into the '70's, although during the last few years it has confined itself entirely to poetry and has been published only once or twice a year.

The boys who wrote for this magazine and those who took part in the debates were learning how to express themselves, and were getting something valuable out of college. The boys who merely absorbed what their professors said were getting very little. These were at their best on the days before vacations when they were not allowed to cut classes. They would stack their suitcases outside the door, enter the room with a brighter glint in their eyes than at any other time during the semester, and keep their ears alert for the ringing of the bell that meant freedom. They convinced me at that hour that they had souls as well as bodies, and I could see in their eyes that they were bubbling over with joy.

I am tempted at this juncture to enumerate a number of students I have had in my classes. If I submitted to the temptation I would fill another book. But I must mention one student who entered as a freshman in September 1927 and graduated in the class of '31. Charles Olson was both a debater and a poet. Hence I saw much of him during his undergraduate years.

He asked me if I would direct him while he wrote a treatise on Melville as an M.A. thesis. I told him I would, but only on one condition —that he agree not to read what other people had written about Melville. I wanted desperately to have Olson receive the same impact I received when I stumbled onto Melville in the stacks of the Bowdoin College library in 1905, when Melville's name was nearly 100 per cent unknown as a writer in America. He consented, and we went through all of Melville's prose chronologically. It was a monumental task, but

Charlie was equal to it. The thesis was his own original estimate of the man and his work. There was a May 1 deadline for master's theses. On about April 10 Charlie called me up at 2:00 A.M. and asked me to come in, if I would, to read a chapter of the thesis so he could finish it. I went in and spent two hours with him. Two weeks later, nearer and nearer to the deadline, he called me up at 3:00 A.M. and asked if I would come in to read a chapter on *Moby-Dick*. Now professors wouldn't do that for many people, but I'm sure if they knew him, they would do it for Charlie.

Later Charlie wanted money to pay his expenses while he traced down the books Melville had had in his personal library. President Mc-Conaughy told me there was no money in the college for research in English, but that there was money lying idle which was marked for economics research, and Charlie could have that. I never ceased to thank McConaughy for this. Olson accepted it, and made a careful search in Brooklyn, in New York, in Pittsfield, and in other places. He rounded up 124 Melville books—95 of which he discovered in the home of one of the writer's granddaughters in East Orange, New Jersey. Reading the many marginal notations Melville had made in these books, Olson deciphered the author's unique shorthand. In the copy of *King Lear* he felt he had found evidence to mark Melville's change of interest from straight sea narrative to symbolic writing. His account of this discovery appeared in Mabel Norman's publication called *Twice-a-Year*. In my opinion this is one of the finest things Charlie ever wrote in prose. This was followed by *Call Me Ishmael*, the book on Melville that made him famous among scholars.

Despite the success of his prose, his major interest was poetry. As an undergraduate in my Modern Poetry course, Charlie wrote me a long paper on W. B. Yeats which was thorough enough for a university thesis. He brushed aside the notion that the poetry of the early Yeats was of little or no value, and made a penetrating study that opened my eyes. I still have that essay, and cherish it. In Professor Alec Cowie's American Literature class, he wrote an essay on George Herbert's influence on the poetry of Ralph Waldo Emerson which was so excellent that Cowie awarded it the only A-plus he ever gave in his life.

Few students ever made on me the impact that Charlie Olson did. He was an original thinker, a stutterer to the stars, and an endless dreamer. I knew him first as a debater. With his height of six feet eight inches and his booming voice, he was so overpowering on the platform that the judges didn't dare give the decision to anybody else! In three years he lost only one debate. That was at Brown University in Rhode Island. He was so humiliated by this defeat that he refused to return to Wesleyan that night. Instead he hired a taxi-driver to take him to his home in Gloucester, Massachusetts. He told the driver that Wesleyan would pay the bill—forty-odd dollars. I went to President McConaughy. "Jim," I said, "he was workin' for the college, and you ought to pay this." McConaughy teased me and needled me—and left me in hell for three weeks, purgatory anyhow. In the end the President paid the bill.

Only once did Charlie show some of his poems to me. That was at the close of his senior year. I read three of them, felt they were too deeply inspired by the work of Pound and Williams, and urged him to give his life to politics and government. I told him that people needed his power, his oratory, his clear thinking; that the greatest lack in politics in America is that politicians don't have imagination—which he did have. But no. He wanted to be a poet first of all.

Years later Charlie came to Middletown begging money for Black Mountain College, of which he was president. And two tires, not one but *two* tires, on his car went flat right in front of the Paradise Café. In undergraduate days he had had a brief love affair with a girl, and they had had a fight about religion at that very spot. She was a Protestant and he was a Catholic. Charlie believed there was a connection between their quarrel and those tires going out at that exact spot.

In December 1939 I decided that his alma mater ought to recognize his achievement and his many services to American prose and poetry. I wrote a long letter detailing his contributions, urging strongly that he be given an honorary degree. But nothing came of my plea. Thirty years later, in 1969, I again urged the college to give him an honorary degree. In response to my plea this time, President Etherington assured me that Charlie was close to the top of his list of men to be honored in June. But death intervened. Charlie left us in January of that year.

He and I had kept in close touch throughout his life. He wrote to me continually; when he didn't write, he called me on the telephone. I felt as if I had lost another son when he died, so close to me was he. There was nobody like him. Each of his visits enriched my life, and he visited me many times. He was great-hearted and sociable.

I remember Dick Wilbur and I once tried to tell him that Robert Frost wasn't so bad as a new anthology made him out; the editor had given Charlie twice as many lines as he had given to Frost. So we spent the afternoon trying to convert him to Frost. One of us read "After Apple Picking," and the other read "Home Burial." We softened him up a great deal. When the women called us for supper, we didn't pay any attention. He was the best of all company. He made friends wherever he went and enriched young men's lives all over America.

On the morning of March 5, 1929, I suffered an irreparable loss. East Hall, where I had my office, the oldest building of the college and an excellent example of early New England architecture, burned to the ground. I was away that night on a lecture assignment, otherwise I might have been found among the ashes in my room on the third floor. The college paper says:

> Professor Snow is believed to have suffered the greatest loss, for numbers of unpublished poems and essays, extensive notes on his life in Utah and Alaska, and most of an elaborate library consisting of many valuable first editions and rare copies were destroyed.

I lost between six and seven hundred books, mostly volumes of English and American poetry and prose. I was buying poetry as rapidly as I could and lost many first editions, some of which are now collectors' items. I lost lecture notes built up over twenty years. Worst of all, I lost ballads that I had gathered in Alaska, southern Utah, Indiana, and other places. This loss hit me hardest, for I had in mind the publication of a book of American ballads—uniquely my own. I began to believe that fire was my enemy. It had taken the house in which I was born, the house I lived in at Spruce Head, and now almost everything I cherished in the form of books and papers went up in the East Hall fire. I felt like rare Ben Jonson when his house and possessions were burned in 1623 and he excoriated the god of fire in his poem "An Execration upon Vulcan":

> And why do this to me, thou lame Lord of fire,
> What had I done that might call on thine ire?
> Or urge they Greedie flame, thus to devoure
> So many my Yeares-labours in an houre?
> I ne'er attempted, *Vulcan*, 'gainst thy life;
> Nor made least line of love to thy loose wife;
> Or in remembrance of thy afront, and scorne
> With Clownes, and Tradesmen, kept thee clos'd in horne. . . .

When I told Dean Nicholson about my loss he said, "Every professor ought to have his lecture notes burned once in twenty years."

The undergraduates, headed by George Bragdon, went around

begging money for me to start a new library. They made me a present of $175 they had collected. With the money I bought new books and put new bindings on old ones that could be salvaged. One trustee, Henry I. Harriman, wanted the college to give me a sum to cover my losses, but other trustees said, "It would be starting a dangerous precedent," and the project fell through.

I will turn aside long enough to say something about two young poets who were stricken by "Death's untimely frost" before they really got started on their promising careers. The first was Marshall Schacht, who came into my English 1 class in 1925 and told me he wanted to be a poet. He asked me to grant him one special favor. I said, "What is the favor?" He replied, "I want to hand in a poem every time there is an assignment." I said, "Do you mean you want to hand in a poem a week for the entire year?" He said, "Yes." I said, "All right; go ahead. But please don't mention it to anybody else. You might get us both in trouble." A poem of his which I put in the first volume of the *Cardinal* shows that he already knew something of his "trade," as Yeats calls it:

SONNET

I never shall have strength enough to hold
The air made beautiful with falling snow—
Like feathers shaken softly down from cold
White wings of angels everywhere I go.
My heart is set to smaller loveliness
That is within the compass of my hand.
I am amazed at grandeur—loneliness.
I love the little things I understand.
Oh, let the windless snow forever fall
From endless sky about our wondering feet!
But I shall dip my hand into a wall
Where snow is, when I walk along the street,
And never look before me nor behind
Lest too much loveliness should strike me blind.

Schacht left Wesleyan at the end of his freshman year. He told me that he wanted courses in art and music that were not given here but were offered by Dartmouth. He was a delightful student and I hated to see him go. In his forties he was told he had leukemia and had only a few years to live. He accepted his fate unflinchingly and died as he was approaching middle age. Although he did not live long enough to "build some lofty parapet of song," as Longfellow once phrased it, a thing he dreamed about and talked about during his freshman year with me, he did publish one fine book of verse entitled *Fingerboard*.

The other young poet was John Ogilvie, a serious, dark-complexioned, lean young man who admired inordinately Stephen Vincent Benét's *Western Star* and wanted to do something comparable to it. He wanted to write this long poem as his senior year "honor work" at Wesleyan, and he wanted me to be his guide. I accepted the assignment, but when I looked over his first five pages of blank verse and found fault with some of his lines, he froze. There we were, he frozen and inarticulate, I bewildered by his attitude. We were to meet once a week for an hour's session, but these hours proved to be the most difficult of my long academic career. No Quaker meeting in America could match our confrontations. If he had had a sense of humor the impasse might have been resolved, but he lacked that one thing needful in such circumstances. I reread *Western Star*, brought it to our weekly meetings, and talked over with him its epic intentions and its limitations. I tried to show where Benét's poem did not measure up to the grand argument the author intended. He listened in silence. So there we were polarized. The only hours I ever knew that went slower were those I experienced in Thursday night prayer meetings at Spruce Head when I was a boy.

After Ogilvie left us he went to Indiana University for graduate study. His M.A. thesis there was on Robert Frost. He entitled it "From the Woods to the Stars." It was so well written that he sold a large portion of it to the *South Atlantic Quarterly*. He also sold poems to such magazines as the *Yale Review* and the *American Scholar*.

One afternoon, a few years later, he came to my home with his wife Olympia, a dark-complexioned girl from the West Indies. "A beauty of deeper glance," as Keats once phrased it. We had a long talk about poetry in general and Robert Frost in particular. He told me he had accepted an excellent offer from Williams College. He was to teach American literature there and work as a member of the English Department. I was happy to see that one of my students was embarked on such a fine literary career. Several months later news of his suicide darkened my day. He had thrown himself out of a second-story window the day before his first baby was born.

His abnormal sensitivity coupled with the absence of a sense of humor was his undoing. The dean of Williams wrote me that he was so sensitive that if a student cut one meeting of his class he took it as a personal insult.

I cannot resist telling about a third student who was not a poet but an excellent critic, Horace J. Kelly. He wrote as his M.A. thesis, under my direction, a long paper on Edward Rowland Sill, a Connecticut poet now forgotten but whose poems such as "The Fool's Prayer" and "Opportunity" were once immensely popular and had a definite influence on Robinson and Frost. Sill was so exasperated by the adverse reception given his first book of verse that he resolved not to publish another during his lifetime—a resolution he adhered to. His favorite magazine, the *Atlantic Monthly*, had a section each month entitled "The Contributor's Club," to which Sill sent pieces under a variety of assumed names. In 1935 the *Atlantic* filled up its seventy-fifth anniversary number by reprinting the best poems, stories, essays, and Contributor's Club items published since its founding. The editors were unaware of the fact that every single one of the pieces reprinted from the Contributor's Club section was written by one man under various pseudonyms, and that man was Edward Rowland Sill. Kelly's research had discovered this and he wrote informing the editors about it. They were so amazed at Kelly's discovery and their own stupidity that they invited him to Boston, gave him a sumptuous dinner, and presented him with a complete edition of Sill's works. It was a red-letter day in Kelly's life, and as his guide in this thesis I shared it with him.

In 1929 I was raised to the status of full professor by the same President who had told me I need not expect ever to attain that exalted position. There was still a catch in my promotion. The catch was in the following sentence: "You are elected full professor *for one year*." This sentence makes it plain that I was regarded in some high places as "Wesleyan's Bad Boy," still on probation.

In 1931 Wesleyan celebrated her hundredth anniversary. On this occasion I entertained Robert Frost. He and his wife came to our home and made us a delightful visit. Wilson Irvine, who had painted my portrait, and Mike Berrien, my most loyal defender and supporter among the trustees, were also our house guests on this memorable week end. The debating team and I as coach contributed our part during that centennial year by winning every debate at home and abroad. That year we even defeated Bates College, an institution which made debating its number one extracurricular activity.

In 1932 my third volume of verse, *Down East*, was published and the critics at last ceased talking about the Robert Frost influence. Most of the reviews this time were plus instead of plus and minus. In a review of the book in *The New York Times* Eda Lou Walton said:

> He has discovered a new frontier, when all frontiers seemed to have vanished, a frontier facing the wilderness of the sea. He has identified himself with a homogeneous and simple people in whom life is still allowed its natural outlet of adventure, just when it seemed that America had no such people left. This is his value as a poet.

The dedication to *Down East* reads:

TO HOMER E. WOODBRIDGE

Yours the unruffled Berkshire hills,
And mine the turbulent Northern sea;
Lulled by the smooth flow of your rills
These tides have learned tranquility.

After my first book came out Homer had urged me to take courses at Yale and get a doctor's degree. More than anyone else he wanted me to stay on at Wesleyan and the only thing that stood in the way was my lack of a doctorate. After my second book came out, however, we took a long walk together and he told me that the lyrics in this second book convinced him that I should not bother any more about a doctor's degree, but go on and write a third book of verse.

I wrote most of this third book, *Down East*, at my summer camp in Maine between the hours of five and eight each morning. This I did in my writing shack, a 12 x 14 building located in a spruce wood on the shore about three hundred feet from my camp. The entire eastern side facing the ocean was of glass with no curtains, and enough of the trees were cut away to give me glimpses of the water. The sunrise out of Penobscot Bay has always been an inspiration to me. Every sunrise is a new creation. No one of them is like any other that has gone before. People who do not see sunrises are missing a great deal of joy and uplift. Here is one poem of the many I have written on the subject:

MORNING BY THE SEA

Give me the morning on Penobscot Bay—
A daybreak when the sun's returning force
Is drying off the rocks whose colors play
More richly in the moisture; let the course
Of tides be low in order that the weirs

> May cast their deepest shadows on the sea,
> And the ebon rock that almost never rears
> His length hold tired shags upon his knee.
> And let it be the morning after rain
> And fog and storm have bullied us a week—
> The glad note in the gulls is here again,
> The driftwood on the shore is new; waves speak
> The madness they have revelled in: each one,
> Breaking upon the beach, shouts to the sun.

At eight o'clock I had breakfast with the family, and was at their disposal for the remainder of the day. We took trips to the Mussel Ridge Islands, to White Head, or to the fishing grounds for cod and haddock out in the bay—all this in the little twelve-foot motorboat which I bought from a Spruce Head neighbor. If ever we were enveloped in banks of swift-moving fog my three years as a lobster catcher stood me in good stead, for I knew the exact sound the waves made on different ledges out in the bay, I knew the smell of different islands, and I knew the condition of the tides at any given hour. All this had been drilled into me from age fourteen to seventeen when I spent the larger part of my days on the water.

Once we were out in the middle of the bay when the cotter pin of our engine played out. There we were stranded in the fog, facing a long, dreary row home with four hungry children to keep in check. Jeannette looked at the engine, saw what was needed, took a pin from her hair, bent it into the shape of a cotter pin, and put it in place. I started the engine, and off it went with a roar! My admiration for my wife's resourcefulness and ingenuity took on added dimensions, and the next morning I did not wake her up to look at the sunrise, as had been my custom.

From my third book the poem "Conflict" has had its title used as the name of a yacht, has been read into a record by the actor Eli Wallach, and has been inscribed on the gravestone of a boy who was killed in Vietnam. It reads:

CONFLICT

> The sea is forever quivering,
> The shore forever still;
> And the boy who is born in a seacoast town
> Is born with a dual will:
> The sunburned rocks and beaches

Inveigle him to stay;
While every wave that breaches
Is a nudge to be up and away.

Another lyric in this book, "Heritage," has had a more interesting history. A welterweight champion boxer, Dick Whalen, had charge of the gymnasium in St. Paul's School just outside Concord, New Hampshire. His fistic days were over. He pinned this poem up on the wall of the gymnasium, and some of the boys read it. One of them, Marshall Dodge, liked it so well that he wanted to use it in one of his "Bert and I" records, but neither he nor Whalen knew who wrote the poem. He asked the people in the English Department of Yale, but they knew nothing about either the poem or the author. Finally Dodge made a call upon Andrew Wyeth's niece, Ann McCoy, one of my most loyal fans, and there he saw my book and discovered the author of "Heritage." He called me up by phone and said he wanted to try out my voice. "A strange request," I thought, "from a stranger." I asked what he meant, and he said he would like to make a record of my poetry including "Heritage," and add it to his "Bert and I" series.

In due time the recording was published and he sent a copy to his old school in Concord. A short time later St. Paul's School asked me to come up and give a reading. I said I would come if they would let me sit beside Dick Whalen. They consented to this request, and at the dinner which preceded the reading I turned suddenly to him and said, "Mr. Whalen, I don't believe you ever bought one of my books of verse." He was noticeably surprised but said, "No, Mr. Snow, I never did." "Then how did you get acquainted with 'Heritage'?" "Do you really want to know?" I answered, "Yes, that's what I came up here for." "Well," he replied, "if you must know, I had a ten-round bout in the Boston Garden. That's over the North Station, you know. I am absolutely certain that I won at least six of those ten rounds, but the referee (they don't have judges in Boston) awarded the bout to my opponent. I was so blue and disappointed that I went down to the slummiest slum in the city, and there I saw an old drunk pacing back and forth across the floor repeating in a loud voice. 'They made their graveyards on the hill!' I was so impressed by his performance that I took a lead pencil and copied the entire poem as he repeated it over and over. He was a well-dressed man who had been wrecked by liquor. I shall never forget him."

So there at last I had Whalen's story. But another question re-

mained unanswered. Where did the drunken man get it? To me the
remarkable part of the story was that he got every word correct.

HERITAGE

They made their graveyards on the hill,
Their houses just below,
And something from the tombs came down
The slope long years ago;

It fastened on the cellar walls,
It climbed the rough-hewn beams
Clear to the attic, back again,
And mildewed in the seams—

Till those who called these dwellings home
Saw the dark spate leave behind
A tiny fringe of graveyard loam
Upon New England's mind.

In 1935 Edwin Valentine Mitchell, the owner and manager of a
bookstore on Lewis Street in Hartford, told me he had faith in the
value of my poetry and wanted to publish a volume of *Selected Poems*
of mine. His selection would include poems from my first three books
plus ten or more new ones that had not yet appeared in book form. I
urged him to contact Harcourt, Brace and secure their permission,
which he did.

Mitchell was something of a writer. He published two books which
showed that he had an interest in the highways and byways of the
literary world. He was also the publisher of a magazine entitled *Book
Notes*. His bookstore on Lewis street was a delightful place to visit.
Here one could meet people who had literary tastes and enjoy good
talk.

Mitchell was a tall, broad-shouldered Westerner who loved books
and literary gossip. Dorothy Parker, whose witty verse and devastating
remarks enjoyed a national circulation, was a frequent visitor. So was
Robert Hillyer, a poet and at that time a professor at Trinity College.
Odell Shepard, whose life of Bronson Alcott won a Pulitzer prize,
dropped in occasionally. Mitchell published a volume of poems by a
local woman whose name was Eleanor Koenig. She was as German as
sauerkraut, but he made her Irish by giving her the middle name
O'Rourke to attract Irish poetry lovers. But, alas, the sales were not
large.

Nor did my book sell as he expected it would. He printed two thousand copies. The book had excellent reviews in *The New York Times*, the *Christian Science Monitor*, and other periodicals, but he sold only about fifteen hundred copies. He was always dead broke, and did not send me any royalties. He was deeply in debt for other purchases he had made and books he had published and was finally forced into bankruptcy. Instead of royalties he presented me with the final four or five hundred copies of my *Selected Poems*. This gift proved to be a godsend. Whenever I desperately needed a few dollars I took a half-dozen copies of this volume to a bookstore in Hartford, Middletown, or New Haven, and sold them for 60 per cent of the published price. My income in this case instead of being 10 per cent was 40 per cent, and these needed dollars tided me over many a rough hour.

In 1935 Connecticut celebrated its three hundredth birthday, and Wilbur Cross, the governor, was anxious to make this a great event. He was a native of Tolland County, a retired dean of Yale University, a man endowed with a keen historical sense. He wanted to make this celebration the high point of his four terms as governor. He persuaded Samuel Fisher, a retired New York lawyer living in Litchfield, to become the chairman of the celebration—an assignment Fisher accepted and carried out magnificently. The Governor also persuaded the legislature to appropriate money to defray the expenses of the affair. There were to be parades, pageants, and exhibitions showing the growth of the state. Each of the various nationalities put on a colorful show revealing the part it contributed to that growth. More than 160 of the 169 towns in the state participated in this great event. For the first time, Connecticut was made aware of its diverse population and realized how much the various nationalities had to offer historically and culturally.

Late in June I had a letter from Colonel Fisher asking me if I would write an ode appropriate for the Tercentenary occasion. I wrote back telling him that Brian Hooker, a straight lineal descendant of Thomas Hooker, the founding father of Connecticut and the man whose famous sermon inspired the writing of the Fundamental Orders, was the man to do the job. I added that young Hooker was a poet and I had read and admired a poem of his recently published in *Harper's Magazine* entitled "The Ballad of the Dreamland Rose." Colonel Fisher sent me a long, vague, bewildering telegram thanking me for my letter and adding the Program Committee still decided I was the man for the job. It seems that they had already asked Brian Hooker to do the ode and he had refused. He told them he was working hard in Hollywood, and was entirely out of touch with the mood of his native state. They did not dare to tell me of this refusal, thinking that if they did I would exercise my poetic temperament and "blow my stack."

I wrote again and told Colonel Fisher that I would attempt the task but insisted that my name be omitted on the program as I might be unable to fill the assignment. A good poem cannot be forced. He agreed to my stipulation. Then I began to read Connecticut history. But no poetry would come. Finally one morning I walked up the hill into the woods above my home and the first strophe came to my mind. After that, it was just a matter of work until the full hundred-odd lines were written. Here is that first strophe:

THE CONNECTICUT TERCENTENARY ODE

What offering can we bring
To the pioneers who made this valley ring
With psalm and sword three centuries ago?
The broadaxe in the river towns proclaimed
Saint George adventuring forth once more to slay
The dragons that were challenging his way
To Liberty and Justice, setting free
Man's urge in separate molds to shape his plea
That Heaven's will be tabernacled here.
Connecticut was Jordan and the clear
Streams flowing to it marked the Promised Land.
Here Hooker, Stone, and Ludlow took their stand
And reared a Western tower that withstood
The dragons of rebellion, fire, and flood.

The big day was October 11. Each performer was taken to a home and cared for. At noon Jeannette and I were guests at the Hartford Club, where an excellent dinner was served, followed by a talk on Connecticut inventions. In the evening we changed our clothes and went to Bushnell Memorial Hall for the big meeting. There the president of Yale read a historical address. Governor Cross followed with a commentary on the early days of the state, an essay compounded of wisdom and humor. I completed the program by reading my Ode. Reporters pressed me for a copy. I said the Ode was not finished to my satisfaction—I wanted to change a few lines. They called me a damn fool, told me that I was missing a front-page headline, but I stuck to my guns. The Ode was finally given first place in a booklet published by the Commission and entitled *The Tercentenary of Connecticut, 1635–1935*; and it was later reprinted in my *Collected Poems*.

The great surprise came a few weeks later when they sent me a check for $250. Nothing had been said about money in connection with this poem, but when all expenses for the celebration were paid, there was some money left over and they sent me a slice of it. It was the largest amount I have ever received for writing a poem.

Unexpected and pleasing as this honorarium was, two letters I received commending my work upon it were even more unexpected and more pleasing. One of them was from George W. Davison, the other from Addison Green—the two trustees of Wesleyan who had wanted my head on a platter in 1924 because I stumped the state for Robert La Follette.

As a result of this experience I felt myself drawn closer to my adopted state. I followed state affairs more closely than ever and ultimately was elected to a state office. And still later I had a part in the making of a new Constitution for Connecticut.

Let me end this chapter on a personal note. During World War II our three oldest boys were with the armed forces in the Pacific; and we had lost our fourth child, Stephen, because of a brain tumor that would not yield to surgery. Our youngest son, Gregory, left alone, could not sleep. My wife thought that another child in the house would cure the trouble. Our church organist at this time was taking temporary care of a homeless boy named Donald. We went to see him, brought him back to our home, and he lived with us thereafter, a well-loved son.

CHAPTER 20

The Robert Frost I Knew

I first met Robert Frost at his fiftieth birthday dinner on March 26, 1925, in the old Brevoort Hotel. The letter of invitation was signed by Amy Lowell, Frederic Melcher, Louis Untermeyer, and Irita Van Doren. The real inspirer and begetter of the dinner was Melcher, who was then the editor and publisher of *Publishers Weekly*. In preparation for the event Melcher asked if I would write an article on "New England in the New Poetry of America," with special emphasis on the contribution of Robert Frost. I agreed, and in my concluding paragraphs on Frost I wrote as follows:

> Of all these poets, Robert Frost, whose fiftieth birthday we are now celebrating, is undoubtedly nearest to the heart of New England. "The love of bare November days before the coming of the snow"; the feel of "the long scythe whispering to the ground"; the fascination of a pasture spring; "the lay of different farms"; the tarbands on the cherry trees; the apples that float before one's eyes after an all-day siege of picking; the wood-pile warming the frozen swamp "with the slow smokeless burning of decay";—these he has looked upon more lovingly than the other poets in this group and written about them with an eye more single to the local colors of the region. In a word, he has struck the rock of the abandoned farm New England with the rod of insight, and water has gushed forth beyond all expectations.

> Frost's first volume, *A Boy's Will*, was a book of promise rather than of achievement. A stubborn honesty may be found in it, and a fine choice of lyric subjects; but it was in the second volume, *North of Boston*, that the accent changed and the poet hit his gait. The accent in this second volume comes from the cadences of the New Hampshire farmers themselves. Their hints, hesitations, half-finished sentences, long meaningful silences, he captured as no one else ever did or ever thought of doing. Other poets, like the two Lowells, for example, working at this same material thought of dialect as the medium; but Frost, knowing the pitfalls of caricature into which a worker of dialect may fall, chose to use conversational but correct English.

These left behind, defeated people Frost neighbored with and farmed with. They, too, were a part of life. Defeated people are people subject to fears of all kinds; and in Frost we read of night fears, fear of adventure, fear of going insane, fear of being found out in an escapade, and a score of others. In the book quoted at the beginning of this essay [*From Whitman to Sandburg* by Bruce Weirick] the author says, speaking of Frost and Robinson, "Neither poet is what is termed social minded: neither one apparently thinks critically of his times." As a matter of fact, is not this portrayal of a defeated people the truest type of social mindedness? In too much of our so-called social injustice he lets the grim facts supply their own moral, as in "The Self Seeker." If the reader is too obtuse to read between the lines, Frost should not be held responsible.

Mountain Interval carried on the accent of *North of Boston* and added to it a number of lyric moods which were new. *New Hampshire*, the latest volume, opens with a racy pcem which is quite different from his other work. He feels free now to talk about himself, his art, and his ideas. He cares less for resiliency in his lines in this poem than anywhere else. We are thankful for this glimpse of Frost even though most of us shy at calling it poetry. Later in this volume there is a group called "Grace Notes" which contains the most finished work of the author. He has returned once again to the more regular lyric form, but he has added a depth of melody, and a variety of color to these lyrics which many never thought him capable of. I can think of no lyric in American literature more certain of immortality than "Stopping by Woods on a Snowy Evening."

That tribute was a favorable one, as birthday greetings ought to be. But it was not altogether uncritical. It was critical of his first book, *A Boy's Will*, perhaps overly critical. At least I think so now. And it shied at calling the poem "New Hampshire" poetry. In spite of this, and before the postprandial speeches had begun, Frost came over to my table and introduced himself. (I was seated at a table with Willa Cather, whom he had already met.) He and I liked each other from the start. He took me by the arm and led me to the back of the room where he said, "Now Louis will be jealous of you but we don't care." I did not know the significance of that remark until much later. He said he liked what I had written in *Publishers Weekly*, but I had not in his opinion paid enough attention to his longer poems in *North of Boston*. He mentioned especially "The Mountain" and asked me to examine it again carefully, for in it I would find his best workmanship. (*North of Boston* had already made an indelible impression on me. I read it at one sitting and came away from it feeling that this book was a permanently durable addition to American poetry. I even felt that he had literally been able to extract blood out of a turnip.) I insisted that "Home Burial," "The Fear," "Mending Wall," and "After Apple Picking" were still my favorites in that book. He laughed and said, "We'll let it go at that, but I want to see more of you. For we have much in common."

Two years before this dinner I had written Frost urging him to come to Wesleyan and give a reading. I added that his second book had made a great impression on me and that I was anxious to meet the author. He replied under date of January 21, 1923, as follows:

> Dear Mr. Snow:
> I'm indebted to you for your good opinion of my work and sometime I must try to repay you by going to Middletown to see you; but I'm afraid it can't be this year. I've been kept away from Michigan too much as it is, by engagements I made before I decided to go back to Michigan this year and by sickness in my family.
> Keep a warm place for me in your heart and some day you shall entertain me.
> I shall be on the lookout for your book. May it have good luck.
> Thanks for having thought of me in the same course with Carl and Vachel.
>
> > Sincerely yours,
> > Robert Frost

In this letter I felt a certain humility in the author which made me more than ever anxious to meet and talk with him. Nothing in this letter squares with the assertive arrogance so many critics have found in his character. One of the students in my course on modern American poetry, Harold Brennan, was doing a paper on Edward Thomas, a poet whom Frost loved more than anybody else he met in England, and I wrote again asking if he would favor my student who himself had written to Frost, and say a few things about Thomas' poetry. The letter he wrote to my student is a little gem. Brennan quoted it in his class paper, which was afterward published in the *Cardinal:*

> Edward Thomas had about lost patience with the minor poetry it was his business to review. He was suffering from a life of subordination to his inferiors. Right at that moment he was writing as good poetry as anybody alive but in prose from where it did not declare itself and gain him recognition. I referred him to paragraphs in his book *The Pursuit of Spring* and told him to write it in verse form in exactly the same cadence. That's all there was to it. His poetry declared itself in

(above) Portrait-photo of the family, ca. 1932: l. to r., Bill, Jeannette, Wilbert holding Stephen, Jack, Nick (photo by Bachrach); (below) At Spruce Head, summer 1932: l. to r., Bill, Wilbert with friend, Nick, Stephen, Jack

(above) Robert Frost and Wilbert Snow at the latter's home, 1960; (below) Reception for Robert Frost at Spelman and Morehouse Colleges, 1954 (photo by Alexander L. Adams)

verse form, and in the year before he died he took his place where he belonged among the English poets.

The fact that Frost was glad to be included in the same league as Carl Sandburg and Vachel Lindsay, two poets I persuaded to come and give readings that year, impressed me further by its modesty.

He had gone to the University of Michigan at Ann Arbor to be poet-in-residence, and it was not easy to get him to come east. I again strongly urged him to come to Wesleyan, and he replied on May 1, 1926, as follows:

Dear Snow

Old devil me, not to write you sooner about the fun it was going to be at Wesleyan in your grand foursquare colonial with you. It's no excuse and the circumstances aren't just ordinary. It's more like an excuse that I haven't had the peace of mind for writing letters or anything else this winter. We've had a long long sickness in the family. Marjorie our youngest and the best poet in the family had to go and give us a scare almost for her life. Good diagnostician as I am (I'm a better diagnostician than critic) I haven't been able to tell what ailed her besides pneumonia, pericarditis and appendicitis, but it may partly have been finding the world too fast among people a little too old for her. There's strain isn't there in outside life-thinking that there never is in inside school thinking.

I suppose you have been scattering poems all over the face of periodicality. I follow no magazines any more to see.

It seems I am about to receive a volume of poetry from Mitchell of Hartford with your compliments. All set—or braced. Tell me about the poetess.

I am going farming again in New England. We've got to get settled near the farmer son.

Not prepared to say yet when I am comng to you. All's up in the air. Best wishes to you and Mrs. Snow.

Always yours,
Robert Frost

Finally he said he would come to Wesleyan and stay with me for two weeks. His letter, dated November 23, 1926, is as follows:

Dear Snow

I couldn't bring myself to haggle about terms beyond a suggestion that I perhaps ought not to be asked to talk all afternoon with the boys on the two days (or is it three) when I am expected to lecture in the evening. So I am afraid you can't have me as free for play as you

would like to ideally. After all what are you dreaming? We ought to think
of this as an intensive two weeks with the boys. We'll get in some time
together. I must go home to the house with you some of the time,
though it seems to be thought best for me to have a headquarters at
the college too. These things are not in my hands.

We'll talk about your book that is and mine that is next to be.

Elinor will write to Mrs. Snow about her coming with me. She can't
get away, I am afraid, till toward the end of the first week.

Ever yours
Robert Frost

Those two weeks were memorable weeks in my life. We sat up
every night until four o'clock in the morning. I had to get up and
meet a nine o'clock class every day, but he slept from four to twelve,
sometimes from four to one, and came down to have "brunch" with
my wife. During that period a poet wrote and asked him to write an
introduction to his newest volume of verse—a request which he gruffly
threw into the wastebasket, saying, "Every tub has to stand on its own
bottom." During that period a famous English photographer arrived
by taxi (my home was five miles from the college) and wanted Frost
to pose many times for him. His name was Hoppé, he had photographed many of the greats of England and was fully aware of his
own reputation. During those hours he photographed my two sons
aged five and six, and did a better job with them than he did with
Frost. During that period we had students and professors out to supper almost every night. One of those students, Lawrence Thompson,
then a sophomore, later became Frost's official biographer.

We talked endlessly about American poetry. To him Emerson was
our greatest poet, our greatest germinal mind. I was inclined to agree,
but I held out for the importance of Whitman. I told him that what
Emerson dared dream of, Whitman dared to do. This annoyed him
because he insisted on the importance of form, and Whitman lacked
form. One poem of Whitman's he acknowledged moved him, the one
entitled "To You," a poem of affirmation of the greatness of a human
being. The others, he said, left him cold. I tried to make him aware
of some of Emerson's atrocious rhymes, such as *date* and *Ararat*, or
zone and *Parthenon*. He winced at the first, but stoutly defended the
second. We had both been to high schools where three years of Greek
was required for a young man who wanted to go to a liberal arts college. "Our Greek teachers," he said, "pronounced the third syllable
of *Parthenon* as a perfect rhyme for *zone*, and you know it." Then he

repeated solemnly those two famous lines: "Earth proudly wears the Parthenon/As the best gem upon her zone."

Of all Emerson's poems the one he cherished most was "Uriel." "The greatest poem written in America," he asserted. To me the poem was autobiographical. That is, Uriel was Emerson himself. This poem expressed the sorrow that was his because he was not permitted to come to Harvard after he had delivered his blasphemous "Divinity School Address." He probably never felt quite so emotionally disturbed before and never would again. The "stern old war gods who shook their heads" were the Protestant ministers of the Establishment around Boston and vicinity upholding the faith of their fathers. They believed "the rash word boded ill to all," and kept him away from their great seat of learning for twenty-five years. To Frost it was all this and much more. It was a poem that dipped into the secret mysteries of life. Like Blake's "Ballad of Heaven and Hell," it declared that "Evil will bless and ice will burn." To him it was a probe into the problem of good and evil expressed, as Frost liked to see things expressed, in "the low tones that decide."

Of the other old New England poets Longfellow was his favorite. The title of his first book was a bow to Longfellow. "You can damn all you want to," he told me, "Bryant, Lowell, Holmes, and Whittier, but keep hands off of Longfellow." Longfellow to him had learned his trade and loved "whatever is well made." He had made the most readable translation of the *Divine Comedy* of Dante, possessed the finest narrative gift of any American poet, wrote a few masterly sonnets and some excellent lyrics, like the one in the "Golden Legend" of Joseph and Mary being held up by robbers during their flight into Egypt. He had found his way into the heart of the American people far more than any other American poet. "Longfellow was the only poet that ever stopped a session of the United States Senate," he told me. It seems that the poet was once sitting in the Senate gallery when he was spied by a senator who admired his work and called for a recess in order that they all might shake his hand.

I was amazed to hear how much stress Frost laid on what he called "trial by market." By this he meant that a poet's business was to write poetry that a common reader would want to buy and enjoy. On the wall of one of the rooms in our rented house at the time there was a framed copy of Edwin Markham's "The Man with the Hoe." He looked up at it and said, "I envy that man. That one poem netted

Markham one hundred thousand dollars." "But, Robert, you are a better poet than Markham and you know it." "Yes," he said, "I suppose that is true. I recognize too that the poem is full of rather loud rhetoric, but I envy him just the same."

We talked at length about his life in England among the poets and critics. He realized what a literary life in the British Isles could mean to a young man. But he regretted that he had to make good in England before he could be recognized in the United States. As his friend Khrushchev would one day say, "That was the bone in his throat." "Don't you do it," he said to me. "Fight it out over here. That's what I wish I had done." He made one grand friend and many delightful acquaintances in England. He said that in some cases he liked the poetry but not the man. In others he liked the man but not the poetry. He gave Yeats as an example of the first and A. E. as an example of the second. In two instances, James Stephens and Walter de la Mare, he said, he liked both the man and the poetry. (I liked Frost so well after that two weeks' visit I hoped I could qualify for the latter category.)

I told him that in my opinion it was the English experience that made him. It was a daring venture but it paid off. He became acquanted with some of the finest writers of the Georgian period; he gained a perspective on those nine years on a New Hampshire farm that he could not have had if he had stayed here in America. I said that his insight was so clear and exact that he discovered perfectly what to make of the life of declining New England. He listened patiently but shook his head.

On his contemporaries he was unusually harsh. He said he could not endure Amy Lowell's poetry, said it was eye-minded verse, red slippers in a shop window or white tables in the Grand Central Station, or white narcissus in a flower garden. He said she had no ear, and reading her poetry strained his eyes and gave him a headache. He said that though Edgar Lee Masters lacked both eyes and ears, *Spoon River Anthology* was a landmark in American poetry; it swept out of existence forever the sentimentalities of James Whitcomb Riley and Will Carleton. He liked nothing else that Masters wrote. I tried to convince him that the poem *Two Lives* by William Ellery Leonard was worth while, that I was deeply moved by it. He said, "There is not one single sonnet in that book that will bear minute inspection." He had a good word to say for Edna St. Vincent Millay's "Renascence" but found nothing very good in her later verse. He was tender toward what he called Ezra Pound's "experiments," for Ezra had befriended him and his poetry in an hour when he needed a friend. He said that Vachel Lindsay had struck a popular note, but that there was too much of the "Tin Pan Alley accent" in him.

A few weeks after his visit to our home in 1926 he took me as his guest to a dinner at the Brevoort in honor of Lizette Woodworth Reese, a Baltimore poet whose work published by Mosher enjoyed Frost's hearty approval. At our table that night were Edwin Markham and his wife. When I told Markham that I had learned the "The Man with the Hoe" by heart, he gave me a big bear hug. Another person at our table whose hugs would have meant much more to me was Elinor Wylie. She was my idea of what Helen of Troy must have looked like. All through the evening she fascinated me. Her iceberg-green eyes were far apart, her forehead wide and high, her bonze-gold hair thick and ample, her shoulders wide, and her bearing majestic. I could easily see why so many men would want to know her and love her. The old men at the Scaean Gate who stood up at the approach of Helen would have stood up for her, I thought, had she been in Helen's shoes. But Frost let me know later that he cared little for her poetry. "It is cold, cold," he said.

Across the table Frost and Markham got to talking about four lines Walter Savage Landor wrote on his eightieth birthday:

> I strove with none; for none was worth my strife.
> Nature I loved and, next to Nature, Art;
> I warmed both hands before the fire of life;
> It sinks, and I am ready to depart.

"Now that is magnificent," said Frost. "Yes, but I have four lines that are better," replied Markham:

> He drew a circle that shut me out—
> Heretic, rebel, a thing to flout.
> But Love and I had the wit to win:
> We drew a circle that took him in.

Frost looked over in my direction and shook his head. The conversation quickly turned to something else.

Frost's dislike for Sandburg disturbed me. I told him American poetry had room for them both, but nothing I said on the matter made much impression. Finally I resorted to teasing him about Carl. One day he said to me, "Why do so many of these college boys want to write poetry?" I answered, "They all want to play Hamlet." "Who wrote that?" he inquired. "Why, Sandburg, of course," I replied, "who else?" Again when we were on the subject of religion, I quoted, "God is the Umpire in a game called on account of darkness." "Did you write that?" he inquired. "No," I replied, "but Carl Sandburg did." "I never knew he wrote anything as good as that," he said. "But whatever Carl is, he is an artist," I ventured. "Yes, but that's all he is."

"Once," he told me, "Carl came to give a reading to the students of the University of Massachusetts, and aside from the hour and a half he was in the Student Building, he spent his time visiting me. He should have got acquainted with the boys. They were paying him. They brought him to Amherst. But he spent just as little time with them as he could."

Of all these living poets Robinson was the one for whom Frost had the greatest admiration and respect. When Robinson was fifty years old in 1919, his publishers sent out a request to poets and critics for letters to make up a brochure that would tell of his great contribution to poetry. Almost everyone responded and sang E. A.'s praise. Frost put the letter in the wastebasket and did not answer. I asked him why not? He replied, "I thought it was merely an advertising dodge." "What of it?" I said. "It was advertising a good product." Robert's refusal to answer offended Robinson and his admirers. Frost told me that earlier they were good friends, drank beer and coffee and had good talks together. From that time on a coolness developed between them. Frost once said to Mark Van Doren, "There can be only one heavyweight champion at a time." And he himself apparently wanted to be that champion.

Robinson did not have any jealousy or enmity toward Frost, for in 1917 when *Mountain Interval* came out, he wrote Robert a letter full of praise for the performance. He said, in part, "In *Snow, In the Home Stretch, Birches, The Hill Wife,* and *The Road not Taken* you seem undoubtedly to have added something permanent to the world, and I must congratulate you." And in 1925, when Robinson and I were given honorary degrees at Bowdoin, we spent two wonderful days together, and he had nothing but fine words to say to me about Frost's poetry. In this case Frost alone seemed to be the ungenerous one.

Shortly before his two weeks' visit with us in 1926, we had engaged a carpenter named Algott to build us two garage doors. He was an extremely busy man and could work for us only on Sundays. He arrived about seven in the morning and began at once. Soon I heard a man's voice calling, "Snow! Snow! Come here." I came to the bottom of the stairs, and standing above me in a long one-piece nightshirt that made him look for all the world like one of the characters in a Mother Goose book, Frost asked, "What is all this carpentering and building going on here? I can't sleep." I replied that I would go see the carpenter at once. I ran to the shed and said, "Algott, this noise must be stopped. We have a guest here who needs sleep and demands quiet."

"O.K.," he said. "I have given up another job to come here for you and I'll try to be more quiet with the work. You know that Sunday is the only free day I have. And that is not really free. I'll be through in an hour." This time the pounding was less violent, but within a few minutes Frost again appeared at the top of the stairs and called out, "Snow! This carpentering and building must be stopped." Again I went to Algott and asked him to cease the pounding. Algott thought of another task I wanted him to do, that is, help adjust and put on four storm windows. He started rather gently to do this new work, which required only a slight amount of pounding. But here for the third time Frost appeared. This time he was in a rage and demanded that no carpenter work of any kind should be done on the premises. So I went back and told Algott that I would pay him the full amount promised if he would only leave, which he did.

That afternoon Frost was the first speaker at an educational parley on the Wesleyan campus. His subject was "The Manumitted Student." But he started off by saying, "I have a new definition for a democrat." The boys who knew of my political activities began to laugh. Frost checked them, held up his right hand, and said, "I mean democrat with a small *d*. A *democrat* is a person who cannot discharge his hired man."

Examine this incident carefully and you will understand much about Frost. The high-strung nervous nature; the mounting exasperation; the annoyance he endured, and yet his mental rumination and pondering and exploration of the experience—with the resulting fresh and thoroughly original definition of a democrat as distinguished from an aristocrat—all this reveals much about the inner life of this unique man.

One bright Sunday morning during this visit the four of us were having a late breakfast. Our two children were playing out in the yard. The conversation turned to the life of a poet in America and the price he had to pay for pursuing his art. My wife spoke up and said, "After all, life comes before art." Thereupon Elinor stood up, walked over to the other side of the table, put her arms around Jeannette, and embraced her warmly. Robert gave me a savage look. His eyes literally exploded and he fell silent. He had made the supreme sacrifice, suffered and compelled his family to suffer, even to the point of malnutrition, that he might pursue singly the life of a poet. He was living what Henry James had written about in his *The Lesson of the Master*. Elinor at that moment at least felt that the price he had paid for his eminence was too great.

At one time later in New Hampshire he told us the family had lived for two weeks on little more than a few potatoes. "One day," he said, "a man from my publishing house arrived. We were just getting up from the table. I somehow managed to glimpse our table through his eyes, and suddenly realized that there was nothin' on the table, just literally nothin'. So I gathered myself together and got a job teaching."

Their early married life together was exceedingly happy. One night when I told him how much I enjoyed his poem "A Tuft of Flowers," he said, "That was the poem that kept us from giving the whole thing up. That was the poem, also, that got me my job at Pinkerton Academy. We knew that one was worth while, and kept on." The way he used the word "we" in connection with his work instead of "I" impressed me deeply. Later they grew apart. She didn't want him to publish a ballad entitled "The Middletown Murder," for example, and she was right. He sold the ballad and had it published in *The Saturday Review of Literature*, but never to my recollection did he include it in any edition of his *Collected Poems*. In his public readings she disliked his little humorous asides that reached only the first three rows of his audiences. Their feeling on this matter was so intense that they made an agreement that she would not attend his lectures, a compact which was fully carried out.

The story of his teaching job at Pinkerton Academy in Derry, New Hampshire, has been told many times, and I will not repeat it here, even though my version differs a little from the versions others have written. Suffice it to say that he coached plays, coached debates, and taught literature to students who were awakened to what literature could offer.

During this period of the '20's there was much discussion as to who was the original Coolidge man. Frost said he couldn't answer that one, but he could tell who was the original Frost man and that was New Hampsire State Superintendent of Schools Morrison. During his rounds of inspection Morrison was obliged to look over private schools as well as public. He said he stopped for five minutes to see what Frost was doing and became so enthralled at his performance that he offered him a hundred dollars to go with him around the state and tell the teachers of English how to teach poetry. Frost needed the money desperately, but he was afraid to face a public audience. He was so nervous about his first appearance before a group of teachers that he put small pebbles in the bottoms of his shoes and walked up and down the street so that the pain of the pebbles would act as a counterirritant to his fear of going on. When he got started talking, he told me, the pain left him and he survived the ordeal. Needless to say he kept on. He kept on until he became one of the finest platform performers in America. Morrison was also responsible for his promotion from Pinkerton Academy to the Plymouth Normal School, where he had a better position with better pay.

During his fortnight with us, students came out to my house night after night—some to show Frost the poems they had written, others just to hear Frost talk. He was very kindly in his attitude toward these undergraduate poets, would hit upon one good line a boy had written, read it aloud and tell the student to bring the other lines up to that one. In only two instances did he seem unkind. In one case a boy showed him a sheaf of three poems he had written. Frost turned to him and asked, "Is that all you have done? It ought to be pouring out of you at your age." Twenty years later I discovered that this student had not yet forgiven Frost for those remarks. In the second instance a student insisted on reading aloud a sonnet he had written. After finishing the boy said, "*Another* poet has written on this same subject." Frost quietly said, "Another poet?" and that was all.

Watching Frost at these difficult maneuvers, I solemnly resolved not to show him any of my own poems, and kept my resolve. One night he took down from the shelf my then newly published book *The Inner Harbor*, and read aloud a poem in it entitled "Advice to a Clam-Digger" and proceeded to show me virtues in the poem that I did not know it possessed. He said, "This is in iambic and iambic is the only meter there is, tight iambic and loose iambic." I disputed him by saying that many of the most popular American poems were

Codline's Child

358   *Codline's Child*

written in trochees, anapaests, and dactyls, citing Poe's "Raven" and "Ulalume," and Longfellow's *Hiawatha* and *Evangeline*. I thought I had him stymied, for I knew well how highly he thought of Longfellow. But he brushed me aside and pointed out that Chaucer's "Prologue," Shakespeare's plays, Milton's "Lycidas," Gray's "Elegy," and Wordsworth's greatest poems were all written in iambic.

He was off on technique again and there was no stopping him. He said, "There are only two lines in poetry that are any good, the lines that talk and the lines that sing," and gave Milton's "Shall I go on? Or have I said enough?" as an example of a talking line, and Tennyson's "Tears, idle tears, I know not what they mean," as an example of a singing line. I argued for a third which I called a *neutral* line, a line that neither sings nor talks, and gave him Coleridge's defense of the dull waste places in Wordsworth's *Prelude*. He listened but was not convinced. He objected to Robinson's long poems because many lines in them neither sang nor talked and so did not justify their existence. But his praise for Robinson's short lyrics was unqualified and glowing. Later in his introduction to Robinson's posthumous poem, *King Jasper*, he didn't say a word about the poem he was introducing, but again sang the praises of the early lyrics.

He told me a few years later that when he heard Robinson was in the hospital he had a hunch he might not come out alive. Frost believed in hunches far more than most men. He said, "I sat down and wrote him a long letter telling him that few if any had made a contribution comparable to his. I told him he had given this country a great number of lyrics that would be cherished as long as we had a country. And I told him much more."

Somehow Frost's letter made me feel that it was written in part at least as an atonement for the way he had acted toward a brother poet he really admired. I wish that letter could be found. It may be yet. But probably either Robinson himself or one of the nurses threw it into the wastebasket.

Frost was out of sympathy with those who write poetry without subjects. He agreed with Emerson that a poem should be a "metre-making argument," that no poet should write pure effusion but should write about something. His introduction to Robinson's *King Jasper* summarizes his objections to the ultramodern abstract poetry about as well as anything he ever wrote.

When he was living and working on his poems in England, he

told me, he made a brief visit to Ireland and got acquainted with Yeats, A.E., James Stephens, and other lesser-known poets. He found the conversation in the region around Dublin the best he had ever known and urged me to make a visit to the old sod. He said he was at a dinner party in Dublin one night where Yeats was the guest of honor. During the meal Yeats spoke up and said to Frost, "You know I was the first in modern times to put that colloquial everyday speech of yours into poetry. I did it in my poetic play *The Land of Heart's Desire.*" Frost, who felt he had a monopoly on plain talking verse, said nothing. Someone at the table said, "Give us an example," at which Yeats replied with a line from that play, "The butter's at your elbow, Father Hart." A lady at the other end of the table, sensing the situation, remarked, "To be realistically natural and up-to-date the line ought to read, 'Your elbow's in the butter, Father Hart.'" Frost told me he was delighted with this revision. It filled him with admiration for a good-looking lady and relieved a tense moment.

During that period it dismayed me to learn that Frost did not believe in the progress of the human race. What we call progress was to him merely another cycle that the race had gone through before. He was amused when I told him that my old history professor assured us that the world would never again experience tyrants like Peisistratus, or Phalaris who burned people to death inside a brazen bull. To him Hitler and Stalin were merely a return to the Tyrannic Cycle. "Fair is foul, and foul is fair:/Hover through the fog and filthy air" summed up his interpretation of the human race.

He told me he thought war was one of the perennial functions of the race and that it would never be outmoded, in spite of my argument that nuclear fission made war obsolete. Men who showed great prowess in battle had an unusual fascination for him. One of his finest poems is a sonnet entitled "A Soldier."

When President Kennedy made the dedicatory address at the Robert Frost Memorial Library in Amherst in 1963, he had to hunt long and hard to find in Frost a poem about the improvement of the human race. He closed his address that day with these lines from a Frost poem:

> Take nature altogether since time began,
> Including human nature in peace and war,
> And it must be a little more in favor of man,
> Say a fraction of one percent at the very least,

> Or our number living wouldn't be steadily more,
> Our hold on the planet wouldn't have so increased.

A fraction of one percent isn't very much, but it was enough to show that the poet had mellowed and grown a bit optimistic since the days of our long powwow.

The religious side of Frost was the most pervasive aspect of his life and in many ways the most attractive. His mother was a deeply religious woman, he told me, a Swedenborgian, who knew her Bible and saw to it that her children should look upon it as the Book of Books. I tried to spoof him once about a poem of his entitled "Sitting by a Bush in Broad Sunlight" and quickly found that I had made a mistake and touched a tender chord. Only later did I learn of his superlative sensitivity. He even told me that he considered the account of man's creation as recorded in the first chapter of Genesis as no more miraculous than the combined factors of air, heat, light, moisture, climate, and other conditions brought into exact harmony to make life upon this planet possible.

His poem concludes:

> God once declared He was true
> And then took the veil and withdrew,
> And remember how final a hush
> Then descended of old on the bush.

> God once spoke to people by name.
> The sun once imparted its flame.
> One impulse persists as our breath;
> The other persists as our faith.

When he read in the paper that there was a professor of biology in one of our Ivy colleges who was not completely convinced of the exactitude of Darwin's theory of evolution, that he wanted first to see the missing link, Frost was immensely delighted. In our conversation about the Scopes trial, which everybody was talking about during those years, his sympathies were all on the side of Bryan and the old Southern farmers who carried their Bibles to the courthouse during the trial. Over and over he kept saying that Clarence Darrow lacked imagination, that he depended too much on rationality to solve the problem of human existence. Frost even believed in witches, and said that in one guise or another they are still with us and still have a useful function to perform.

When he was pressed by his friends to essay a larger canvas, he turned to the Bible and wrote two masques—one a "Masque of Justice," the other a "Masque of Mercy." The entire problem of justice versus mercy intrigued him. In the 1930's he sat up until well past midnight many times in our house denouncing mercy and lauding justice. My wife and I pled the cause of mercy and pointed out the mercies which filled the pages of the New Testament. He retorted that he was an "Old Testament Christian" who feared the softening effect of mercy. Justice as laid down in Deuteronomy delighted him, and once when he was coming to our house he wrote ahead and warned me to read Deuteronomy before he arrived. His case against the New Deal was that it was putting mercy too much above justice, and was in danger of wrecking all we have achieved in our American experiment.

Religion was so deep a part of his nature that he could turn a curse into a prayer. When J. J. Lankes, the artist who did the woodcuts for Frost's New Hampshire volume, was dying, he sent for Frost to come and see him. Frost found him dying of cancer in a corner of a room in a drab convalescent home. He put his two hands in the hands of the invalid and said, "Now you say these words over with me: 'God, damn it all to hell.'" Lankes got excited, took a tighter grasp on Frost's two hands, and the two of them repeated in unison, "God, damn it all to hell." Although he brightened up and seemed to enjoy the exercise and the prayer Frost told him to repeat, within a half-hour Lankes was dead. Who but Frost could do a thing like that and transform a common curse into an uncommon but appropriate prayer? When Frost told me this, I wondered what the people in the nearby beds thought of this performance.

One night he said, "Let's look at the country preachers, and see if they are doing more good or more harm." I'd tell him about our March revival meetings in Maine, how they stirred the village up, how they would bring sinners to the altar—and then, as soon as the revivalists had gone, the converts would begin to backslide. He could match any revival story I had with one of his own. I think he was much more sympathetic toward these preachers than I was, but he would not commit himself either to condemnation or approval. His early religious training influenced him to give the clergy the benefit of the doubt.

The stars interested him more than almost anyone I ever knew. We would sit up until 4:00 A.M. each night, and if the night was clear he would say, "Let's have a look at the stars and see if the Pleiades,

Taurus, and Orion got across the sky all right." Out we would go and he would just look and say nothing.

Those nights when we looked at the stars showed me a Frost I had not known—a Frost more sensitive than ordinary everyday people can really understand. Before that time I had been rough with him and expected him to be rough with me. One night during the early part of our visit I told him that the poem "Provide, Provide" was unworthy of him, especially the stanza:

> Better to go down dignified
> With boughten friendship at your side
> Than none at all. Provide, provide!

"Why does a poet want to be dignified?" I asked. I added that of all people in the world who did not need "boughten friendship," or who would not really enjoy "boughten friendship" when purchased, he was my prime example. My criticism of this fine poem must have sunk deep, for at readings all over the country he would bring this matter up, call my name out in meeting, and chastise me. Friends of mine would write in and tell me about it. One man, Vincent Godfrey Burns, who could take down shorthand, wrote and sent me the exact wording of his comment. Burns wrote:

> In 1962 I heard Frost speak at the National Poetry Festival in Washington, and transcribed his remarks. Here is what he said about you:
> "Wilbert Snow is a poet, a friend of mine, Governor of Connecticut once, and a professor. A great friend of mine for many years. He's very radical and a great pleasure to me. I call him 'Wild Bill'—he's wild. And he came all the way, miles, to protest against that poem 'Provide, Provide!' He said, 'It was unworthy of you!' I said, 'Bill, you're taken care of in that poem. See! Some have relied on what they knew—that's professors. Others on being simply true—that's their wives. That's your wife and you.' And he went home with his tail between his legs."

He just could not bear criticism. Wanting to be his friend more than his critic, I learned my lesson and laid off. Critics can be had for a dime a dozen—especially poetry critics—but friends like Robert Frost happen only once in a lifetime.

The examples I have enumerated may possibly give the reader a glimpse of those fourteen days, but I fear they give only a glimpse. For to have been in the same room with Frost for a fortnight until four in the morning at each session; to have felt the sparkle and sensitivity of his personality; to have noted the changes that came and went in his expressive blue eyes; to have felt the warmth of his outgoing intellectual curiosity; to have discussed endlessly the land we both loved and the life on earth we found fascinating—all this was an experience I would not have missed, or exchanged for wealth and honors.

He was tough on his contemporaries, but when he was concerned, he acknowledged their virtues. He was a man of sorrows and acquainted with grief, but he managed to take Sorrow in as a November guest and accept what she had to offer. In religion he, like Tennyson, could only "faintly trust the larger hope." "There may be a little or much beyond the grave,/But the strong are saying nothing until they see"—as Frost says in his poem "The Strong Are Saying Nothing." At the close of these sessions, however, he told me that life on earth is not enough for a fellowship like ours. We need more. Man, he felt, is a creature of Eternity as well as a creature of Time. His personality, like Franklin's key, attracted whatever lightning there happened to be in the vicinity. I wish his detractors could have caught a glimpse of him at those early morning hours. They would then have seen clearly what I have attempted dimly to express.

Truth compels me to end this visit on a mundane note. When Frost left he said he had no money with him and my wife let him have $25 to get home on. Money with us at that time was a pressing matter. Our salary was only about $2500 a year; our family was rapidly growing; and at this moment we had spent far more in entertainment than we could possibly afford. We needed the money so desperately that my wife, after some weeks, wrote to Frost reminding him of the loan. A few nights later, Frost called me up by telephone from Mount Holyoke College, where he was giving a reading, and apologized for the delay. He had forgotten all about the money, he said, but would send it to Jeannette at once, which he did.

He came to our college again in 1928. The president of the college wanted him to stay at the guest house this time, and not at our home. I saw him only briefly on this visit, and all he seemed to want to talk about at that time was the Democratic National Convention that nominated Al Smith, the Happy Warrior, for President. He feared the effect of the Catholic issue on the country. His real fear was for the American experiment. He didn't want it to fail.

In 1931 I tried to get him to the campus again, for this was a big year at Wesleyan University. The college was preparing for its centennial, and I was pressing to have Frost receive one of the honorary degrees at that celebration. Frost wrote me as follows the last week in February:

Dear Bill:

It's shameful the way I don't write. One of my excuses is I let myself in for too much of everything these days. I feared I was going to be afraid of the New School course and so to sink it into less significance I took one lecture before and after each New School lecture. And I says to myself See how you like that you unbreakable old fraid-cat.

I got some fine poems from you and I didn't even acknowledge them. The egotist in me probably thought it was enough that I liked them. It didn't matter whether you knew it or not.

I'm trying to persuade your revered president to have me for March 29–30–31 after my worst lecturing is over. I'd bring Elinor with me to see the family.

> Ever yours
> Robert Frost

Robert's sickness coupled with the illness of his children compelled him to cancel this engagement. But he did come in October and the college conferred upon him the degree of Litt.D.

A letter from Mrs. Frost before their arrival (dated October 2) will give the reader a glimpse into their home life, as will another from her (dated October 25) after they got home.

Dear Bill Snow,

Robert and I will enjoy staying with you and Jeanette very much. We were sorry that Robert was too ill for our visit last spring.

We are planning to reach Middletown from Amherst by train Sunday afternoon or evening. We will wire you exact time Saturday afternoon. Then we can stay on with you Monday night, and can have a good talk after the excitement of the great celebration is over.

Now will it be possible for you to provide Robert with a cap and gown. He always borrows one. His measurements are

> Head size—7½
> Chest about 42
> Height—5 ft. 10½ in.

If there seems to be nothing available, can you tell me some place where such things are sold? I have heard there is some place in Albany, but do not know the address—

Robert and I are quite well now, and have been traveling in the west this summer—to Colorado and California.

We are looking forward to seeing you both, and the children, too—

Sincerely
Elinor Frost

My dear Jeannette,

Every day I have wanted to write—to you—but the days have been crowded with things to do. We stayed in Amherst a week, much longer than we had expected to, because we got our minds on buying a house there. We are quite tired of taking furnished houses belonging to professors who are away from home for one reason or another. We got foolishly excited about buying a 4 acre lot on a bit of a hill right in town with such big trees that you couldn't *see* the houses on the forked roads below. But, alas! you could *hear* them, especially as one of the roads is a main-travelled one. With lots of trucks. For half a day we thought the place might do instead of a farm up here. There was a grand house on it—once, which burned down fifteen years ago.

Since coming home last Tuesday I have been busy, together with a strong young girl from the village. Cleaning up the house. We had some plastering done just before leaving home, and the front part of the house was dirty with a thin but tenacious film of white dust. Well, everything looks nice now. I expect Lesley here to spend the night with her two babies on her way up to Woodstock, either tonight—or tomorrow night.

Robert and I had a delightful time in Middletown, and you were all so kind to us. You and Bill must have been exhausted afterward with looking after so many guests in your house. It was a really impressive occasion that Monday morning outdoors, which I shall always remember. I only hope none of the men on the terrace took cold, and especially that the death of that trustee wasn't in any way to be attributed to the exposure.

We have had mild pleasant weather since returning home, until today, which is not cold, but we have had frequent hard showers.

You must come and see us on your way to Maine next summer. I think we could scatter enough cots around the place to make the children comfortable.

Affectionately yours
Elinor Frost

In 1932 my third book of poems *Down East* was published by Gotham House. It was well received by the reviewers. To my great relief the reviewers this time ceased saying that my verse was an echo of Frost. I was delighted with all these warm reviews but not one of them warmed me quite as much as a letter I received from Frost the following spring. I doubt if any young poet ever received a more encouraging message. It filled me with courage to go on and "beat my music out."

Dear Bill,

For me specially Etching, The Hungry Shark, January Thaw, Wave Music and so on through the lyrics and sonnets. It need not bother you that those against anything or anybody such as An Indiana Pioneer, The Ballad of Jonathan Coe, The Evangelist, Heritage, and The Flood are less to my taste. Your attitude of a political agitator has to be allowed for. You wouldn't be you if you suspected as I suspect that there is really nothing the matter with anybody. We are a sad lot, rather than a bad lot. My mind goes back to how true Turgenev holds the balance between protagonists in the death of Bazarov in Fathers and Sons. He is perfect in his non-partizanship. I never quite like to hear a wife turned on against a husband or vice versa. They know too much about each other and they are not disinterested. They lack, what they should lack, detachment. Maybe it bothers me as a breach of manners. But if manners count so much with me, then why don't I answer people's letters or properly acknowledge their books. I'll tell you in a minute. But first I want to finish with you where we are. The Evangelist reminds me not too painfully of Sinclair Lewis and a song we used to sing fifty years ago.

> O my God I'm feeling blue
> For I'm six months overdue.

Only in this case

> It was from a grey haired drummer
> Who was round here all last summer.

As George Meredith says we girls are not so much betrayed by evangelists and drummers however: "We are betrayed by what is false within."

But here I go quarreling with you about your tenets when it wasn't more than a week ago I was saying in public that in verse as on the trapeze and tennis court performance is all.. And that's why nothing around college absolutely nothing is as near poetry and the arts in general as the sports of the stadium. The Greeks agreed with me, or they wouldn't have had drama and games at the same time and place.

And all through the book you satisfy me with your performance. You are a going poet and no mistake. I'm happy to be of your audience and proud to be remembered with a complimentary ticket now and then.

Which brings me back to why I didn't acknowledge your fine book as soon as I got it. Well I got it for last Christmas didn't I? I thought it would be a poetical idea if I gave you a letter of thanks for it next Christmas. Honestly! And I should have carried out the idea if I could have stood the strain of being misjudged by you a whole year and liable to one of your narrow condemnations.

Dust to dust and salt of blood back to salt of sea. I may be tempted to steal that some day. But if I do steal it it won't be unknowingly: the source is too deeply stamped in my memory.

Love to you all,
R. F.

In the fall of 1934 I tried to get him to come to our campus again, and sent him a long philosophical poem I had written entitled "Tides" which is too long to summarize here but which the reader may find, if he is curious, in my *Collected Poems*, pages 229–234. His reply reads:

Jimminy criquetts Bill,
I don't know whether I want any more lectures than I have bit off this year. I'd like damn well to see you and correct your aberration of heat and cold. I don't want you to get too far from the abnormal. I say to myself if I can only keep Bill Snow fresh and wild I don't care how intelligible an old age Gertrude Stein decays into.

Your long poem goes all right for me. I mean it hears all right and I get sights out of it. But as you once took too much stock in Haeckel; so you now take too much stock in Eddington. I can't bear you should be wrong twice. Because if you were, I should have to class you with the out-boys on the New Republic who once fondly believed in art for art's sake but have been lately maladjusted by Moscow to a belief in art for the state's sake. If you want someone to follow, follow me. Let me tell you something I have just found out by experimenting in the back shed. A circle representing rest has but one centre. But the minute it comes to life, begins practising law (natural), the minute it starts going round or anything starts going round it, it elongates into an ellipse and shows two centres, one imaginary, one substantial, mind and matter, Haeckel and Eddington. Of the two foci of the earth's orbit, the sun, the one made manifest, is possibly the less determinative in our destiny. So much we may safely affirm. There are things in your poem as I say. But it sticks in my mind that they might be better by themselves. I may be prejudiced in favor of the old you.

We are going south till March or April to see if it won't change our luck back to what it always was before. Any letter of protest will be forwarded from Amherst, Mass. Don't mind anything I may say or do; we're really very fond of you folks.

R. F.

In 1936 I tried again to get him to come to Wesleyan. He had just accepted the Charles Eliot Norton Lectureship of Poetry at Harvard and it worried him. It worried him most of all because he had to sign a document promising to publish these Norton lectures in book form. And that was one thing, he told me, he did not want to do. His letter was written in Florida just before he came north to deliver the introductory lecture. It goes:

> Dear Bill:
>   You see where your letter has been—everywhere but to where we were in Coconut Grove, Florida hanging on till the last moment for a little brownth against all we are in for this spring.
> * I know who my true friends are, which come first in time and importance, and if I haven't paid any attention to your letters of invitation it was because I didn't want to say no. I'm awfully slow about saying no. I ought to say no now. But I didn't say it to Harvard when perhaps for reasons of strength and health I should have said it; so I simply won't say it to you. I'll come to see you, Woodbridge and McConaughy if you'll wait till late April or early May. I can get the visit in when I go to Yale for my fellowship duty. I can't do a whole lot of hard work though. Suppose I give you two nights and one day. You'll have to take care of me. I've had lots on me lately, and obligations to the public multiply. If I had thought beforehand that writing a few poems would lead to all this—The proof that I didn't expect much lies in the fact that I didn't begin with an epic.
>   We'd both love to see you and Jeannette, but I don't promise you Elinor can come. She is sick tonight and has been terribly down all the last year.
>
> Forever yours
Robert
(arrived last night)
> First lecture (The Old Way to Be New) begins at 8 Wednesday night

A banner year in our family life was 1937, when we made the trailer swing around the country which I detailed in an earlier chapter. When we returned home from that lengthy trip, Frost wanted me to come to Amherst and tell the whole story. Here is his letter, dated October 17, 1937:

> Dear Bill:
>   Look! You are dealing (Old Style) with old friends, to be sure, but worse than that with old stagers in their last stages. We have had a terribly discouraging time about Elinor's health this fall; and though she is better now after a serious operation in the Hospital, I am taking her nowhere till we turn south late next month and am going nowhere

except to keep engagements already made and for the shortest time I can fulfill them in. I have only four or five lectures to do and then no more for me this year. I wish you could come up to Amherst on tennis or hockey or skiing teams (faculty, of course); we could have a rousing talk about your wild west explorations. I was afraid you would fall off that narrow road to Mexico City. Did you? And if so, how are you back here with no losses to lament? Your letter sounds intact. I tell you what to do. Don't come to my reading but come to the reception afterwards and monopolize me regardless of manners. Talk about your travels though. None of your class room gossip about Amyednacarlvachel Masters. Because I personally hate such pickled tripe, and if you want to please me you will keep off it in favor of plain tales from the road. Even so you won't have time, you take so long to pass a given point. You'll have to run up to Amherst for a meal with me in a hotel and sit around for an afternoon and evening.

Ever yours
Robert Frost

I was unable to accept this kindly and generous invitation, but did see him a few weeks later and told him about our trailer trip. I discovered that he was no so much interested in the trip as he was in rediscussing the old subject of Justice vs. Mercy. He was putting the finishing touches on his two masques, "The Masque of Reason" and "The Masque of Mercy," and he gave me the feeling that he hoped these two poems would be his major achievement. He said he loved the masque form and that Milton's "Comus," written in that form, had always fascinated him.

Unfortunately these two poems are not among his major achievements, but in the first one on the Book of Job he handles the tone of the talking line about as well as he ever did.

A letter written from Florida in January 1938 reveals some of the thoughts that were haunting him at the time. It is perhaps the longest letter he ever wrote to me.

Bill Bill

Use your brains a moment while we brush up your vocabulary. You simply must not quibble in a serious matter like a win-at-any-cost public debater. Don't pretend you don't know what Milton meant when he said mercy was always first. You know your Milton and your Puritanism. He used it in the sense of first aid to what? To the deserving? No, to the totally depraved and undeserving. That's what we are and have been since the day Eve ate the rotten apple. I bet it was rotten. Eve wouldn't have known the difference. It was probably her first apple.

(There you get a genuine first) And look what a city person will eat for an apple from never having seen one on a tree. "In Adam's fall We sinned all." Mercy ensued. There could be nothing for us but mercy first last and all the time from the point of view of the religious pessimist. Milton's first is only relative. It is very like Adam and Eve's being first and yet finding the daughters of men as wives for Cain and Abel. There is the presupposition of a whole set up of sin, failure, judgment, and condemnation. Mercy comes in rather late to prevent execution—sometimes only to delay it. It is too easy to understand Milton. He faced and liked the harshness of our trial. He was no mere New Testament saphead. (I should like to think Christ was none; but have him your own way for the time being. You'd better have read up on your Deuteronomy before I see you again.) Milton loved Cromwell for his Ironsides and Michael for licking the Devil. He had a human weakness for success; he wanted the right to prevail and was fairly sure he knew what right was. Within certain limits he believed in the rewards of merit. But after all was said for the best of us he was willing to admit that before God our whole enterprise from the day we put on fig leaves and went to work had been no better than pitiful.

I'm like that with a class in school. I see the boys as comparatively good and bad but taken as a job lot in the absolute so really good for nothing that I can bring myself to mark them with nothing but mercy and I give them all A or at worst B. Your sense of justice is shocked. You can hardly credit my claim to godlike illogical kindness. I have always been a prey to it. The office where justice sits with the scales over her eyes has never approved of me. I never go there except to try to get a scholarship or a fellowship for some poor fool you probably would have flunked out; particularly a Rhodes Scholarship because I'd rather sacrifice a bad man than a good to the seductions of Cecil Rhodes. There I go distinguishing between the good and bad but I don't readily see how I can avoid it, do you old Tops (plural as a praise word)?

Illogical kindness—that is mercy. Only those are likely to act on it who know what it is in all its subordination. It was just and logical that a man's body should be taken in slavery when he went beyond his depth in debt. It was illogical that his creditor couldn't take him in slavery and the state should take him merely as a prisoner. It was another step in illogic when it was decided his person should never again be taken at all. Another when it was decided that he shouldn't be reduced by the sheriff below a certain amount of personal property. At every step there were warnings from the conservative that character would be demoralized by the relaxation of strict logical justice. People would go in debt on purpose it was feared to abuse the rich and thrifty. We are now in our lifetime seeing a great step taken in this long story of debt—and it will be something if it is all that comes of your New Deal. It is going to be settled once for all that no man's folly or bad luck can ever reduce him to no income at all. A chicken is hatched with enough yolk in its guts to last it several days. Henceforth not only the rich but everybody born is to be sure of at least a few dollars a week as long as he lives. Never more quite down to the quick. That is in America—and while we can afford it. We are all going to fetch in and make that come true. But don't call that social justice. Keep your words in their places. It is illogical kindness. It is mercy. And you and the Lord have mercy on my argument.

Ever yours

R. F.

In April 1938 Frost's wife died rather suddenly. He had taken her to Gainesville, Florida, for her health, but she continued to grow worse. She said before she died that she wanted her ashes strewn on the fields of Derry, New Hampshire, where she had spent her happiest hours. "After he became famous," Elinor once said to my wife, "outsiders constantly seeking him came between us." She thought during the last years of her life that her own children should have become as famous as Robert. Looking around for a reason or an excuse for her disappointment, by some mental quirk she hit upon Franklin D. Roosevelt as the villain and spent hours inveighing against him and his New Deal. All this made Robert's burden harder to endure.

He sent me a telegram asking me to be an honorary pallbearer at her funeral, which I of course accepted. My wife and I were both very fond of Elinor. She had visited us, and we had had happy visits at her homes in South Shaftsbury, Vermont, and at Amherst. When she and her husband once saw that we were going to spend a summer camping in Maine in one tent, she insisted that we accept the gift of another tent to provide more living room. There was a brisk exchange of letters between Elinor and Jeannette. On one of our visits Elinor confided to Jeannette her deep remorse, castigating herself for letting their daughter Marjorie die of childbed fever in Montana when she should have taken action at once and carried her off by plane to the Mayo Brothers Clinic in Minnesota. To lose the gifted Marjorie—a poet in her own right—was burden enough without the added sense of guilt. Elinor was a gentle, sensitive, and lovable woman. We were both mourners at her funeral.

Upon hearing of Elinor's death, President King of Amherst took a plane to Gainesville and tried to bring some sympathy and comfort to the bereaved man. Robert was living through one of his darkest hours, and said to the President, "I don't think I am making much of any contribution to Amherst. I think perhaps I ought to resign." King replied, "We'll not talk about that now." Robert said that one word *now* sank so deeply into his heart that within twenty-four hours he had sent in his resignation. A telling example of the extreme sensitivity this man had to live with.

Hearing of his resignation, friends and admirers of Frost put up the money and established the Ralph Waldo Emerson Chair of Poetry at Harvard with the proviso that Robert Frost be the first occupant. This chair he accepted with the understanding that he would not occupy the post more than two years. I called on him several times during these years, once to comfort him when his son had committed suicide. The inevitable question, Why, why did he do it? was troubling him. The boy had failed in several business ventures; was also lamentable, the father told me, in his attempt to be a poet like his father. Robert said, "I had just settled a monthly income on him. Perhaps that was the last straw. His pride couldn't take it."

I was with him at another time during this period when the boys on the Harvard *Advocate* were getting out an issue honoring Wallace Stevens. One of these *Advocate* boys was a devoted admirer of Stevens. Others were bewildered by his impressionistic abstract poems and didn't want to concur in the project without Frost's endorsement. So Frost wrote out, "I hereby declare that Wallace Stevens is a good and great poet. Signed R. F." This shows how generous he could be at times toward one of his rival poets.

In 1938 Frost visited us for three days. He came at the moment when Hitler was making his drive into Vienna. To Frost that drive was simply an attack on Sigmund Freud and all he stood for. "To think that Hitler and I have that in common! If I could help it I would not want that man to have one thing in common with me. But there it is." He had the same dislike of Freud that Nabokov expresses so vividly in his autobiography: "I reject completely the vulgar, shabby, fundamentally medieval world of Freud, with its crankish quest for sexual symbols (something like searching for Baconian acrostics in Shakespeare's works) and its bitter little embryos spying, from their natural nooks, upon the love life of their parents."

During that visit we had a dinner party to which we invited a distinguished man of letters and two couples from Wesleyan University. When the dinner was well under way the man of letters drew out of his pocket a sheet of paper on which was typed a paragraph from one of Hawthorne's notebooks describing a forgotten woodpile, a paragraph something like the last poem, "The Wood-Pile," in Frost's *North of Boston,* and proceeded to read it:

> In a wood a heap or pile of logs and sticks that had been cut for fire-wood, and piled up square, in order to be carted away to the house when convenience served—or, rather, to be sledded in sleighing time. But the moss had accumulated on them, and leaves falling over them from year to year and decaying, a kind of soil had quite covered them, although the softened outline of the woodpile was perceptible in the green mound. It was perhaps fifty years—perhaps more—since the wood-man had cut and piled those logs and sticks, intending them for his winter fires. But he probably needs no fire now. There was something strangely interesting in this simple circumstance. Imagine the long dead woodman, and his long dead wife and family, and the old man who was a little child when the wood was cut, coming back from their graves, and trying to make a fire with this mossy fuel.

After he had finished reading the paragraph a silence fell upon the table somewhat similar, I suspect, to the silence that fell upon Heaven in the Book of Revelations when the Seventh Seal was opened. Whether this strange act was done out of jealousy to needle Frost for plagiarism, or whether the perpetrator felt that the dinner party might lag and would need perking up, I was never able to make out. Frost gave me a look that I will never forget that somehow made me feel I was a party to the plot. It was a combination of inquiry, quizzicality, humor, acidity, and wonder. People who knew Frost well knew that he could convey as much by his eyes and facial expression as most people could impart in a long speech. When the silence had grown rather unbearable, a woman at the table asked Robert if he had ever read the passage, at which he replied, "I don't recall that I ever did." And the matter ended there.

The two items have little in common except that they both deal with the same subject. Hawthorne pictured in general terms a wood-pile that had been neglected for over fifty years or more, and ruminated that the woodchopper might some day return from the dead and warm himself by it. Frost, after sixteen preliminary lines, pictured in exact terms a cord of neglected wood left by some individual who apparently had the habit of moving casually from place to place. He climaxes his poem not about someone returning from the grave but about the woodpile itself trying "To warm the frozen swamp as best it could/ With the slow smokeless burning of decay."

In 1952 the people of Derry, New Hampshire, had built a magnificent new school, the Hood Memorial Junior High School, on the site of the original Hood Milk Farm. To dedicate it properly they decided that they would ask their old friend and neighbor and teacher at Pinkerton Academy to celebrate the occasion by reading his poetry. They asked me to come and give the introduction and said they would give me $50 for my part. Frost would take nothing, for he had got to the place where he wanted a big fee or none at all.

Frost telephoned me and said he would go if I could come up, drive him to Derry, stay all night, and drive him back to Cambridge the following day. Inasmuch as he was about the best company in the world, I agreed. The date was December 11 and he was worried about the weather. But I pulled out the *Old Farmer's Almanac* and read to him over the phone what the prognostication of that date was. That proved to be a clincher. He said, "All right, I'll go."

In my introduction I attempted to describe the farm background of Frost, and said among other things that his farm poem "A Blue Ribbon at Amesbury" is not only a fine description of a fine bird, but unconsciously gives us Frost's own place among American poets:

> The roost is her extent of flight,
> But once she rises to the height,
> She shoulders with a wing so strong
> She makes the whole flock move along.

"His poetic flights," I said, "do not soar into the Empyrean, nor do they give us 'light dissolved in star showers,' as the poetry of Shelley does. It does tell us in unforgettable speech-tones the inner weather of neglected people. We have all felt the strength of his mighty wing." I added that he achieved the effect of dialect without using dialect, for if a poet uses dialect he is too prone to caricature people when he should be characterizing them. (I found out later that this remark robbed him of one poem he had planned to read that night, "The Axe Helve," one of the very few poems of his that uses dialect.) In closing I spent a little time on his dark side, quoting: "He moves in darkness as it seems to me/Not of woods only and the shade of trees."— and quoted five other like items portraying the tragic aspect of his Muse.

This ending displeased him very much, he told me the next day. "That may be a minority report of me, I suppose, but I don't want it emphasized." (At his Eighty-Fifth Birthday Dinner at the Waldorf-

Astoria seven years later, Lionel Trilling was the one and only speaker, and his entire speech was devoted to this tragic side of Frost's vision of life. One felt as he spoke that this side and this side only revealed to us the great Frost. The listeners on that occasion sat at their tables like "People in a parlor all silent and all damned," as another poet might phrase their bewilderment.)

Robert began his part of the program that evening at Derry by telling them that he had been a farmer for nine years. "I was not an expert farmer," he said, "but I observed some of the rules of the farm game. For instance, I milked my cows, as a farmer should, twelve hours apart—that is, I milked them at twelve o'clock noon and at twelve o'clock midnight." The old farmers in the front seats who knew little about poetry but much about Frost's farming nodded their heads and smiled, and from that time on he had his audience and held them spellbound. He kept pretty much to the poems of the farm and farm people, and when the meeting broke up they crowded around him in a gathering that reminded me of Old Home Week, or Old Settlers' Day in the Middle West. "What became of this one, and that one, this family and that family?" he asked, with sly characterizations and happy memories that kept them there until midnight. It was a memorable occasion full of nostalgia and good cheer.

In 1953–1954 I was asked by the John Hay Whitney Foundation to be Visiting Professor at Spelman and Morehouse—two Negro colleges in Atlanta, Georgia. I accepted the offer and lived on the campus at Morehouse. While there I wrote to Frost and Sandburg asking them to come and give readings. Frost said he would come but Sandburg said that he was too crowded with things that ought to be done and could not accept. Frost was coming to Agnes Scott College, a girls' school at nearby Decatur, and on leaving that institution would come to us.

The final letter of acceptance, written by Kay Morrison, Frost's secretary (and in my opinion one of the most dedicated and unselfish secretaries any man ever had), reads as follows:

> By now you will have received the various messages and telegrams and know that R. F. will come to you after leaving Agnes Scott. I have asked that Agnes Scott change his reservations in Miami from January 29 to Monday January 31. This is terribly important so be an angel and be sure nothing has slipped up. He must be put on that through train to Miami and not left standing at some little junction in the early hours of the morning.

When news got around that Frost was coming to town, some enterprising reporter put a headline on the front page of the Atlanta *Constitution* which read:

ROBERT FROST COMING TO SPELMAN AND AGNES SCOTT

That morning early an unreconstructed Southerner, chairman of the English Department at Agnes Scott, set my telephone to ringing and roused me out of bed. An angry voice asked, "Why did you put that headline in the *Constitution* this morning?" I had not seen the paper, knew nothing about the article, so all I could say was, "I have not read the paper this morning and know nothing about the matter." The lady replied, "We are paying him a thousand dollars for this visit and we want Agnes Scott to be the focal point of his visit here." I said, "I don't care about headlines; I just want the boys and girls here at Morehouse and Spelman to get a taste of Frost and his poetry." "Are you paying him? And how much?" I fell back on an answer given by one of "The Two Black Crows" and replied, "A certain amount." (As a matter of fact I had wangled $100 from Spelman and $100 from Morehouse for his appearance.)

When he finally got ready to come to us, I went over to Agnes Scott to fetch him, and his host there wanted him to come over to Morehouse and Spelman, make his address, and return the same evening. They wanted to keep his baggage. But Frost himself came to the rescue and said, "Bill can take care of me, put the luggage aboard." Which they did.

On Sunday evening, January 30, Frost appeared before a large audience including many white people in Sisters Chapel at Spelman and read his poems. In introducing him I needled him a bit by calling him Robert Lee Frost and reminded the large audience that he did not use that middle name up North. He interspersed his poems with a talk on the paradox of coupling "liberty" and "equality"—two words that were to him antithetical. Next he discussed "liberty" and "authority," saying that each must limit the other, not to injure our common human rights. After the meeting we had an informal gathering with him in the lounge of the Chemistry Building at Morehouse—a gathering that did not break up until the wee small hours of the morning. It was a fitting climax to his visit. I never knew appreciation quite equal to that of Spelman and Morehouse for Frost's presence among them. If I had done nothing else for those two colleges during that year but bring Frost to the campus, that would have been enough; I would have amply earned my salary.

One afternoon while he was there we took a walk over to the Joel Chandler Harris house, now a museum. He told me that while he was in England one loquacious Englishman told him that Harris was the best of all American writers—that his Uncle Remus saga was the best writing that ever came out of America. Frost did not agree, but he did say that the Uncle Remus stories were the only things Harris ever did that were worth reading. I told him that one of my finest Spelman students in American literature was writing a paper on Harris but that the women in charge of the Musuem refused to let her go in because she was colored. (Like Uncle Remus himself!)

On the walk back I said something nice about Yeats' poem "Sailing to Byzantium." He turned rather savagely toward me and said, "We'll stop right here. Are you another of those damned fools who think the early Yeats was no good, that only the late Yeats is worth anything?" I answered him by repeating from memory that lyrical passage of twelve lines in "The Land of Heart's Desire" which begins "The wind blows out of the gates of the day,/The wind blows over the lonely of heart," adding that in those lines I realized that English poetry had found an entirely new and original voice.

"That's better. Now we'll go on." We finished our walk home without further interruption.

The following day he asked me to drive him back to Agnes Scott, where a dinner was planned for the two of us, and where I could meet a wonderful old retired judge who might possibly convince me that the Supreme Court decision of May 17, 1954, was a mistake. I listened to the charming gentleman but came away unconvinced.

At the end of Frost's visit I felt that he belonged with the Agnes Scott group rather than with the Spelman-Morehouse group. He defended his white Southern friends there as men of good will, honestly wishing to find a solution to a difficult problem but not knowing how to do it. And he had nothing but praise for the liberating work in the South of Frank Graham of North Carolina.

A few weeks after he had gone I gave a reading of my own poetry to some of the students and faculty of the University of Georgia at Athens. The reading was preceded by a dinner with several members of the faculty. One faculty member drew me aside and told me that Frost would hurt himself in the South if he should keep up the program he put on at Spelman and Morehouse. He said, "Frost was raking in some big fees down here; and it didn't hurt him to let it be known that his middle name was Lee." I felt somewhat guilty and disturbed about these remarks and wrote to Frost about them. He replied:

Dear Bill

Nothing to it. My audiences have been crowdeder than ever in the South. The presidents have been more personal than ever. They sit on the platform with me. Twice since I was at Spelman I have been drawn out of my way to Birmingham Southern—a new one for me—to please Pres. Snavely. I don't know the kind of thing you're telling about. Is it meant to hurt me, hurt the South, or help some cause? Smearish I call it, but dinne ye fash yersel laddie about it.

Fine to hear from you. Requite your sentiments with all my heart.

I shall be looking for Gregory at Bowdoin. Have him speak to me.

I'm doing too much for a lazy man. I'm off to see the Catholics in Chicago right this minute. . . .

Wish I could see you. Must soon.

I'm going to England in May for myself mostly but partly for the State Department. Gee is an abbreviation for what?

Robert

Looking back upon those fourteen long nights of 1926, I realize that an amazing amount of our time was spent considering the American experiment. Washington was Frost's first American hero. He insisted that Washington had a much more difficult task than Lincoln, for Lincoln had the industrial strength of the North at his command, while Washington had only a raggle-taggle army plus a handful of unusually intelligent leaders.

Frost had drunk deep from the springs of Emerson, knew the *Journals* thoroughly, and had absorbed and accepted Emerson's distrust of reformers. One paragraph of the *Journals* he had taken to heart:

The reforms whose fame now fills the land with Temperance, Anti-Slavery, Non-Resistance, No Government, Equal Labor—fair and generous as each appears, are poor bitter things when prosecuted for themselves as an end. . . . I say to you plainly there is no end to which your practical faculty can aim so sacred or so large that, if pursued for itself, will not at least become an offense to the nostrils.

To one who had become a "New Dealer" twenty-five years before the word was invented, this antireform attitude was hard to take. To one who had been kicked out, eased out, and frozen out of many American colleges because of his New Deal proclivities, Frost's attitude was almost incomprehensible. His father's enthusiasm for and support of the Democratic Party of Grover Cleveland and Samuel J. Tilden, together with his father's early death, by some twist that Freud could explain and emphasize, led him toward the rock-ribbed Republican persuasion of Vermont. Born under the Grant administration and brought up under the regime of cutthroat competition, he had decided that competition was better than all wild-eyed reforms. Over and over again he asked me to defend such items as minimum wage, medicare, social security, labor union legislation, and the like.

Luckily for me, I had coached college debating teams for nearly twenty years on both side of these questions and could satisfy him somewhat. He insisted, however, that minimum wages would end with everybody being reduced to the minimum, that labor unions would end by labor's taking the place of the capitalists of the '80's and '90's, that medicare would fill our hospitals with women who had little or nothing to do and lower our nation's high medical achievement by attracting an inferior caliber of person into the profession. He had seen people suffer under two great depressions when the country was dependent on an inelastic bond-secured currency, and said he did have some sympathy with unemployment insurance that would keep people from starving. In spite of his conservative attitude I reminded him that he spent an undue amount of his time consorting with New Dealers like Henry Wallace, Senator Mahoney, Judge Frankfurter, and myself. When I told him that I regarded his poem "Build Soil" as an anti–New Deal document, he scolded me and said, "Read it again." As a result of his early training in California with his father, he could not shake off his interest in politics. This side of him came as a surprise to me.

Although I had served fifteen years on the Town Committee, and later became lieutenant governor of Connecticut for two years and governor for two weeks, I had no such absorbing interest in politics as he had. When I ran for lieutenant governor in 1944 and a colleague of mine in the Wesleyan English Department, Stewart Wilcox, became my local manager and money collector, Frost sent him one of the most charming letters imaginable. It read:

> Dear Friend of Bill Snow's:
> In enclose my check for five dollars. I hope Bill will think that is my share of enough to pay for the Lieutenant Governorship of a state like Connecticut. I am willing to buy anything Bill cries for. I should be glad next time to join a Thousand Dollar Club and be one of a

legion to contribute a thousand dollars (one grand) apiece to get him made President of the United States. That would come to a Great Deal of money: ten million dollars. It seems as if it ought to do the trick. Bill has had an ideal pure past for a candidate for office. There would be very little we would have to hide or keep still about in the campaign except that he is a poet and a good one. That he is such a good one is the worst of it. Some enthusiast for the poet in him might lose self-control and write a letter to the papers, giving him away on the eve of the election. Then where would the faithful be? It would constitute another Burchard incident. Of course once he was elected there would be no harm in coming out with him in his true colors. We poets would be one up on the philosophers and scientists with one of our number on the President's throne. I should feel differently about a poet. I should be agreeable to having his administration last long enough to take rank in history as a reign. Pardon me if I seem to talk big about having a thousand dollars to spend on politics. I am not now in the thousand dollar class I have to admit. But four years from now or at most eight who can tell? Meanwhile let's put Bill in the Charter Oak Chair. I always wished my hardest for the election of Cross to the Governorship—not because he was a poet himself but because he was one of the best friends of poets this Democratic Republic has ever had.

Sincerely yours and Bill's
Robert Frost

A month after I was elected lieutenant governor I received the following letter: ·

Dear Bill
    The important thing is that you shouldn't forget the dinner party that was to reward me for having got you elected. I might ask for a Cabinet position. Have you a secretaryship of Commerce to dispose of? But never mind the honors, all I ask of the New Deal is a Square Deal.

R.F.

I replied that I might consider him for the position of boxing commissioner if he would come and take up residence in Connecticut.

He visited Wesleyan during my term as lieutenant governor, and once when he left I drove him to Springfield to catch a Boston train. I had inherited from my outgoing predecessor a seven-passenger Buick, and traveling over the state I made it a point to take on board hitchhikers of all kinds and descriptions. I did this to keep my ear close to the ground so that I might learn what Connecticut people were thinking. On this particular drive I took in two teen-age boys. Frost asked them if they knew whom they were riding with and they answered "No." He embarrassed both the boys and myself by letting them know they were riding with Connecticut's lieutenant governor. After I let the boys out I told him that I would never think of asking boys such a question. He replied, "Think these youngsters ought to have respect for public office. That's why I did it."

I told him that my own grass-roots experience with Connecticut boys had taught me a lot, that I was amazed to discover how indifferent to politics the "swamp Yankees" were. All they wanted to talk about when I gave them rides was the luck of the Red Sox or the Yankees, or the excitement of Sunday afternoon professional football games. In contrast, the Polish and Italian boys I took aboard often told me what they would do if they were the governor. The indifference of these "natives" appalled me, as much as the intense interest of the immigrant offspring delighted me. Like Harry Truman, Frost had a tremendous regard for American public office. This came out most strongly toward the end of his life when he got himself tied up with the Kennedy Administration.

When I ran for governor of Connecticut in 1946 he followed the campaign with interest. Two polls indicated that Democrats in 1946 had no chance, that fourteen years with one party in office was quite enough. After my defeat he sent me, along with his annual Christmas card, the following note:

Dear Bill:
    I too was sore at your defeat. Nevertheless I won't deny I think it serves you somewhere near right for having neglected religion for politics lately and put your trust in the votes of men and women instead of where Jay Gould's daughter, on her deathbed, told her father to let the tramps put theirs. Haven't I warned you again and again? You may take comfort in the Latin that it was a case of *civium ardor prava jubentium*. By you should have let Bowles suffer the fury of the mob. He was asking for it.

                                R.

I was delighted with this letter, but immensely surprised to find out how much he knew about what was going on in Democratic circles in Connecticut.

The Kennedy Administration was not the only government body that took notice of Frost. In 1950, when he was approaching his seventy-fifth birthday, the Senate, under the leadership of Robert

Taft, passed a resolution which, after the usual "Whereases," ended with these words: "RESOLVED that the Senate of the United States extend him felicitations of the Nation which he served so well."

A few months later (on October, 6, 7 and 8, 1950) Kenyon College in Ohio put on a conference in honor of Frost and I went there as a delegate from Wesleyan. One afternoon Frost and I left the conference and went to an upstairs room in the president's house to listen to a World Series baseball game, an ungracious thing for the two of us to do but an excellent opportunity to be alone together for a few hours. Then he gave me a first-hand report of what happened in Washington. In the first place, he was invited to the White House to meet the President. When he got there, the Chief Executive had been called away and he was left in the hands of a man who knew little about either Frost or poetry. "It was pathetic," he said. But the incident in the Senate was even more pathetic. After the reading of the resolution, several senators arose and made brief comments. One singled out *North of Boston* as a masterly acievement; another repeated a Frost lyric; still another read a few lines of epigrammatic value such as "Good fences make good neighbors." The climax came when a senator from his own New England countryside arose and chided his brethren because in all their remarks they had omitted any reference to the best of all Frost's poems: "Let me live in a house by the side of the road/And be a friend to man."—a poem by Sam Walter Foss whose quality is as far removed from Frost's work as James Whitcomb Riley's verses are from the poetry of John Milton. As he told me this, I could see in his eyes a flash of humor coupled with plain disgust.

The climax of his political activity came in 1961, when he read "The Gift Outright" at President Kennedy's Inaugural. It seemed ironical to me that a man who had spent a part of his talking life damning the New Deal should end by espousing the cause of an out-and-out liberal. But Kennedy had a marvelous personal charm, and he was a New Englander through and through. That was enough for Robert.

I happened to be in Frost's Cambridge home when he was putting final touches on *A Witness Tree*, the book that contains "The Gift Outright." The last line of this poem reads "Such as she was, such as she would become." That evening he was trying to decide whether to use the words "might become" or "would become." I told him that if he

used the word "might" it would indicate that he entertained doubts
about the great American experiment. When I reviewed the book
for the *New York Herald Tribune* some weeks later and drew attention to this particular poem, I was happy to see that he had used
"would become." But at the inauguration President Kennedy, who possessed a deep-rooted faith in the American experiment, wanted Frost
to go a step further and use the words "such as she *will* become." On
the day he delivered the poem Frost used both "would" and "will,"
which indicated that he was not too happy with the President's choice.

A political friend told me that when the inaugural platform was
being built, a man said to Kennedy, "What do you plan to do with
Frost?" Kennedy replied, "Let him read his poems, but don't let him
make a speech." "Why not a speech?" the man asked. "Because if we
did, he would steal the show," the President replied.

His reading at the Inauguration made him a national figure over
and beyond anything he had ever known. So the next Frost Birthday
Dinner was arranged to be held in the Pan-American Building in
Washington on March 26, 1962, with members of the President's Cabinet and the Supreme Court gracing the occasion. Secretary Udall,
who was largely responsible for his participation in the inaugural
ceremonies, was the toastmaster and Judge Felix Frankfurter one of
the principal speakers. The acoustics of this building were so poor
that anyone beyond the first four rows might as well have been listening to one of the silent speeches of Harpo Marx. Frost waited in a
backstage room, looking very tired, and not hearing anything that
was being said in his praise. An immense crowd seated at tables around
the room, unable to hear much of anything that was going on, conversed among themselves.

That afternoon he had personally presented the President with
a copy of his new book of poems, *In the Clearing*, and many in the
audience that night were hoping that the President would make an
appearance at the gathering, but he didn't. Earlier in the evening I
had taken Frost aside and asked him if he liked all this adulation and
glorification that was being heaped upon him. He replied, "I don't
know, Bill, what to think about it. It tires me. But it may do something
for the cause of Poetry." I thought to myself, "There's the old New
England dominie coming out in a man who is supposed to be wary
and skeptical about all preaching and propaganda."

Many people think the culmination of Frost's political activity was his trip to Russia as Cultural Ambassador and Special Representative of President Kennedy. And he himself would concur. He thought the trip constituted the best service he had rendered his country.

A few weeks before he died he gave a poetry reading at Trinity College in Hartford, and while there was a guest of Bacon Collamore, a literary collector. I dined there and talked with him for two evenings about his Russian experiences. "It was the greatest experience of my life," he said to me. "Khrushchev and I looked each other in the eye, and believe it or not, Bill, we liked each other. We both had come up from the soil and had that in common. He had something of the great man in him, but he was rough and probably ruthless. Not so ruthless as Stalin, but ruthless nevertheless. He was solicitous about my health and was genuinely interested in our country. 'We are two great nations,' I said to him, 'and ought to be friendly rivals, rivals like great athletic teams,' I said. I felt I had made some impression on him—hoped I had. I left the country feeling that we will grow more like Russia and Russia will grow more like us. Out there somewhere our political aims will incline to be more and more alike. They still have a long way to go, but they have the energy and the ambition and are on their way."

"And why are you," I asked, "an anti–New Dealer, so immensely wrapped up in the Russian experiment?"

"Just stalking life," he replied, "just stalking life." And that, I concluded, was the real Frost; immensely and curiously interested in man's life upon earth. He was a traveler who knew that "it is better to travel than to arrive." As he said in his poem "Neither Out Far Nor In Deep:

> They cannot look out far,
> They cannot look in deep,
> But when was that ever a bar
> To any watch they keep?

He was forever "keeping watch o'er man's mortality," and found the watching endlessly interesting.

CHAPTER 21

Other Poets

Carl Sandburg

THE other poet I knew best was Carl Sandburg, of whom I have written much in earlier chapters. We were brought together by our love of American ballads. I had aroused an interest in ballads at Indiana University, and when I left they felt compelled to employ a ballad man, Stith Thompson, as my successor. I had Sandburg down to the University and he made a great hit with the students with his guitar, his ballad singing, his deep resonant voice, and his workingman's costume. When I came to Wesleyan in 1921 I made an effort to bring him to the college. He was more than anxious to come because Caleb T. Winchester, one of the great English teachers of America, had already written an essay on modern American poetry in which he praised Sandburg's work beyond others. In this essay he said:

> In the whole body of our new poetry there is none more spontaneous and impassioned than this. And more than that, for all its coarseness and crudity, none represents more forcibly social and industrial conditions that are growing to be nationwide today. It means something and it means it intensely.

Carl had read this, and consequently it was not difficult to get him to come to Wesleyan where Winchester had taught.

In fact, I brought him here twice in one year. During those visits, he and Arthur Sutherland and a few other boys sat up all night putting together material for his *American Songbag*. When he was having an appearance in a nearby town, he would come to our home to spend the night. On one of these occasions, Mrs. Elizabeth McConaughy had presented me with a gallon of wine which she had made during the Prohibition era. I brought the gallon up out of the cellar, and Carl drank it from nine o'clock that night until two in the morning.

385

We had cordial fights over the subject of free verse, and he told me once that he would rather have the raw notes out of which Edna St. Vincent Millay wrote the sonnets in her book *Fatal Interview* than to have the finished sonnets themselves. I reminded him that his ballads such as "Casey Jones" and "Jay Gould's Daughter" had both rhyme and meter. He said, "Yes, but that is poetry on a lower level. Pure poetry ought to move in a world above rhyme and meter." I said, "Can you name a purer poem than Milton's *Lycidas*, which has both rhyme and meter?" That silenced him.

He thought the New England poets were dying or dead. He spoke disparagingly of Robinson, and when he did I repeated Robinson's powerful poem on George Crabbe, which begins:

> Give him the darkest inch your shelf allows,
> Hide him in lonely garrets, if you will,—
> But his hard, human pulse is throbbing still
> With the sure strength that fearless truth endows.

It affected him so strongly that he said, "Maybe you're right."

Sandburg was given a degree by Wesleyan for his six magnificent volumes on Abraham Lincoln. A few hours later, Jeannette and I drove him across the state, and on that entire journey he cursed Wesleyan, saying, "God damn that gang to hell! Don't they know I'm a poet? The author of *The People, Yes?* Any long-haired professor with a Ph.D. could research and write a good biography of Lincoln, but nobody but myself could write *The People, Yes*."

He had some strange ideas about art. He believed that photography was greater than painting, that his own brother-in-law, Steichen, was as great as Rembrandt. I tried to argue him out of this, saying that a great portrait painter talks with his subjects and gets insights into their inner life which no photographer's plate could ever record. To keep the peace, we had to drop the subject.

Carl was very kind to us, gave us two of his books for a wedding present, gave us autographed copies of many of his other books. When my second book *The Inner Harbor* was published, he reviewed it at length for the Chicago *Daily News*:

A MAINE POET

Wilbert Snow is a poet who has straddled bronchos on a cattle ranch, who has shipped on tramp steamers and who has lived among the Eskimos. Having had all these things in his life, he is settled now as an instructor in English in Wesleyan University at Middletown, Conn.

We offer these items about Mr. Snow's career and works in the past because of the publication this week of "The Inner Harbor," (Harcourt) designated by the author as "more Maine coast poems." It is an interesting book, perhaps the commentary counts for more if we add that seldom does a book of poetry come along to our desk which we open, glimpse through casually and then start and read from the first page to the last.

Naturally, in this case, it makes a difference that we know Mr. Snow, that we have sung songs and told stories till late hours in the morning with him, that before he went east we saw him down at Indiana University, and that once he visited Chicago and brought over to this advertising office an advertising man named O'Connor, who works in the advertising division of a Chicago department store and between ads is reckoned one of the foremost among Cook County ornithologists.

On some pages Mr. Snow gives us portraits of Maine people, such as the barber, who left the customer with one side of the face shaved, and made a beeline for his seine and dory. On returning he had words with the customer, ending:

> I know I left
> Without much ceremony—but if you think
> I'd let a chance to get a school of mackerel
> Slip through my fingers for a ten-cent shave
> You're mightily mistaken—I'd a'thought
> You'd have the sense to scrape the rest yourself.
> And as for summer folks, just listen here,
> They're spoiling half the people of this island:
> Now all the girls must dress like rich men's girls;
> The men turn into beggars figurin' out
> An easy way to live off summer people;
> Our women ain't content to stay at home,
> But must make trips to Boston or New York.
> I wish to God you'd never set your foot
> Among us—and furthermore, for you,
> I guess I won't shave off the other side.
> It wouldn't be quite safe the way I'm feelin'.

What Zeb Kinney has to say about college professors who come to the coast of Maine to summer is gossip with a salt tang. The sketches "Country Dance," and "Prayer Meeting" are spare, well-done short stories, the one on the prayer meeting being of sure touch and profound sympathy.

Over the years I had many letters from Carl, which I have cherished. The following, dated November 15, 1921, is typical:

Brother Snow:

It seems as though my Massachusetts engagements are entirely in the hands of The Players, 162 Tremont St., Boston. Write to George N. Whipple who is in charge there about my date in Hartford in February and any arrangements he chooses to make will be okeh with me.

Congratulations on getting onto Harcourt's list. You could not be surer about a good handling of your book. Thank you for a live letter. When February comes we ought to have an old time talk, arriving maybe at a decision about our prospects for the afterworld, whether we go to heaven with Bryan or to hell with Darwin.[1]

Sandburg was a great friend and a delightful though sometimes cantankerous companion. He always had a chip on his shoulder because some people whose opinions he cherished insisted that his contribution to America was not in poetry but in his life of Lincoln.

Edwin Arlington Robinson

Although I knew and admired other poets of the '20's, I never spent long hours with them as I did with Frost and Sandburg. My only close contact with Edwin Arlington Robinson was the two days we spent together at Bowdoin in 1925. My admiration for his best lyrics and sonnets was boundless, beginning in 1905 when as students in college my cousin and I discovered *Captain Craig*.

For about ten years thereafter Robinson was my hero. He could match Tennyson's melodious Victorian lines such as "laborious orient ivory, / And the mellow ousel fluting in the elm"—as he proved when he praised Virgil in "The White Lights":

> When first the pearled, alembic phrase
> Of Maro into music ran—
> Here there was neither blame nor praise
> For Rome, or for the Mantuan.[2]

When this poem was written, Robinson, William Vaughn Moody, and Percy MacKaye dreamed of doing for Broadway what the great dramatists of the past had done for Athens, Rome, and London. He could write closet dramas suitable for reading like those of Browning, as he showed in his *Porcupine* and *Van Zorn*. But these were not his

[1]Used by permission of Greenbaum, Wolff & Ernst, attorneys for the heirs of Carl Sandburg.

[2]From *The Town Down the River*, by Edwin Arlington Robinson, copyright © 1910 by Charles Scribner's Sons. Used by permission of Charles Scribner's Sons.

forte. His character sketches in lyric form such as "Mr. Flood's Party," "Miniver Cheevy," and "Luke Havergal" have never been surpassed by any American poet. He also added new dimensions to the sonnet form, as one can discover in such examples as "George Crabbe," "Charles Carville's Eyes," "Aaron Stark," and a dozen others. Nor do I despise the long poems, as critics urge us to do. *Isaac and Archibald* to me is one of the gems of our literature. *Rembrandt on Rembrandt* is really Robinson on Robinson. *The Man Who Died Twice* contains a confession of the author's bout with King Alcohol that to me is memorable. Of his three Arthurian narratives, *Merlin* is probably the best, but the others have passages here and there that one ought not to miss. His other long narratives have lines that neither talk nor sing. They are dull chores that will soon be forgotten. But I confidently predict that his best short lyrics will have a long life in American literature.

Edna St. Vincent Millay

In the winter of 1912–1913 I remained at home, troubled with a duodenal ulcer that every now and then gave me great annoyance. On the street in Rockland one day I introduced myself to Edna St. Vincent Millay, and told her how much I enjoyed her poem "Renascence" that came out in Mitchell Kennerly's *The Lyric Year*. Several other times I stopped and talked with her about poetry.

One night I induced her and her sister Norma to spend an evening with my freshman roommate in college, Ensign Otis, and his attractive wife Betty. A few days previously I had bet Betty's brother Nathan a box of chocolates that Miss Millay would smoke cigarettes. He appeared at his sister's home that evening, eager to see who was going to win. We hadn't been seated in the parlor more than five minutes when Edna turned to Betty and said, "Do you mind if I smoke a cigarette?"

I told her I had a copy of her high school graduation poem and liked it. It was a rambling poem of eighty-odd lines entitled "La Joie de Vivre" and was full of happiness. Four typical lines read:

> The world and I are young!
> Never on lips of man,
> Never since time began
> Has gladder song been sung.[3]

[3]From "La Joie de Vivre" by Edna St. Vincent Millay. By permission of Norma Millay Ellis.

But she had grown a lot since June 1909, and wanted me to give her my copy of the poem. I told her I would think it over. But I still have it.

She read us that night an early draft of a sonnet about a woman who had just lost her husband and was now hanging onto a strap in a trolley car, carefully reading all the advertisements pasted along the walls. The contrast between the sorrow of the woman and the silliness of the ads made it a poem which a listener, hearing her gentle voice reciting it, would never forget. The poem she read that night ultimately became one of her finer sonnets. It reads:

> If I should learn, in some quite casual way,
> That you were gone, not to return again—
> Read from the back-page of a paper, say,
> Held by a neighbour in a subway train,
> How at the corner of this avenue
> And such a street (so are the papers filled)
> A hurrying man—who happened to be you—
> At noon to-day had happened to be killed,
> I should not cry aloud—I could not cry
> Aloud, or wring my hands in such a place—
> I should but watch the station lights rush by
> With a more careful interest on my face,
> Or raise my eyes and read with greater care
> Where to store furs and how to treat the hair.[4]

I told her again how much I enjoyed her "Renascence." But I did not fall in love with her. I was too sick with ulcers to fall in love with anyone. (Edmund Wilson once said that so many men fell in love with Edna that they ought to form a club and have regular meetings.)

I followed her career closely, bought all her books as they appeared, and was proud of the fact that she was born and grew up on the coast of Maine.

Twice later she appeared before the Hartford Poetry Society and I got closer to her then. After one of these readings a group gathered at the home of Robert Hillyer to finish off the evening with much talk and many drinks. At one point Edna sat down on the floor at my feet, looked up at me thoughtfully, and said in a low voice no man could possibly imitate, "I have all your books." At that moment I realized how effective she could be with a poor weak male. Her voice, her informal manner, the naïve expression in her blue eyes made her irresistible, and I knew what Edmund Wilson was talking about.

[4]From *Collected Poems*, Harper & Row. Copyright © 1917, 1945 by Edna St. Vincent Millay. By permission of Norma Millay Ellis.

On the second occasion I was the one chosen to introduce her. Before going on she and I met backstage where she told me her troubles. The war had stopped her husband's import business and she had to support the family. Her health was unreliable and often when she was weary and extremely nervous, she had to force herself to step out and face an audience. As she spoke, she drank her third highball, "as a bracer," she said. She was a most unhappy woman. Two lines of Wordsworth came to my mind with added force: "We poets in our youth begin with gladness / But thereof come in the end despondency and sadness."

She had a most sympathetic audience that night and did well in spite of her inner feelings. During the reading all I could think of was the contrast between the bubbly joy of the commencement poem and her present state of mind. Compare "La Joie de Vivre" with the later sonnets in her *Fatal Interview*. The latter breathe not joy but bleak despondency. It has been rumored that *Fatal Interview* records an extramarital love affair of hers. I doubt that. I believe it is a retelling of her early love for Arthur Davison Ficke. Santayana says, "One love suffices for eternity," and this, I believe, was hers.

Wallace Stevens

My first meeting with Wallace Stevens probably came through his wife. In the early '20's I spent much time advocating the modern American poets and giving talks on them. One of these was at the Hartford Bard and Sage Club, of which Mrs. Stevens was a member. I read some of Wallace's poetry and praised the workmanship, especially of his poem "Susanna and the Elders." She came up to me at the end of the hour and said, "That's the first time that anybody ever mentioned my husband's poetry in public." I looked at her and understood why she was chosen by Adolph A. Weinman to model for the bust on our "Mercury" dime.

I called up Stevens a short while later and invited him to have luncheon at the Heublein. There he bewailed the fact that America's "wild men" like myself were spending their hours in politics instead of poetry. I countered by saying that American politics needed more men of imagination. We soon drifted onto our favorite subject, poetry. But he kept going back to politics. He said, "What is all this talk about the 'First International,' the 'Second International'? What does it mean? And now they are talking about the 'Third International.'" I said, "I'm not a Marxian and cannot help you out. But I do know that American corporations are getting bigger and bigger, and I dread the outcome. America was built by small farms and small businesses. And both are now on the way out."

"But what frightens me," he said, "is all this talk among intellectuals about the Third International. If this keeps on I'm going to leave America and go abroad to live." "Where are you going?" I asked. "Sweden," he said. "Why Sweden?" I asked.

He went on to tell me of a beautiful Swedish rug he had bought in New York. He examined it carefully and on the underside he discovered the name and address of the woman who made it. He struck up a lively correspondence with her. She told him that a better and more beautiful rug was on exhibit in Chicago. He was inclined to go out to Chicago and buy it, but this correspondence with the Swedish lady had incurred the jealousy of his wife. She wouldn't have liked the rug.

On another occasion Wallace came to the table with a copy of *Hound and Horn* which contained an article by R. P. Blackmur on Stevens' use of words—an exposition of his rich, unique, and extensive vocabulary. He threw the magazine on the table and said, "Snow, am I as dull as that?" Luckily for me I had already seen the article and I replied, "You certainly are not. But I must say you make no concessions to the common reader." "Why should I?" he asked.

This set me off on a favorite topic. "Well, because I agree with Dr. Johnson that the common reader is the deciding factor in what poetry is going to last. Dr. Johnson concludes his chapter on Thomas Gray in the *Lives of the Poets* by lavishing praise on the 'Elegy in a Country Churchyard.' 'Poetry,' he says, 'that is loved and cherished by the common reader will outlast poetry built upon the "refinements of subtlety" and "the dogmatism of learning." ' Your 'Peter Quince at the Clavier' is, in my opinion, a good example."

He said, "But you are more interested in verse than you are in poetry."

I knew what he was thinking and said, "Yes, but a verse-writer becomes a poet after he is dead just as a politician becomes a statesman after he is dead. Look at Hogarth, for example. Critics of the eighteenth century looked upon him as a hack. But he could paint a portrait that could match the best of those painted by Sir Joshua Reynolds. Or look at Robert Burns writing verses all over the place. He was loved for his 'routh of rhymes,' but the critics during his lifetime rated him as a verse-writer, not as a poet."

"Well, that's what he was," Wallace replied.

I didn't agree, but thought it was time to change the subject. So I asked, "Why do you send your poems to such magazines as *Furioso, Others,* and *Compass,* which have only a handful of readers? Your poetry has color and magnificent control of meters and ought to reach a larger audience."

A few weeks later he stopped me on Main Street in Hartford and said, "I sold a poem to one of your popular magazines." "What one?" I asked. "*Harper's Bazaar,*" he replied with a smile. "How much did they pay you?" I asked. "Seventy-five dollars," he replied. "That would be a godsend to me," I answered, "but to you as the vice-president of a Hartford insurance company I suspect it's a good deal of a joke." I could see, though, that it gave him great satisfaction.

A month or two later he stopped me on Prospect Street and told me he had reached deeper into the "common reader" and had sold a poem to *The New York Times.* At that time I was selling many verses to the *Times* and didn't have to ask how little they paid. But I could plainly see that this sale did give him a certain pleasure.

When his *Man with the Blue Guitar* came out, I was so enthusiastic about it that I wrote Bliss Perry, a member of the Pulitzer Prize Committee, urging that Stevens be given the poetry prize. In one paragraph of that letter I said:

> If you had come down I was going to regale you again with the virtues of Wallace Stevens as a poet. His book *The Man with the Blue Guitar* strikes me as an excellent volume of poetry, and I am anxious to see him reach a larger group of readers than he has ever known. Some one told me recently that you are on the Pulitzer Prize Committee for poetry; and if that is so, I hope you will sometime be able to convince your colleagues on that committee that Stevens is a real poet deserving of a much wider recognition than he has ever achieved. If this paragraph is unorthodox, I appreciate your kindness well enough to know that you will forgive my enthusiasm.

Perry answered that he knew and appreciated Wallace Stevens' poetry, and added that I should know the final decision was made not by the Committee but by the Trustees of Columbia University. I followed my first letter by another, but nothing came of it at that time; Stevens did not win his Pulitzer Prize until 1955.

In 1941 I started a campaign to give him an honorary degree at Wesleyan. The Honorary Degree Committee shied away from my enthusiasm. One member told me that Stevens was too difficult and too obscure. When this same member learned that Wallace came from Pennsylvania Dutch stock, he himself, a Pennsylvania Dutch descendant, turned completely around and became his number one booster.

In June 1947 I had the honor of presenting Stevens to the University President to receive the degree of Doctor of Letters. When President Butterfield invited him to the campus to receive the degree—his first—Wallace wrote the following reply to a letter from me:

> Thanks for your note. When Mr. Butterfield first wrote to me, I took it for granted that you had a finger in the pie. I am pleased no end. We shall see you—look you up. I know nothing about these things and do not know how free I shall be. There is a dinner at one o'clock and after that an interval until six and I assume that we can come to see you during that interval. By the way, I hope I am not expected to speak. I am relaxing in that idea.[5]

When I presented him for his degree, I said:

> Mr. President, I have the honor of presenting Mr. Wallace Stevens, a poet who has enlarged the boundaries of our nation's literature by flashing more vivid colors before the eyes of those who would like "to catch tigers in red weather"; by insisting upon the imagination as "the only reality in this imagined world"; and by emphasizing the value of poetry for its own sake in a land where utilitarian values are all too apparent. I present him, Mr. President, in order that you may induct him into the fraternity of "gray grammarians in golden gowns," and bestow upon him the degree of Doctor of Letters.

Wallace and Mrs. Stevens stayed at our house during the two days of Commencement, and we had grand talks together. I was glad that Wesleyan had given him his first honorary degree, and I urged him to brace himself "because a dozen other colleges and universities will follow in our train."

That year the Beta boys were giving a Commencement dance, and my third son Nick had brought a Powers model up from New York to be his partner. She was a beautiful girl and her picture had appeared that month on the cover of a popular magazine. Wallace was smitten with her beauty. He liked the way she walked and the way she looked. To use an old worn-out expression, he couldn't keep his eyes off her.

---

[5]Used by permission of Holly Stevens.

In the afternoon the two of us and our wives took a walk around the college campus. On the way we came across Nick and the girl, who were strolling leisurely toward us on the other side of High Street. Wallace said to me, "Let's cross over. I want to get another look at your son's girl." His wife and Jeannette were walking behind us. He said, "My wife will give me hell. But I don't care. Let's cross over." I said, "O.K.," and across we went. I never found out what Mrs. Stevens said when they arrived back in Hartford. I do know that women who marry poets must realize that male pursuit and contemplation of beauty is not confined within the walls of home.

At the dinner before the Commencement exercises our Pennsylvania Dutch professor asked me if he could sit beside Stevens. I said, "Go ahead," and went to the other end of the table to join Kay Butterfield, my colleague on the School Board. I overheard Wallace say, "Snow knows only my first volume *Harmonium*." It is true that nothing he wrote later hit me so hard as "Sunday Morning," "Susanna and the Elders," and "Monocle of Mon Oncle," all in the first book. Imagine how pleased I was years later to read in one of his published letters a confirmation of my judgment: "I like a few things in *Harmonium* better than anything I have done since."

A few days after returning to Hartford Wallace sent our adopted boy an excellent camera; and to me, an autographed copy of his *Transport to Summer* plus a bottle of choice imported liquor. With these came the following letter:

> Mrs. Stevens and I appreciated your kindness to us and your hospitality, last Sunday, and even imported language could not say more. Mrs. Stevens is writing separately. In the meantime, she wants to send a Kodak to the boy whom you have taken into your family, Donald, I believe, and I am adding a bottle of Hine's and a copy of *Transport to Summer*. The cognac is a superb variety, if you care for that sort of thing. If you insist on using it with ice (which is the last thing in the world you ought to do), select the soda with greatest care. If you are driving through Boston on your way to Maine, stop at Pierce's and see if you can get some Schweppe's. Good luck and many thanks. And this, of course, goes for Mrs. Snow too.
>
> One of the girls from the office is unfortunate enough to come from Middletown and that is how I am able to send these to you directly: through the kindness of Miss Flynn.[6]

In *Transport to Summer* I was happy to find this:

[6]Used by permission of Holly Stevens.

SKETCH OF THE ULTIMATE POLITICIAN

He is the final builder of the total building,
The final dreamer of the total dream,
Or will be. Building and dream are one.

There is a total building and there is
A total dream. There are words of this,
Words in a storm, that beat around the shapes.

There is a storm much like the crying of the wind,
Words that come out of us like words within,
That have rankled for many lives and made no sound.

He can hear them, like people on the walls,
Running in the rises of common speech,
Crying as that speech falls as if to fail.

There is a building stands in a ruinous storm,
A dream interrupted out of the past,
From beside us, from where we have yet to live.[7]

These lines call up the ghost of Abraham Lincoln, who is my ideal politician. I told Stevens that this poem stood head and shoulders above the others in the volume, although I felt sure that the critics would call "Notes Toward a Supreme Fiction" the grandest poem in the book, and his major contribution to American poetry.

Toward the end of his life Stevens became interested in writing abstract poetry. One day at Mount Holyoke College, when he was the main speaker at a meeting of the New England English Teachers Association, he spent the whole hour reading his abstract verse. The teachers listened politely but without enthusiasm. When he had finished, I went up to him and said, "Wallace, why didn't you read 'Peter Quince at the Clavier'? The teachers would have lapped it up." He answered, "No, I'll leave that to Frost and the hillbillies." Should I tell Frost what he had said? That was the question. Homer Woodbridge, my best friend at Wesleyan, said, "Go ahead and tell him. I want to hear Frost's answer. I know it will be a good one." But my wife said, "No. It will hurt him too much." I followed my wife's advice, but I was often tempted to get Robert's reaction. Frost and Stevens were rivals, and they were alike in that neither had much enthusiasm for the poetry of Eliot and Pound.

Stevens was kind to me though he was anything but kind to other poets I knew. One of these called him up and wanted to meet and talk with him. Wallace said, "I'm busy. Call again in ten years." Another man brought a poet friend from Cambridge to Hartford, called Wallace, and said, "I have a poet here with me. I would like to bring him to see you." "Who is your poet?" Wallace asked. The name was given. "He is not a poet in my book," said Wallace as he slammed down the receiver.

The truth is that Stevens wanted all his evenings to himself. He allowed himself and his wife very little social life and only went out when symphony orchestras were playing at the Bushnell Memorial.

In my talks with him I was amazed to see what a deep impression French culture had made on him, even though (as he stated in one of his published letters) he never visited France. He was affected by the Dadaist movement and looked on Paris not only as the "chrysalis of the nocturnal butterfly" but as the art center of the modern world. He told me he had a standing order at a Paris bookstore to send him anything new coming out in French poetry. He also employed an art critic to pick out and send him from time to time original works of art —watercolors and oils. After his death these pictures were put on display, but they certainly were not very impressive as works of art, although they cost him thousands of francs.

Whether we like it or not, this French influence can be traced throughout his poetry. He never completely recovered from the effects of Dada. To me, I hasten to say, his poetry is better than any other that came out of the Dadaist movement. His skill with the five-beat line in "Sunday Morning" and "Monocle of Mon Oncle" is superior to that of any other poet of our generation. His mastery of the four-beat line in *The Man with the Blue Guitar* cannot be matched anywhere in American poetry. He labored over his lines with the exquisite workmanship employed by old seamen who built miniature full-rigged ships and anchored them inside bottles.

Once I told him that "Sunday Morning" was an excellent poem but it was hitting below the belt when he used such grand Elizabethan lines as "The holy hush of ancient sacrifice," carrying the tone of the Book of Common Prayer, to play down and denigrate the Christian religion. He replied, "I don't care too much for 'Sunday Morning.'" "What poem in *Harmonium* is better?" He answered, "Earthly Anecdote." This preference, to me, is one more example of a creative man's inability to judge well of his own work.

He believed with Matthew Arnold that poetry was going to take the place of religion, and it is significant to me that his most religious poem was never published during his lifetime. Here it is:

BLANCHE McCARTHY

Look in the terrible mirror of the sky
And not in this dead glass, which can reflect
Only the surfaces —the bending arm,
The leaning shoulder and the searching eye.

Look in the terrible mirror of the sky.
Oh, bend against the invisible; and lean
To symbols of descending night; and search
The glare of revelations going by!
Look in the terrible mirror of the sky.
See how the absent moon waits in a glade
Of your dark self, and how the wings of stars,
Upward, from unimagined coverts, fly.[8]

His daughter Holly has wisely put it first in her excellent selection of her father's poems. To many of us who knew him, Connecticut is poorer and less colorful since he left.

Vachel Lindsay

Lindsay's appearance at Indiana University made such a deep impression on me that I resolved to bring him to Wesleyan at the first opportunity. I have already mentioned how exciting and outgoing he was. Although we had never met before, we felt at once that we had been friends for years. During that Indiana visit he handed me a new poem he had written entitled "Johnny Appleseed" and asked me to criticize it and cut it. "It is too long," he said, "and needs to be trimmed." I worked over the poem all night and cut out sixteen lines. It was the most difficult thing I had ever done for a fellow-writer. When the poem was finally published in book form, I noticed that all my sixteen cut-out lines had been restored. I realized then that I was not an Ezra Pound, and neither did I have a meek T. S. Eliot to deal with.

My first attempt to bring Lindsay to Wesleyan failed. An engagement had been set, but he wrote me a letter on January 30, 1923, which read:

I am very sick and must cancel our date. I am indeed sorry but dare not travel a step further this year. I am hoping I may postpone our date just one year. Meanwhile I urge as more than substitutes—Frost or Sandburg.[9]

(His praise of two other poets in the last sentence, along with Frost's kind words about Sandburg and Lindsay in Chapter 20, make one think that the 1920's were a good time to be alive and writing poetry. I share this feeling because my own first books were issued in the '20's and my publisher, Alfred Harcourt, treated me as if I were a prince. This was all changed when Eliot's *Waste Land* and Pound's *Cantos* won over the professors and critics and American poetry began heading for a long, dark night.)

The above letter was written from a girl's junior college in Gulfport, Mississippi, whose president, Richard Cox, had been a college mate and friend of Lindsay's at Hiram College. Cox urged him to teach one course in poetry, settle down, and rest—which he did. The Southern girls made a powerful impression on this worn-out, tired bachelor. He fell deeply in love with one of them and proposed marriage. She was eighteen and he was forty-three. She wisely rejected his offer and he sank into deeper gloom.

While in this depressed state he decided that the American Northwest was where he belonged. In 1921, with an Englishman named Stephen Graham, he had taken a six-weeks' tramping trip through Glacier National Park and had fallen in love with the area. He felt himself a part of the westward movement of America and was sure he would be well and happy in that region. So, as soon as he was able, he set out for Spokane.

One of the leading lawyers of that city, Benjamin H. Kizer, had read and admired Lindsay's first two collections of poetry as well as his prose book on preaching the Gospel of Beauty, and wanted him to settle down in Spokane and be a sort of "poet in residence" for the city. Kizer secured him a room at the Davenport Hotel for $75 a month. Lindsay was to pay $35 and the lawyer, unknown to the poet, was to pay the other $40.

He became a cultural addition to the city and gave readings and talks to many different organizations. At one of these gatherings he met and fell in love with one of the most attractive women I have ever

[9]Used by permission of Professor Nicholas C. Lindsay.

known, Elizabeth Conner. After a brief courtship they were married. They decided to spend their honeymoon on a tramping trip through Glacier National Park.

The first night on the road was one of the weirdest in history. As they were about to retire Vachel was taken with an epileptic fit. His bride watched him fall to the ground with a thud. He had never told her that there was epilepsy in his family and the girl was thoroughly frightened. There she was, hundreds of miles from doctor or hospital. Long afterward she told me about that night, and I could not keep back the tears of sympathy. She was twenty-six and he forty-seven at the time, and for the next six years she had to be a nurse as well as wife and companion. Luckily she adored him fully, and nobody ever admired his poetry more than she.

I have thought many times of that first night in the mountains and connected it with Vachel's father, "Old Mohawk." Vachel said of his father, "He had a fear and a dread and a loathing of venereal disease beyond anybody I ever knew. He kept me chaste and made me live the life of a monk. He said this talk of gonorrhea being no worse than a bad cold is the biggest lie that ever was perpetrated on this planet. 'It gets in your blood,' he told me, 'and stays there. And if "606" cures a man of syphilis, he can still, after being cured, transmit the disease to his offspring.' I once came away from one of his sessions in a lather of sweat brought on by fear. On this subject there was no one who could be compared with him. How about yours?"

I said to him, "My father, being a New Englander, didn't talk much about such things. He never expressed himself vehemently on the subject. But his attitude was much like that of your 'Old Mohawk.' " I recalled one saying my father had repeated often: "Treat a girl the way you would like to have a boy treat your sister." His only other caution was this: "If you expect to have children, keep away from girls of easy virtue. Too often they are diseased."

Vachel and I discovered that we both had lived womanless lives during adolescence and after. This we had in common. I never felt inclined to talk about sex as he did, however. He was an extrovert beyond any man I ever met. I believed in the sublimation of sex and as a young man worked off my energy hunting and fishing and sailing boats. He worked off his by taking long walks all over America.

He was a Midwest Puritan when I first knew him—no alcohol, no tobacco. He was officially a lecturer for the Anti-Saloon League for over a year. By the time he got around to writing a poem on Carrie Nation, he had changed a great deal and would smoke a cigarette or drink a glass of wine. "The Saloon Must Go" is to be taken by the reader humorously—at least in part. But Vachel was always a great admirer of Carrie Nation and her crusade.

After the marriage he and his wife rented an apartment on the outskirts of Spokane and settled down for a while. They proceeded promptly to have two children, a daughter Susan and a son Nicholas. Vachel kept his room at the Davenport Hotel where he could be alone and write. He neglected his family and at times his wife had no money to buy the children's milk.

In the fall of 1928 he came to Harvard and I tried once more to get him to come to Wesleyan. I told him that I had acquainted the boys with his poems and they were eager to see him. I offered a fee of $150. Here is his reply:

> Thanks for your letters and wires. They have all come to hand at last.
>   I have wired you today:—
> "Can come November 22 on condition there are at least two high school assemblies the same day making the total days work four times your fee. Stop. Wire care W. B. Feakins, James Building, New York City."
>   In short my minimum fee is $200, for a day's work for you. I am at Keuka College, Keuka Park, Nov. 20, and may be addressed there for final arrangements. I will be at Lakeville, Connecticut, Hotchkiss School for Boys Nov. 24. Please move up my fee toward the standard $500 as near as you can. I can recite all day if I may sleep in between and am *not* entertained. I am willing to work but must have wages.[10]

To understand this jockeying for more pay, the reader must know that Edna St. Vincent Millay had just received $500 for one reading in Montclair, New Jersey, and this big fee made news. The poets (Vachel among them) whose fees were usually $100 or $200 were envious of this large honorarium and wanted for themselves as much as "that girl" could get!

Illness again prevented his appearance at Wesleyan. In the meantime word drifted down from Harvard about an appearance he made in an American literature class there. Uninvited and unnoticed, he came in and sat down in a back seat. The professor was talking about Thomas Holley Chivers. About two-thirds of the way through his lecture, sensing the indifference of his students, he said, "I don't suppose any of you

---

[10]Used by permission of Professor Nicholas C. Lindsay.

ever heard of Thomas Holley Chivers." Whereupon Lindsay arose and repeated by heart about forty lines from Chivers' poems. (Lindsay's voice was immensely resonant and the audience was thrilled.) At the close of this performance by an unknown visitor, the professor said one word—"Remarkable!"—and dismissed the class.

In 1930 Wesleyan succeeded in landing him. Our college paper gave him a big buildup before he arrived. This time he came as a married man and stayed at our house. When we took him to his room he opened his dress-suit case, took out three large photographs, and arranged them on the bureau to suit him. The pictures were of his daughter, his son, and between them, his wife Elizabeth. He stood off and looked at them. I looked and shared his admiration.

He first told me about his previous night. A meeting in behalf of some cause had been held in a hall in New York City. Ten or twelve American poets and novelists were on the stage where the assembled crowd could look at them. He found himself beside a famous Negro writer, James Weldon Johnson. Sometime during the evening he invited Johnson to come west and visit him. Johnson replied, "You white folks always invite me to come see you, but you really don't mean it. You wouldn't know what to do if my wife and I should drop in on you." To show that he really meant it, Vachel took out his notebook, penned him a written invitation, signed it "Vachel Lindsay," and handed it over.

We talked for hours that night and the next day. Lindsay was full of strange theories. He had much in common with William Blake, as a comparison of stanzas from poems by each will show. Blake's four lines read:

> I will not cease from Mental Fight
> Nor shall my Sword sleep in my hand,
> Till we have built Jerusalem
> In England's green & pleasant land.

Here is a quatrain by Lindsay:

> We should build parks that students from afar
> Would choose to starve in, rather than go home,
> Fair little squares with Phidian ornament,
> Food for the spirit, milk and honeycomb.[11]

[11]From "On the Building of Springfield" by Vachel Lindsay, copyright © 1913 by Macmillan Publishing Company, Inc. Reprinted from *Collected Poems* of Vachel Lindsay by permission of Macmillan Publishing Company, Inc.

The desire to create new and wonderful nations out of their homelands was a ruling passion of these two poets. Both men felt the need of using drawings to illustrate their poems, although Blake was far superior to Lindsay as an artist. Both men felt that the present day was an impoverished period and that the Golden Age was in some distant past. Lindsay's Golden Age was the America of the pioneers, the westward-moving people intent upon finding a better life. To him these people disappeared with the buffalos, and his "Ghost of the Buffalos" is perhaps one of his finest poems.

Because he was a mystic, many of the ideas he regaled me with will not stand logical analysis. For example, he told me that it was not by mere chance that he happened to be in Saskatoon, Saskatchewan, on the day that Tutankhamen's tomb was discovered in Egypt. These combinations of vowels and consonants conveyed something to his spirit that never reached me. Another example which did interest me was his idea that there was a compelling magic in the lines of popular songs which made them important and which poets should study—unforgettable American songs such as "After the ball was over," "In the shade of the old apple tree," "Shine on, harvest moon," "There'll be a hot time in the old town tonight." He used this last line in a poem of his own. He called the poem "The Village Improvement Parade," and slavishly followed the meter and line of the popular song to prove his point. But one must say that this poem of his was inferior and a refutation of his theory.

He told me that many people thought of him as a new and later Whitman and that the *New Republic* had asked him to write an essay on Whitman, which he did. (It was perhaps the poorest of all his poor performances.) He said, "Of course, I admired Whitman like we all do, and I used lines of Whitman at the beginning of every chapter in my *Litany of Washington Street*. But Whitman is not my poet—*Poe is*. It was Poe who could see the golden Greek showers over the trees and pastures and fields of America. He was the Master Builder, the music maker I wanted to follow, not Whitman." He continued by quoting some lines from a poem he had written in praise of Poe, entitled "The Wizard in the Street":

> Useful you are. There stands the useless one
> Who builds the haunted Palace in the sun.
> Good tailors, can you dress a doll for me
> With silks that whisper of the sounding sea?

One moment, citizens,—the weary tramp
Unveileth Psyche with the agate lamp.
Which one of you can spread a spotted cloak
And raise an unaccounted incense smoke
Until within the twilight of the day
Stands dark Ligeia in her disarray,
Witchcraft and desperate passion in her breath
And battling will, that conquered even death?[12]

"Ah, that's the poet for me," he said. "I could never write anything like that about Whitman, great as I believe he was."

When I told him that cranks always fascinated me, he said, "You are on the right trail. People like Carrie Nation, sockless Jerry Simpson, General Coxey, Bernarr McFadden, Thomas Holley Chivers, and Elihu Burritt the learned blacksmith, are the real Americans, not the acknowledged great. They are on the lookout for what lies 'beyond the ranges'; never forget that."

Like Charlie Olson he had definitions that were uniquely his own. One I remember was his definition of a Virginian. His father's people came from Virginia and his heart was divided by the Mason-Dixon Line. To him a Virginian was a man who was gallant and courageous and radiated personal charm. I asked him how he came upon that wonderful contrast between the Babbitts and the Virginians in his poem beginning:

Babbit, your tribe is passing away.
This is the end of your infamous day.
The Virginians are coming again.[13]

He said, "I don't know." "Your answer," I said, "reminds me of a statement by Plato in one of his essays. Searching for the source of creative thinking, Plato questioned philosophers, theologians, and local sages. They gave him nothing but vague, nebulous theories. At last he went to the poets, the acknowledged creative thinkers, and found that they knew least of all!"

On an afternoon walk with Vachel around Middletown I noticed

[12]From "The Wizard in the Street" by Vachel Lindsay, copyright © 1913 by Macmillan Publishing Company, Inc. Reprinted from *Collected Poems* of Vachel Lindsay by permission of Macmillan Publishing Company, Inc.
[13]From "The Virginians Are Coming Again" by Vachel Lindsay, copyright © 1929 by Macmillan Publishing Company, Inc. Reprinted from *Collected Poems* of Vachel Lindsay by permission of Macmillan Publishing Company, Inc.

a book bulging out of his side pocket and asked him what it was. He replied, "*The Walled City*, by Ralph Adams Cram"—the architect of the Cathedral of St. John the Divine, whom he admired intensely. What he liked best in Cram was his high regard for the medieval cities of Europe which vied with one another in marks of distinction. He wished our American cities likewise to compete with one another in their architecture, music, drama, and art. Lindsay himself was constantly preaching the "Gospel of Beauty," with the same emphasis as Cram. He suggested, for instance, that Middletown, since it had a fine example of Italian architecture in the Church of St. Sebastian, could make Sebastian its patron saint. In tiny Union Park off South Main Street he saw the bronze bust of Henry Clay Work (which has since been moved to South Green). Work was a native of Middletown and the composer of such popular songs as "Marching Through Georgia" and "Nicodemus the Slave." Lindsay looked long at Work's rugged features and said, "Why couldn't your city set apart one day each year as a memorial to this man, and on that day set the whole town singing his songs?"

Among the students, Lindsay's appearance was a great success. The college theatre was full and the reading lasted two and a half hours. The listeners had never before heard such a performance, and most of the people were enthralled by his stage antics and his voice. Here are some extracts from the long account that appeared in the next issue of the *Argus*:

> Before a large audience . . . Vachel Lindsay gave a reading of his poetry, interjecting from time to time a little humor, a few interpretations of the meanings of certain poems and explanations of how they came to be written. . . .
>
> Mr. Lindsay firmly believes that poetry is a spoken, rather than a written, art, and many of his poems are not comprehensible unless read aloud by one who understands just what they mean. Such poems as "The Congo" and "General William Booth Enters into Heaven" take on new meaning under his handling. In the reading of his poetry, Mr. Lindsay departed from all orthodox methods and alternately sang, shouted, chanted and declaimed. He punctuated his words with waving arms, rolling head, and rapid strides up and down the stage. . . .
>
> In all his remarks Mr. Lindsay gave the impression that he is completely absorbed in his art. His love for poetry was reflected in everything he said. He takes it seriously, and wants others to do the same. Nothing, he said, infuriates him more than to have people think that his poems are experiments, or to quote Christopher Morley, "nice, delicate casting of verbal dice."

Lindsay could completely capture and hold the attention of a college audience. Some of the best term papers I ever had from students were written about him. Heywood King wrote his entire paper in verse, and good verse at that; he called it "The Litany of Vachel Lindsay." Allie Wrubel became so fascinated by one of the poet's lines—"I know all this when gypsy fiddles cry"—that he composed a song entitled "Gypsy Fiddles," the sale of which started him on a successful career as a Broadway and Hollywood songwriter. Horace Kelly, after he had gone on to graduate school at Pennsylvania, planned a study of Lindsay's life and work as his thesis.

It is hard for people of today to realize what an impact Lindsay made on his audiences. He was the William Jennings Bryan of American poetry (one of his best poems is titled "Bryan, Bryan, Bryan, Bryan"). Those who have heard him in action are emotionally moved by the mere recollection of his performance. There was never anything like it in America, and probably never will be again. He wore himself out before his audiences, ruined his health, and died a body-sick, mind-sick, broken man.

In one of his early prose books Lindsay wrote: "Democracy has the ways of a jackdaw. Every once in a while a changeling appears, not like any of the people around, a changeling whose real ancestors are aristocratic souls forgotten for centuries." He was fascinated by such people because he himself was one of those rare offshoots. He wrote a poem about a bronco that would not be broken but preferred to die rather than accept harness. He was also that bronco, and his dramatic and violent death affirms it. He was our William Blake, overendowed with imagination; but unlike Blake, he had a wild streak in him that was peculiarly American. I never again expect to see such an exciting person.

Poe, in his autobiography, characterized Thomas Holley Chivers as "one of the best and one of the worst poets in America." If someone should put together a complete collected edition of Lindsay's poetry (which I hope will never be done), the same might well be said of him. But I shall leave the last word to Edwin Arlington Robinson, who wrote on January 16, 1932, to John S. Mayfield of Dallas a letter which the recipient subsequently issued in a private, limited edition. Here is the text as printed:

> When a man's work is of sufficient importance to arouse controversy, contemporary criticism can only search in a fog of conjecture for the

place that time will ultimately find for it. But I am one of those who believe that the best of Vachel Lindsay's work will live for a long time; for there is nothing else like it, and the best of it has a spontaneity and a mark of the inevitable that comes only by what we have to call genius. He will be easy to remember, and as difficult to forget.[14]

I cannot leave this poet without speaking a little about his widow, Elizabeth Conner Lindsay. Early in 1933, when she was at Mills College, I wrote her to re-establish a contact that had so far existed only at one remove, to urge that she herself write the official biography of her husband, and to ask if she could make some of the unpublished materials available to Horace Kelly for his study.

Her warm and gracious reply—two closely typed pages—told me that the authorized life had already been written by Edgar Lee Masters at the joint agreement of Macmillan (which was to publish it), Harriet Monroe, Hazleton Spencer, and most profoundly herself; also that Kelly was welcome to inspect the eight large cabinets of Lindsay materials stored in Springfield, but they were too bulky to ship. She added that there were eight manuscript volumes of unpublished poems, "mostly early stuff rejected by Vachel himself," which both his publisher and Miss Monroe thought would add nothing to his reputation. For, she said, "Vachel had always kept his good new things in circulation; and although he had six months' leisure a year, in which to write, during the years I knew him; and part of the time, a full year, he was not well, nervously, and the gradual merging into a new strength of utterance that I had hoped for him did not come about." She said that the children, then five and seven, were well and happy, both in school, both showing musical talent. As to herself:

> Work here is a bit strenuous. I was quite worn out when I arrived, what with the shock of Vachel's death, a literary executorship with its heavy responsibilities, the effort to put in order an estate consisting of about $4,000 of debts; to try to arrange for an adequate memorial beginning in Springfield, for Vachel; working with Lee on the biography; and meantime continuing my various teaching, secretarial, and organizing jobs, to take care of the present needs of the family, plus locating myself with a view to better equipment for the future. I went to work here last June, four days after I arrived and moved into a cottage with the babies and our colored nurse; and have been working ever since: academic secretary to the School of Fine Arts, as executive and publicity

[14]Reprinted from Mr. Mayfield's private edition. Used by permission of Professor David S. Nivison on behalf of the heirs of E. A. Robinson.

secretary for the Summer Session, a full-time job in itself as it covers three departments and the entire United States for a mailing list, and the College has not been able to give stenographic help regularly; as teaching fellow in the Department of English, 18 hours a week; and as candidate for an M.A. in Latin, my former major at this, my Alma Mater, with 17 units of graduate work completed this year. I don't know whether it's "congenial" or not; it's forward-moving and necessary, but the main adjective is "strenuous"; a thesis with a vengeance.[15]

The letter ended with a further reference to Masters' biography, which she hoped would be published soon, "and once this is done, I am sure the way should be clear for others."

The Masters work, issued in 1935, turned out to be wholly inadequate as a life of Lindsay; it was largely a tirade against America for the shabby way it treats its poets, using Vachel as an outstanding illustration. There was more need than ever for a good biography, and I hoped that Horace Kelly would do it, but he tired of academic life and went into his father's business. It was not until Eleanor Ruggles' *The West-Going Heart* that we got a good life of the poet.

I entered upon a lively correspondence with Mrs. Lindsay which lasted until she died. She left Mills College in California and went to work at a private school in Hartford. As president of the Connecticut Association of Boards of Education I got her a paying engagement to lecture at one of our annual meetings, and I appeared on the same platform with her in Hartford one night when she read "The Chinese Nightingale" dressed in a beautiful Chinese costume. We had many good talks about Vachel and his poetry, many good hours together. As Richard Steele once said about a woman of the eighteenth century, "Just to know her was a liberal education." I was sorry when she accepted a call to Cambridge, Massachusetts, and left us. Her daughter Susan married a son of Bertrand Russell, and one of their sons will undoubtedly inherit the peerage when he comes of age. I have wondered a hundred times what Vachel would think of that! Each of her children grew up to be a blessing to her. And she herself was a blessing to everyone who knew her. The way she buckled down and paid off Vachel's debt of $4000; the way she took it when Vachel, on the night of his death, writhing in agony from the poison he had taken, railed at her, accusing her of robbing him of his virginity and destroying his creative gift; the way they lived in an apartment in Spokane at times almost

15Used by permission of Professor Nicholas C. Lindsay.

penniless with two little children while he was occupying a large room in the Davenport Hotel and holding forth to visitors in the lobby—all this increased my love and admiration. She seemed to be able to walk triumphantly over all the obstacles of this life.

A Handful of Others

I am loath to bring this chapter to an end. I would like to say a good word for Alfred Kreymborg, who wrote a history of American poetry entitled *Our Singing Strength* and followed it with an anthology as a supplement. He heroically started a magazine called *Others*, which published poems the established periodicals would not print. I had him up twice at the college and the boys greatly enjoyed his talk on poetry and his music on the "mandelute."

I would also like to say a word in behalf of Sara Teasdale, whose poetry and personality fascinated me. (At one period they fascinated Vachel Lindsay too, and his 1923 *Collected Poems* was dedicated to her.) Some of her verses seemed to call for musical settings—and some got them, though I know of none that achieved popularity as a song.

Sara had a lively love affair with Vachel Lindsay. He met her in 1914, fell madly in love with her, and wanted to buy her an engagement ring. But she hesitatingly said "No." He visited her in St. Louis twice and courted her violently, mostly by forcing his poems upon her. She fully recognized his genius, and helped him add a softer touch to several of his poems, such as "The Chinese Nightingale" and "The Santa Fe Trail." When Lindsay's genius was first recognized in New York City, he and she had a wonderful week together. He wanted her to say "Yes," but she finally decided to marry her businessman lover back in St. Louis. When Vachel died, she showed her love for him in a poem she wrote to his memory which closes with these words:

> Fly out, fly on, eagle that is not forgotten *
> Fly straight to the innermost light, you who loved
>   sun in your eyes—
> Free of the fret, free of the weight of living,
> Bravest among the brave, and gayest among the wise.[16]

I must add Genevieve Taggard to the list of poets I admired. It was she who discovered a new lover for Emily Dickinson and who wrote a fine book on Emily's life and work. She came to Wesleyan to lecture on Emily and stayed at our house. In those days a number of our rooms, including the guest room she occupied, did not have electricity. In her room we had placed a kerosene lamp, a Rochester burner with round wicks, and left it lighted while we were having supper. Before long we smelled smoke and saw a black cloud descending the stairs. We rushed up, turned off the light, and opened the windows. The wick had been turned up too high and clouds of smoke had filled the room with webs of soot. Miss Taggard's two finest dresses were covered in black smudge. But she took the disaster in her stride and pitched in helping us to clean up. We got rid of the soot, but the odor remained. She slept in that room all night, for we had no other guest room. A year or so later she and I were judges at a poetry contest and she laughed again about the mishap. She had forgiven us completely. Many years later, I wrote her the following:

VILLANELLE TO GENEVIEVE TAGGARD

The high cheek bones of Genevieve—
(How many men have felt their height?)
Aroused me on a mild May eve:
'Twas Holyoke's annual lyric night;
Our task, to judge the verse aright—
I judged the cheeks of Genevieve!
Hawaiian waters brownish-white
Had left on her a wave-capped light
That dazzled me that mild May eve.
Her sister poets' loftier flight,
Like Elinor's cold *bas-relief*,
Or Sara's wistful, gentle weave,
Or Edna's daring lyric might,
Surpassed her own. But, friends, believe
Her own seemed best that mild May eve.
All four have left earth's bloom and blight:
I loved them all, but most I grieve
The high cheek bones of Genevieve
That charmed and won me that May eve.

How can I leave out Anna Hempstead Branch, who once served with me as a judge of a Mount Holyoke poetry contest? As the senior member of the judges' committee, she was to read all the student poems first and send them on to the other two judges. Two weeks passed, then three. No word from Anna. Miss Ada Snell, in charge of the affair, was driven frantic. Anna finally confessed that *she* had lost the whole batch. I sent her a letter containing two lines from her most famous poem, "The Monk in the Kitchen": "Order is a lovely thing, / On disarray it lays its wing." She promptly sent me a note containing just one word: Touché!"

I would like to say a word about Mark Van Doren, who lived to become the grand old man of American poetry. He kept up the pastoral tradition with a vein of verse uniquely his own. In addition to being a poet, he had been an editor, a critic, and a teacher. As editor of *The Nation* he gave several of my poems their first hearing.

Another poet with whom I spent many happy hours was Robert P. Tristram Coffin, a fellow Bowdoin man and a localist with a vengeance, who once said that "Maine is not a state, but a state of grace." He could tell a tall tale with gusto and spin a salty yarn about as well as anyone I ever knew.

"Tomorrow to fresh woods and pastures new," but the woods and pastures of politics can never measure up to the excursions I have made on the hills and valleys of poetry.

CHAPTER 22

Politics and Public Life

MY interest in government began at my father's table. He talked about Grover Cleveland, William McKinley, and William Jennings Bryan in such a way as to give us the feeling that the government in Washington, D.C., was somehow a part of our own lives. He bought a life of James A. Garfield, which he couldn't afford, from a traveling book agent, and I read it through several times. I have already told the story of the small boy Wilbert, who walked before breakfast eight miles of dirt road barefoot, his shoes in his hands, to hear Bryan speak at eight-thirty in the morning at the Rockland Court House. I have told of my work for Wilson in 1912, and my campaigning for Cox and the League of Nations in 1920.

The number one influence, however, came from my work in argumentation and debate. For thirty years I carried the debating courses and coached the debating teams in several colleges. I paid little attention to the oratorical part of the work, and concentrated on a detailed study of both sides of whatever question was before us. In this way I became thoroughly acquainted with current state and national issues.

When I had survived two threats of dismissal from the college and finally achieved tenure, I felt settled at Wesleyan. The town itself attracted me. The population was made up of six layers—Connecticut Yankees, Irish immigrants, Scandinavians, Italians mostly from Sicily, Poles, and about twenty black families. Two of these black families, the Hunters and the Moodys, lived on our street. Their children spent so much time in our house that we felt we had had a share in their upbringing. On second thought, this was not so, for the black children had better manners than our own. When Jeannette called the children to supper, it was Charley Moody who made the boys put away their playthings and clean up the room before leaving. I was pleased to think that we were living in a neighborhood that was a good cross section of

America. I also liked Middletown because it was not too big or too small—some 25,000 people during our first decade there.

I decided to get well acquainted with the intricacies of the grassroots political scene, joined up with John Tynan, and learned the goings-on in a "smoke-filled room." I became an active member of the Democratic Town Committee for fifteen years. John was the local boss and a good one. For himself, he settled upon the job of Middletown tax assessor, a steady post that was not affected by elections. At that time he cared much more about winning a city election than he did about winning a state or a national campaign. I carried my portable typewriter to meetings of the inner circle, made up propaganda letters for the *Middletown Press*, and even helped newly elected officials to write their acceptance speeches. Through all this, John and I became great friends.

In addition to politics, we both were replenishing the earth's population. Every time I would get a boy he would have a girl. Nobody on this planet ever wanted a daughter more than I did, and few people ever wanted to have a son and heir more than John. To make a long story short, he ended up with seven girls and I with five boys.

He enjoyed doing favors for people, some of which had strings attached to them; others did not. As an example of a "did not," I recall the case of a Republican's son, home on a vacation from law school, desperately needing to earn money. John landed him a job when everybody else, including big shots in his father's own party, failed. John was the old-fashioned type of boss, brilliantly depicted in the autobiography of Lincoln Steffens. He insisted on getting much gravy for himself and his inner circle of friends. But when a great need of the town was at stake John could be counted on. The outstanding illustration of this is the story of a standpipe needed at the south end of the town. The water pressure there was so low that, when a fireman trained his hose on a burning building, he could obtain only a trickle and had to stand there and watch the house burn. The need of a standpipe to increase the pressure was great, but the cost meant a million dollars levied on the taxpayers. Some of us urged that we put the demand for a standpipe in our plaform. An old pro spoke up and said, "If you do, you will lose the election." The debate grew hot and ugly. Finally John settled the matter by saying, "All right. Let's put it in the platform and lose the election. The need is too great to ignore." We did put it in the platform, we did lose the election, but we awakened the town to the need of the standpipe as we never could in any other way. Within three years a million-dollar standpipe at the south end was on its way toward completion. The town seemed to appreciate our sacrifice, and we won the next election overwhelmingly.

Those early contacts with the inner side of the political party organization opened to me a new world that at times was amusing and at other times frightening. John had a custom once a year of throwing a dinner for the leaders of the "minority" groups, where they could acquaint us with their *grievances,* which they did with a vengeance. Our object as a party was to be fair to all minority groups and get their votes, but we sometimes fell short! I shall never forget my first "grievance" dinner. After the dessert and coffee, John arose and asked them to air their complaints. One Pole stood up and told us that we had given all the gravy to the Italians. He was desperately in earnest as he said, "See what you have done for them. You gave them the job to run the elevator in the City Hall. You gave them jobs for two men on the city dump; you gave *them* a job to watch a manhole on Court Street. You even put one of them on the City Council. And what have you done for us?" He reached out his right hand, spread wide his fore and middle fingers in Churchill fashion, and yelled out at the top of his voice, "And what have you done for us? Two GARBAGE COLLECTORS!!"

This startled and amused me so much that I pretended to retrieve a napkin and dropped my knee to the floor to hide my laughter. The man was deadly serious, as much in earnest as if he had inside knowledge of the Day of Judgment. John kept a straight face, but he was more amused by my reaction than by the speech itself. These gripes were new to me but were "old hat" to him.

John did not make many mistakes as a politician, but like Mayor La Guardia, when he did make one it was a "beaut." In 1940 the Republicans put up Bert Spencer for mayor. He was a good public servant, had served as chairman of the School Board and in several other offices, and had always done an excellent job. Our candidate that year was not a charismatic vote-getter. John saw by the advance votes of the schoolchildren that we were losing the election and he grew fearful. Without consulting any of us, he issued a statement saying that Bert Spencer was anti-Catholic. He could not have done anything more harmful to our ticket. The Catholic priests of the town rose to Spencer's defense and he was swept into office by an overwhelming majority. John realized later what a big mistake he had made and said, "I got what I deserved."

At Mayor Bielefield's suggestion John put me on the Town School Board and I was a member of that body for over thirty years and chairman for eleven years. We had two school boards, one for the four square miles of the inner city and one for the forty-four square miles outside, known as the "town." The town wanted to retain its own identity. Even after we wrote a new City Charter in an attempt to unite the two, the town insisted on retaining the office of first selectman to handle the affairs of the outlying districts. The two small districts, South Farms and Westfield, also insisted on keeping their own private fire departments, relics of our dual government that still exist.

Our first selectman for many years was Ray Wilcox, a man who knew everybody in town and was undefeatable at the polls. When Ray sensed my curiosity about all town affairs, he took me around and showed me something of the night life of the city. We went down along the river to see the "Light House," where Ray introduced me to "Mamie," who ran the establishment. Mamie took in roomers regardless of condition or caste and could readily make accommodations for the sex-starved males of Middletown and vicinity.

We finished the evening with a visit to the city jail. That night the police were holding an intoxicated "lady" behind iron bars. While I was there she pounded on the bars and cried out to the policeman on duty, "Officer, officer, come here." Mike O'Shaughnessy went over and called out in a gruff voice, "What do you want?" She replied, "Send one of the boys across the street to get me a box of Kotex." "Look here, lady," he said, "tomorrow morning you will eat corn flakes just like all the other prisoners. I'll not be after cooking up any special dishes for the likes of you!"

In 1930 John Tynan asked me to run for state senator on the Democratic ticket. I didn't want the post, for I was working on a third book of verse and wished to finish it. My friend Lane Lancaster of the Government Department at Wesleyan had run for that position in 1926 and lost. George Gilbert, author of *Forty Years as a Country Preacher*, had run in 1928 and lost. So John Tynan insisted that it was now my turn. The G.O.P. had made a pitch for the heavy Italian vote by nominating a young Italian lawyer named Don Cambria. I kept thinking of what a frustrated life I would lead if I won. I would belong to a very small and powerless minority in the legislature. Only one Democrat in the entire state was elected to the Senate in 1926. However, I would still have a voice; I could speak in that assembly. John saw that I was weakening and asked me to have a conference with the Democratic State

Central Committeeman, J. Harry Fagan. This was necessary before my name could be presented to the Senatorial Convention for nomination, and I would have to take my chances with other aspirants for the job. A few days later I joined Mayor Bielefield, Fagan, John, and one or two others in the smoke-filled room.

I was delighted with Fagan. He was a middle-aged man with blue eyes and a head of bushy, curly hair which the undergraduates of today would look upon with envy. He loved politics for its own sake, and the more exciting the campaign the better he liked it. He had a hearty contagious laugh. He also had a lovely daughter who was the joy of his life. She was a charmer whom I had already noticed at a number of Democratic meetings.

When the conference began I was rather sober. I didn't have any money to put into the campaign, and told them so. I was still mourning over the seven hundred books and manuscripts I had lost in the East Hall fire one year earlier. I also carried daily in my briefcase the manuscript of my third book of verse almost ready for publication. At first I was reluctant, but Fagan's enthusiasm, humor, stories of other campaigns, and spirit of goodwill won me over. I thought perhaps a change into political life and a chance to put into state law some of those reforms that I had been debating for years would lift me out of the doldrums and do me good. So before the conference broke up we were slapping each other on the back and girding ourselves for the fray.

The campaign got off to a slow start. At that time our senatorial district consisted of three towns, Middletown, Cromwell, and Middlefield. I visited Cromwell once and never went to Middlefield at all. Near the close of the campaign, the League of Women Voters got busy and staged a debate between Cambria and myself in the Town Hall, with every seat taken and scores of people standing in the corridors outside.

Mrs. Leroy Howland, president of the League, took charge of the meeting and introduced me first. I showed that the G.O.P. state boss, J. Henry Roraback, was a lobbyist for the New Haven Railroad at a stipend of $5000 a year, that he was the leading public utilities tycoon in the state, and that holding these positions he could stymie any reforms in these areas. I made a strong plea for the abolition of the "rotten borough" system in the state, a system that let two representatives from the small town of Union with under 200 inhabitants carry as much weight as two representatives from Hartford with over 164,000 people.

I dwelt on the need for old age pensions—which was a plank in our state platform. My opponent, Mr. Cambria, ignored my arguments for the "rotten borough" reform and old age pensions and dwelt mostly in generalities, stressing the importance of good sound government.

Election Day in Middletown was an exciting time for the party workers. For a number of years we had one big headquarters for all districts except the two small ones. The six or seven telephones were in use all the time—"Have you voted?" "May we send a car for you?" Girls bent over the lists of voters, checking off every hour the names of those who had voted. Some workers had their streets well canvassed. They had tramped from house to house, speaking a word for the Party and offering rides to the polls or baby-sitters if needed. Other workers had a desultory grasp of the streets assigned to them. All this was carefully noted by the leaders in the smoke-filled room. A few boys from the college drove voters to the polls, shared our coffee and sandwiches, and enjoyed immensely all the coming and going, the reckoning and the hullabaloo. One professor's wife told me she had the best time of her life on one of these strenuous days when our party was successful.

Early on one Election Day word came to headquarters that a man on the west side of the town had committed suicide. He was a registered Democrat, and the big question at headquarters was whether he had or had not voted before committing the terrible deed!

Late in the afternoon John Tynan would show up, look over the charts, and call out, "Who is covering Hanover Street? These people haven't voted at all. Give me two drivers. GET ON THE JOB!" There would be much scurrying around and Hanover Street would be taken care of.

When the polls closed at eight o'clock in the evening we all gathered around the telephones. Every worker was there, and people drifted in from the street until we were packed in like straphangers on a subway. News from the First District soon reached us. This district was heavily populated by Italians, and we could tell by the number voting there how we were going to fare. A big turnout meant a big Democratic vote and we could feel fairly sure that we would carry the city. On this evening we carried the First District, but the margin of victory was not large enough to blot out a heavy Republican vote in the Second. When all the votes were counted I carried Middletown by 72 votes. I might possibly have carried the other two towns if I had visited them. The final tabulations around the state showed that twenty

Republicans and fifteen Democrats were elected to the Senate. I was not among them.

After the election the local paper, the *Middletown Press*, although strongly Republican, wanted to say something nice of both winners and losers. Of me and my campaign it said, "It may be some balm to him to know he kept the majority figure down to its lowest figure in twenty years."

As Mayor, Fred Bielefield had done an excellent job. Among other things he had tackled for the first time in many years the question of paying off the city's indebtedness. When he retired from the rough-and-tumble of city politics and took the position of city postmaster, I initiated a testimonial dinner in his behalf at Stueck's Tavern. One of our workers asked me if he could help out by standing at the door and taking the money for the tickets. I readily consented. There were about seventy people present. In the midst of the postprandial speeches in behalf of the honored guest and his work, our ticket-taker got up and left the room. He also left town, absconding with all the dinner money. We did not want to become the laughing stock of the opposition party, so we all chipped in quietly and paid the tavern bill.

Out of this election I received a new insight into things needing to be done in Connecticut, such as (1) the removal of sweatshops; (2) better labor and management relations; (3) liquor legislation; (4) old age pensions; and more. My work with the debating teams became more detailed and more intense. In 1931 we celebrated Wesleyan's one hundreth birthday by winning every debate at home and away with teams on both sides of the questions. The Debating Banquet which closed the season was unusually well attended this year, for few things sharpen undergraduate interest like success. Debaters of other days came back to college to help in the celebration. They had amusing stories to tell of past victories. One returned veteran recalled a night when Williams and Wesleyan were debating the subject of government ownership and operation of railroads. One boy on the Williams team said among other things that government ownership could not succeed in this country because there were too many foreigners straight out of Europe engaged in railroad work here. In rebuttal the Wesleyan man said, "My opponent objects to *too many foreigners* working on railroads in this country. Let me remind the opposition that government owner-ship and operation has been a success in Europe, and over there they are *all foreigners!*" I need not tell you who won the debate.

Our record of winning in 1931 pleased President McConaughy so much that he gave me a semester off on full pay—a sabbatical that I had never known before in all my years of teaching. I had never stayed long enough in one college to earn one. Instead of going abroad I elected to go to Spruce Head, Maine, and acquaint my sons with the life I knew as a boy—a life of smelting, cod-fishing, boating, and hunting. They would attend the same ungraded one-room school where I spent my seventh to my fourteenth years.

When the summer visitors had left and the fishermen had moved back to the village from their island fishing camps and all the houses were occupied again, the village came alive with friendly warmth. There was much visiting from house to house, and the coffeepot was always on the stove. As Christmas drew near and we saw no particular preparation made for its celebration, I decided to revive the communal Christmas I knew as a boy. The people responded to the idea and helped in every detail. The village chapel was opened, cleaned, and heated. Rehearsals for a Christmas play went forward. On Christmas Eve a snowstorm prevented the minister from coming down from Rockland, and I had to give the Bible reading and prayer. The snow did not prevent the village folk from filling the chapel. We started with a procession of children holding lighted candles, singing as they marched down the central aisle to an improvised altar on the stage. Our boy Jack recited "The Night Before Christmas." The play was a great success. Last of all, Santa Claus distributed gifts. Each family had brought one gift for each child and put it on the tree. Such a happy time!

We almost achieved the honored status of "home folks" rather than the contemptuous use of "summer folks" ("summer complaints" was the favorite term). Our promotion in social status showed up in a letter from a village boy to one of our sons along in May, after we had returned to Middletown. The letter read: "When are you coming home?"

At the same election at which I was defeated for state senator, Wilbur Cross, the grand old dean of Yale, was elected governor. Politically he was the loneliest man in the state. The lieutenant governor was a Republican, all the other elective state officers were Republicans, the Senate and House were overwhelmingly Republican. What could he do? Fortunately for him, there were some appointments that did not require approval by either the House or the Senate. They were his alone. But now came "the most unkindest cut of all"—the Roraback hierarchy was determined to take these appointments away from him.

They introduced a bill that would have made all the governor's appointments subject to confirmation by the Senate—which, if it did not approve his nominees, could substitute its own. It never got beyond the Judiciary Committee, because the rank-and-file Republicans would not go along with the leaders. Cross asked one question: "Why is it that constitutional doubts concerning these appointments disturbed no one until the election of a Democratic governor?" He succeeded in making his own appointments, getting approval also of those requiring confirmation. It should be said that he appointed as many Republicans as Democrats to the various judgeships and commissions. He normally sent his appointments to the Assembly in twos—one a Democrat and one a Republican. He was quickly "learning the ropes."

A real gain I got out of political activity was an acquaintance and friendship with Governor Cross. He was a gifted raconteur. He loved a good story and could tell one to the queen's taste. If the queen was not in the room he could tell an amusing off-color story. Cross was a man to know. He had written a life of Henry Fielding that put this all-round man of letters of the eighteenth century in a higher niche than earlier critics had given him. The American writer he loved best was Mark Twain, and he could quote him endlessly. He kept on his desk a quotation from Twain which read, "Always do right. This will gratify some people, and astonish the rest." Talk about Twain inevitably led us to Joan of Arc. I told him that my publishing house had put on the market the complete story of the trial of Joan of Arc. He became interested, wrote me a letter which said, "Will you review the Joan of Arc book for me? I will pay you $10." I wrote the notice, and he published it immediately in the *Yale Review*. A section went as follows:

> We are certain to be thrilled by the story—one of the most vivid in world history. On one side, sixty learned judges, armed with theological and ecclesiastical statutes and decisions stretching over hundreds of years, feeling themselves the defenders and preservers of the Church Militant against heretical error; egged on to do their duty by the University of Paris; the dark shadow of Bedford (brilliant brother of Henry the Fifth) lurking in the background. On the other side, a country virgin of nineteen, armed with peasant shrewdness, simplicity, naïve candor, and her "Voices," facing these judges without counsel, and burdened by heavy iron chains. Her responses are so superb, and her conduct so appealing, that she confounds her judges, fascinates and wins over to herself the imagination of France and of the world, and opens up new and unrealized possibilities in human nature. She becomes, in the phrase Whitman applied to another, "The sweetest, dearest soul of all our days and lands."

In a letter dated December 5, 1932, Cross wrote as follows:

I was perfectly delighted with your Jeanne D'Arc review which I read in galley proof. I wish indeed that I might find time to read the Trial. I congratulate you on your rapid progress in your literary work, on the good reviews you are getting. . . .

He not only wrote me this good letter, but he also gave me a bigger stipend than he had promised.

In June 1932 Wesleyan conferred on Cross the honorary degree of LLD. Although he belonged to the opposite party, President McConaughy's admiration for the Yale dean and state governor was unbounded. He asked me to present him for the degree, which I happily did.

Cross knew that there was nothing he could do to change the Lower House to a Democratic body. As governor he was facing difficulties. He once said to me, "If I lose the state by 70,000 votes, the vote in the Lower House will be Republican by 6 to 1; if I win by 70,000, the vote in the Lower House will be Republican by 3 to 1. That shows how hopeless the situation is." But he thought he might bring the Senate into the Democratic column, and he went to work on that problem.

He knew a veterinarian named Dimock in Tolland County who took care of everybody's cats and dogs, and never sent out a bill asking for payment. He called on this man and asked him to run for the State Senate on the Democratic ticket in a district that was 6 to 1 Republican. The man consented and was elected. Cross said to me, "Who would dare to vote against a man who had taken care of all their dogs and cats without asking for pay?"

He hated racetrack gambling in all forms. He thought that betting would teach young people that life itself was a gamble and that nothing they could do for themselves counted for much—vicious doctrine. He was confident that the racetrack gambling bill could be defeated in the Senate but he was uncertain about the House. So he called an early morning session of the House to vote on the bill. He knew that many of these legislators would still be in their beds when the vote was taken, while many independent Republicans were with him on this issue. The racetrack gambling bill was defeated by a slim majority.

Cross's leadership began to show itself at the end of his first term, and the State Senate in his second term was 18 to 17 in favor of the Democrats. That majority of one was slim and the Lower House was still overwhelmingly Republican. But he maneuvered a few good laws through both houses, such as widow's pensions, and many independents all over the state were singing his praises.

He sailed right through four two-year terms but was defeated when he came up for a fifth. A new party, followers of Father Coughlin of Detroit, who had no gubernatorial candidate of their own, endorsed Baldwin, the Republican, as their candidate, managed to get on the ballot (illegally, some thought), and polled just enough votes to defeat Cross. Later he said, "Sometimes I wish I had challenged the legitimacy of Father Coughlin's party." "Why did you want a fifth term?" I asked. "Well, you know," he said with a smile, "if you die in office you are assured of a bigger and better funeral!"

My next venture into public life was an attempt to secure public housing for the city of Middletown. This effort extended over a period of years. It began in 1932 when the Congress of the United States, moved by the "Bonus Army" marching on Washington, decided that something ought to be done for the housing of veterans of World War I. Late in that session a bill was enacted which would provide Federal money for housing for people of low incomes. The contractors of the West, taking advantage of the Federal handout, began to build houses by the hundreds, but the conservative East was slow to act. In 1937, when Charles Schaeffer was mayor, my wife and I investigated the slum dwellings of Middletown. We found apartments with cold water only, no central heat, a toilet in the kitchen, rats running across the floor, and cold winds blowing through holes in the plaster. My wife was a social worker before we were married and had a genius for uncovering sore spots!

I went to the Mayor's office and asked him if Middletown could apply for public housing. Schaeffer was conservative by nature, slow to react, but finally, with the consent of the Common Council, he sent the application to Washington. Months later, for the wheels of government grind slowly, our request was granted. We were promised four hundred units, and three-quarters of all the expense was to be taken care of by the Federal government. The Mayor immediately set up a Housing Authority with ex–Representative William Citron as chairman, aided by a group of public-minded citizens. I was named publicity director for the project.

All was well until we began to look around for a suitable site. When the *Press* announced that the open meadows north of Bow Lane were acceptable both to the Authority and to the Federal Office of

Slum Clearance in Boston, what an uproar exploded! We had not expected to meet such violent opposition. As publicity director I wrote for the *Press* enough material on public housing to make a small book. At the various service clubs questions were thrown at me that a Philadelphia lawyer could not answer. "Will the tenants keep coal in the bathtubs? Will the buildings last long enough to pay for themselves? What will compensate the city for the loss of revenue from these tax-free buildings?" I was invited to address practically all of the service clubs in town. At the close of each address they were loaded for bear. Many of them knew far more about building houses than I did, and their detailed questions, hurled in anger, often made me wretchedly miserable. They treated me so roughly at the Rotary Club that Charles Hoover, a colleague at Wesleyan, Club president at the time, although belonging to the opposite party, came to my defense and said, "You are altogether too rough on Bill. How do you expect him to have an exact answer to all these intricate technical questions?" I have never forgotten Hoover's kindness to me on that occasion.

The Authority held meetings in the Municipal Building, where every phase of the question was discussed. At one of these meetings a faculty wife defended a wealthy spinster whose income came largely from rents from slum houses. She took $50 rent from each family that was squeezed into her buildings and she put nothing back in repairs. The faculty wife rose and asked, "If this program goes through, what will people like Connie Howard do for an income?"

The businessmen of the city had one main objection—the project would be tax-free. Ours was then a poor town and the picture of four hundred new tax-free houses and at the same time no rents coming in from the empty slum houses was more than they could stand. But when they discovered that "towns with a housing shortage" did not have to tear down their substandard buildings but merely repair and improve them, they ceased their opposition. We could then breathe easier, for that opposition was formidable.

The bankers who had money invested in the slums kept quiet, but would sign no petitions on our side. We tried to get the Board of Health to condemn the existing structures. But the Board replied, "We cannot turn these people out, for there is no place for them to go." Finally the Bow Lane residents secured an injunction halting construction and we had to look for another site.

In the midst of this we had the 1940 city election, mentioned ear-

lier, in which Bert Spencer was overwhelmingly elected and the Town
Council went Republican on his coattails. The chairman of the Council was a young Italian named Cubeta who was deadly opposed to
public housing. On Christmas Eve Cubeta succeeded in securing from
the City Council a vote abrogating the entire housing program. That
was a sad Christmas Eve for me, and I didn't sleep at all that night. I
did write a grim letter about the Christmas present which Cubeta and
his Council had given the poor people of this town. But that wouldn't
help the cause so I tore it up.

One Polish young man on the Council, a Democrat whom we
thought we could rely upon, betrayed us that night and voted with
Cubeta. The vote was 5 to 4, so that one vote would have saved the
day for the new housing. I dropped everything I was doing and went
and called upon the Polish priest of the town, Father Piechocki. He
saw that I looked haggard and distressed, gave me a warm handshake,
and invited me to come in. I noticed an excellent fishing rod standing
in the corner. I asked the Father if he ever used it. He said, "Yes, every
chance I get." So before coming to the business of the hour we talked
of flies, lines, hooks, and Connecticut streams and discovered that we
were both members of the Izaak Walton Club. I then told him my
errand, started to describe the slum houses. He interrupted me, "Yes,
yes! I know, I know! Some of my people are living in those run-down
places." I asked him to talk with his parishioner on the Council and
beg him to change his vote. Father Piechocki shook my hand warmly
and said, "I'll take care of that at once." The same night the Polish
councilman called me up and gave me the greatest bawling out of my
life. He said, "You — —— —— son of a bitch! Why didn't you call
me? Why did you have to go to Father Piechocki? If you have anything again to say to me, call me up. Don't go to somebody else to get
what you want." I said, "I'm sorry, but after all the months I've put
upon this low-income housing I couldn't bear to see it ruined now."

Another man on the Council, a Republican, went to Aaron Palmer,
a lawyer who was one of our inner Democratic circle and later became
a distinguished Superior Court judge. He proposed a deal: "I'll vote
for your damned housing if you'll give me a variance on Union Street
for a shop I want to put up in a semiresidential district." Aaron agreed
to the proposition, so we now had two extra votes, one more than we
needed to reverse the abrogating vote of the Council. Beyond all this,
Mayor Spencer said to me, "While I don't believe in government hous-

ing myself, Mayor Schaeffer has committed the town to it and we have gone so far that as mayor I would never agree to see it abrogated now." So before the twelve days of Christmas were over my worries ceased and the housing program was on its way.

We found a good stretch of open land in South Farms east of the Linus Baldwin property. The people of that region did not want slum dwellers brought out to their neighborhood. They gave the same objections we had at Bow Lane. They organized, hired a lawyer, and wrote endless letters to the *Press*. A well-dressed man and woman said to me, "We don't care how many Negroes you put in the housing, but we don't want you to bring any Italians out here."

One has not gone very far in public life in America before he begins to realize this ugliness of racial antagonism. He sees that the ingredients of the melting pot fail to melt. When the G.O.P. in town got tired of losing the city election in Middletown they put up for mayor a fine Italian businessman named Santangelo and he swept the city. Italian Democratic girls working for our party that day, and getting good wages, slipped guiltily out when the opportunity offered, went to the polls, and voted Republican. Our city then had two representatives in the state legislature. Both parties fell into the habit of naming one Italian and one Pole for these posts.

In the state the Democrats at one close election put a Pole on the ticket as a candidate for congressman-at-large and won with Polish candidates from that time on until the Party got reckless and named a New Haven Italian for congressman-at-large. The Poles showed their resentment as well as their power by going to the polls and soundly defeating him.

In those days when the leaders of either party compiled a state ticket they gave careful attention to race and religion. In religion we have made great advances toward tolerance. When I came to Connecticut in the early '20's, the politicians told me it would be a long time before there would be a Catholic in high office. When Bill Citron and I stumped eastern Connecticut for Al Smith, some Protestant Democrat town chairmen would not let us have a hall for our meeting, and we had to speak in the open streets. When I went to Connecticut College for Women in New London to make a speech for Smith, the professor who invited me there wrote, "You will have to come in the back door, for it is not quite respectable here to be for Al Smith." Since that time we have had a Catholic President, and in Connecticut, two Catholic governors. The wheels of democracy move slowly in these matters—but they move.

In Middletown the wheels were still rolling, for while the opposition to low-income housing was strong, support from influential citizens was growing stronger. The project needed support, for a crisis was now at hand.

Kicked out of the second location, the Authority decided to use land owned by the city near the abandoned poorhouse. There were no neighbors there to object, for the land was way over and down the hill beyond the state mental hospital. However, we immediately ran into another hazard—by hook or crook we had to get sewer and water to the site. This would cost more than $50,000, and at that time according to our city charter, anything that cost over $50,000 would have to go through a referendum. The opposition said, "We've got you now!" because in a referendum they felt sure that the vote would be NO!

Our problem now was how to avoid a referendum. (Not exactly a democratic attitude!) Three of us went to Washington, D.C., and talked with Mr. Wiley, the head man in Low Income Housing, telling him of our desperate situation. He thought it over a while, asked a good many questions, and finally said, "Rather than let the whole project go by the board, I can promise you that the Federal government will take care of the water and sewer." We threw our caps in the air. What a relief! At long last we could begin construction.

In addition to these outside obstacles we had internal differences among the Housing Authority members that were often painful and took a lot of our time to resolve. An Irish member of the Authority said one night, "I don't want to see any Negroes in those nice apartments. If we let them in they'll reduce them to shambles." The chairman, Bill Citron, spoke up and said, "But that's what public housing is for. These people have never had good houses. Here is our chance to help them." The argument went back and forth for an hour. Finally someone said, "Let's call up Boston. The man there is in charge of this whole New England region." So we called up Boston and got a firm answer: "You must take them in regardless of race or color. That is in the Housing Act." "All right," the Irishman said, "but let's put them all in one section." This was agreed to, and we put the Negroes in the top row of apartments. That was the finest location, and it afforded the best view of the Connecticut River at its loveliest spot. But the Negroes were not satisfied. Little by little, one by one, as vacancies occurred, they moved into the lower circles with the whites and finally had no one spot for their homes any more than the Italians, Poles, or Yankees.

As publicity man I was obliged to accept a small monthly check. I put the money in a separate savings account. When the project was finished and occupied, I purchased for the central recreation room the finest radio and record player I could find in Hartford, together with a collection of popular records. For three weeks the radio and the records were enjoyed by the tenants who came into the recreation room. At the end of twenty-one days someone broke into the room and stole the record player and all the records.

This long experience was an education for me. The way people hired lawyers and kicked us off of Bow Lane and South Farms astonished me. The lower the people were in the economic and social scale, the harder they would fight to keep what they called the bilge water of the ship of state from running over their property.

I realized all over again how patient one must be to get anything accomplished through the democratic process. We got the housing but we spent more than two years getting it. The prices during these years of argument kept on going up and up and up, and when we finally settled, we erected 205 apartments using wooden buildings instead of the 400 brick units we planned for and were promised. This is a good example of the gospel of the half-loaf, the real gospel of democracy. With all its faults it is better than dictatorship.

A dozen years, the '30's and early 40's, passed quickly. I was teaching at the college, writing and publishing books of poems, and keeping my hand in Democratic town politics. Imagine my surprise when in 1944 John Tynan asked me if I would consider running for governor of the state. Homer Cummings, he said, had sent him to sound me out. "Well," I said, "this will take some thinking over." "Sure," John said, "take your time. But will you meet Cummings this Saturday at the Garde Hotel in New Haven just to talk things over?" I agreed.

I had never met Cummings, but I had read and admired his powerful keynote speech at the Democratic National Convention of 1920. It summarized in excellent English the achievements of Woodrow Wilson more succinctly and more effectively than they had ever been expressed before—or since. This speech could only be matched by the "Plumed Knight" speech of Robert G. Ingersoll extolling the greatness of James G. Blaine at the Republican National Convention of 1876.

Cummings had known me as the author of many poems published

in *The New York Times* and as an acquaintance of Brien McMahon of Norwalk, who was ambitious to become United States senator, and who had been trying to make himself known to Democratic circles in eastern Connecticut. Cummings had been national chairman of the Democratic Party and had served six years as attorney general in the cabinet of Franklin Roosevelt. He was the man who had appeared before the Supreme Court to convince the judges of that body of the reasonableness and legality of many startling New Deal measures—some of which were rejected. He was also the man who defended F.D.R. in his attempt to enlarge that body—popularly known as "packing the court"—one of the most unpopular measures F.D.R. ever conceived.

Cummings told me of the wonderful work Brien McMahon had done as one of his most trusted lieutenants in the attorney general's office. He wanted to repay Brien by getting him nominated for senator. He said, "Brien is a Catholic in the western part of the state. To balance the ticket we need for governor a Protestant from the eastern part of the state. Would you be interested?"

I answered, "I have never thought of such a thing." I told him that I wasn't a very ambitious man, and that whatever ambition I did have ran toward poetry rather than politics. I added that I did have an acquaintance with public questions inasmuch as I had coached debaters in different colleges for many years. "What better preparation could any man have?" he asked. "You made a good run," he said, "for the State Senate." He seemed to know all about me.

"But," I said, "I only did that because no one else would allow his name to be on the ticket." "Well, think it over. Now let's talk poetry." To my immense surprise I discovered that he was more interested in poetry than he was in politics. For an hour we forgot all about politics and surveyed the American literary scene.

I went home and told Jeannette what Homer Cummings wanted. She was as surprised as I was and finally said, "Perhaps a change of interest will be good for you. Let's follow it up."

I followed it up at Cummings' suggestion by making the acquaintance of the three leading Democratic bosses of the state: John Golden of New Haven; Cornelius Mulvihill of Bridgeport; and Thomas J. Spellacy of Hartford. I discovered that their political thinking was on a different level from mine. One of the three, Spellacy, had some vision. As mayor of Hartford he had got some needed things done, such as a dike that would keep the spring floods from overflowing into the city.

He was also the only one of the three that I could have a good talk with. He was witty, a good conversationalist, and therefore a delightful table companion. But like the other two his major interest was spoils— the spoils of office.

One of these men, John Golden, was determined to nominate Robert Hurley for governor. Golden controlled the 74 delegate votes of New Haven, and about 74 more in the small towns thereabouts. What support I gathered, in a few weeks of vigorous campaigning, came almost wholly from the Second Congressional District (the four counties east of the Connecticut River). I had neither time nor money to campaign elsewhere.

Convention day arrived. On a Friday evening the delegates gathered in Bushnell Memorial Hall to listen to an eloquent defense of F.D.R.'s New Deal by John O. Pastore, governor of Rhode Island. The speech was a "rip-roarer" but it did not reach the ears of the city bosses, who were secreted in the upper rooms of the Bond Hotel, trying to line up the ticket which they would direct the delegates to nominate the next day. Democracy in action! John Tynan was there with the other leaders, but I was not even told that such a meeting was in progress.

At the hotel the delegates milled around the corridors until the early morning hours snatching at what bits of gossip they could hear, trying to find out who would get what. At midnight everything seemed to be in doubt. Hurley was reported to have said, "Tynan has got me over a barrel." At 1:00 A.M. Mike Connor came to me and said, "Snow, you have got this nomination if you really want it. Your only tough contender is Hurley and a great many of these delegates don't want him again. He has Golden and that's about all." I went to bed thinking that I had a fair chance to be nominated for governor.

The next morning Brien McMahon was nominated for the office of United States senator. Then began the nominating speeches for the candidates for governor, starting with Hurley. My friend Hugh Brockunier sat in the front row ready to make a nominating speech for me. At this critical moment John Tynan hurried up to me and said, "Bill, I'm sorry, but Homer says you haven't enough strength to be nominated as governor. He wants you to take second place. Tell Brockunier to hold it now and shift his speech to lieutenant governor."

That was a stunning blow to me, and I was inclined to hold out. But Tynan wanted me to give in. The town chairman, Angelo De Toro, wanted me to give in, and they both worked on my wife until she advised me to do so. "What can you do without your home town support?" she asked. I surrendered, and the Convention settled by putting me on the ticket as the nominee for lieutenant governor.

As we left the hall feeling not too happy, McMahon's wife Rosemary stopped us and said, "Bill, you have been the victim of a legitimate double cross." "I didn't know that a double cross could be legitimate," I answered. "Yes," she said, "Homer has been playing the game of politics according to the rules." I understood then that Cummings had set me up to give himself trading power in that game. He had my support to give to Hurley to pay for Hurley's support of Brien!

Robert Hurley, Golden's choice, was given the nomination for governor. Shortly after, at a meeting of all the candidates, Hurley asked me to act as "hatchet man" during the campaign. I refused, saying that such a position would be out of keeping with my entire nature. Whatever success I had in public life was gained by persuasion. Vituperation and damnation were not my weapons. I could dispense honey better than I could vinegar. So John L. Sullivan became the hatchet man, and he did the job so well that we used him again in that capacity two years later.

People who have never traveled over Connecticut highways in October have escaped one of the real horrors of running for a state office. In the fall of the year the soil is still warm, and on a chilly autumn night the cold air meeting with warm earth creates a heavy mist that makes motoring hazardous. Driving a car on these nights is like sailing a boat on a foggy sea. (I would rather take my chances on the sea.) Campaigning, one has to go out every night no matter what the weather is and no matter how one feels. Worse still, he has to accept it all with a smile. "A smiling public man," Yeats calls him. At times on these trips I could not see the white line that marked the road. At the murkiest moments my wife had to get out, find the edge of the road, and walk ahead, guiding me. I mention this because people who are sleeping comfortably in their beds don't realize what office seekers have to contend with! When I was alone on long trips, desperately exhausted and in danger of dozing, I used to sing hymns that I learned as a boy in the Spruce Head chapel. Those old hymns, which I thought in my clearer hours to be grim and dolorous and devoid of poetry, really gave me comfort and kept me awake.

On Election Day Jeannette and I voted early and then used our station wagon to haul people to the polls. At seven o'clock that evening the election results began to pour into our headquarters. Raymond Baldwin, the popular Republican candidate for governor, was running well ahead of Hurley, and I, for lieutenant governor, was running better than Hadden, my Republican opponent. (The two offices were not then wired together as they were later.) As the excitement mounted, Ed Shugrue, a party worker, and a few Wesleyan undergraduates put me in Ed's car and carried me off to WTIC headquarters in Hartford. The man in charge at WTIC that night was Leonard Patricelli, a former student of mine at Wesleyan. He said, "Bill, I think you are going to be elected lieutenant governor. Take this paper, write out a short acceptance speech, and we'll put you on the air." I wrote a few sentences and handed them over for his approval. But I added, "Pat, I don't go on until I am sure. Call up Hadden and see if he concedes."

He called Hadden and heard my opponent say, "Concede? If Ray was elected, then I was elected." The boys kept tally of the votes as they came in. When all the votes of three-quarters of the 169 towns had been reported, they found I had a plurality of 18,000. At about three o'clock I was finally convinced I had won. Patricelli handed me the short speech I had written. On the outside of the paper he had marked a big "B—." I said, "What's this B— for?" He replied, "That's the highest grade you ever gave me in your class, and you gave that to me only once." The students laughed and called out, "Give it to him, Pat!" "What a memory!" I said. I took the paper, went to the mike, and read the customary felicitations and the usual platitudes.

I was entering on a new experience. Two-thirds of the Wesleyan student body had gone to war. The college had been turned into a training school for the armed services. The professors in the humanities were set to teaching the Morse code, the combustion engine, wig-wag, and hand signals. The subject assigned to me was aerology.

We had been doing this as best we could since September. Our students were mainly poor boys who had never been to college and never expected to go. Some of them were better college material than we had been getting at the school. All this came to me like an awakening. I saw then and there that the country was losing something valuable by not educating these young men. (The junior or community college movement had not then been started, but when it did come I saw it as the answer to what I was looking for.)

Just before I was inaugurated in January a "directive" came from

Washington to the English Department asking us to cease what we were doing and turn our efforts toward giving the boys a thorough course in English grammar and composition. We hailed this directive with glee and went back to teaching subjects we knew something about. I wanted to be in on this new program and did not resign from the college. I felt that I could handle both jobs—lieutenant governor and college teacher. My wife was a far better drillmaster in English grammar than I ever was, and she taught my class whenever I had to be in Hartford. She could teach the boys the correct use of "shall" and "will," something I was never able to master.

My first impression of the Legislature on opening day was a favorable one. I went into the lieutenant governor's office, and sitting there were the members of the Superior Court in robes, waiting and ready to swear us all in. They were really a superior group of men, and they made me feel confident of the welfare of the state. I kept thinking of a statement of Giordano Bruno, who said, "A nation has nothing to fear as long as it has an incorruptible judiciary."

My job was to preside over the Senate. I went to the rostrum and carefully looked over the chair made of wood from the Charter Oak— the chair I was supposed to occupy. I soon learned, however, that the lieutenant governor stands throughout each session while he is presiding, and that the elaborately carved oak chair is merely something to look at and admire. I was also pleased that my party had a working majority in the Senate. While political rivalry between the two parties was sometimes brushed aside when bills for the betterment of the state were under consideration, it was safer to have a working majority of your party at least in the Senate, if not in the House.

Some of the early maneuvers of my party amused me immensely. For example, we had in the Senate a few subordinates who were known as "cloakroom attendants." These were a hangover from the eighteenth century, a relic of Old England whose lawmakers dressed in long dark broadcloth coats and tall hats and needed servants to remove these stately garments and care for them. Reformers in the state had proposed that these attendants be abolished. "We have outgrown all that," they said. The men who performed this Senate function were party hangers-on who disliked manual labor but who loved all the gossip and maneuvering of party politics in the statehouse. They were paid $700 a session for this "labor." One of the Democratic senators in a closed session in my office said, "Isn't it about time that these attendants were dropped out? All they do is stand around and chew the rag." Whereupon Al Coles, a senator from Bridgeport, arose and made an eloquent speech in behalf of keeping them. He said, "The Republicans have kept these ward-heelers on the payroll for years, and why should we wipe them out? They have all done good work for us in their home towns. The cost to the state is very small and these men enjoy their jobs. I move that we keep them on and do our reforming on more important matters." Al's speech, at times amusing and at times serious, was always eloquent. The vote to keep them carried the day, and the cloakroom attendants were safe for one more session.

The senators at first treated me as a "literary man" who knew nothing about legislation. They had had such a person in Odell Shepard, who had been lieutenant governor from 1941 to 1943. Shepard was a masterful prose writer. He had written a scholarly article on the unicorn which was as readable as a good novel. He had written a book entitled *The Harvest of a Quiet Eye*, the record of a walking trip across Connecticut, which gave pleasure to thousands of readers. It was this book that led Governor Hurley to choose him as his running mate in 1940. But Shepard had no acquaintance with the subject matter of the two thousand bills pending in the Legislature, and he refused to dig in and master the world of economics and politics. He just wasn't interested. He did master the details of *Robert's Rules of Order*, and some of his decisions on procedural matters made Senate history. I cared nothing about *Robert's Rules of Order* myself, but I had a clerk named John L. Sullivan who was a master of protocol and procedure and who saved me from a hundred pitfalls during my term in office.

My main interest was in bills like the "Little Wagner Act" for labor; the two educational bills, one appropriating $2,000,000 for building new schools in the state, the other an equalization bill that would assure teachers in the country towns salaries commensurate with those in the large cities; and welfare legislation, including my own pet project, a Medicare bill.

The people in the Governor's office said to me, "You can have the two-million-dollar building bill or you can have the equalization bill, but you can't have both." That was the edict from the G.O.P. Directing Committee, headed of course by J. Henry Roraback, but in the end we got both. The credit should go to two good Democratic workers on the Education Committee, Benny Leipner and Margaret Hurley.

I had no vote, but I could talk on the floor after sessions and I could testify at hearings. When I wanted to introduce a bill providing medical care for the poor and the aged, I had a hard time finding a representative or senator to put his name on it. Medicare at this time was a touchy subject. The American Medical Association was pretty solidly against it. Finally Senator Perry Barbour agreed to introduce the bill. "His goose is cooked!" was the comment on Capitol Hill. I am pleased to record that Barbour is now a Superior Court judge. While this issue was being tossed back and forth (mostly back!) a Dr. Wentworth invited me to his home to discuss Medicare with fifteen or twenty doctors. I accepted, as I was not afraid to submit myself to their questions. One of them said, "How did you get this crazy idea?" I answered, "At Spruce Head where a large percentage of my three hundred neighbors did not have a doctor until they were about to die. The doctor would come, see that the man was at death's door, then 'take a-holt and drag him through' as one wag put it." I read excerpts from the *Ethics* of Aristotle which said that a state should want good healthy men for soldiers in the army, and consequently the state ought to take over the medical needs of its citizens. "Today," I said, "we want not only to serve the needs of the army, but to build a good life for all our citizens. That cannot be realized with our hospitals and asylums filled beyond capacity all over the country, and thousands outside needing care they are not getting." The doctors could not deny this. We ended the evening without coming to blows. As I left, Dr. Wentworth opened a window and showed me a deep snowdrift just outside. "We planned, if the discussion got rough, to throw you out there, sending Snow back to snow!"

This session of the Legislature ended as so many others had done, in a wild scramble to get the important bills passed before the deadline, midnight, June 6. When twelve o'clock came and no appropriation bill had been passed, someone set the clocks back three hours. The appropriation bill and a number of others were hustled through. No one stopped to read these bills, or to find out if they had been properly given a hearing and the endorsement of a committee.

The good things the Legislature did in the session of 1945—the Little Wagner Act, two educational bills, veterans' aid, etc.—were smothered by the wrangle over the appointments of local judges. In forty-nine cases the two parties were deadlocked. They finally and reluctantly left these forty-nine appointments in the hands of Governor Baldwin. It was this wrangle that stole the headlines.

Along in the summer the attorney general ruled that Governor Baldwin would have to call a special session of the Legislature to validate the bills that were passed after midnight on June 6. The governor at first wished to limit the session to the validation of the faulty bills. I hoped that we might do something for the defense workers and the returning veterans. I thought that Connecticut ought to support and implement the Kilgore Bill then before Congress. Some states that had attracted large numbers of workers from other states to their defense plants refused to pay unemployment insurance to men who, now that the plants were discharging workers, wanted to return home. If they left that state where they had been employed, they could draw no insurance. The Kilgore Bill would right this unfair situation. I went to Washington and testified in favor of the bill and wrote a letter which was printed in *The New York Times* on September 9, 1945.

I was more active these two years than I had ever been before. I continued my teaching at Wesleyan and kept my place on the Town School Board. I was trying to make something out of the office of lieutenant governor. A New Haven paper said editorially when I was elected that the office of lieutenant governor did not serve any good purpose and ought to be abolished. This editorial challenged me and I was out to refute it. I was not gunning for the gubernatorial nomination; I was trying to make something of what I had.

As titular head of the Party (highest ranking official) I was called on to be the speaker at all sorts of Democratic gatherings. Now it was a clambake in Waterbury. Again it was a testimonial dinner in New London (these testimonial dinners were supposed to honor some active party worker, but they really were devised merely to build up the fortunes of the Party).

Aside from the political talks, I was asked to speak before such groups as the Zontas, the Soroptimists, the Rotary Clubs, Kiwanis groups, Chambers of Commerce, and so on. In addition to all this a small radio station called WONS, which is Snow spelled backwards, came to my home every Sunday night to broadcast a fifteen-minute talk on such subjects as "The Connecticut Farmer," "Taxes," "Our Penal Institutions," and "Education."

Sometimes the old pros in the political game, in a teasing manner, put me through embarrassing situations. Dr. Satti one day put me on a very spirited black stallion he owned just to see if I could stay on. Fortunately for me, I had ridden horseback almost every day during

World War I, when I was in the horse-drawn 329th Field Artillery. That experience saved me. The stallion was a mean one, and had it not been for this Army training I would have been thrown off within twenty seconds. As it was I had a difficult time, but I succeeded in riding completely around the corral.

A more embarrassing time came when some of these old pros invited me to go with them to a new and very good restaurant, so they said. When we went in I saw at a glance what kind of place it was. Many "ladies of the evening" with next to nothing on were walking around the room and occasionally planting themselves down on some man's lap. My friends saw to it that a very attractive blonde should plant herself in mine. These old pros wanted to see me squirm. I found the girl rather easy to talk with—asked her where she came from and how long she had been here and other commonplace questions. She laughed and we talked freely while my friends were looking disappointed because I neither hustled her upstairs nor pushed her away. The situation reminded me of two lines spoken by a floozy in "The Jolly Beggars" by Robert Burns: "I once was a maid though I cannot tell when / And still my delight is in proper young men." When I suggested that the verse applied to her she said, "Yes, that's me!" We got along well together but both were relieved when I had to depart for another engagement.

On January 12, 1946, the United Nations voted to make their permanent headquarters in the United States. I immediately wrote a letter to the *Press* urging that their headquarters be located in Fairfield County in Connecticut. I said they would add color and distinction to our state. We could offer a beautiful, peaceful countryside "far from the madding crowd" yet near enough to New York City to use its facilities. My letter troubled the Republicans, for I was a step ahead of them. The next day Governor Baldwin, who was given state and nationwide radio coverage, urged that the organization be located here. Two towns, Greenwich and Stamford, got busy and opposed our plan. The decision was finally made when John D. Rockefeller offered an $8,500,000 site on the East River in New York City. That settled it. Thanks to Governor Baldwin, a group from the United Nations did have one meeting with us in Connecticut. We all dined together, and never in my life have I felt so deeply the need of language equipment. At the dinner party I sat between a Russian and a Frenchman, both of whom had a smattering of English. We talked about the differences between Russian humor, French humor, and American. We had a grand time, and I came away wishing more than ever that the United Nations might settle in Connecticut. But who could make any headway against an eight-million-dollar gift?

On June 14, Flag Day, I made a speech on the United Nations before a Middletown group composed of Elks, soldiers, and the American Legion. I indulged in a little prophecy. I believed that the United Nations would have a flag with a blue design on a white ground as a symbol of peace. Although the U.N. never heard of me and my prophecy, when they did adopt a flag on October 20, 1947, they chose the colors I had suggested.

My extracurricular activities sometimes required an entire day. One of these was the funeral of U.S. Senator Francis Maloney of Meriden. A member of the State Police called for me and drove me to the Maloney home, where a large crowd had already assembled. I expressed my sympathy to Mrs. Maloney and then mingled with the others. Funerals often turn into family reunions and are enjoyed as such. The Maloney funeral turned into a political family reunion. Who was there and who failed to show up were questions of the hour. A woman grasped my arm and said, "Which is Clare Boothe Luce? They say she is here." I glanced around and there was Mrs. Luce, very beautiful and flawlessly dressed. I pointed her out, to the complete satisfaction of my questioner. Another friend came along and asked, "Have you seen Jim Farley? I'd like to get a look at him." In the next room the family reunion had turned into a reception for Big Jim. The crowd around him was testing his reputation for remembering names.

We repaired to the church for a Requiem Mass which took an hour and a half. At its close a distinguished-looking prelate arose and said, "It is not customary in this church to make eulogistic remarks in addition to the Mass for the Dead, but this man warrants an exception." He proceeded for about an hour to extoll the virtues of the deceased senator.

We were driven to the cemetery for the final rites. It was a bitter cold and windy day. A priest at the graveside urged us to keep our hats on. We were glad when all the prayers were ended and we could seek the shelter of the 1823 Inn and partake of a belated dinner. We heard Senator David Walsh, an unusually eloquent man, pay tribute to his friend. He called him a senator's senator, enumerating incidents of Maloney's resourcefulness in the dark days of the Great Depression when he was both mayor of Meriden and United States senator.

Not to be outdone, our own Governor Raymond Baldwin, a member of the opposite party, arose and climaxed the meeting with a tribute to the departed brother, wonderfully well expressed, closing with two lines from *Hamlet*: "Good night, sweet prince; / And flights of angels sing thee to thy rest!"

I was driven home in the late afternoon, and had no more than got seated when a telephone rang and I was informed that I had been chosen as the person to write a memorial tribute to Senator Maloney to be placed in the records of this session of the Connecticut Legislature.

It was a pleasure to do this chore for Francis Maloney, for he was a man I admired. His entire life was given up to public service. In the Great Depression he inaugurated a "make-work" program for the unemployed of Meriden which was later taken over by the Federal government. He had a sharp sense of humor and a great fund of good stories, of which this is one:

One Irishman was conversing with another on a Sunday afternoon. Pat said, "Did you hear about John Danaher going over to the Republicans?" Mike replied, "It's a damn lie! I saw him at Mass this morning."

A second long day was spent at the Eastern Orthodox Church in New Britain. The occasion was the burning of the mortgage on a Ukrainian church which the congregation had bought from the Roman Catholics two years earlier. Governor Baldwin, perhaps knowing how much time this assignment would consume, palmed it off on me. Arriving at the parish hall just before noon, I was ushered to the head table and introduced to the Bishop of the Ukrainian Orthodox Church, who was presiding. He was the big attraction of the day and people came from all over the state to see him. He was a Russian of about forty and his Byzantine church robes, together with his beard, made him look stately and very impressive. He was slow of speech, enunciating every syllable of every word much in the manner of Carl Sandburg. In fact, he reminded me of Carl in many ways. I tried to talk Byzantine art with him but he was not interested. He fascinated the women, who waited on him constantly, and I suspected that he enjoyed their veneration. I told him I came as a messenger from our Governor to extend the greetings and congratulations of the state. He said, "We'll have that later. Now sit down and eat."

I began to see that I was in for a protracted meeting. I feared the burning was going to occupy as much time as was spent in paying off the mortgage.

I asked the Bishop to tell me about the Ukraine. This waked him up and he cut loose: "I want to tell you that we Ukrainians long for our freedom as much as you Americans ever did. We have the makings of a great country—the soil, the people, the climate—all are the best in the world. But we are tied to Russia and Russia won't let us go. Groups that you never heard of start freedom movements with what result? They are brutally wiped out. Freedom does not dare to raise its head, but we want liberty as much as you. You got your independence because England was three thousand miles away. My greatest hope in the world is freedom for the Ukraine. But how can we get it with the might of Russia at our doorstep?" All this was made more effective by the deliberate slowness of his speech.

More courses kept coming onto the tables, and more Russian Orthodox groups kept coming in from all over the state. As a large group from Norwalk strolled in at about three-thirty, I said to the Bishop, "This doesn't seem fair to the women out there in the kitchen. Why didn't these people all come on time?" He replied, "Slavs are not like Americans. They don't believe as you do that punctuality is the courage of Time. They like to defy Time and show they are not its slaves. These women have many children to feed and dress; their husbands like to stay in bed Sunday morning. So they are late." I watched the women come in from the kitchen, clear a large table, and set it up again for the newcomers. Their good humor and the supply of food seemed inexhaustible. I asked the Bishop, "How can these workers be joyful! What do they get out of it?" He said, "When all are fed, we call them in and give them a hearty round of applause. That's their pay."

At long last a group of four men came in and set up on a platform a big bronze brazier. The local priest placed the documents on the brazier and cautioned, "Don't light the match just yet!" There were three or four speeches praising everyone who had had a part in paying the debt on the church—and prayers of thanks to God. Then the Bishop lighted the match and we all watched the papers reduced to ashes. The calloused workingmen's hands holding the big brazier made a tremendous impression on me. They were the rock on which this church was built. I finally extended the greetings and congratulations of the State, and left the hall. It was past supper time when I got home.

Two special senatorial banquets were held during each session of the legislature, the first given by the senators in honor of the lieutenant governor; the second given by the lieutenant governor to honor the senators. I shall speak only about the second, for that was my financial responsibility and I was extremely shy on finances. One lieutenant governor had served the senators a sumptuous dinner on gold plates, an affair frightening for me to think about. How could I give a good party and still cut down the expenses? I finally decided to bring the group to Middletown and entertain them in the banquet room on the street floor of the college Downey House. Walter Heideman, the man in charge of the college buildings, agreed to have white birch logs burning in the baronial fireplace that evening. Small tables would be covered with red-checkered cloth and a rib roast of beef dinner would be served. John Tynan contributed an improvised bar together with a congenial and articulate bartender for the event. (The bartender assured me that he would be delighted to serve the senators as a favor to me.) Edward Fenn, a Republican, who was owner and manager of the Pickwick Arms of Greenwich, and two or three other well-to-do senators offered to pay for the liquor, the most expensive item of the entire evening. Four large angel cakes, made by my wife and served with ice cream, climaxed the dinner. The postprandial program was unplanned and rather casual. Political differences were forgotten and good fellowship marked the evening. After the dessert we toasted each other and reminded each other that

> It's always fair weather
> When good fellows get together
> With a stein on the table
> And a good song ringing clear.

Nicholas Spellman went to the piano and struck up popular songs which we all joined in singing. Sam Malkan, the president pro tem of the Senate, arose and exhibited the hat I had been wearing, called it a disgrace. He said it was the most disreputable hat ever worn by an officer of the state. He threw the hat on the floor and trampled on it. He closed by presenting me with a new, flawless, beautiful hat and threw my old one into the fire amid the cheers of my colleagues. Not content with this present, Leon Riscassi, the majority leader of the Senate, made a short speech about my virtues and defects and presented me with a large silver platter on which were engraved the names of all the senators, in their own handwriting, a present which I cherish.

It was not easy to respond to all this generosity. I said I believed they were making a good record and doing something to improve the state, and that was really our main business. As they left for home that night I gave each one a copy of my *Selected Poems*. With the help of generous friends I had cleared this hurdle without going into bankruptcy!

At the Jackson Day Dinner in 1945 I made a plea for the returning veterans. I must have been in good form that night, judging by the laughter and applause that kept interrupting me. From that time on people in the small towns were urging me to run for governor. The big cities, especially New Haven and Bridgeport, wanted nothing to do with me. John Golden of New Haven, Cornelius Mulvihill of Bridgeport, and Tom Spellacy of Hartford wanted a candidate who had money. They were all out for Chester Bowles. John Bailey, who was battling for the leadership of the Hartford Democratic Committee, wanted to make complete his break with the old leader of the city, Tom Spellacy. He attempted to win the eighty Hartford delegates for me. At first nearly one-third were for me, a few were for Dodd, and the Spellacy faction was for Bowles.

A month before the Convention I had a telephone call urging me to come to Wallingford, where the C.I.O. was having a luncheon meeting. Arriving there at noon, I was escorted to the head table and introduced to Walter Reuther. I had admired his way of getting things done among the auto workers and was glad of a chance to meet him. He was a man with a mop of reddish hair, keen blue eyes, sharp distinctive features. He was in early middle life and his movements showed him to be on the young side. He was dynamic and yet calm. It was easy to see how he could climb to the top of a labor organization. He told me he wanted me to drop out of the gubernatorial campaign and run for the office of United States senator. He said that labor wanted Chester Bowles to be governor. I told him I was as good a friend of labor as Bowles. As lieutenant governor I had succeeded in putting the Labor Act as the number one bill on the roster: I had gone over the wording of it with attention to every sentence, and had succeeded in getting two weasel-worded sentences changed. I told him we had passed a Fair Employment Practices Act in the State Senate, as well as an anti-child-labor act. Both of these were killed in the Lower House. He listened carefully and seemed pleased with what I said. But he still came back and pointed out that Bowles was more aggressive, that labor leaders wanted him for governor, and that I would do a better job as United

States senator. While this talk was going on I watched two newspaper men across the hall straining to hear what we were discussing. They heard enough to get a story. Connecticut papers next day announced that labor wanted me to pull out of the gubernatorial contest and throw my weight to Chester Bowles. I had no notion of quitting. The small towns of the state would never have forgiven me. As I thought it over I said to myself, "How little outsiders know about the mood of a town or a state!" I figured that forty years of residence in the state and more than two years of travel through most of the 169 towns should count for something.

On the morning of the Convention we found Bushnell Memorial solidly decorated with Bowles banners. They hung from the rail of the balcony way across the hall. Piles of banners nailed to short sticks were stacked in the corners ready for what was expected to be a Bowles victory parade.

The noisy crowd after several appeals was persuaded to sit down and listen to the nominating speeches. The name of Bowles was placed before the convention amid the shouts and cheers of his supporters.

Jack Everett, a young philosophy professor at Wesleyan, had been chosen to nominate me. His speech was a masterpiece. He acted the part of a shy young man who knew nothing about politics and was totally unacquainted with the customary "a man who" brand of nominating speeches. He did say that I had a few things to recommend me for the position and reluctantly dug them up one by one until he had enumerated more virtues than I or anybody else ever dreamed I might have. He made my experiences as a lobster catcher in Maine and a reindeer agent in Alaska look like acts of high adventure rather than lowly chores. The way he dramatized his own unfitness for the task was something new in Connecticut politics. Jack won the audience completely. When he had finished the whole convention was on its feet and banners marked "Vote for Snow" were carried around the hall. It was the exciting moment of the day, and for me something entirely new.

Then came the voting. It was generally agreed that Bowles would win the nomination on the first ballot. The midnight edition of the Hartford *Courant* came out with a big headline on the first page— "Bowles Nominated. The Professor Slinks Back to the Cloistered Halls of Wesleyan," or words to that effect. John Bailey said if he could stop Bowles from getting a majority on the first ballot he could get me the nomination. He begged other towns that did not want to vote for me to vote for Dodd or some favorite son—which they did. On the first ballot, and before the final results were announced, I had 545 votes, Bowles had 480, and Dodd had 195. Seeing how things were going, several town chairmen, headed by John L. Sullivan of New Britain, hurried to the rostrum to change their votes from Bowles to Snow. They wanted to be on the bandwagon; the one unforgiveable sin in politics is to fail to jump on the bandwagon. Francis Smith, the Waterbury leader, had promised his delegates that in the final hour he would have them all on the bandwagon. He failed, and some never forgave him. Bowles walked to the rostrum, pushed aside all those who were trying to get to the microphone, and moved that the Convention make the decision for Snow unanimous. For the first time in years the small towns had made themselves felt, and the bosses of the big cities, especially Golden and Mulvihill, went off to sulk in their tents. Bailey's handling of the Hartford delegation and his influence on other delegations was mainly responsible for my getting more votes than Bowles on the first ballot.

At the summit conference to raise money for the campaign, I donated $500, money I borrowed from a local bank. In spite of the smallness of my contribution, I did have a large campaign fund—large for those days. People who normally do not give money to campaign funds contributed generously to mine. This was because people regarded me as an amateur—or a nonpolitical politician. A young Wesleyan instructor, Stuart Wilcox, sent out a form letter begging for contributions and raised a few hundred dollars. The smallest contribution on this list was fifty cents donated by one of my colleagues in the English Department! Robert Frost sent $5 and added a letter which I consider a masterpiece and which can be found in this book on page 379. Allie Wrubel, the song writer and an old student of mine, composed words and music for a theme song entitled "Vote for Snow," which was used on radio throughout the campaign. I gathered $650 locally and reported an expenditure of $1150 for this vicinity at the end of the campaign. From over the state John Bailey told me we had received $93,000, the largest campaign fund the Party had ever collected. Then he showed me the Roper polls indicating that I would lose the state by 100,000 votes. With this showing, John asked me if he could take a few thousand and start permanent headquarters for the State Democratic Party at 525 Main Street, Hartford. I said, "You are the boss. Go ahead." While writing this memoir I asked Bailey how much he took out for the operation.

He did not remember the exact figure, but wrote, "We didn't need much because prices were not high then."

The organization had money enough to hire Eliot Janeway to write my speeches. He was interested in economic and political theory and in fact has had a notable career as a writer on economic and business matters and an advisor to corporations. When I talked with him I found his mind running toward abstract theories, Dow-Jones averages, Keynes economics, trade balances and all such lingo that meant so much to him and so little to me. I had taught my children that the one and only purpose of the financial pages of a daily paper was to start a fire in the fireplace. (This was one of the seventeen mistakes I made in bringing up my children, according to their own estimate of me as a father.)

When I saw one of Janeway's speeches that I was supposed to deliver, I was dumbfounded. It didn't sound like me, and if I had read it over the networks I would have sounded like a reluctant eight-year-old boy trying to stumble through an essay in a class of third-readers.

When Janeway and I met to talk things over, we seemed unable to make contact with each other. His wife, an attractive novelist, often appeared in the same room with us; I felt certain that if she and I were cooperating on my speeches instead of her husband, there would have been a much better rapport in the speech department.

One day I asked him if I could have one of his speeches and make it over to sound like myself. He immediately said, "No." I asked why. He replied, "I can only work well under pressure, and I can get a speech finished just before you are to deliver it." That foretold disaster.

I reported my predicament to John Bailey, and he got Jeannette to go into the room where Janeway was writing and see if she could not look over his prose, page by page as he wrote, and bring it closer to my style. Janeway endured this for some minutes, then in exasperation left the room. After he came back, his wife and Barbara Bailey entered and invited Jeannette to come and have tea with them. She did not at the time realize that this was Janeway's attempt to get rid of her, and she answered, "No, thank you. I'd better stick with the speech." Poor Janeway struggled on. I knew I had supporters who expected me to be different, but here I was, spouting the old haranguing line. "So he's just another ordinary politician!" my friends would conclude.

Some of the speeches were merely a damnation of the opposition party, and I hated to deliver them. One night I left the broadcasting studio after one such speech and walked back to headquarters swearing at myself, "Damn, damn, God damn!" until Jeannette, walking along beside me, could stand it no longer and refused to walk with me.

"Why don't you let me write my own speeches as I did when I was campaigning for the nomination?" I asked. Then I would write out a fifteen-minute speech, hand copies to the reporters, and then go on the platform and talk for thirty minutes. I would improvise enough to double any speech I wrote. The reporters didn't like my improvisations, which made extra work for them, and they complained about them, but the audiences thought that my laterals were the best part of the evening's performance.

Toward the end of the campaign Bailey said, "Go ahead and write your own speeches," which I gladly did. But the damage had already been done and I felt thwarted. It is true that I was often bluntly indiscreet, and Bailey didn't want me as a candidate for governor to go on the air unbridled, but if I had been left free I feel certain that I would have obtained a larger vote.

The campaign was not at first an exciting one. My opponent was James L. McConaughy, whom I had known for years. In our early twenties we were both instructors in the English Department of Bowdoin College. He was a natural conservative and I was a born Celtic liberal, one who thought that standing still was going backward. In spite of our wide differences we became warm friends and had many happy hours of conversation together. Moreover, we belonged to the same fraternity and that strengthened the bond. I would rather have had as my opponent any other Republican in Connecticut. He was also my chief, being president of Wesleyan, and I was merely one more Indian in the tribe.

I wanted no guttersnipe tactics in this campaign; I welcomed a more civilized form of rivalry. In one speech McConaughy said, "When I am elected governor I am going to make Snow poet laureate of Connecticut!" This was said in a tone of gentle mockery toward poets. In reply I reminded him that there were enough people writing poetry in Connecticut to swing an election and that he'd better be careful about making fun of poets. This response brought me many favorable telephone calls, and fairly represents just how bloody the battle was!

McConaughy had delivered a speech in behalf of birth control a few years earlier, which had met with a fiery and wrathful response in the *Catholic Transcript*. My advisors wanted to use this *Transcript* material to discredit my opponent and I said, "No, don't use it. I believe in birth control myself." It is hard for readers today to realize what a touchy subject birth control was in Connecticut politics a generation ago. The Catholics were dead against it, and they constituted a majority of the voting population of the state. John Bailey said to me, "Bill, you lack the killer instinct," an accusation that was all too true, and doubly true with Jim as my opponent.

The Republicans played up two issues that were more effective than the rest. The first was "Had enough?"—a reminder that America had had fourteen years of one-party rule, and it was time for a change. The other was the "red issue"—a spurious affair, but immensely effective. Senator Joe McCarthy of Wisconsin had poisoned America with this issue. He spread fear throughout the country. He succeeded in having four of the best men in the State Department dismissed and their careers wrecked because they saw the China situation clearly and wanted us to take heed of the new leaders of China and negotiate with them as well as with Chiang Kai-shek. Anybody who was a homosexual, a progressive, a liberal, or even a nudist was included in his definition of Communist. His performance made people realize that "it could happen here" if a bunch of demagogues should reach out to grab control of America in a time of depression and confusion. I was a consistent liberal and therefore I was one of those creatures who were suspect.

In late October Clare Boothe Luce came to Connecticut and made two statewide broadcasts, in both of which she pictured me as one who could not throw off the little red bug of Communism that was crawling around inside of me. The first one was a vicious speech against me, and the second one was delivered on Hallowe'en and said that the liberal Democrats like myself were aiding the Communist conspiracy in America. I tried to answer it by saying that this diatribe of Mrs. Luce's was timed to coincide with the hour when ghosts and goblins were filling the air and old hags were riding from place to place on broomsticks! But my humor was lost, for many people were inclined to believe that liberals in the Democratic Party were largely responsible for the growth of "the Communist conspiracy" in the United States. The issue of Communism and the fact that the Democratic Party had held the reins of government for fourteen years led to our defeat. That year two of the best vote-getting Democrats in America—Lehman of New York and Louche of Ohio—were unable to stand the onrushing Republican tide. In the election the enemy won national control of both the House and Senate and I, a mere Connecticut Indian, was defeated by my chief, President James L. McConaughy, by 95,000 votes.

If I could portray what happened in our home on the night of my defeat I would make this chapter come alive beyond all others. We had no sooner carried the supper dishes from the table than the first wave of friends began to arrive. I quickly saw that we were in for a wake— a wake unlike any that I had attended during the two years I was in office. Some of these guests expressed their sympathy and drove off. Others settled down for the evening. I had won big in Middletown, a 1754 plurality. All our local candidates were elected. Muriel McCormick Hubbard, granddaughter of John D. Rockefeller, a near neighbor, arrived with two dozen bottles of Mumm's Extra Dry champagne— enough for all the guests, and a relief to us who were not prepared to entertain. Mrs. Hubbard, a Republican, had voted for me, but she had hired nearly all the available cabs in the town to carry people to the polls to vote against our judge of probate, Leonard Ryan. (Ryan had thwarted her every attempt to adopt children.) She was out to defeat him, but he was swept back into office on my coattails. At our home that evening she carried in her hand a copy of Rudyard Kipling's poem "If." She wanted to read it to me to cheer me up. As soon as she got started on the first two lines—"If you can keep your head when all about you / Are losing theirs and blaming it on you"—someone from Hebron, or Bozrah, or Meriden would break in, reach out his hand, and express his sympathy. Mrs. Hubbard would start again and reach the third line but then there would be a call, "Snow, Snow! Telephone!" These interruptions occurred about twenty-five times during the evening before Mrs. Hubbard was able to get me over in the corner and recite the poem. I did not tell her that I already knew it by heart!

The New York *Sun* called me up during the wake and asked me to give my version of the defeat. I dictated the following (people were all around me at that moment and I made it as brief as I possibly could): "We are in for some reaction, but it is by action and reaction that the purposes of democracy are fulfilled." To my great surprise other papers took that sentence up and said nice things about it. Shall I be immodest enough to quote one example? Dave Boone of the Paterson *Evening News*, in New Jersey, wrote: "I didn't hear a wiser, more sportsmanlike or truly American comment by a defeated candidate from any other spot in America."

Of course I was disappointed. I wanted to be the governor who laid more stress on education than had any who had come before me. There were things I wanted to do for the state. The one thing that really hurt me that evening was the reaction of my ten-year-old son

Gregory. When he learned that McConaughy had won, tears came to his eyes and he said, "I can't go to school tomorrow." I assured him that I would go with him. His father was his hero and he could not bear to hear the boys laughing and hooting at him in his defeat. I drove Greg to school. When the children in the yard saw me standing there, calm, smiling, and undismayed, the taunts they no doubt had ready to sling at Greg were stilled.

Later in the morning I went out into my study and found one reporter, whom I shall not name, drunk and asleep on the floor with his boots on, and all his photographic apparatus beside him on the rug.

It took me a little time to recover from this ordeal. But the campaign was not a total loss, for I was able to renew my friendship with Governor Cross, who was running for the short-term senate seat. Cross loved good food and would seek out and find the best restaurants in any given city. He would begin the meal with a glass of wine or beer. If he felt extremely tired (he was then eighty-five), he would indulge in a Scotch and soda but that occurred only a few times during the campaign. As lieutenant governor I was automatically a member of the Yale Corporation and attended all their meetings. I told him I was impressed by such men as Henry Sloan Coffin, Senator Taft, and President Seymour. His own favorite was Professor Lounsbury, who had gone abroad with him when he was working on the English novelists of the eighteenth century. Cross told me that solid scholars like Professor Tinker held a secret resentment against Yale's widely known and popular Professor William Lyon Phelps. Once Phelps brought Gene Tunney, the heavyweight boxing champion, to his class at Yale to give a lecture on Shakespeare. That was almost too much for a Yale scholar. Tinker, in a back room nursing his wrath, said, "Next week I'm going to bring Gertrude Ederle to my class to give a talk on Keats." (Gertrude Ederle, as the reader may recall, was a butcher's daughter who covered her body with thick grease and swam across the English Channel in 1926.) Cross also told me that Phelps once had George Lyman Kittredge, the famous English teacher of Harvard, as his guest at a Princeton-Yale football game. At one exciting moment of the game a Princeton player named Poe broke away from the scrimmage and ran for a touchdown. Kittredge turned to Phelps and asked, "Is he any relation to the great Poe?" Before Phelps could answer, a Yale undergraduate sitting behind them tapped Kittredge on the back and said, "This *is* the great Poe."

Sometimes we would have minor candidates at the restaurant to fill us in on the local situation, and that would turn Cross toward political talk. He knew the state thoroughly. He told us that when he started campaigning in 1930 there were many towns that didn't even know who the Democratic town chairman was. "I had to start from scratch," he said. "It was a long pull, but it finally paid off."

He always closed the dinner with a good cigar, and nobody ever enjoyed a cigar more. He relished every moment of it, and kept the conversation at a high level. Traveling with him was in itself something of an education.

There were still many calls for speeches and many consolation letters to answer. There were still clubs and organizations all over the state asking me to come and address them.

At Christmastime Governor Baldwin sent to the Secretary of State his resignation as governor. He had been elected United States senator on two ballots—one for the unexpired portion of the late Senator Maloney's term, the other for a new six-year period. As a senator in Maloney's place, he could go to Washington and be sworn in at once. This would give him seniority advantage over newly elected senators all over the country, whose terms would not begin until January 8, 1947. In Washington it is the committees of Congress that do the work, and the higher one stands on the totem pole of any given committee, the more influence he can wield.

Governor Baldwin's action not only elevated his senatorial standing but it left me as governor for two weeks, until governor-elect McConaughy could be inaugurated on January 8.

Those thirteen days as governor began with my own inauguration. Friends crowded the office and my neighbor, Mrs. Muriel Hubbard, saw to it that flowers were all over the room. Chief Justice Maltbie swore me in, whereupon I received many handclasps from men and many kisses from women.

Beneath this festive mood I was pestered by a sense of futility. The General Assembly was not in session. To call a special session would be absurd, particularly since both houses were overwhelmingly Republican. Two weeks were too short a time for any bill to go through the assembly. Things we had in our platform would not be achieved. All the changes that I dreamed of such as improved education, increased payment for state employees, fair employment practices laws, etc., would have to be put aside until a more favorable time.

Jack Zaiman reported in the Hartford *Courant* that my family had moved into the governor's mansion. How ridiculous. I did visit the people in charge there three times. I told them I wanted to give a dinner party for the candidates who had run on the Democratic ticket with me. The Finance Commissioner gave his approval. The date was set for New Year's Eve. All the guests arrived. We forgot our defeat and had a grand time. Governor Cross was in particularly fine form as a storyteller. Our candidate for attorney general brought his wife, who was on the verge of having a baby. John Bailey and his wife helped to make the evening lively. It was a snowy, blustery, stormy evening. The attorney general candidate and his wife started home for Bridgeport, then turned back and stayed in the mansion all night. I wanted the baby to be born in the mansion that night, so that we could have a cheerful headline for the papers next morning. But alas! The baby wasn't born until two days later.

The chef did put on a magnificent dinner. I sat at one end of the table, Jeannette at the other. The butler stood immediately behind her awaiting orders. This ceremonial made it appear like a "state dinner" of some importance! With us it was merely an amusing interlude in our lives. The state paid the expenses for this party on all items except the liquor. This old Puritan New England state made it clear that such doubtful extravagance as booze was not to be paid out of taxpayers' money!

Letters of all descriptions came to the governor's office. Here is one from a boy who wanted to go fishing in a pond owned by the state and used for drinking:

> Congratulations and good luck. I wish to take this opportunity to obtain from the Governor of the State of Connecticut, a written permit to do ice fishing in the Middletown State Hospital Reservoirs. Under former Governor Hurley, I had the pleasure of having such permit. Knowing that you also like to fish, I feel confident that you will grant me such permission for myself and a few friends.

And this, from Fairfield State Hospital:

> This letter and my previous one I want you please to send to State's Attorney W. Hadden for action. The longer I am kept prisoner here the farther the consequences will reach. I have no intention of letting a group of venal officials in this crime to label me with the unutterably horrible stigma of mental incapableness.

Many of the letters contained requests for jobs. They got a brief reply: "Please write again to the new governor coming next week."

John Bailey told me I should have a secretary to handle these letters. He had a woman for the job. She had turned her own town from the Republican to the Democratic column, had a picture of me in her handbag, and had listened to all my radio addresses. What an achievement! Surely deserving of a reward. She wanted to be my secretary. I interviewed her and found out that she could not use a typewriter, take dictation, or answer any of the letters that came pouring into the governor's office. She hung around the outer office a few days, then gave up and left for home. When my time was up I was told that she came back with a bill for two weeks' work. Luckily for me, Governor Baldwin's secretaries were still at the office every day and I could use them.

Francis H. Wessell, who had charge of the secretaries, was a charming man who served as aide to ten governors of both political parties. He saw at once how forgetful I was, and often as I left the office he would call me back to put on my rubbers or pick up a briefcase I had laid on his desk. One incident I shall never forget. I told him I wanted to dictate a letter and asked him to send me a good stenographer. I went into the office and stretched out horizontally on a long couch. (I had found out during my years as lieutenant governor that I could think better, phrase and dictate better, when I was flat on my back.) When the girl came into the room I stretched out my arm to indicate the chair where she might sit. She misunderstood my gesture, turned quickly and left the room. Wessell assured her that I had no "untoward intentions" and sent her back. She was an excellent stenographer and a fine girl. We became good friends.

There was little I could do except *talk*, and talk I did. I used my brief "open door" with the press to urge once more the abolition of the "rotten borough" system in Connecticut. Before the Beta Pi fraternity of the University Club of Hartford I said:

> Here in Connecticut we have let matters drift that should have been corrected. Our political leaders have taken no account of the shifts and drifts in population for over a hundred years. A few voices crying in the wilderness have told us of the evils of the rotten borough system, but like the rich man in the story of the Good Samaritan, we have passed by on the other side.
>
> To those who really believe in democracy it is disturbing to realize that the people in fourteen of our smallest towns, who, taken together, comprise one-half of one per cent of the state's population, have equal power and influence in the Lower House of the General Assembly with the total number of persons living in eleven of our greatest cities.
>
> To those who really believe in democracy the fact that one man's vote

in one town is equal in value to 131 other men's votes in another town seems a far cry from democratic representation.

Another parting shot I delivered was a protest against betting on horseraces and state lotteries. I feared that these activities would bring into the state a "Mafia group" of undesirables. More than that, I feared that we would teach our youngsters that life is a gamble.

I also sounded off against a sales tax, calling it a blackmailing program against low-income people. I had already shown my interest in an income-tax program for the state, but the people of major influence in both parties looked upon a state income tax with horror. I still think it is only a matter of time before we have an income-tax measure based on the ability to pay—the only fair tax for any state or nation.

I did take a hand in the appointment of two commissioners whose terms expired. On December 31 I reappointed two men—one, J. William Hope, the finance commissioner, and the other, Dr. John Satti, workmen's compensation commissioner. Before he left for Washington Governor Baldwin had already appointed Hope, a Republican, but had repudiated Dr. Satti, a Democrat, and in his place had appointed Charles Jewett, Republican. This struck me as politics at its worst. I argued that the appointment of Jewett was filling a vacancy where there was no vacancy and would not be until the end of the year. On December 31, I filled the vacancy, for then there was one. Dr. Satti had done a good job. As commissioner he was closer to the workmen than Jewett, and I thought he deserved a reappointment. The matter was finally put to the courts and after an appeal to the Supreme Court it was decided that Governor Baldwin's early appointment was legally admissible and that Jewett could belatedly take over the job of compensation commissioner. At a press conference on the subject I said:

> I believe Governor Baldwin erred when he reached beyond his term of office and made the Workmen's Compensation Commissioner's appointment in the Second District which became vacant within my short term of office.
>
> I would not make the appointment if I was not convinced it would in the long run be a misfortune as well as a detriment to the State to have one Governor dip into the future and invade another Governor's province and take away another Governor's prerogatives. In view of the fact that the term of Dr. C. John Satti as Workman's Compensation Commissioner in the Second District expires on December 31, I am reappointing Dr. Satti to that office for a term of five years, beginning January 1, 1947, in accordance with the state statutes.

Dr. Satti has conducted that office capably and efficiently and has earned his reappointment. Five of his decisions have been submitted to the courts on appeal and he has been sustained in each case. This in itself is eloquent testimony to his capabilities and qualifications for the office.

Inauguration Day came clear and cold. I rode with Governor Mc-Conaughy from the old Capitol to the new, escorted by the Horse Guard in their red suits and plumed hats.

The Foot Guard took charge of the evening ball with all its ritual and splendor. At the close of the ball my wife and I took leave of the McConaughys, wished them success and happiness, and then drove home to the writing and teaching still ahead of me.

One would think that I had had enough of politics, but no, "the old hoss was still rarin' to go." In 1950 I decided to make one more venture—I would run for the United States Senate. Senator Ray Baldwin, after three years in Washington, had resigned his seat for personal reasons. Bowles, then governor, appointed William Benton, his friend and business partner, to fill the one year of Baldwin's unfinished term. If he wanted to continue the remaining two years he would have to face an election. Benton had made an excellent record in his one year. He had dared to stand up four-square against Senator Joe McCarthy, that poisoner of American life, and I admired his courage. But he was a stranger in Connecticut politics, while I had twenty-five years of residence and of work with the Party from the grass roots up; hence I had a claim on this post.

Someone started a rumor that President Truman was coming to Connecticut and would speak for Benton. I knew that if this happened, I would have no chance. So I wrote to the President asking him if he would stay out of the Connecticut campaign. He answered with the following note, dated July 18, 1950:

Dear Mr. Snow:

I read your letter of June twenty-first with a great deal of interest.

Of course, my knowledge of Connecticut politics is very limited and naturally I would not interfere in any local situation. Senator Benton has made a very able and capable addition to the Senate, however.

I traveled over the state and found that many small towns, especially in the eastern sections, were for me. Fannie Dixon Welch of Columbia, who did so much for the election of Governor Cross, was 100 per cent for me. But the bosses in the cities wanted nothing to do with a candidate who was "as poor as a church mouse." (I could never understand why a church mouse who delighted in the leavings of all the church suppers and bazaars should be considered more underprivileged than other mice!) John Tynan, whom I had worked with for years, came out against me as a candidate. That was the deadliest blow of all, for a man must have the backing of his own town delegates to get anywhere. John examined all the potential delegates to the State Convention and exacted from them a promise that they would vote for Benton. Some of the old regulars who were always delegates to the Conventions, such as Leonard Ryan and Mrs. Sheedy, refused to be delegates if they couldn't vote for me, so they were excluded and others were substituted. I would have the humiliating experience of going to the State Convention seeking a nomination with my own delegation wholly against me. John was now emerging as one of the big league of Democratic leaders, and I judge he did not want to do anything that would jeopardize his relationship with the big city bosses. They had all picked a man with money as their candidate and I, the church mouse, was left without a crumb.

When the Democratic Town Committee met to elect the previously selected delegates to the State Convention, John Tynan made a speech against me. In seeking nomination for a high office I had committed serious blunders—I ignored protocol, I lacked stature, I was aiming too high. Benton had the keen intellect and aggressiveness needed in a senator. Nothing could be done for me! I took this rebuke of John's in my stride and we remained friends. I could make a distinction between the personal and the political and knew John was doing what he did for legitimate political preferment. But Jeannette, like almost all other women I ever knew, could not separate the political from the personal. "He made you appear an irresponsible child or a halfwit," she stormed, when we were home. She resigned as vice-chairman of the Town Committee where she had been a tower of strength.

On the morning of the Convention, while the preliminary clearing of the decks was in order, I went to John Bailey and said, "John, if I had two men who would work for me to capture this nomination one-half as hard as you worked for me in 1946 when I was to be the gubernatorial candidate, I would sweep this convention." "But Bill," said John, "you can't run a political organization without money, and you ought to know it." When the voting was about one-third over, I could

(above) Governor Cross and Governor-to-be Snow (photo by Coviello, Waterbury *Democrat*); (below) Middletown delegates to the Democratic State Convention, 1968: l. to r., John J. Tynan, Lawrence Cacciola, Raymond J. Dzialo, James M. Kelly, Josephine Licitra, Marion Newberg, Carl P. Fortuna, Kenneth J. Dooley, Wilbert Snow, John F. Pickett (photo courtesy of Mr. Pickett)

Penobscot Bay, late afternoon

see I was overwhelmed. I arose and withdrew my name and urged the Convention to make the nomination of my opponent unanimous.

The loss of this nomination did not injure me. I had something dearer to me than politics to turn to, and I also knew that if Benton were elected, he would prove an excellent senator. He had already shown this in his previous senatorial activities, and I was glad to help him throughout his campaign. Happily, he won the Senate seat and served the remainder of Baldwin's six years.

It is no pleasure for me to record the way I was treated by John Tynan, but in this autobiography I am trying to tell the truth, and I want to warn any young men who are desirous of making their life in law and politics to realize that politics as practiced in America is a rugged and often brutal activity. I hope they will keep in mind the words of Daniel Webster in a letter to a young man who was interested in making such a career: "Young man, remember this: Law is uncertain and politics is altogether vanity."

After the 1950 attempt, I withdrew from active political life. However, I found that I could not entirely pull out. Whatever happened in the town, in Connecticut, or in the nation was still my concern. I had been subscribing to four daily papers and found it hard to break the habit. In fact I haven't broken it yet.

Poetry still held first place in my life and always would. So I left the hustings with few regrets. Next to poetry was education, and whatever happened new in that field was certain to catch and hold my attention. I was one of the "founding fathers" of the Connecticut Association of Boards of Education (C.A.B.E.) and served two terms as its president. I rejoiced to see it grow and become one of the foremost organizations in our state. It has done more than any other one body to improve Connecticut education.

In 1957 I wrote a letter to the local *Press*, urging the establishment of a community college in Middlesex County—our county. The School Board looked with disfavor on my proposal; hence I got together an *ad hoc* committee to work on the project. On my committee were Derry D'Oench, the editor of the local paper; Richard O'Brien, manager of Radio Station WCNX; Dr. Carl Harvey, a tower of strength on the town School Board when I was chairman of that organization; and two or three others. We explored what three other states—California, Iowa, and Florida—were doing with community colleges, and began our long trek. It was seven years later before both parties' candidates for mayor of Middletown heeded our call and started the program. Even then I felt like Jacob when he worked seven years for Rachel and was given Leah instead, for the new state committee in charge of community colleges made ours a subsidiary of the Manchester Community College rather than an independent body of our own. But this remained true only a few years, and then we were given our independence. For five years I was president of the Advisory Council of this body, and nothing I have ever done in public life ever gave me so much satisfaction as the development and growth of Middlesex Community College. We now (1973) have nineteen hundred full-time and part-time students, and our three new buildings are a joy to everyone who visits our campus.

Twice I was pulled out to resume public activity—once as a special envoy of the State Department in 1951–1952 doing propaganda work for the United States in twenty-one countries of Europe, Asia, and the Near East, and again as a member of the convention that built a new Constitution for Connecticut in 1965. These two items, in abbreviated form, will be the subjects of my next chapters.

CHAPTER 23

Overseas for the State Department

EARLY in 1951 I got a call from the State Department, asking if I would spend a year in Helsinki as a Fulbright professor at the University. I politely declined, for I had my own writing to do and thought I had had enough of public life for a while. Two or three days later the Department called again and said, "Here's something we don't think you'll refuse. We would like to have you go to twenty-one countries of Europe, Asia, and the Near East as a special envoy to give lectures on American life and literature." They explained that I would act as a goodwill ambassador and would be received everywhere as a V.I.P. (which I was not). My audiences would often be university people, though I would also address secondary schools, binational institutes, Rotary Clubs, and other cultural bodies. (I feel sure that Senator Benton was the prime mover behind that offer.)

Nobody could turn down such an opportunity, so I said, "All right, I'll go." I was asked to write a series of ten lectures on the broad theme of the United States: her culture; her poetry; her men of vision such as Emerson, Whitman, and Thoreau; her attempts at federation; her bouts with the Four Freedoms; and the expression of her life as revealed in American folk songs and ballads. I submitted drafts to the Department for consideration and criticism; they came back with a few untactful remarks cut out but otherwise little changed.

The Department people expected that I would travel alone, but Jeannette was anxious to go and I wanted her with me. In that case, they said, I would have to advance $3000 to cover her air travel to India and back. I was able to borrow this amount against a government insurance policy which I had kept up since World War I. (Later on, in Sweden, a traveling American Congressman offered to show me how I could sneak these costs onto my bi-weekly expense account, but I

said, "Never mind, I'll handle it somehow.") We had to have inocula-
tions against everything from housemaid's knee to bubonic plague, or
so it seemed—a necessity but also a torture.

We started our trip from New York to Southampton, first class on
the *Queen Elizabeth*—a sharp contrast to the steerage crossing we had
made three decades earlier on the *paquebot Paris*. There, everything
had been crowded, intimate, warm-hearted life among poor folk of a
dozen national origins and cultures; here, we did not make one single
close contact. If you would get at the human bedrock, never travel
first class!

In Southhampton, still full of the rubble from German bombings, I
had my first taste of keen audience criticism when I addressed the
Rotary Club on "What Is American?" There was more lively discussion,
largely of Poe and Whitman, when I spoke in London on the contrasts
between English and American literature. I really caught it at Glas-
gow, where my theme was "The Four Freedoms as They Exist in
America." What of our treatment of Negroes, the sharply critical listeners wanted to know. I could only admit our shortcomings and at the
same time point out the great strides that had recently been made.

Norway was beautiful, civil, calm, and keen-minded, its students
very much like those I had had at Wesleyan. But German devastation
had been massive, especially in the northern coastal towns; the country
was desperately poor and people were working hard to rebuild.

Sweden had escaped all that—she had stayed neutral in both
World Wars—but the people did not seem to feel quite right about it.
The graduate students at the University of Stockholm, with whom I
met one afternoon, preferred the new "Waste Land" poetry to that of
Frost, and thought that such prose writers as Caldwell, Mailer, Faulkner, and James Jones represented America more truly than "old fogies"
like Emerson, Melville, and Thoreau. For all that, they couldn't get
enough of Carl Sandburg!

In Stockholm we lodged in a hotel facing the royal palace, where
my Wesleyan colleague Heinrich Schwarz had lived as the King's guest
when he arrived, a penniless refugee, from Nazi-occupied Vienna.
Later, at the University of Göteborg, we called on another colleague,
Alexander Cowie, who was giving courses in American literature as a
visiting professor. There, and again at the universities of Lund and
especially Uppsala, we were deeply impressed by the reverence the
Swedish people showed for men of learning. The professor in Sweden

ranked above the doctor, the preacher, the lawyer, or the businessman; and he carried himself with a dignity and formality unknown to American teachers. Sweden made me proud to belong to such a guild.

We went on to Denmark, to the Netherlands (in some circles, you would be rebuked for calling the country Holland), to France, Switzerland, Italy. We had opportunities for sightseeing and took full advantage of them: the Rijksmuseum in Amsterdam, where Rembrandt's "Night Watch" had a masterfully illuminated wall to itself; the impressive church in Soro, Denmark, where Bishop Absalon, founder of Copenhagen, is buried; the Coliseum and St. Peter's in Rome, the birthplace of Columbus in Genoa, the canals and palaces of Venice. We saw also many signs of the war so recently over, and of the Cold War then at its height: economic depression in Denmark's dairy-based economy, the polders of Holland only now being reclaimed from the sea which had rushed in when retreating German troops blew the dikes. Political unrest and doubt were evident everywhere. Some intellectuals and students, as well as workers, saw the Soviet Union as "that great light in the east," and to such the Marshall Plan was merely a clever American attempt at domination. But many more, I believe, truly appreciated what our country was doing to help Europe rebuild herself.

My own talks as a rule went well. Best received everywhere was that on ballads, beginning with "Barbara Allen" and coming down to the present day. Often enough, with a little nudging from me, the audience would respond by singing folk ballads of their own. But when I spoke on our national life and ideals, I was sure of close and sometimes hostile questioning. Our treatment of Indians and Negroes, the just-exposed relations between certain Federal officers and organized crime, the first evidences of the drug problem—all these gave me some difficult moments. And throughout Europe, as in Sweden, I found that such books as *Tobacco Road, The Naked and the Dead,* and the novels of William Faulkner were generally taken as true revelations of American life. A reporter at The Hague had what struck me as a sound explanation of this belief. Europeans, he said, read and absorbed this pessimistic, ugly view of life not because it was specifically American, but because it tallied with their own despair after the terrible slaughter of two world wars in one generation.

Our flights between cities were smooth enough, with a single shattering exception on the leg from Geneva to Rome. Our plane, a discarded American C–47 now used by Alitalia, was routed by way of Nice in order to skirt the high Alps where stormy weather was brewing. We took off at five o'clock—the date was November 17—and darkness fell soon after. Suddenly the plane began to jerk from side to side, then tipped tail down and plummeted toward earth. Her sides buckled, and I feared she was disintegrating in midair. We hastily fastened our seat belts; our stomachs caved in and we gasped with the sickening sensation of falling, falling through space. Nobody said a word; nobody prayed or cursed, as they might have done in a novel. There was nothing we could do but hold on and watch the lights of the village below us grow larger and brighter. The propellors made a horrible clatter, slower and slower, then suddenly stalled. A crash seemed inevitable. But almost immediately the engines roared on again and we began to climb. Later the co-pilot told us we had run into a cumulus cloud with a fierce downdraft and that we had dropped 4000 feet before pulling out of it. Our destination was the Eternal City; but we had missed the City Eternal by something between 100 and 150 yards!

In all these goings and comings, among all the sights seen and the people met, there is one that lingers in memory more vividly than any other. That was an afternoon I spent in Rome visiting George Santayana. Years earlier, as a young instructor at Williams, I had known him and had walked the Berkshire Hills in his company. Now, nearing his ninetieth year, he was living on the outskirts of Rome in a hospital conducted by the Blue Sisters. I found him clad in pajamas and a faded blue dressing gown, seated in a comfortable lounging chair. He was thinner, much thinner, than in 1910, but despite his apparent frailty, his brown eyes had lost none of their magnificent luster.

We talked about poets and poetry—his own "Columbus" sonnet (the first poem he ever wrote, he told me) and his "Minuet at Fifty." We spoke of poetry in general and of my cavalier disdain for rhetoric. "All poetry is rhetoric in a way," he told me. He spoke with some scorn of Ezra Pound, who had known him for twenty years but did not call on him until, as he phrased it, Pound found himself "in a jam" over his pro-Fascist activities and broadcasts during the war.

Inevitably, we discussed Santayana's widely read novel *The Last Puritan*. I insisted that his New Englander had a Spanish mentality, and that he was a bit hard on America. He said he was surprised by the book's success, but that Americans had a tendency to read novels that were severe on them. "A good trait," he thought. Questioning him closely about some of the passages in that work, I found he had largely forgotten it. In the end, he was talking of old friends—Bentley Warren of Williams, whom I had also known, and especially William James. "He did not agree with me," said the old poet-philosopher, "but he had a large outlook on life and was far more generous in his judgments than most men. And he had gusto, a quality that I was not endowed with."

Walking back to my hotel, I decided this last remark was not exactly true. Santayana had always lived apart, but he took a lively interest in the world. I was never to see him again, for he died the following year—still not wholly reconciled to the Catholic faith of his forebears, still unable to sever completely that powerful umbilical cord. Subsequently I wrote a full account of this interview, which was published in the *American Mercury*.

We spent the Christmas week end in Greece, where I had no lectures scheduled. Nonetheless I did meet with a group of Athens university students one afternoon; and nowhere else did I encounter people who so greatly appreciated what America had done for their country. Greece, worn down by years of German occupation and civil war, was ripe for Communist plucking, and only the Marshall Plan and Truman's Point Four program saved her from disappearing behind the Iron Curtain. These students knew that, and their expressions of gratitude were so voluble that I was embarrassed.

Our official contacts in Athens were few: a Christmas dinner with my former Wesleyan student Bob Lewis, now a vice-consul; and another dinner with the consul-general, who had served in China and had much to say about why Lattimore, Vincent, and Service were wrong in advocating our acceptance of Mao's successful revolution. We also had to call on the Egyptian consul-general, since that nation was next on my schedule but my visa had expired. A new visa proved hard to get; I had a visa for Israel, which *a priori* made me persona non grata to Egypt. It took me three long mornings to convince Mr. Naguib that I was no enemy of Arabs, and finally I got the visa.

Meanwhile, we did much sightseeing, especially around the Acropolis. Even in its ruins, the Parthenon was immensely impressive, its long line of Doric columns massive, well proportioned, and majestic. Seen in the purple evening light spilling across Mount Hymettus to the sea, the dream of Phidias became a reality. I was conscious, too, of how great a legacy classical Greece had left to our Western culture—in literature, in philosophy, in sculpture and architecture, in the political ideals on which our democratic governments are based. (I have often thought that if this Greek heritage had been imparted to Russia as well, the terrible misunderstandings of the Cold War might never have occurred.)

Yet in truth I was somewhat disappointed in Greece, no doubt because I had expected too much. There was much poverty, much evidence of wartime destruction. In the streets of Athens I found not living counterparts of Apollo Belvidere and Venus de Milo, but a barrage of miserably clad old men, women, and ragged children with hands out whining for drachmas. It was impossible to shake them off, and they destroyed my peace of mind.

Our introduction to Egypt had a touch of the Arabian Nights about it. We reached Cairo airport late in the evening, spent several hours clearing customs, and then were driven by a piratical-looking Egyptian with tarboosh and heavy beard to the Semiramis Hotel on the banks of the Nile. As we checked in—at 3:00 A.M.—the desk clerk said we must have a bite to eat. "At this hour?" I asked. "Certainly, we will have it brought to your room at once." Fifteen minutes later into our room came a man in a tuxedo, carrying nothing except a broad smile of goodwill. Behind him was an Egyptian giant bearing aloft a large silver tray exquisitely wrought. He was six feet three or more, massive of body, dressed in a red tarboosh and a long white gown with a red sash. Here was a man fit to serve Scheherazade! The sight of him was enough to make good digestion wait on appetite. Such a display of grandeur, such dignity and solemnity for a bit of tea and toast, surpassed anything in our experience.

This was one face of Egypt, but the country had other aspects which were somewhat terrifying. Britain's long suzerainty was nearing its end; the playboy King Farouk sat on a shaky throne, supported only by a handful of pashas who owned 75 per cent of the land; a war against Israel had been lost three years earlier; there was still sporadic fighting along the Suez Canal; the city masses and the country fellaheen alike were seething with discontent. Everywhere one could sense a hatred of everything Western and a fierce, growing sense of Arab nationalism. We knew nothing of it at the time, but already the Society of Free Officers was preparing the swift coup that brought first Naguib and then Nasser to power not six months after our departure.

What we saw was not the details of Egyptian politics but the unrest in the streets. The abandoned British barracks were being torn down; two bronze lions on a Nile bridge, symbols of British authority, were marked for destruction. We ourselves, taking moving pictures of a crowded street scene, were physically threatened and reported to the police by two saturnine men, and had to escape by ducking into a nearby restaurant and out through a back door. Again, we were turned back by a mob as we left the American College for Girls, and had to be rescued by a government car. We were warned to keep out of the slum districts of Alexandria as no one could be responsible for our safety there. People on the streets hissed "Inglese" at us, and once I was attacked by a fanatic. We did not dare go out of our hotel at night, and toward the end of our stay we felt uneasy even in broad daylight.

Yet Egypt was undeniably colorful and fascinating, the streets of Cairo like nothing else on earth. Here were men in tarbooshes and long, graceful galabias of many colors; donkey carts carrying chattering veiled women; beggars imploring "baksheesh"; street vendors with their wares spread out on the sidewalk; trolley cars alive with people hanging on all four sides; everywhere tall camels striding along, their proud heads thrown back. Over it all was a vast medley of sounds—wagon wheels, beating hoofs, shouting crowds, and the long-drawn cries of the muezzin on his minaret (now carried through loud-speakers). We had time, too, for the usual tourist sights: the Pyramids of Giza, whose construction truly boggles the mind; the Sphinx, who has not weathered the years very well (he looks somewhat like a punch-drunk prizefighter in the last round); ancient tombs with their frescoes; the stone-and-marble waterfront of Alexandria; a Bedouin camp out in the desert; and not far from it, the barbed wire, broken axles, and rusted gasoline drums left behind by Rommel and Montgomery in their desert war.

With all this, I had my scheduled lectures—at the American University and the College for Girls in Cairo, at Alexandria in a private house (the cultural officer there did not dare hold the advertised public meeting, so tense was the atmosphere); at the Y.M.C.A. in Cairo, where "The Four Freedoms" aroused a storm of controversy. I met also with representatives of the Arab League, who told me stories of Israeli atrocities that matched the German atrocities at Lidice.

In all, we liked Egypt, its land, its animals, its people; and it impressed us as a country of potential riches crying out for development. But the tension was such that, when the time came to leave for Iran, we were glad to get away. Two days after we had left, the mob erupted and destroyed Shepheard's Hotel by fire.

The flight to Teheran was not without incident. We touched down briefly at Damascus, then took off for a scheduled landing at Baghdad. But a combined sandstorm and snowstorm forced the pilot to turn back, so in the end we spent a night and a morning in the Syrian capital. Then we were off for Baghdad once more, this time landing without difficulty. Here we had to lay over since Teheran's airport was iced in. This gave us a night at the Tigris Palace Hotel, whose gardens abut that famous river, and a day for seeing such sights as the tomb of King Feisal, the Golden Mosque, and above all the impressively bearded men of Baghdad—tall, stately, lean, and handsome in their magnificent turbans, like true descendants of the caliphs of the Arabian Nights. I was tempted to join a group of them sipping coffee at a sidewalk café; but Jeannette would not have been welcome in that all-male group and I certainly couldn't leave her standing in the street.

Finally making it to Teheran on the next day, I moved into a full round of lectures. The local U.S.I.S. had me scheduled to speak every night, with tape-recording machines at each session. At these lectures we saw how poetry-conscious the Iranians were. On Monday I spoke on American poetry to an audience of 250; on Tuesday, when the United Nations was my subject, only 75 showed up; but Wednesday's talk on Walt Whitman drew the entire 250 back to their seats. Even the chief streets of Teheran were named for poets—Ferdosi Avenue, Hafiz Street, Saadi Avenue. I asked, "Why no Omar Khayyam Street?" "No," they answered, "he was too much of an unbeliever."

At that time there was much anti-Western propaganda broadcast from Russia to Iran, some of it in English; and it was working. One boy told me that my talk on "What Is American" was the first that had ever made him question what he heard on Moscow radio. Another boy, just back from the States, answered one question for me to my complete satisfaction. I was asked, "How do the Negroes live in America?" He spoke up and said, "A little better than the Shah of Iran"—a reply that would have been terrible from me, but from him it was a smash hit.

Karachi in Pakistan was our next scheduled stop but it was not easy to get there. We had plane tickets on K.L.M., but that airline was no longer serving Teheran. We ended by taking a train to Khorram-shahr at the head of the Persian Gulf—a two-day ride over the majestic Zagros Mountains—and from there on the British-India steamer *Dara* to Karachi. This sea voyage provided a rest period that was not in our official schedule, but one we desperately needed.

On the pier at Karachi we were met by American cultural officers, and by something not nearly so pleasant to behold: a large band of coolies waiting to unload the ship, some of whom had been standing in line since midnight. Here was our first sight of Pakistan's desperate unemployment. Since the partition from India only a few years earlier—in effect, a religious war between Moslem and Hindu in which millions died—both countries had known a refugee problem almost unparalleled in human history. The outer streets of Karachi were cluttered with the miserable huts of these people: patchwork structures of straw and poles that offered little protection from the weather and no sanitary facilities at all. The gutters and vacant lots served both as public toilets and as playgrounds for the naked children who swarmed everywhere.

Not all of Karachi was like that, of course. Large and imposing government buildings were being erected in various parts of the city; and there remained, too, some sturdy structures from the days of British rule. The streets were almost as picturesque as those of Cairo, swarming with three-wheeled pedicab rickshaws, horse-drawn victorias, a few taxis and other motor vehicles, and everywhere stately camels with bells at their knees, here used as draft animals.

While in Karachi we stayed in a new hostelry called the Nazli, where pure drinking water was delivered each day from the U. S. Embassy. Otherwise, it was a somewhat strange place. The bathroom fixtures—tub and so on—were molded in concrete, and their drain pipes stopped just above a hole in the floor to catch the waste water; so if the water flowed too fast, it failed to connect and poured out over the floor. For bedding, each person was allowed one sheet and one scratchy blanket. Jeannette begged for a second sheet; a servant searched the entire hotel and returned with a tablecloth. The next night I too asked for a second sheet and was rewarded with a thin white window curtain. The food, however, was satisfactory as Oriental food goes (all sorts of curries with rice), and we remained at the Nazli for the duration of our visit.

Since we had been delayed in reaching Pakistan, my schedule was crowded, with two or even three addresses in a single day. I talked on the teaching of poetry to the teachers at a Parsee high school, and got embroiled in a lengthy and somewhat pointless argument about T. S. Eliot with one of the audience there. I talked on English poetry to the students of a private college for girls run by British Catholic nuns. I gave an evening lecture on American folklore and ballads, which I ended by asking those present to sing some of their own folk songs; but a man from Radio Pakistan hurried me away for an impromptu interview on the air.

We had been scheduled to visit Lahore but could get no reservation by either train or plane. Moreover, we had appointments in India, which demanded that we move on. The day we left, I received a telegram from Chester Bowles, ambassador to India and concurrently minister to Nepal, offering us his house and car during our one-week stay in New Delhi (he would be in Katmandu at the time). A welcome offer indeed, since our recent hotel accommodations had been somewhat primitive to say the least.

I was considerably upset by another message that reached me at the airport. It was a letter from President Butterfield of Wesleyan, telling me that, as of June 1952, I would be retired from the faculty because I had reached the mandatory age limit of sixty-eight. I had known this was coming, but the day was darkened for me all the same.

India—vast, sprawling, heavily populated, full of poverty and hope, superstition and sublime faith—is a difficult land to speak of in short space. We saw the dark side you have read about: the predatory monkeys, the sacred cows, the flies, the dirt, the poverty, the ritual bathings in the Jumna River in which some of the faithful would inevitably drown. We saw too the beautiful broad avenues of New Delhi with their lovely gardens and impressive public buildings. We saw the new industrial village of Nilokheri, eighty miles from the capital, where in only four years some six thousand Hindu refugees from Pakistan had built a thriving community of homes, factories, and schools in what had formerly been a snake-infested swamp. This was the dream and the accomplishment of a man named C. J. Dey—an accomplishment so successful that Prime Minister Nehru, seeing it, cried out, "I want ten thousand Nilokheris!" We saw a somewhat similar but larger-scale project at Ferinidab, where a disciple of Gandhi named Ghosh, with the help of Rs. 25 million in government loans, had built up a complex of manufacturing and agricultural communities that gave work and housing to thirty thousand refugees. We saw at Agra the most wonderful of all sights in India, the Taj Mahal, that too-faultless architectural gem which at sunset seems spectral and unreal, like the embodied spirit of twilight floating in the twilight itself. We saw the dreamy, drowsy beauty of Bangalore, whose fertile soil and excellent climate have made it a garden spot and a favorite retirement place for businessmen and sometime officers of the British Army in India. At Mysore we saw the palace of the Rajah, one native potentate who was a great benefactor to his people and really enjoyed their goodwill.

At this same city I caught a glimpse of the most beautiful woman I have ever seen—a slim, golden-brown Untouchable of about twenty-five, whose plum-colored silk sari clung gracefully to her shapely body. She wore silver anklets and bracelets exquisitely wrought, with golden rings in her ears. On her head she carried two shiny brass water pots, one above the other, balancing them with the ease of a good rider on a spirited horse. Her piercing eyes, dark and slanting, made me realize what Keats meant by "beauties of deeper glance." She haunted me for days.

Meanwhile I had my mission to perform, and it began on a note of high—or low—comedy. I was asked to speak at the University of New Delhi on Walt Whitman, and did so before an audience of two or three hundred students—but in the front rows I noticed a number of military officers in full uniform, and I wondered why they were there. Midway in my lecture a troubled student came to the platform and handed a note to the Dean, who had introduced me. He merely chuckled in amusement. But at the talk's end another student shook a copy of the New Delhi *Times* in my face and told me that my announced subject was "War Equipment," not "Walt Whitman." That explained the officers! I could only laugh it off and retire to the Dean's office for coffee. My Passage to India had been launched in rare style.

At Mysore the subject was English and American literature. At Bangalore I gave my ballad lecture one evening, and on another I had to lecture twice on the Four Freedoms—to university students and to the British Indian Cultural Society. The students were the brightest we met in the Orient, and they asked hard questions—such as why, if we believed so deeply in democracy, we gave aid money to dictators like Tito and Franco.

There were of course personal contacts too. I remember vividly a talk with V. K. H. V. Rao, director of the New Delhi School of Economics. He was recently back from a visit to Red China; and while not converted to Mao-style Communism, he had been mightily impressed. We got into a hot argument and almost came to blows. At last he burst out, "What have America and Russia to teach Mother India? Our wisdom antedates and outweighs them both." I could only reply that the struggle was not between East and West, but between dictatorial slavery and nondictatorial freedom, adding that America's experience of democratic government outdated India's by 175 years.

Best of all, I remember a Washington's Birthday reception given by Chester Bowles, now back from Nepal. Scores of people from all the embassies were there; so too were President Prassed, Prime Minister Nehru, and his sister Madame Pandit. (If Nehru's daughter Indira was present, I didn't know it.) Nehru, smaller than his pictures would indicate, was most affable and greatly amused by my "Walt Whitman–War Equipment" contretemps, of which he had heard; but I could not draw him out on political matters. Madame Pandit, on the other hand, talked freely on world affairs from first-hand knowledge. She had already served as India's ambassador to the United Nations, the United States, and the Soviet Union, and she had filled these posts with marked success. Her general viewpoint I found to be much like that of the average American liberal. At this party it was manifestly clear that the post of American ambassador was an influential one, and that Bowles was magnifying its importance in building better relations between the two countries.

Israel had always drawn me as a lodestone draws iron filings. For here had lived and died Jesus Christ—to me, the central figure in human history—and a trip to the Holy Land had long been one of my cherished dreams. The actuality, as we saw it in 1952, was and still is difficult to evaluate. Then as now, feeling in the Near East ran high and all too easily took on violent overtones. Our impressions were too brief and too kaleidoscopic to permit any over-all analysis or judgment, even if I felt inclined to make one.

Our first impression, oddly enough, was one of cold and rain. We had boarded the through plane in New Delhi's stifling heat and brilliant sunshine; nine hours later we landed at Tel Aviv in a frigid downpour, the first rain we had seen in five months. There a cultural attaché met us and took us to the Ramat-Aviv, a cottage hotel whose room rate was virtually doubled by extra charges—for an electric heater, for Saturdays, for a seat in the lounge while we drank tea, for a "house charge" that was never fully explained, and so on. A clerk told me that these extras were necessary because the government-set base rate was too low to cover costs, so the place could not function without them.

The next day we went to Jerusalem—at that time half in Israel and half in Jordan. I gave my ballad program to a good response at the University in the Jewish city; but the splendid library of 600,000 volumes was in the Jordanian sector and unavailable to professors and students. Worse for us, the Biblical city also lay in Jordan, and we had no time to get a visitor's permit, which would take two weeks. We could only look down into the old city from the spire of a church atop Mount Zion, where Jeannette ran off some twenty feet of movie film. The place swarmed with Israeli border guards, one of whom tried to confiscate her film (how did he know we were not Arab spies seeking good emplacements for machine guns?). But after much questioning and many phone calls, we were released with film intact.

That night I spoke at Pehah-Tiqva on the Four Freedoms. When I had finished, a translator repeated my speech in Hebrew, with editorial additions and harsh comments of his own, for which he was twice rebuked by the chairman. The question period was lively and my questioners well informed.

They were well informed, too, at the Rotary Club in Haifa, from whose members I learned much of the economic problems of Israel. At that time food, particularly meat, was a major problem. Swarms of immigrants had been admitted into the new Jewish state, and too many of these had crowded into the cities or into refugee centers, where they lived in army tents while waiting for jobs and better quarters. The agriculture of the nation, as it then stood, could not support so large an urban population, and for political reasons it was impossible to import food from the surrounding Arab states. Hence the government was engaged in a desperate effort to increase food production—by irrigation, by ground-clearing, by encouraging the immigration of farmers while discouraging nonfarmers.

Some of this we were told, some of it we saw in traveling about the country. We visited a kibbutz near the Sea of Galilee, where we dined rather sumptuously on homegrown foods. Elsewhere we met people whose usual fare was boiled fish three times a day—no oil or butter for frying for a change, no meat of any sort. Bread, oranges, and other fruits were in good supply, jam and margarine nonexistent. Everywhere there was feverish activity—new houses and towns being built, new sewers and waterways, new roads and bridges. Such determination was really inspiring.

But over all hung the menace of Arab hostility. We could see it in Haifa's oil refinery, which had once been supplied by pipeline from Iraq but now ran at one-third capacity, using crude oil brought by tanker all the way from Venezuela. We could see it in public attitudes and in small "incidents" created by young hotheads. The world has since then seen it on a larger scale in the Suez affair of 1956 and the "six-day war" of 1967. In 1973, it would take a bold man to predict the end.

Beneath all this turmoil of settlement, building, and political menace lay the ancient wonders of the Holy Land which we had so much wanted to see. Old Jerusalem, as I stated, was off limits for us; but we did go by car up a miserable track to the summit of Mount Carmel, where Elijah had overcome the 450 priests of Baal. We passed through Cana, where Christ performed His first miracle—a little town of low stone houses and winding streets, with nothing of the Oriental splendors depicted in Veronese's famous painting. We went to the Sea of Galilee, saw the wherrylike fishing boats, inspected the fishermen's catches—mostly, I thought, varieties of bass. We walked about in Nazareth, where Jesus had dwelt with Mary and Joseph. It was a town of old houses surrounded by ancient olive groves, with narrow, twisting streets just wide enough to accommodate a fully laden pack mule—a sight that we saw every few minutes, one that Christ must have seen many times two millennia ago. Guides showed us the cave (now surmounted by a church) where Mary is said to have lived with her parents at the time of the Annunciation; also another cave (again with a church above it) said to have been the childhood home of Jesus. There were cheap trinkets and crude olivewood carvings on sale everywhere, and too many overzealous guides; but Nazareth, more than any other town, suggested the reality of Biblical times.

Our flight path from Tel Aviv to Istanbul led through Nicosia, Cyprus, where we made a dangerous landing late in the evening through a drenching thunderstorm. As transit passengers we were put up for the night at a miserable hotel where we could not even get a cup of tea. The next morning we had a few hours to see the city and savor its patina of English language, currency, and manners superimposed on a Greek culture. Most interesting to us was an ancient building called a *khan* into which we stumbled by chance. It was a huge, forbidding, windowless structure of stone, its walls pierced by a single arched passageway. Inside, we found ourselves in a large courtyard circled by balconies that one reached by ancient stone staircases —a secure little medieval community given over to horses, cattle, and mules on the ground level, while the upper stories were dwellings. At midday we were in the air again on the four-hour flight to Istanbul.

At this great city, one of the world's crossroads, we had a day to ourselves, together with a car and an English-speaking guide supplied by the cultural officer. Naturally, we headed at once for Hagia Sophia, the marvelous domed Byzantine church erected by Justinian, later converted to a mosque by Turkish conquerors, and at the time of our visit in process of reconversion (at Kemal Ataturk's order) to a national museum. So the original Byzantine mosaics and frescoes depicting Christian images were once more coming into view, as the superimposed layers of plaster with their Moslem patterns of intricate scrolls, stylized flowers, and the like were being scraped away. Hagia Sophia has often been described by others, in great detail; it is enough to say here that it is truly the glory of the Byzantine world.

We left that same evening by overnight train to Ankara, where my work would begin. The Anatolian countryside, as we saw it in the morning, was not unlike our own West—little farming villages, open rolling land, cattle grazing in the fields, wide acres of wheat, trees newly planted in even rows (reforestation was a deep concern of the government). Many of the houses were mud or stone, others unpainted two-story structures of wood. The people seemed warmly clad and well fed, and most of the women had discarded the veil. This was a feature of Ataturk's modernization program; another was the substitution of the Latin for the Arabic alphabet; and a third was a decree that everyone under twenty-five must learn to read and write. One is tempted to speak at length of this remarkable man and his accomplishment, for virtually single-handed he turned Turkey from a weak, backward Oriental despotism into a strong, progressive modern nation and a staunch ally of America.

Modern Ankara and its University were also his creations. Here I put on my ballad program, and as usual ended it by calling on my listeners to sing ballads of their own. At first they were quite shy; but after some prodding, four boys sang a plaintive prison song. Then a group of girls sang a love song. People began to stray in from other rooms to join the singing, and in the end we had a wonderful two-hour session. The following day my subject was American poetry. The story of the ballad singing had got around, and the audience was much larger than anticipated. There was a lively discussion period, and someone asked, "Why can't we have a course in American poetry here?" At which the department head, an Englishman, was on his feet at once, explaining that the curriculum was already overcrowded and any addition was out of the question. After the success of the ballad program, this was a shrewd blow; but such were the ups and downs of the trip.

To complete our Turkish assignment we returned by train to Istanbul. I spoke twice at the girls' college, on Walt Whitman and on American poetry—a talk I repeated at Robert College. The English Department teachers there, recruited from leading American institutions, were a young and lively group, and their differing opinions of modern American literature delighted us. Then there were two appearances at the University of Istanbul, one on ballads and one on American poetry. After each session I noticed that the girls participated as freely as the boys in questions and discussion—fresh evidence of how emancipated Turkey's young people were.

Yet there were glimpses of an older, more leisurely Turkey. Going into a bank to cash a traveler's check, I was ushered into a side room where an officer greeted me graciously, seated me in an easy chair, and regaled me with thick Turkish coffee and cigarettes—with apologies that they were not an American brand. We sipped and smoked and chatted of Ataturk, of America, of the world situation—and only after a proper social interval did he cash my ten-dollar check. I can't imagine that he made money by this transaction; the coffee and cigarettes alone must have absorbed his entire profit.

Jeannette too, on days when I had writing to complete, saw something of the more traditional Turkey. Wandering around the city in trolley cars, she rode through the narrow streets by the Seraglio Palace, Hippodrome Square, and so to the Grand Bazaar. In this labyrinth of covered streets and small shops it was easy to get lost, but she always managed to find her way home, bringing a copper tray or a brass plate inlaid with silver. She greatly enjoyed these excursions and was treated with fine courtesy everywhere. But she noticed that Turkish women did not always receive such mannerly treatment; one afternoon, in fact, she saw a stout grimy laborer push a pale, shabby woman aside and triumphantly sit down in the vacant seat she had been trying to reach. This may have been an isolated instance of male rudeness, but no one on the trolley seemed surprised or offended by it.

If I felt one misgiving about Turkey, it concerned the general indifference to religion. (Here again was the influence of Ataturk, whose viewpoint was entirely practical and materialistic.) Not even our Turkish guide—herself a Moslem—knew the difference between a *minbar* (high pulpit) and a *migrab* (prayer niche facing Mecca). But we found young people at the universities who responded immediately to the idealism of Emerson and Thoreau, and we felt that they were the hope of the future.

A K.L.M. plane took us from Istanbul to a brief stopover in Munich, then on to Vienna. Here we landed behind the Iron Curtain; for the Austrian Republic, although established and self-governing since the war's end, was still divided into occupation zones held by the Big Four Allies, and the airport lay in the Soviet sector. The city itself, an island in the Russian zone, was also divided into four occupation sections. Residents could move freely throughout the city but not into the Russian-held countryside.

We were met by a woman from the American Embassy and driven along a road heavily patrolled by Russian troops to the Bristol Hotel on the "Ring." This hostelry had been taken over by the State Department and was excellently maintained—good beds, bright lights, private baths, comfortable furniture. But we promptly learned that, for good eating, it was better to seek out Vienna's famous exotic restaurants.

My first lecture was at the University of Vienna, on those ultra-modern American poets who follow the melancholy banner of Pound and Eliot. My remarks were decidedly critical, and I expected violent protests from the audience of bright young students. No sooner had I finished, however, than the chairman made a few gracious remarks and dismissed the class. Obviously, in this institution, students were not to argue; they were merely to listen, learn, and go home.

Happily, that rule did not apply elsewhere. There was a luncheon given by the chargé d'affaires at which one Frau Doktor, a historian, recalled at length the good old days under Emperor Franz Joseph, then launched into a denunciation of President Wilson's Fourteen Points. The one concerning self-determination, she held, had destroyed the Austro-Hungarian Empire, and things had never been right in Europe since then. An evening talk on Whitman to the University Students' Union brought on a lively discussion period, generally favorable to the spirit of Emerson and Whitman, especially the latter's as expressed in his line, "O America, because you build for mankind, I build for you." Why, they wondered, had this spirit disappeared from recent American writing? On another evening I spoke to an international-relations group on the United Nations idea in American history, and here the criticism was really sharp. These students had made a deep study of the U.N. charter, they had ferreted out all its weaknesses, and they demanded an early revision. But they forgave my faith in the organization's future because I was an American and therefore a natural optimist.

As usual, the ballad program was the best received of all. It was first given one afternoon for a group of young people of high school age. At the close, I got them to singing their native songs and ballads, and they did it so well, with such beautiful harmony and musicianship, that one would have thought they were a practiced choir—which they were not at all. When we repeated the program two days later at the Austrian-American Institute, there was no audience singing; they were ready for it, but an adult class in basic English was waiting for the hall, and every other room in the building was filled by other classes —an indication of the Austrian thirst for learning.

Meanwhile we were seeing the sights of the city, still full of charm despite much bomb damage. Its restaurants were incomparable; its cafés were afternoon centers for coffee-sipping, lounging, gossip—and some said Russian espionage. We saw operas by Strauss and Verdi (the latter much more satisfying); the beautiful blue Danube, which was neither beautiful nor blue; the famous Vienna Woods, a high mountainous park with lovely great trees and deep ravines; the house that Goethe and Grillparzer shared during some of their most creative days.

From Vienna we went by train through the Russian zone to Salzburg. The charm of this picture-book town took my breath away. Its narrow streets wound between the Salzach River on one side and steep gray cliffs crowned by a castle-fortress on the other. In one of its houses Mozart was born—his cradle, his first violin, his earliest compositions, might still be seen there—and his musical genius seemed to dominate the place. My only talk here was on ballads, and as one might expect, the audience was much more interested in the music than in the history or poetry of this folk material.

In Linz, an industrial town on the upper Danube, I had two addresses to give—one on English and American literature to a lively group of young people, who adjourned the discussion period to a nearby clubroom where we talked over coffee and beer; the other on "What Is American" to a large, responsive audience of mixed ages at the Austrian-American Society. This city was on the edge of the Soviet zone—the Russians controlled the bridge—and it was associated with Hitler's early years, a fact of which the citizens were not proud.

We had but one further destination in Austria, the most beautiful of all—Innsbruck in the Tyrol, dominated by glorious snow-capped mountains on every side. For decades it has drawn tourists from all over the world—in recent years mostly skiers, but it is associated too with such great literary names as Browning, Heine, Goethe, and Schiller. My one talk here was on Poe, who had a fascination for Europeans beyond any other of our poets. My audience was a fine one, and their informed, intelligent comments during the discussion period showed that the choice was a happy one.

In all, we loved Austria—to us, the land of music and charm. Yet we could not help feeling disturbed about her future; for in those days of hot war in Korea and Cold War elsewhere, the Russian occupation was all too evident, and we feared that what the Bear had once grasped, he would never let go. In this case, the Bear did let go several years later, but not before exacting millions in crude oil and other goods in the name of "reparations payments."

Our last scheduled country on this marathon trip was the Federal Republic of (West) Germany, the key nation of Europe. Technically, it had been a self-governing state since 1949, but it was still divided into British, French, and American control zones. We checked in at Frankfurt, a heavily bombed city, where the United States High Commission for Germany (HICOG) maintained headquarters in the vast former I. G. Farben building. Right away there was trouble over my travel orders; they were dated June 15, 1951, were good for nine months only, and here we were in April 1952. The military mind found it hard to cope with this dilemma. But I had a letter from the State Department outlining my trip from September to May. HICOG finally accepted this interpretation, gave us military railroad passes, and let us stay at military hotels where available.

Mike Barjansky, the cultural officer who met us, had already arranged a series of one-night stands for me throughout Bavaria, capped by several days in Berlin. The first was in Wurzburg, which in prewar days had been one of the most beautiful of German cities but had suffered vast bomb damage—some said 85 per cent destruction—when the Nazi gauleiter refused to surrender to the advancing Allies. A few of its old monuments still survived, including the *Residenz* with its magnificent architecture by Balthassar Neumann and its ceiling frescoes by Tiepolo. For the rest, the people were rebuilding as fast as they could. Some of the streets looked quite normal, but around the corner you would find roofless walls filled with rubble or a row of new one-story shops overtopped by jagged walls and gutted church towers. In this city I talked at the Amerika Haus, a combination library, reading room, and lecture hall maintained by U.S.I.S. My subject was the United Nations idea in American history, and a lively discussion followed. The people made me feel that they had had enough of militant nationalism —they had seen in two world wars where it led—and they seemed to agree that the political indifference of most cultivated Germans was largely to blame.

We moved on to Ingolstadt, a charming fourteenth-century city untouched by bombs, where my ballad program at the Amerika Haus was a great success—especially its aftermath, when an attractive woman refugee from Silesia led the audience in hearty singing of German folk songs. Next we went to Straubing on the Danube, which had known the tramp of Roman legions and was now an American army base. My talk on the Four Freedoms led to the usual hostile-cynical questions about our treatment of Indians and Negroes. One woman asked, "Would you let Negroes come into your own home?"—and when I replied that my sons' black friends came and went as freely as anyone else, her expression showed that she didn't believe me. Someone else asked if we would not now return to our former isolationist stance; and when I said No, a voice called out, "What about Robert Taft?" At this I recalled the recent New Hampshire primary, stuck my neck out, and predicted that the nomination would go to Eisenhower.

So it went for the next several days—Munich for a week end of relaxation among its museums and theatres; Lichtenfels for a sight of the wonderful white-and-gold Church of the Fourteen Saints, the most beautiful Baroque structure in Europe; Nuremberg, full of bomb destruction and rebuilding and memories of Albrecht Dürer (his house had been leveled to the ground but had already been restored, though his mammoth bronze statue in the nearby square was miraculously undamaged).

On the train to Regensburg we passed through a wide rural landscape, freshly green and splashed with flowers. Many people were at work in the fields, plowing behind horses or more often oxen, scattering manure with pitchforks, planting potatoes by hand. I was told that in northern Germany they used modern farm machines, but here in Bavaria the old ways predominated.

At Regensburg my subject was again the Four Freedoms, followed by the usual questions plus some fresh ones. Would America experience a postwar inflation as Europe had done? Would we go Communist within twenty-five years? What about the marriage of Catholics and

Protestants, a problem of great concern in this city? This one surprised me, for I had thought that all of South Germany was Catholic; but I now learned that some cities, like this one, were largely Protestant. Most embarrassing, they asked if I would like to live in Germany. I could only squirm out of that one on the old ground that "East, West, home is best." The next day there was a May Day parade, which I expected would be a Communist demonstration. But no: the marching workers carried only German flags, and their posters bore such demands as the forty-hour week and free Saturday afternoons. The emphasis was entirely on labor conditions and national unity. We ended that Sunday with a boat trip up the Danube to Mariaort and a rousing song-fest in a beer garden, among men in *lederhosen* and horn-buttoned flannel jackets, women in white blouses with green bodices, full blue skirts, and pink aprons. Here was German *gemütlichkeit* in full flower!

That evening we left by overnight train for Berlin, isolated 120 miles within the Russian zone. What a spectacle met our eyes the next morning! Mile after mile of roofless buildings, rubble heaps, whole blocks of tangled steel and broken concrete, other whole blocks cleared of debris and ready for reconstruction. Here indeed was the abomination of desolation, but there were signs of rebirth—new buildings rising, the shops on the best streets full of cheerful display, the people hard at work, and the striking modernistic monument to our Airlift fliers already in place at Tempelhof Airport.

It was not so in Communist East Berlin, which we visited twice (the Wall was not yet in existence). Over there, amid garish monuments to Russian glory and posters of Stalin, one found gray, grinding poverty among the people, only a few tawdry goods in the stores, and armed Vopos—the dreaded paramilitary police—on every other corner. Here too was the rubble of bomb destruction, which "volunteers" from factories and offices spent Saturday afternoons removing with their bare hands. We did manage to talk confidentially with some of the people, many of whom listened to the American Sector radio when they could —or read the West Berlin newspaper *Neue Zeitung*—or got Free World news from the moving electric sign (like that in New York's Times Square) which overlooked the Potsdammer Platz on the border of the Russian zone. They also relieved their tensions with black-humor jokes like this: "Why were Adam and Eve the first Communists?" "Because they had no clothes and no shelter, but they were living in Paradise."

Berlin in those days was a battleground of propaganda, and I felt that our side was holding its own. I did my part by speaking at Amerika

Haus on our poets, before a fine and intelligent crowd. At the dinner which preceded the talk I met a German who had admired the Führer and had belonged to the Hitler Youth. In those days, he told me, he had been impatient with the slow, compromising ways of democracy, and had seen only two choices—Fascism or Communism. Now he had learned by experience the corruption that absolute power brings; it was now clear to him that, for all its limitations, the way of democracy was best.

After Berlin, I had but two engagements left. One, in Bayreuth, was official, and in that musical shrine I naturally spoke on ballads. The second took place on May 6 at the Sorbonne in Paris, by request of the students, and the subject was Robert Frost. The audience seemed to prefer our "wild men"—Whitman, Mencken, Pound, Sandburg—but they could still appreciate Frost's splendid contribution.

That evening seemed a fitting close to a strenuous tour—so much so that I turned down an invitation to address the English-Speaking Union at Stratford-on-Avon three weeks later. Instead, we went to Cherbourg and sailed for home on the *America*.

Looking back on it, I feel that this propaganda excursion was the largest assignment I ever undertook, the most important public service I ever rendered. The America I presented was that of Lincoln, Emerson, Whitman, and Wilson. It was the America I myself believed in, and my audiences sensed that fact. It convinced me, too, that folk songs, spirituals, and ballads of any nation constitute the best means of reaching the people of other lands. Left to myself, I would have discarded all my other talks and concentrated on this one; but in foreign university towns the leaders wanted Whitman and Poe, and I tried to give them what they wanted.

Back in Washington I gave three talks on my work and observations to increasingly large audiences. Who these people were I didn't know, probably understrappers of the State Department or similar government staffers or spies. Two men called me in and asked if I would be willing to undertake a similar assignment in South America. I said Yes, I would—but only if the schedule were less crowded and only after a period of rest. Early in November, after the Presidential election, they wrote me a note: "We think you understand that the management of the United States Information Service will now fall into new hands."

CHAPTER 24

Constitutional Convention

My last attempt to serve the state came in 1965 when I was chosen to be a member of the Constitutional Convention. Forty-two Republicans and forty-two Democrats were assigned the task. But non-party voters, who in Connecticut outnumbered registered Republicans, got no representation at all.

First of all, we wanted to avoid the errors of the last Constitutional Convention of 1902 and come up this time with a Constitution that would be acceptable to the people. At that former attempt the membership of the convention was suspiciously unbalanced, with 122 Republicans and 44 Democrats. The majority group wanted to keep the "rotten borough" system that gave them political ascendency in the Lower House year after year. That grip on Connecticut was like the Democratic grip on the states of the "Solid South," and although this majority often acted wisely they did not act democratically. When the 1902 constitution was put to a popular vote, the document was overwhelmingly repudiated.

This time we put a planning commission in charge, and they were so anxious to keep the parties equal that even the research assistants were divided equally between the two parties.

During the summer months we held open meetings around the state to learn what people wanted us to include in the document. At each meeting there appeared a woman who wanted us to make fluoridation of drinking water unconstitutional. She granted that fluoridation would be helpful to children's teeth, but she said it was poisonous to the intestines of grown-ups. No matter where we held our meetings, this lady would appear and tell the same story. After four appearances Governor Baldwin, our presiding officer, told her we already had heard her recommendation and urged her not to speak unless she had something new to add. She would invariably say, "I do have something new to add." Thereupon she would start off with two new sentences, then slide back into the identical arguments we had heard before! Another pest kept telling us that our procedure was illegal and unconstitutional. He regaled us with the correct way to call a convention, and ended by urging us to disband and go home. I was never able to follow the ramifications of his legalistic argument.

Other people who came to these preliminary meetings showed a live interest in our objective beyond our expectations and offered many excellent suggestions for the new document.

Our first regular session was held in the Old State House in Hartford. The building is a Bulfinch masterpiece and an inspiration to almost everybody who enters and examines it. I wish all our meetings could have been held there. But, unluckily, no room in the building was big enough for our purpose, and we held all our subsequent large meetings in the Hall of the Lower House.

In true schoolboy style I prepared myself for the work ahead by reading and taking detailed notes on Carl Van Doren's *The Great Rehearsal*, which describes the activities of the men who built our first national Constitution in 1787. It was amazing to learn how many similarities marked the concerns of these two groups working two hundred years apart. First, the main business that called the Convention of 1965 together was the "one man, one vote" decision of the Supreme Court. The National Convention of 1787 was also concerned with the question of voting. It decided to count in three-fifths of the Negro population of the Southern states in determining the number of representatives to Congress allowed each state. At that time all the Negroes were totally disenfranchised. In our own day under the "rotten borough" system where one man's vote in a city was equal to 1/116 of another man's vote in a country town, we had not total but semi-disenfranchisement. To correct that was the main business of the 1965 Convention.

The second similar concern was the relation of the smaller units of government to the larger body above them. In 1787 each one of the thirteen states wanted to run its own affairs. The people from the various states were distrustful and suspicious of the Federal government. They finally got it settled that matters not specifically assigned to the Federal government were left to the disposition of the individual states.

In 1945, when I was presiding over the State Senate, few things annoyed me more than this same struggle for power between the state and the towns. The state kept a strong hold over the smaller units. Hundreds of bills concerned with questions such as these choked the Legislature: "Would the town of Cromwell be permitted to build a sewer?" "Would the city of Hartford be permitted to add to its water supply by linking up with the Metropolitan District Commission?" I asked myself, "Why should the state decide such purely local matters?" Holding onto such decisions was merely a clutch for power on the part of the state, like parents who want to run the lives of their children.

In the Constitution we were writing, some of us fought for more home rule for towns and boroughs. Here is a section of Article 10 which shows that the majority of the Convention gave in a little on home rule, but to some of us they did not go far enough:

> After July 1, 1969, the General Assembly shall enact no special legislation relative to the powers, organization, terms of elective offices or form of government of any single town, city or borough, except as to (a) borrowing power, (b) validating acts, and (c) formation, consolidation, or dissolution of any town, city or borough, unless in the delegation of legislative authority by general law the General Assembly shall have failed to prescribe the powers necessary to affect the purpose of such special legislation.

Take a good look at the words *except* and *unless* and see how anxious the group was to centralize the power in Hartford and not in the individual towns.

This excerpt from Article 10 will also give the reader an example of the English exhibited in our new Constitution. It is permeated with the phrasing of lawyers. Reading it is like walking through soft mud with slippers on. Lawyers' documents are usually so downright heavy in their sentence structure that only another lawyer can make out what is meant. I was not on the phrasing committee, but at one plenary session I attempted to effect a slight correction in the English of Article 3, which decides when we shall hold legislative sessions: "If such Monday falls on a holiday the session shall begin on the *next following* day." I rose and asked if they would take out the word *next* or the word *following*, either one would suit me. But no, they must have both— *next following* day. I told them it was a good example of a lawyer's habit never to use one word when four or five would suit his purpose. It reminded me, I said, of an old man in my home village who was complaining about a teen-ager's swearing. The old man said, "He cursed, and swore, and used profanity." That old man should have been a lawyer!

In spite of heavy English with its trailing syntax, we built a good

Constitution. First of all, we corrected the inequities of voting—the major reason for our being called together.

We made a start toward home rule—a more feeble start than I realized at the time. We straightened out the status of a lieutenant governor when a governor dies or quits his office—a matter which was foggy under our old Constitution. We forestalled the recurrence of another "rotten borough" situation by demanding the revision of our elective officeholders occasioned by changes of population every ten years. We thought we had prevented the possibility of any gerrymandering of our local and district lines for elective offices, but the votes of two judges out of three in our latest reapportionment attempt indicates that the spirit of Elbridge Gerry is still very much alive.

We gave more power to the governor by making his veto stand unless two-thirds of both houses overrode it.

A few of the younger members of the Convention wanted a unicameral legislature. I made a speech against it and recalled a dispute on the subject between Alexander Hamilton and George Washington in 1787. Hamilton was all for a unicameral body and Washington was soundly against it. During the interchange of views Washington said, "Why, when you drink tea, do you pour it out in the saucer before putting it to your lips?" (That was the custom in the eighteenth and well into the nineteenth century.) Hamilton replied, "Why, to cool it off, of course." Whereupon Washington said, "There's the reason why we need two houses instead of one." Settling upon two houses resolved the vexed dispute of state representation in our Federal government. Only one of the fifty states voted to get along with one house, and that was Nebraska. Some Nebraskans have urged one house on other states, but their eloquence has never obtained results. Nebraska is like the fox in Aesop's fable who had his tail cut off. He called a gathering of the other foxes, and urged them to follow his example for the new style, but got nowhere. When I visited Lincoln, Nebraska, in 1937, I was told that the state's one legislative house was run by one political leader. The people who want one house are like Alexander Hamilton, who could not endure the long, patient process required in a democracy. (He wanted a king to rule over us.) But democracy is a government that calls for endurance rather than speed, and the people who want to "put a girdle around the earth in forty minutes" have little patience with it.

I made an attempt to put a Commission of the Arts into the Constitution. My resolution read as follows:

Constitutional Convention Resolution No. 57. By Mr. Snow of Middletown, entitled "Resolution concerning an Amendment to the Constitution to Create the Office of Commissioner of the Arts." To see that the state takes a more active part in the art life, to reward achievement in the arts as we now reward science, business and stagecraft; to raise the standards of artistic accomplishment, and to enlarge the cultural activities for our ever and ever increasing leisure hours.

I wanted Connecticut to be the first state to have such a department. My speech in behalf of this measure was unusually well received. I pointed out what such a department could do to save many magnificent buildings. I cited the Return Jonathan Meigs house in Middletown which had paneling such as I had never seen in any other American house; it was torn down to make room for Route 9. I also cited the Governor Coffin house with its magnificent pillars, which was the chief monument of our Main Street; it was torn down to be replaced by a redevelopment program. These would have been saved if a strong Arts Commission with sufficient power had been in charge. These two items in my town could be duplicated in many other towns of the state. "The Seven Arts," I said, "are the crowning glory of any civilization and they should be fostered, nourished, and cultivated here in America as they are in many countries of the Old World. Let us be pioneers in the arts here in Connecticut and make a beginning that other states will follow." No speech I ever made was better received, but when it came to a vote I got only thirteen out of eighty-four members of the Convention. One more lost cause in my life, alas! The leader of the Republican contingent, Meade Alcorn, did make an appeal to curb the unlimited powers of the Highway Commission to cut through our lawns, disturb our homes, and wreck our peace. He cited my speech to buttress his argument. He succeeded in bringing his case before the electorate as a part of our referendum, and secured an unusually large vote to back his case, but it was short of a majority.

The day we achieved the "one man, one vote" redistricting alignment fulfilled the purpose that brought us together. As soon as the vote was announced I arose and said, "This is to me a day for rejoicing. One thing I had long dreamed of and hoped for has at last come true. The people in the cities of our beloved state will no longer be semi-disenfranchised."

The Democrats, or at least most of them, applauded but the Republicans looked rather glum. One of their leaders arose and assaulted my arguments. He said the word "rotten borough" was a word out of old England and did not belong in Connecticut. He said that the record of the Connecticut General Assembly was one of the finest in the country. "We have given this state a sound government and that is something we all ought to be proud of." His speech was followed by another in the same vein. And after this a third. What was I to reply? We had won our point and this was no time to gloat over it. So I arose and said, "If I have said anything insulting or detrimental or offensive to the members on the other side of the aisle, I want to ask their pardon. I don't want this convention to end on a sour note. I have lived in Connecticut for forty years and I love the Nutmeg State. Again I ask the pardon of any member here whom I have offended."

In spite of this and a few other squabbles, the eighty-four members worked harmoniously. Congenial groups had Dutch-treat luncheons together, and discussed endlessly the new baby they were borning. The most difficult spot for harmony was this main object of readjusting the lines of the six Congressional districts and the local lines for senators and representatives. Too much praise cannot be bestowed on John Bailey and Searle Pinney, the political leaders of the two major parties, for the magnificent way they handled this most difficult chore. During the seven months we made acquaintances and friends who have enriched our lives and endeared us more than ever to the constitution state; we all felt a great deal of relief on December 14 when the citizens of the state showed their approval of what we had done by a vote of 178,426 to 84,219 in favor of accepting the new Constitution. It was proclaimed adopted by Governor John Dempsey on December 30, 1965.

At the close of the session the state graciously presented to each of us a small tree, a descendant of the famous Charter Oak—each one of which was to be planted in our home town. I planted mine at an elementary school on Wadsworth Street in Middletown.

WHEN a man is pressing ninety and still has good health and a clear mind, he is besieged by people who ask him how he did it. Replies vary. Some say, "By drinking a pint of whiskey a day." Others say, "By never touching a drop of intoxicating liquor." Bernard Shaw thought he did it by being a vegetarian. Bronson Alcott drew the string tighter, eating vegetables that develop and ripen in the sun and eschewing those like potatoes, carrots, and beets that grow entirely underground. The very old people I have known personally give the credit to long-lived ancestors. A goodly number of the Snows lived to be over ninety.

The answers often cancel each other out and the questioner is as bewildered at the end as he was at the beginning.

Old age is one subject people never tire of talking about, and this is because they themselves are inching toward it every day of their lives.

Browning looked toward old age as an exhilarating experience. He explodes with:

> Grow old along with me!
> The best is yet to be,
> The last of life, for which the first was made.

He says this with so much earnestness that he carries the reader along in his wake.

His fellow Victorian, Matthew Arnold, went to the other extreme. In the poem "Growing Old" he says:

> It is to spend long days
> And not once feel that we were ever young;
> It is to add, immured
> In the hot prison of the present, month
> To month with weary pain.

Happily for many of us, this is not true. It almost seems as if in anger
Arnold is determined to discredit his fellow Victorian.

The common reader remembers the lines of Browning in "Rabbi
Ben Ezra" but forgets completely what Arnold wrote in "Growing Old."

The third Victorian I was brought up on, namely Tennyson, had a
tremendous love for life on earth. In an early poem he cried out:

> Whatever crazy sorrow saith,
> No life that breathes with human breath
> Has ever truly long'd for death.
> 'Tis life, whereof our nerves are scant,
> O life, not death, for which we pant;
> More life, and fuller, that I want.

He sobered somewhat when he wrote *Tithonus* (the man who
asked the gods to let him live on earth forever, but forgot at the same
time to ask for eternal youth. As a result, he shriveled up like a grass-
hopper.) In that poem he says:

> Why should a man desire in any way
> To vary from this kindly race of men,
> Or pass beyond the goal of ordinance
> Where all should pause, as is most meet for all?

In "goal of ordinance" he is thinking, I suspect, of the Ninetieth
Psalm which fixes man's life on earth at seventy years. This psalm, I
think, has probably hurried thousands of people into their graves before
their times. David, or whoever wrote it, has a good deal to answer for
in my opinion, for many of us have had some of the fairest and finest
days of our lives in years past our seventieth birthday.

One who is mulling over this line of thought cannot resist looking
at Shakespeare's *As You Like It*, and seeing what he had to say about
old age. In his "Seven Ages of Man" (Shakespeare was in a bad mood
when he wrote these lines—he couldn't even find something nice to say
about a baby!) he writes:

> Last scene of all,
> That ends this strange eventful history,
> Is second childishness and mere oblivion,
> Sans teeth, sans eyes, sans taste, sans every thing.

His judgment of old age here is as negative as Matthew Arnold's.

In this same play, Shakespeare shows his tenderest attitude towards
the subject in his story of Old Adam. Adam has had enough of the

wicked Duke Frederick, the usurper, and wants to leave his service. During his long life he has saved five hundred crowns. He offers it all to Orlando if he can be permitted to spend his last days with him. Adam says:

> I have five hundred crowns,
> The thrifty hire I saved under your father,
> Which I did store to be my foster-nurse
> When service should in my old limbs lie lame
> And unregarded age in corners thrown:
> Take that; and He that doth the ravens feed,
> Yea, providently caters for the sparrow,
> Be comfort to my age: Here is the gold;
> All this I give you. Let me be your servant:
> Though I look old, yet I am strong and lusty:
> For in my youth I never did apply
> Hot and rebellious liquors in my blood,
> Nor did not with unbashful forehead woo
> The means of weakness and debility;
> Therefore my age is as a lusty winter,
> Frosty, but kindly: let me go with you;
> I'll do the service of a younger man
> In all your business and necessities.

Orlando replies:

> O good old man, how well in thee appears
> The constant service of the antique world,
> When service sweat for duty, not for need!

Shakespeare had another word to say about old age, and this tells a cheerful story. In *Macbeth* he writes:

> And that which should accompany old age
> As honour, love, obedience, troops of friends.

Here is a pronouncement that makes old age exhilarating, and something one can proudly look forward to.

In my teens I somehow got hold of a copy of Benjamin Franklin's autobiography. Its materialism was such a contrast to the Bible that it made a great hit with me. His rules for correct living, such as "Eat not to heaviness, drink not to elevation," made an indelible impression. I have been wondering as I come to the close of this autobiography whether my own rules for living would interest the reader.

One who retired twenty years ago and is still active probably should share his secrets with others. I am not sure there are any secrets.

I do physical work for a half-hour each morning. In the winter I saw three armsful of wood for my stove. I like the heat and the smell of burning wood. In spring and summer I work in the garden and rose garden. I drink a cup of hot water tinctured with lemon juice each morning and during the day drink about twice as much as the average man of ginger ale to help keep my intestinal tract in order. I learned this from a "crank doctor" named White, in Boston, when I was a college undergraduate.

I have told the college boys many times that they must keep their waistlines from bulging. (At the age of fifty-two, mine was thirty-two inches.) I have urged the boys to avoid a second helping whether it be a magnificent dinner or a magnificent lady that they are enjoying. I have told them that the two major joys of the male animal are women and liquor. Both exact such excessive and often terrible prices for what they have to give that I have urged the boys to cultivate the minor joys of life such as walking, skiing, sailboating, mountain climbing, etc., etc. These are not only good substitutes for the two major joys, but they will enable one to enjoy this green earth much longer. To some, of course, eating is one of the major pleasures. This has never been true for me. The table to me is primarily a place for talk. Eating is secondary, although I enjoy it. I make it a point never to eat anything between meals. I make up for that strict abstinence by drinking every soft drink in the supermarket. As an eater I usually avoid meat and cleave to seafood. How could it be otherwise for a man who was born on an island surrounding by herring, mackerel, cunners, flounder, cod, and haddock—not to mention clams and lobsters, both of which were circling that island in abundance? I never bought a cookbook, but if I should buy one it would be one didicated to seafood. I think there is a certain resiliency in one who feeds mainly on fish. I was confirmed in my unusual belief when I observed the people for an hour or two at the fish market in Bergen, Norway. A Nordic strength was in those people and I couldn't help noticing it.

One more item: always have a project ahead of the one you are working on. This will not only help you to complete the job you are now on, but it will be an incentive for you to tackle the dreamed-of next chore.

Last of all, it is important to work on something that cannot be brought to perfection. If you aim at a lesser objective, you may reach it and arrive. Always keep in mind that he who arrives is lost. Those who collect the signatures of the men who signed the Declaration of Independence and fail to find the signature of Button Gwinnett never realize how lucky they are.

Here is the final glory of religion and the arts. They are always working in the world of uncertainty and imperfection. A scientific demonstration of the certainty of immortality would be ruinous to the prophets. The arts never reach final perfection. Both insist that man is a creature of Time and of Eternity. To those of us who believe with Emerson that "Time is the false reply" to the riddle of human life, Eternity beckons convincingly.

Working in the fields of art and religion and pondering them, you will always fall short of perfection. You will not make port, furl sails, and put down your anchor. You will always be out in the open sea alone with God where you belong.

As I finish this book I feel a great sense of relief, I feel almost as sentimental as Tiny Tim in Dickens' *A Christmas Carol* when he cried out, "God bless us, every one."

One New Year's Day in the midsummer of my life I got to thinking of the coming on of life's winter and wrote the following. Let it be my parting salute.

NEW YEAR

Sad is the farewell of another year
When youth has passed the Tropics and must steer
Into the northern straits of chilling Age
Where icebergs loom to mock and spur the rage
That rises in us as we contemplate
Their monumental beauty, and the fate
That winnowed all our early dreams to dust;
We only say farewell because we must.
Currents of wind and tide are setting strong
Into the Arctic where the nights are long
And cold and deep, where resolution fails
To rouse us for a trek on icy trails,
And all ambitions merge themselves in one:
To chart the unbuoyed course beyond the sun.